CASH FOR BLOOD

The Baltimore to New Orleans Domestic Slave Trade

By
Ralph Clayton

HERITAGE BOOKS
2007

HERITAGE BOOKS

AN IMPRINT OF HERITAGE BOOKS, INC.

Books, CDs, and more—Worldwide

For our listing of thousands of titles see our website
at
www.HeritageBooks.com

Published 2007 by
HERITAGE BOOKS, INC.
Publishing Division
65 East Main Street
Westminster, Maryland 21157-5026

Portions of several stories published in this book originally
appeared in the *Baltimore Chronicle* of January 1998, v.25
no.10 and December 2000, v.28, no.9

Other books by the author:

Black Baltimore, 1820-1870

Slavery, Slaveholding, and the Free Black Population of Antebellum Baltimore

CD: African-Americans in Anne Arundel County and Baltimore, Maryland

CD: Black Baltimore, 1820-1870

CD: Free Blacks of Anne Arundel County, Maryland 1850

CD: Slavery, Slaveholding and the Free Black Population of Antebellum Baltimore

International Standard Book Number: 978-0-7884-2235-5

For Alma and Detria
"Love never fails"
1Cor. 13.8

"We notice in an Easton Paper that a wholesale dealer announces his ability, at all times, to advance as much cash as will purchase all the human blood that is to be found in fifty carcasses."

Niles Register, July 21, 1821

Contents

List of Illustrations vii
Acknowledgments ix
Introduction: Birth of the Final Passage xi

1. Auctions of Slaves 1
2. Agencies and Intelligence Offices 15
3. Dockside Sales 23
4. Hotels, Taverns and Inns 29
5. Children as Victims of the Trade 35
6. Baltimore's Early Coastwise Domestic
      Slave Trade 43
7. The Baltimore/Alexandria Market 53
8. Baltimore's Major Slave Traders 59
      Austin Woolfolk-Early King of the Trade 59
      Austin Woolfolk's Rise to Supremacy 69
      A Chronology of Austin Woolfolk's
         New Orleans Trade 78
9. Hope Hull Slatter, Heir to the Throne 83
      The Pearl 92
      A Chronology of Hope Hull Slatter's
         New Orleans Trade 98
10. Other Local Traders 103
      Joseph S. Donovan 103

A Chronology a Joseph S. Donovan's
    New Orleans Trade   106

James Franklin Purvis   109

John N. Denning   111

Jonathan Means Wilson   112

Bernard Moore Campbell   112

A Chronology of Bernard Moore Campbell's
    New Orleans Trade   120

11. Baltimore's Banner Years 1840-1849   125

Epilogue   131

Index to Inward Bound Slave Manifests
    into the Port of New Orleans from Baltimore
    and Other Maryland Ports   133

Index to Vessels Transporting Slaves   621

Appendix 1:
    The Largest New Orleans Shipments   641

Appendix 2:
    The Wharves and Docks of Baltimore   658

Notes   659

Bibliography   671

Index   673

About the Author   681

List of Illustrations

Reading Bodies   facing 14
The Auction   facing 15
General Wayne Inn   facing 34
Spear's Wharf   facing 42
Edmondson Sisters   facing 98

Acknowledgements

A large portion of the research for the opening text of this work was conducted in the Enoch Pratt Free Library, Maryland's State Library Resource Center, located in Baltimore. As always the staff of the Pratt have provided assistance in a number of ways.

The holdings of that institution's Maryland Department provided resources helpful to this endeavor. I would like to extend a special note of thanks to Jeff Korman, Eva Slezak and Layne Bosserman for their assistance.

The vast holdings of the Pratt Library's Periodicals Department afforded access to numerous newspapers, special collections, and documents crucial to the project. A special note of thanks to department head Marcia Dysart for her editorial suggestions.

The staffs of the Maryland Historical Society, Washington D.C. Historical Society, and National Archives offered their professional assistance. The resources of their institutions proved to be crucial to the body of this work.

I'd like to thank friends and associates Philip J. Merrill and Uluaipou Aiono of Nanny Jack and Co. for their encouragement and support.

Mrs. Marion B. W. Holmes, Ed. D., a direct descendant of Emily Edmondson, graciously granted permission to use the image of her family members in this book.

I'd like to extend my appreciation to Mary Kay Ricks who provided helpful information concerning the Edmondson family.

Bob Brown, a distant relative of Austin Woolfolk's, was helpful in introducing me to little known details concerning the Woolfolk's heritage and personal life.

Last, but not least, I'd like to thank my wife Alma and daughter Detria who put up with my nonsense for the past five years.

Introduction

By the first decade of the nineteenth century the populations of the South and the Southwest had begun to increase dramatically. The invention of the cotton gin and the consequent expansion of cotton plantations throughout the South brought about a greater demand for slave labor. Merchants, as they had been for several decades, continued to import substantial numbers of African slaves into southern ports such as Mobile, Savannah, and New Orleans. The rigorous demands placed on the health of slaves by an ever expanding cotton and sugar production led to shortened life spans and a constant need of re-supply in the Southern market. This seemingly insatiable hunger for labor, while bringing fortunes to a select few, brought misery in the form of separation, loss of identity, and even death to many enslaved Africans.

Before the end of the first decade of the nineteenth century the United States Congress, after much debate, voted to abolish the African slave trade. As of January 1, 1808 it became illegal for merchants to import slaves from Africa into ports in the United States. Although the illegal slave trade continued to operate for six more decades, the number of African slaves brought into southern ports declined considerably. The Southern economy, desperate for a continuing re-supply of inexpensive labor, sought out new means of reaching its' goal. One of the states that offered a solution to the shortage in the labor market was Maryland.

For several decades Maryland and Virginia had been experiencing major changes in their respective agricultural economies. During the Colonial period there had been an emphasis, throughout both states, on a tobacco dependent agricultural economy. This brought about a substantial demand for slave labor, a fact reflected in the large slave populations still in place in both states by the turn of the nineteenth century. By this time, however, the trend in a number of counties in Maryland and Virginia had moved to an agricultural economy based on cereal farming as well. The breakup of a number of tobacco plantations into smaller, less labor intensive wheat, corn, and oat farms led to what was known as a "superabundance" of slaves.

Slaveholders faced with excess laborers were left with three possible solutions. The first was to hire out their slaves for a period of time. Most contracts placed responsibility for the servant's keep with the individual who had hired the slave. The most favored contract was one where the slave was hired out by the year. This enabled the slaveholder to retain ownership while benefiting from the payments received from the hirer.

A second option was to manumit the slave, a term which meant to free the slave. This was performed by deed or will. Such manumissions became widespread in Maryland by the end of the first decade of the nineteenth century. When slaves were freed they often moved to larger towns and cities seeking employment. This phenomenon led directly to Baltimore becoming the city with the largest free African American population anywhere in the United States by 1810.

A third option was the sale of the slave. Numerous slaves were sold in the state of Maryland during the period from 1800-1860. As a result the city of Baltimore, with a wealth of access to waterways, and eventually rail access, became a major center or clearing-house for a large number of those sales.

Newspaper advertisements of sales are an invaluable source for determining how variable and widespread the market for slaves continued to be for many decades. Auctioneers handled estates or promoted private sales while agents or brokers sold slaves as middlemen, providing hundreds of sources for the buyer. Dockside sales occurred in which captains, sailing vessels from the Eastern shore of Maryland, sold slaves on board ship while moored in the inner harbor basin. Public sales were held in the market places around the city while private sales and auctions occurred in the enclosed yards of slave trader's pens. Sales in inns, taverns and hotels pervaded Baltimore's early commercial district for decades.

Speculators, sensing an opportunity to make their fortunes buying low in Maryland and selling high in the Southern market made their way to Baltimore from Kentucky, Virginia, Georgia, Tennessee, and other states. They plied their trade from the many hotels and inns west of Jones Falls, south of Market Street, east of Cove Street, and the inner harbor basin. Some, the traveling traders, remained for a season before moving on to markets in Petersburg, Norfolk-Portsmouth, Alexandria and Richmond. Others remained, constructed slave pens, and set up their base of operations in Baltimore.

Thousands of families and individuals were shipped from the city on their "final passage" and almost certain separation in the South. The market was vast, the players plentiful, and the victims plenteous. This is their story.

Author's Note: The author has attempted to maintain the original integrity of all copied ads as well as names recorded in primary source materials. Incidents of misspelled names as well as grammatical errors are evident in a number of those entries.

Chapter 1
Auctions of Slaves

It was a beautiful spring day in Baltimore. The weekend had arrived and with it a great deal of activity in and around the markets and shops in the city. Families traveled from the surrounding counties throughout the morning and into the early afternoon, checking out the current bargains in the stalls along Center Market Space. The sounds of carts and drays driven over the cobblestone street mixed with the calls of merchants advertising their wares.

The fish market, close to the northern end of the stalls, needed no call. The smell of fresh cod, perch and catfish filled the air. Throughout the market the odors of roasted peanuts, fresh produce and fish, mixed with the smells emanating from the numerous taverns that lined the area. With the weather so warm numerous merchants had opened the doors of their establishments.

Everyone seemed to be enjoying the festive atmosphere always apparent on market day. Slaves, dressed in their finest clothes, shopped for their masters side by side with people of all ethnic and social classes. As always the marketplace offered a small sense of freedom for them, an opportunity to meet friends, share conversation, and find out the latest rumor. Not far from the market another type of business was about to begin, one that was the subject of conversation among the free Blacks and slaves mingling along the waterfront.

Several blocks away a large crowd had been gathering for some time behind the courthouse. At least six of the city's slave traders had positioned themselves close to the auction block in the courtyard. Most of them, smoking cigars and gesturing emphatically among themselves as though doing so would make their point ever more clear, mixed their posturing with occasional fits of laughter. Soon, however, the mood became decidedly somber and the pontificating, so often accompanying such events, ceased.

It was 10 a.m. and there was a sense amongst those gathered that the auction was about to begin. Before long a woman and her four little children were led out of the courthouse and up the steps to the block. The woman was decidedly beautiful, or at least would have seemed so in any other arena but this. She pushed back a lock of hair from her face with one hand, and laid the other upon the shoulder of her eldest, a child of seven. As the auctioneer began to perform his duty the bidding for the five human beings became feverish. With each rise of the auctioneer's hand the excitement of those present increased in intensity. The air grew stagnant with the odor of plumes of cigar smoke that now hung like clouds near the block. The woman, now holding her youngest child to her breast, began to cry. Within minutes all of the family *had been sold. The mother, her heart now broken, wept openly as they were led away.[1]*

uctions of slaves were held in many cities throughout the South. Although the extent and number of auctions of slaves in Baltimore never reached the level that it had in New Orleans there were clear similarities in their function. Specifics of the auction process were covered extensively in magazine and newspaper accounts of the day. A number of historians have examined the intricacies of the events leading up to the sale itself. The entire process appeared almost ritualistic to the careful observer.

Most auctions were held in the morning hours, sometime between 9 A.M. and noon. Before the auction took place, those individuals who would become potential buyers were allowed to look at the *"stock."* There were several phases to the process, each holding importance for the slave and potential buyer.

The questioning period allowed the individual bidders to seek information directly from the slave. In this manner they were able to filter out fiction that often accompanied the sellers reasoning for sale. Questions of age, family history, special abilities, health, and reason for being sold were often asked.

The examination period could be extensive and often humiliating. The men were often stripped, squeezed for muscularity, checked for hernias, and searched for marks of whipping or beating. Such marks were associated with trouble making and would often keep the price of the individual down. Their heads were pushed back and teeth examined to determine the condition of their gums.

Women and children were also subject to close scrutiny before the sale. Women could, at the request of a potential buyer, be viewed naked from the waist up and were sometimes subjected to squeezing and pinching of personal areas on the pretence of seeking muscular firmness and ability.

Upon request a female could be examined below the waist in order to determine if a hernia or venereal disease was present. An attending physician generally performed this type of exam in a private room or behind a curtained stall.[2]

In his excellent study on the slave market in New Orleans Walter Johnson described the examination process his research revealed as "reading bodies."

"Buyers ran their hands over the bodies of slaves, rubbing their muscles, fingering their joints, and kneading their flesh...The buyers were searching for taut muscles and hidden problems-broken bones, ossified sprains, severed tendons, internal injuries and illnesses." [3]

During a tour of the South Charles R. Weld, an English barrister, observed auctions and wrote:

"Personal examination (of women) was confined to the hands, arms, legs, bust and teeth. Searching questions were put respecting their age and whether they had children. If they replied in the negative, their bosoms were generally handled in a repulsive and disgusting manner." [4]

In early March 1853 a traveler passing through Richmond, Virginia stopped long enough to view several auctions that were occurring at the time. Distressed by what he witnessed he wrote a letter to a friend at the offices of the New York Tribune, which is reprinted here, in part.

"The slave depots are in one of the most frequented streets of the place, and the sales are conducted in the building on the first floor, and within view of the passers-by. There are small screens behind which the women of mature years are taken for

*inspection; but the men and the boys are publicly examined in
the open store, before an audience of full one hundred each
scar or mark is dwelt upon with great minuteness-its cause, its
age, its general effect upon the health, etc, are questions asked
and readily answered. I saw full twenty men stripped this
morning and not three or four of them had clean backs. One
was so cut (by the whip) that I am sure you could not lay your
finger on any part of his back without coming in contact with
a scar. These marks damaged his sale. although only about 45
to 50 years old he only brought $450".* [5]

Such tactics would be used at auctions in Baltimore as
well. During the summer of 1822 Nicholas Strike sold two
small children at auction, by order of the Orphans' Court. The
sale was scheduled to take place in front of Garland Burnett's
Tavern, near the head of Center Market. Before the sale *"all
who were interested could inspect the children."* The
advertisements alerting the public to this event claimed that
the children's characters were *"unexceptional."* At 10 o'clock
in the morning the twelve-year old boy and eight-year old girl
were sold to the highest bidder. [6]

Auctions like those aforementioned were periodically held
in Baltimore at the trader's pens, in the businesses of local
auctioneers, on the steps of the penitentiary or courthouse, or
in front of the local taverns and inns. Trader's agents kept their
eyes and ears open for news of impending sales.

Auctioneer Thomas Chase advertised one of his regular 10
o'clock sales in the Vendue warehouse on the corner of
Second and Frederick Streets. After the summer of 1813
several auctions were planned for the shoppers and merchants
who would be making their way into the city in order to find a
bargain. The first auction, which was scheduled to begin at 10
o'clock, offered a variety of dry goods, which were to be *"sold
for cash without reserve."* [7]

Prior to the second auction, which was to begin at noon, the auctioneer offered a special sale. At 11:30 a sixteen-year-old female slave was brought to the block and offered to the highest bidder for a term of years. The auctioneer claimed that she was *"used to housework."* Shortly after the gavel fell the third auction began, offering barrels of sugar, coffee, cocoa, cognac brandy, Holland Gin and a few bales of cotton.[8]

Several weeks later one of Chase's major competitors, John Wood, held a similar auction at the Exchange auction rooms on the corner of Commerce and Water Streets. The first sale at 11:30, offered beds, bedding, mattresses, chairs, dining tables and looking glasses. Immediately following the first sale, at noon, a *"very valuable Negro woman, a slave for life."* was sold to the highest bidder.[9]

Two days later Wood handled an estate auction at the intersection of Great York and Caroline Streets. Once again desks, tables, china, chairs, bedsteads, blankets, clocks and beds were offered at the onset of the sale. The furniture sale was followed by an auction of a *"Negro boy, a slave for life."* Wood encouraged buyers to consider that the slave was.*" brought up chiefly to the care of horses and working in an extensive garden."* [10]

During the second week of October Wood offered a variety of household furniture, which included beds, mattresses, bookcases, tables, and chairs. Immediately following the auction of furniture he sold a *"young Negro woman"* to the highest bidder. *"She is desirous of being sold to a good family in or near the city"* he exclaimed. *"She comes highly recommended, both for her good disposition and qualification as a house servant."* [11]

Keeping a feverish pace of sales, only three days had passed when Wood offered at private auction *"a Negro girl, accustomed to housework, a slave for life."*[12] The following month he again offered another woman *" a female servant who can be highly recommended."* [13]

During the last week of November Wood's auction house had received damaged flannels for auction. On the third of December, at 11:00 a.m. promptly, the flannels were sold to the highest bidder after which a *"Negro man, 35 years of age"* was auctioned. *"He is from the country"* Wood declared ... *"accustomed to farming and a slave for life."* [14]

Yet another Orphans' Court sale was directed to Wood's establishment when, two weeks later, he offered *"two valuable Negro girls and sundry articles of household furniture"* for auction. [15]

Continuing the brisk business that often accompanied the Christmas season Wood sponsored a number of major auctions during the last week and a half of December. On the morning of 21 December he was offering several separate auctions, one that touted furniture and *"Negroes"* ordered sold by the Orphans' Court. The second auction would contain *"an additional quantity of furniture and a valuable Negro woman."* Although auctions continued throughout the week prior to Christmas, Wood insisted that there would be no auction on December 25th in order to honor *"the anniversary of the nativity."* [16]

The month of December had seen the auction of a number of human beings as well as dry goods and furnishings. To close out the year Wood offered one last opportunity for those who might have missed the Christmas week sales.

A Valuable Negro Girl for Sale by Auction

On Friday next, at the Old Exchange at 12 o'clock immediately after the sale of Dry Goods, will be sold a stout healthy Negro Wench, 17 years old, recently from the country. Any person wishing to possess a

*valuable servant will do well to embrace the
present opportunity.*[17]
John Wood, Auctioneer

The following holiday season many of Wood's
competitors offered cash for blood on the auction block. The
Yates and Harrison auction house located on O'Donnel's
Wharf, offered stiff competition for other merchants in the
area. (The wharf is the current site of the National Aquarium-
Mammal building complex at the foot of Frederick Street). On
1 December the establishment offered at auction, for a term of
three years, a *"Negro woman, about 30 years old."* Yates and
Harrison insisted in the ad that she had been *"used to ironing,
washing, and cooking."* [18]

Auctioneers William Vance and Co. held a huge sale
during the first week of December that offered sugar, coffee,
Tenerife wine, rice, molasses, salt, gunpowder, flour, red
wood, Port wine, flints and Cassia buds. Also up for bidding
was the seven-year term of a *"Negro woman."* The
auctioneers claimed her owner was offering her because she
was *"removing from this country."* [19]

Auctioneers in Baltimore realized the importance of
promoting the fact that slaves had been reared on Maryland's
Eastern Shore. The hardy farm work experience that many
slaves on the shore had endured made them prime candidates
for sale.

Two days after the aforementioned Vance auction Thomas
Chase sold, from his store on the corner of Second and
Frederick Streets, molasses, coffee, teas, upland cotton, rice,
salt, and Spanish cigars. Prior to the sale of the groceries
Chase offered a young boy at auction. Note how many
attributes he credits the boy with having.

*"Previously to the sale of groceries
will be sold a very valuable Mulatto boy,
slave, extremely hale and well grown, recently
turned 14 years of age, and is manumitted to
be free at 35. He has just arrived from the
eastern Shore-said to remarkably docile and
free from vice, and for a boy of his age well
acquainted with the farming business, to
which he has been soley accustomed."*
Thomas Chase, Auct. [20]

Four weeks later Chase preceded another sale of a variety of groceries with the auction of a young boy. Once again we can clearly see Chase's style, which was to compact into a relatively small ad the many good qualities of the boy.

*"Previous to the sale of the groceries
at 12 o'clock, will be sold a valuable well
grown Black boy, between 12 and 13 years of
age, to serve until 35 years. He is a smart
active lad, of excellent disposition, and
brought up exclusively to waiting."*
Thomas Chase, Auct. [21]

John Wood, O. II. Neilson, and Samuel Cole repeatedly auctioned everything from groceries, furniture, and humans into the early months of 1816. In January Neilson, who held his regular auctions on Tuesdays at his rooms on 71 Water Street, offered dry goods, furniture, time pieces, and a *"Mulatto boy, about 18 years old."* This young man would have brought a good price. Not only was he proclaimed to be *"stout, active, and healthy"* he had been *"taught the trade of a shoemaker."* [22]

Three weeks later John Wood offered at auction, by order of the Orphans' Court, articles of household furniture and *"a very handsome bright mulatto boy, who can be highly recommended.* " [23]

The following month Samuel Cole auctioned a large copper boiler and two slaves. The first was advertised as *"a Negro girl, 20 years of age, recently from the country."* The second was *"a Negro boy, 13 years of age, to serve 13 years from 1st of September last."* Both slaves were sold on condition that the purchasers offer security that neither would be sold *"to be removed out of the state of Maryland."* [24]

During the autumn of 1816 auctioneer W. Simpson was operating from the Exchange auction rooms where he was offering tables, chairs, mirrors, clocks, glasses and at private auction *"a female house servant and her 2 male children, slaves for life."* [25]

Whenever trades could be mentioned as a talent of a slave the price steadily rose during the sale. One much sought after trade already largely performed by Blacks in Baltimore, slave and free, was caulking. Considering that some of the best shipbuilders in the eastern seaboard were located in Baltimore it is not hard to imagine that the following ad brought a great response in the weeks before Christmas. The auction room of Charles R. Green was offering a *"stout likely Negro Man, 20 years old"* that had been *"latterly employed as a caulker, for which he is a good hand."* [26]

During the same month Green auctioned off a *"Negro Woman, 25 years of age, a slave for life...a good house servant and well recommended."* The sale was scheduled to take place at the Horse Market where one could also bid on *"a number of very fine horses."* [27]

Business continued to be brisk for Green as the New Year began. Once again Green was about to offer a slave with two talents very much in demand. On the morning of January 24, 1817 at 11 o'clock, a *"Negro man, 30 years old, a slave for life"* was auctioned. He was touted as an *"excellent farmer and a good rough carpenter."* [28]

Green was also willing to sell a slave directly when it fit his needs. In the summer of 1816 he had become angry with his nineteen-year old slave for his *"bad conduct while driving my carriage."* His punishment was to be sold to another owner. Although Green had expressed his anger in the advertisement he loaded the young man down with praise *"He has been brought up on a farm, and latterly employed as a coachman and Ostler - he is an excellent hand in the stable, and is perfectly sober and honest."* [29]

In 1818 Samuel & John Cole, Auctioneers, advertised the sale of a twenty-three year old woman and her three-year old son. *"If not previously disposed of by private sale, they will be sold at auction on Thursday, the 9th instant, at our auction room, at 11 o'clock."* [30]

Cole, a resident of Milk Lane in Fells Point would also occasionally offer a slave by direct sale. During the summer of 1816 he offered *"Negro Charles for Sale."* Charles, a slave for life, was advertised at a price of $600 in Cole's own words *"To save trouble."* [31]

Marsh Market Center, also known as Center Market, was not the only marketplace in Baltimore where slaves were auctioned. Several weeks before Christmas, 1818 auctioneer Nicholas Strike was hired by the administrator of Elizabeth Fry's estate to sell her slaves. The chosen location for the auction was the market house in Fells Point. Broadway, also known as Market Street was the heart of the Point. The heavy foot traffic made the location perfect for the public sale. At three o'clock in the afternoon, on the ninth of December the fate of Elizabeth's two female slaves was sealed as the auctioneer's gavel fell. [32]

The pace of auctions remained high for a number of years. During January of 1823 Nathaniel Hynson, keeper of the Maryland Penitentiary, offered Ned Linn for public auction on the steps of the institution. Linn, advertised as a manumitted slave, was sold for five years, six months, and twenty-three days.[33]

The next year Hynson advertised the impending auction of Charles Bowen, a slave for life, at the institution. The sale was to occur on Saturday, January 10, 1824 at 10 o'clock.[34]

In April of 1824 the death of Elizabeth Elliott brought about a course of action by her executor. In light of the fact that the woman had died intestate the executor of her estate, George T. Dunbar, advertised an Orphans' Court sale of Elizabeth's property. Handling the auction of the deceased woman's belongings was Harrison Dawes of Green Street. Everything in Ms. Elliott's house on the southwest corner of Howard Street and cider alley was to be auctioned; *"furniture, rugs, kitchen utensils, one 40 year old female slave and a twenty year old female slave and her child."* [35]

During the late spring of the same year James Horton, commission agent and auctioneer with offices on Commerce Street opposite the Exchange offered *"Three likely young Negro girls who understand housework."* [36]

On numerous occasions the auctioneer was asked by the Orphans' Court to handle the auction on site at the estate to be sold. During the late summer of 1824 auctioneer Elisha Randall placed the possessions of Elizabeth Smith on the block from her house at 20 High Street. All of the household and kitchen furniture was offered as well as *"A Negro Woman to serve 9 years, a Negro girl, 4 years old, to serve 21 years and a Negro Boy, 9 years old, to serve 15 years."* They were available on *"credit for one third cash, with a balance on a credit of six months."* [37]

Another on site auction handled by Elisha Randall transpired during the summer of 1825 in Fells Point, at the corner of Ann and Lancaster Streets. The personal estate of Davis McCaughan, administered by Daniel McCaughan, was auctioned at 10 A.M. on Friday, July 22. Among the items auctioned by Randall were beds, bedsteads, tables, chairs, carpets, crockery, iron, and one *"Negro female slave."* The ad concluded *"Terms of sale cash."* [38]

Auction scenes were commonplace in Baltimore throughout the first half of the nineteenth century. The air around taverns, Court Houses, trader's pens, and auction houses was often filled with the smell of liquor, burning cigars, the vulgarities of bidders and the sobs of sorrowing victims.

There was another method of slave transfer that proved to be more extensive than auctions and more extensive than historians have ever considered. Brokerage houses, also known as Intelligence Offices or Agencies proved to be functionally important in the transfer of human beings in Baltimore's slave market.

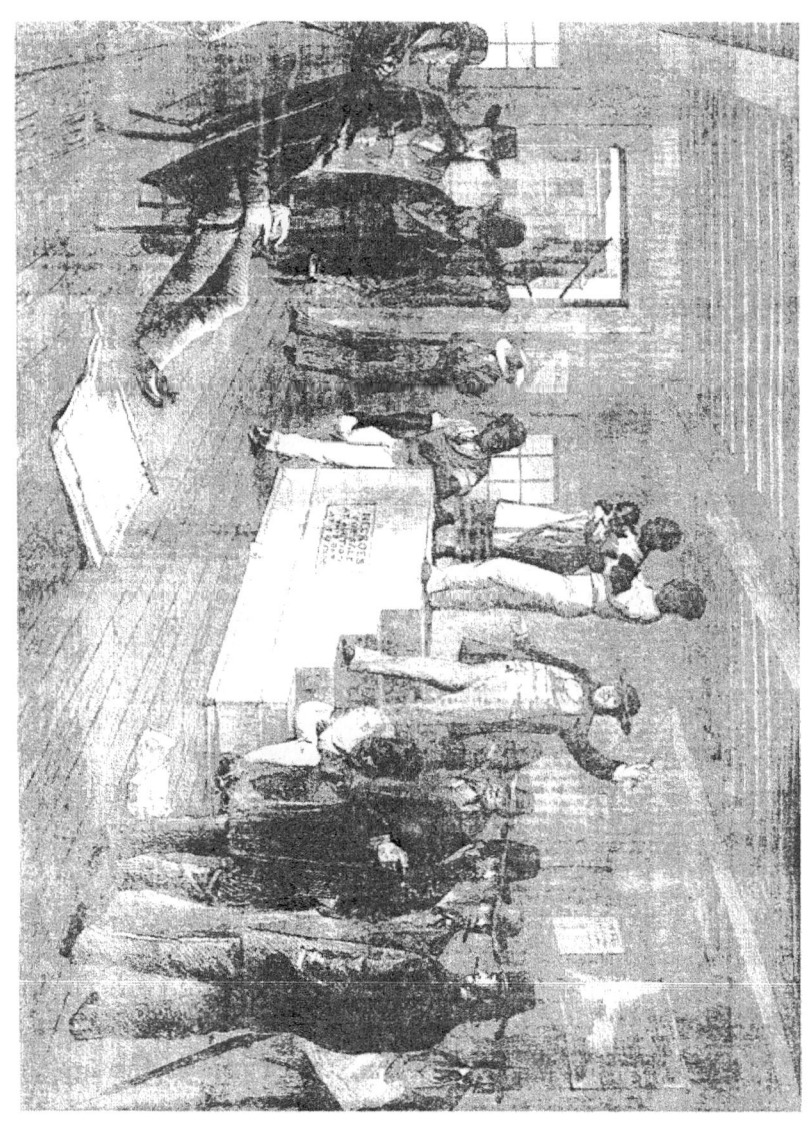

The Auction

Reading Bodies

Chapter 2
Agencies and Intelligence Offices

A nother popular method for the transfer of slaves in Baltimore was through intelligence offices or agencies. These agencies operated in a similar fashion to contemporary employment agencies. They acted as the "middlemen" or brokers in employer-employee relationships. Their reward for services rendered was a finder's fee, generally paid by the job recipient and the employer.

An additional service provided by these agencies was to act as brokers for perspective slave sellers. Numerous individuals in the market for selling slaves refused to be bothered with the particulars and were willing to pay a fee to have an agency handle the advertisement and sale of their slaves. Additionally agencies offered to provide slaves for hire, acting as middlemen for the hirer and the slaveholder.

One of the numerous intelligence offices was located at the southwest corner of Gay and Market Streets in the early 1820s. During the summer of 1821 the General Intelligence Office ran the following advertisement.

A Negro Woman for Sale

*Has four years to serve, a first rate
woman in every branch appertaining to*

*housework. A Negro boy about 17 years of
age, for life, a first rate waiter. Men, women
and children of various ages for sale, not to be
taken out of the state. Slaveholders who wish a
good interest for their domestics can hire them
out at excellent wages, as at this moment the
demand is so great for hirelings.*

     *Wanted, two colored boys to wait on
table: two Negro women for cooks: Two
Negro men for farming. A most excellent wet
nurse on hand. Apply at the General
Intelligence, southwest corner of Gay and
Market Streets.*[1]

Another typical add placed by the same office (also known
as the Register Office) advertised

    *"A number of valuable slaves of both sexes for sale-among
them cooks, chambermaids, hostlers, carriage drivers, etc."*

The advertisement continued by noting *"The expense is
very trifling to obtain all the information required."*[2]

Other examples of the extensive sale of humans by this
particular office during a nine-week period include:

    *"A girl 30 years of age; a boy 10 years of age; a girl 26
years of age; a boy 12 years of age (for sale or will be
exchanged for a middle aged woman of good character)."*[3]

    *"A Negro woman, about 40 years of age; a man slave, 23
years of age (a first rate farmer, and is considered a good
boatman and pilot in the bay)."*[4]

"A first rate Negro man for sale, 26 years of age. Also slaves bought and sold for this state only." [5]

"A Negro girl (about 18) for sale; for hire a woman, slave, about 40 years old; also (another) Negro girl about 18 years of age for sale...fond of children." [6]

"A Negro girl for sale, about 18 years of age, with a fine child 2 years old. This girl would make an excellent farm servant.
N.B. A number of servants of all ages and sexes for sale." [7]

"Valuable slaves for sale man 36 years of age; boy 13 years of age; woman 25 years of age; woman 50 years of age; woman 40 years of age (wants merely a proper master)." [8]

By August of 1825 the Maryland Intelligence Office had become so busy that they opened a second office on Gay Street, opposite Frederick Street. In their first ad after expansion proprietor Edward M. Greene sought to sell *"A servant, 20 years of age, who is an excellent waiter."* [9]

In September Greene offered a fourteen year old female to serve *"till she is 24 years old."* [10]

Ten days later he advertised a *"Negro boy"* twenty years old and a woman, twenty-seven years of age. [11]

Some of the ads reflected the willingness on the part of the original owners of slaves to exchange when sale might not be preferred. In September of 1826 the Maryland Intelligence Office offered, *" A Black boy (who) will be sold for a term of years, or exchanged for a Black girl, capable of attending to children."* [12]

Register Offices and other intelligence agencies were extensive. One of the most prolific dealers in human flesh through such agencies was Lewis F. Scott, who operated his business over a three-decade period at several locations in the city. In the early 1830's his agency was located at No. 2 west Lombard St. (in the basement of Barnum's City Hotel) where, in 1833 he advertised a *"very likely Negro man 32 years of age."* [13]

The following decade his agency, now known as "Scott's General Slave Agency and Intelligence Office" was located at 10 Exchange Place. [14]

By the early 1850s he had moved once again, now located at 18 East Lombard St. over the bridge opposite Clagett's Brewery. [15]

The lengths to which Scott would go to provide services for a profit were incredible. Not only was his business known as a *"Slave Agency"* but he copied deeds, wills, leases, collected accounts, wrote letters of agreements, created insolvent papers, gave business advice, rented and sold houses, and procured employment. [16]

Because the temptation for profit was great on all sides many dealers in the slave trade hierarchy found themselves mired in litigation as defendants or claimants. Scott became embroiled in an interesting case during the spring of 1844, which showed the great lengths that the courts might go to in order that justice was exacted.

A young boy by the name of John Harris complained to Justice Pennington that his own stepfather (Jacob P. Hynson) had attempted to kidnap him to the southern states. When the facts in the complicated case became clear it seems that the boy's mother and stepfather had applied to Lewis F. Scott for assistance in binding their son out to some employer.

Young Harris, apparently unwilling to participate in his parents' plan, was arrested at the insistence of his mother and stepfather and temporarily placed in the slave pen of Bernard Campbell (on Conway). Samuel Oaks, a *"Negro Dealer"* whose offices had been located over the Scott agency claimed he had found a farmer in the country to whom he had been able to indenture the boy.

Justice Cloud and King, who agreed to Harris's release from the pen had in fact, been deceived by Oaks. John Harris was placed on board a vessel called the *European*, bound for Charleston with a number of slaves. When the Customs Officer checked the ship's manifest he learned that a number of the slaves were convicts from the Baltimore jail, and refused clearance for Charleston. At this point Harris was taken back to Scott's agency where he was placed under lock and key in the room in the back of the business, which was reserved for slaves to be sold or hired.

In a bizarre twist of events the boy escaped. A man in the process of delivering a stove had unlocked the door. It was then that Harris lodged a formal complaint against his stepfather, believing him to be involved in the entire affair. When the complaint was examined there was no compelling evidence to warrant the arrest of Hynson and the case was dismissed.[17]

Another popular agency during the early 1840s was the City Agency, on Baltimore and Frederick Streets, managed in 1842 by A. R. Day. His advertisements reflected, as Scott's did, the great variety of services that would be provided for a nominal fee.

*Wanted-At the City Agency Office,
corner of Baltimore and Frederick Streets;
Overseers, Farmers, Clerks, Porters, Waiters,
coachmen, draymen, a man who has a wife,
apprentice boys, cooks, chambermaids,
nurses. For Sale-A colored boy 17 years old,
for a term of years; and several slaves for life;
Champagne wines, raisins, soap, Gold and
silver watches, farms, houses, and several
lots. For Rent-A farm of 130 acres, 20 miles
from Baltimore, also, one 10 miles out on the*

York road. Cash To Loan Out, in sums to suit
the wants of the applicants.

A.R.Day [18]

In a show of humanitarianism Henry H. Wood, a former grocer who now operated the Real Estate and Intelligence Office on Light Street, offered his services to receive donations for the poor. He also opened his office as a place to bring lost children where parents would be received and *"restored to their children free of any expense."* [19]

Mr. Wood's ability to afford such efforts came, in part, as a result of the sufferings of others. Among the items he brokered for profit were farms, houses, bank stocks and the sales of human beings. A month before his generous offer to aid the poor he had sought to buy good servants *"for sale for life."* [20] A week later he offered to sell a twenty-three year old woman and her two and seven year old children *"separately or together as may best suit the purchaser."* [21]

Although the operations of interstate slave traders had a substantial impact on families and local economies the business generated by slave agencies in the city of Baltimore has never been explored. Careful scrutiny of the agencies' advertisements indicates that, in total, a significant number of human beings were sold intrastate (as well as some with the intentions of being carried beyond the boundaries of Maryland).

Scott, for example, from his offices in the basement of Barnum's City Hotel advertised for a large number of slaves during the second half of January 1841.

Wanted to Purchase Immediately
20-30 Good house servants of good character, of both
sexes, from 13 to 22 years of age, slaves for life, for a very
extensive hotel in the city of New Orleans, there they will be
well treated...They are expressly for the gentleman's own use,

and not for speculation, and a fair cash price will be given on application to Lewis F. Scott's General Slave Agency and Intelligence office, old establishment No.2 West Fayette Street, basement of the City Hotel. [22]

Scott had no aversion to selling and buying young children and separating them from their families. On the same day that he advertised for the servants needed in New Orleans he sought to buy *"a young girl, 12 to 15 years of age, a slave for life, for a gentleman." She will have a good home"* he promised and *"will be well treated."* The advertisement made it clear that the family of the gentleman was about to leave for Virginia and that *"a fair cash price will be given."* [23]

On the same day Scott advertised for sale a sixteen year old servant boy, *14 years to serve "very smart and active, and a good waiter"* [24] and a *"A Black girl, 15 years of age...well grown, and a house servant."* [25]

A visitor arriving on board a vessel in Baltimore's Inner Harbor might have witnessed another form of sale, not quite as extensive as auctions or agencies. Vessels arriving from Maryland's Eastern Shore occasionally carried slaves, purchased by the captain on speculation, in the hope of making a profit through sale when the vessel docked in Baltimore.

Chapter 3
Dockside Sales

During the antebellum decade a strange sight could occasionally be witnessed near the docks in Baltimore's Inner Harbor basin, a free black man marching slaves along Pratt Street. The slaves, purchased from vessels moored in the basin, would be led through a tunnel at the Light Street Wharf to a pen located several blocks west of the harbor. The trader for whom the man worked would then auction the slaves or jail them until a manifest was filled.[1]

Sales of slaves from dockside were not uncommon events during the first half of the nineteenth century. Captains or owners of packet ships making their run from the "slave rich" eastern shore of Maryland would often purchase slaves and sell them at the docks in Baltimore to make an extra profit.

Just before Christmas, 1815 you could *"if applied for immediately"* purchase a *"valuable Negro man"* at Bowly's Wharf. He was touted in advertisements as a good seaman and vessel steward and was being sold *"Only to gratify his wish of going by water."* [2]

In late February 1816 the **Easton Packet** docked on the lower end of the County Wharf. A *"Black man about 19 years of age"* was being offered for sale on board the vessel. The advertiser noted, *"He will not be sold to go out of state."* [3]

The following week Captain Vickars, docking another of the Easton packets at the county wharf offered a woman and her two children for sale. The woman, described by Vickars as *"likely"* was to be sold along with her two young sons. Vickars, hoping to attract a larger number of potential buyers added, *"She is a good washer, ironer and plain cook."* On the same vessel the captain offered a male who he proclaimed *"a first rate hewer and sawyer."* All four slaves could be viewed by coming on board the **Easton Packet**.[4]

Ten days later the **Queenstown Packet** arrived in port with a number of slaves for sale. A woman, touted as a *"first rate cook"*, was offered for sale along with a child, seven years of age. Also on board and for sale was the woman's husband (the child's father). Three more human beings were offered on the same vessel; a woman who was advertised as a *"good house servant"* was for sale along with her two children, one seven years of age and the other eighteen months. Particulars could be obtained on board the vessel or by inquiring at *"Mr. Beal's hotel."* [5]

Nine days before Christmas of the same year a *"stout, healthy Negro boy, about 21 years of age"* could be obtained by applying to Captain Lemeul Legg at Cheapside. (The Cheapside Hotel was also known as Sinner's Hotel). [6]

Several days later, a *"likely young Negro man, about 18 years old"* could be seen on board the schooner **Sally and Betsey** at the Light Street Wharf. Interested applicants were asked to see Captain Jarboe at the vessel.[7]

Occasionally advertisements went to great lengths to answer all of the questions that were generally asked of the slave during the questioning and body reading period before purchase. In the following ad the captain addressed the health, length of service, and special work qualifications of the slave. He completed the ad by informing the potential buyer of the reason why the owner found himself forced to sell.

> *A Valuable Servant For Sale*
> *A very handsome healthy mulatto Boy,*
> *of general good character, nineteen years of*
> *age, and has seventeen years to serve. He has*
> *been accustomed to farm work and the*
> *management of horses-he would make an*
> *excellent coachman or waiter. He is the*
> *property of an insolvent debtor, and must be*
> *sold. Enquire on board of the Easton Packet,*
> *at Bowly's Wharf.* [8]

During the summer of 1823 the **Chestertown Packet**, anchored at the Commerce Street Dock had two slaves on board that *"anyone willing could apply to purchase."* According to the owner one of the slaves, thirty years of age, was *"accustomed to farming and taking care of horses."* The other, a nineteen year old was *"brought up to farming."* Both were slaves for life.[9]

Upon arriving at the Commerce Street Wharf in the summer of 1825, the **Chestertown Packet** had on board a twenty year old male slave for sale who was advertised as *"healthy and strong, and has been accustomed to farm work."* [10]

Captain Henry Legg's packet from Kent Island, docked at Bowly's Wharf in mid September of 1826 with *"two likely Negro boys, slaves for life, one aged 14 years, the other 12."* Their purchase was conditional... they could not be sold by the new owners to *"go out of state."* [11]

When the **Easton Packet** arrived in Baltimore during the late summer of 1828 the vessel was pulled into the Frederick Street Dock. On board, and for sale to a good master was a *"likely young Negro man to be sold low if immediate* *application be made to Captain Auld.*" He had thirteen years to serve and was said to be "*active and healthy.*" [12]

The following month Captain Auld offered a sixteen year old girl for sale for a term of ten years. She was to be sold "*for no fault.*" Anyone interested in seeing her could apply to the captain on board the **Easton Packet** once again lying at the Frederick Street Dock.[13]

A week later Samuel Kennard on Patterson's Wharf, Fells Point, had a twenty-one year old male slave for sale "*lately from the Eastern shore.*" The slave, according to Kennard, had "*five years and six months to serve.*" [14]

Several days before Christmas, Edward Lloyd offered to sell a twenty year old man, a slave for life. He could be seen on board the **Easton Packet** at the Frederick Street Dock. "*He is accustomed to farming*" Lloyd continued "*smart, active, and healthy.*" In a continuation of the ad Lloyd also offered "*prime Eastern Shore corn fed pork.*" [15]

During the late summer of the following year John Carter had for sale, on board the schooner **Araminta Elizabeth**, lying at Bowly's Wharf a "*Negro Boy, about 14 years of age.... to be sold without reserve.*" [16]

Although the prior listed ads are just a small sampling of the extensive dockside sales that could be seen throughout the period there were also ads that indicated that the slaves had been off loaded and transported to a hotel or inn a short distance from the docks. Some captains preferred to keep their chattel close by when they took a room in town. Many such advertisements reflected this form of transportation and sale.

For Sale-Three Smart Negroes

*Lately from the Eastern Shore, one girl
and two boys; one of the boys for a term of
years, the other two for life. They are not to be
sold out of state. Apply at the Sinner's Hotel
in Water Street.* [17]

Negroes for Sale

*For life one likely Negro man aged 35 years,
two likely house women aged 28 years, two
likely Boys and one boy for a term of years,
(Not to be taken out of state) arrived this day
from the Eastern Shore. Inquire in Water
Street, at the Sinner's Hotel.* [18]

Hotels and Inns provided an important function for the local and coastwise trader. They became the regular meeting places for the purchase and sale of slave labor throughout the South.

Chapter 4
Hotels, Taverns, and Inns

As the need for slave labor in Maryland decreased the resultant slave market that developed depended on an intricate network of agents, brokers, and contacts. As slaveholders and traders descended on Baltimore to consummate deals, hotels and inns provided important means of rendezvous.

Hotels, taverns, and inns were used as contact points for the purchase and sale of slaves. Planters, in town on business, as well as speculators and traveling traders used the establishments effectively to consummate their deals. As a result a system of agents and brokers developed throughout the city, individuals who were paid commissions by the traders.

Bartenders were often used as agents. Their exposure to numerous travelers extending their stay in the city at the local inns placed them in an ideal position to act as go-betweens. A number of ads often reflected the seller or buyer's desire to have information left *"at the bar."*

The use of taverns and inns as the meeting places for the slave trade was evidenced through a number of advertisements in local newspapers. Many hotels in the South provided rooms where slaves could be locked up between sales.[1]

Sales could draw a great deal of attention. An example of such a sale occurred in February of 1855 when fugitive slave

Anthony Burns (incorrectly reported as Arthur Burns), was sold at Barnum's Hotel:

Arthur Burns, the fugitive slave whose trial excited so much attention in Massachusetts about six months ago, was yesterday in this city, and took the cars last evening for Philadelphia, with the intention of proceeding North as far as Massachusetts. It appears that his master did not wish to part with him, but finally agreed to do so, whereupon he was purchased by Mr. McDaniel for $900. The gentleman yesterday reached here, and effected a sale of Burns to Rev. Lloyd A. Grimes, of Massachusetts, for the sum of $1,325. The transaction took place at Barnum's Hotel, and was evidenced by Colonel Houston, one of the clerks. Burns excited considerable attention during the few hours he was here. Upon his arrival North a grand demonstration will be made. [2]

Evidence of sales from and to residents of local hotels is abundant in much earlier records of Baltimore's major newspapers.

An unnamed trader advertised, during the autumn of 1815, to pay cash for *"25 or 30 likely Negroes."* The subscriber was asked to apply at Mr. Lilly's Tavern, Howard Street. [3]

On the same day another unnamed dealer required *"10 or 12 healthy young Negroes of both sexes"* with instructions to apply at Fowler's Tavern near the New Market, Lexington Street. [4]

Several weeks later John Freeman, taking up residence at John H. Barney's Fountain Inn on Light Street, asked for *"a few young Negroes between the ages of 8 and 20 years."* [5]

In January of 1816 Thomas Ragland, naming his contact as available at the Sinner's Tavern (head of Cheapside), offered cash for fifteen or twenty *"likely, young Negroes."* [6]

In the spring of the same year Jon Davis offered the highest prices for fifteen or twenty *"likely young Negroes."* while residing at Mrs. Kirk's, the Sign of the Three Kegs.[7]

In early 1817 Caleb Eubank, of Columbia County Georgia offered *"cash for Negroes"* at William Fowler's, near the Circus in the Old Town sector.[8]

In July of 1817 Robert B. Wilson offered *"cash for Negroes"* from John Cugle's, sign of General Wayne, head of Market Street. He sought a few *"likely young Negroes"* from ten to twenty years as well as two men between twenty and twenty-seven years of age *"provided they are not bad characters."* [9]

The summer of 1822 brought a request from David Cobbs on behalf of a *"gentleman from Kentucky"* for a few *"Negro boys of good character".* Mr. Cobbs noted that he could be found at the Columbian Hotel, North Howard Street near Market Street for *"12 or 15 days."* [10]

During January of 1824 Joseph Meek sought eight *"likely Negroes, if immediate application is made at the Sinners Hotel, near the exchange."* [11]

The same month John S. Hutcherson, of Caswell County, North Carolina was in town advertising for slaves from eight to twenty years of age and requesting that word is left at the *"bar of the Globe Hotel, opposite the exchange."* [12]

The next day Joseph Meek used the Globe Hotel, opposite the exchange, as his contact point when he asked for *"a few likely Negroes."* [13]

One week later J. A. Dollerhide was anxious to purchase a *"few likely Negroes"* if the seller would only apply at the bar of the Globe Hotel, opposite the exchange.[14]

Auctions sanctioned by local county courts were also held at taverns or inns, a congregating point for substantial numbers of potential buyers. On February 11, 1824 a trustee's sale was held at Knight's Tavern, on the York Turnpike Road. The terms were cash at sale or six months credit with interest and approved security. Available at auction through the estate trustee A. L. Cook were: *"one Negro Man, 1 Negro woman, 1 horse, 500 rails, 1 stack of hay, a quantity of fodder, fourteen barrels of corn, timothy seed, farming tools, paneled doors and Venetian shutters."* [15]

In September of 1824 Benjamin Chambers, homesick after weeks of advertising to buy slaves from Cugle's Tavern at the head of Market Street (Baltimore Street) offered

Cash For Negroes

> *Having nearly completed my purchase and being desirous to return to North Carolina I will give liberal prices for 12 or 15 young slaves of both sexes. Those wishing to sell would do themselves justice to call on the subscriber, at the head of Market Street ..Cugle's Tavern* [16]

In November of 1829 *"four handsome Negroes from the Eastern Shore of Maryland, among the number a girl accustomed to housework"* were offered for sale by applying at Mr. David Barnum's bar (The City Hotel) for terms. [17]

Several days later a woman and her two young children, brought up in St. Mary's County and *"sold for no fault"* were offered on the condition that they would *"not be sold to go out of the state."* [18]

By no means were the sales of slaves restricted to hotels in Baltimore. Throughout the state buyers and sellers could be located, on a regular basis, doing business at local inns and taverns.

Grabbing reader's attentions by mentioning the one commodity most major traders had to work with, an unnamed speculator offered.

Cash! Cash!

The highest prices in Cash will be given for a few likely young Negroes; Application to be made at the Western Inn, Hagerstown. [19]

During the spring of 1831 Henry Lowe sought to purchase fifty servants *"of both sexes, of the ages from 12 to 25"* from the Union Tavern in Frederick County. According to his advertisement they had to come with *"certificates suitable to introduce them into the state of Louisiana."* [20]

One week before Christmas 1834 William Hooper asked for *"one hundred Negroes"* and continued *"all communications will be promptly attended to if left at James Hunter's Hotel, Annapolis, at which place the subscriber can be found."* [21]

Long before his association with the infamous Baltimore trader Jonathan M. Wilson, G. H. Duke sought to purchase *"fifty servants, of both sexes, from the age of 12 to 25"* from Turnbutt's Hotel in Frederick, Maryland. [22]

During the mid 1840s A. C. Wheeler, an agent working for Bernard Campbell and Company advertised that he was willing to give the highest cash prices for *"Negroes of both sexes and all ages."* He asked for those persons having *"Negroes for sale"* to call on him at J. H. Burroughs Hotel, in Port Tobacco. [23]

Charles Willigman, a speculator operating out of Cambridge in the mid 1840s offered to purchase *"Negroes of*

Both sexes that are slaves for life." He could be found at all times at John Bradshaw's Hotel, in Cambridge.[24]

"In many cities of the South there was a pyramidal network of information gathering and slave selling that stretched from the slave pens through the city's hotels and barrooms a network in which every bartender was a potential broker and every broker tried to control every bartender." [25]

The General Wayne Inn, corner of Paca and Baltimore Streets. For many years the General Wayne Inn was among the numerous hotels and inns in Baltimore where slaves were purchased or sold by travelers.

Photo courtesy of the Maryland Historical Society, Baltimore Md.

Chapter 5
Children as Victims of the Trade

As the slave market and the domestic trade developed in Baltimore the practice of offering "cash for blood" not only impacted the slave family through separation but the free Black family as well.

Although it was quite common to see slave children sold separately from their families once they reached the age of six, free Black children in Baltimore were also suffering as the victims of kidnapping and sale.

The following ads are reflective of the types of sales of children that brought about separation from loved ones. A number of the ads will reveal how pressing the problem of kidnapped free children became as the hungry South continued to operate under an ever increasing need for slave labor as the nineteenth century unfolded.

Children were often the subject of shipment, sale and separation throughout the history of the domestic trade (and in the slave market in general) in Baltimore. In December of 1820 a local newspaper advertised for sale a *"Negro boy about 12 years of age, slave for life, being healthy and of good disposition."* [1]

During the late spring of 1824 *"two Negroes from the Eastern shore, a healthy strong boy, twelve years old, and a healthy likely Negro girl thirteen years old"* were for sale by

Patrick McNeil The ad indicated that the *"Negroes could be seen at 22 Chatham Street."* [2]

In October of 1827 a *"Black girl twelve years of age and very fond of children"* was to be sold but not outside the state of Maryland.[3]

In the spring of 1847 John Walter, of Second Street, was offering, *"an active, industrious colored servant boy, between thirteen and fourteen years of age who (he continued) understands the management of horses."* [4]

In January 1849 a woman and her ten year old female child were offered for sale as slaves for life. Also for sale was a thirteen year old mulatto boy (apparently not related to the woman), who had *"twelve years to serve."* The ad ended with further particulars *"he is just from the country, and every satisfaction can be given. Apply at the Sun office."* [5]

In March of 1852 John Cooper, 5 North High Street, offered for sale *"a Woman thirty-two years of age, with a male child one year old."* The same advertised a separate sale of two girls one *"twelve years of age, and one seven years of age, slaves for life."* [6]

One slaveholder couldn't decide on specifics before he placed his add in early March of 1824 *"for sale-Three or four young Negroes, slaves for life, from nine to fifteen years of age-Enquire at this office."* [7]

It was not uncommon for children to be hired. An owner residing at 556 West Lexington Street, in early 1859, offered *"four Negro Boys-slaves eighteen, sixteen, fourteen and seven years of age. Three of them good house servants, or suitable as drivers; one a good farm hand."* [8]

Several years earlier a resident of 61 East Baltimore Street had for hire *"a colored Boy, aged ten years, a place in the country preferred."* [9]

In March of 1855 a slaveholder at 18 Dover Street (near Pine) advertised, *"two Servant Girls For Hire-Aged ten and twelve years, accustomed to nursing children."* [10]

In cases where a sale might not be possible, trades were encouraged. In September of 1826 The Maryland Intelligence Office offered *"for sale or exchange- a Black Boy will be sold for a term of years, or exchanged for a Black girl, capable of attending to children."* [11]

In March of 1853 a resident of North High Street offered *"for Sale Or Exchange For A Girl, a Negro Boy, suitable for a servant. Both are smart, active and healthy."* [12]

Age was certainly no barrier to the slave trader when profits could be made. When the brig *Hyperion* left port in May of 1822 one of the forty-four slaves on board was four-day old George, belonging to Alex De Valcourt.[13]

When the Christmas Eve shipment of 1827 was loaded on board the Baltimore built ship *Jefferson* at Prices' New Wharf, two month old Margaret Boyd and Bob Couch as well as twenty day old Lindy Berry were on board.[14]

Two month old triplets Jackson Green, Jesse Green, and Rachel Green were on board the *Arctic* when it left Gibson's Wharf in January of 1829.[15]

During the fall of 1831 one month old Mary Butler and Henry Stafford were on board the 150-ton brig *Ann and Leah*, captained by Samuel Goldsmith.[16]

Two month old George Bennet and three month old Dennis Dutton were received on the brig *Orbit*, captained by Philip Riley, on April 13, 1825.[17]

Charles Butler, Emeline Chase, Alfred Chew, John Driver, Dennis Moore, George Ranking, Kitty Snowden, Nicholas Baker, John Johnson, William H. Matthews, Emeline Owens, James Smith, James Thomas, Judy Cooper, and Abram Mitchell were additional slaves shipped to the New Orleans market who held the dubious distinction of being between four days and three months of age. Of course children this young were, almost without exception, accompanied by their mothers.

Young children, specifically those between the ages of six and twelve, were often the targets of kidnappers in Baltimore. It was a great deal easier to kidnap a child from the streets of the city, falsify ownership papers, and sell the victim to a trader than it was to kidnap an adult (although those kidnappings succeeded on occasion).

Disappearances, particularly of Black children, were commonplace during the evolution of the slave trade in the city. During the summer of 1823 a small boy named Moses left his house on an errand and was never seen again. The editors of the *American and Commercial Daily Advertiser* who, ironically, did not hesitate to profit from the placement of ads selling young children, seemed to be moved by this particular case. A major ad, at the expense of the editors, ran during the third week of August of that year.

Lost Child
Supposed to have been kidnapped

On Thursday morning last, about 8
o'clock, a small colored boy named Moses,
left his home in the upper part of this city, on
an errand, and has not since been heard of; as
he is well acquainted with that part of the city,
there is but little doubt that he has been
kidnapped! he is about seven years of age,
very dark, quite active for his age-has a scar
under one of his eyes, (supposed the right) and
another on his knee, caused by a burn-he had
on a yellow nankeen jacket with short sleeves,
and coarse linen pantaloons with the letter
L.(manufacturer's mark) stamped on them.
Any information left at this office, respecting

*said boy, will be thankfully received by his
distresssed mother.*

*Editors throughout this and Southern
States will serve the cause of humanity by
giving the above a few insertions.* [18]

The following spring of 1824 Rachel Cooper, the mother of fifteen year old Perry Cooper asked the editors of the *American and Commercial Daily Advertiser* to run an add informing the public about the disappearance of her son. The add, placed without charge by the editors, began *"to the humane and benevolent"* Following a detailed description of the boy the editor continued

"Left his home on Sunday last and has not since been seen or heard of. As it is supposed he has been kidnapped, any person possessing any knowledge relative to the above youth, will benefit society in general, and relieve the feelings of an unfortunate mother and a distressed family by leaving information at this office." [19]

Three months later a seven year old *"colored boy by the name of Talbot Hayes"* was reported missing. He and his mother had come to Baltimore from the country to shop in Marsh Market and was believed to have strayed or been kidnapped. The following afternoon he had not yet been located when a reward was offered for his return.[20]

During the summer of 1828 the mayor's office was seeking information concerning the suspicious disappearance of Priscilla Blake, a fourteen year old free Black female whose parents resided near High Street, Old Town. Foul Play (kidnapping) was clearly on the minds of those placing the ad, which indicated, *"as she took no clothes but those she had on, it is feared that she has been carried off."* [21]

Henny, a six year old *"small colored girl"*, disappeared after being sent to the store to buy yeast in the summer of 1835. A reward was being offered by the subscriber, George S. Eichelberger, for her delivery to his residence in Pitt Street, near the Shot Tower.[22]

A fifteen year old *"free Black boy"* was reported missing during the spring of 1836. Samuel Childs, who had placed the advertisement on behalf of the young man's aunt, hinted at a suspicion of kidnapping when he stated *"His uniform good conduct leaves no doubt of his forcible detention somewhere."* [23]

Jane Harris, a ten year old, disappeared during the first week of January 1853 near her home on Saratoga Street opposite the Black Bear Tavern. She was described as having.... *"very large eyes and lips, a black josey, blue figure dress, black calico apron and dark gingham bonnet."* [24]

Slave manifests would occasionally note the fact that free persons of color were being shipped south to New Orleans. The schooner **Lapwing**, which sailed from Baltimore the last week of March 1822 had on board when arriving in New Orleans *"a black woman with free papers."* [25]

Slave trader David Anderson, while shipping twelve slaves on the 119-ton brig **Franklin**, from Craigg and Barron's Wharf during the autumn of 1819, included forty-five year old Hetty. The Customs Collector in New Orleans reported at the bottom of the **Franklin's** manifest *"I have seen the certificate of freedom in possession of the above named woman (Hetty)."* [26]

Although traders were known to accept and ship kidnapped Blacks there were occasions when they received a small taste of their own medicine. During the summer of 1847 George Schwartz and Edward Miller hired a free woman of color, Mary Whiting, from Chambersburg, Pennsylvania. After bringing her to Baltimore on the pretense of business they attempted to sell her as a slave to Hope Hull Slatter. When their ruse was discovered they were arrested and charged with attempting to defraud Slatter. Mary Whiting was released and sent back to Pennsylvania.[27]

Kidnapping was prevalent in the vicinity of Baltimore despite the fact that the crime carried stiff penalties if those guilty were discovered. During the autumn of 1821 Levin Anderson was sentenced to the penitentiary in Baltimore for five years for kidnapping *"Two free Negroes."* The report appearing in the *Genius of Universal Emancipation* indicated that it was not certain whether or not Anderson had *"sold them into bondage before he was apprehended."* [28]

This is Spear's Wharf, west side of the Gay Street Dock. A number
of vessels were used to carry slaves to New Orleans from Gay Street
as well as numerous other docks along Baltimore's harbor. Notice
the auction and commission merchants' houses that extended along
the docks in the Inner Harbor.

Photo courtesy of the Maryland Historical Society, Baltimore Md.

Chapter 6
Baltimore's Early Coastwise Domestic Slave Trade

Just before sunrise a procession of slaves reached the foot of Bowly's Wharf in Baltimore's inner harbor basin. It was the morning of the twenty-first of November 1821 and the manifest of the Good Hope was being prepared for departure for its journey to New Orleans.

Before long a Customs officer arrived and checked the manifest of slaves against the captain's report. After the vessel was cleared to sail, lines were tied between the sloop and a steamer moored at the foot of the dock. The tow of the vessel off Fells Point was completed in short order. Now the captain and crew awaited a favorable wind to begin their journey south.[1]

The voyage of the sloop *Good Hope* was one of the dozens of shipments that occurred in the early history of the domestic trade in Maryland.

Although individual manifests reflecting shipments of slaves from Baltimore prior to 1818 have not survived it is clear that the domestic trade had been active in the city since the end of the War of 1812. During the July 1816 term of the Grand Jury for Baltimore County a portion of the report, covered by the *American and Commercial Daily Advertiser* pointed to the evils of the domestic slave trade already existent in the city.

"There are, in this city, houses appropriated to this trade, as prisons for the reception of the Negroes intended to be carried to other states. Slaves are crowded together, male and female, in one common dungeon. They are loaded with irons, confined in their filth, and subjected to various species of cruelty and tyranny from their keepers." [2]

In the early years of the domestic slave trade Baltimore became an important shipping center for several of the more prolific traders. Between December 1818 and December 1822 David Anderson of Kentucky shipped 223 slaves to New Orleans from Baltimore. Anderson traveled throughout the Maryland and Virginia region, placing ads, purchasing slaves, and shipping them from a variety of ports.

One of the favored bases of operations for Anderson while in Baltimore was the New Bridge Hotel, in the Old Town district. In 1818 while staying at the hotel he advertised *"persons having Negroes of either sex to dispose of will meet with ready cash and liberal prices by applying at the New Bridge Hotel."* [3]

Anderson's prominent customer in the South was Hector McClean, a merchant residing in the city of New Orleans. In December of 1818 Anderson placed nine slaves on the brig **Temperance** consigned to McClean. Less than four months later he placed another nine slaves, this time on the ship **Superb**, bound for New Orleans and, once again, consigned to McClean. By December of 1822 Anderson had made a number of separate shipments from Baltimore to New Orleans, exclusively for Hector McClean and Co.

Gideon T. King, a resident of Baltimore Street, west of Hammond's Alley, also shipped consignments of slaves to

New Orleans merchants. In November of 1821 King placed nineteen slaves on the Baltimore brig *Budget*, consigned to William T. Gorham, a merchant in New Orleans (as well as five additional slaves for David Anderson).

Traders like Joseph Isnard, Barthalomew Accinelly and Edwin Lee contributed to the more than 1,400 slaves shipped to New Orleans from Baltimore in the four years between the autumn of 1818 and the autumn of 1822. This was a substantial number considering that there were other ports of entry also being used.

The earliest surviving record of a slave shipment to New Orleans from Baltimore was on the brig *Temperance*, captained by James Beard. The twenty-four slaves, boarded by six different shippers, were brought to the dock over a four day period in December 1818. This provides revealing evidence of a pattern that was to be repeated numerous times. Between 1818-1856 slaves were loaded on board ship at different times by different owners. As a result there were slaves who might spend several days in the hold of a ship waiting for departure.[4]

The shipments that followed reflected the cycle of the market. Most shipping occurred between September and April, after the planting, growing and harvesting was completed.

Although a number of slaves were shipped as a result of transmigration, the records reflect the fact that traders shipped the vast majority. A look at the four leading slave traders in Baltimore's history will confirm this pattern.

Of the Woolfolks' seventy-one shipments listed in the surviving New Orleans manifests, only four were shipped in the period between May and August. The other three trading firms list as follows: Hope Hull Slatter three out of sixty shipments; Joseph S. Donovan eight out of sixty-five shipments; Bernard Moore Campbell four out of sixty shipments. More than 92 percent of the major trader's shipments followed the harvest and preceded the growing season.

The period of the final passage often varied as a result of numerous mitigating factors. Weather conditions, stop-off for additional passengers or slaves, type of vessel, and tonnage would adversely impact time to destination.

On January 6, 1819 the brig *Emilie,* captained by Benjamin Godfrey cleared the port of Baltimore with passengers, merchandise, and twenty slaves (most of who were being shipped by David Anderson on behalf of Hector McClean in New Orleans). Twenty-four days later the vessel cleared customs in New Orleans.[5]

On April 7, 1819, the ship *Superb* cleared Barron's Wharf with fifteen slaves ranging in age from six months to thirty-five years. After an uneventful journey of just over three weeks the vessel landed in New Orleans on April 29.[6]

The 176-ton brig *Actress* cleared Baltimore on November 8, 1819 captained by Thomas Parker and carrying sixteen slaves for David Anderson and James Garsicles. Once again Anderson's eleven slaves were consigned to merchant Hector McClean and Co., of New Orleans. The brig landed in New Orleans on November 28, after a voyage of twenty days.[7]

Packet shipments that carried slaves to New Orleans were not always incident free. Upon arrival in New Orleans some manifests had grown due to birth taking place while at sea.

Female slaves in the advanced state of pregnancy were subject to New Orleans shipments. After the brig *Emilie* loaded thirty-seven slaves at Tenant's Wharf in late March of 1821 the captain sailed with orders to make a stop in Norfolk. Somewhere between the vessel's departure from Norfolk and arrival in New Orleans one birth had been recorded and confirmed by Customs Officers in Louisiana.[8]

When the brig *Clio* left Baltimore during the third week of March 1819 the vessel had one less slave than upon arrival in New Orleans where the *"birth of one child"* had been recorded.[9]

The schooner *Lapwing*, captained by Thomas Kennedy, left Baltimore early in the fourth week of March 1822. Upon arrival in New Orleans on April 18 the Customs Collector recorded *"one child born."* [10]

This practice was not uncommon to other ports in the upper South. In February 1819 the brig *Planter* left Norfolk with a shipment of slaves bound for the New Orleans market. Upon arrival the Customs Officer noted that the manifest was correct *"except that a child has been born."* [11]

When the schooner *Fanny and Mary Seabury* arrived in New Orleans from Richmond in March of 1820 Edith, a twenty-nine year old slave had been recorded as *"giving birth to a child on the passage."* [12]

Although deaths were a rare event on the vessels there is evidence that they did occur. The 127-ton brig *Eros*, which had departed Baltimore near the end of June 1822 carried, amongst a cargo of forty slaves, fifteen month old Carlos who died during the voyage.[13]

Apparently a disease had infected the slaves of George Milligan before boarding the ship *Balloon* the week before Christmas 1821. Upon arrival in New Orleans January 18, 1822 fifteen-year old Andrew and forty-year old Hannah had died and their bodies were missing (presumed buried at sea). Eleven-year-old John and nine-year-old George, also slaves belonging to Milligan, were listed as very sick. Four other slaveholders had contributed to the shipment of 113 slaves on board. So concerned had the owners become that they agreed to decree that *"all are in good health"* on board. [14]

In a rare late spring shipment in 1822 the brig *Eros*, of Baltimore, shipped five slaves from William Knight of Kent County and ten slaves from George W. Oldham, of Louisiana, on behalf of John Clay, a merchant in New Orleans. On the same ship David Anderson sent ten slaves to a New Orleans merchant. Upon the arrival of the *Eros* in New Orleans Customs Officer John Daly commented *"I have examined the*

within list and found Harriet, a child missing." A closer
scrutiny of the manifest notes that six month old Harriet, a
child of twenty one year old Nancy (on board) had died during
the voyage and apparently been buried at sea.[15]

Voyages were not always safe from incursions by pirates
on the high seas. The manifest of the brig *Aurilla,* which
weighed anchor from the Frederick Street Dock (current site of
the national Aquarium and Mammal building in Baltimore's
Inner Harbor) in late April of 1822, is an excellent example.
Charles Warfield, Austin Woolfolk, Leon Chabert, and
Stephen A. Wikoff swore by notary that they had shipped the
slaves on board the *Aurilla* from the port of Baltimore. The
Notary's statement in the manifest concludes:

*"On the said voyage from Baltimore from this port (New
Orleans), the said brig Aurilla was taken by pirates. Was
robbed of most of her cargo and one of said slaves, and also
of all the papers and letters or forms including said manifest
and these appearing do further swear that there were no other
slaves on board said brig on said voyage." Signed Beverly
Chew, New Orleans June 11, 1822.*[16]

As the Atlantic seaboard slave trade developed, packet
ships loaded with cabin passengers, slaves and wholesale
goods made their way from Baltimore with increasing
regularity. As a result of the potential for similar incidents
some of the ships were armed for protection against pirates.
The 152-ton brig *Intelligence* was one such vessel.

During a journey in April of 1823 the brig was loaded at
Jackson's Wharf with twenty-seven slaves belonging to Austin
Woolfolk as well as two additional slaves shipped by private
owners. Henry Thompson, the merchant handling the
shipment, advertised openly in the newspaper that the
Intelligence was *"completely armed against pirates."* Captain
Benjamin Godfrey, who often mastered the *Intelligence,*

sailed her to St. Mary's county where an additional twenty-nine slaves were shipped to New Orleans on behalf of owner John R. Plater Jr.[17]

From time to time packet ships that would otherwise normally transport slaves for the interstate traders had other plans for their cargo holds. Merchants occasionally advertised that slaves would not be taken on board. In such circumstances exceptions would be made for individual owners traveling to New Orleans with their own personal chattel. Thomas Tenant, the merchant handling the November 1820 sailing of the brig *Hyperion* advertised *"she has superior accommodations for passengers, whom she will take, and freight if offered in time. No slaves will be taken except the servants of passengers."* [18]

When Joseph Saul boarded the brig on November 8th he had with him his thirty-three year old female slave Sarah. Also on Board was George Y. Kelso with his three male and three female slaves.[19]

During the next eighteen months the *Hyperion* was used by a number of major traders to ship a total of seventy-nine slaves for the Southern Market.

In the autumn of 1819 merchant Henry Thompson, handling the cargo of the brig *Decatur* ended his advertisement by noting, *"no slaves can be taken, except the servants of passengers."* [20] True to his word, when the brig sailed during the last week of October only Tobias E. Stansburg and his wife, of Louisiana were on board with their slaves twenty-five year old Hannah Hollins, twenty year old Louisa Johns, Louisa's five year old son Hercules, and eighteen year old Betty.[21]

The vessels of choice most often used as packet ships were barques and brigs. By the 1820's the pattern had become a familiar one. Vessels loaded with goods from New Orleans would dock in the basin or Fells Point, advertise their merchandise for sale, and take on passengers, products or slaves for the Southern market.

In December 1822 the 204-ton brig *Orion* brought in cognac, rum, Madeira Cordials, Irish Whiskey, pig iron, steel stoves, hollow ware, mountain green coffee and other products, docking at Spear's Wharf on the west side of the Gay Street Dock. Before long Austin and Richard Woolfolk, as well as George W. Oldham began loading a total of thirty-eight men, women, and children on board. By early January the captain of the *Orion* was sailing the vessel to New Orleans once again.[22]

In February of 1824 the 185-ton brig *Robert Reade*, lying at Water's Wharf, between Fell and Thames, had just been unloaded and awaited cargo for the return trip. By the time the vessel's hold had been emptied of molasses eleven of Austin Woolfolk's slaves, between the ages of nine and twenty-nine, had been placed below deck. Captain Samuel Smith weighed anchor for the return trip during early March.[23]

During the autumn of 1827 the 230-ton brig *Sultana* had the 2,000 bushels of coarse salt removed from the vessels hold at Gibson's Wharf near the foot of Ann and Fell Streets. On board, upon departure, were cabin passengers, merchandise and three slaves headed for New Orleans.[24]

At times the larger ships leaving Baltimore would have unusual mixtures of cargo; merchandise, the wealthy boarding in staterooms, and the slaves in a separate area of the cargo hold.

The ship *Tippecanoe*, which was used a number of times by interstate slave traders for shipments, was a prime example of this. Once the ship reached New Orleans and unloaded its human cargo it would often continue up the Mississippi, pulled in tow by steamboat, the nineteenth century version of tugboat duty. During the autumn of 1841 merchants Clark and Kellog, handling such a shipment on the *Tippecanoe* advertised *"large and splendid accommodations, having two separate cabins for ladies and gentlemen, with commodious staterooms.   Steam taken up the river (Mississippi) as usual.* " [25]

Although the ship, docked at Fenby's Wharf and captained by Adam Gary, only carried six slaves for the purpose of transmigration there were at least four other trips when the *Tippecanoe* carried large numbers of slaves for local traders.

In December of 1840 William Harker, the partner of James Franklin Purvis, and Hope Hull Slatter shipped twenty-one slaves to New Orleans on the *Tippecanoe*. Also on board were slaves owned by James W. Zacharie and Greenbury Pearce. [26]

The following March the ship, docked at Fenby's Wharf, received twenty-three slaves for Hope Hull Slatter, James Franklin Purvis, and James Biscoe. [27]

The largest recorded shipment of slaves for the New Orleans market on board the *Tippecanoe* occurred in January 1842. James Franklin Purvis, Joshua Staples, and Hope Hull Slatter shipped 112 of the 115 slaves boarded at Chase's Wharf (Fells Point at the foot of Thames). Slaves owned by Adam Gray (the captain), John F. Strohn, and J. W. Chenowith were also boarded. [28]

In April of 1844 the ship carried forty-one slaves (again from Chase's Wharf) for Theophilus Bangs, William Harker, and Hope Hull Slatter. [29]

The *Tippecanoe* was not the only vessel carrying slaves for traders as well as sporting fine accommodations for travelers heading to New Orleans on business or pleasure. Many of the brig, barques, and ships offered to carry a striking combination of human and inanimate cargo.

The ship *Margaret Forbs*, loading at Chase's Wharf in November of 1838 boarded thirty-five slaves for Hope Hull Slatter. [30] The advertisements for the vessel claimed *"Fine accommodations for passengers."* [31]

The barque *Irad Ferry*, boarding at the Frederick Street Dock in January of 1840, received thirty-seven slaves (seven

of them children under ten years of age) for C. T. Maddox,
Hope Hull Slatter, and A. Clendenin.[32]

The 299-ton vessel, captained by J. J. Stevens and shipped
by merchants Clark and Kellog was advertised *"for freight or
passage having handsome accommodations."* [33]

During the autumn of 1847 the 343-ton barque **Kirkwood**,
docked at Flannigan's Wharf, received cabin and steerage
passengers as well as a shipment of 166 slaves owned by
traders Joseph S. Donovan and Ebenezer Rodbind.[34]
Advertisements for the barque, placed by merchants B. Buck
and Sons touted *"Built expressly for a packet between this
port and New Orleans. Has superior stateroom
accommodations for both cabin and steerage passengers."*
Once the cargo was unloaded at New Orleans *"She will take
steam up the Mississippi."* [35]

Chapter 7
The Baltimore/Alexandria Market

During the decades of the 1830s and 1840s major dealers such as James H. Birch, William H. Williams, Joseph W. Neal, and George Kephart (among others) were operating substantial businesses in the Washington city, Alexandria, Baltimore corridor.

Locally, up and coming traders Hope Hull Slatter, James Franklin Purvis (Isaac Franklin's nephew), Joseph S. Donovan, Bernard Moore Campbell, John N. Denning, William Harker, Moses Hindes, and Jonathan Means Wilson were among the several dozens of men operating in the realm of "cash for blood."

The 1830s brought about significant changes in the slave trade hierarchy of Maryland and Virginia. Although records are incomplete it appears the Baltimore-New Orleans trade had lessened significantly during that decade. The total numbers of slaves shipped and reflected in surviving manifests indicate a drop from 3,749 during the decade of the 1820s to 2,116 during the decade of the 1830s. Woolfolk's chattel had dropped from 2,139 during the decade of the 1820's (fifty-seven percent of the trade) to 441 during the 1830's (20 percent). Missing manifests notwithstanding, the leading trader in Baltimore had obviously lost a great deal of his business.

There are probably a combination of reasons for the slackening of the trade, one of which was the quality and quantity of the competition in the region. In 1828 one of the leading slave trade firms in the history of the domestic slave trade opened for business in Alexandria, Virginia. The owners were Isaac Franklin and John Armfield, both of whom brought buying power and prestige to the business. They quickly moved to scour the Virginia, Maryland region buying and shipping large numbers of slaves to the southern market.

Between 1830 and 1836 their trade became *"far in the lead of all other traders in Maryland, Virginia, and the District."* [1] The Franklin-Armfield business was said to be sending more than 1,000 slaves a year to the Southwest by 1834.[2]

So vast was the Alexandria based firm that between 1828 and 1835 they acquired or had built at least four vessels for the trade: The brig **United States,** 158-tons burthen, captained by Henry C. Bell; the brig **Tribune**, captained by Samuel C. Boush; the brig **Uncas,** 155-tons burthen, captained by Nathaniel Boush; and the brig **Isaac Franklin**, captained by William Smith.

One of the few surviving descriptions of the type of storage and sleeping arrangements that Franklin and Armfield had placed below decks in their brigs is quoted in William Jay's *Miscellaneous Writings on Slavery*

"Her name is the Tribune. The hold is appropriated to the slaves, and is divided into two apartments. The after hold will carry about eighty women, and the other about one hundred men. On either side were two platforms running the whole length; one raised a few inches, and the other half way up the deck. They were about five or six feet deep. On these slaves lie, as close as they can stow away." [3]

The Baltimore built brig *Isaac Franklin* was a *"square stern brig with one deck, two masts, a bast head, but no galleries."* The vessel measured eighty-nine feet five inches in length, twenty- three feet in width, and ten feet four inches in depth.[4]

After their retirement in 1836, Franklin and Armfield sold the *Isaac Franklin* as well as their headquarters in Alexandria to George Kephart.

Kephart shipped on several occasions from Baltimore's docks during the latter 1830s. The most notable of those shipments was the one that left Fells Point during the late summer of 1838.

During the final week of September 1838 the *Isaac Franklin* was docked at Craigg's wharf. Traveling trader George Kephart and Baltimore based Hope Hull Slatter delivered their shipments of slaves through Fells Point, to the foot of Thames and Lancaster on the eastern end of the docks. Eighty-eight of the 170 slaves on board belonged to Slatter, who had moved men, women and children from his pen on Pratt Street near Howard. Forty-seven of his consignment, or slightly more than half, were women.

Making their way down the narrow wooden steps into the darkness of the vessel's hold was forty-five year old Sandy Thompson, twenty-two year old John Thompson and eighteen year old Caroline Thompson. Following them was thirty-two year old Charlott Thomas carrying three month old James Thomas. Walking close behind Charlott was sixteen year old Priscilla and four year old William Thomas.

Seven members of the Johnson family, teenagers George and Richard Kennard, Mary Dorsey and her one year old son Thomas, Cora and Elias Bruner along with four year old Manuel and eight year old Clary slipped into the darkness. Several moments later Emily, Harriet and Mary Bright followed.

A number of children held the hands of, or were carried by the juveniles and adults as they made their way on board. Mary Arthur and Claiborne Baker, both two years old; one year old Thomas Dorsey and infant George Franklin; two year old Nancy Morris and twenty-five year old Lear Chew carrying her six month old child.

George Kephart began to board his eighty-two slaves, almost half of who were female. There were nine members of the Baker family, five of whom were eight years of age or less; four members of the Gant family; six members of the Harris family; five members of the Jackson family as well as five members of the Rolfs family. Also boarding were eleven year old Dealy Bun, nine month-old Catherine Miles, and four year-old William Wirt. [5]

The major interstate traders had a number of advantages over the less active speculators in the market. The large trading firms were almost always able to offer cash up front for their purchases. This was important to the seller who had immediate needs and did not want to become involved in promissory notes or contracts.

In Baltimore the prominent operating firms had their own slave jails. Although traders typically paid the city annual licensing fees for the right to operate their pens (generally about $400 per annum), a number of possibilities for income were generated when jails were owned outright. [6]

Traders owning their own jails could gather significant numbers of slaves in a secure environment while awaiting shipment. They could, and often did, rent out space to their competitors (the traveling traders or their agents) who needed security for their slaves after making local purchases.

Runaways or slaves who were suspected of committing felonies were often arrested and placed by the city in private jails until the status of their cases was determined. All placements of individual slaves not owned by the trader brought the standard fee of 25 cents a day. Even private owners, wishing to secure their slaves while out of town on business or pleasure, would often rent space in the local trader's pen. Only the wealthiest or most powerful traders could afford to operate the jail on a regular basis. Ownership, in fact, became an important status symbol.

The larger trading firms in Baltimore also owned or rented jails in New Orleans. There the agents or business partners (often relatives) managed the sales on the southern end of the market. During the entire run of Hope Slatter's business in Baltimore his firm's pen in New Orleans was operated from the corner of Esplanade and Moreau Streets by son Henry or brother Shadrack.[7] After the firm's move to Mobile in 1851 they could be found at Hewlett's Exchange, Common Esplanade where Slatter was listed as a slave trader.[8]

In 1851 Jonathan M. Wilson's pen was operating at 15 Esplanade where he was listed as a slave trader.[9]

Down the street, on the corner of Esplanade and Moreau Streets Walter Lewis Campbell, Bernard's brother and business partner, could be found at their pen.[10] Bernard Campbell's business had been located on Moreau Street for years, even pre-dating his initial shipments from Baltimore. The 1842 New Orleans city directory indicates that his slave pen was on 12 Moreau Street.[11]

Further evidence that Moreau Street was a popular slave market is reflected by the fact that even the *"justly celebrated"*

Austin Woolfolk had operated his pen at 14 Moreau, next door to the eventual site of Bernard Campbell's jail.[12]

Chapter 8
Baltimore's Major Slave Traders

Austin Woolfolk, Early King of the Trade

*D*uring the spring of 1816 a tall, nineteen year old man entered the port of Baltimore and made his way to an area, near the Western Precinct Market, known as William Fowler's (Sign of the Sunflower). After taking a room he approached the local newspapers with an ad that would offer

> *"Cash and High Prices for twenty or thirty*
> *likely Negroes of both sexes."* [1]

The following January he returned, advertising *"cash for Negroes"* and indicating that he was willing to give liberal prices for *"fifty or sixty Negroes."* This time word could be left at *"William Fowler's near the Circus."* [2]

During the following summer he had once again returned to Baltimore, staying at Anthony Egan's, opposite the Circus, Old Town. It was the content of this ad that gave some clue to where his business had been based prior to this point.... *"twenty Negroes wanted to go to Georgia, for which I will give more than any other Georgiaman in Baltimore."* [3]

By the following year he could be reached by leaving a message at the tavern of Mrs. Green, in Marsh Market (Center Market).

His name was Austin Woolfolk.

Negroes Wanted

> *Cash and liberal prices will be given,*
> *for a number of NEGROES. Apply at Mrs.*
> *Green's tavern, sign of the green tree,*
> *opposite the marsh market.*
>   *A. Woolfolk*[4]

Austin Woolfolk was one of the earliest major speculators in slaves to work the domestic trade in the Maryland region. As was typical with many slave traders in the upper South, he decided to use local taverns and hotels as his contact points while he tested the waters of the local market.

Among the contact points he used were the Three Tuns Tavern on the corner of Paca and Baltimore streets, Sinner's Hotel on Water Street, and the Sign of the Green Tree in Marsh Market Space.

Although some of Woolfolk's earlier manifests for New Orleans have been lost it is apparent that his business was not locally based for the first several years. During the summer of 1821 he moved from the Sign of the Green Tree in Marsh Market to a house on the north side of Pratt Street, west of Cove. It is here that he began operating a slave jail and trading by sea in earnest.

The appearance of Woolfolk's abode was a deceptive one. Trees in front of the white frame house, often mentioned in his advertisements, provided what seemed to be an idyllic setting. One passerby wrote to a local editor

"We remember Woolfolk's den. It was pointed out to us as we passed through Baltimore. A pretty house in front, presented a smiling aspect. The small grated windows of his prison in the rear-the chains, fetters, and miserable objects of suffering there concealed, chilled the blood with horror ". [5]

In November of 1821 the sloop **Good Hope**, moored at Bowly's Wharf and captained by Paul Wing, carried fifty-four slaves to New Orleans for the Woolfolk family. Assisting Austin in the shipment were nephew Richard T. Woolfolk and his brother Samuel M. Woolfolk.[6]

By 1822 Woolfolk's business had increased dramatically. In Harford County his purchases that year amounted to over $4,700.[7] In total, the Woolfolk business shipped 255 slaves to the New Orleans market during the year.

One of the numerous sources of supply for the interstate traders was the community jail. When a person was arrested on the suspicion of being a runaway he or she was incarcerated and an ad run in the local newspaper, periodically for at least six weeks. The owner was given the opportunity to claim his property and pay the fines levied by the sheriff. Unfortunately (or fortunately for the sheriff) some of those jailed were not claimed and subsequently sold according to state law. Although the sale was intended to help pay the $50 per week fine levied against the suspected runaway the local government, as well as the sheriff, received a portion of the sale's proceeds.

On the twentieth of December 1821 Gabriel Diggs, suspected as a runaway, was committed to jail in Baltimore County by Sheriff Sheppard C. Leakin. The twenty-three year old, 5 foot 6 inch Diggs claimed to belong to John Read Magruder of Prince George's County, near Upper Marlboro. When arrested he had on *"a pair of drab cassimere pantaloons, one course roundabout jacket, fine linen shirt, coarse shoes, fine hat and stockings."* [8]

Not long after arresting Diggs, Sheriff Leakin began running the advertisement giving particulars about the suspect. Unfortunately for the prisoner, Magruder probably never saw the ad. On March 22, 1822 Diggs' new owner, Austin Woolfolk, placed him on the 141-ton brig *Harriet*. The brig, moored at Jackson's Wharf (near Thames and Bond) and captained by William Diamond, sailed for New Orleans several days later with sixty-four additional slaves bound for the Southern market.[9]

Another source of slaves for traders was the acceptance of kidnapped free Blacks as slaves for the market. Woolfolk was implicated in an unlawful case of such a kidnapping in 1822.

During the summer of 1822 the Woolfolk business was indirectly involved in a kidnapping that was covered in a local Baltimore newspaper. The kidnapping involved a legally manumitted twenty-five year old ex-slave known by the name of Fortune Lewis. On the evening of the twenty fifth of July he was mugged at night, while walking home in the vicinity of Pratt Street extended.

During the period of time he was in a dazed state the men bound him by the hands and feet. When he came to his senses two white men were carrying him like a *"bale of goods"*. He was confined in a white house that he said was *"situated on the north side of Pratt Street extended, where the Washington Turnpike Road intersected it."* (This is a description of Woolfolk's house).

Within less than an hour he was placed, with two other Black men, in a carriage, and driven at high speed throughout most of the night. As dawn approached the men were placed in a jail within the boundaries of Washington City.

Several days later, after being informed by his jailer that he had been arrested as a suspected runaway, he produced a certificate of freedom that had been cleverly concealed in his clothes. Upon inspecting the papers, the jailer left the cell to confer with associates. After nearly an hour the jailer returned, unlocked the cell, and informed him that he was free to go.

During the mugging the men had searched his pockets in order to steal his money as well as destroy any evidence that he was a free man. Now he found himself alone, in a strange city, unable to afford a way back to Baltimore. Fortunately he was able to hire his services out to a carpenter for four days, thereby earning the price of a ticket home.[10]

A reflection of the irony of life in a slave market could not have been more clearly stated than in two advertisements placed side by side in a Baltimore newspaper on New Years Day, 1824. Austin Woolfolk offered cash for slaves from his residence on Pratt Street. The following advertisement, placed below his, noted special festivities to occur that evening:

Abolition of the Slave Trade

The sixteenth annual anniversary of the abolition of the slave trade will be celebrated by an exhibition of scholars at the African Bethel Church, Fish Street January 1st, 1824. Tickets to be had at the church; price of admission 12 1/2c.[11]

Had the scholars remained in the area for a short period of time they would have witnessed an odd sight on Pratt Street before sunrise the following morning.... Austin Woolfolk marching eleven of his slaves, all between the ages of eight and nineteen, to the ship ***Hamlet*** docked at Ramsay's Wharf.[12]

Woolfolk placed a number of advertisements in the local newspapers during the first half of 1824 in an attempt to purchase slaves to fill an order from the South. During the month of February he sought *"fifty Negroes"* by the 1st of

March in order to fill an order for that specific number in New Orleans.[13]

Through the month of March the Woolfolk clan continued to seek to fill the order by placing additional advertisements. The response apparently fell short of their expectations. As a result Joseph B. Woolfolk tried a different tact. In March, when he sought to purchase *"fifty Negroes"* he added *"they are intended for the state of Tennessee and not for sale."* [14]

They were apparently never able to fill the complete order. Their April 7th shipment on the ***Hamlet*** (the last bound for New Orleans until the autumn season) carried a total of only twenty-three slaves for Joseph and Austin.[15]

After several weeks the Woolfolks resumed their quest for additional laborers for the Southern market *"the subscriber wishes to purchase by the 15th of May 30 Negroes."* [16]

One month later Austin Woolfolk claimed *"the subscriber wishes to purchase, as soon as possible, twenty Negroes, and will give liberal prices as he has nearly completed his purchases for the present."* [17]

After four weeks, when Woolfolk repeated the ad it was his uncle Joseph who added in the same day's issue *"liberal prices for a few likely Negroes."* For particulars those interested were asked to call at the bar of the Globe Hotel, opposite the Exchange.[18]

For several years the Woolfolks' trade and the domestic slave trade in general had caught the attention of Baltimore resident Benjamin Lundy. Lundy, publisher of the abolitionist newspaper *Genius of Universal Emancipation*, used his monthly publication to expose the horrors of slavery. During the months of June and July 1825 Lundy focused on a six-week period of the local domestic trade, highlighting the Woolfolk business.

During the latter part of March the 239-ton brig ***Lady Monroe*** (captained by Edwin Bailey), carried a shipment of slaves for Austin and Joseph Woolfolk. Lundy reported that the vessel, owned by Thomas Tennant, had shipped ninety-nine slaves from Baltimore (the number was actually 115).[19] Although those shipped were as young as four weeks old, 67 of the 110 (whose ages were discernable) were between twelve and thirty years of age. That represented almost 61 percent of the total. Twenty-one of the remaining slaves (19 percent) were between newborn and ten years of age.[20]

Lundy later ran a copy of an advertisement the Woolfolks had placed in a New Orleans newspaper.

Ninety-Eight Negroes For Sale

The subscriber has just received by brig lady Monroe, from Baltimore, Ninety-Eight Negroes; amongst which, are a number of prime field hands; a blacksmith; a rough carpenter; a bricklayer; carriage drivers; house servants; seamstress and washerwomen. All of which will be sold low for cash, or on a short credit for good paper, by John Woolfolk
                    122 Chartress St.[21]

Several days after the **Lady Monroe** sailed the 183-ton brig **Statira**, captained by William Patton, shipped twenty-eight slaves from Smith's Dock on behalf of Dr. James Smith. Although twenty-one of the slaves (75 percent) were thirty years of age or under this was probably a case of transmigration and not sale for profit. The remaining 7 slaves ranged in age from thirty-six to fifty-five. The presence of such superannuated slaves, the fact that Dr. Smith was involved in only one recorded shipment, and a notation in the custom house records indicating that his slaves were *"not for sale"* leads us to such a conclusion.[22]

On April the 13th the 199-ton brig **Orbit** (Philip Riley, master) was loaded with forty-eight slaves, setting sail three days later. Austin and Joseph Biggers Woolfolk owned twenty-seven of the slaves.[23]

Three weeks later the 260-ton brig **Alfred**, captained by Paul A. Oliver, was loaded with passengers, merchandise and twenty-three slaves at Ramsay's Wharf. The Woolfolk family had shipped all of the slaves. In forty-three days the port of Baltimore had cleared four vessels shipping 214 slaves to the port of New Orleans.[24]

By the end of 1825 shippers operating out of Baltimore had sent 2,240 slaves to the port of New Orleans during the period beginning with December 1818. The Woolfolks' business represented almost 41 percent of the total positioning them as the premier Baltimore based traders in the early domestic slave trade.

By understanding the methods of shipment and movement of slaves by Woolfolk we can see how local and southern economies would have been impacted on a number of levels by the trade.

By 1825 Austin Woolfolk had a representative of his family living in the Cambridge area. Cambridge had become one of the centers of the slave market on the Eastern Shore of Maryland. The inns and taverns became a focal point for deals involving the transfer of slaves. Auctions in the area provided numerous sources for the purchase of servants from the slave rich communities surrounding Cambridge.

Woolfolk's favored means of transport was to ship by waterway whenever possible. Purchases from the Eastern Shore of Maryland would have made that a simple procedure.

Auctions were often preceded by the production of handbills and the advertisement in local newspapers as to place and time and particulars of the upcoming sale. The auction house sponsoring the sale expected to profit from the fee of each individual sale. The auctioneer's services would have been hired for his particular ability in such sales.

When Woolfolk's representative purchased a *"lot"* of slaves from such auctions it was important for the agent to secure them until shipment. Several local newspapers of the day complained about the fact that sheriffs were allowing traders to place their slaves in the jail, for a fee, until shipment. Numerous inns and hotels throughout the state had locked rooms for the temporary control of slaves.

While the slaves were incarcerated the agent made arrangements for a packet ship to transfer his purchase to Baltimore. The vessels owner and, or the commission merchant handling the vessel's shipments made a profit from such an arrangement.

When the slaves were brought to Baltimore they were moved from the wharf to the head of Pratt Street, just west of Cove (known as Freemont since the mid-1840s). There they were placed in Woolfolk's pen and confined until a shipment could be arranged.

Local merchants were then consulted and space on board their packet ship purchased for the transfer of the slaves to New Orleans. On the day the slaves were boarded a Customs Officer was present to perform the roll call, checking the manifest that had been prepared by the trader to make sure that his human shipment complied with the law. For his efforts the officer was paid a fee of $1.50. If the manifest was deemed correct, the vessel was cleared to sail.

The packet ship was often towed out of its berth by one of the large steamers that anchored at the foot of the docks along the inner harbor basin. Once the vessel was towed down river it either set sail or anchored, so as not to clog the sea-lanes, and await favorable conditions.

When the vessel arrived in New Orleans a Customs Officer would board the vessel and check the manifest once again, performing another roll call. Assuming the manifest was correct the vessel was cleared to land and the Customs official was paid $1.50 for his services.

On land the slaves were now transferred to a consignee or a pre-designated agent (often a relative) of Woolfolk. The slaves were walked to the pen on Moreau Street (owned by the Woolfolk business). There they were incarcerated until an order was filled, a private sale was held, or a public auction initiated. If the slaves found themselves at auction once again (as they sometimes did) the auction house in New Orleans would make a profit from each sale.

Once a slave was purchased by the new owner he or she might be found in a number of places; working in the sugar cane or cotton fields of the South, as a carriage driver or house servant, or resold again and shipped up the Mississippi's intercoastal highway to the market in Natchez.

This scenario, which occurred on numerous occasions, brought direct and indirect profits to a number of individuals and businesses throughout the upper and lower South.

Not only did the transactions of these slave sales and movements bring profits to local economies the labor they performed literally helped to build the South. Slaves provided labor in the fields, in shops, stores, warehouses, and throughout almost every facet of Southern life.

Recently historians have more fully examined another way in which slaves bodies were used as collateral for mortgages. Historian Walter Johnson has noted

"The entire economy of the antebellum South was constructed upon the idea that the bodies of enslaved people had a monetary value...Slaves were regularly used as collateral in credit transactions...When they borrowed money, many slaveholders simply wrote out a bill of sale for a slave who would actually be transferred only if they failed to pay their debt." [25]

As a result in some parishes in Louisiana slaves accounted for almost 80 percent of security offered for recorded mortgages.[26]

Profits from the slave trade allowed dealers like Woolfolk to make investments in properties throughout Baltimore and in several Southern states. Traders like James Franklin Purvis channeled money from "cash for blood" into banking and brokerage businesses in the city. A portion of that money was certainly used for loans provided for local businesses and manufacturers. In short, the blood stained money found its way into many areas of the local economy.

Austin Woolfolk's Rise to Supremacy

Woolfolk's probe for profits continued to take him or his agents into the surrounding counties. County court records alone indicated the extent of the Woolfolk brothers' business in the immediate vicinity of Baltimore. Between May 18 and July 28, 1825 they were recorded with purchases totaling more than $22,400 (for 84 slaves this represented a median price of about $270 each).[1]

Between 1818 and 1830 Woolfolk and Co. purchased forty slaves from the Harford County area for a total of $10,992 (this represented a median price of about $275 each).[2]

After purchasing a number of slaves in Harford County during the autumn of 1822 the Woolfolk brothers shipped them all on the schooner *Susan Miller* from Baltimore.[3] Of the ninety-one slaves on board belonging to the Woolfolks eleven had been purchased from the following owners, all from Harford County:

Robert (Bob) (thirty years old)-price $335 former owner
    George Henderson
Maria (seventeen years old) and Hannah (eighteen months
    old)-price $350 former owner John Kenny Sr. (note: their
    ages in the manifests are recorded as eighteen and one
    respectively)
Abraham (nineteen years old), and Jacob (twenty-one years
    old)-price $850 former owner Aquilla Nelson
Abraham (fifteen years old), and Rosetta (fifteen years old)-
    price $640 former owner Isaac Wilson
Pinkey (seventeen years old) -price $475 former owner Elijah
    Davis
John (twenty-eight years old), Robert (twenty-three years old),
    Winston (twenty years old)-price $1,262 former owner
    Edward Hall.[4]

Other traders took advantage of such sales, traveling
through a county, purchasing slaves, taking them to local jails
for temporary incarceration, transporting them overland or by
ship to Baltimore, placing them in slave pens and shipping
them to New Orleans.

New Orleans trader Leon Chabert purchased a number of
slaves from inhabitants of Harford County during a visit in
1825. Isaac, sold by Acquilla McComas, brought $300 while
Hannah (thirty-five years old), Hamp (nine years old), and
Mint (five years old) were purchased together for $320 from
Sarah Mitchell. In another bargain Betty (seven years old),
Margaret (twelve years old), and Lucy (ten years old) were
purchased from John Kean for $450.[5]

On April 16th, 1825 the 199-ton brig *Orbit*, captained by
Philip Riley and departing from Baltimore carried all who had
been purchased to New Orleans on behalf of Chabert.[6]

Woolfolk's rise to supremacy in the domestic slave trade
was not without its difficulties. During the early spring of
1826 a series of events surrounding the trade of the Woolfolk

clan was to bring Austin Woolfolk and local abolitionist publisher Benjamin Lundy into a direct confrontation that was to nearly cost Lundy his life.

In late April 1826 Austin Woolfolk led thirty-one slaves, most bound in chains, down Pratt Street. They made their way, under the cloak of darkness, to Philpot Street and along the wharves in Fells Point. There they were placed on board the schooner *Decatur*. Later that day, as a good wind blew up, the vessel set sail for the city of New Orleans. The lives of everyone on board were about to change dramatically.

Walter R. Galloway had left his Whiskey Alley residence after saying goodbye to his wife and three children. As the captain of the *Decatur*, he was about to embark on yet another sea voyage that required the transportation of slaves to a Southern port.

By the time he reached the ship, he was informed that all of the ship's cargo, slaves included, had been loaded. Several hours later, the captain ordered the anchor pulled and the sails set for the journey down the Chesapeake.

One of the male slaves on board was known as William Bowser (alias William Hill). Born at West River, the twenty-four year old slave of the Harrison family had lived his entire life in the vicinity of Baltimore County. His journey to the *Decatur* had been by a most unusual route. An unsuccessful attempt at escape from his owners had led him to the city jail where he remained until Austin Woolfolk spotted him.

Woolfolk often made the rounds of the jail attempting to obtain slaves whose offences made them subject to sale. Bowser, along with several other slaves purchased by Woolfolk, was moved to the trader's pen on Pratt Street. There he was shackled by the leg with a heavy chain and forced to wait four weeks until the *Decatur* shipped.

Five days out to sea Captain Galloway awoke to pleasant weather and a ship's speed of six knots. Shortly after 9 a.m. a seaman entered the captain's cabin, expressing his concern about the procedure of allowing small parties of slaves, unchained, above deck. Galloway, experienced in transporting slaves, offered reassurances to the sailor.

A short time later the captain made his way above deck for the inspection. During the tour he noticed a great deal of mud on the anchor stocks and took a seat astride the rail to scrape it away. Suddenly, from beyond his field of vision, two slaves, Thomas Harrod and Manuel Wilson, rushed toward him, seized his legs, and threw him overboard.

Below deck, William Porter heard a series of loud, unusual noises emanating from above. He made his way topside and rushed toward the rail, where the noise was loudest. As he looked over the rail he saw the captain struggling in the water below. Just then three slaves attacked him from behind and tossed him into the sea.

Crewmember James Brown, awakened from his sleep by the sounds of screaming, rushed up the steps to investigate. As he approached the rail several slaves restrained him from making any attempt to help his crewmates. The slaves then took possession and all of its holdings. It was 10 a.m., and the insurrection on board the *Decatur* was complete.

The insurrectionists gave command over to a crewmember whose attempts to steer the ship proved futile. Ironically they had killed the two men with the most sailing experience. As a result the ship meandered off the Eastern seaboard for five days.

On May 2nd, the crew of the *Constitution*, a whaling ship bound for Nantucket, spotted the *Decatur*. In need of supplies, the *Constitution's* captain pulled alongside the schooner and asked permission to board.

Outclassed and fearing that they would not be able to outrun the larger ship, the slaves ordered the *Decatur's* surviving crew to allow the intrusion. It was not until a seaman from the *Decatur* reached the *Constitution* that he felt safe enough to tell the truth.

The *Constitution's* crew re-boarded the *Decatur*, armed with muskets and side-arms, and successfully recaptured the schooner from the slaves. Although seventeen slaves were taken on board the *Constitution* (eight women, two men, and seven children), the remaining fourteen male slaves were left on board the *Decatur* with the ship's crew.

Three days later, on May 5th, the brig *Rooke* fell in with the *Decatur* and took the remaining fourteen slaves on board. Not long after the brig's arrival in the port of New York, in an amazing turn of events, all fourteen slaves escaped into the city. Although great effort was expended to recapture them, only one, William Bowser, was apprehended. After his capture at West Chester, New York, he was returned to New York City to await trial.

Bowser was found guilty of the murder of the two men and sentenced to hang in the late autumn. According to several sources, Austin Woolfolk was in attendance at the execution (a fact that he denied). Given a last opportunity to speak William Bowser looked directly at Woolfolk and told him that he forgave him for all the injuries he had brought upon him and that he hoped to meet him in heaven. It was December 15, 1826.

When word of the execution reached Benjamin Lundy in Baltimore he wrote a scathing report, attacking the character of Woolfolk. Calling him a "monster in human shape" for his conduct at the execution of Bowser, Lundy completed the column by stating, "Hereafter, let no man speak of the humanity of Woolfolk." When Woolfolk learned of the comments he was incensed and went looking for Lundy.

According to Lundy he was heading toward the post office to mail some letters when Woolfolk found him. An argument ensued, during which Woolfolk, the much stronger of the two men, knocked Lundy to the ground. Although Lundy offered no resistance he was savagely choked and beaten by Woolfolk. Only the quick intervention of several bystanders saved Lundy's life.

Lundy was later to write, "With a brutal ferocity that is perfectly in character with his business, he choked me until my very breath was nearly gone, and stamped me in the head and face, with the fury of a very demon."

The following month Woolfolk's trial for assault took place in Baltimore. During the trial he denied having been present at the trial of Bowser and brought several witnesses into the court in his defense. Nevertheless Woolfolk was found guilty.

When Woolfolk rose to hear the sentence that Judge Brice had decided upon, many in the court were stunned to learn that it was to be a fine in the amount of only one dollar. [7]

After the trial Lundy continued his work for the abolitionist cause, managing to steer a clear distance from Woolfolk. As for the seventeen slaves delivered to the port of Boston, apparently nothing further was ever reported.

Undaunted by his experience with Lundy, Woolfolk continued to make regular shipments to New Orleans. In the fall of 1826, he contributed to one of the largest shipments of slaves to leave Baltimore by placing 141 souls on board the *Hibernia*. The 327-ton, Baltimore built ship, captained by Matthew Robinson, carried 188 slaves in total. [8]

In February of 1827, the 107-ton schooner *Lapwing* carried fifty slaves for the Woolfolk clan. [9]

Seven weeks later the 191-ton brig *Jasper*, captained by Oliver Colbourn, left Tenant's Wharf carrying thirty-five souls. [10]

During his final shipment that spring, Woolfolk sent fourteen men, women and children on the 207-ton brig *Lady Richmond*.[11]

Business picked up later in the fall with the shipment of 138 slaves on the Baltimore built, 290-ton brig *States*.[12]

Shortly after the brig sailed the 306-ton Baltimore built ship *Jefferson* arrived at Price's new wharf, Fells Point. The long journey from Amsterdam had been a fruitful one. Gay Street merchant Charles W. Karthaus advertised a number of goods that could be found on board; Holland gin and potatoes, boxes of Coney wool, Holland sail cloth, and brass kettles were but a few of the items for sale.[13] As the weeks passed merchants and passengers booked space on board the Jefferson, with the next port of call scheduled to be New Orleans. Among those preparing to ship Christmas week were the Woolfolks. In the business of slave trading, greed observed no holiday.

On the night of 23 December the candles burned later than usual in the establishment of Austin Woolfolk, on Pratt Street, near Cove. Austin and his brother Joseph were copying slave manifests they had drawn up several days earlier. These were the copies that would be presented to the master of the Jefferson, the brig that would carry their shipment of slaves to New Orleans on Christmas Eve.

Behind the white frame house, in the smaller attached jail with barred windows, a few of the slaves slept. Others lay in the chill and darkness of their locked cells, waiting for the moment when the march was scheduled to begin.

For the men and larger boys, separated from the women and younger children, all aspects of family life had ended. Now that the shipment was about to occur, they would be segregated below the deck of the *Jefferson* in compartments apart from their wives and mothers. For some, the journey would be made alone, without the accompaniment of other family members on board.

Several hours before sunrise, on the morning of Christmas Eve, those who had managed to sleep were awakened and, along with the others, ordered to prepare for their departure.

The men and larger boys were chained together in two's, as was customary. The women and smaller children were allowed to remain unchained. All were then led into the street, forming one long line that stretched forward toward their destination.

In all there were 97 souls, 33 of which were children twelve years of age and under. Among them were eight members of the Johnson family, eight members of the Boyd family, Clem and Amy Thomas and their seven month old son, Charlotte Griffin and her three children, and Lindy Berry with her twenty day old daughter Lindy.

Later that morning, after each slave had been checked against the list the Woolfolks had made, the Customs Collector signed the manifest and cleared the ship to sail.

During the evening, when favorable conditions prevailed, the anchor was weighed and the ship set sail on its journey to New Orleans.[14]

The following year was Woolfolk's best in the New Orleans trade. More than 520 slaves were shipped, 123 of which were children ten years of age and under. Woolfolk's shipments of children were notoriously high. At least 18.6

percent of the more than 2,500 slaves for whom we have records were children under the age of eleven.

During the next two years the Woolfolk family business began to decline. In spite of his decreasing trade, notwithstanding the quality of the competition, Woolfolk was not hurting for money. As one visitor stated in 1835 he had *"made himself very rich by this trade."* [15] With six properties in Baltimore, large parcels of land in several southern states, and a major sugar plantation in Bayou Grosse Tete, Louisiana, Woolfolk had passed his "cash for blood" into profit in land.

In 1842 Woolfolk left the trade in Baltimore and moved to his beloved plantation in Louisiana. There he had become recognized as one of the largest sugar planters in the state. Although he continued to travel to Baltimore for business his slave trading days were all but over. His final recorded shipment to New Orleans was September 12, 1846. [16]

During 1846 Woolfolk's health had begun to fail. He suffered with a case of consumption (tuberculosis). In early 1847, fatigued and losing strength, he shortened a business trip to Baltimore and attempted to reach his uncle's house in Georgia. He never did. Death came to Austin Woolfolk on February 10, 1847, in a tavern in Auburn Alabama where he had spent the last days of his life. His uncle John Woolfolk, who was with him at his death, wrote to Woolfolk's wife that, *"he lingered for a long time and ate nothing, scarcely for some days previous to his decrease, being reduced to a mere skeleton."* [17] His obituary which, appeared in the *Columbus (Georgia) Times* on February 23rd said in part:

"In Auburn, Macon County, Alabama, on the 10th instant. Austin Woolfolk, on his way from Baltimore to his home and family in Louisiana. In the fond hope of reaching them ere death had laid his icy hands upon him, he struggled on from place to place, against the advice of friends, and the ruthlessness of his disease, notwithstanding he was utterly

*unfit to bear the fatigue of traveling, and the unavoidable
exposure to an inclement season. He died about 50 years of
age, after an illness of two years duration.* " [18]

A Chronology of Austin Woolfolk's New Orleans Trade

12/9/18- Temperance (brig) (4 slaves)
4/6/19- Superb (ship) (1 slave) Barron's Wharf
11/22/19- Triton (ship) (1 slave) Kerr's Wharf
*11/16/21- Good Hope (sloop) (54 slaves) Bowly's
        Wharf (*5 shipped by Richard T. Woolfolk) (*16
        shipped by Samuel M. Woolfolk)*
3/23/22- Harriett (brig) (56 slaves) Jackson's Wharf
4/6/22- Aurilla (brig) (22 slaves) Frederick Street Dock
5/10/22- Hyperion (brig) (7 slaves)
*10/25/22- Susan Miller (schooner) (91 Slaves) (*25
        shipped by Richard T. Woolfolk) (*28 shipped by
        Samuel M. Woolfolk)*
11/23/22- North America (ship) (39 slaves)
*12/20/22- Intelligence (brig) (30 slaves) Jackson's
        Wharf*
*12/30/22- Orion (brig) (7 slaves) Spear's Wharf (*3
        shipped by Richard T. Woolfolk)*
3/6/23- Harriett (brig) (13 slaves) Ramsay's Wharf
4/5/23- Intelligence (brig) (27 slaves) Jackson's Wharf
5/9/23- Lawrence (schooner) (21 slaves)
*10/14/23- North America (ship) (18 slaves) Water's
        Wharf*
11/18/23- Virginia (brig) (7 slaves)
1/2/24- Hamlet (ship) (9 slaves) Ramsay's Wharf
1/28/24- Eros (brig) (37 slaves) Ramsay's Wharf
2/28/24- Robert Reade (brig) (11 slaves) Water's Wharf
*4/7/24- hamlet (ship) (23 slaves) Ramsay's Wharf (*11
        shipped by Joseph Biggers Woolfolk)*

*10/30/24- Mars (brig) (*139 slaves) Water's Wharf (* 28 shipped by Joseph Biggers Woolfolk)*

12/20/24- North America (ship) (39 slaves) Water's Wharf

1/18/25- Alfred (brig) (30 slaves) Ramsay's Wharf

3/25/25- lady Monroe (brig) (97 slaves) (*19 shipped by Joseph Biggers Woolfolk)

4/16/25- Orbit (brig) (27 slaves) (*9 shipped by Joseph Biggers Woolfolk)

5/7/25- Alfred (brig) (23 slaves) Ramsay's Wharf (*9 shipped by Joseph Biggers Woolfolk)

9/29/25- Lady Monroe (brig) (32 slaves)

11/28/25- States (ship) (22 slaves)

12/19/25- Virginia (brig) (36 Slaves) (*shipped by Joseph Biggers Woolfolk)

1/5/26- Algerine (brig) (20 slaves) (*8 shipped by Joseph Biggers Woolfolk)

3/8/26- States (ship) (43 slaves) (*3 shipped by Joseph Biggers Woolfolk)

3/25/26- Algerine (brig) (14 slaves)

4/24/26- North America (ship) (12 slaves) Mezick's Wharf (*10 shipped by Joseph Biggers Woolfolk)

12/5/26- Hibernia (ship) (141 slaves)

2/15/27- Lapwing (schooner) (50 slaves) (*7 shipped by Joseph Biggers Woolfolk)(*18 shipped by Samuel M. Woolfolk)

4/7/27- Jasper (brig) (35 slaves) Tenant's Wharf

4/30/27- Lady Richmond (brig) (14 slaves)

11/21/27- States (ship) (138 slaves) (*24 shipped by Joseph Biggers Woolfolk)

12/24/27- Jefferson (ship) (97 slaves) Price's Wharf (*16 shipped by Joseph Biggers Woolfolk)

2/13/28- Billow (brig) (93 slaves) Frederick Street Dock (*37 shipped by Joseph Biggers Woolfolk)

3/31/28- Virginia (brig) (5 slaves)

4/14/28- States (ship) (76 slaves) Mezick's Wharf

4/29/28- Betsey (schooner) (47 slaves)

5/15/28- Arctic (brig) (20 slaves)

10/18/28- Lafayette (ship) (211 slaves) (*30 shipped by Joseph Biggers Woolfolk) (* 67 shipped by Richard T. Woolfolk)

11/12/28- Liberator (brig) (27 slaves) Chase's Wharf

12/4/28- Henry Clay (ship) (41 slaves) Price's Wharf

12/6/28- Climax (schooner) (3 slaves) Spear's Wharf

1/8/29- Julia (brig) (44 slaves)

1/24/29- Arctic (brig) (15 slaves) Gibson's Wharf

3/3/29- Catharine (brig) (23 slaves) Tenant's Wharf

3/11/29- Hope and Hannah (schooner) (15 slaves) Frederick Street Dock

4/20/29- Topaz (brig) (39 slaves) O'Donnell's Dock

1/1/31- Mechanic (brig) (26 slaves)

1/15/31- Catharine (brig) (8 slaves)

3/26/31- Pandora (brig (16 slaves)

4/2/31- Sarah (brig) (3 slaves)

4/14/31- Catharine (brig) (1 slave)

10/11/31- Brunswick (ship) (148 slaves) Water's Wharf

11/1/31- Ann and Leah (brig) (85 slaves)

11/12/31- Signal (sloop) (33 slaves)

2/10/32- Julia (brig) (11 slaves) Smith's Dock

9/10/33- Bourne (brig) (2 slaves)

11/4/35- Hector (brig) (4 slaves)

11/26/36- Caspian (ship) (70 slaves) Kerr's Wharf

12/14/36- Hortensia (barque) (18 slaves)

2/27/39- Russell (brig) (15 slaves) Bowly's Wharf

10/27/41- Caledonia (ship) (4 slaves)

9/30/43- Scotia (ship) (2 slaves)

10/7/43- Mary (barque) (4 slaves)

9/12/46- Victorine (brig) (4 slaves) Smith's Dock

Austin Woolfolk & Co. organized seventy-one shipments between December 1818 and September 1846 (sixty-eight of these shipments were initiated while a resident of Baltimore). The number of slaves varied from 2 to 211 per shipment. Fifteen of the shipments carried fifty or more slaves for Woolfolk. Of those whose age was discernable 18.6% were children eleven years of age and under. The total number shipped to New Orleans was 2,601 (36+ average per shipment)

Chapter 9
Hope Hull Slatter, Heir to the Throne

Hope Hull Slatter was born in Clinton Georgia in 1790 to Solomon and Nancy Slatter. Records indicate that, as early as the late 1820s, Slatter was involved in the transfer of slaves while still residing in Georgia.[1]

By 1835 competition in Baltimore had become keen. Most of the buyers operated out of the city either as inter-state traders, auctioneers, commission merchants, or exchange brokers. Between January 1835 and the late summer of the same year James Franklin Purvis, Austin Woolfolk, Hope Hull Slatter, J. Bates Jr., Nat Austin, John Busk, David H. White, and E. G. Abbott were some of those advertising to buy in the city.[2]

Slatter arrived in Baltimore in early 1835 taking up residence on Baltimore Street extended.[3] Not long after his arrival he began advertising his wish to purchase slaves. When a visitor to the city spoke with the fledgling trader during his first summer in Baltimore Slatter was very forthcoming with information on the market in the area. According to Slatter *"likely fellows"* were worth $500-$650 and girls of the same age $300-$500.

Although slaves were scarce that summer Slatter felt that the reason was slaveholders unwillingness to sell until after the crops were harvested and that *"hands will be plenteous in a few weeks when the harvest is Over."* [4]

During their conversation Slatter, believing that the visitor was an interested planter, offered *"a little girl-bright mulatto-seven years old"* for $250.[5]

Of all the traders dealing in "cash for blood" in Baltimore more information is known about the appearance and operation of the slave jail of Hope Hull Slatter than any others.

In 1837 Slatter applied to municipal authorities for permission to build a slave jail on Pratt Street.[6] Slatter extensively advertised the jail, which was completed in the summer of 1838. The establishment was located one door from Howard Street, on the north side of Pratt Street. He preferred to call the cells where the slaves were kept apartments and made it clear that *"male and female apartments"* were completely separate. The apartments were claimed to be *"light, large, airy, and completely above ground."* [7]

During the course of the ad Slatter invited the potential customer to house their slaves at his pen for 25 cents per day. Also included was the invitation to ship slaves to the New Orleans market or to *"any other place, at the request of the owner."* [8]

Slatter was well known for the pride he took in his establishment, often inviting visitors to tour his pen. Accounts of these tours offer insight into the operation of the jail. One such tour occurred in the spring of 1840 when eight abolitionists from a New England conference visited Baltimore. They reported their experience to the *Wesleyan Observer*. Their findings were later reprinted in the *National Anti Slavery Standard* copied here in part.

"Through the intervention of a friend, while at Baltimore, we visited the above establishment ".(here they reflect upon an add of Slatter's placed in the local papers). "We were conducted through the entire premises by the proprietor himself. This abode of unrighteousness and misery we shall

*attempt to describe. The prison itself is situated in the rear of
the mansion and office of the owner. The yard fronting the
prison encloses an area, as near as we can judge, of about 20
by 25 feet square. The walls around it built substantially of
brick, are about 20 feet high. We entered the yard through an
iron- grated door, the key of which was kept by a black man,
probably a slave. Mr. Slatter informed us that during an
absence of two months at the South, this man had the entire
care of the prison and of all the slaves within it. Back of the
prison yard stood the goal, in which the slaves are kept during
the night. The windows are as strongly grated with iron, and
the rooms appeared to be every way as secure as most of our
country goals. They were perfectly clean, so indeed was the
entire establishment. Motives of interest if no other, would
induce the owner to keep it in this state. The pantry was well
supplied with hams and potatoes. The utensils for cooking and
eating were much like those used by seaman in our navy, and
soldiers in our army. Back of the prison secured by a chain
and a strong iron gate, was a large blood hound, whose deep
terrific guttural growl and appearance indicated that he had
been bred for a specific purpose."* [9]

Nine months later two distinguished guests, Joseph Sturge
and poet John Greenleaf Whittier, while visiting Baltimore,
were courteously received by Slatter at his infamous pen. They
were surprised by the cleanliness and order in the jail along
with the fact that only about six slaves were locked in the jail.
Slatter informed them that not many days before their arrival
he had sent a shipment to New Orleans. (Slatter had boarded
thirty-five slaves on the schooner ***Ewarkee*** at Fenby's Wharf
on March 4, 1841) [10]

During their visit the anti-slavery activists observed the
open courtyard where the slaves exercised as well as other
living conditions. Slatter informed them that his jail keep (also
known as a cicerone) was his male slave. As a reward he had

freed the slave's wife and intended to free him if he conducted himself well "a few years longer". Just before his departure from the slave business in Baltimore in 1848 Slatter freed his only male slave Basil Tyler. There is a high degree of likelihood that Tyler was Slatter's cicerone.[11]

In the first week of November, 1843 Slatter shipped eighty-eight men, women and children to New Orleans on the 523-ton ship **Superb**.[12] The day after the captain weighed anchor and the ship left Tenant's Wharf Slatter guided several abolitionists, visiting from Philadelphia, on a tour of his pen.

The men visited five "apartments" in the prison, the first of which had *"six or eight males, from ten to perhaps about forty or fifty years of age."* [13] Slatter introduced the ten year old boy and commanded him to do a dance called "Jumping Jim Crow". While they watched the spectacle Slatter informed the men how much the slaves loved to jump, dance and fiddle...in short, how happy they were with their lives.

As the tour continued another apartment was opened, revealing a beautiful woman who was ironing clothes. She was a prisoner in the jail, awaiting a court decision that might possibly free her. She had been sold to Slatter from Virginia. He in turn, sold her to a local slaveholder, contrary to Maryland law. (It was unlawful to bring slaves into the state of Maryland with the intention of reselling them for a profit within the boundaries of the state).

In yet another apartment the men came upon a heart rending scene: *"a Mother, with six little children clinging to her, the oldest, perhaps, not more than ten years of age."* According to the one of the visitors *"the fear of being separated from those dear objects of her love, seemed to drive her almost mad."* There were a few bedclothes lying on the floor, in the corner of their room, which served as their bed.

The last room Slatter showed his guests was the storeroom where ham, rice, coffee, molasses, and other foods were stored for the slave's consumption. Interestingly there were several apartments that Slatter did not allow the men to visit.[14]

In 1846 yet another visitor was kindly greeted by Slatter and given the tour of his jail. The visitor described the courtyard where the *"stock"* was allowed to exercise and play games during the day. At night they were locked in the barred building at the back of the yard. In spite of the claims by Slatter that his establishment was airy one of his assistants told the visitor that at night it was *"hot as hell in there."* [15]

The slaves were expected to do their own wash in tubs that sat near the back of the front house (Slatter's quarters). Rope was strung across a portion of the yard where clothes were hung to dry.[16]

There was an auction block on one side of the courtyard with a large stove for cooking on the other. There were no trees, shrubs or grass in the yard. The high compound walls did not allow for a healthy airflow in the summer. As a result conditions on hot, muggy days must have been intolerable.

Another fascinating addition that Slatter added to his pen was the construction of a two block long tunnel that led from his pen to the dock at Light Street. Rezin Williams, a free man of color residing in the city at the time recounted his story of the tunnel in the slave narratives collected during the WPA project in the 1930s.

Rezin was considered a good judge of healthy slaves and, as a consequence, often accompanied purchasers to the Baltimore slave markets.

"He told of having been taken by a certain slave master to the Baltimore wharf, boarded a boat and after the slave dealer and the captain negotiated a deal, he, Williams, led a group of some thirty or forty blacks, men, women, and children, through a dark and dirty tunnel for a distance of several blocks to a slave market pen, where they were placed on the auction block.

He was told to sort of pacify the black women who set up a
wail when they were seperated from their husbands and
children. It was a pitiful sight to see them, half naked, some
whipped into submission, cast into slave pens surrounded by
iron bars." [17]

Close scrutiny of the slave traders in Baltimore clearly
indicate that the only major pen that fit the description set
forth by Williams was Slatter's pen. (It was the only pen
exactly two blocks from the Light Street Dock) Further
evidence that the tunnel was Slatter's was to come from the
unlikeliest of sources.

During the late summer of 1937 while city workers were
digging to lay electric conduits they struck a hard masonry
object in Camden Street near Hanover. As they continued to
dig they uncovered a huge tunnel that apparently led from the
harbor to Slatter's pen. Residents and businessmen of the area
were unanimous in claiming it to be Slatter's old tunnel, the
one *"through which slaves were transported between the mart*
and the harbor." [18]

The newspaper report continued by elaborating on the
business operations of Slatter and reporting that *"It was the*
custom to bring the slaves into the harbor aboard ship, unload
them at the Light Street pier and transport them to the mart
through the tunnel." [19]

Slatter used a number of modes of transportation as he
moved his slaves to the packet ships. There are times when he
marched his slaves in the open light of day down Pratt Street.
During the autumn of 1839 he boarded a large number of
slaves on board the ***Solomon Saltus***. An eyewitness later
reported in the *Liberator*:

"We are informed that Hope H. Slatter, not long since,
marched in open day, a gang of one hundred and thirty slaves

(the actual number was 114) through Pratt Street, in Baltimore, to a slave ship bound for New Orleans. " [20]

Slatter was also known to hire transportation to carry his slaves to the waiting packet ships. In December of 1843 a caravan of twenty-four coaches was seen moving down Pratt Street, filled with slaves.[21]

Ship manifests indicate that a shipment of slaves had been loaded on the 211-ton brig **Kirkwood** at Smith's Wharf (east side of the Gay Street Dock) two days before Christmas. On board were 22 of Joseph Donovan's slaves and the 69 slaves Slatter had driven by caravan.[22]

When J. Peters and company began to run a new line of omnibuses in the city during the autumn of 1844 another means of transport became available to the trader.[23] Omnibuses were large, horse drawn, enclosed vehicles with a series of windows on the sides and a single door for entry and exit at the rear. This mode of transportation offered Slatter greater security and control. Families and friends often attempted to walk along with the mini coffles and offer a word or a touch to a loved one. When it came time to move the slaves, traders accepted no interference. They and their assistants followed on horseback, whips in hand, to beat away any attempted goodbye.

The numerous travelers and ship workers that congregated along the Pratt Street corridor often watched these caravans of sorrow. One such eyewitness in the autumn of 1847 recorded his experience in the Leeds Anti-Slavery series.

"Hope H. Slatter, the notorious dealer in God's image, has made a shipment of a large number of men, women, and children, for the rich swamps of the far South.

The General Pinckney, the vessel which took this freight of bodies and souls, cleared several days previous to sailing, and lay anchored off the point, and in real slave-trading style, at the appointed time weighed anchor, dropped into her birth, took in her cargo, and immediately sailed. Slatter's slave prison is about two miles from the Point. He generally, as in this case, treats his goods to an omnibus ride from their public house to the vessel; and in the free, enlightened, Christian city of Baltimore, third city of the only republican and free country on earth, on Tuesday, January 19, 1847, might have been seen a train of omnibuses crowded with human beings, "made a little bit lower than the angels", torn from all that makes life desirable, without crime or offence, and hurried off to toil beneath the burning sun of a Southern plantation, without reward, with no man to care for their souls. Following the train, was a tall, gray-headed old man, of sixty, on horseback.

The traders heart was callous to the wailings of then mother for her child. He heeded not the sobs of the young wife for her husband. The sister, whose grief was insupportable, as she heard the last farewell, faintly uttered, from an only brother, as he hurried on board the accursed vessel, moved not the adamantine heart of this human trafficker. These connections may not have existed as I have stated them; but friendship in every relation is severed by these horrible transactions. I saw a mother whose very frame was convulsed with anguish for her first-born, a girl of eighteen, who, not withstanding her master was under bond, to the amount of two thousand dollars, not to sell any of his family out of the state, had been sold to this dealer, and was among the number then shipped. I saw a young man who kept pace with the carriages, that he might catch one more glimpse of a dear friend, before she was torn forever from his sight. As she saw him, she burst into a flood of tears, and was hurried out of his sight, sorrowing most of all that they should see each others' faces no more." [24]

On December 29, 1846 the ***General Pinckney*** arrived after a four-day journey from Charleston. On board was cotton and lumber for the firm of merchant John K. Randall. For the next three weeks the vessel lay docked at 104 Smith's Wharf, at the east end of the Gay Street Dock.[25]

The 194-ton vessel received goods and passengers in the final days before departure. On board by January 19 were 140 slaves, 83 of whom belonged to Hope Hull Slatter. Also shipping on the brig was Bernard Moore Campbell and Thomas Williams. Thirty-eight of the traders' slaves were children, twelve years of age and under.[26]

Among the unwilling passengers were Charlotte Chambers and her one year old daughter Ann; Delia Cornish and her infant son Samuel; Harriett Duffin and her infant son Joe; Betty Ann Dyer and her daughters Lucy (two years old) and Mary (three years old); Jane Evard and her five year old son Frank, eight year old daughter Dolly, and her infant daughter Mary Jane.[27]

On January 19th the vessel, with Captain Gayle in command, began its fourteen-day journey to the port of New Orleans.

By 1848 Slatter had made the decision to sell his business in Baltimore and head with his family to Mobile, Alabama. A deal between Slatter and slave traders Bernard Moore and Lewis Campbell was made to transfer the pen on Howard Street over to the two brothers when the Georgia native left Baltimore in mid summer.

One of Hope Slatter's last transactions involved the acquisition of approximately thirty of the seventy-seven slaves who attempted to escape from Washington D.C. on the schooner *Pearl*.

The Pearl

Word that waterman Daniel Drayton had assisted a woman and her five children in their escape to Frenchtown had spread through the slave community in the District. A free man of color (by the name of Daniel Bell) approached Drayton, on his subsequent visit to Washington, with a request for assistance. He was willing to pay Drayton if he agreed to help him secret his wife and eight children out of the District and to freedom in Pennsylvania.

Approximately eight weeks later Drayton hired the services of the owner of the schooner *Pearl*. On board when they made their daring trip to the Washington docks were Drayton, Captain Edward Sayres, and the first mate, Chester English. Although they had landed on the thirteenth of April the schooner's human cargo was not scheduled to arrive until the late evening of the fifteenth.

The city was in revelry as a result of the news that the first French Republic had been declared after a revolution that had expelled Louise-Phillipe. It was under the cover of this distraction and the subsequent planned events of the fifteenth of April that the ship would carry its human cargo to safety.

By the night of the planned departure not only had Bell and his family arrived at the schooner, but dozens of other slaves desperate to escape. Among the remaining slaves were members of the Edmondson family, a respected slave family in the District area. In total, seventy-seven men, women, and children made their way below deck during the course of the night.

Shortly after midnight Sayres weighed anchor and set the schooner out into the channel. They had not traveled far when the wind died and the decision was made to anchor south of Alexandria and wait for favorable conditions.

Before sunrise the *Pearl* began its fateful journey down the Potomac. As the new day dawned word spread quickly through the community that a number of slaves had escaped during the night. A posse was formed as excited slaveholders searched for a clue to what had happened. The men, upon learning the name, description, and general sailing direction of the escaping vessel, chartered a steamer and the chase was on.

As the *Pearl* approached the place where the Potomac emptied into the Chesapeake a great wind blew up. The captain realized that he carried an unusually heavy cargo and could not safely maneuver the schooner into the bay. As a consequence he pulled into Cornfield Harbor and anchored for the night. During the night the captain of the steamer, on a hunch that the schooner might not have attempted the journey in foul weather pulled into Cornfield Harbor. The *Pearl* had been discovered!

The armed men quickly took the schooner's inhabitants by surprise. Sayres, English, and Drayton, along with the seventy-seven runaways, were placed under guard. The *Pearl*, now being towed by the steamer, was quickly returned to the docks in Washington.

The three whites, as well as the seventy-seven slaves (children included) were incarcerated in separate cells at the city jail. In less than a week, and according to the laws of the state of Maryland and the District, the majority of the runaways were sold to traders to be shipped south. The names of the runaways (along with the names of their owners), published by the *Baltimore Sun* shortly after their incarceration are recopied here in their entirety. The owners' names are indicated first followed by their slaves' names: [28]

Mrs. Armistead (slaves: Andrew, George Bell, Mary
    Bell, Caroline, Caroline's 2 children, Ellen, Harriet,
    Mary, Mary Bell's 2 children)
Mr. Armistead (slave: Daniel Bell)

Mrs. Lisle (slaves: Augusta, Nat, Hannibal)

Dr. Causin (slave: Jane Brent)

John Downing (slave: John B.B. Brooke)

O. B. Brown (slave: John Calvert)

Mr. Swann (slave: Gabriel Cambell)

R. B. Nally (slave: George Craig)

Vincent King (slave: Augustus Chase)

W. Horman (slave: Philip Crowley)

Mr. Waters (slave: Minn Davis)

Charles Fletcher (slave: Mary Day)

Ignatius Mudd (slaves: Elizabeth, Anderson Marshall, Matthew)

Mrs. Corcoran (slave: Ellen)

Ms. Culver (slaves: Emily, Ephraim, John Evans, Mary, Reuben, Sara)

A. Hoover (slave: Frank, Joe)

Dr. Triplett (slave: Grace)

S. Brereton (slave: Henry Graham)

Mrs. Sarah Crane (slave: Perry Gross)

William H. Upperman (slaves: Harriet, Pricella Queen, Precilla)

Mrs. McDaniel (slave: Isaac)

Ms. Dick (slaves: Jane, Kitty, Sam, William)

John M. Young (slave: Joe)

Mr. Kirkwood (slave: Edward King)

Jonathan Y. Young (slaves: Leonard King, Mary Letha King, Mary Dotson)

F. Dodge (slaves: Priscilla King, Priscilla's 2 children)

B. F. Middleton (slave: John Knox)

John H. Smith (slaves: Louisa Washington, Louisa's 3 children, Minerva Washington)

Mrs. Madison (slave: Mary)

J. J. Stull (slaves: Mary Ann, Mary Ann's 2 children)

W. Mayo (slave: Plumer Matthews)

L. Storm (slave: Newman)
General Hunter (slaves: Daphne Pavre, Daphne's child)
George C. Howard (slave: Madison Pitts)
Colonel Carter (slave: Alfred Pope)
Mr. Connelly (slave: Peter Rix)
Mr. Frozel (slave: George Shanklin)
W. Jackson (slave: Henry Smallwood)
James Barnill (slave: William Thompson)
Mr. Lyons (slave: Samuel Turner)
Mr. Bell (slave: William)
Mrs. Irwin (slave: Madison Young)

Although a variety of stories have evolved, whose facts dispute one another, it is clear that a number of the slaves ended up in Baltimore's slave pens.

In all probability the fact that Baltimore had regular Morse telegraph communication with Washington allowed the news of the attempted escape to reach the city in short fashion. Traders Bernard Campbell and Hope Slatter knew they had to move quickly if they hoped to get a good deal on some of the runaways.[29]

Although they had been rivals in the business for more than four years the cooperation between the traders made perfect sense. After all, Bernard and his brother Lewis were finalizing plans to purchase Slatter's stand upon his departure in July. Slatter and several of his assistants boarded the train for Washington.

During the visit Slatter, on behalf of himself and Campbell, managed to buy at least thirty of the *Pearl* fugitives (as well as a number of other slaves unrelated to the case). On 21 April the slaves were marched from the jail to the railroad depot by Slatter and his assistants. Once on board the rail car the male slaves were left in irons for the journey back to Baltimore.

At each end of the car Slatter had positioned two men, with large canes in their hands.

> Relatives and friends of the slaves struggled for a last glimpse or touch of their loved one, but to no avail. Both inside and outside the train the weeping and wailing of the broken hearted filled the air. One man climbed up to a window of the car in an attempt to embrace his wife. She reached her hand toward him but Slatter warned the husband not to continue. Both husband and wife implored Slatter to give them a few last moments together. Slatter, in a rage, knocked the husband down from the window and ordered him away.[30]

Once Slatter and his men returned to Baltimore the slaves were deposited in at least two different pens. Much of the details of what happened over the next several weeks are unclear. There are indications that at least one of the slaves from the *Pearl* was taken to Campbell's pen and that a number of others were shipped to New Orleans by Baltimore based slave trader Joseph Donovan.[31]

Several of the slaves shipped by Donovan were the members of the aforementioned Edmondson family. Slave manifests indicate their names and ages as Emly (15), Mary (17), Ephrim (30), John (26), Richard (20), and Samuel (21).[32]

Paul and Emily Edmondson had raised a large family. Of the fifteen children they had together fourteen were still living at the time of the attempted escape.[33]

His owner had freed Paul, a former slave from Montgomery County twenty-eight years earlier (at the age of forty-two). At the time of the children's birth Amelia, Paul's wife, was a slave. As a consequence of state law all of the Edmondson children were born into slavery.[34]

The Edmondson's were highly respected throughout Montgomery County and in and around the area of the District of Columbia. The news of the six Edmondson children's attempted escape shocked many in the community.

Word of the details of the Edmondson's connection with the escape became clearer as the weeks and months after the incident had passed.

Upon learning that the members of the Bell family were attempting an escape twenty-one year old Samuel Edmondson approached sister Emily with the plan. She promised to go along if her brother could talk sister Mary into accepting the plan. Mary agreed and so did three additional brothers.

After the slaves' capture the Edmondsons were purchased by the Alexandria firm of Bruin and Hill. A number of weeks later they were sent to Donovan's pen and then eventually to New Orleans on the brig *Union*.

Approximately three weeks after their placement in the New Orleans pen the Edmondsons were sent back to Baltimore in order to keep them from contacting the yellow fever that was running rampant in the city.

Within several weeks, during what was now the latter part of August, Bruin and Hill arrived in Baltimore to transport them once again back to their Alexandria pen.

The girl's father traveled to New York and, with the assistance of a number of clergymen, raised the funds to buy his daughters freedom as per his agreement with Mr. Bruin.

During the first week of November the girls were finally set free. Their odyssey had lasted six months.

Emily and Mary were sent to school in New York, under the care of Harriet Beecher Stowe and Reverend Henry W. Beecher. In the spring of 1852, four years after their attempted escape, they were reunited with their mother who had traveled to the city for the joyous occasion.

A daguerreotype of the sisters was taken during their mother's visit. It is the photo that appears on the cover of this book. Mary Edmondson died the following year of consumption (tuberculosis).[35]

During his thirteen and one half year stay in Baltimore Hope Hull Slatter had become one of the leading traders in the history of the South. His trade, along with those of Austin Woolfolk, Joseph Donovan and Bernard Moore Campbell sent thousands of families and individuals on their final passage to the Southern market.

After the sale of his pen to the Campbell brothers, Slatter and his family moved to Mobile Alabama where Slatter continued to hire out and sell slaves but on a much smaller, localized scale. Shortly after his relocation in Alabama his son Henry, who had assisted him in his trade, died at the age of thirty-one.

Shadrack Slatter, Hope's brother and assistant in the trade died July 6, 1861 in Mississippi. He was sixty-one years of age.

Hope Hull Slatter died in Mobile on September 23, 1853, at the age of sixty-three, of yellow fever.

A Chronology of Hope Hull Slatter's New Orleans' Trade

11/16/35- Palestine (ship) (47 slaves) Water's Wharf
1/10/38- Uncas (brig) (43 slaves)
4/3/38- Uncas (brig) (5 slaves)
9/28/38- Isaac Franklin (brig) (88 slaves) Craigg's Wharf
10/11/38- Glasgow (20 slaves) Water's Wharf

Edmondson Sisters

Mary and Emily Edmondson were two of the six Edmondson children who attempted to escape from Washington on the schooner *Pearl* in April 1848.

Photo (circa 1852) courtesy of the Historical Society of Washington, D.C. and with permission of Dr. Marion B. W. Holmes, a direct descendant.

11/28/38- *Margaret Forbs (ship)* (35 slaves) *Chase's Wharf*

12/19/38- *Glasgow* (2 slaves)

12/19/38- *Seaman (ship)* (24 slaves)

3/1/39- *Russell (brig)* (31 slaves) *Bowly's Wharf*

3/25/39- *Seaman (ship)* (49 slaves*) *Bowly's Wharf* (*31 slaves shipped by Shadrack Slatter)

10/7/39- (114 slaves)

1/22/40- *Irad Ferry (barque)* (4 slaves) *Frederick Street Dock*

10/9/40- *Eliza (barque)* (48 slaves) *Frederick Street Dock*

11/25/40- *Gannicleffi (brig)* (36 slaves) *Tennant's Wharf*

12/16/40- *Tippecanoe (ship)* (12 slaves)

1/18/41- *Bostonian (barque)* (32 slaves)

3/4/41- *Ewarkee (schooner)* (35 slaves) *Fenby's Wharf*

4/1/41- *Tippecanoe (ship)* (12 slaves) *Fenby's Wharf*

4/24/41- *Splendid (brig)*(26 slaves) *Fenby's Wharf*

5/20/41- *Architect (brig)* (15 slaves) *Frederick Street Dock*

1/17/42- *Tippecanoe (ship)* (67 slaves) *Chase's Wharf*

10/21/42- *Burlington (ship)* (76 slaves)

11/16/42- *Peres (barque)* (18 slaves)

12/9/42- *Irad Ferry (barque)* (44 slaves) *Fenby's Wharf*

1/24/43- *Catharine (brig)* (32 slaves)

2/13/43- *Architect (brig)* (16 slaves)

2/26/43- *Northumberland (brig)* (33 slaves)

3/25/43- *Lafayette (schooner)* (31 slaves) *Frederick Street Dock*

9/30/43- *Scotia (ship)* (72 slaves)

11/1/43- *Superb (ship)* (88 slaves) *Tennant's Wharf*

12/23/43- *Kirkwood (brig)* (69 slaves) *Smith's Dock*

3/9/44- *Victorine (brig)* (46 slaves) *Smith's Dock*

4/15/44- *Tippecanoe (ship)* (29 slaves) *Chase's Wharf*

1/4/45- *Kirkwood (brig) (*36 slaves)

2/8/45- *Margaret Hugg (barque) (*20 slaves) *Corner's Wharf*

3/1/45- *Victorine (brig) (*36 slaves) *Smith's Dock*

3/22/45- *Home (barque) (*34 slaves)

4/11/45- *Kirkwood (brig)* (60 slaves) *Frederick Street Dock*

5/14/45- *Victorine (brig)* (41 slaves)

9/9/45- *Paoli (barque)* (61 slaves) *Frederick Street Dock*

10/16/45- *Kirkwood (brig)* (89 slaves) *Frederick Street Dock*

11/10/45- *General Pinckney (brig) (*39 slaves)

12/17/45- *Victorine (brig) (*81 slaves)

1/14/46- *Kirkwood (brig) (*30 slaves)

2/21/46- *General Pinckney (brig) (*32 slaves)

3/14/46- *Victorine (brig) (*30 slaves)

4/4/46- *Kirkwood (brig) (*18 slaves)

9/12/46- *Victorine (brig) (*30 slaves) *Smith's Dock*

9/28/46- *Salvadora (brig) (*51 slaves)

10/28/46- *Hermitage (barque)* (48 slaves) *Frederick Street Dock*

12/10/46- *Kirkwood (brig)* (42 slaves) *Frederick Street Dock (*Shipped by Henry F. Slatter)*

12/31/46- *Victorine (brig)* (45 slaves) *Smith's Dock (*Shipped by Henry F. Slatter)*

1/19/47- *General Pinckney (brig) (*83 slaves) *Smith's Dock*

2/16/47- *Zoe (*61 slaves)

3/27/47- *Phoenix* (16 slaves)

7/26/47- *Union (brig)* (50 slaves) *O'Donnell's Wharf*

9/15/47- *Pioneer (barque)* (49 slaves) *Flannigan's Wharf*

10/11/47- *Louisa (barque)* (28 slaves) *Wilson's Wharf*

11/7/47- *W.H.D.C.Wright* (9 slaves) *Flannigan's Wharf*

*11/30/47- E.H.Chapin (*barque*) (*72 slaves*)*

Hope Hull Slatter & Co. organized sixty shipments between November 1835 and November 1847. The number of slaves varied from 2 to 114 per shipment. Seventeen of the shipments carried fifty or more slaves for Slatter. Of those whose age was discernable 15.4 percent were children ten years of age and under. The total number shipped to New Orleans was 2,533 (42+ average per shipment)

Chapter 10
Other Local Traders

Joseph S. Donovan

For a number of years, in the early 1830s, Joseph S. Donovan worked as the keeper of the Vauxhall Gardens. Little did anyone in Baltimore realize that the man with such mundane beginnings would soon become one of the nations leading slave traders.

The Maryland native's first recorded shipment of slaves to the New Orleans market was in early November 1843 when he placed twenty-nine slaves on board the 523-ton ship *Superb* at Tennant's Wharf.[1]

Donovan's initial advertisement for the purchase of slaves was placed in the *Baltimore Sun* during the second week of October. He offered *"cash for Negroes"* from the slave jail, on Pratt Street, formerly owned by Austin Woolfolk.

Cash For Negroes

The subscriber wishes to purchase likely young Negroes, for which he will give the highest prices. Persons having Negroes for sale, will please call at the old establishment formerly occupied by Austin Woolfolk, Esq,

Pratt Street, near Cove. Negroes received and
safely kept at 25Cts. per day
       Joseph S. Donovan [2]

Donovan continued to operate his business from the pen on West Pratt Street until the autumn of 1846 (Donovan's last ad from Woolfolk's pen was printed in the third week of September). The trader's new base of operations was from a pen on 13 Camden Street, between Light and Charles Streets.[3]

The new location was directly adjacent to the end of a rail line that could deposit slaves a short distance from the front door of his establishment. He often advertised *"persons bringing Negroes by the cars will find it very convenient as it is only a few yards from where the passengers get out."* [4] Also nearby (merely fifty yards to the east) were the steamboat landings along the Light Street Wharves.[5]

In the autumn of 1858 Donovan's newly erected slave jail was completed and ready for business. The pen was located on the southwest corner of Eutaw and Camden Streets.[6]

Of all of the major inter-state slave traders operating out of Baltimore Donovan maintained the lowest percentage of children shipped to the New Orleans market (males and females twelve years of age and under). Less than 9 percent of his manifests represented children of the aforementioned age group.

Although Donovan would never hesitate to sell children for profit separately or with their mothers his trade seemed to focus more on adults for the cotton and sugar plantations of the South and Southwest. During the summer of 1847, while collecting slaves for shipment to New Orleans in the autumn he advertised:

Negroes Wanted

> *The highest cash prices will be given
> for Negroes. I wish to purchase a large lot of
> Negroes for sugar and cotton planters. I will
> also give the largest sort of prices for house
> servants or mechanics. Those having such for
> sale will find it by their interest to call at my
> office, Camden Street, in the rear of the
> railroad depot.*
>
> J. S. Donovan[7]

That autumn Donovan shipped his largest single shipment to New Orleans on the 343-ton barque **Kirkwood** from Flannigan's Wharf. When the vessel was loaded on October 26th there were 166 slaves on board...141 belonging to Donovan.[8]

Like most of the major traders in Baltimore, Donovan had agents in the field. One of the most lucrative markets in Maryland was to be found on the Eastern Shore. Agents often used hotels and inns as contact points. During the post harvest period, and continuing through the shipping season, ads reflecting the slave trade were often placed in the newspapers such as the *Cambridge Chronicle*:

> *Cash For Negroes*
> *I wish to purchase for the New Orleans
> market, likely young Negroes. those having
> Negroes for sale will find their interest
> promoted by calling at John Bradshaw's
> Hotel..Cambridge or addressing me by mail at
> Baltimore.*
>
> J. S. Donovan[9]

During the mid 1840s Donovan operated in the Baltimore area with the assistance of agent Jonathan M. Wilson. By the summer of 1849 their partnership was dissolved and notice given in the *Baltimore Sun*.[10] Both Donovan and Wilson continued to trade, however, making their names known throughout the South.

Joseph Donovan's death in the spring of 1861 was received with little fanfare in the local press, considering the degree of prominence he had attained in the domestic slave trade. On April 16, 1861 the *Baltimore Sun* reported:

Deceased-Joseph S. Donovan, Esq. A well known slave dealer, and extensively known throughout the South, died yesterday morning, after a short illness, at his residence, southwest corner of Eutaw and Camden Streets, in the 60th year of his age.[11]

A Chronology of Joseph S. Donovan's New Orleans Trade

11/2/43- Superb (ship) (29 slaves) Tennant's Wharf
12/23/43- Kirkwood (brig) (22 slaves) Smith's Wharf
2/10/44- Sabine (20 slaves)
3/23/44- Kirkwood (brig) (23 slaves) Smith's Wharf
5/22/44- Victorine (brig) (60 slaves)
10/25/44- Victorine (brig) (8 slaves)
11/21/44- Colonel Howard (barque) (10 slaves)
1/4/45- Kirkwood (brig) (62 slaves)
1/18/45- Catharine (brig) (49 slaves) Smith's Wharf
2/8/45- Margaret Hugg (14 slaves)
3/1/45- Victorine(brig) (7 slaves)
3/22/45- Home (barque) (30 slaves)

4/15/45- Kirkwood (brig) (39 slaves) *Frederick Street Dock*

5/14/45- Victorine (brig) (26 slaves)

9/29/45- Victorine (brig) (108 slaves)

10/16/45- Kirkwood (brig) (5 slaves) *Frederick Street Dock*

11/10/45- General Pinckney (brig) (35 slaves)

11/29/45- St. Mary (brig) (41 slaves)

12/17/45- Victorine (brig) (13 slaves)

1/14/46- Kirkwood (brig) (15 slaves)

2/21/46- General Pinckney (brig) (29 slaves)

3/14/46- Victorine (brig) (9 slaves)

4/4/46- Kirkwood (brig) (12 slaves)

4/25/46- Architect (brig) (19 slaves) *Flannigan's Wharf*

5/30/46- Leda (barque) (5 slaves)

9/28/46- Kirkwood (brig) (82 slaves) *Frederick Street Dock*

10/28/46- Hermitage (barque) (19 slaves) *Frederick Street Dock*

12/10/46- Kirkwood (brig) (91 slaves) *Frederick Street Dock*

12/31/46- Victorine (brig) (33 slaves) *Smith's Wharf*

1/20/47- Frances Amy (brig) (66 slaves) *Flannigan's Wharf*

2/16/47- Zoe (35 slaves)

3/9/47- Kirkwood (brig) (36 slaves) *Frederick Street Dock*

3/27/47- Phoenix (26 slaves)

10/9/47- Louisa (barque) (46 slaves) *Wilson's Wharf*

10/26/47- Kirkwood (barque) (141 slaves) *Flannigan's Wharf*

12/2/47- E.H.Chapin (barque) (26 slaves)

5/13/48- Union (brig) (46 slaves) *O'Donnel's Wharf*

7/3/48- Louisa (barque) (2 slaves) *Flannigan's Wharf (shipped by Walter Lewis Campbell)*

8/28/48- E.H. Chapin (barque) (2 slaves)

10/14/48- Kirkwood (barque) (95 slaves) Flannigan's Wharf

10/28/48- Henry A. Barling (schooner) (8 slaves) Flannigan's Wharf (shipped by Walter Lewis Campbell)

11/18/48- Elizabeth (barque) (75 slaves) Flannigan's Wharf

12/16/48- Union (brig) (63 slaves) Frederick Street Dock

3/17/49- Union (brig) (8 slaves) Frederick Street Dock

5/12/49- Elizabeth (barque) (4 slaves) Flannigan's Wharf

8/11/49- Henry A. Barling (schooner) (2 slaves)

10/6/49- Elizabeth (barque) (17 slaves) Flannigan's Wharf (11 slaves shipped by Walter Lewis Campbell)

10/27/49- Southerner (barque) (81 slaves) Frederick Street Dock

11/28/49- Kirkwood (barque) (39 slaves) Flannigan's Wharf

1/2/50- Elizabeth (barque) (43 slaves) Jackson's Wharf

1/21/50- Southerner (barque) (22 slaves) Frederick Street Dock

3/21/50- Elizabeth (barque) (17 slaves) Flannigan's Wharf

10/24/50- John C. Calhoun (ship) (93 slaves) Henderson's Wharf

11/27/50- Narragansett (ship) (32 slaves) Henderson's Wharf

1/21/51- Cora (barque) (5 slaves)

2/24/51- Henry A. Barling (schooner) (21 slaves) Henderson's Wharf

4/3/51- Waverly (brig) (8 slaves) Henderson's Wharf

4/23/51- Charles (ship) (16 slaves)

5/17/51- Henry A. Barling (schooner) (4 slaves)
  Henderson's Wharf
11/13/51- Eliza F. Mason (ship) (57 slaves)
12/18/51- Henry A. Barling (schooner) (11 slaves)
1/5/52- Southerner (barque) (26 slaves) Brown's Wharf
2/12/52- Nathaniel Hooper (ship) (24 slaves) Brown's
  Wharf
6/12/52- Pampero (2 slaves)
12/2/52- Justina (barque) (22 slaves)

Joseph S. Donovan & Co. organized sixty-five shipments between November 1843 and December 1852. The number of slaves varied from ? to 141 in number per shipment. Thirteen of the shipments carried 50 or more slaves for Donovan. Of those whose age was discernable 8.7 percent were ten years of age or under. Total number shipped to New Orleans was 2,113 (32+ average per shipment)

James Franklin Purvis

James Franklin Purvis was born in Tennessee in 1808. During the early 1830s he began acting as an agent for his uncle Isaac Franklin, of the slave trading firm Franklin and Armfield in Alexandria.[12]

His residence (as well as his slave pen) was located on Harford Road near the intersection of Aisquith Street. The 1835/36 city directory of Baltimore lists him as a *"dealer in Negroes, Harford Road North of the church."* [13]

Although a friendly rivalry grew between Purvis and Hope Hull Slatter they were known to occasionally ship together to New Orleans. The Purvis advertisements for his slave jail often took advantage of the negative reputation that Slatter's jail had for being *"hot as hell"* in the summertime.

"The subscriber's establishment is located on Harford Avenue, in one of the highest and most healthy parts of the city, having a free circulation of air, and a yard for exercise through the day must necessarily be more healthy than in the center of the city, especially in hot weather." [14]

For a number of years his advertisements had noted that the potential seller could locate him, his brother, or his agent through the jail itself or his two other locations in the downtown Baltimore area. The city locations were Number 2 south Calvert Street, adjoining Hutchison and Weart's Stage Office (several door south of Baltimore Street) and the Whitman's Eagle Hotel, opposite the Baltimore and Philadelphia railroad office.[15]

One of the unanswered mysteries of the slave manifests recorded by Customs Collectors in Baltimore is why Purvis, who handled slaves from his Harford Road location from at least late 1832, is never shown shipping to New Orleans until February 1841.[16]

His agent in the trade, who managed the Calvert Street office, was William Harker. Harker was to remain in the business long after Purvis, advertising for the trade as late as 1859.[17]

The Harker-Purvis shipments noted in surviving New Orleans manifests total only 308 for a 5 1/2 year period (1841-46) many times lower than the actual number probably was.

With the money made from "cash for blood" James Franklin Purvis was able to become involved in the banking and exchange brokerage business that he operated until his retirement in 1868. He and his family then moved to a farm in Freedom District, Carroll County where he died during the spring of 1880, at the age of 72. Nowhere in the obituary of

Purvis was there mention of how he made the funds to become involved in the banking business. His remains were interred in Greenmount Cemetery (in Carroll County) on April 26, 1880.[18]

John N. Denning

Although slave manifests reflecting the shipments of John N. Denning are mysteriously absent from the surviving records it is clear that he had a significant trade in Baltimore. During the 1840s Denning's trade operated from his establishment at 104 N. Exeter Street (near the Methodist Episcopal Church).[19]

He was often in the habit of making incredible claims in his advertisements that would have been impossible to keep. He asked for large or small families, or *"single Negroes"* offering in the same breath the promise "families never separated". [20] In another ad he wished to purchase *"any number of Negroes with good titles."* [21]

Cash, of course, was always a major drawing card when attempting to purchase slaves. Within Denning's insertions in the *Baltimore Sun* he would often promise cash two or three times in the same add. *"I will pay the highest prices in cash"* he claimed, followed several lines later with *"I am always in the market with the cash."* [22]

In October of 1849 Denning moved his establishment to a pen at 18 South Frederick Street, Between Baltimore and Second Streets. He continued to operate from the house *"with trees in front"* for a number of years.[23]

Jonathan Means Wilson

Although Jonathan Wilson became noted for his slave trade throughout the South little is known about his business.

As early as 1839 Wilson was operating as an agent for Hope Slatter. During the latter 1840s he had switched allegiance to Joseph Donovan. It was not until the summer of 1849 that Donovan dissolved his association with Wilson, allowing him to expand in the trade under his own name.[24]

Wilson's pen was located on Camden Street, several doors from Light Street. Early in his operation from this location he associated himself with long time trader G. H. Duke, an association that was to last until June of 1856.[25]

Six months later Wilson took a new partner under his wing, son-in-law Moses Hindes, a partnership that was to continue until the Civil War interrupted the domestic slave trade nationwide.[26] As a consequence Wilson and Hindes' final ads for slaves appeared during the last of May 1861.[27]

It is interesting to note that within the entire body of surviving New Orleans slave manifests Wilson's trade is strangely absent. He is shown as shipping only two slaves on an 1851 shipment to that city.[28]

Adding to the mystery of his absence from these records is the fact that he was known to have participated in the slave trade, particularly to New Orleans, in a major way.

Bernard Moore Campbell

Two of the more prominent Baltimore based traders were Bernard Moore Campbell and his brother, and junior partner, Walter Lewis Campbell. The earliest surviving record of a

New Orleans slave shipment by the Campbells from Baltimore was during the third week of March 1844. The 211-ton Baltimore built brig **Kirkwood**, moored at Smith's Dock, had loaded 69 slaves for a total of one non resident and three resident traders. On board were 16 slaves belonging to the Campbell brothers.[29]

During their first four years of trading in the city the Campbell slave pen was located at 26 Conway Street (Several door west of Hanover Street on the south side of Conway). Across the street and down the block was the Otterbein Church.[30]

The Campbells quickly came to the realization that agents were an important part of any slave trade establishment. One such agent working the Southern Maryland market for the Campbells was John G. Campbell who began running ads on behalf of the brothers in the *Port Tobacco Times* as early as 1845. He often sought *"young Negroes, whose owners have good titles and are slaves for life."* [31]

Seeking slaves for life was perfect for the New Orleans Market, a market that literally consumed the lives of thousands of the enslaved in the cotton and sugar cane fields of the hot, humid South. John Campbell would often end his ads identifying himself as *"the agent for B. M. Campbell."* [32]

During their first four years in business the Campbells' New Orleans trade was modest at best. Between the spring of 1844 and the early summer of 1848 the brothers only shipped 271 slaves to the southern port. When the Campbells purchased *"Slatter's old stand"* upon his departure from Baltimore in 1848 business picked up quickly. The brothers now had one less major trader to contend with and were permitted to use Slatter's name in their ads for a number of years.[33]

Between the late summer of 1848 and the autumn of 1849 the Campbells shipped 311 slaves to New Orleans, more than they had shipped in their first four years in the business. And business was about to get better.

Between 1850 and 1853 the brothers shipped an additional 619 slaves to the New Orleans Market. Although the records of slave manifests that have survived are scanty after 1853 it is apparent that the Campbells' business flourished as well as or better than most of the remaining traders in Baltimore.

In his excellent book *Slave Trading in the Old South* Frederic Bancroft indicated, *"The height of the success of the Campbells was near the end of the decade (1850's)."* [34]

So successful had the Campbells become that they established a farm eighty miles north of New Orleans where any slaves not sold by June were acclimated to the Southern Market. When shipments began again in earnest during the autumn season the Campbells already had a large group of these acclimated slaves to pick from. [35]

By May of 1861 the Civil War had all but ended the slave trade business flowing to the South out of Baltimore. The Campbells were able to continue to make money while boarding slaves for the city (suspected runaways) or for slaveholders fearful of losing their property to the Union.

By 1862 emancipation of slaves in the District of Columbia was well on its way to becoming a reality. During the spring of that year President Lincoln signed an act *"for the release of certain persons held to service or labor in the District of Columbia by reason of African descent."* [36]

Congressional hearings were held in late spring to determine the true value of a slave in order that the slaveholder might be fairly compensated after emancipation. The slave trader invited to testify as to the value of each slave was Bernard Moore Campbell. [37]

The signing of the act had caused an exodus of slaves to arrive in the District expecting to be freed. This action prompted a number of slaveholders in Maryland, in fear of their slaves running away, to compensate Campbell for jailing their slaves for safekeeping.[38] Campbell was making money on both ends of the deal.

A number of the incarcerated slaves, once able to have some movement of freedom on the plantation, quickly grew restless in their new jail surroundings. One week before Campbell was to leave for Washington to testify the slaves in the Pratt Street pen revolted.[39]

It was customary for slaves in Campbell's pen to have free movement in the courtyard until 7:00 p.m. every night. After that hour they were locked in their apartment until 5:00 a.m. the following day.[40] This allowed them time for socializing, cooking, washing their clothes, and playing games during daylight hours.

On Saturday night, May 31, when Campbell attempted to make the slaves go to their apartments they refused. Campbell was forced to leave the yard for fear of injury from the increasingly unruly captives, seventy-two in number.

After the police arrived and entered the yard of the slave jail a near riot resulted. Fights broke out between the police and a number of the male slaves who used anything they could get their hands on the strike the officers.

During the fray a "stout athletic Negro named Copely" struck Campbell on the back part of the face and head. More than twenty police were required to finally subdue the slaves and force them into their apartments. The men were handcuffed during the night to avoid any further complications. In all, the near riot had lasted for half an hour.[41]

When Campbell arrived in Congress to testify, *"a red and still angry welt slashed across his forehead, and his swollen black eye was black and blue."* [42]

The following summer the streets of Baltimore were filled with scenes of excitement as soldiers poured into the city after the battle of Gettysburg.

The Campbells' pen became the center of attention as Union troops approached the jail with orders to free the male slaves.

As Union troops, under the command of Colonel William Birney, marched toward the intersection of Howard and Pratt Streets, a large crowd of local citizens had begun to gather. In the aftermath of the hostilities at Gettysburg three weeks earlier there had been no shortage of excitement in the streets of Baltimore.

Birney arrived, with orders in hand, making his way towards the unobtrusive two-story brick building. Word had spread quickly throughout the crowd that something momentous was about to occur.

Colonel Birney walked forward, showing a document to the man who had unlocked the door of the establishment. He was delivering special order #202, an action by the government giving him the authority to free the slaves held in trader's pens throughout the city.

Although Bernard Moore Campbell and his brother Lewis (proprietors of the jail) were absent from the city, the prison's steward allowed Colonel Birney to enter without hesitation. As the soldiers passed the jail keep they moved through to the back of the building and into the yard of the compound.

Portions of the east and west sides of the courtyard were home to the buildings where the slaves were kept locked during the night. The air in the yard, trapped by the high walls surrounding the compound, was stagnant and almost suffocating. In all there were fifty-six men, women and children milling about the yard.

Susan Collins, of Ellicott Mills, held her four month old son Willie to her breast. She had spent twenty-four months in the pen, becoming pregnant and giving birth to him during her incarceration. Also impregnated during her fifteen month stay in the prison was Matilda Shipley of Montgomery County. She stood in the blazing heat of the yard holding her eight month old son Henry close to her body.

Without exception none of the inmates were owned by the Campbells but had been placed there for safekeeping. Each slave's imprisonment brought the ex-traffickers in human flesh 25 cents each per day, for a total of $98 per week.

Sixteen of the men before them were shackled, by twos, with heavy irons on their ankles. One individual stood, legs chained to one another, while a separate chain, connected to the leg irons, was suspended to his waist. Birney had called for the blacksmith who was already present and proceeding to remove the men from their encumbrances.

As the freed slaves made their way onto Pratt Street many of the friends or family greeted the women and children. The adult males who had been freed willingly marched with Birney's soldiers the short distance to the Colonel's headquarters on Camden Street. There they proceeded to take an oath and enlist into the service of the Union Army under Birney's second U.S. Colored troops. It was July 27th, 1863 and the pen, which had housed thousands of slaves over a period of twenty-five years, had been officially put out of business.[43]

The following is a list of those slaves who were freed from Bernard-Campbell's slave pen by the Union Army. The slave's name is indicated first, followed by the names of the owners (in parenthesis), the area, and the number of months, days, or years of incarceration. The slaves who joined the Union Army are asterisked.

William (Williams) Baltimore 23 days

Baden, Sophia (William Contee) Prince George's 5 months

Banks*, Dan (William Ammison) Annapolis 30 months

Bell*, Edward (Phillip E. Berry) Georgetown 17 months

Bond, Henrietta (Owen Gardner) Relay House 8 months

Brooks, Jane (James Chalbut) Prince George's 15 months

Clark, Martha (Thomas E. Berry) Prince George's 12 months

Chisler*, James C. (James C. Gustaw) St. Mary's 8 months

Clark*, Daniel (Thomas E. Berry) George's 11 months

Clark*,Robert (John Higgins) Prince George's 13 months

Collins, Susan (Hammond Doucy) Ellicott Mills 24 months

Collins, Willie (4 months old) (Hammond Doucy) Ellicott Mills born in prison

Coucy, Jane (John C. Cook) Washington D.C. 16 months

Davis*, Samuel (William H. Clagget) Prince George's 4 months

Debtor, Martha (Washington Duval) Montgomery 12 months

Dent*, James (Alfred Osborne)   Prince George's 22 months

Dickson*, Andrew (William Anderson) Annapolis 13 months

Dorm, Harriett (Robert E. Turner) Baltimore 9 months

Dorry*, Charles (Thomas Worthington) Baltimore 10 days

Dorsey*, Charles (James Reynolds) Baltimore 6 months

Elliott, Mary (Charles R. Duvall) Annapolis Junction 13 months

Fletcher*, Michael (Charles Hill) Prince George's 14 months

Fletcher*, Stephen (Charles Hill) Prince George's 14 months

Foote*, Charles (Dr. Thomas Ristar) Baltimore 15 months

Foote*, Perry (Dr. Thomas Ristar) Baltimore 15 months

Foster, Jane (Frederick Talbot) Baltimore 3 months

Foster, Louisa (John Talbot) Baltimore 23 months

Foster, Philip (2 years old) (John Talbot) Baltimore 23 months

Hammond*, George (Reese Hammond) Anne Arundel 24 months

Harrod, Lenah (Dr. S. Makel) Georgetown 15 months

Harrod, Rachel (6 years old) (Dr. S. Makel) Georgetown 15 months

Ivens, Jane (Thomas Baldwin) Baltimore 19 months

Johnson, Eliza (Maj. Rupel- McClellan's staff) Washington D.C. 4 months

Kittle, Maria (Washington Bell) Prince George's 7 months

Langly, Mary Jane (Henry Langly) St.Mary's 7 months.

Lee*, Pat (Alfred Roby) Alexandria 17 months.

Lincoln*, Abraham (Thomas T. Welch) Anne Arundel 15 months.

Lincoln*, Dan (Thomas T. Welch) Anne Arundel 15 months.

Parker, Mary J. (Samuel Dorsey) Baltimore 12 months.

Queen, Ellen (William Hill) 9 months.

Robertson, Ellen J. (Uriah Hessett) Washington D.C. 15 months.

Scott, Francis (Benjamin A. Flurry) Baltimore 15 months.

Sewell*, Marwin (James H. Alby) St. Mary's 15 months.

Shipley, Henry (8 months old) (Washington Duval) Montgomery born in prison.

Shipley, Matilda (Washington Duval) Montgomery 15 months

Simmons, Sophia (William B. Hill) Malburn 12 months

Simms*, William (Nancy Counter) Prince George's 17 months

Snow, Hannah (Emanuel Wade) Baltimore 15 months

Sparr, Willis (William Brogden) Anne Arundel 4 months

Stevenson, Elisa (Samuel E. Brooks) Baltimore 12 months

Thomas*, James (John N. Smoot) Georgetown, Del.18 months

Thomson*, Phillip (Michael Allender) Baltimore 17 months

Toodles*, Henry (George Ranskin) Baltimore 4 months

Toodles*, John F. (James Mulligan) Prince George's 3 years

Walker*, James (William Ammison) Annapolis 16 months

Ward, Betsey (Dr. Snyder) Georgetown 23 months

Wells, Mother (William B. Hill) Malburn 12 months

West, Virginia (William Claggett) Prince George's 7 months [44]

With the closing of the Campbells' pen one of the darkest hours in Baltimore's history, the domestic slave trade, had come to an end.

A Chronology of Bernard Moore Campbell's New Orleans Trade

3/23/44- Kirkwood (brig) (16 slaves) Smith's Dock
11/30/44- Margaret Hugg (barque) (20 slaves) Corner's Wharf
1/4/45- Kirkwood (brig) (12 slaves)

2/8/45- Margaret Hugg (barque) (15 slaves) Corner's Wharf

3/1/45- Victorine (brig) (17 slaves) Smith's Dock

3/22/45- Home (barque) (12 slaves)

4/15/45- Kirkwood (brig) (30 slaves) Frederick Street Dock

11/29/45- St. Mary (brig) (7 slaves)

12/17/45- Victorine (brig) (2 slaves)

12/27/45- Paoli (barque) (6 slaves)

1/14/46- Kirkwood (brig) (10 slaves)

3/14/46- Victorine (brig) (1 slave)

4/4/46- Kirkwood (brig) (14 slaves)

4/25/46- Architect (brig) (6 slaves) Flannigan's Wharf

5/18/46- Louisa (barque) (6 slaves)

9/7/46- Globe (brig) (2 slaves)

12/10/46- Kirkwood (brig) (18 slaves) Frederick Street Dock

12/31/46- Victorine (brig) (8 slaves) Smith's Dock

1/19/47- General Pinckney (brig) (32 slaves) Smith's Dock

2/16/47- Zoe (9 slaves)

3/9/47- Kirkwood (brig) (21 slaves) Frederick Street Dock

10/9/48- Union (brig) (14 slaves) Frederick Street Dock

10/14/48- Kirkwood (barque) (52 slaves) Flannigan's Wharf

11/18/48- Elizabeth (barque) (45 slaves) Flannigan's Wharf

12/1/48- Delanarian (barque) (26 slaves) Frederick Street Dock

12/16/48- Union (brig) (41 slaves) Frederick Street Dock

3/7/49- Union (brig) (20 slaves) Frederick Street Dock

3/31/49- Louisa (barque) (13 slaves) Flannigan's Wharf

4/19/49- *Henry A. Barling (schooner)* (13 slaves)
Flannigan's Wharf

5/12/49- *Elizabeth (barque)* (8 slaves) *Flannigan's Wharf*

10/29/49- *Southerner (barque)* (9 slaves) *Frederick Street Dock*

11/5/49- *Louisa (barque)* (17 slaves) *Flannigan's Wharf*

11/17/49- *Union (brig)* (18 slaves) *Frederick Street Dock*

11/28/49- *Kirkwood (barque)* (13 slaves) *Flannigan's Wharf*

1/2/50- *Elizabeth (barque)* (17 slaves) *Jackson's Wharf*

1/20/50- *Southerner (barque)* (9 slaves) *Frederick Street Dock*

3/21/50- *Elizabeth (barque)* (30 slaves) *Flannigan's Wharf*

4/20/50- *Union (brig)* (9 slaves) *Frederick Street Dock*

11/27/50- *Narragansett (ship)* (17 slaves) *Henderson's Wharf*

12/18/50- *Charles (ship)* (32 slaves) *Henderson's Wharf*

1/20/51- *Cora (barque)* (11 slaves)

2/8/51- *Sarah Bridge (barque)* (38 slaves) *Henderson's Wharf*

2/14/51- *Henry A. Barling (schooner)* (15 slaves) *Henderson's Wharf*

3/10/51- *Edward Everett (ship)* (22 slaves) *Henderson's Wharf*

4/3/51- *Waverly (brig)* (16 slaves) *Henderson's Wharf*

4/23/51- *Charles (ship)* (9 slaves)

10/18/51- *Edward Everett (ship)* (8 slaves) *Henderson's Wharf*

11/18/51- *Mary Broughton (barque)* (36 slaves) *Henderson's Wharf*

12/18/51- Henry A. Barling (schooner) (39 slaves)

1/5/52- Southerner (barque) (26 slaves) Brown's Wharf (formerly Craigg's Wharf)

2/12/52- Nathaniel Hooper (ship) (27 slaves) Brown's Wharf (formerly Craigg's Wharf)

4/28/52- Abbott Lord (barque) (37 slaves) Henderson's Wharf

10/15/52- Brandywine (ship) (6 slaves) Henderson's Wharf

10/18/52- Helen A. Miller (ship) (105 slaves)

11/1/52- Jane Henderson (18 slaves) Henderson's Wharf

11/20/52- John S. Gittings (brig) (36 slaves) Henderson's Wharf

6/1/53- Patrick Henry (schooner) (15 slaves)

7/12/53- Seguin (brig) (17 slaves)

11/26/53- Tangier (barque) (25 slaves)

11/15/56- P.R. Hazeltine (barque) (8 slaves) Henderson's Wharf

Bernard Moore and Walter Lewis Campbell 60 shipments between March of 1844 and November 1856 (all but one of these shipments occurred between March 1844 and November 1853) Of those whose age was discernable 12.1 percent were ten years of age or under. Total number shipped to New Orleans was 1,279 (21+ average per shipment)

Chapter 11
Baltimore Traders' Banner Years
1840-1849

*D*uring the decade of the 1840s at least 144 vessels carrying slaves sailed from Baltimore to New Orleans. More than 60 percent were major shipments for the Southern Market. The number of slaves gleaned from surviving records for the decade reached 5,712. Clearly the city had become the leading exporter of slave labor in the upper South. One of the major reasons for the shift in emphasis to Baltimore was the introduction of at least four major trading firms, other than Hope Hull Slatter's, that had been non existent prior to 1840: Joseph S. Donovan, Bernard and Walter Campbell, Jonathan M. Wilson and John S. Denning.

The four major available vessel types were used to transport the valuable human cargo. Brigs and barques, most averaging 180-350 tons burthen were the vessels used more often than any other for the packet lines that regularly plied their trade from Baltimore. Vessels as small as 119-tons or as large as 708-tons were also used. Anything moving over water with available space in the cargo hold could and would be used.

Major competitors made a number of significant shipments in the trade. In January of 1842 the 444-ton ship *Tippecanoe* was towed out of her berth at Chase's Wharf. Captained by

Master Adams Gray, the vessel carried 115 slaves, most shipped on behalf of James Franklin Purvis, Hope Hull Slatter, and Joshua Staples. Captain Gray shipped his forty year old slave Dolly Harris, J. W. Chenowith took twenty-four year old Nathaniel Morton and John F. Strohn placed twenty-eight year old Ben on board.[1]

In the autumn of 1842 the 534-ton ship **Burlington** received eighty slaves, seventy-six of which were owned by Hope Hull Slatter.[2]

During the early autumn of 1843 the 560-ton ship **Scotia**, captained by Henry Leslie, weighed anchor with ninety-seven slaves, owned by William Harker and Hope Hull Slatter. Although the youngest slave on board was twelve months old, most were young adults probably destined for the cotton and sugar cane plantations of New Orleans.[3]

Less than five weeks later the 523-ton ship **Superb**, docked at Tennant's Wharf, received 117 slaves on board. Captained by John G. Gatchel, the vessel carried its human cargo for Hope Hull Slatter and Joseph S. Donovan.[4]

The following month the 211-ton brig **Kirkwood** received ninety-one slaves at Smith's Wharf. Captained by Hugh Martin the vessel took consignments for Hope Hull Slatter and Joseph S. Donovan.[5]

Between February and December of 1844 four hundred forty-three slaves were carried during thirteen packet shipments to New Orleans. The decade's greatest shipments were, however, still to come.

Between 1845 and 1847 Slatter, Donovan, and Campbell shipped slaves to New Orleans in record numbers. Baltimore transferred 3,059 souls to the southern queen of the slave market. The three interstate giants shipped all but 439 slaves.

The most productive fifty-two week period in the trade occurred between December 20, 1844 and December 17, 1845. At least 1,251 slaves were shipped from Baltimore to the New Orleans market. In the course of the twenty-two shipments brigs were the vessel of choice fifteen times while barques were used on seven occasions.

The 239-ton brig *Victorine* shipped twenty-four slaves during the third week of December 1844. Captained by J. B. Sanner, the vessel carried fifteen slaves for Thomas Williams and nine for Richard S. D. Gardiner. Among those on board were six members of the Hall family ranging in age from four months to forty-eight years of age.[6]

During the same week the 363-ton barque *Georgia* left the port under the guidance of Captain James Otis with forty souls on board owned by Robert J. Brent. Eighteen were children between nine months and ten years of age.[7]

The first week of January 1845 brought what was to be one of the four largest shipments of the period. The 211-ton brig *Kirkwood*, captained by Hugh Martin had 110 slaves below deck. Among those shipping were Bernard Campbell, Joseph S. Donovan, and Hope Hull Slatter. Twenty-seven of the souls on board were children, ten years of age and under.[8]

On January 18th one 199-ton brig *Catharine* left Smith's Wharf with forty-nine slaves on board shipped by Joseph S. Donovan. Eight were children ten years of age and under.[9]

Bernard Campbell, William Harker, Joseph S. Donovan and Hope Hull Slatter shared space of the 327-ton barque *Margaret Hugg* when the vessel weighed anchor the second week of February, from Corner'sWharf. Captained by William H. Litton the vessel carried 53 slaves, seven of whom were children ten years of age and under.[10]

Not all of the shipments by traders were great in number. Ten days after the shipment of the *Margaret Hugg* the 345-ton barque *Nancy W. Stevens*, loading at McElderry's Dock (current site of Baltimore's Power Plant), shipped 7 slaves, between the ages of four and thirty-five, for traveling trader Ebenezer Rodbind.[11]

On the first day of March the brig *Victorine*, newly arrived from New Orleans, received cargo while anchored at Smith's

Dock. Ebenezer Rodbind, Hope Hull Slatter, Joseph S. Donovan, and Bernard Campbell shipped 82 slaves, sixteen of whom were children ten years of age and under.[12]

Three weeks later the 377-ton barque *Horne*, captained by W. J. Watts received ninety-nine slaves on behalf of shippers George V. Hollins, Bernard Moore Campbell, Joseph S. Donovan, Ebenezer Rodbind, and Hope Hull Slatter. Fifteen of those carried on board were children ten years of age and under.[13]

During mid April the Baltimore built brig *Kirkwood*, being prepared for the second New Orleans shipment of the year, received one 127 slaves on board at the Frederick Street Dock. Once again Bernard Moore Campbell, Ebenezer Rodbind, Hope Hull Slatter, and Joseph S. Donovan placed their consignment of human cargo on the same vessel. Twenty-two of the slaves were children ten years of age and under.[14]

Four weeks later the brig *Victorine*, being loaded for the vessel's third journey to New Orleans in five months, received ninety slaves for shippers Joseph S. Donovan, Ebenezer Rodbind, and Hope Hull Slatter. Nine of the slaves on board were children ten years of age and under.[15]

The autumn shipping season began with a vengeance when 382 slaves were carried in a two month period between the second week of September and the second week of November. Among the vessels were the barque *Paoli*, the brig *Victorine*, the brig *P. Soule*, and the brig *Kirkwood*. Two of the vessels weighed anchor from the Frederick Street Dock while the other two weighed anchor from Flannigan's Wharf and Smith's Dock respectively. Thirty-four of those shipped were ten years of age and under.

In all, during the fifty-two week period ending December 27, 1845, two hundred of those shipped to New Orleans were children ten years of age and under.

The following year 911 slaves were carried to New Orleans. The shipping season from September of 1846 to

March of 1847, a period of only six months, was one of the busiest in Baltimore's history.

One of the shipments during this period was that of the barque *Hermitage*. Built by Baltimore shipbuilders Cooper and Abrams, the owners boasted of a one hundred-three foot long deck length, breadth of twenty-six feet, and depth of hole as twelve feet, five inches.[16]

The vessel, completed in 1844, was used only once to carry slaves to the port of New Orleans. Space on the vessel had been hired during the autumn of 1846 to carry a total of ninety slaves, most of whom belonging to Hope Hull Slatter, Joseph S. Donovan, and traveling trader Thomas Williams. On October 28th the roll call was completed and the barque, under the direction of Captain John H. Frey, began its twenty-six day voyage to New Orleans.[17]

In the seven-month season eleven shipments by major inter-state slave traders had forwarded more than 1,042 slaves to the Southern capital of the slave market. Of those, 502 souls were sent on the "final passage" during a period of less than six weeks. And still, the voracious labor market of the South cried for more.

During July of 1847 a rare summer shipment of slaves left O'Donnell's Wharf, captained by Edward Hooper. The shipment was rare in that the entire manifest, transported on behalf of slave trader Hope Hull Slatter, carried only five children twelve years of age or under in its total of fifty slaves. The 180-ton brig *Union*, chosen for the shipment, was moored at O'Donnell's on the eastside of the Frederick Street Dock.[18]

Seven weeks later another shipment of fifty slaves, this time aboard the 346-ton barque *Pioneer*, left Flannigan's Wharf. Forty-nine of the human cargo belonged to Hope Hull Slatter. Of those only four were twelve years of age and under. Slatter was beginning to ship adults with greater frequency.[19]

Roll call was performed on the 316-ton barque *Louisa* on October 11th. On board Captain F. A. Gunby supervised the placement of the twenty-eight slaves belonging to Hope Slatter below deck. Two days earlier Joseph S. Donovan had placed forty-six slaves on the *Louisa*.[20]

Throughout the final two years of the decade numerous additional shipments were made under the direction of Baltimore based slave traders.

Among those shipments some of those of significant number were: the *Kirkwood* (168 slaves), the *E.H. Chapin* (101 slaves), the *Union* (46 slaves), the *Union* (64 slaves), the *Kirkwood* (147 slaves), the *Elizabeth* (139 slaves), the *Union* (139 slaves), the *Union* (42 slaves), the *Southerner* (94 slaves), the *Union* (65 slaves), and the *Kirkwood* (59 slaves).

A number of historians believe that the New Orleans market probably received about seventy to seventy-five percent of the entire shipments of slaves leaving Baltimore and ports in Virginia. A record of the Customs House in Baltimore, copied in Harriet Beecher Stowe's *Key to Uncle Tom's Cabin*, seems to confirm that figure. According to the report 1,043 slaves were shipped from Baltimore to Southern ports between January 6, 1851 and November 20, 1852. Of that number 742 (seventy-one percent) were shipped to New Orleans. The top two runners-up were Norfolk with 261 (nineteen percent) and Charleston with 68 (6.5 percent).[21]

Epilogue

The insatiable demand for slave labor in the South led to the sales of thousands of families and individuals in Maryland after the turn of the nineteenth century. Baltimore, with its central location and excellent shipping industry became the focal point for an ever-expanding slave market. Slave traders and speculators searched the countryside for slaves, brought them in chains into the port, and transported them on packet ships for resale in New Orleans and other cities.

Men, women and children, heartbroken and afraid, were shipped on their final passage. The death of separation became commonplace as the voracious southern economy swallowed their identities and, in many cases, their lives.

For a season "cash for blood" became the cry of the men of dark deeds. Baltimore's holocaust consumed thousands of mothers, fathers, daughters and sons as their bodies were used for labor and collateral to build businesses throughout the South.

Index to Inward Bound Slave Manifests
Into the Port of New Orleans
From Baltimore and Other Maryland Ports
1818-1856

The heart of this work is the following index of inward bound slave manifests to the port of New Orleans. The bulk of the surviving records that have been indexed cover a period between 1818 and 1853.

Of the records relating to Maryland (most of which indicate departure from the city of Baltimore) the full names of more than 8,000 slaves were discernable. The first names of another 3,550 slaves were discernible in the manifests. Of the total, the names of 416 slaves were neither discernible by first nor last name.

Whenever possible the author attempted to remain faithful to the spelling (whether correct or incorrect) visible in the documents. This process proved extremely difficult in some cases, particularly where records were faded. Many examples of the incorrect spellings of names could be mentioned here. For the sake of brevity, however, the author points to the excellent example of the name Harriet the variations of which were: Hariet, Harriet, Harriett, Harriot, and Harriott.

It is this portion of the reference work presented here that the author labored over for the better part of a year. Names are sacred in that they are the symbols of the human entity to which they were given. Outside of the manifests collected during the domestic slave trade, the vast majority of the following names have never appeared in print before this listing.

The original manifests are stored in record group 36 of the National Archives in Washington D.C. The index is organized as follows:

Column 1: Surname: This is the surname of the slave when indicated (and discernable).

Column 2: First Name: This is the given name of the slave (when discernable)

Column 3: Age: This is the age of the slave recorded in a variety of ways. i.e. days, weeks, months, years.

Column 4: Ship: The name of the vessel on which the slave was placed for transportation.

Column 5: O/S: Record of the owner/shippers of said slaves. This category is helpful in determining trends in shipments of identified major inter-state traders. It also affords us with a study of one-time shippers...those often shipping for purposes of transmigration (relocation).

Column 6: Date: The recorded dates when the Customs Collector called the roll and checked the slaves actual bodies and descriptors (also indicated in the document) against the manifest that had been prepared by the owner shipped. After it was determined that information matched the manifest the document was signed by the Customs official, the captain, and the owner or shipper.

Column 7: Depart: The port from which the vessel departed. Although more than 98% of this index is representative of Baltimore shipments there were several occasions when shipments originated in another location or when Baltimore vessels made stops to pick up additional slaves. These stop-offs or shipments from Anne Arundel or St.

Mary's counties were clearly the result of transmigration (relocation) and not the work of inter-state traders.

Surname	First Name	Age	Ship	O/S	Date	Depart
Abed	Treacy	26	Bostonian	Slatter, Hope Hull	Jan. 18, 1841	Balto.
Abed		infant	Bostonian	Slatter, Hope Hull	Jan. 18, 1841	Balto.
Aby	Lewis	24	Tippecanoe	Slatter, Hope Hull	Dec. 16, 1840	Balto.
Acers	John	17	Victorine	Rodbinc, Ebenezer	Dec. 31, 1846	Balto.
Acwith	Levi	26	Tippecanoe	Slatter, Hope Hull	Apr. 15, 1844	Balto.
Adams	Alexander	18	Kirkwood	Donovan, Joseph S.	Oct. 26, 1847	Balto.
Adams	Andrew	32	Henry A. Barling	Marriott, William H.	Oct. 28, 1848	Balto.
Adams	Caleb	28	Southerner	Campbe_, Bernard M.	Jan. 20, 1850	Balto.
Adams	Daniel	19	Union	Sheckles, Gannon	March 17, 1849	Balto.
Adams	Dinah	1	Mary Broughton	Campbe_l, Bernard M.	Nov. 18, 1851	Balto.
Adams	Garrison	28	Elizabeth	Campbell, Bernard M.	Jan. 2, 1850	Balto.
Adams	Henry	26	Elizabeth	Campbell, Bernard M.	Jan. 2, 1850	Balto.
Adams	Hester	16	Louisa	Slatter, Hope Hull	Oct. 11, 1847	Balto.
Adams	John	21	Victorine	Donovan, Joseph S.	Sept. 29, 1845	Balto.
Adams	Malinda	22	Kirkwood	Slatter, Henry F.	Dec. 10, 1846	Balto.
Adams	Nathan	27	Kirkwood	Williams, Thomas	Apr. 4, 1846	Balto.
Adams	Rutha	20	Mary Broughton	Campbell, Bernard M.	Nov. 18, 1851	Balto.
Addison	Benjamin	22	Hibernia	Woolfolk, Austin	Dec. 5, 1826	Balto.
Addison	Christy A.	18	St. Mary	Williams, Thomas	Nov. 29, 1845	Balto.
Addison	Edward	47	Harriet	Carroll, Charles	Dec. 7, 1836	Balto.
Addison	Ephraim	26	Zoe	Slatter, Hope Hull	Feb. 16, 1847	Balto.
Addison	Fanny	17	Hibernia	Woolfolk, Austin	Dec. 5, 1826	Balto.
Addison	Isaac	21	Victorine	Rodbind, Ebenezer	March 1, 1845	Balto.
Addison	Isaiah	18	Kirkwood	Donovan, Joseph S.	Sept. 28, 1846	Balto.
Addison	Joseph	18	Sarah Bridge	Campbell, Bernard M.	Feb. 8, 1851	Balto.
Addison	Mary Ann	20	Osprey	Tilletson, S.R.	Nov. 11, 1847	Balto.

Surname	First Name	Age	Ship	O/S	Date	Depart
Addison	Moses	47	Harriet	Carroll, Charles	Dec. 7, 1836	Balto.
Addison	Nancy	16	Kirkwood	Donovan, Joseph S.	Jan. 4, 1845	Balto.
Addison	Priscilla	18	Osprey	Tilletson, S.R.	Nov. 11, 1847	Balto.
Adison	Moses	24	Splendid	Slatter, Hope Hull	Apr. 24, 1841	Balto.
Adison	William	26	Splendid	Slatter, Hope Hull	Apr. 24, 1841	Balto.
Aerns	Ann	15	Catharine	Slatter, Hope Hull	Jan. 24, 1843	Balto.
Aerns	Margaret	14	Catharine	Slatter, Hope Hull	Jan. 24, 1843	Balto.
Ailsy	Ellis	22	Edward Everett	Campbell, Bernard M.	March 10, 1851	Balto.
Airs	Peter	20	Abbott Lord	Campbell, Bernard M.	April 28, 1852	Balto.
Akins	James	16	Russell	Slatter, Hope Hull	March 1, 1839	Balto.
Alcorn	Phillip	25	Brunswick	Woolfolk, Austin	Oct. 11, 1831	Balto.
Aldridge	Alfred	18	Solomon Saltus	Slatter, Hope Hull	Oct. 7, 1839	Balto.
Alen	Dominic	18	Kirkwood	Slatter, Hope Hull	Dec. 23, 1843	Balto.
Alexander	Ailsey	31	Isaac Franklin	Kephart, George	Feb. 1, 1839	Balto.
Alexander	Billy	39	Delawarian	Campbell, Bernard M.	Dec. 1, 1848	Balto.
Alexander	Caroline	33	Pharsalia	Daniel, Edward	Jan. 10, 1855	Balto.
Alexander	Elizabeth	17mon.	Isaac Franklin	Kephart, George	Feb. 1, 1839	Balto.
Alexander	Ellen	15	Pharsalia	Daniel, Edward	Jan. 10, 1855	Balto.
Alexander	Hetty	4	Isaac Franklin	Kephart, George	Feb. 1, 1839	Balto.
Alexander	Hillery	26	Elizabeth	Donovan, Joseph S.	Jan. 2, 1850	Balto.
Alexander	James	13	Pharsalia	Daniel, Edward	Jan. 10, 1855	Balto.
Alexander	Jube	23	Isaac Franklin	Kephart, George	Feb. 1, 1839	Balto.
Alexander	Julia	11	Pharsalia	Daniel, Edward	Jan. 10, 1855	Balto.
Alexander	Linda	3	Pharsalia	Daniel, Edward	Jan. 10, 1855	Balto.
Alexander	Sandy	20	Union	Donovan, Joseph S.	May 13, 1848	Balto.
Alfred	Solomon	18	Kirkwood	Slatter, Hope Hull	Jan. 14, 1846	Balto.

Surname	First Name	Age	Ship	O/S	Date	Depart
Allden	Robert	23	General Pinckney	Donovan, Joseph S.	Feb. 21, 1846	Balto.
Allen	Albert	19	Elizabeth	Donovan, Joseph S.	Jan. 2, 1850	Balto.
Allen	Alexander	14	Brunswick	Woolfolk, Austin	Oct. 11, 1831	Balto.
Allen	Amos	21	Kirkwood	Slatter, Hope Hull	Oct. 16, 1845	Balto.
Allen	Anthony	24	Union	Sheckles, Gannon	March 17, 1849	Balto.
Allen	Charles	14	Kirkwood	Slatter, Hope Hull	Jan. 4, 1845	Balto.
Allen	Charles	17	Kirkwood	Donovan, Joseph S.	Oct. 26, 1847	Balto.
Allen	Charloitte	19	States	Woolfolk, Austin	Apr. 14, 1828	Balto.
Allen	David	20	Kirkwood	Slatter, Hope Hull	Apr. 4, 1846	Balto.
Allen	Debby	20	Sarah Bridge	Campbell, Bernard M.	Feb. 8, 1851	Balto.
Allen	Elizabeth	17	Salvadora	Slatter, Hope Hull	Sept. 28, 1846	Balto.
Allen	George	9	Southerner	Donovan, Joseph S.	Jan. 5, 1852	Balto.
Allen	James	25	Union	Williams, Thomas	Oct. 9, 1848	Balto.
Allen	James	25	Victorine	Donovan, Joseph S.	May 22, 1844	Balto.
Allen	James	22	Waverly	Campbell, Bernard M.	Apr. 3, 1851	Balto.
Allen	Jane	30	Burlington	Slatter, Hope Hull	Oct. 21, 1842	Balto.
Allen	Mary	25	Mary	Lee, John	March 3, 1840	Balto.
Allen	Milly	13	Home	Rodbind, Ebenezer	March 22, 1845	Balto.
Allen	Nace	24	Scotia	Harker, William	Sept. 30, 1843	Balto.
Allen	Nancy	17	Jefferson	Woolfolk, Austin	Dec. 24, 1827	Balto.
Allen	Sarah Jane	15	Superb	Slatter, Hope Hull	Nov. 1, 1843	Balto.
Allen	Spencer	25	Kirkwood	Slatter, Hope Hull	Oct. 16, 1845	Balto.
Allen	Susan	19	Russell	Lee, John	Feb. 28, 2839	Balto.
Allen	William	21	Kirkwood	Donovan, Joseph S.	March 23, 1844	Balto.
Allen		infant	Sarah Bridge	Campbell, Bernard M.	Feb. 8, 1851	Balto.
Allensworth	David	20	Elizabeth	Donovan, Joseph S.	Nov. 18, 1848	Balto.

Surname	First Name	Age	Ship	O/S	Date	Depart
Allin	Eliza	12	Catharine	Slatter, Hope Hull	Jan. 24, 1843	Balto.
Allin	Notley	20	Tippecanoe	Slatter, Hope Hull	Apr. 1, 1841	Balto.
Allin	Sarah Ann	13	Irad Ferry	Slatter, Hope Hull	Dec. 9, 1842	Balto.
Allis	John	15	Shamrock	Guyton, Elisha	March 11, 1840	Balto.
Allison	James	21	Elizabeth	Donovan, Joseph S.	May 12, 1849	Balto.
Alton	Jesse	24	Elizabeth	Campbell, Bernard M.	Nov. 18, 1848	Balto.
Altor	Maria	17	Eliza F.Mason	Donovan, Joseph S.	Nov. 13, 1851	Balto.
Always	Anthony	30	Lafayette	Woolfolk, Joseph B.	Oct. 18, 1828	Balto.
Alzens	Penton	22	Kirkwood	Slatter, Hope Hull	Oct. 16, 1845	Balto.
Ambush	Cassy	35	Osprey	Rodbind, Ebenezer	Nov. 11, 1847	Balto.
Ambush	Eliza	16	Isaac Franklin	Kephart, George	Sept. 28, 1838	Balto.
Ambush	James	35	Hermitage	Slatter, Hope Hull	Oct. 28, 1846	Balto.
Ames	Polly	16	Irad Ferry	Wilson, J.W.	May 6, 1839	Balto.
Amley	Thomas	22	Salvadora	Slatter, Hope Hull	Sept. 28, 1846	Balto.
Amos	Joshua	22	Lapwing	Woolfolk, Samuel M.	Feb. 15, 1827	Balto.
Anderson	Albert	22	Victorine	Slatter, Hope Hull	Sept. 12, 1846	Balto.
Anderson	Alexander	21	Victorine	Donovan, Joseph S.	May 22, 1844	Balto.
Anderson	Ann	25	Irad Ferry	Slatter, Hope Hull	Dec. 9, 1842	Balto.
Anderson	Bland	30	Victorine	Kendall, James.B	Dec. 9, 1843	Balto.
Anderson	Christiana	14	Victorine	Slatter, Hope Hull	May 14, 1845	Balto.
Anderson	David	28	Sarah Ann	Reich, Isaac	Oct. 15, 1836	Balto.
Anderson	Elijah	23	Superb	Slatter, Hope Hull	Nov. 1, 1843	Balto.
Anderson	Eliza	13	Kirkwood	Donovan, Joseph S.	Oct. 26, 1847	Balto.
Anderson	Elizabeth	14	Elizabeth	Campbell, Bernard M.	March 21, 1850	Balto.
Anderson	Esther	10	Solomon Saltus	Slatter, Hope Hull	Oct. 7, 1839	Balto.
Anderson	Fanny	19	Catharine	Woolfolk, Austin	March 3, 1829	Balto.

Surname	First Name	Age	Ship	O/S	Date	Depart
Anderson	Fanny	25	Gamicleftt	Slatter, Hope Hull	Nov. 25, 1840	Balto.
Anderson	George	infant	E.H.Chapin	Donovan, Joseph S.	Dec. 2, 1847	Balto.
Anderson	Henderson	21	Kirkwood	Donovan, Joseph S.	Sept. 28, 1846	Balto.
Anderson	Henry	25	Isaac Franklin	Slatter, Hope Hull	Sept. 28, 1838	Balto.
Anderson	Hester	46	Lafayette	Woolfolk, Austin	Oct. 18, 1828	Balto.
Anderson	Isaac	28	E.H.Chapin	Donovan, Joseph S.	Dec. 2, 1847	Balto.
Anderson	Jackson	14	Kirkwood	Slatter, Hope Hull	Jan. 14, 1846	Balto.
Anderson	Jacob	24	Lafayette	Woolfolk, Austin	Oct. 18, 1828	Balto.
Anderson	James	20	Kirkwood	Rodbind, Ebenezer	Apr. 15, 1845	Balto.
Anderson	James	19	Waverly	Campbel., Bernard M.	Apr. 3, 1851	Balto.
Anderson	Jane	12	Kirkwood	Slatter, Hope Hull	Dec. 23, 1843	Balto.
Anderson	Jenny	24	Hibernia	Woolfolk, Austin	Dec. 5, 1826	Balto.
Anderson	John	16	Brunswick	Woolfolk, Austin	Oct. 11, 1831	Balto.
Anderson	John	14	Gamicleftt	Slatter, Hope Hull	Nov. 25, 1840	Balto.
Anderson	John	25	Kirkwood	Donovan, Joseph S.	Dec. 23, 1843	Balto.
Anderson	John	34	Superb	Slatter, Hope Hull	Nov. 1, 1843	Balto.
Anderson	Louisa C.	17	Victorine	Donovan, Joseph S.	Dec. 31, 1846	Balto.
Anderson	Mariah	25	E.H.Chapin	Donovan, Joseph S.	Dec. 2, 1847	Balto.
Anderson	Mary	13	Victorine	Slatter, Hope Hull	May 14, 1845	Balto.
Anderson	Matilda	16	Kirkwood	Donovan, Joseph S.	Jan. 4, 1845	Balto.
Anderson	Matilda	17	Southerner	Donovan, Joseph S.	Jan. 5, 1852	Balto.
Anderson	Milly	16	Victorine	Slatter, Hope Hull	Dec. 17, 1845	Balto.
Anderson	Nathan	22	Kirkwood	Donovan, Joseph S.	Oct. 26, 1847	Balto.
Anderson	Peter	10	Kirkwood	Slatter, Henry F.	Dec. 10, 1846	Balto.
Anderson	Peter	30	Scotia	Harker, William	Sept. 30, 1843	Balto.
Anderson	Priscilla	15	Architect	Purvis, James Franklin	Feb. 3, 1841	Balto.

Surname	First Name	Age	Ship	O/S	Date	Depart
Anderson	Rebecca	20	Lady Monroe	Woolfolk, Austin	March 25, 1825	Balto.
Anderson	Rebecca	18	Southerner	Donovan, Joseph S.	Oct. 27, 1849	Balto.
Anderson	Samuel	18	Victorine	Donovan, Joseph S.	Sept. 29, 1845	Balto.
Anderson	Sarah	14	Kirkwood	Slatter, Hope Hull	Dec. 23, 1843	Balto.
Anderson	Susan	40	Kirkwood	Campbell, Bernard M.	Jan. 4, 1845	Balto.
Anderson	Thomas	16	Kirkwood	Slatter, Hope Hull	Jan. 14, 1846	Balto.
Anderson	Thomas	13	St. Mary	Donovan, Joseph S.	Nov. 29, 1845	Balto.
Anderson	Tom	21	Isaac Franklin	Kephart, George	Feb. 1, 1839	Balto.
Anderson	Warren	25	Northumberland	Slatter, Hope Hull	Feb. 27, 1843	Balto.
Anderson	Washington	20	Kirkwood	Donovan, Joseph S.	Nov. 28, 1849	Balto.
Anderson	William	25	Algerine	Woolfolk, Joseph B.	Jan. 6, 1826	Balto.
Anderson	William	19	Kirkwood	Slatter, Hope Hull	Jan. 14, 1846	Balto.
Anderson	William	22	Superb	Donovan, Joseph S.	Nov. 2, 1843	Balto.
Anderson	William	19	Victorine	Rodbind, Ebenezer	Dec. 31, 1846	Balto.
Anderson	William	infant	Ganniclefft	Slatter, Hope Hull	Nov. 25, 1840	Balto.
Ann	Grace	18	Gazelle	Staples, Joseph	Feb.28, 1842	Balto.
Anness	Mary	16	Union	Sheckles, B.O.	Nov. 17, 1849	Balto.
Anthony	Joseph	18	John C. Calhoun	Donovan, Joseph S.	Oct. 24, 1850	Balto.
Anthony	Thomas	24	Hibernia	Woolfolk, Austin	Dec. 5, 1826	Balto.
Archer	John	22	Southerner	Rodbind, Ebenezer	Jan. 21, 1850	Balto.
Aren	Rachel	13	Colonel Howard	Donovan, Joseph S.	Nov. 21, 1844	Balto.
Armstrong	David	21	Uncas	Slatter, Hope Hull	Jan. 10, 1838	Balto.
Armstrong	Lewis	25	Scotia	Slatter, Hope Hull	Sept. 30, 1843	Balto.
Armstrong	Pere	30	Pioneer	Slatter, Hope Hull	Sept. 15, 1847	Balto.
Armstrong	Silvey	18	Victorine	Slatter, Hope Hull	Sept. 12, 1846	Balto.
Arnold	George	21	Hermitage	Williams, Thomas	Oct. 28, 1846	Balto.

Surname	First Name	Age	Ship	O/S	Date	Depart
Arnold	Matilda	14	Union	Campbel, Bernard M.	Dec. 16, 1848	Balto.
Arnold	Spencer	14	Elizabeth	Donovan, Joseph S.	Nov. 18, 1848	Balto.
Arnolds	Charlotte	12	Bostonian	Slatter, Hope Hull	Jan. 18, 1841	Balto.
Arthur	Maria	24	Isaac Franklin	Slatter, Hope Hull	Sept. 28, 1838	Balto.
Arthur	Mary	2	Isaac Franklin	Slatter, Hope Hull	Sept. 28, 1838	Balto.
Arthur	Montgomery	11	Southerner	Donovan, Joseph S.	Jan. 21, 1850	Balto.
Arts	Rebecca	19	Helen A. Miller	Campbel, Bernard M.	Oct. 18, 1852	Balto.
Asbury	David	20	Kirkwood	Donovan, Joseph S.	Oct. 26, 1847	Balto.
Asbury	George	17	Kirkwood	Donovan, Joseph S.	Oct. 26, 1847	Balto.
Asbury	Jane	16	Kirkwood	Donovan, Joseph S.	Oct. 26, 1847	Balto.
Asbury	William	17	Kirkwood	Donovan, Joseph S.	Oct. 26, 1847	Balto.
Asbury	Washington	20	Isaac Franklin	Slatter, Hope Hull	Sept. 28, 1838	Balto.
Ash	Charity	20	Hermitage	Williams, Thomas	Oct. 28, 1846	Balto.
Ash	Rachael	26	Tangier	Campbel, Bernard M.	Nov. 26, 1853	Balto.
Ashby	William	22	Elizabeth	Donovan, Joseph S.	Nov. 18, 1848	Balto.
Askew	Henry	22	Helen A. Miller	Campbell, Bernard M.	Oct. 18, 1852	Balto.
Askins	Daniel	19	Margaret Hugg	Campbell, Bernard M.	Feb. 8, 1845	Balto.
Ates	Aggy	27	Kirkwood	Williams, Thomas	Apr. 4, 1846	Balto.
Ates	Jackson	21	Kirkwood	Williams, Thomas	Apr. 4, 1846	Balto.
Ates	John	21	Kirkwood	Donovan, Joseph S.	Apr. 15, 1845	Balto.
Atkins	David	24	Kirkwood	Donovan, Joseph S.	March 9, 1847	Balto.
Atkins	Harrison	30	Louisa	Donovan, Joseph S.	Oct. 9, 1847	Balto.
Atkinson	Eliza	19	States	Woolfolk, Austin	Apr. 14, 1828	Balto.
Atkinson	Elizebeth	20	Pioneer	Slatter, Hope Hull	Sept. 15, 1847	Balto.
Atkinson	Jane	23	Kirkwood	Donovan, Joseph S.	Dec. 23, 1843	Balto.
Atkinson	Philip	15	Abbott Lord	Campbell, Bernard M.	April 28, 1852	Balto.

Surname	First Name	Age	Ship	O/S	Date	Depart
Austim	William	23	States	Woolfolk, Austin	Nov. 21, 1827	Balto.
Austin	Margaret	16	Bostonian	Slatter, Hope Hull	Jan. 18, 1841	Balto.
Austin	Mariah	10	Catharine	Donovan, Joseph S.	Jan. 18, 1845	Balto.
Ayers	Daniel	21	Kirkwood	Donovan, Joseph S.	Oct. 14, 1848	Balto.
Ayres	Isaac	17	Jefferson	Woolfolk, Austin	Dec. 24, 1827	Balto.
Ayres	Tom	17	States	Woolfolk, Austin	Nov. 21, 1827	Balto.
Backus	James	18	Victorine	Donovan, Joseph S.	Dec. 31, 1846	Balto.
Bacon	Bassil	21	Union	Donovan, Joseph S.	May 13, 1848	Balto.
Bacon	Sesiner	17	Margaret Forbs	Slatter, Hope Hull	Nov. 28, 1838	Balto.
Badeau	Henry	20	Tangier	Campbell, Bernard M.	Nov. 26, 1853	Balto.
Bailey	Anne	20	States	Woolfolk, Austin	Nov. 26, 1825	Balto.
Bailey	Benjamin	30	Architect	Slatter, Hope Hull	May 20, 1841	Balto.
Bailey	Charles	25	John S. Gittings	Campbell, Bernard M.	Nov. 20, 1852	Balto.
Bailey	Charlotte	22	Margaret Hugg	Campbell, Bernard M.	Nov. 30, 1844	Balto.
Bailey	Delphia	18	Union	Slatter, Hope Hull	July 26, 1847	Balto.
Bailey	Francis	20	Northumberland	Slatter, Hope Hull	Feb. 27, 1843	Balto.
Bailey	George	10	Liberator	Woolfolk, Austin	Nov. 12, 1828	Balto.
Bailey	Henry	20	Algerine	Woolfolk, Austin	March 25, 1826	Balto.
Bailey	Henry	18	Burlington	Slatter, Hope Hull	Oct. 21, 1842	Balto.
Bailey	Hester	20	Margaret Hugg	Campbell, Bernard M.	Feb. 8, 1845	Balto.
Bailey	John	22	General Pinckney	Slatter, Hope Hull	Jan. 19, 1847	Balto.
Bailey	Louisa	35	Venus	Harker, William	Nov. 17, 1845	Balto.
Bailey	Samuel	22	Tippecanoe	Harker, William	Dec. 16, 1840	Balto.
Bailey	Sarah	35	Margaret Hugg	Campbell, Bernard M.	Feb. 8, 1845	Balto.
Bailey	Simon	17	Kirkwood	Donovan, Joseph S.	Oct. 26, 1847	Balto.
Bailey	Stephen	22	Colonel Howard	Harker, William	Nov. 21, 1844	Balto.

Surname	First Name	Age	Ship	O/S	Date	Depart
Baily	Betsy Ann	16	Victorine	Donovan, Joseph S.	Oct. 25, 1844	Balto.
Baitz	William	21	Victorine	Donovan, Joseph S.	Sept. 29, 1845	Balto.
Baker	Charles	6	Kirkwood	Donovan, Joseph S.	Jan. 4, 1845	Balto.
Baker	Clabourn	2	Isaac Franklin	Slatter, Hope Hull	Sept. 28, 1838	Balto.
Baker	Emaly	11	Kirkwood	Donovan, Joseph S.	Dec. 10, 1846	Balto.
Baker	George	24	Victorine	Rodbind, Ebenezer	Dec. 31, 1846	Balto.
Baker	Harriet	19	Victorine	Rodbind, Ebenezer	Dec. 31, 1846	Balto.
Baker	Henry	14	Kirkwocd	Slatter, Hope Hull	Oct. 16, 1845	Balto.
Baker	Hester	19	Kirkwocd	Campbell, Bernard M.	Oct. 14, 1848	Balto.
Baker	John	21	Home	Donovan, Joseph S.	March 22, 1845	Balto.
Baker	John	23	Irad Ferry	Slatter, Hope Hull	Dec. 9, 1842	Balto.
Baker	John	8	Isaac Franklin	Kephart, George	Sept. 28, 1838	Balto.
Baker	John	27	Isaac Franklin	Kephart, George	Sept. 28, 1838	Balto.
Baker	Leitha	19	Paoli	Slatter, Hope Hull	Sept. 9, 1845	Balto.
Baker	Lewis	23	Isaac Franklin	Kephart, George	Sept. 28, 1838	Balto.
Baker	Mariah	7	Kirkwood	Donovar, Joseph S.	Jan. 4, 1845	Balto.
Baker	Mimy	27	Isaac Franklin	Kephart, George	Sept. 28, 1838	Balto.
Baker	Moses	19	Helen A. Miller	Campbell, Bernard M.	Oct. 18, 1852	Balto.
Baker	Moses	6	Isaac Franklin	Kephart, George	Sept. 28, 1838	Balto.
Baker	Moses	3	Kirkwood	Donovan, Joseph S.	Jan. 4, 1845	Balto.
Baker	Nicholas	3 mon.	Isaac Franklin	Kephart, George	Sept. 28, 1838	Balto.
Baker	Rachel	20	Isaac Franklin	Kephart, George	Sept. 28, 1838	Balto.
Baker	Richard	infant	Kirkwood	Donovan, Joseph S.	Jan. 4, 1845	Balto.
Baker	Sally	4	Isaac Franklin	Kephart, George	Sept. 28, 1838	Balto.
Baker	Thomas	25	Helen A. Miller	Campbell, Bernard M.	Oct. 18, 1852	Balto.
Baker	Thomas	4	Isaac Franklin	Kephart, George	Sept. 28, 1838	Balto.

Surname	First Name	Age	Ship	O/S	Date	Depart
Baker	William	21	John C. Calhoun	Donovan, Joseph S.	Oct. 24, 1850	Balto.
Baker	William	30	Salvadora	Slatter, Hope Hull	Sept. 28, 1846	Balto.
Baker		infant	Kirkwood	Campbell, Bernard M.	Oct. 14, 1848	Balto.
Baldwin	Harry	23	Kirkwood	Donovan, Joseph S.	Oct. 26, 1847	Balto.
Baldwin	Tyler	35	Intelligence	Anderson, David	Dec. 20, 1822	Balto.
Bales	Clarecy	9	Union	Donovan, Joseph S.	Dec. 16, 1848	Balto.
Bales	Pheny	8	Union	Donovan, Joseph S.	Dec. 16, 1848	Balto.
Ball	Ben	22	Abbott Lord	Campbell, Bernard M.	April 28, 1852	Balto.
Ball	Margaret	18	Abbott Lord	Campbell, Bernard M.	April 28, 1852	Balto.
Ball	Martha	16	Kirkwood	Donovan, Joseph S.	Sept. 28, 1846	Balto.
Ball	Robert	19	Victorine	Donovan, Joseph S.	May 14, 1845	Balto.
Ball	Rosetta	25	Julia	Woolfolk, Austin	Jan. 8, 1829	Balto.
Ball	Warner	21	Southerner	Donovan, Joseph S.	Oct. 27, 1849	Balto.
Ball		infant	Abbott Lord	Campbell, Bernard M.	April 28, 1852	Balto.
Ballad	Agnes	10	Southerner	Donovan, Joseph S.	Oct. 27, 1849	Balto.
Ballard	David	20	Union	Campbell, Bernard M.	Apr. 20, 1850	Balto.
Ballard	George	40	Home	Slatter, Hope Hull	March 22, 1845	Balto.
Ballinger	Peter	21	Cora	Donovan, Jospeh S.	Jan. 21, 1851	Balto.
Balten	Frederick	21	Eliza F.Mason	Donovan, Joseph S.	Nov. 13, 1851	Balto.
Baltimore	Lord	8	General Pinckney	Slatter, Hope Hull	Jan. 19, 1847	Balto.
Baltimore	Sally	16	Kirkwood	Crow, William	March 23, 1844	Balto.
Baltimore	Susan	14	Kirkwood	Slatter, Hope Hull	Oct. 16, 1845	Balto.
Balwin	Milly	8	Kirkwood	Slatter, Hope Hull	Dec. 23, 1843	Balto.
Banas	Mary Ann	17	Victorine	Donovan, Joseph S.	May 22, 1844	Balto.
Bangs	Henry	10	Louisa	Campbell, Bernard M.	March 31, 1849	Balto.
Bangs	James	23	Jefferson	Woolfolk, Austin	Dec. 24, 1827	Balto.

Surname	First Name	Age	Ship	O/S	Date	Depart
Bangs		19	Billow	Woolfolk, Joseph B.	Feb. 23, 1828	Balto.
Banion	Joseph	18	Kirkwood	Donovan, Joseph S.	March 9, 1847	Balto.
Banister	Rachel	26	Kirkwood	Donovan, Joseph S.	Oct. 14, 1848	Balto.
Bankitt	Daniel	21	Elizabeth	Donovan, Joseph S.	Nov. 18, 1848	Balto.
Banks	Alfred	26	Pioneer	Slatter, Hope Hull	Sept. 15, 1847	Balto.
Banks	Debby	16	Gannicleftt	Slatter, Hope Hull	Nov. 25, 1840	Balto.
Banks	Eleanor	16	Kirkwood	Campbell, Bernard M.	March 9, 1847	Balto.
Banks	Elisa	14	States	Woolfolk, Austin	Apr. 14, 1828	Balto.
Banks	Emeline	16	Burlington	Slatter, Hope Hull	Oct. 21, 1842	Balto.
Banks	Garrett	24	General Pinckney	Slatter, Hope Hull	Nov. 10, 1845	Balto.
Banks	George	21	Kirkwood	Donovan, Joseph S.	Oct. 26, 1847	Balto.
Banks	Grace	14	Architect	Crow, William	Feb. 3, 1841	Balto.
Banks	Hetty	17	Southerner	Rodbind, Ebenezer	Jan. 21, 1850	Balto.
Banks	James	22	Southerner	Donovan, Joseph S.	Oct. 27, 1849	Balto.
Banks	Jim	30	Abbott Lord	Campbell, Bernard M.	April 28, 1852	Balto.
Banks	John	14	Kirkwood	Williams, Thomas	Apr. 4, 1846	Balto.
Banks	John	16	Victorine	Slatter, Hope Hull	March 14, 1846	Balto.
Banks	Lewis	17	Zoe	Slatter, Hope Hull	Feb. 16, 1847	Balto.
Banks	Louisa	13	Gannicleftt	Slatter, Hope Hull	Nov. 25, 1840	Balto.
Banks	Maria	18	Kirkwood	Harker, William	March 23, 1844	Balto.
Banks	Maria	19	Margaret Hugg	Harker, William	Nov. 30, 1844	Balto.
Banks	Martha	10	Abbott Lord	Campbell, Bernard M.	April 28, 1852	Balto.
Banks	Mary	20	Isaac Franklin	Kephart, George	Sept. 28, 1838	Balto.
Banks	Matilda	45	Abbott Lord	Campbell, Bernard M.	April 28, 1852	Balto.
Banks	Peter	10	Kirkwood	Williams, Thomas	Apr. 4, 1846	Balto.
Banks	Sarah	32	Burlington	Slatter, Hope Hull	Oct. 21, 1842	Balto.

Surname	First Name	Age	Ship	O/S	Date	Depart
Banks	Sarah Jane	22	Home	Slatter, Hope Hull	March 22, 1845	Balto.
Banks	Susan	16	Abbott Lord	Campbell, Bernard M.	April 28, 1852	Balto.
Banks	William	21	General Pinckney	Slatter, Hope Hull	Jan. 19, 1847	Balto.
Banler	Anderson	13	General Pinckney	Slatter, Hope Hull	Jan. 19, 1847	Balto.
Banling	Eliza	18	General Pinckney	Slatter, Hope Hull	Jan. 19, 1847	Balto.
Banning	Israel	18	Eliza F.Mason	Donovan, Joseph S.	Nov. 13, 1851	Balto.
Banton	Hager	18	Kirkwood	Slatter, Hope Hull	Apr. 15, 1845	Balto.
Bantum	Samuel	19	Abbott Lord	Campbell, Bernard M.	April 28, 1852	Balto.
Barber	Ann	18	Irad Ferry	Clendenin, A.	Jan. 16, 1840	Balto.
Barber	Catherine	20	Irad Ferry	Clendenin, A.	Jan. 16, 1840	Balto.
Barber	David	17	Tweed	Bowling, John D.	Oct. 20, 1836	Town Creek
Barber	John	30	Seaman	Freeman, Theophilus	March 25, 1839	Balto.
Bard	Charles	22	E.H. Chapin	Campbell, Walter L.	June 7, 1848	Balto.
Bardins	Frank	30	Splendid	Slatter, Hope Hull	Apr. 24, 1841	Balto.
Barker	Sandy	21	Victorine	Rodbind, Ebenezer	May 14, 1845	Balto.
Barker	Winnie	47	Louisa	Waggaman, John H.	June 30, 1848	Balto.
Barkley	Littleton	20	General Pinckney	Slatter, Hope Hull	Feb. 21, 1846	Balto.
Barnes	Abeline	30	Brandywine	Campbell, Bernard M.	Oct. 15, 1852	Balto.
Barnes	Alexander	4	Brandywine	Campbell, Bernard M.	Oct. 15, 1852	Balto.
Barnes	Ann	28	Isaac Franklin	Slatter, Hope Hull	Sept. 28, 1838	Balto.
Barnes	Caroline	25	Ganniclefft	Slatter, Hope Hull	Nov. 25, 1840	Balto.
Barnes	Charles H.	23	Union	Williams, Thomas	Oct. 9, 1848	Balto.
Barnes	Charlotte	18	Victorine	Donovan, Joseph S.	May 14, 1845	Balto.
Barnes	Donna	21	Margaret Hugg	Wilson, Thomas C.	Nov. 30, 1844	Balto.
Barnes	Donna	21	Margrett Hugg	Wilson, Thomas C.	Nov. 30, 1844	Balto.
Barnes	Eliza	16	Isaac Franklin	Slatter, Hope Hull	Sept. 28, 1838	Balto.

Surname	First Name	Age	Ship	O/S	Date	Depart
Barnes	Fanney	10	Mary	Harker, William	Feb. 10, 1844	Balto.
Barnes	George	16	Arctic	Woolfoll, Austin	Jan. 24, 1829	Balto.
Barnes	George	infant	Brandywine	Campbell, Bernard M.	Oct. 15, 1852	Balto.
Barnes	Henry	8	Brandywine	Campbell, Bernard M.	Oct. 15, 1852	Balto.
Barnes	Henry	28	Hermitage	Williams, Thomas	Oct. 28, 1846	Balto.
Barnes	Henry	20	Kirkwood	Donovan, Joseph S.	Oct. 26, 1847	Balto.
Barnes	Henry	23	Victorine	Donovan, Joseph S.	Sept. 29, 1845	Balto.
Barnes	John	30	Paoli	Slatter, Hope Hull	Sept. 9, 1845	Balto.
Barnes	Louisa	40	General Pinckney	Slatter, Hope Hull	Jan. 19, 1847	Balto.
Barnes	Mary	21	Sarah Bridge	Campbell, Bernard M.	Feb. 8, 1851	Balto.
Barnes	Minerva	18	Southerner	Donovan, Joseph S.	Oct. 27, 1849	Balto.
Barnes	Sandy	20	Isaac Franklin	Kephart, George	Feb. 1, 1839	Balto.
Barnes	Sarah	19	Helen A. Miller	Campbel , Bernard M.	Oct. 18, 1852	Balto.
Barnes	Surina	12	Brandywine	Campbel , Bernard M.	Oct. 15, 1852	Balto.
Barnes	Susan	16	Zoe	Slatter, Hope Hull	Feb. 16, 1847	Balto.
Barnes		infant	Gannicleftt	Slatter, Hope Hull	Nov. 25, 1840	Balto.
Barnett	Aaron	16	Lapwing	Woolfolk, Austin	Feb. 15, 1827	Balto.
Barnett	James	18	Home	Donovan Joseph S.	March 22, 1845	Balto.
Barns	Brisk	15	Victorine	Slatter, Hope Hull	March 1, 1845	Balto.
Barns	Zovey	19	States	Woolfolk, Austin	Apr. 14, 1828	Balto.
Barrac	Nancy	17	Lapwing	Woolfolk, Joseph B.	Feb. 15, 1827	Balto.
Barrac	Perry	24	Lapwing	Woolfolk, Joseph B.	Feb. 15, 1827	Balto.
Barrac	William	21	Lapwing	Woolfolk, Joseph B.	Feb. 15, 1827	Balto.
Barrad	James	20	Bostonian	Slatter, Hope Hull	Jan. 18, 1841	Balto.
Barrett	Taylor	23	States	Woolfolk, Austin	Apr. 14, 1828	Balto.
Barrick	Abraham	25	Eliza F.Mason	Donovan, Joseph S.	Nov. 13, 1851	Balto.

Surname	First Name	Age	Ship	O/S	Date	Depart
Barroll	John	16	Ann & Leah	Woolfolk, Austin	Nov. 1, 1831	Balto.
Barron	William	14	E.H.Chapin	Slatter, Hope Hull	Nov. 30, 1847	Balto.
Barrow	Mark	27	Lafayette	Woolfolk, Austin	Oct. 18, 1828	Balto.
Barton	Alex	19	Fidelia	McCracken, John	May 13, 1843	Balto.
Barton	Andrew	27	Burlington	Slatter, Hope Hull	Oct. 21, 1842	Balto.
Barton	Basil	35	Zoe	Slatter, Hope Hull	Feb. 16, 1847	Balto.
Barton	Francis	16	Union	Sheckles, Gannon	March 17, 1849	Balto.
Barton	Rose	16	E.H.Chapin	Donovan, Joseph S.	Dec. 2, 1847	Balto.
Barton	William	20	Union	Sheckles, Gannon	March 17, 1849	Balto.
Bassett	Burrell	36	Liberator	Woolfolk, Austin	Nov. 12, 1828	Balto.
Bastion	William	10	E.H.Chapin	Slatter, Hope Hull	Nov. 30, 1847	Balto.
Bates	Austin	20 mon.	Union	Williams, Thomas	Oct. 9, 1848	Balto.
Bates	Delia	28	Union	Williams, Thomas	Oct. 9, 1848	Balto.
Bates	Henry	28	Union	Williams, Thomas	Oct. 9, 1848	Balto.
Batson	Ann	20	Kirkwood	Donovan, Joseph S.	Oct. 14, 1848	Balto.
Batson	John	28	Elizabeth	Campbell, Bernard M.	Nov. 18, 1848	Balto.
Baxton	Perdy	21	Hibernia	Woolfolk, Austin	Dec. 5, 1826	Balto.
Bayler	Gabriel	37	Pioneer	Stuart, William R.	July 20, 1848	Balto.
Bayley	Julian	7	Southerner	Donovan, Joseph S.	Oct. 27, 1849	Balto.
Bayley	Mary	18	Architect	Donovan, Joseph S.	Apr. 25, 1846	Balto.
Bayley	Rachel	5	Southerner	Donovan, Joseph S.	Oct. 27, 1849	Balto.
Bayley	Sarah	23	Southerner	Donovan, Joseph S.	Oct. 27, 1849	Balto.
Bayley	Warner	17	Edward Everett	Campbell, Bernard M.	March 10, 1851	Balto.
Bayly	John H.	19	Victorine	Rodbind, Ebenezer	May 14, 1845	Balto.
Baynard	Anthony	20	Mary Broughton	Campbell, Bernard M.	Nov. 18, 1851	Balto.
Baynard	Celia	18	Louisa	Campbell, Bernard M.	Nov. 5, 1849	Balto.

Surname	First Name	Age	Ship	O/S	Date	Depart
Baynard	George	17	Superb	Donovan, Joseph S.	Nov. 2, 1843	Balto.
Baynard	Henry	30	Henry A. Barling	Campbell, Bernard M.	Dec. 18, 1851	Balto.
Bazell	Henry	18	Palestine	Slatter, Hope Hull	Nov. 16, 1835	Balto.
Beadly	Henry	22	Henry A. Barling	Donovan, Joseph S.	Dec. 18, 1851	Balto.
Beall	Maria	10	General Pinckney	Slatter, Hope Hull	Jan. 19, 1847	Balto.
Beals	Brigget	17	Billow	Woolfolk, Austin	Feb. 23, 1828	Balto.
Bean	Daniel	27	Kirkwood	Donovan, Joseph S.	Oct. 26, 1847	Balto.
Bean	John	24	Solomon Saltus	Slatter, Hope Hull	Oct. 7, 1839	Balto.
Bean	John B.	9	Topaz	Woolfolk, Austin	Apr. 20, 1829	Balto.
Bean	Louisa	11	Topaz	Woolfolk, Austin	Apr. 20, 1829	Balto.
Beandos	Kitty	18	Union	Slatter, Hope Hull	July 26, 1847	Balto.
Beans	George	17	Lafayette	Woolfolk, Austin	Oct. 18, 1828	Balto.
Beans	Henrietta	16	Brunswick	Woolfolk, Austin	Oct. 11, 1831	Balto.
Beard	Charles	30	Elizabeth	Campbell, Walter L.	Oct. 6, 1849	Balto.
Beard	Isaac	24	Brunswick	Woolfolk, Austin	Oct. 11, 1831	Balto.
Beccus	Celia	18	Kirkwood	Slatter, Henry F.	Dec. 10, 1846	Balto.
Beccus	Eliza	infant	Kirkwood	Slatter, Henry F.	Dec. 10, 1846	Balto.
Beck	Maria	15	Victorine	Slatter, Hope Hull	March 9, 1844	Balto.
Beck	Robert	9	Irad Ferry	Clendenin, A.	Jan. 16, 1840	Balto.
Becker	George	18	Delawarian	Campbell, Bernard M.	Dec. 1, 1848	Balto.
Beckett	Henry	24	Paoli	Slatter, Hope Hull	Sept. 9, 1845	Balto.
Beckley	Ann	13	Paoli	Slatter, Hope Hull	Sept. 9, 1845	Balto.
Beckley	Elizabeth	20	Paoli	Slatter, Hope Hull	Sept. 9, 1845	Balto.
Bedford	Frederick	20	Jane Henderson	Campbell, Bernard M.	Nov. 1, 1852	Balto.
Bedford	Hack	19	Catharine	Slatter, Hope Hull	Jan. 24, 1843	Balto.
Bedford	Hannah	16	States	Woolfolk, Austin	Nov. 21, 1827	Balto.

Surname	First Name	Age	Ship	O/S	Date	Depart
Bedford	Samuel	22	Victorine	Donovan, Joseph S.	Sept. 29, 1845	Balto.
Bell	Andrew	26	Paoli	Slatter, Hope Hull	Sept. 9, 1845	Balto.
Bell	Ann	17	Kirkwood	Donovan, Joseph S.	Dec. 23, 1843	Balto.
Bell	Benjamin	17	Elizabeth	Donovan, Joseph S.	Nov. 18, 1848	Balto.
Bell	Caroline	22	Eliza	Slatter, Hope Hull	Oct. 9, 1840	Balto.
Bell	Charles	16	Kirkwood	Donovan, Joseph S.	Oct. 26, 1847	Balto.
Bell	David	22	Kirkwood	Donovan, Joseph S.	Sept. 28, 1846	Balto.
Bell	Elizabeth	24	Victorine	Donovan, Joseph S.	Dec. 31, 1846	Balto.
Bell	Enoch	23	Home	Slatter, Hope Hull	March 22, 1845	Balto.
Bell	Harriet	infant	Union	Donovan, Joseph S.	Dec. 16, 1848	Balto.
Bell	Harriet	32	Union	Donovan, Joseph S.	Dec. 16, 1848	Balto.
Bell	Henry	21	Victorine	Meredith, William	Dec. 21, 1844	Balto.
Bell	James	18	Kirkwood	Campbell, Bernard M.	Oct. 16, 1845	Balto.
Bell	Joshua	26	Abbott Lord	Campbell, Bernard M.	April 28, 1852	Balto.
Bell	Julia	15	Lafayette	Woolfolk, Richard	Oct. 18, 1828	Balto.
Bell	Letty	15	Henry A. Barling	Campbell, Walter L.	Oct. 28, 1848	Balto.
Bell	Lewis	12	Kirkwood	Donovan, Joseph S.	Sept. 28, 1846	Balto.
Bell	Margaret	20	Isaac Franklin	Kephart, George	Feb. 1, 1839	Balto.
Bell	Maria	18	Tippecanoe	Staples, Joshua	Jan. 17, 1842	Balto.
Bell	Maria	5	Union	Donovan, Joseph S.	Dec. 16, 1848	Balto.
Bell	Mary	19	Kirkwood	Donovan, Joseph S.	Oct. 14, 1848	Balto.
Bell	Mary	16	Victorine	Slatter, Henry F.	Dec. 31, 1846	Balto.
Bell	Mary Jane	9	General Pinckney	Slatter, Hope Hull	Jan. 19, 1847	Balto.
Bell	Nancy	26	John S. Gittings	Campbell, Bernard M.	Nov. 20, 1852	Balto.
Bell	Nathan	12	Union	Donovan, Joseph S.	Dec. 16, 1848	Balto.
Bell	Rachel	15	Kirkwood	Donovan, Joseph S.	Dec. 23, 1843	Balto.

Surname	First Name	Age	Ship	O/S	Date	Depart
Bell	Rachel	infant	Kirkwood	Donovan, Joseph S.	Oct. 14, 1848	Balto.
Bell	Richard	11	General Pinckney	Williars, Thomas	Jan. 19, 1847	Balto.
Bell	Robert	22	John S. Gittings	Campbell, Bernard M.	Nov. 20, 1852	Balto.
Bell	Samuel	22	Kirkwood	Slatter, Hope Hull	Jan. 4, 1845	Balto.
Bell	Sandy	28	Southerner	Donovan, Joseph S.	Jan. 21, 1850	Balto.
Bell	Susan	19	Tippecanoe	Staples, Joshua	Jan. 17, 1842	Balto.
Bell	William	24	Paoli	Slatter, Hope Hull	Sept. 9, 1845	Balto.
Belt	Henry	20	Burlington	Slatter, Hope Hull	Oct. 21, 1842	Balto.
Belt	Winney A.	17	General Pinckney	Williams, Thomas	Jan. 19, 1847	Balto.
Belts	Henrietta	16	Tippecanoe	Slatter, Hope Hull	Apr. 15, 1844	Balto.
Belts	Lenora	13	Kirkwood	Slatter, Hope Hull	Dec. 23, 1843	Balto.
Belts	Phillip	17	Kirkwood	Slatter, Hope Hull	Dec. 23, 1843	Balto.
Ben	Priscilla	20	Isaac Franklin	Kephart, George	Sept. 28, 1838	Balto.
Ben		6 mon.	Isaac Franklin	Kephart, George	Sept. 28, 1838	Balto.
Bennet	Cassey	14	States	Woolfolk, Austin	Apr. 14, 1828	Balto.
Bennet	Priscilla	10	States	Woolfolk, Austin	Apr. 14, 1828	Balto.
Bennett	Charlotte	20	Virginia	Woolfolk, Joseph B.	Dec. 19, 1825	Balto.
Bennett	George	2 mon.	Orbit	Woolfolk, Austin	Apr. 16, 1825	Balto.
Bennett	Hannah	18	Orbit	Woolfolk, Austin	Apr. 16, 1825	Balto.
Bennett	James	15	Kirkwood	Slatter, Hope Hull	Oct. 16, 1845	Balto.
Bennett	James W.	12	Henry Clay	Woolfolk, Austin	Dec. 4, 1828	Balto.
Bennett	Josiah	18	Irad Ferry	Clendenin, A.	Jan. 16, 1840	Balto.
Bennett	Mariah	16	Helen A. Miller	Campbell, Bernard M.	Oct. 18, 1852	Balto.
Bennett	Rosetta	22	Julia	Woolfolk, Austin	Jan. 8, 1829	Balto.
Bennett	Samuel		Eliza F.Mason	Donovan, Joseph S.	Nov. 13, 1851	Balto.
Bennett	Susan	18	Margaret Hugg	Campbell, Bernard M.	Feb. 8, 1845	Balto.

Surname	First Name	Age	Ship	O/S	Date	Depart
Benson	Alfred	20	Pioneer	Stuart, William R.	July 20, 1848	Balto.
Benson	Ben	30	Hope & Hannah	Woolfolk, Austin	March 11, 1829	Balto.
Benson	Betsey	15	Hope & Hannah	Woolfolk, Austin	March 11, 1829	Balto.
Benson	Eliza	1	Nathaniel Hooper	Campbell, Bernard M.	Feb. 12, 1852	Balto.
Benson	Henry	infant	Charles	Campbell, Bernard M.	Dec. 18, 1850	Balto.
Benson	James	20	Kirkwood	Campbell, Bernard M.	Oct. 16, 1845	Balto.
Benson	John	30	Nathaniel Hooper	Campbell, Bernard M.	Feb. 12, 1852	Balto.
Benson	Lucinda	22	Nathaniel Hooper	Campbell, Bernard M.	Feb. 12, 1852	Balto.
Benson	Nathan	22	States	Woolfolk, Austin	Apr. 14, 1828	Balto.
Benson	Perry	21	Algerine	Woolfolk, Joseph B.	Jan. 6, 1826	Balto.
Benson	Robert	11	Lafayette	Woolfolk, Austin	Oct. 18, 1828	Balto.
Bentley	Daniel	21	Kirkwood	Donovan, Joseph S.	Oct. 16, 1845	Balto.
Bentley	Matilda	16	John S. Gittings	Campbell, Bernard M.	Nov. 20, 1852	Balto.
Bentley	William	23	Susan Miller	Woolfolk, Austin	Oct. 25, 1822	Balto.
Bently	Betsey	24	Jefferson	Woolfolk, Austin	Dec. 24, 1827	Balto.
Bently	Henry	5	Jefferson	Woolfolk, Austin	Dec. 24, 1827	Balto.
Bently	Maria	3	Jefferson	Woolfolk, Austin	Dec. 24, 1827	Balto.
Bently	Rachel	18	Jefferson	Woolfolk, Austin	Dec. 24, 1827	Balto.
Berrey	Warren	23	Hermitage	Slatter, Hope Hull	Oct. 28, 1846	Balto.
Berry	Allen	21	St. Mary	Donovan, Joseph S.	Nov. 29, 1845	Balto.
Berry	Anne	16	Henry A. Barling	Donovan, Joseph S.	Feb. 24, 1851	Balto.
Berry	Caroline	22	Uncas	Slatter, Hope Hull	Jan. 10, 1838	Balto.
Berry	Charles	21	Irad Ferry	Wilson, J.W.	May 6, 1839	Balto.
Berry	Flora	infant	Kirkwood	Donovan, Joseph S.	March 9, 1847	Balto.
Berry	James	23	Scotia	Slatter, Hope Hull	Sept. 30, 1843	Balto.
Berry	Joshua	23	Phoenix	Donovan, Joseph S.	March 27, 1847	Balto.

Surname	First Name	Age	Ship	O/S	Date	Depart
Berry	Lindy	20 days	Jefferson	Woolfolk, Joseph B.	Dec. 24, 1827	Balto.
Berry	Lindy	18	Jefferson	Woolfolk, Joseph B.	Dec. 24, 1827	Balto.
Berry	Margaret	21	Liberator	Woolfolk, Austin	Nov. 12, 1828	Balto.
Berry	Margeret	17	Kirkwood	Donovan, Joseph S.	Oct. 26, 1847	Balto.
Berry	Ned	2	Liberator	Woolfolk, Austin	Nov. 12, 1828	Balto.
Berry	Sam	8	Ballcon	Milligan, George	Dec. 17, 1821	Balto.
Berry	Sam	3	Liberator	Woolfolk, Austin	Nov. 12, 1828	Balto.
Berry	Samuel	20	Elizabeth	Campbell, Walter L.	Oct. 6, 1849	Balto.
Berry	Sophia	18	Kirkwood	Donovan, Joseph S.	March 9, 1847	Balto.
Berry	Strother	21	Scotia	Slatter, Hope Hull	Sept. 30, 1843	Balto.
Berry	William	20	Lafayette	Woolfolk, Austin	Oct. 18, 1828	Balto.
Berryman	Cecilia	18	Nathaniel Hooper	Campbell, Bernard M.	Feb. 12, 1852	Balto.
Berryman	Spencer	24	Nathaniel Hooper	Campbell, Bernard M.	Feb. 12, 1852	Balto.
Berrymore	Notus	22	Isaac Franklin	Kephart, George	Sept. 28, 1838	Balto.
Best	Stephen	19	Osprey	Tilletson, S.R.	Nov. 11, 1847	Balto.
Betts	Tom	18	Hibernia	Woolfolk, Austin	Dec. 5, 1826	Balto.
Bevans	Milly	26	Victorine	Slatter, Hope Hull	March 14, 1846	Balto.
Beverly	Jerrey	25	John S. Gittings	Campbell, Bernard M.	Nov. 20, 1852	Balto.
Beverly	Juliana	18	Salvadora	Slatter, Hope Hull	Sept. 28, 1846	Balto.
Beverly	Watson	20	John S. Gittings	Campbell, Bernard M.	Nov. 20, 1852	Balto.
Bevesly	John	20	Kirkwood	Crow, William	Jan. 14, 1846	Balto.
Bias	Elizabeth	infant	St. Mary	Donovan, Joseph S.	Nov. 29, 1845	Balto.
Bias	Frances	21	St. Mary	Donovan, Joseph S.	Nov. 29, 1845	Balto.
Bias	Frances	28	St. Mary	Donovan, Joseph S.	Nov. 29, 1845	Balto.
Bias	Hester	17	Kirkwood	Donovan, Joseph S.	Oct. 14, 1848	Balto.
Bias	Lucinda	18	Kirkwood	Donovan, Joseph S.	Oct. 14, 1848	Balto.

Surname	First Name	Age	Ship	O/S	Date	Depart
Bias	Maria	12	Victorine	Donovan, Joseph S.	Dec. 31, 1846	Balto.
Bias	Samuel	32	St. Mary	Donovan, Joseph S.	Nov. 29, 1845	Balto.
Bias	William	20	Victorine	Slatter, Hope Hull	Sept. 12, 1846	Balto.
Biays	Bob	22	Algerine	Woolfolk, Austin	March 25, 1826	Balto.
Bigum	Daniel	21	Narragansett	Donovan, Joseph S.	Nov. 27, 1850	Balto.
Billingster	Henry	20	Phoenix	Donovan, Joseph S.	March 27, 1847	Balto.
Billingster	John	23	Phoenix	Donovan, Joseph S.	March 27, 1847	Balto.
Billingster	Samuel	21	Phoenix	Donovan, Joseph S.	March 27, 1847	Balto.
Bingham	Delana	20	Southerner	Rodbind, Ebenezer	Jan. 21, 1850	Balto.
Bingham	Leancy	20	Isaac Franklin	Kephart, George	Feb. 1, 1839	Balto.
Bird	Abraham	21	Zoe	Slatter, Hope Hull	Feb. 16, 1847	Balto.
Bird	Charles	16	Union	Slatter, Hope Hull	July 26, 1847	Balto.
Bird	Henry	17	Kirkwood	Donovan, Joseph S.	March 9, 1847	Balto.
Bird	Jane	15	Architect	Crow, William	Feb. 3, 1841	Balto.
Bird	Margritt	16	Victorine	Slatter, Hope Hull	Dec. 17, 1845	Balto.
Bird	Thomas	20	Kirkwood	Donovan, Joseph S.	March 9, 1847	Balto.
Birkhead	Anne	12	Hibernia	Woolfolk, Austin	Dec. 5, 1826	Balto.
Biscoe	Eliza	23	Julia	Woolfolk, Austin	Jan. 8, 1829	Balto.
Biscoe	George	infant	Julia	Woolfolk, Austin	Jan. 8, 1829	Balto.
Bishop	John	34	Virginia	Pearce, James Alfred	March 27, 1828	Balto.
Bishop	Margrett	25	Victorine	Slatter, Hope Hull	May 14, 1845	Balto.
Bishop	Milly	25	Kirkwood	Donovan, Joseph S.	Nov. 28, 1849	Balto.
Bishop	Thomas	21	Pamphylia	Maddox, T.	March 30, 1853	Balto.
Bisio	Eliza	20	Isaac Franklin	Kephart, George	Sept. 28, 1838	Balto.
Bitser	George	24	Superb	Slatter, Hope Hull	Nov. 1, 1843	Balto.
Bivins	Lewis	18	Abbott Lord	Campbell, Bernard M.	April 28, 1852	Balto.

Surname	First Name	Age	Ship	O/S	Date	Depart
Black	Bill	40	Kirkwood	Campbell, Bernard M.	Oct. 16, 1845	Balto.
Black	Celiua	4	Lady Monroe	Woolfolk, Austin	March 25, 1825	Balto.
Black	Charles	16	Elizabeth	Campbell, Bernard M.	May 12, 1849	Balto.
Black	Joseph	25	Jane Henderson	Campbell, Bernard M.	Nov. 1, 1852	Balto.
Black	Nackey	11	Southerner	Donovan, Joseph S.	Oct. 27, 1849	Balto.
Black	Nathan	22	Union	Donovan, Joseph S.	Dec. 16, 1848	Balto.
Black	Phoebe	35	Intelligence	Colt, R.L.	Sept. 18, 1821	Balto.
Black	Susan	13	Union	Campbell, Bernard M.	Oct. 9, 1848	Balto.
Black	Tom	17	Intelligence	Anderson, David	Dec. 20, 1822	Balto.
Blackburn	Francis	18	Elizabeth	Donovan, Joseph S.	Nov. 18, 1848	Balto.
Blackburn	Maria	25	General Pinckney	Slatter, Hope Hull	Jan. 19, 1847	Balto.
Blackeston	Delia	18	Louisa	Campbell, Bernard M.	March 31, 1849	Balto.
Blackiston	Charles	22	Hermitage	Slatter, Hope Hull	Oct. 28, 1846	Balto.
Blackiston	Jerry	14	Henry A. Barling	Campbell, Bernard M.	Apr. 19, 1849	Balto.
Blackiston	Rachael	18	Union	Campbell, Bernard M.	Nov. 17, 1849	Balto.
Blackley	Juliain	30	Ganniclefft	Slatter, Hope Hull	Nov. 25, 1840	Balto.
Blackson	John	10	Northumberland	Slatter, Hope Hull	Feb. 27, 1843	Balto.
Blackston	Delosia	25	Sarah Bridge	Campbel, Bernard M.	Feb. 8, 1851	Balto.
Blackston	Eliza	18	Elizabeth	Donovan, Joseph S.	Nov. 18, 1848	Balto.
Blackston	Horace	infant	Elizabeth	Donovan, Joseph S.	Nov. 18, 1848	Balto.
Blackston	Thomas	21	Elizabeth	Donovan, Joseph S.	Nov. 18, 1848	Balto.
Blackston	Thomas	16	Southerner	Donovan, Joseph S.	Oct. 27, 1849	Balto.
Blackston	William	19	Elizabeth	Donovan, Joseph S.	Nov. 18, 1848	Balto.
Blackwell	Alford	22	Helen A. Miller	Campbell, Bernard M.	Oct. 18, 1852	Balto.
Blackwell	Betsey	11	Kirkwood	Campbell, Bernard M.	Jan. 14, 1846	Balto.
Blackwell	Betsey	5	Kirkwood	Donovan, Joseph S.	Jan. 4, 1845	Balto.

Surname	First Name	Age	Ship	O/S	Date	Depart
Blackwell	Daniel	4	Kirkwood	Donovan, Joseph S.	Jan. 4, 1845	Balto.
Blackwell	Isaac	25	Kirkwood	Donovan, Joseph S.	Jan. 4, 1845	Balto.
Blackwell	Isaac	34	Kirkwood	Donovan, Joseph S.	Jan. 4, 1845	Balto.
Blackwell	James	12	Kirkwood	Donovan, Joseph S.	Jan. 4, 1845	Balto.
Blackwell	Lindsay	24	Pioneer	Slatter, Hope Hull	Sept. 15, 1847	Balto.
Blackwell	Nancy	30	Kirkwood	Donovan, Joseph S.	Jan. 4, 1845	Balto.
Bladen	Nick	20	Hibernia	Woolfolk, Austin	Dec. 5, 1826	Balto.
Blake	Ann	1	States	Woolfolk, Austin	Nov. 21, 1827	Balto.
Blake	Bill	40	Clio	Starnsburg, William	March 22, 1819	Balto.
Blake	Dorcas	12	States	Woolfolk, Austin	Nov. 21, 1827	Balto.
Blake	Emory	9	Jefferson	Woolfolk, Austin	Dec. 24, 1827	Balto.
Blake	George	19	Union	Campbell, Bernard M.	Dec. 16, 1848	Balto.
Blake	Jenny	33	States	Woolfolk, Austin	Nov. 21, 1827	Balto.
Blake	John	21	Eliza F. Mason	Donovan, Joseph S.	Nov. 13, 1851	Balto.
Blake	Mary	5	States	Woolfolk, Austin	Nov. 21, 1827	Balto.
Blake	Minty	16	Northumberland	Slatter, Hope Hull	Feb. 27, 1843	Balto.
Blake	Perry	17	States	Woolfolk, Austin	Nov. 21, 1827	Balto.
Blake	Philip	1	States	Woolfolk, Austin	Nov. 21, 1827	Balto.
Blake	Rachel	10	States	Woolfolk, Austin	Nov. 21, 1827	Balto.
Blake	Sam		States	Woolfolk, Austin	Nov. 21, 1827	Balto.
Blake	Sarah	3	States	Woolfolk, Austin	Nov. 21, 1827	Balto.
Blanch	Mary	17	Billow	Woolfolk, Austin	Feb. 23, 1828	Balto.
Bland	Alfrad	20	Kirkwood	Rodbind, Ebenezer	Oct. 26, 1847	Balto.
Blaxton	Joseph	21	Louisa	Donovan, Joseph S.	Oct. 9, 1847	Balto.
Blaxton	William	23	Louisa	Donovan, Joseph S.	Oct. 9, 1847	Balto.
Blay	Lavenia	17	Victorine	Slatter, Hope Hull	March 9, 1844	Balto.

Surname	First Name	Age	Ship	O/S	Date	Depart
Bloxton	George	25	Hibernia	Woolfolk, Austin	Dec. 5, 1826	Balto.
Blue	Ann	23	Victorine	Rodbind, Ebenezer	May 14, 1845	Balto.
Blue	Emily	18	Kirkwood	Slatter, Hope Hull	Jan. 4, 1845	Balto.
Blue	Fanny	48	Victorine	Rodbind, Ebenezer	May 14, 1845	Balto.
Blue	James	13	Victorine	Donovan, Joseph S.	May 22, 1844	Balto.
Blue	Mary	20	Tippecanoe	Slatter, Hope Hull	Jan. 17, 1842	Balto.
Blue	Wallace	25	Victorine	Rodbind, Ebenezer	May 14, 1845	Balto.
Boadley	Charles	24	Brunswick	Woolfolk, Austin	Oct. 11, 1831	Balto.
Boadley	Elisabeth	15	Brunswick	Woolfolk, Austin	Oct. 11, 1831	Balto.
Boadley	Matilda	infant	Southerner	Donovan, Jospeh S.	Jan. 5, 1852	Balto.
Boadley	Sarah	17	Southerner	Donovan, Jospeh S.	Jan. 5, 1852	Balto.
Boadly	Maria	22	Julia	Woolfolk, Austin	Jan. 8, 1829	Balto.
Boaman	Henry	25	Victorine	Rodbind, Ebenezer	Dec. 31, 1846	Balto.
Boardley	George	28	Justina	Donovan, Joseph S.	Dec. 2, 1852	Balto.
Boardly	Bill	18	Seamar	Purvis, James Franklin	Apr. 8, 1842	Balto.
Boardly	John	20	Pioneer	Slatter, Hope Hull	Sept. 15, 1847	Balto.
Boardly	Richard	17	Pioneer	Slatter, Hope Hull	Sept. 15, 1847	Balto.
Boardly	Susan	12	General Pinckney	Campbell, Bernard M.	Jan. 19, 1847	Balto.
Boardman	Eliza	18	Victorine	Gardiner, Richard S.D.	Dec. 21, 1844	Balto.
Boardman	Henrietta	16	Victorine	Gardiner, Richard S.D.	Dec. 21, 1844	Balto.
Bohen	William	22	Elizabeth	Donovan, Joseph S.	Nov. 18, 1848	Balto.
Boice	Charles	17	Kirkwood	Donovan, Joseph S.	Oct. 14, 1848	Balto.
Bold	William	26	Margaret Forbs	Slatter, Hope Hull	Nov. 28, 1838	Balto.
Boles	John	18	Union	Donovan, Joseph S.	Dec. 16, 1848	Balto.
Boley	Tom	28	States	Woolfolk, Austin	Nov. 21, 1827	Balto.
Boley	W.H.	26	Russell	Slatter, Hope Hull	March 1, 1839	Balto.

Surname	First Name	Age	Ship	O/S	Date	Depart
Boman	Gustus	25	General Pinckney	Slatter, Hope Hull	Feb. 21, 1846	Balto.
Boman	Jane	16	Victorine	Slatter, Hope Hull	March 14, 1846	Balto.
Boman	Richard	35	Tippecanoe	Purvis, James Franklin	Jan. 17, 1842	Balto.
Boman	Sarah	16	Brunswick	Woolfolk, Austin	Oct. 11, 1831	Balto.
Boman	William	20	General Pinckney	Slatter, Hope Hull	Feb. 21, 1846	Balto.
Boman	Woody	37	Victorine	Harker, William	March 14, 1846	Balto.
Bonaparte	James	14	Victorine	Slatter, Hope Hull	May 14, 1845	Balto.
Bonaparte	Jerome	33	Solomon Saltus	Slatter, Hope Hull	Oct. 7, 1839	Balto.
Bond	Angelina	30	Victorine	Slatter, Hope Hull	May 14, 1845	Balto.
Bond	Ann	20	Victorine	Slatter, Hope Hull	Dec. 17, 1845	Balto.
Bond	Ben	45	Tweed	Sothoron, William H.	Oct. 20, 1836	Town Creek
Bond	Charles	22	States	Woolfolk, Austin	Nov. 21, 1827	Balto.
Bond	Charles	14	Tweed	Sothoron, William H.	Oct. 20, 1836	Town Creek
Bond	Eliza	16	Southerner	Donovan, Jospeh S.	Jan. 5, 1852	Balto.
Bond	Joe	18	Helen A. Miller	Campbell, Bernard M.	Oct. 18, 1852	Balto.
Bond	John	21	Kirkwood	Campbell, Bernard M.	Oct. 14, 1848	Balto.
Bond	John	20	States	Woolfolk, Austin	Nov. 21, 1827	Balto.
Bond	John	12	Tweed	Sothoron, William H.	Oct. 20, 1836	Town Creek
Bond	Joshua	17	States	Woolfolk, Austin	Apr. 14, 1828	Balto.
Bond	Laura	14	General Pinckney	Slatter, Hope Hull	Feb. 21, 1846	Balto.
Bond	Mary	18	Elizabeth	Donovan, Joseph S.	Nov. 18, 1848	Balto.
Bond	Mary	13	Tweed	Sothoron, William H.	Oct. 20, 1836	Town Creek
Bond	Mary Jane	18	General Pinckney	Slatter, Hope Hull	Nov. 10, 1845	Balto.
Bond	Nancy	38	Tweed	Sothoron, William H.	Oct. 20, 1836	Town Creek
Bond	Sarah	infant	General Pinckney	Slatter, Hope Hull	Nov. 10, 1845	Balto.
Bond	Sarah	26	General Pinckney	Slatter, Hope Hull	Nov. 10, 1845	Balto.

Surname	First Name	Age	Ship	O/S	Date	Depart
Bond	Sydney	17	Scotia	Slatter, Hope Hull	Sept. 30, 1843	Balto.
Bond	Tom	6	Tweed	Sotheron, William H.	Oct. 20, 1836	Town Creek
Bond	William	infant	General Pinckney	Slatter, Hope Hull	Nov. 10, 1845	Balto.
Bond	William	9	Tweed	Sotheron, William H.	Oct. 20, 1836	Town Creek
Bond	William	infant	Victorine	Slatter, Hope Hull	Dec. 17, 1845	Balto.
Bond	William	22	Signet	Woolfolk, Austin	Nov. 12, 1831	Balto.
Bonda	Alexander	infant	Elizabeth	Donovan, Joseph S.	March 21, 1850	Balto.
Bonda	Rosena	18	Elizabeth	Donovan, Joseph S.	March 21, 1850	Balto.
Bonde	Ceaser	23	Elizabeth	Donovan, Joseph S.	March 21, 1850	Balto.
Boon	Edward	21	Helen A. Miller	Campbell, Bernard M.	Oct. 18, 1852	Balto.
Boon	Peter	15	Southerner	Donovan, Joseph S.	Oct. 27, 1849	Balto.
Boon	Samuel	37	Margaret Hugg	Donovan, Joseph S.	Feb. 8, 1845	Balto.
Boone	Pheobe	15	Eliza F Mason	Donovan, Joseph S.	Nov. 13, 1851	Balto.
Boone	Sarah	14	Uncas	Slatter, Hope Hull	Jan. 10, 1838	Balto.
Booth	Bill	22	Missouri	Cook, James K.	March 2, 1819	Balto.
Borey	Matilda	14	Irad Ferry	Wilson, J.W.	May 6, 1839	Balto.
Bossy	Jane	18	Victorine	Rodbird, Ebenezer	Dec. 31, 1846	Balto.
Bosten	Andy	16	Abbott Lord	Campbell, Bernard M.	April 28, 1852	Balto.
Boston	Authur	20	Victorine	Slatter, Hope Hull	Dec. 17, 1845	Balto.
Boston	Benjamin	24	Scotia	Harker, William	Sept. 30, 1843	Balto.
Boston	Daniel	21	Isaac Franklin	Slatter, Hope Hull	Sept. 28, 1838	Balto.
Boston	John	25	Kirkwood	Campbell, Bernard M.	Apr. 15, 1845	Balto.
Boston	Kier	21	Julia	Woolfolk, Austin	Jan. 8, 1829	Balto.
Boston	Mary	22	E.H.Chapin	Slatter, Hope Hull	Nov. 30, 1847	Balto.
Boston	Mulvina	13	Home	Donovan, Joseph S.	March 22, 1845	Balto.
Boston	Romey	21	Salvadora	Slatter, Hope Hull	Sept. 28, 1846	Balto.

Surname	First Name	Age	Ship	O/S	Date	Depart
Boswell	Abraham	29	Isaac Franklin	Slatter, Hope Hull	Sept. 28, 1838	Balto.
Boswell	Eliza	15	Union	Williams, Thomas	Oct. 9, 1848	Balto.
Bouldin	Amanda	16	Victorine	Donovan, Joseph S.	May 14, 1845	Balto.
Bouldin	Betsey	14	Kirkwood	Donovan, Joseph S.	Jan. 4, 1845	Balto.
Boulding	Corbin	21	Victorine	Donovan, Joseph S.	March 14, 1846	Balto.
Boures	George H.	20	Union	Williams, Thomas	Oct. 9, 1848	Balto.
Bowdin	Morris	35	Splendid	Slatter, Hope Hull	Apr. 24, 1841	Balto.
Bowdle	James	10	Narragansett	Donovan, Joseph S.	Nov. 27, 1850	Balto.
Bowen	Catherine	19	Union	Williams, Thomas	Oct. 9, 1848	Balto.
Bowen	Edward	5	Henry A. Barling	Campbell, Bernard M.	Dec. 18, 1851	Balto.
Bowen	Elias	8	London	Ringold, J.	Nov. 6, 1840	Balto.
Bowen	Jacob	24	Victorine	Slatter, Hope Hull	May 14, 1845	Balto.
Bowen	Jane	26	Henry A. Barling	Campbell, Bernard M.	Dec. 18, 1851	Balto.
Bowen	Narcissas	15	Osprey	Rodbind, Ebenezer	Nov. 11, 1847	Balto.
Bowen	Shadrick	22	Julia	Woolfolk, Austin	Jan. 8, 1829	Balto.
Bowen	Silvia	23	London	Ringold, J.	Nov. 6, 1840	Balto.
Bowen	Stephen	21	London	Ringold, J.	Nov. 6, 1840	Balto.
Bowen	Thomas	6	Henry A. Barling	Campbell, Bernard M.	Dec. 18, 1851	Balto.
Bower	John	18	Russell	Woolfolk, Austin	Feb. 27, 1839	Balto.
Bowers	Francis	24	Home	Donovan, Joseph S.	March 22, 1845	Balto.
Bowers	Lucy	40	Zoe	Donovan, Joseph S.	Feb. 16, 1847	Balto.
Bowers	Sam	15	Union	Rodbind, Ebenezer	Dec. 16, 1848	Balto.
Bowers	Wesley	25	Union	Rodbind, Ebenezer	Dec. 16, 1848	Balto.
Bowes	Maria	16	Kirkwood	Donovan, Joseph S.	Sept. 28, 1846	Balto.
Bowie	Adam	17	Kirkwood	Donovan, Joseph S.	Sept. 28, 1846	Balto.
Bowie	Ann	17	John C. Calhoun	Donovan, Joseph S.	Oct. 24, 1850	Balto.

Surname	First Name	Age	Ship	O/S	Date	Depart
Bowie	Elijah	18	Union	Sheckles, Gannon	March 17, 1849	Balto.
Bowie	John	28	Paoli	Slatter, Hope Hull	Sept. 9, 1845	Balto.
Bowie	John	20	Southerner	Donovan, Joseph S.	Oct. 27, 1849	Balto.
Bowie	Lloyd	9	Irad Ferry	Wilson, J.W.	May 6, 1839	Balto.
Bowie	Louisa	12	Irad Ferry	Wilson, J.W.	May 6, 1839	Balto.
Bowie	Mary	18	Elizabeth	Campbell, Bernard M.	Jan. 2, 1850	Balto.
Bowie	Nancy	28	Irad Ferry	Wilson, J.W.	May 6, 1839	Balto.
Bowie	Nathaniel	20	Nathaniel Hooper	Donovan, Jospeh S.	Feb. 12, 1852	Balto.
Bowie	Sarah	18	Irad Ferry	Purvis, James Franklin	Feb. 5, 1842	Balto.
Bowie	Singleton	18	Kirkwood	Donovan, Joseph S.	Oct. 14, 1848	Balto.
Bowie	Thomas	18	Kirkwood	Donovan, Joseph S.	Apr. 15, 1845	Balto.
Bowie	William	22	Paoli	Slatter, Hope Hull	Sept. 9, 1845	Balto.
Bowis	Richard	18	Kirkwood	Slatter, Hope Hull	Oct. 16, 1845	Balto.
Bowley	Ann	22	Southerner	Donovar, Joseph S.	Jan. 21, 1850	Balto.
Bowley	Charles	infant	Southerner	Donovan, Joseph S.	Jan. 21, 1850	Balto.
Bowley	John	infant	Southerner	Donovan, Joseph S.	Jan. 21, 1850	Balto.
Bowling	Eliza	18	Mary Broughton	Campbell, Bernard M.	Nov. 18, 1851	Balto.
Bowling	William	18	Sarah Bridge	Campbell Bernard M.	Feb. 8, 1851	Balto.
Bowman	David	22	General Pinckney	Slatter, Hope Hull	Nov. 10, 1845	Balto.
Bowman	Edward	15	Union	Rodbind, Ebenezer	Dec. 16, 1848	Balto.
Bowman	Larry	26	Union	Rodbind, Ebenezer	Dec. 16, 1848	Balto.
Bowman	Mary Ann	infant	Victorine	Donovan, Joseph S.	Dec. 17, 1845	Balto.
Bowman	Milly	28	Union	Rodbind, Ebenezer	Dec. 16, 1848	Balto.
Bowman	Prissilla	18	Kirkwood	Donovan, Joseph S.	Oct. 14, 1848	Balto.
Bowman	Rachel	2	Victorine	Donovan, Joseph S.	Dec. 17, 1845	Balto.
Bowman	Robert	20	Union	Donovan, Joseph S.	May 13, 1848	Balto.

Surname	First Name	Age	Ship	O/S	Date	Depart
Bowman	Winney	23	Victorine	Donovan, Joseph S.	Dec. 17, 1845	Balto.
Bowser	Betsey	16	Irad Ferry	Slatter, Hope Hull	Dec. 9, 1842	Balto.
Bowser	Charles	25	Elizabeth	Donovan, Joseph S.	Jan. 2, 1850	Balto.
Bowser	Delia	17	John C. Calhoun	Donovan, Joseph S.	Oct. 24, 1850	Balto.
Bowser	Dick	27	Harriet	Carroll, Charles	Dec. 7, 1836	Balto.
Bowser	Emaline	17	Kirkwood	Slatter, Hope Hull	Apr. 4, 1846	Balto.
Bowser	James	21	Superb	Slatter, Hope Hull	Nov. 1, 1843	Balto.
Bowser	Robert	21	Pioneer	Slatter, Hope Hull	Sept. 15, 1847	Balto.
Bowser	William	21	Elizabeth	Donovan, Joseph S.	Nov. 18, 1848	Balto.
Bowyer	Frederick	21	Lapwing	Woolfolk, Samuel M.	Feb. 15, 1827	Balto.
Boy	Carsey	20	Ann & Leah	Woolfolk, Austin	Nov.1, 1831	Balto.
Boy	Emeline	20	General Pinckney	Donovan, Joseph S.	Feb. 21, 1846	Balto.
Boyd	Alley	10	Jefferson	Woolfolk, Austin	Dec. 24, 1827	Balto.
Boyd	Benjamin	25	E.H.Chapin	Slatter, Hope Hull	Nov. 30, 1847	Balto.
Boyd	Charles Henry	infant	Victorine	Donovan, Joseph S.	Oct. 25, 1844	Balto.
Boyd	Fenton	38	E.H.Chapin	Slatter, Hope Hull	Nov. 30, 1847	Balto.
Boyd	Frank	28	Emilie	Anderson, David	Jan. 5, 1819	Balto.
Boyd	George	3	Jefferson	Woolfolk, Austin	Dec. 24, 1827	Balto.
Boyd	George	20	Jefferson	Woolfolk, Austin	Dec. 24, 1827	Balto.
Boyd	George	22	Julia	Woolfolk, Austin	Jan. 8, 1829	Balto.
Boyd	Harriott	17	Victorine	Donovan, Joseph S.	Oct. 25, 1844	Balto.
Boyd	Margaret	2 mon.	Jefferson	Woolfolk, Austin	Dec. 24, 1827	Balto.
Boyd	Maria	4	Jefferson	Woolfolk, Austin	Dec. 24, 1827	Balto.
Boyd	Mary	9	E.H.Chapin	Slatter, Hope Hull	Nov. 30, 1847	Balto.
Boyd	Robert	12	Jefferson	Woolfolk, Austin	Dec. 24, 1827	Balto.
Boyd	Sally	30	Jefferson	Woolfolk, Austin	Dec. 24, 1827	Balto.

Surname	First Name	Age	Ship	O/S	Date	Depart
Boyd	Susan	4	E.H.Chapin	Slatter, Hope Hull	Nov. 30, 1847	Balto.
Boyd	William	8	Jefferson	Woolfolk, Austin	Dec. 24, 1827	Balto.
Boyd		18	E.H.Chapin	Slatter, Hope Hull	Nov. 30, 1847	Balto.
Boyer	Caroline	13	Virginia	Boyer, Lucy	Nov. 18, 1823	Balto.
Boyer	Emily	9	Virginia	Boyer, Lucy	Nov. 18, 1823	Balto.
Boyer	Henry	28	St. Mary	Rodewell, Frederick	Nov. 29, 1845	Balto.
Boyer	James	16	Tippecanoe	Purvis, James Franklin	Apr. 1, 1841	Balto.
Boyer	Lucy	45	Virginia	Boyer, Lucy	Nov. 18, 1823	Balto.
Boyer	Neal	11	Henry Clay	Woolfolk, Austin	Dec. 4, 1828	Balto.
Boyman	John	24	Kirkwood	Slatter, Hope Hull	Dec. 23, 1843	Balto.
Bracken	William	17	Zoe	Slatter, Hope Hull	Feb. 16, 1847	Balto.
Braddick	Peter	19	Ann & Leah	Woolfolk, Austin	Nov.1, 1831	Balto.
Bradford	George	22	Isaac Franklin	Slatter, Hope Hull	Sept. 28, 1838	Balto.
Bradley	Lewis	20	Uncas	Slatter, Hope Hull	Jan. 10, 1838	Balto.
Brady	Clarasy	20	Kirkwood	Donovan, Joseph S.	Oct. 26, 1847	Balto.
Brady	Jane	infant	Kirkwood	Donovan, Joseph S.	Oct. 26, 1847	Balto.
Brady	Mary	12	Northumberland	Slatter, Hope Hull	Feb. 27, 1843	Balto.
Brady	Mary Ann	16	Kirkwood	Donovan, Joseph S.	Apr. 4, 1846	Balto.
Brady	Ned	10	Tippecanoe	Purvis, James Franklin	Jan. 17, 1842	Balto.
Brady	Rachel	18	Victorine	Slatter, Hope Hull	March 1, 1845	Balto.
Brady	Washington	16	Tippecanoe	Purvis, James Franklin	Jan. 17, 1842	Balto.
Braizer	Henry	19	Victorine	Donovan, Joseph S.	Sept. 29, 1845	Balto.
Bran	Ann	22	Kirkwood	Donovan, Joseph S.	Apr. 15, 1845	Balto.
Branagin	Fanny	32	Tippecanoe	Slatter, Hope Hull	Apr. 15, 1844	Balto.
Branagin	Hellen	16	Tippecanoe	Slatter, Hope Hull	Apr. 15, 1844	Balto.
Branagin	Jacob	4	Tippecanoe	Slatter, Hope Hull	Apr. 15, 1844	Balto.

Surname	First Name	Age	Ship	O/S	Date	Depart
Branch	Len	24	Union	Campbell, Bernard M.	Nov. 17, 1849	Balto.
Branch	Thomas	22	Union	Campbell, Bernard M.	Nov. 17, 1849	Balto.
Braningham	Jacob	27	Victorine	Slatter, Hope Hull	Dec. 17, 1845	Balto.
Brannon	Solomon	25	Kirkwood	Donovan, Joseph S.	Dec. 10, 1846	Balto.
Branor	Elijah	35	Billow	Woolfolk, Joseph B.	Feb. 23, 1828	Balto.
Bransom	Henry	21	Elizabeth	Campbell, Bernard M.	May 12, 1849	Balto.
Branson	Charlotte	17	Kirkwood	Campbell, Bernard M.	Nov. 28, 1849	Balto.
Branson	Mary	16	Abbott Lord	Campbell, Bernard M.	April 28, 1852	Balto.
Branum	Robert	21	Elizabeth	Donovan, Joseph S.	Nov. 18, 1848	Balto.
Brashears	Jane	19	Nathaniel Hooper	Donovan, Joseph S.	Feb. 12, 1852	Balto.
Brawner	Felix	20	Southerner	Campbell, Bernard M.	Oct. 27, 1849	Balto.
Braxon	Sarah Ann	12	Tippecanoe	Slatter, Hope Hull	Jan. 17, 1842	Balto.
Braxton	Alford	25	Henry A. Barling	Campbell, Bernard M.	Feb. 24, 1851	Balto.
Braxton	George	18	Southerner	Donovan, Joseph S.	Oct. 27, 1849	Balto.
Braxton	Joe	18	Louisa	Donovan, Joseph S.	Oct. 9, 1847	Balto.
Brayton	Thomas	21	Southerner	Donovan, Joseph S.	Oct. 27, 1849	Balto.
Brenager	Lloyd	8	Kirkwood	Campbell, Bernard M.	Oct. 14, 1848	Balto.
Brent	Harriet	17	Nathaniel Hooper	Donovan, Jospeh S.	Feb. 12, 1852	Balto.
Brent	Otho	16	Victorine	Williams, Thomas	Dec. 20, 1844	Balto.
Brewer	Emily	15	Arctic	Woolfolk, Austin	Jan. 24, 1829	Balto.
Brewer	Sarah Ann	19	Kirkwood	Donovan, Joseph S.	Apr. 15, 1845	Balto.
Brian	Harriett	22	Kirkwood	Donovan, Joseph S.	Oct. 14, 1848	Balto.
Brice	Ellis	22	General Pinckney	Slatter, Hope Hull	Nov. 10, 1845	Balto.
Brice	John	11	Arctic	Woolfolk, Austin	Jan. 24, 1829	Balto.
Bridge	Curry Tilghman	13	Northumberland	Slatter, Hope Hull	Feb. 27, 1843	Balto.
Briegs	Moses	23	Lafayette	Woolfolk, Austin	Oct. 18, 1828	Balto.

Surname	First Name	Age	Ship	O/S	Date	Depart
Briggs	Emeline	8	Burlington	Slatter, Hope Hull	Oct. 21, 1842	Balto.
Briggs	Emily	2	Burlington	Slatter, Hope Hull	Oct. 21, 1842	Balto.
Briggs	Jacky	36	Burlington	Slatter, Hope Hull	Oct. 21, 1842	Balto.
Briggs	Nelly	14	Kirkwood	Slatter, Hope Hull	Apr. 15, 1845	Balto.
Briggs	Samuel	6	Burlington	Slatter, Hope Hull	Oct. 21, 1842	Balto.
Bright	Emaline	20	Hermitage	Slatter, Hope Hull	Oct. 28, 1846	Balto.
Bright	Emily	13	Isaac Franklin	Slatter, Hope Hull	Sept. 28, 1838	Balto.
Bright	George	17	Irad Ferry	Slatter, Hope Hull	Dec. 9, 1842	Balto.
Bright	Harriet	12	Isaac Franklin	Slatter, Hope Hull	Sept. 28, 1838	Balto.
Bright	Mary	25	Isaac Franklin	Slatter, Hope Hull	Sept. 28, 1838	Balto.
Brim	Louisa	11	States	Woolfo k, Austin	Nov. 21, 1827	Balto.
Brinkley	Henry	21	Burlington	Slatter, Hope Hull	Oct. 21, 1842	Balto.
Brisco	Joseph	25	Billow	Woolfolk, Austin	Feb. 23, 1828	Balto.
Briscoe	Benjamin	10	States	Woolfolk, Austin	Apr. 14, 1828	Balto.
Briscoe	Caroline	16	Irad Ferry	Purvis, James Franklin	Feb. 5, 1842	Balto.
Briscoe	Daniel	23	Clio	Turner, John S.	March 20, 1819	Balto.
Briscoe	Dennis	27	Southerner	Donovan, Joseph S.	Jan. 21, 1850	Balto.
Briscoe	Eleanor	15	Tweed	Sothoron, William H.	Oct. 20, 1836	Town Creek
Briscoe	Gabriel		Topaz	Woolfolk, Austin	Apr. 20, 1829	Balto.
Briscoe	John	22	Elizabeth	Rodbind, Ebenezer	Nov. 18, 1848	Balto.
Briscoe	Martha	17	Helen A. Miller	Nally, William	Oct. 18, 1852	Balto.
Briscoe	Matilda	17	Margaret Hugg	Donovan, Joseph S.	Feb. 8, 1845	Balto.
Briscoe	Nace	28	Henry A. Barling	Campbell, Bernard M.	Dec. 18, 1851	Balto.
Briscoe	Samuel	23	Victorine	Slatter, Hope Hull	March 9, 1844	Balto.
Briscoe	Sarah Ann	15	Tippecanoe	Slatter, Hope Hull	Jan. 17, 1842	Balto.
Briser	James	16	Victorine	Donovan, Joseph S.	Sept. 29, 1845	Balto.

Surname	First Name	Age	Ship	O/S	Date	Depart
Brisker	Stephen	21	Victorine	Rodbind, Ebenezer	Dec. 31, 1846	Balto.
Britton	Margaret	22	Elizabeth	Campbell, Bernard M.	Nov. 18, 1848	Balto.
Britton		infant	Elizabeth	Campbell, Bernard M.	Nov. 18, 1848	Balto.
Brock	Margaret	20	General Pinckney	Slatter, Hope Hull	Nov. 10, 1845	Balto.
Brogden	John	22	Union	Campbell, Bernard M.	Nov. 17, 1849	Balto.
Brogden	Mary	18	Louisa	Campbell, Bernard M.	March 31, 1849	Balto.
Brogden	Rachael	30	Ganniclefft	Slatter, Hope Hull	Nov. 25, 1840	Balto.
Brogden	William	3	Ganniclefft	Slatter, Hope Hull	Nov. 25, 1840	Balto.
Brook	Letty	15	Salvadora	Slatter, Hope Hull	Sept. 28, 1846	Balto.
Brook	Sophia	28	Salvadora	Slatter, Hope Hull	Sept. 28, 1846	Balto.
Brooke	Mary	18	Bostonian	Slatter, Hope Hull	Jan. 18, 1841	Balto.
Brooks	Abram	32	Kirkwood	Donovan, Joseph S.	March 23, 1844	Balto.
Brooks	Alfred	28	Home	Rodbind, Ebenezer	March 22, 1845	Balto.
Brooks	Alfred	21	Victorine	Slatter, Hope Hull	March 9, 1844	Balto.
Brooks	Ann	16	Home	Rodbind, Ebenezer	March 22, 1845	Balto.
Brooks	Ann	35	Victorine	Slatter, Hope Hull	Dec. 17, 1845	Balto.
Brooks	Bazzell	50	W.H.D.C.Wright	Rodbind, Ebenezer	Nov. 7, 1847	Balto.
Brooks	Charity	19	Elizabeth	Rodbind, Ebenezer	Nov. 18, 1848	Balto.
Brooks	Charles	18	Kirkwood	Donovan, Joseph S.	Jan. 4, 1845	Balto.
Brooks	David	23	Charles	Campbell, Bernard M.	Dec. 18, 1850	Balto.
Brooks	Ellis	18	Victorine	Slatter, Hope Hull	Dec. 17, 1845	Balto.
Brooks	Enoch	18	Sabine	Donovan, Joseph S.	Feb. 10, 1844	Balto.
Brooks	Fanny	3	Home	Rodbind, Ebenezer	March 22, 1845	Balto.
Brooks	Francis	20	Phoenix	Donovan, Joseph S.	March 27, 1847	Balto.
Brooks	George	10	E.H.Chapin	Donovan, Joseph S.	Dec. 2, 1847	Balto.
Brooks	George	20	Splendid	Slatter, Hope Hull	Apr. 24, 1841	Balto.

Surname	First Name	Age	Ship	O/S	Date	Depart
Brooks	Green	18	Mary Broughton	Campbell, Bernard M.	Nov. 18, 1851	Balto.
Brooks	Harriett	15	Victorine	Harker, William	March 9, 1844	Balto.
Brooks	Harriett	45	W.H.D.C.Wright	Slatter, Hope Hull	Nov. 7, 1847	Balto.
Brooks	Henrietta	19	Southerner	Rodbind, Ebenezer	Oct. 27, 1849	Balto.
Brooks	Henry	28	Charles	Campbell, Bernard M.	Dec. 18, 1850	Balto.
Brooks	Henry	19	Kirkwood	Donovan, Joseph S.	March 9, 1847	Balto.
Brooks	Henry	8	Lafayette	Woolfolk, Richard	Oct. 18, 1828	Balto.
Brooks	Hilary	10	Union	Williams, Thomas	Oct. 9, 1848	Balto.
Brooks	Hinson	30	Tippecanoe	Slatter, Hope Hull	Jan. 17, 1842	Balto.
Brooks	Isaac	22	Superb	Donovan, Joseph S.	Nov. 2, 1843	Balto.
Brooks	Jacob	25	Margaret Hugg	Campbell, Bernard M.	Nov. 30, 1844	Balto.
Brooks	James	19	Margaret Hugg	Wilson, Thomas C.	Nov. 30, 1844	Balto.
Brooks	Jerry	20	John C. Calhoun	Donovan, Joseph S.	Oct. 24, 1850	Balto.
Brooks	John	21	Mary	Harker, William	Feb. 10, 1844	Balto.
Brooks	John	18	Topaz	Woolfolk, Austin	Apr. 20, 1829	Balto.
Brooks	John	23	Union	Williams, Thomas	Oct. 9, 1848	Balto.
Brooks	Letha	17	Kirkwood	Donovan. Joseph S.	Dec. 10, 1846	Balto.
Brooks	Lewis	21	Margaret Hugg	Campbell, Bernard M.	Nov. 30, 1844	Balto.
Brooks	Lilly	35	Home	Rodbind, Ebenezer	March 22, 1845	Balto.
Brooks	Lucinda	14	Victorine	Harker, William	March 9, 1844	Balto.
Brooks	Mariah	16	Kirkwood	Donovan, Joseph S.	Apr. 15, 1845	Balto.
Brooks	Martha	20	Sarah Bridge	Campbell, Bernard M.	Feb. 8, 1851	Balto.
Brooks	Mary	16	Brunswick	Woolfolk, Austin	Oct. 11, 1831	Balto.
Brooks	Mary	18	Phoenix	Rodbind, Ebenezer	March 27, 1847	Balto.
Brooks	Mary Ellen	18	Zoe	Slatter, Hope Hull	Feb. 16, 1847	Balto.
Brooks	Mary Jane	11	E.H.Chapin	Slatter, Hope Hull	Nov. 30, 1847	Balto.

Surname	First Name	Age	Ship	O/S	Date	Depart
Brooks	Nancy	15	Union	Williams, Thomas	Oct. 9, 1848	Balto.
Brooks	Nelly	31	General Pinckney	Slatter, Hope Hull	Jan. 19, 1847	Balto.
Brooks	Rachel	20	E.H.Chapin	Donovan, Joseph S.	Dec. 2, 1847	Balto.
Brooks	Rachel	16	Home	Rodbind, Ebenezer	March 22, 1845	Balto.
Brooks	Roger	22	Union	Williams, Thomas	Oct. 9, 1848	Balto.
Brooks	Sansan	16	Victorine	Donovan, Joseph S.	March 14, 1846	Balto.
Brooks	Sarah	13	Phoenix	Rodbind, Ebenezer	March 27, 1847	Balto.
Brooks	Sarah	17	Victorine	Slatter, Hope Hull	March 14, 1846	Balto.
Brooks	Susan	28	Architect	Slatter, Hope Hull	May 20, 1841	Balto.
Brooks	Susan	18	Kirkwood	Donovan, Joseph S.	Oct. 26, 1847	Balto.
Brooks	Susan	15	Phoenix	Rodbind, Ebenezer	March 27, 1847	Balto.
Brooks	Thomas	25	Isaac Franklin	Kephart, George	Feb. 1, 1839	Balto.
Brooks	Tom	19	Jefferson	Woolfolk, Austin	Dec. 24, 1827	Balto.
Brooks	Townson	35	John C. Calhoun	Donovan, Joseph S.	Oct. 24, 1850	Balto.
Brooks	Washington	22	Charles	Donovan, Joseph S.	Apr. 23, 1851	Balto.
Brooks	Washington	21	Victorine	Donovan, Joseph S.	Sept. 29, 1845	Balto.
Brooks	William	30	Charles	Campbell, Bernard M.	Dec. 18, 1850	Balto.
Brooks	William	25	Colonel Howard	Harker, William	Nov. 21, 1844	Balto.
Brooks		infant	Sarah Bridge	Campbell, Bernard M.	Feb. 8, 1851	Balto.
Broom	Charity	10	Union	Williams, Thomas	Oct. 9, 1848	Balto.
Broom	George	22	Hermitage	Williams, Thomas	Oct. 28, 1846	Balto.
Broom	Jane	9	Union	Williams, Thomas	Oct. 9, 1848	Balto.
Broome	Cornelia	infant	Kirkwood	Campbell, Bernard M.	Dec. 10, 1846	Balto.
Broome	Dinah	18	Kirkwood	Campbell, Bernard M.	Dec. 10, 1846	Balto.
Broome	William	infant	Kirkwood	Campbell, Bernard M.	Dec. 10, 1846	Balto.
Broughton	Vachel	22	Hibernia	Woolfolk, Austin	Dec. 5, 1826	Balto.

Surname	First Name	Age	Ship	O/S	Date	Depart
Brown	Abraham	25	John C. Calhoun	Donovan, Joseph S.	Oct. 24, 1850	Balto.
Brown	Abraham	18	Kirkwood	Donovan, Joseph S.	Oct. 14, 1848	Balto.
Brown	Abraham	18	Victorine	Donovan, Joseph S.	Sept. 29, 1845	Balto.
Brown	Adam	20	Victorine	Slatter, Hope Hull	March 14, 1846	Balto.
Brown	Adeline	15	Jefferson	Woolfolk, Austin	Dec. 24, 1827	Balto.
Brown	Agness	18	General Pinckney	Donovan, Joseph S.	Feb. 21, 1846	Balto.
Brown	Amos	13	Margaret Forbs	Slatter, Hope Hull	Nov. 28, 1838	Balto.
Brown	Andrew	24	Nathaniel Hooper	Campbell, Bernard M.	Feb. 12, 1852	Balto.
Brown	Andrew	infant	Zoe	Slatter, Hope Hull	Feb. 16, 1847	Balto.
Brown	Ann	18	Eliza F. Mason	Donovan, Joseph S.	Nov. 13, 1851	Balto.
Brown	Ann	17	Elizabeth	Donovan, Joseph S.	Nov. 18, 1848	Balto.
Brown	Ann	20	Isaac Franklin	Slatter, Hope Hull	Sept. 28, 1838	Balto.
Brown	Ann	15	Victorine	Rodbind, Ebenezer	Dec. 31, 1846	Balto.
Brown	Anne	11	Louisa	Donovar, Joseph S.	Oct. 9, 1847	Balto.
Brown	Ben	18	Brunswick	Woolfolk, Austin	Oct. 11, 1831	Balto.
Brown	Ben	18	Helen A. Miller	Campbell, Bernard M.	Oct. 18, 1852	Balto.
Brown	Ben	23	Kirkwood	Williams, William H.	Jan. 14, 1846	Balto.
Brown	Ben	20	Union	Rodbind, Ebenezer	Dec. 16, 1848	Balto.
Brown	Betsey	30	Solomon Saltus	Slatter, Hope Hull	Oct. 7, 1839	Balto.
Brown	Bill	20	Kirkwood	Rodbind, Ebenezer	Apr. 15, 1845	Balto.
Brown	Caroline	20	Helen A. Miller	Campbell, Bernard M.	Oct. 18, 1852	Balto.
Brown	Caroline	20	Solomon Saltus	Slatter, Hope Hull	Oct. 7, 1839	Balto.
Brown	Cassey	28	Zoe	Slatter, Hope Hull	Feb. 16, 1847	Balto.
Brown	Cassy	18	Lapwing	Woolfolk, Austin	Feb. 15, 1827	Balto.
Brown	Catherine	15	St. Mary	Donovan, Joseph S.	Nov. 29, 1845	Balto.
Brown	Caty	45	Tippecanoe	Slatter, Hope Hull	Jan. 17, 1842	Balto.

Surname	First Name	Age	Ship	O/S	Date	Depart
Brown	Cealy	15	Lafayette	Woolfolk, Richard	Oct. 18, 1828	Balto.
Brown	Charity	23	Victorine	Donovan, Joseph S.	May 22, 1844	Balto.
Brown	Charles	23	Ganniclefft	Slatter, Hope Hull	Nov. 25, 1840	Balto.
Brown	Charles	20	General Pinckney	Donovan, Joseph S.	Nov. 10, 1845	Balto.
Brown	Charles	25	Hermitage	Slatter, Hope Hull	Oct. 28, 1846	Balto.
Brown	Charles	16	Lafayette	Woolfolk, Austin	Oct. 18, 1828	Balto.
Brown	Charles	5	Solomon Saltus	Slatter, Hope Hull	Oct. 7, 1839	Balto.
Brown	Charles	23	William and Mary	King, Gideon T.	Oct. 9, 1821	Balto.
Brown	Charlott Ann	25	Kirkwood	Campbell, Bernard M.	Oct. 14, 1848	Balto.
Brown	Charlotte	9	Kirkwood	Slatter, Hope Hull	Apr. 15, 1845	Balto.
Brown	Charlotte	19	Superb	Slatter, Hope Hull	Nov. 1, 1843	Balto.
Brown	Charlotte	13	Union	Rodbind, Ebenezer	Nov. 17, 1849	Balto.
Brown	Cissy	26	Louisa	Donovan, Joseph S.	Oct. 9, 1847	Balto.
Brown	Cornelius	21	Scotia	Slatter, Hope Hull	Sept. 30, 1843	Balto.
Brown	Course	23	Virginia	Woolfolk, Joseph B.	Dec. 19, 1825	Balto.
Brown	Daniel	22	Kirkwood	Donovan, Joseph S.	Nov. 28, 1849	Balto.
Brown	David	17	Narragansett	Donovan, Joseph S.	Nov. 27, 1850	Balto.
Brown	Dorcas	17	E.H.Chapin	Slatter, Hope Hull	Nov. 30, 1847	Balto.
Brown	Edward	48	Elizabeth	Donovan, Joseph S.	Oct. 6, 1849	Balto.
Brown	Eleanor	15	Jasper	Woolfolk, Austin	Apr. 7, 1827	Balto.
Brown	Eliza	18	Glasgow	Slatter, Hope Hull	Oct. 11, 1838	Balto.
Brown	Eliza	19	Irad Ferry	Slatter, Hope Hull	Dec. 9, 1842	Balto.
Brown	Eliza	12	Louisa	Donovan, Joseph S.	Oct. 9, 1847	Balto.
Brown	Eliza	12	Victorine	Slatter, Hope Hull	March 9, 1844	Balto.
Brown	Elizabeth	22	General Pinckney	Donovan, Joseph S.	Nov. 10, 1845	Balto.
Brown	Elizabeth	14	Union	Donovan, Joseph S.	Dec. 16, 1848	Balto.

Surname	First Name	Age	Ship	O/S	Date	Depart
Brown	Elizebeth	14	Victorine	Slatter, Hope Hull	Dec. 17, 1845	Balto.
Brown	Ellen	20	Edward Everett	Campbell, Bernard M.	March 10, 1851	Balto.
Brown	Ellen	19	Kirkwood	Slatter, Hope Hull	Apr. 4, 1846	Balto.
Brown	Ellen	25	Solomon Saltus	Slatter, Hope Hull	Oct. 7, 1839	Balto.
Brown	Ellen	24	Victorine	Slatter, Hope Hull	Sept. 12, 1846	Balto.
Brown	Emanuel	60	Union	Donovan, Joseph S.	Dec. 16, 1848	Balto.
Brown	Enoch	30	Uncas	Slatter, Hope Hull	Jan. 10, 1838	Balto.
Brown	Fanny	18	Aurilla	Warfield, Charles	Apr. 26, 1822	Balto.
Brown	Fanny	20	Henry Clay	Woolfolk, Austin	Dec. 4, 1828	Balto.
Brown	Fanny	23	Kirkwood	Donovan, Joseph S.	March 23, 1844	Balto.
Brown	Frances	17	Kirkwocd	Crow, William	Jan. 14, 1846	Balto.
Brown	Frances	15	Victorine	Slatter, Henry F.	Dec. 31, 1846	Balto.
Brown	Frances Ann	20	Kirkwood	Donovan, Joseph S.	Jan. 14, 1846	Balto.
Brown	Frederick	20	Union	Donovan, Joseph S.	March 17, 1849	Balto.
Brown	George	20	Architect	Harker, William	Feb. 15, 1840	Balto.
Brown	George	24	Elizabeth	Donovan, Joseph S.	Jan. 2, 1850	Balto.
Brown	George	24	Henry A. Barling	Donovan, Joseph S.	Feb. 24, 1851	Balto.
Brown	George	22	Kirkwood	Donovan, Joseph S.	Oct. 14, 1848	Balto.
Brown	George	24	Northumberland	Slatter, Hope Hull	Feb. 27, 1843	Balto.
Brown	George Washington	13	Catharine	Donovan, Joseph S.	Jan. 18, 1845	Balto.
Brown	Godfrey	38	Victorine	Donovan, Joseph S.	March 14, 1846	Balto.
Brown	Hannah	20	Kirkwood	Donovan, Joseph S.	Dec. 10, 1846	Balto.
Brown	Harriott		Victorine	Donovan, Joseph S.	Sept. 29, 1845	Balto.
Brown	Henney	16	General Pinckney	Rodbind, Ebenezer	Feb. 21, 1846	Balto.
Brown	Henrietta	2	Colonel Howard	Harker, William	Nov. 21, 1844	Balto.
Brown	Henrietta	18	Union	Donovan, Joseph S.	Dec. 16, 1848	Balto.

Surname	First Name	Age	Ship	O/S	Date	Depart
Brown	Henry	5	Colonel Howard	Harker, William	Nov. 21, 1844	Balto.
Brown	Henry	20	General Pinckney	Donovan, Joseph S.	Nov. 10, 1845	Balto.
Brown	Henry	25	Isaac Franklin	Slatter, Hope Hull	Sept. 28, 1838	Balto.
Brown	Henry	19	Lafayette	Woolfolk, Austin	Oct. 18, 1828	Balto.
Brown	Henry	infant	Phoenix	Donovan, Joseph S.	March 27, 1847	Balto.
Brown	Henry	20	Sabine	Donovan, Joseph S.	Feb. 10, 1844	Balto.
Brown	Henry	12	Scotia	Slatter, Hope Hull	Sept. 30, 1843	Balto.
Brown	Henry	22	Solomon Saltus	Slatter, Hope Hull	Oct. 7, 1839	Balto.
Brown	Henry	30	Solomon Saltus	Slatter, Hope Hull	Oct. 7, 1839	Balto.
Brown	Henry	18	Union	Slatter, Hope Hull	July 26, 1847	Balto.
Brown	Henry	21	Victorine	Donovan, Joseph S.	Dec. 31, 1846	Balto.
Brown	Henry	23	Victorine	Rodbind, Ebenezer	May 14, 1845	Balto.
Brown	Henson	42	Nathaniel Hooper	Donovan, Joseph S.	Feb. 12, 1852	Balto.
Brown	Isaac	30	Victorine	Slatter, Hope Hull	Dec. 17, 1845	Balto.
Brown	Jack	19	Henry Clay	Woolfolk, Austin	Dec. 4, 1828	Balto.
Brown	Jain	14	Victorine	Donovan, Joseph S.	Sept. 29, 1845	Balto.
Brown	James	30	Catharine	Donovan, Joseph S.	Jan. 18, 1845	Balto.
Brown	James	23	Kirkwood	Slatter, Hope Hull	Dec. 23, 1843	Balto.
Brown	James	20	Margaret Hugg	Wilson, Thomas C.	Nov. 30, 1844	Balto.
Brown	James	23	Orbit	Woolfolk, Austin	Apr. 16, 1825	Balto.
Brown	James	16	Solomon Saltus	Slatter, Hope Hull	Oct. 7, 1839	Balto.
Brown	James	17	Southerner	Donovan, Joseph S.	Jan. 5, 1852	Balto.
Brown	James	10	Southerner	Donovan, Joseph S.	Oct. 27, 1849	Balto.
Brown	James	22	Victorine	Donovan, Joseph S.	Sept. 29, 1845	Balto.
Brown	Jane	18	Elizabeth	Donovan, Joseph S.	Nov. 18, 1848	Balto.
Brown	Jane	22	Irad Ferry	Clendenin, A.	Jan. 16, 1840	Balto.

Surname	First Name	Age	Ship	O/S	Date	Depart
Brown	Jerry	22	Tippecanoe	Purvis, James Franklin	Jan. 17, 1842	Balto.
Brown	Jesse	20	Lapwing	Woolfolk, Austin	Feb. 15, 1827	Balto.
Brown	Joe	25	Southerner	Campbell, Bernard M.	Jan. 5, 1852	Balto.
Brown	John	22	Aurilla	Warfield, Charles	Apr. 26, 1822	Balto.
Brown	John	21	Catharine	Donovan, Joseph S.	Jan. 18, 1845	Balto.
Brown	John	18	Kirkwood	Donovan, Joseph S.	Apr. 15, 1845	Balto.
Brown	John	8	Lafayette	Woolfolk, Austin	Oct. 18, 1828	Balto.
Brown	John	22	Louisa	Campbell, Bernard M.	May 18, 1846	Balto.
Brown	John	25	Solomon Saltus	Slatter, Hope Hull	Oct. 7, 1839	Balto.
Brown	John	23	Superb	Anderson, David	Apr. 6, 1819	Balto.
Brown	John	26	Victorine	Rodbind, Ebenezer	March 14, 1846	Balto.
Brown	John	19	Victorine	Slatter, Hope Hull	March 9, 1844	Balto.
Brown	John	21	Victorine	Donovan, Joseph S.	Sept. 29, 1845	Balto.
Brown	John		Zoe	Donovan, Joseph S.	Feb. 16, 1847	Balto.
Brown	John Baptist	23	General Pinckney	Slatter, Hope Hull	Nov. 10, 1845	Balto.
Brown	Joseph	25	John C. Calhoun	Donovan, Joseph S.	Oct. 24, 1850	Balto.
Brown	Joseph	13	Kirkwood	Donovan, Joseph S.	Sept. 28, 1846	Balto.
Brown	Josiah	22	Tippecanoe	Purvis, James Franklin	Jan. 17, 1842	Balto.
Brown	Julia	14	Henry A. Barling	Campbell, Bernard M.	Feb. 24, 1851	Balto.
Brown	Julia	30	Nathaniel Hooper	Donovan, Jospeh S.	Feb. 12, 1852	Balto.
Brown	Julia	19	Victorine	Rodbind, Ebenezer	March 14, 1846	Balto.
Brown	Julia Ann	20	States	Woolfolk, Austin	Nov. 21, 1827	Balto.
Brown	July ?	19	Kirkwood	Donovan, Joseph S.	Oct. 26, 1847	Balto.
Brown	Lafayette	infant	Nathaniel Hooper	Donovan, Jospeh S.	Feb. 12, 1852	Balto.
Brown	Leonard	35	Catharine	Slatter, Hope Hull	Jan. 24, 1843	Balto.
Brown	Letty	25	Union	Sheckles, B.O.	Nov. 17, 1849	Balto.

Surname	First Name	Age	Ship	O/S	Date	Depart
Brown	Levina		Superb	Slatter, Hope Hull	Nov. 1, 1843	Balto.
Brown	Levy	16	General Pinckney	Rodbind, Ebenezer	Feb. 21, 1846	Balto.
Brown	Lewis	15	Catharine	Donovan, Joseph S.	Jan. 18, 1845	Balto.
Brown	Lloyd	21	Margaret Hugg	Wilson, Thomas C.	Nov. 30, 1844	Balto.
Brown	Louisa	16	States	Woolfolk, Austin	Nov. 21, 1827	Balto.
Brown	Loyd	13	Louisa	Donovan, Joseph S.	Oct. 9, 1847	Balto.
Brown	Lucinda	16	Eliza F.Mason	Donovan, Joseph S.	Nov. 13, 1851	Balto.
Brown	Lucinda	11	Russell	Slatter, Hope Hull	March 1, 1839	Balto.
Brown	Mahala	18	States	Woolfolk, Austin	Apr. 14, 1828	Balto.
Brown	Mandy	16	Kirkwood	Donovan, Joseph S.	Dec. 10, 1846	Balto.
Brown	Margaret	14	Zoe	Slatter, Hope Hull	Feb. 16, 1847	Balto.
Brown	Margrett	18	Kirkwood	Donovan, Joseph S.	March 9, 1847	Balto.
Brown	Margrett	18	Victorine	Slatter, Hope Hull	March 9, 1844	Balto.
Brown	Maria	23	Brunswick	Woolfolk, Austin	Oct. 11, 1831	Balto.
Brown	Maria	17	Union	Campbell, Bernard M.	Dec. 16, 1848	Balto.
Brown	Maria	infant	Victorine	Slatter, Hope Hull	March 9, 1844	Balto.
Brown	Mariah	10	Southerner	Donovan, Joseph S.	Jan. 21, 1850	Balto.
Brown	Mariah	22	Union	Campbell, Bernard M.	March 17, 1849	Balto.
Brown	Marinda	18	Louisa	Slatter, Hope Hull	Oct. 11, 1847	Balto.
Brown	Marshall	infant	Nathaniel Hooper	Donovan, Joseph S.	Feb. 12, 1852	Balto.
Brown	Martin	24	Southerner	Donovan, Joseph S.	Oct. 27, 1849	Balto.
Brown	Mary	17	Ann & Leah	Woolfolk, Austin	Nov.1, 1831	Balto.
Brown	Mary	15	Catharine	Woolfolk, Austin	March 3. 1829	Balto.
Brown	Mary	13	Elizabeth	Donovan, Joseph S.	March 21, 1850	Balto.
Brown	Mary	15	Henry A. Barling	Campbell, Bernard M.	Dec. 18, 1851	Balto.
Brown	Mary	20	Sarah Bridge	Campbell, Bernard M.	Feb. 8, 1851	Balto.

Surname	First Name	Age	Ship	O/S	Date	Depart
Brown	Mary Ann	15	Victorine	Slatter, Hope Hull	Dec. 17, 1845	Balto.
Brown	Mary Catharine	18	General Pinckney	Slatter, Hope Hull	Nov. 10, 1845	Balto.
Brown	Mary Ellen	infant	Kirkwood	Crow, William	Jan. 14, 1846	Balto.
Brown	Matilda	26	Colonel Howard	Harker, William	Nov. 21, 1844	Balto.
Brown	Matilda	25	Louisa	Donovan, Joseph S.	Oct. 9, 1847	Balto.
Brown	Matilda	infant	Supet	Slatter, Hope Hull	Nov. 1, 1843	Balto.
Brown	Matilda	10	Union	Rodbird, Ebenezer	Dec. 16, 1848	Balto.
Brown	Milly	18	General Pinckney	Rodbird, Ebenezer	Feb. 21, 1846	Balto.
Brown	Milly	25	Henry A. Barling	Campbell, Bernard M.	Apr. 19, 1849	Balto.
Brown	Mima Ann	18	General Pinckney	Campbell, Bernard M.	Jan. 19, 1847	Balto.
Brown	Molan	19	Hibernia	Woolfork, Austin	Dec. 5, 1826	Balto.
Brown	Moses	28	Southerner	Donovan, Joseph S.	Oct. 27, 1849	Balto.
Brown	Oliver	12	Kirkwood	Donovan, Joseph S.	Jan. 14, 1846	Balto.
Brown	Patrick	20	Margaret Hugg	Harker, William	Feb. 8, 1845	Balto.
Brown	Perry	26	Southerner	Campbe l, Bernard M.	Jan. 20, 1850	Balto.
Brown	Peter	20	Kirkwood	Slatter, Hope Hull	Oct. 16, 1845	Balto.
Brown	Philip	27	Tippecanoe	Slatter, Hope Hull	Jan. 17, 1842	Balto.
Brown	Polly	30	Colonel Howard	Harker, William	Nov. 21, 1844	Balto.
Brown	Priscilla	18	Hope & Hannah	Woolfolk, Austin	March 11, 1829	Balto.
Brown	Quincy	17	Kirkwood	Donovan, Joseph S.	Oct. 26, 1847	Balto.
Brown	Rachel	15	Eliza F.Mason	Donovan, Joseph S.	Nov. 13, 1851	Balto.
Brown	Rachel	20	Victorine	Slatter, Henry F.	Dec. 31, 1846	Balto.
Brown	Rebecca	18	Union	Williams, Thomas	Oct. 9, 1848	Balto.
Brown	Robert	26	Garnicleft	Slatter, Hope Hull	Nov. 25, 1840	Balto.
Brown	Robert	23	Kirkwood	Slatter, Hope Hull	Oct. 16, 1845	Balto.
Brown	Robert	23	Kirkwood	Donovan, Joseph S.	Oct. 26, 1847	Balto.

Surname	First Name	Age	Ship	O/S	Date	Depart
Brown	Robert	22	Southerner	Donovan, Joseph S.	Jan. 21, 1850	Balto.
Brown	Robert	16	Victorine	Slatter, Henry F.	Dec. 31, 1846	Balto.
Brown	Rosetta	20	Union	Donovan, Joseph S.	Dec. 16, 1848	Balto.
Brown	Sam	22	Billow	Woolfolk, Joseph B.	Feb. 23, 1828	Balto.
Brown	Sam	15	Porpoise	Purvis, James Franklin	Dec. 11, 1841	Balto.
Brown	Sam	9	States	Woolfolk, Austin	Apr. 14, 1828	Balto.
Brown	Samuel	23	Scotia	Slatter, Hope Hull	Sept. 30, 1843	Balto.
Brown	Samuel	60	Solomon Saltus	Slatter, Hope Hull	Oct. 7, 1839	Balto.
Brown	Samuel	30	Superb	Slatter, Hope Hull	Nov. 1, 1843	Balto.
Brown	Samuel	20	Victorine	Slatter, Hope Hull	March 9, 1844	Balto.
Brown	Samuel	11	Zoe	Slatter, Hope Hull	Feb. 16, 1847	Balto.
Brown	Sarah	15	Zoe	Donovan, Joseph S.	Feb. 16, 1847	Balto.
Brown	Scott	30	St. Mary	Donovan, Joseph S.	Nov. 29, 1845	Balto.
Brown	Shadrack	10	Brunswick	Woolfolk, Austin	Oct. 11, 1831	Balto.
Brown	Susan	25	Ganniclefft	Slatter, Hope Hull	Nov. 25, 1840	Balto.
Brown	Susan	18	Victorine	Slatter, Hope Hull	Sept. 12, 1846	Balto.
Brown	Susana	11	Union	Donovan, Joseph S.	Dec. 16, 1848	Balto.
Brown	Sylva	28	Union	Slatter, Hope Hull	July 26, 1847	Balto.
Brown	Thomas	16	General Pinckney	Donovan, Joseph S.	Nov. 10, 1845	Balto.
Brown	Thomas	21	Louisa	Slatter, Hope Hull	Oct. 11, 1847	Balto.
Brown	Thomas	18	Margaret Hugg	Wilson, Thomas C.	Nov. 30, 1844	Balto.
Brown	Thomas	14	Superb	Slatter, Hope Hull	Nov. 1, 1843	Balto.
Brown	Thomas	20	Tippecanoe	Slatter, Hope Hull	Jan. 17, 1842	Balto.
Brown	Thomas	36	Topaz	Woolfolk, Austin	Apr. 20, 1829	Balto.
Brown	Thornton	21	Helen A. Miller	Campbell, Bernard M.	Oct. 18, 1852	Balto.
Brown	Tom	13	Seaman	Rush, George Jr.	Dec. 16, 1841	Balto.

Surname	First Name	Age	Ship	O/S	Date	Depart
Brown	Townley	26	Southerner	Donovan, Joseph S.	Oct. 27, 1849	Balto.
Brown	Warsen	11	Zoe	Slatter, Hope Hull	Feb. 16, 1847	Balto.
Brown	Washington	30	Kirkwood	Donovan, Joseph S.	Dec. 10, 1846	Balto.
Brown	Washington	22	Paoli	Slatter, Hope Hull	Sept. 9, 1845	Balto.
Brown	William	19	Edward Everett	Campbell, Bernard M.	March 10, 1851	Balto.
Brown	William	10	Jefferson	Woolfolk, Austin	Dec. 24, 1827	Balto.
Brown	William	24	Lapwing	Woolfolk, Joseph B.	Feb. 16, 1827	Balto.
Brown	William	9	Louisa	Donovan, Joseph S.	Oct. 9, 1847	Balto.
Brown	William	15	Shamrock	Guyton Elisha	March 11, 1840	Balto.
Brown	William	24	Southerner	Donovan, Joseph S.	Jan. 21, 1850	Balto.
Brown	William	24	Tippecanoe	Slatter, Hope Hull	Dec. 16, 1840	Balto.
Brown	William	22	Tippecanoe	Slatter, Hope Hull	Jan. 17, 1842	Balto.
Brown	William	8	Zoe	Slatter, Hope Hull	Feb. 16, 1847	Balto.
Brown	Willson	11	Ann & Leah	Woolfolk, Austin	Nov. 1, 1831	Balto.
Brown		infant	Edward Everett	Campbell, Bernard M.	March 10, 1851	Balto.
Brown		27	Emilie	Coalman, Henry E.	Aug. 21, 1819	Balto.
Brown		21	Kirkwood	Donovan, Joseph S.	Dec. 10, 1846	Balto.
Brown		19	Phoenix	Donovan, Joseph S.	March 27, 1847	Balto.
Brown		infant	Solomon Saltus	Slatter, Hope Hull	Oct. 7, 1839	Balto.
Browner	Adaline	15	Victorine	Donovan, Joseph S.	Sept. 29, 1845	Balto.
Browner	Eliza	17	Victorine	Donovan, Joseph S.	Sept. 29, 1845	Balto.
Browner	Johanna	16	Victorine	Donovan, Joseph S.	Sept. 29, 1845	Balto.
Brozier	Mary Ann	18	Margaret Hugg	Harker, William	Feb. 8, 1845	Balto.
Bruce	George	28	Henry A. Barling	Campbell, Walter L.	Oct. 28, 1848	Balto.
Bruce	Iatecia	18	Kirkwood	Slatter, Hope Hull	Apr. 15, 1845	Balto.
Bruce	Maria	12	Victorine	Rodbind, Ebenezer	May 14, 1845	Balto.

Surname	First Name	Age	Ship	O/S	Date	Depart
Bruce	Mary	17	Kirkwood	Rodbind, Ebenezer	Oct. 26, 1847	Balto.
Bruice	Lloyd	30	Peru	Slatter, Hope Hull	Nov. 16, 1842	Balto.
Bruill	Thomas	19	Ann & Leah	Woolfolk, Austin	Nov.1, 1831	Balto.
Brummell	David	23	Liberator	Woolfolk, Austin	Nov. 12, 1828	Balto.
Bruner	Clary	8	Isaac Franklin	Slatter, Hope Hull	Sept. 28, 1838	Balto.
Bruner	Cora	30	Isaac Franklin	Slatter, Hope Hull	Sept. 28, 1838	Balto.
Bruner	Elias	33	Isaac Franklin	Slatter, Hope Hull	Sept. 28, 1838	Balto.
Bruner	Elias	18	Kirkwood	Slatter, Hope Hull	Oct. 16, 1845	Balto.
Bruner	Manuel	4	Isaac Franklin	Slatter, Hope Hull	Sept. 28, 1838	Balto.
Bryan	Alexander	25	Cora	Donovan, Jospeh S.	Jan. 21, 1851	Balto.
Bryan	Ellen	26	Paoli	Slatter, Hope Hull	Sept. 9, 1845	Balto.
Bryan	Lewis	22	Kirkwood	Donovan, Joseph S.	Oct. 26, 1847	Balto.
Bryan	Mary	18	Hibernia	Woolfolk, Austin	Dec. 5, 1826	Balto.
Bryan	Mary	25	Southerner	Donovan, Joseph S.	Jan. 21, 1850	Balto.
Bryan	Sam	22	Lapwing	King, Gideon T.	March 22, 1822	Balto.
Bryand	Jane	21	Home	Donovan, Joseph S.	March 22, 1845	Balto.
Bryant	Eliza	17	Elizabeth	Campbell, Bernard M.	Jan. 2, 1850	Balto.
Bryant	Emily	16	Abbott Lord	Campbell, Bernard M.	April 28, 1852	Balto.
Bryant	Jane	13	Tippecanoe	Slatter, Hope Hull	Jan. 17, 1842	Balto.
Bryant	Milton	24	Helen A. Miller	Campbell, Bernard M.	Oct. 18, 1852	Balto.
Buchanan	Abraham	22	Tippecanoe	Slatter, Hope Hull	Jan. 17, 1842	Balto.
Buchanan	Bushrod	26	Lafayette	Harker, William	March 25, 1843	Balto.
Buchanan	Dorcus	22	Victorine	Slatter, Hope Hull	Sept. 12, 1846	Balto.
Buchanan	Edward	20	Victorine	Slatter, Hope Hull	Sept. 12, 1846	Balto.
Buchanan	George	infant	Frances Amy	Donovan, Joseph S.	Jan. 20, 1847	Balto.
Buchanan	George	20	Topaz	Woolfolk, Austin	Apr. 20, 1829	Balto.

Surname	First Name	Age	Ship	O/S	Date	Depart
Buchanan	Jane	18	Frances Amy	Donovan, Joseph S.	Jan. 20, 1847	Balto.
Buchhannon	Henry	27	Alfred	Woolfolk, Austin	May 7, 1825	Balto.
Buck	George	10	States	Woolfolk, Austin	Apr. 14, 1828	Balto.
Buck	James	25	Irad Ferry	Purvis, James Franklin	Feb. 5, 1842	Balto.
Buck	Matilda	20	States	Woolfolk, Austin	Nov. 21, 1827	Balto.
Buckhanan	Robert	38	Kirkwood	Williams, Thomas	Apr. 4, 1846	Balto.
Buckner	William	19	Isaac Franklin	Kephart, George	Sept. 28, 1838	Balto.
Buckram	Redna	infant	Kirkwood	Slatter, Hope Hull	Apr. 15, 1845	Balto.
Buckram	Sarah	26	Kirkwood	Slatter, Hope Hull	Apr. 15, 1845	Balto.
Bucktrout	Louisa	21	Seaman	Slatter, Hope Hull	March 25, 1839	Balto.
Bullas	Lewis	23	Budget	Spraggins, Samuel M.	Nov. 27, 1821	Balto.
Bullen	Margaret	15	Victorine	Donovan, Joseph S.	Sept. 29, 1845	Balto.
Buller	James	23	Lafayette	Woolfolk, Austin	Oct. 18, 1828	Balto.
Buller	James	18	Southerner	Donovar, Joseph S.	Jan. 21, 1850	Balto.
Bullet	Louisa	15	Delawaran	Campbell, Bernard M.	Dec. 1, 1848	Balto.
Bun	Dealy	11	Isaac Franklin	Kephart, George	Sept. 28, 1838	Balto.
Bunger	Edwin	11	Ann & Leah	Woolfolk, Austin	Nov.1, 1831	Balto.
Bunkley	Ned	20	Seaman	Slatter, Hope Hull	March 25, 1839	Balto.
Buonaparte	Polly	30	Solomon Saltus	Slatter, Hope Hull	Oct. 7, 1839	Balto.
Buonaparte		infant	Solomon Saltus	Slatter, Hope Hull	Oct. 7, 1839	Balto.
Buoneparte	Mary Ann	7	Solomon Saltus	Slatter, Hope Hull	Oct. 7, 1839	Balto.
Buoneparte	Susan	8	Solomon Saltus	Slatter, Hope Hull	Oct. 7, 1839	Balto.
Buoneparte	William	4	Solomon Saltus	Slatter, Hope Hull	Oct. 7, 1839	Balto.
Burch	Charles	23	Superb	Slatter, Hope Hull	Nov. 1, 1843	Balto.
Burges	Charity	16	Union	Slatter, Hope Hull	July 26, 1847	Balto.
Burges	Thomas	20	Elizabeth	Donovan, Joseph S.	Nov. 18, 1848	Balto.

Surname	First Name	Age	Ship	O/S	Date	Depart
Burgess	Ann	23	Kirkwood	Slatter, Hope Hull	Dec. 23, 1843	Balto.
Burgess	Louisa	18	Architect	Harker, William	Feb. 16, 1843	Balto.
Burgess	Reason	25	Architect	Slatter, Hope Hull	May 20, 1841	Balto.
Burk	Lucinora	17	General Pinckney	Williams, Thomas	Jan. 19, 1847	Balto.
Burke	George	22	Kirkwood	Donovan, Joseph S.	Dec. 23, 1843	Balto.
Burke	Henry	19	Kirkwood	Crow, William	March 23, 1844	Balto.
Burke	Richard	20	Elizabeth	Campbell, Bernard M.	Nov. 18, 1848	Balto.
Burke	Robert	23	Seaman	Slatter, Hope Hull	Dec. 19, 1838	Balto.
Burley	Julia	19	Elizabeth	Campbell, Bernard M.	May 12, 1849	Balto.
Burlez	Dilsey	16	Colonel Howard	Donovan, Joseph S.	Nov. 21, 1844	Balto.
Burnes	James	16	Kirkwood	Donovan, Joseph S.	Jan. 4, 1845	Balto.
Burns	Charles	22	Tippecanoe	Purvis, James Franklin	Jan. 17, 1842	Balto.
Burns	James	30	Elizabeth	Donovan, Joseph S.	Nov. 18, 1848	Balto.
Burns	Luke	20	Hermitage	Slatter, Hope Hull	Oct. 28, 1846	Balto.
Burris	Amanda	18	Mary Broughton	Campbell, Bernard M.	Nov. 18, 1851	Balto.
Burt	Joshua	28	Isaac Franklin	Slatter, Hope Hull	Sept. 28, 1838	Balto.
Burton	Betsey	19	Lady Monroe	Woolfolk, Austin	March 25, 1825	Balto.
Burton	Hannah	18	Lapwing	Woolfolk, Samuel M.	Feb. 15, 1827	Balto.
Burton	James	19	Colonel Howard	Donovan, Joseph S.	Nov. 21, 1844	Balto.
Burton	Samuel	18	Alfred	Woolfolk, Austin	May 7, 1825	Balto.
Bush	Ally	40	Victorine	Slatter, Hope Hull	March 9, 1844	Balto.
Bush	Isaac	12	Victorine	Donovan, Joseph S.	Sept. 29, 1845	Balto.
Bush	Mahala	16	Victorine	Donovan, Joseph S.	May 22, 1844	Balto.
Bush	Phebe	20	Hermitage	Williams, Thomas	Oct. 28, 1846	Balto.
Bush	Samuel	18	Architect	Harker, William	Feb. 16, 1843	Balto.
Bush	Venora	4 mon.	Victorine	Donovan, Joseph S.	May 22, 1844	Balto.

Surname	First Name	Age	Ship	O/S	Date	Depart
Bushrod	Harriet	16	Union	Donovan, Joseph S.	Dec. 16, 1848	Balto.
Butcher	Mathias	19	Victorine	Donovan, Joseph S.	May 22, 1844	Balto.
Butler	Alfred	20	Zoe	Slatter, Hope Hull	Feb. 16, 1847	Balto.
Butler	Amelia	17	Zoe	Williams, Thomas	Feb. 16, 1847	Balto.
Butler	Ann E.	23	Union	Rodbird, Ebenezer	Nov. 17, 1849	Balto.
Butler	Anne	20	Lafayette	Woolfolk, Austin	Oct. 18, 1828	Balto.
Butler	Baszil	23	General Pinckney	Donovan, Joseph S.	Nov. 10, 1845	Balto.
Butler	Charles	2 mon.	Brunswick	Woolfolk, Austin	Oct. 11, 1831	Balto.
Butler	Charles	20	Brunswick	Woolfolk, Austin	Oct. 11, 1831	Balto.
Butler	Charles	17	Victorine	Gardiner, Richard S.D.	Dec. 21, 1844	Balto.
Butler	Eliza	16	Elizabeth	Donovan, Joseph S.	Nov. 18, 1848	Balto.
Butler	Emanuel	20	Superb	Donovan, Joseph S.	Nov. 2, 1843	Balto.
Butler	Emily	23	General Pinckney	Campbell, Bernard M.	Jan. 19, 1847	Balto.
Butler	Fanny	18	States	Woolfolk, Austin	Nov. 21, 1827	Balto.
Butler	Frances	3	E.H.Chapin	Slatter, Hope Hull	Nov. 30, 1847	Balto.
Butler	George	25	Catharine	Slatter, Hope Hull	Jan. 24, 1843	Balto.
Butler	George	17	Helen A. Miller	Campbell, Bernard M.	Oct. 18, 1852	Balto.
Butler	George	22	Hermitage	Williams, Thomas	Oct. 28, 1846	Balto.
Butler	George	22	Southerner	Campbell, Bernard M.	Jan. 20, 1850	Balto.
Butler	George	16	Union	Rodbind, Ebenezer	Nov. 17, 1849	Balto.
Butler	George Edward	20	Southerner	Donovan, Joseph S.	Oct. 27, 1849	Balto.
Butler	H.	22	States	Woolfolk, Austin	Nov. 21, 1827	Balto.
Butler	Hanibal	17	John C. Calhoun	Donovan, Joseph S.	Oct. 24, 1850	Balto.
Butler	Hanson	19	Helen A. Miller	Campbell, Bernard M.	Oct. 18, 1852	Balto.
Butler	Harriet	17	Brunswick	Woolfolk, Austin	Oct. 11, 1831	Balto.
Butler	Harriett	7	General Pinckney	Slatter, Hope Hull	Nov. 10, 1845	Balto.

Surname	First Name	Age	Ship	O/S	Date	Depart
Butler	Harriett	20	Sabine	Donovan, Joseph S.	Feb. 10, 1844	Balto.
Butler	Henny	18	Ann & Leah	Woolfolk, Austin	Nov. 1, 1831	Balto.
Butler	Henrietta	16	Kirkwood	Donovan, Joseph S.	Sept. 28, 1846	Balto.
Butler	Henrietta	22	Seguin	Campbell, Bernard M.	July 12, 1853	Balto.
Butler	Henry	23	States	Woolfolk, Austin	Nov. 21, 1827	Balto.
Butler	James H.	18	Scotia	Slatter, Hope Hull	Sept. 30, 1843	Balto.
Butler	Jane	infant	General Pinckney	Slatter, Hope Hull	Nov. 10, 1845	Balto.
Butler	Jane	infant	Kirkwood	Slatter, Henry F.	Dec. 10, 1846	Balto.
Butler	Jarrett	17	Union	Williams, Thomas	Oct. 9, 1848	Balto.
Butler	John	18	Brunswick	Woolfolk, Austin	Oct. 11, 1831	Balto.
Butler	John	16	Hope	Brooks, Gorhan	Sept. ?, 1834	Balto.
Butler	John	23	Julia	Woolfolk, Austin	Feb. 10, 1832	Balto.
Butler	John	9	Kirkwood	Slatter, Henry F.	Dec. 10, 1846	Balto.
Butler	John	12	Kirkwood	Slatter, Hope Hull	Dec. 23, 1843	Balto.
Butler	John	16	Kirkwood	Donovan, Joseph S.	Oct. 14, 1848	Balto.
Butler	John	4	Seguin	Campbell, Bernard M.	July 12, 1853	Balto.
Butler	John	30	Solomon Saltus	Slatter, Hope Hull	Oct. 7, 1839	Balto.
Butler	John H.	18	Scotia	Slatter, Hope Hull	Sept. 30, 1843	Balto.
Butler	Josephine	17	Salvadora	Slatter, Hope Hull	Sept. 28, 1846	Balto.
Butler	Kitty	18	Glasgow	Slatter, Hope Hull	Oct. 11, 1838	Balto.
Butler	Lewis	24	Tippecanoe	Purvis, James Franklin	Jan. 17, 1842	Balto.
Butler	Lucy Ann	17	Kirkwood	Donovan, Joseph S.	Jan. 14, 1846	Balto.
Butler	Lydia	22	Kirkwood	Campbell, Bernard M.	Nov. 28, 1849	Balto.
Butler	Madison	28	Seguin	Campbell, Bernard M.	July 12, 1853	Balto.
Butler	Mahala	14	Tangier	Campbell, Bernard M.	Nov. 26, 1853	Balto.
Butler	Major	21	Union	Donovan, Joseph S.	May 13, 1848	Balto.

Surname	First Name	Age	Ship	O/S	Date	Depart
Butler	Margrett	40	E.H.Chapin	Slatter, Hope Hull	Nov. 30, 1847	Balto.
Butler	Margrett	16	Kirkwood	Slatter, Hope Hull	Apr. 15, 1845	Balto.
Butler	Margrett	14	Kirkwood	Donovan, Joseph S.	Sept. 28, 1846	Balto.
Butler	Maria	16	Ann & Leah	Woolfolk, Austin	Nov.1, 1831	Balto.
Butler	Mary	1 mon.	Ann & Leah	Woolfolk, Austin	Nov.1, 1831	Balto.
Butler	Mary	19	Glasgow	Slatter, Hope Hull	Oct. 11, 1838	Balto.
Butler	Matilda	6	Victorine	Rodbind, Ebenezer	Dec. 31, 1846	Balto.
Butler	Maurice	22	Solomon Saltus	Slatter, Hope Hull	Oct. 7, 1839	Balto.
Butler	Milly	16	Elizabeth	Donovan, Joseph S.	Nov. 18, 1848	Balto.
Butler	Nelly	24	Scotia	Slatter, Hope Hull	Sept. 30, 1843	Balto.
Butler	Ousbourn	28	General Pinckney	Slatter, Hope Hull	Feb. 21, 1846	Balto.
Butler	Rachel	18	Kirkwood	Slatter, Hope Hull	Oct. 16, 1845	Balto.
Butler	Rosetta	27	Kirkwood	Slatter, Henry F.	Dec. 10, 1846	Balto.
Butler	Rosetta	17	Kirkwood	Campbell, Bernard M.	March 9, 1847	Balto.
Butler	Samuel	16	Kirkwood	Slatter, Henry F.	Dec. 10, 1846	Balto.
Butler	Sarah Ann	26	General Pinckney	Slatter, Hope Hull	Nov. 10, 1845	Balto.
Butler	Walter	35	St. Mary	Donovan, Joseph S.	Nov. 29, 1845	Balto.
Butler	William	15	Kirkwood	Donovan, Joseph S.	Sept. 28, 1846	Balto.
Butler	William	16	Union	Donovan, Joseph S.	Dec. 16, 1848	Balto.
Butler		14	John C. Calhoun	Donovan, Joseph S.	Oct. 24, 1850	Balto.
Butler		25	John C. Calhoun	Donovan, Joseph S.	Oct. 24, 1850	Balto.
Butt	Samuel	24	Hibernia	Woolfolk, Austin	Dec. 5, 1826	Balto.
Butten	John	33	Henry A. Barling	Campbell, Walter L.	Oct. 28, 1848	Balto.
Button	Samuel	30	Elizabeth	Campbell, Walter L.	Oct. 6, 1849	Balto.
Butts	Fanny	14	Colonel Howard	Harker, William	Nov. 21, 1844	Balto.
Butts	Hannah	16	Southerner	Campbell, Bernard M.	Jan. 5, 1852	Balto.

Surname	First Name	Age	Ship	O/S	Date	Depart
Butts	William	22	Solomon Saltus	Slatter, Hope Hull	Oct. 7, 1839	Balto.
Byas	Robert	20	Burlington	Slatter, Hope Hull	Oct. 21, 1842	Balto.
Byers	Charity Ann	11	Zoe	Slatter, Hope Hull	Feb. 16, 1847	Balto.
Bywater	William	22	John C. Calhoun	Donovan, Joseph S.	Oct. 24, 1850	Balto.
Cabrith	Henry	23	Charles	Campbell, Bernard M.	Dec. 18, 1850	Balto.
Cain	Adam	23	Victorine	Donovan, Joseph S.	Sept. 29, 1845	Balto.
Cain	Elisa	16	Ann & Leah	Woolfolk, Austin	Nov.1, 1831	Balto.
Cain	Ellen	6	Ann & Leah	Woolfolk, Austin	Nov.1, 1831	Balto.
Cain	Esther	18	Brunswick	Woolfolk, Austin	Oct. 11, 1831	Balto.
Cain	George	15	Ann & Leah	Woolfolk, Austin	Nov.1, 1831	Balto.
Cain	Ibby	3	Ann & Leah	Woolfolk, Austin	Nov.1, 1831	Balto.
Cain	John	22	Architect	Slatter, Hope Hull	May 20, 1841	Balto.
Cain	John	17	Jefferson	Woolfolk, Austin	Dec. 24, 1827	Balto.
Cain	Joseph	30	Ann & Leah	Woolfolk, Austin	Nov.1, 1831	Balto.
Cain	Joseph Jr.	16	Ann & Leah	Woolfolk, Austin	Nov.1, 1831	Balto.
Cain	Leah	24	Strafford	Harker, William	Nov. 22, 1843	Balto.
Cain	Nelly	35	Ann & Leah	Woolfolk, Austin	Nov.1, 1831	Balto.
Cain	Phill	25	Brunswick	Woolfolk, Austin	Oct. 11, 1831	Balto.
Cain	Priscilla	9	Ann & Leah	Woolfolk, Austin	Nov.1, 1831	Balto.
Cain	Thomas	20	Ann & Leah	Woolfolk, Austin	Nov.1, 1831	Balto.
Cain	William	19	Scotia	Harker, William	Sept. 30, 1843	Balto.
Calhoun	George	20	Bostonian	Slatter, Hope Hull	Jan. 18, 1841	Balto.
Callafer	George	13	Kirkwood	Slatter, Hope Hull	Dec. 23, 1843	Balto.
Calvert	Augustus	23	Kirkwood	Donovan, Joseph S.	March 23, 1844	Balto.
Calvert	Henrietta	15	Elizabeth	Campbell, Bernard M.	Nov. 18, 1848	Balto.
Calvert	Richard	19	Kirkwood	Slatter, Hope Hull	Apr. 4, 1846	Balto.

Surname	First Name	Age	Ship	O/S	Date	Depart
Calvert	Tom	35	Kirkwood	Rodbind, Ebenezer	Apr. 15, 1845	Balto.
Calvert	William	19	Kirkwood	Rodbind, Ebenezer	Apr. 15, 1845	Balto.
Calvert	William	20	Narragansett	Campbell, Bernard M.	Nov. 27, 1850	Balto.
Camel	Celia	19	Kirkwood	Slatter, Hope Hull	Dec. 23, 1843	Balto.
Cammel	Leon	23	Jefferson	Woolfolk, Joseph B.	Dec. 24, 1827	Balto.
Campbell	Ann	17	Burlington	Slatter, Hope Hull	Oct. 21, 1842	Balto.
Campbell	Ann	20	Southerner	Donovan, Joseph S.	Oct. 27, 1849	Balto.
Campbell	Augusta	19	Kirkwood	Campbell, Bernard M.	Dec. 10, 1846	Balto.
Campbell	Charles	24	Phoenix	Donovan, Joseph S.	March 27, 1847	Balto.
Campbell	Ellin	35	Kirkwood	Donovan, Joseph S.	Oct. 14, 1848	Balto.
Campbell	Frank	24	Kirkwood	Slatter, Henry F.	Dec. 10, 1846	Balto.
Campbell	George	17	Elizabeth	Campbell, Bernard M.	March 21, 1850	Balto.
Campbell	James	26	General Pinckney	Slatter, Hope Hull	Jan. 19, 1847	Balto.
Campbell	John	25	Kirkwood	Campbell, Bernard M.	Apr. 4, 1846	Balto.
Campbell	John	18	Kirkwood	Campbell, Bernard M.	Oct. 14, 1848	Balto.
Campbell	Mary	28	Saldana	Harker, William	Feb. 27, 1844	Balto.
Campbell	Peter	7	Saldana	Harker, William	Feb. 27, 1844	Balto.
Campbell	Richard	35	Hermitage	Slatter, Hope Hull	Oct. 28, 1846	Balto.
Campbell	Ruth	3	Kirkwood	Donovan, Joseph S.	Oct. 14, 1848	Balto.
Campbell	Sarah	4	Southerner	Donovan, Joseph S.	Oct. 27, 1849	Balto.
Campbell	Susan	14	Abbott Lord	Campbell, Bernard M.	April 28, 1852	Balto.
Campbell	Virginia	12	Victorine	Rodbind, Ebenezer	Dec. 31, 1846	Balto.
Campbell	William	27	Victorine	Campbell, Bernard M.	Dec. 31, 1846	Balto.
Camper	Anne	9	Margaret Hugg	Harker, William	Nov. 30, 1844	Balto.
Camper	Bob	19	Hibernia	Woolfolk, Austin	Dec. 5, 1826	Balto.
Camper	Charles	11	Margaret Hugg	Harker, William	Nov. 30, 1844	Balto.

Surname	First Name	Age	Ship	O/S	Date	Depart
Camper	Dennis	20	Brunswick	Woolfolk, Austin	Oct. 11, 1831	Balto.
Camper	Ebin	22	Burlington	Slatter, Hope Hull	Oct. 21, 1842	Balto.
Camper	Henry	21	Ewarkee	Purvis, James Franklin	March 4, 1841	Balto.
Camper	John	30	Victorine	Slatter, Hope Hull	May 14, 1845	Balto.
Camper	Josephine	6	Margaret Hugg	Harker, William	Nov. 30, 1844	Balto.
Camper	Joshua	22	Lafayette	Woolfolk, Joseph B.	Oct. 18, 1828	Balto.
Camper	Malinda	23	Helen A. Miller	Campbell, Bernard M.	Oct. 18, 1852	Balto.
Camper	Margaret	16	Brunswick	Woolfolk, Austin	Oct. 11, 1831	Balto.
Camper	Martin	18	Sarah Bridge	Campbell, Bernard M.	Feb. 8, 1851	Balto.
Camper	Richard	24	Lapwing	Hall, Francis	March 22, 1822	Balto.
Camper	Rosanna	25	Margaret Hugg	Harker, William	Nov. 30, 1844	Balto.
Camper	Rose	9	Henry Clay	Woolfolk, Austin	Dec. 4, 1828	Balto.
Camper	William	26	Kirkwood	Slatter, Hope Hull	Oct. 16, 1845	Balto.
Camphor	Henry	22	Home	Donovan, Joseph S.	March 22, 1845	Balto.
Canady	George	28	Pioneer	Slatter, Hope Hull	Sept. 15, 1847	Balto.
Cane	Abraham	13	Southerner	Campbell, Bernard M.	Jan. 5, 1852	Balto.
Cane	Charles	20	Lafayette	Woolfolk, Austin	Oct. 18, 1828	Balto.
Cannedy	Rachel	30	Margaret Forbs	Slatter, Hope Hull	Nov. 28, 1838	Balto.
Canoles	Jack	19	Henry Clay	Woolfolk, Austin	Dec. 4, 1828	Balto.
Cant	Basil	16	Kirkwood	Donovan, Joseph S.	Oct. 26, 1847	Balto.
Canterbury	William	20	Seaman	Slatter, Hope Hull	Dec. 19, 1838	Balto.
Canton	Jim	15	Victorine	Harker, William	March 9, 1844	Balto.
Car	Minty	22	Splendid	Slatter, Hope Hull	Apr. 24, 1841	Balto.
Carey	Isaac	15	Seaman	Rush, George Jr.	Dec. 16, 1841	Balto.
Carey	Jane	17	Nathaniel Hooper	Donovan, Jospeh S.	Feb. 12, 1852	Balto.
Carey	Reuben	15	Architect	Crow, William	Feb. 3, 1841	Balto.

Surname	First Name	Age	Ship	O/S	Date	Depart
Carey	Sam	13	Delawarian	Campbell, Bernard M.	Dec. 1, 1848	Balto.
Carier	Emily	15	Tippecanoe	Slatter, Hope Hull	Jan. 17, 1842	Balto.
Carolus	Dotti	16	Julia	Woolfolk, Austin	Jan. 8, 1829	Balto.
Carpenter	Allen	3	Home	Donovan, Joseph S.	March 22, 1845	Balto.
Carpenter	Kitty	12	Elizabeth	Donovan, Joseph S.	Nov. 18, 1848	Balto.
Carr	Benjamin	18	Union	Donovan, Joseph S.	May 13, 1848	Balto.
Carr	Emaline	8	Margaret Hugg	Wilson, Thomas C.	Nov. 30, 1844	Balto.
Carr	Henry	21	Lafayette	Harker, William	March 25, 1843	Balto.
Carrin	Henry	22	Catharine	Slatter, Hope Hull	Jan. 24, 1843	Balto.
Carrington	Henry	14	Kirkwood	Donovan, Joseph S.	Nov. 28, 1849	Balto.
Carrington	Hilery	15	Kirkwood	Donovan, Joseph S.	Nov. 28, 1849	Balto.
Carrol	John	18	Hyperion	Thompson, Hugh	Nov. 12, 1821	Balto.
Carroll	Benjamin	35	Margaret Hugg	Wilson, Thomas C.	Nov. 30, 1844	Balto.
Carroll	Charity	22	Union	Sheckles. B.O.	Nov. 17, 1849	Balto.
Carroll	Charles	17	Narragansett	Campbell, Bernard M.	Nov. 27, 1850	Balto.
Carroll	Charles	21	Victorine	Donovan, Joseph S.	May 14, 1845	Balto.
Carroll	Clancy	17	Union	Sheckles, Gannon	March 17, 1849	Balto.
Carroll	Clem	10	Narragansett	Campbell, Bernard M.	Nov. 27, 1850	Balto.
Carroll	Edward	22	Victorine	Donovan, Joseph S.	May 14, 1845	Balto.
Carroll	George	21	Catharine	Donovan, Joseph S.	Jan. 18, 1845	Balto.
Carroll	Henry	15	Henry A. Barling	Campbell, Bernard M.	Apr. 19, 1849	Balto.
Carroll	Isaac	15	General Pinckney	Williams, Thomas	Jan. 19, 1847	Balto.
Carroll	John	19	Architect	Donovan, Joseph S.	Apr. 25, 1846	Balto.
Carroll	Lenard	19	Eliza F.Mason	Donovan, Joseph S.	Nov. 13, 1851	Balto.
Carroll	Maria	18	Margaret Hugg	Slatter, Hope Hull	Feb. 8, 1845	Balto.
Carroll	Robert	8	Delawarian	Campbell, Bernard M.	Dec. 1, 1848	Balto.

Surname	First Name	Age	Ship	O/S	Date	Depart
Carroll	Sarah	22	Mary Broughton	Campbell, Bernard M.	Nov. 18, 1851	Balto.
Carroll	Sarah	2	Union	Sheckles, B.O.	Nov. 17, 1849	Balto.
Carroll	Sophia	25	Eliza	Slatter, Hope Hull	Oct. 9, 1840	Balto.
Carroll	Susan	2	Delawarian	Campbell, Bernard M.	Dec. 1, 1848	Balto.
Carroll	Violetta	22	Delawarian	Campbell, Bernard M.	Dec. 1, 1848	Balto.
Carroll	Warren	25	Irad Ferry	Wilson, J.W.	May 6, 1839	Balto.
Carroll	Willis	20	Delawarian	Campbell, Bernard M.	Dec. 1, 1848	Balto.
Carroll		infant	Delawarian	Campbell, Bernard M.	Dec. 1, 1848	Balto.
Carter	Aaron	20	John S. Gittings	Campbell, Bernard M.	Nov. 20, 1852	Balto.
Carter	Aaron	22	Justina	Donovan, Joseph S.	Dec. 2, 1852	Balto.
Carter	Albert	18	Narragansett	Donovan, Joseph S.	Nov. 27, 1850	Balto.
Carter	Ann Mariah	17	Kirkwood	Donovan, Joseph S.	Jan. 14, 1846	Balto.
Carter	Benedick	26	General Pinckney	Slatter, Hope Hull	Nov. 10, 1845	Balto.
Carter	Catherine	18	Frances Amy	Donovan, Joseph S.	Jan. 20, 1847	Balto.
Carter	Catherine	16	St. Mary	Donovan, Joseph S.	Nov. 29, 1845	Balto.
Carter	Cena	12	Patrick Henry	Campbell, Bernard M.	June 1, 1853	Balto.
Carter	Charles		Kirkwood	Donovan, Joseph S.	March 9, 1847	Balto.
Carter	Charles	17	Pioneer	Slatter, Hope Hull	Sept. 15, 1847	Balto.
Carter	Charlotte	14	States	Woolfolk, Austin	Apr. 14, 1828	Balto.
Carter	Culwell	21	Union	Williams, Thomas	Oct. 9, 1848	Balto.
Carter	Elihu	12	Lafayette	Woolfolk, Richard	Oct. 18, 1828	Balto.
Carter	Emily		Union	Rodbind, Ebenezer	Nov. 17, 1849	Balto.
Carter	Fanny	35	Victorine	Slatter, Hope Hull	Sept. 12, 1846	Balto.
Carter	Henry	22	Salvadora	Slatter, Hope Hull	Sept. 28, 1846	Balto.
Carter	Hester Ann	17	Kirkwood	Donovan, Joseph S.	Apr. 4, 1846	Balto.
Carter	James	22	Union	Williams, Thomas	Oct. 9, 1848	Balto.

Surname	First Name	Age	Ship	O/S	Date	Depart
Carter	John	18	Ewarkee	Purvis, James Franklin	March 4, 1841	Balto.
Carter	Letty	25	Victorine	Slatter, Hope Hull	May 14, 1845	Balto.
Carter	Levi	30	Union	Sheckles, B.O.	Nov. 17, 1849	Balto.
Carter	Lucy	18	Architect	Donovan, Joseph S.	Apr. 25, 1846	Balto.
Carter	Mary Jane	17	Frances Amy	Donovan, Joseph S.	Jan. 20, 1847	Balto.
Carter	Mary Jane	15	Henry A. Barling	Campbell, Walter L.	Oct. 28, 1848	Balto.
Carter	Minta	19	Hibernia	Woolfolk, Austin	Dec. 5, 1826	Balto.
Carter	Randolph	40	Union	Sheckles, B.O.	Nov. 17, 1849	Balto.
Carter	Richard	18	Elizabeth	Campbell, Bernard M.	Nov. 18, 1848	Balto.
Carter	Robert	17	Kirkwood	Slatter, Hope Hull	Jan. 4, 1845	Balto.
Carter	Robert	9	States	Woolfolk, Austin	Apr. 14, 1828	Balto.
Carter	Sam	19	Union	Williams, Thomas	Oct. 9, 1848	Balto.
Carter	Sarah	12	States	Woolfolk, Austin	Apr. 14, 1828	Balto.
Carter	Simon	22	Lafayette	Woolfolk, Richard	Oct. 18, 1828	Balto.
Carter	Solomon	36	Elizabeth	Campbell, Bernard M.	Nov. 18, 1848	Balto.
Carter	Susan	24	Edward Everett	Campbell, Bernard M.	March 10, 1851	Balto.
Carter	Thomas	38	Kirkwood	Donovan, Joseph S.	March 9, 1847	Balto.
Carter	Thomas	20	Southerner	Donovan, Joseph S.	Oct. 27, 1849	Balto.
Carter	Tom	21	Union	Williams, Thomas	Oct. 9, 1848	Balto.
Carter	Walker	17	Kirkwood	Donovan, Joseph S.	Nov. 28, 1849	Balto.
Carter	William	20	Kirkwood	Donovan, Joseph S.	Oct. 26, 1847	Balto.
Carter		infant	Edward Everett	Campbell, Bernard M.	March 10, 1851	Balto.
Cartnail	Wesley	19	Tippecanoe	Slatter, Hope Hull	Apr. 15, 1844	Balto.
Cartright	John	25	Architect	Slatter, Hope Hull	May 20, 1841	Balto.
Cary	Jackson	infant	Catharine	Donovan, Joseph S.	Jan. 18, 1845	Balto.
Cary	Peter	2	Catharine	Donovan, Joseph S.	Jan. 18, 1845	Balto.

Surname	First Name	Age	Ship	O/S	Date	Depart
Cary	Sally	27	Catharine	Donovan, Joseph S.	Jan. 18, 1845	Balto.
Cary		37	Catharine	Donovan, Joseph S.	Jan. 18, 1845	Balto.
Cassell	Elias	11	Victorine	Donovan, Joseph S.	Sept. 29, 1845	Balto.
Cassell	Hannah	18	Victorine	Donovan, Joseph S.	Sept. 29, 1845	Balto.
Cassell	Harriet	16	Kirkwood	Donovan, Joseph S.	Jan. 14, 1846	Balto.
Castle	Joe	50	Shamrock	Guyton, Elisha	March 13, 1840	Balto.
Catharine	Mary	16	John S. Gittings	Campbell, Bernard M.	Nov. 20, 1852	Balto.
Catherin	Mary	infant	Tippecanoe	Slatter, Hope Hull	Apr. 15, 1844	Balto.
Catherine	Harriett	10	Kirkwood	Harker, William	March 23, 1844	Balto.
Caton	James C.	30	Triton	Caton, Richard	Dec. 20, 1819	Balto.
Cator	Joseph	21	Scotia	Harker, William	Sept. 30, 1843	Balto.
Caution	Abram	22	Superb	Slatter, Hope Hull	Nov. 1, 1843	Balto.
Caution	Parker	26	Architect	Slatter, Hope Hull	May 20, 1841	Balto.
Ceasar	Elizabeth	24	Victorine	Slatter, Hope Hull	Sept. 12, 1846	Balto.
Cedas	Elizabeth	infant	Zoe	Slatter, Hope Hull	Feb. 16, 1847	Balto.
Cedas	Julia	24	Zoe	Slatter, Hope Hull	Feb. 16, 1847	Balto.
Cefus	William H.	21	Home	Rodbind, Ebenezer	March 22, 1845	Balto.
Ceny	Susan	20	Sarah Bridge	Campbell, Bernard M.	Feb. 8, 1851	Balto.
Cephas	Abraham	25	Arctic	Woolfolk, Austin	Jan. 24, 1829	Balto.
Cephus	Charles	19	Ann & Leah	Woolfolk, Austin	Nov.1, 1831	Balto.
Chace	Phill	19	Brunswick	Woolfolk, Austin	Oct. 11, 1831	Balto.
Chamberlain	Finch	25	Ganniclefft	Slatter, Hope Hull	Nov. 25, 1840	Balto.
Chamberlain	Robert	26	Gannicleftt	Slatter, Hope Hull	Nov. 25, 1840	Balto.
Chamberlain	Thomas	18	Gannicleftt	Slatter, Hope Hull	Nov. 25, 1840	Balto.
Chambers	Ann	1	General Pinckney	Campbell, Bernard M.	Jan. 19, 1847	Balto.
Chambers	Berry	21	Splendid	Slatter, Hope Hull	Apr. 24, 1841	Balto.

Surname	First Name	Age	Ship	O/S	Date	Depart
Chambers	Bill	3	Balloon	Milligan, George	Dec. 17, 1821	Balto.
Chambers	Charlotte	24	General Pinckney	Campbell, Bernard M.	Jan. 19, 1847	Balto.
Chambers	Dianna	18	Kirkwood	Campbell, Bernard M.	Oct. 14, 1848	Balto.
Chambers	Francis	16	Eliza	Slatter, Hope Hull	Oct. 9, 1840	Balto.
Chambers	Hester	18	Victorine	Slatter, Hope Hull	May 14, 1845	Balto.
Chambers	Joshua	19	Burlington	Slatter, Hope Hull	Oct. 21, 1842	Balto.
Chambers	Perry	20	Elizabeth	Campbell, Bernard M.	March 21, 1850	Balto.
Chambers	Perry	32	General Pinckney	Slatter, Hope Hull	Feb. 21, 1846	Balto.
Chambers	Samuel	15	Kirkwood	Donovan, Joseph S.	March 23, 1844	Balto.
Chambers	Tom	23	Catharine	Woolfolk, Austin	March 5, 1829	Balto.
Chambers	Tom	3	States	Woolfolk, Austin	Nov. 21, 1827	Balto.
Chambers	Washington	23	Burlington	Slatter, Hope Hull	Oct. 21, 1842	Balto.
Chandler	July Ann	25	Kirkwood	Slatter, Hope Hull	Oct. 16, 1845	Balto.
Chapman	Basil	26	Union	Campbell, Bernard M.	Oct. 9, 1848	Balto.
Chapman	Charles	17	Kirkwood	Slatter, Hope Hull	Apr. 15, 1845	Balto.
Chapman	Daphney	18	Hermitage	Williams, Thomas	Oct. 28, 1846	Balto.
Chapman	David	24	Henry A. Barling	Campbell, Bernard M.	Dec. 18, 1851	Balto.
Chapman	David	22	Victorine	Donovan, Joseph S.	Sept. 29, 1845	Balto.
Chapman	Elizabeth	14	General Pinckney	Campbell, Bernard M.	Jan. 19, 1847	Balto.
Chapman	Elizabeth	24	Union	Campbell, Bernard M.	March 17, 1849	Balto.
Chapman	Harriet	18	Arctic	Woolfolk, Austin	Jan. 24, 1829	Balto.
Chapman	Letty	11	Victorine	Rodbind, Ebenezer	March 14, 1846	Balto.
Chapman	Margaret	20	Louisa	Campbell, Bernard M.	Nov. 5, 1849	Balto.
Chapman	Milly Ann	18	General Pinckney	Campbell, Bernard M.	Jan. 19, 1847	Balto.
Chapman	Randolph	26	Lafayette	Woolfolk, Richard	Oct. 18, 1828	Balto.
Chase	Ann	23	Ann & Leah	Woolfolk, Austin	Nov.1, 1831	Balto.

Surname	First Name	Age	Ship	O/S	Date	Depart
Chase	Anthony	21	Kirkwood	Donovan, Joseph S.	Oct. 26, 1847	Balto.
Chase	Augustus	23	Union	Donovan, Joseph S.	May 13, 1848	Balto.
Chase	Basil	34	Topaz	Woolfolk, Austin	Apr. 20, 1829	Balto.
Chase	Benjamin	24	Bostonian	Slatter, Hope Hull	Jan. 18, 1841	Balto.
Chase	Charles	10	Harriet	Carroll, Charles	Dec. 7, 1836	Balto.
Chase	Charles	18	Waverly	Campbell, Bernard M.	Apr. 3, 1851	Balto.
Chase	Daniel	21	Elizabeth	Donovan, Joseph S.	Nov. 18, 1848	Balto.
Chase	Dick	21	Harriet	Carroll, Charles	Dec. 7, 1836	Balto.
Chase	Easter	19	Kirkwood	Slatter, Henry F.	Dec. 10, 1846	Balto.
Chase	Emeline	2 mon.	Hope & Hannah	Woolfolk, Austin	March 11, 1829	Balto.
Chase	Harriett	19	Hope & Hannah	Woolfolk, Austin	March 11, 1829	Balto.
Chase	Joe	27	Helen A. Miller	Campbell, Bernard M.	Oct. 18, 1852	Balto.
Chase	John	43	Kirkwood	Donovan, Joseph S.	Oct. 14, 1848	Balto.
Chase	Kitty	15	Kirkwood	Donovan, Joseph S.	Dec. 10, 1846	Balto.
Chase	Peter	25	Union	Rodbind, Ebenezer	Dec. 16, 1848	Balto.
Chase	Phillip	25	Ewarkee	Purvis, James Franklin	March 4, 1841	Balto.
Chase	Rachel	9	Hibernia	Woolfolk, Austin	Dec. 5, 1826	Balto.
Chase	Richard	26	Helen A. Miller	Campbell, Bernard M.	Oct. 18, 1852	Balto.
Chase	Solomon	15	Abbott Lord	Campbell, Bernard M.	April 28, 1852	Balto.
Chase	Washington	19	John C. Calhoun	Donovan, Joseph S.	Oct. 24, 1850	Balto.
Chase	William	20	Narragansett	Donovan, Joseph S.	Nov. 27, 1850	Balto.
Chase	Wilson	23	Phoenix	Rodbind, Ebenezer	March 27, 1847	Balto.
Chaser	Asbury		John C. Calhoun	Donovan, Joseph S.	Oct. 24, 1850	Balto.
Chaser	Ezekiel	22	John C. Calhoun	Donovan, Joseph S.	Oct. 24, 1850	Balto.
Chaulk	Henery	24	Kirkwood	Donovan, Joseph S.	Apr. 15, 1845	Balto.
Chaulk	Hester	25	Kirkwood	Donovan, Joseph S.	Apr. 15, 1845	Balto.

Surname	First Name	Age	Ship	O/S	Date	Depart
Chears	Henry	45	Hope	Knight, James M.	March 26, 1834	Balto.
Cheatham	Levin	35	Southerner	Campbell, Bernard M.	Jan. 20, 1850	Balto.
Cheisley	Hannon	18	Louisa	Slatter, Hope Hull	Oct. 11, 1847	Balto.
Chesley	Sandy	27	St. Mary	Donovan, Joseph S.	Nov. 29, 1845	Balto.
Chester	Fanny	30	Russell	Woolfo k, Austin	Feb. 28, 2839	Balto.
Chester	John	20	Henry A. Barling	Donovan, Joseph S.	Feb. 24, 1851	Balto.
Chester	Mary	27	Lafayette	Woolfolk, Austin	Oct. 18, 1828	Balto.
Chester	Susan	17	Union	Rodbind, Ebenezer	Dec. 16, 1848	Balto.
Chester	William	22	Kirkwood	Slatter, Hope Hull	Apr. 15, 1845	Balto.
Chew	Alfred	2 mon.	Arctic	Woolfo k, Austin	May 15, 1828	Balto.
Chew	Charles	22	Arctic	Woolfolk, Austin	May 15, 1828	Balto.
Chew	George	15	Kirkwood	Slatter, Hope Hull	Oct. 16, 1845	Balto.
Chew	Henny	35	Arctic	Woolfolk, Austin	May 15, 1828	Balto.
Chew	Henry	19	Arctic	Woolfolk, Austin	May 15, 1828	Balto.
Chew	Lear	25	Isaac Franklin	Slatter, Hope Hull	Sept. 28, 1838	Balto.
Chew	Lorenso	6	Arctic	Woolfolk, Austin	May 15, 1828	Balto.
Chew	Nelson	3	Arctic	Woolfolk, Austin	May 15, 1828	Balto.
Chew	Philip	18	Billow	Woolfolk, Austin	Feb. 23, 1828	Balto.
Chew	Priscilla	15	Arctic	Woolfolk, Austin	May 15, 1828	Balto.
Chew	Robert	5	Arctic	Woolfolk, Austin	May 15, 1828	Balto.
Chew	Roy	10	Arctic	Woolfolk, Austin	May 15, 1828	Balto.
Chew	William	35	Architect	Slatter, Hope Hull	May 20, 1841	Balto.
Chew		6 mon.	Isaac Franklin	Slatter, Hope Hull	Sept. 28, 1838	Balto.
Chine	Thomas	30	Victorine	Donovan, Joseph S.	May 22, 1844	Balto.
Chisly	John	25	Sarah Bridge	Campbell, Bernard M.	Feb. 8, 1851	Balto.
Christen	William	17	Billow	Woolfolk, Austin	Feb. 23, 1828	Balto.

Surname	First Name	Age	Ship	O/S	Date	Depart
Christy	Henry	24	Hibernia	Woolfolk, Austin	Dec. 5, 1826	Balto.
Christy	Tom	14	Tippecanoe	Purvis, James Franklin	Jan. 17, 1842	Balto.
Chubb	Catherine	25	Gannicleftt	Slatter, Hope Hull	Nov. 25, 1840	Balto.
Chum	Elly	20	Elizabeth	Campbell, Bernard M.	Nov. 18, 1848	Balto.
Churchman	Frances	16	Jefferson	Woolfolk, Austin	Dec. 24, 1827	Balto.
Cipress	Jim	18	Lapwing	Woolfolk, Austin	Feb. 15, 1827	Balto.
Clagett	Jerry	19	Kirkwood	Williams, William H.	Jan. 14, 1846	Balto.
Clagett	Lewis	21	Kirkwood	Donovan, Joseph S.	Jan. 14, 1846	Balto.
Clagget	Levenia	5	Victorine	Rodbind, Ebenezer	March 1, 1845	Balto.
Clagget	Martha	23	Victorine	Rodbind, Ebenezer	March 1, 1845	Balto.
Clagget	Tom	3	Victorine	Rodbind, Ebenezer	March 1, 1845	Balto.
Claggett	Caroline	17	General Pinckney	Slatter, Hope Hull	Nov. 10, 1845	Balto.
Claggett	Ellen	17	Zoe	Slatter, Hope Hull	Feb. 16, 1847	Balto.
Claggett	Richard	18	Paoli	Slatter, Hope Hull	Sept. 9, 1845	Balto.
Clanican	Henry	28	Margaret Hugg	Poindexter, T.B.	Nov. 30, 1844	Balto.
Clark	Amelia	17	Elizabeth	Donovan, Joseph S.	Jan. 2, 1850	Balto.
Clark	Amos	19	Kirkwood	Slatter, Hope Hull	Dec. 23, 1843	Balto.
Clark	Ann Maria	15	Union	Donovan, Joseph S.	Dec. 16, 1848	Balto.
Clark	Ann Maria	14	Victorine	Slatter, Hope Hull	March 9, 1844	Balto.
Clark	Caroline	16	Home	Rodbind, Ebenezer	March 22, 1845	Balto.
Clark	Caroline	infant	Kirkwood	Slatter, Hope Hull	Oct. 16, 1845	Balto.
Clark	Charles	19	Superb	Slatter, Hope Hull	Nov. 1, 1843	Balto.
Clark	Charlotte	18	Hermitage	Donovan, Joseph S.	Oct. 28, 1846	Balto.
Clark	Eliza	19	Margaret Hugg	Campbell, Bernard M.	Nov. 30, 1844	Balto.
Clark	Ellin	8	Northumberland	Slatter, Hope Hull	Feb. 27, 1843	Balto.
Clark	George	19	Lapwing	Woolfolk, Samuel M.	Feb. 15, 1827	Balto.

Surname	First Name	Age	Ship	O/S	Date	Depart
Clark	Henderson	21	Henry A. Barling	Donovan, Joseph S.	Dec. 18, 1851	Balto.
Clark	Henny	14	Orbit	Woolfolk, Austin	Apr. 16, 1825	Balto.
Clark	Joan	9	Northumberland	Slatter, Hope Hull	Feb. 27, 1843	Balto.
Clark	John	20	Henry A. Barling	Campbell, Bernard M.	Apr. 19, 1849	Balto.
Clark	John	21	Kirkwood	Donovan, Joseph S.	Oct. 26, 1847	Balto.
Clark	Joseph	20	Nancy W. Stevens	Rodbinc, Ebenezer	Feb. 18, 1845	Balto.
Clark	Joshua	22	Gannicleftt	Slatter, Hope Hull	Nov. 25, 1840	Balto.
Clark	Joshua	19	Margaret Hugg	Campbell, Bernard M.	Nov. 30, 1844	Balto.
Clark	July?	26	Victorine	Donovan, Joseph S.	Sept. 29, 1845	Balto.
Clark	Littleton	1	Lafayette	Woolfolk, Austin	Oct. 18, 1828	Balto.
Clark	Louisa	25	Kirkwood	Slatter, Hope Hull	Oct. 16, 1845	Balto.
Clark	Mariah	13	Northumberland	Slatter, Hope Hull	Feb. 27, 1843	Balto.
Clark	Mary	35	Northumberland	Slatter, Hope Hull	Feb. 27, 1843	Balto.
Clark	Mary	20	Solomon Saltus	Slatter, Hope Hull	Oct. 7, 1839	Balto.
Clark	Mary Ann	18	Mary	Purvis, James Franklin	Feb. 8, 1841	Balto.
Clark	Mary Ann	16	Orbit	Woolfolk, Austin	Apr. 16, 1825	Balto.
Clark	Nace	20	Victorine	Donovar, Joseph S.	May 22, 1844	Balto.
Clark	Nancy	17	Brunswick	Woolfolk, Austin	Oct. 11, 1831	Balto.
Clark	Ned	10	Lady Richmond	Woolfolk, Austin	Apr. 30, 1827	Balto.
Clark	Pendleton	19	Kirkwood	Donovan, Joseph S.	Oct. 14, 1848	Balto.
Clark	Phoebe	23	Lafayette	Woolfolk, Austin	Oct. 18, 1828	Balto.
Clark	Sarah Ann	6 mon.	Northumberland	Slatter, Eope Hull	Feb. 27, 1843	Balto.
Clark	Sylvester	13	Uncas	Slatter, Eope Hull	Jan. 10, 1838	Balto.
Clark	Tom	31	Lapwing	Spraggins, Samuel M.	March 22, 1822	Balto.
Clark	William H.	17	Orbit	Woolfolk, Austin	Apr. 16, 1825	Balto.
Clark		infant	Mary	Purvis, James Franklin	Feb. 8, 1841	Balto.

Surname	First Name	Age	Ship	O/S	Date	Depart
Clarke	Ellen	16	Victorine	Donovan, Joseph S.	May 14, 1845	Balto.
Clarke	John	14	Victorine	Donovan, Joseph S.	May 14, 1845	Balto.
Clarke	Lewis	23	Union	Campbell, Bernard M.	March 17, 1849	Balto.
Clarks	Samuel	17	Kirkwood	Donovan, Joseph S.	March 9, 1847	Balto.
Clarkston	Frances	infant	Zoe	Slatter, Hope Hull	Feb. 16, 1847	Balto.
Clarkston	George	6	Zoe	Slatter, Hope Hull	Feb. 16, 1847	Balto.
Clarkston	Jane	40	Zoe	Slatter, Hope Hull	Feb. 16, 1847	Balto.
Clavert	Charles	24	Phoenix	Rodbind, Ebenezer	March 27, 1847	Balto.
Clayton	Charity	18	Union	Campbell, Bernard M.	Dec. 16, 1848	Balto.
Clayton	Darcus	21	Burlington	Slatter, Hope Hull	Oct. 21, 1842	Balto.
Clayton	Juliann	21	Victorine	Slatter, Hope Hull	March 14, 1846	Balto.
Clayton	Kitty	16	Lafayette	Woolfolk, Austin	Oct. 18, 1828	Balto.
Clayton	Nathan	22	Colonel Howard	Donovan, Joseph S.	Nov. 21, 1844	Balto.
Clayton	Perry	20	Lafayette	Woolfolk, Austin	Oct. 18, 1828	Balto.
Clayton	Resby	17	Kirkwood	Donovan, Joseph S.	Dec. 10, 1846	Balto.
Clem	Charles	14	Abbott Lord	Ruark, Alex	June 29, 1850	Balto.
Clemments	Ellen	15	Union	Rodbind, Ebenezer	Dec. 16, 1848	Balto.
Clemmons	Ann	15	Architect	Donovan, Joseph S.	Apr. 25, 1846	Balto.
Cleneston	Mary	17	Margaret Hugg	Poindexter, T.B.	Nov. 30, 1844	Balto.
Clifton	Lloyd	21	Paoli	Slatter, Hope Hull	Sept. 9, 1845	Balto.
Clinton	Beckey	10	States	Woolfolk, Austin	Apr. 14, 1828	Balto.
Clinton	Cary	21	Kirkwood	Donovan, Joseph S.	Dec. 10, 1846	Balto.
Clinton	Floreah	30	States	Woolfolk, Austin	Apr. 14, 1828	Balto.
Clinton	Henny	15	States	Woolfolk, Austin	Apr. 14, 1828	Balto.
Clinton	Richard	22	Helen A. Miller	Campbell, Bernard M.	Oct. 18, 1852	Balto.
Clos	Charlotte	27	States	Kelso, George G.	March 8, 1826	Balto.

Surname	First Name	Age	Ship	O/S	Date	Depart
Clure	William	19	Triton	Anderson, David	Dec. 21, 1819	Balto.
Coakly	Edward	17	Victorine	Donovan, Joseph S.	May 22, 1844	Balto.
Coal	Catharine	28	Victorine	Donovan, Joseph S.	Sept. 29, 1845	Balto.
Coale	Isha	25	Brunswick	Woolfolk, Austin	Oct. 11, 1831	Balto.
Coamel	David	22	Lady Monroe	Woolfolk, Austin	March 25, 1825	Balto.
Coarsey	John	10	Tippecanoe	Slatter, Hope Hull	Jan. 17, 1842	Balto.
Coarsey	Sarah	27	Tippecanoe	Slatter, Hope Hull	Jan. 17, 1842	Balto.
Coates	Daniel	23	Justina	Donovan, Joseph S.	Dec. 2, 1852	Balto.
Coates	Mary	18	Union	Slatter, Hope Hull	July 26, 1847	Balto.
Coates	Moses	21	Burlington	Slatter, Hope Hull	Oct. 21, 1842	Balto.
Coates	Nancy	17	Hermitage	Donovan, Joseph S.	Oct. 28, 1846	Balto.
Coates	Susan	22	Bostonian	Slatter, Hope Hull	Jan. 18, 1841	Balto.
Coats	Elisha	22	General Pinckney	Rodbind, Ebenezer	Feb. 21, 1846	Balto.
Coats	Henry	18	Victorine	Donovan, Joseph S.	May 22, 1844	Balto.
Coats	Richard	22	Irad Ferry	Slatter, Hope Hull	Dec. 9, 1842	Balto.
Coats	Washington	19	Catharine	Slatter, Hope Hull	Jan. 24, 1843	Balto.
Cobb	Edward	6	Kirkwood	Slatter, Hope Hull	Apr. 4, 1846	Balto.
Cobb	William	3	Kirkwood	Slatter, Hope Hull	Apr. 4, 1846	Balto.
Cocks	Jim	35	Lady Monroe	Woolfolk, Austin	March 25, 1825	Balto.
Cody	John	20	Kirkwood	Slatter, Hope Hull	Dec. 23, 1843	Balto.
Coe	Wilson	21	Eliza F. Mason	Donovan, Joseph S.	Nov. 13, 1851	Balto.
Coffer	Armstead	22	Union	Donovan, Joseph S.	Dec. 16, 1848	Balto.
Coffer	Hanna	60	Union	Donovan, Joseph S.	Dec. 16, 1848	Balto.
Coffer	Nicholas	60	Union	Donovan, Joseph S.	Dec. 16, 1848	Balto.
Coiles	Booker	23	Kirkwood	Slatter, Hope Hull	Apr. 4, 1846	Balto.
Coiles	Preston	14	Kirkwood	Slatter, Hope Hull	Apr. 4, 1846	Balto.

Surname	First Name	Age	Ship	O/S	Date	Depart
Colage	Mary Jane	20	Phoenix	Rodbind, Ebenezer	March 27, 1847	Balto.
Colbert	Alexander	21	Kirkwood	Donovan, Joseph S.	Oct. 26, 1847	Balto.
Colbert	Harry	35	Arctic	Thompson, Henry	Oct. 5, 1827	Balto.
Colbourn	Levin	40	Elizabeth	Campbell, Bernard M.	March 21, 1850	Balto.
Colbourn	Stephen	17	Abbott Lord	Campbell, Bernard M.	April 28, 1852	Balto.
Colder	George	19	Solomon Saltus	Slatter, Hope Hull	Oct. 7, 1839	Balto.
Cole	Ann	20	Zoe	Campbell, Bernard M.	Feb. 16, 1847	Balto.
Cole	Anna Maria	20	Solomon Saltus	Slatter, Hope Hull	Oct. 7, 1839	Balto.
Cole	Basil	24	Scotia	Harker, William	Sept. 30, 1843	Balto.
Cole	Charles	11	Kirkwood	Slatter, Henry F.	Dec. 10, 1846	Balto.
Cole	Cyrus	22	Lapwing	Woolfolk, Samuel M.	Feb. 15, 1827	Balto.
Cole	George	10	Elizabeth	Chaplain, J. Bond	Nov. 18, 1848	Balto.
Cole	Henrietta	17	John C. Calhoun	Donovan, Joseph S.	Oct. 24, 1850	Balto.
Cole	Henrietta	18	Mary Broughton	Campbell, Bernard M.	Nov. 18, 1851	Balto.
Cole	James	16	Brunswick	Woolfolk, Austin	Oct. 11, 1831	Balto.
Cole	Lewis	20	Elizabeth	Donovan, Joseph S.	Jan. 2, 1850	Balto.
Cole	Margaret	45	North America	Cole, Margaret	Oct. 14, 1823	Balto.
Cole	Mary	9	Kirkwood	Donovan, Joseph S.	Oct. 26, 1847	Balto.
Cole	Matthew	22	Victorine	Slatter, Hope Hull	Sept. 12, 1846	Balto.
Cole	Murray	23	Helen A. Miller	Campbell, Bernard M.	Oct. 18, 1852	Balto.
Cole	Samuel	23	General Pinckney	Slatter, Hope Hull	Jan. 19, 1847	Balto.
Cole	Sarah Ann	18	Kirkwood	Slatter, Henry F.	Dec. 10, 1846	Balto.
Cole	Susannah	18	Jefferson	Woolfolk, Austin	Dec. 24, 1827	Balto.
Cole	William	23	Kirkwood	Slatter, Hope Hull	Oct. 16, 1845	Balto.
Cole		infant	Zoe	Campbell, Bernard M.	Feb. 16, 1847	Balto.
Coleman	Alfrad	19	Union	Williams, Thomas	Oct. 9, 1848	Balto.

Surname	First Name	Age	Ship	O/S	Date	Depart
Coleman	Ann	18	Elizabeth	Campbell, Bernard M.	March 21, 1850	Balto.
Coleman	George	23	States	Woolfolk, Austin	Nov. 21, 1827	Balto.
Coleman	George	18	Victorine	Slatter, Hope Hull	Sept. 12, 1846	Balto.
Coleman	James	24	Architect	Crow, William	Feb. 3, 1841	Balto.
Coleman	Malinda	16	Kirkwood	Donovan, Joseph S.	Oct. 14, 1848	Balto.
Coleman	Teny	20	Southerner	Donovan, Joseph S.	Oct. 27, 1849	Balto.
Collier	Martha	8	Irad Ferry	Slatter, Hope Hull	Dec. 9, 1842	Balto.
Collier	Mary	15	Tippecanoe	Slatter, Hope Hull	Jan. 17, 1842	Balto.
Collins	Abraham	25	Ann & Leah	Woolfolk, Austin	Nov.1, 1831	Balto.
Collins	Abraham	6	Solomon Saltus	Slatter, Hope Hull	Oct. 7, 1839	Balto.
Collins	Charlotte	18	Kirkwood	Slatter, Hope Hull	Apr. 15, 1845	Balto.
Collins	Charlotte	18	Kirkwood	Slatter, Hope Hull	Apr. 15, 1845	Balto.
Collins	Fanny	18	Solomon Saltus	Slatter, Hope Hull	Oct. 7, 1839	Balto.
Collins	George	32	Superb	Slatter, Fope Hull	Nov. 1, 1843	Balto.
Collins	Henry	4	Solomon Saltus	Slatter, Fope Hull	Oct. 7, 1839	Balto.
Collins	Hester	17	Brunswick	Woolfolk, Austin	Oct. 11, 1831	Balto.
Collins	Mary	40	Solomon Saltus	Slatter, Hope Hull	Oct. 7, 1839	Balto.
Collins	Mary Ann	21	Solomon Saltus	Slatter, Hope Hull	Oct. 7, 1839	Balto.
Collins	Moses	19	Southerner	Donovan, Joseph S.	Oct. 27, 1849	Balto.
Collins	Peter	30	Kirkwood	Donovan, Joseph S.	March 23, 1844	Balto.
Collins	Rachel Ann	14	Solomon Saltus	Slatter, Hope Hull	Oct. 7, 1839	Balto.
Collins	William	9	Solomon Saltus	Slatter, Hope Hull	Oct. 7, 1839	Balto.
Colman	Emory	25	Julia	Woolfolk, Austin	Jan. 8, 1829	Balto.
Colman	Stewart	20	Architect	Slatter, Hcpe Hull	Feb. 13, 1843	Balto.
Colson	George	20	Charles	Campbell, Bernard M.	Apr. 23, 1851	Balto.
Colson	Robert	30	Victorine	Donovan, Joseph S.	May 22, 1844	Balto.

Surname	First Name	Age	Ship	O/S	Date	Depart
Colvert	John	24	Victorine	Slatter, Hope Hull	Sept. 12, 1846	Balto.
Colvert	Thomas	20	Elizabeth	Donovan, Joseph S.	Jan. 2, 1850	Balto.
Comages	James	25	Lafayette	Woolfolk, Austin	Oct. 18, 1828	Balto.
Comages	John	23	Lafayette	Woolfolk, Austin	Oct. 18, 1828	Balto.
Combs	Charles	35	Irad Ferry	Clendenin, A.	Jan. 16, 1840	Balto.
Comfort	Maria Green	14	States	Woolfolk, Austin	Apr. 14, 1828	Balto.
Compte	Alford	20	Louisa	Campbell, Bernard M.	March 31, 1849	Balto.
Compte	Moses	20	Louisa	Campbell, Bernard M.	March 31, 1849	Balto.
Comptee	Susan	18	Kirkwood	Campbell, Bernard M.	Oct. 14, 1848	Balto.
Compton	Ben	35	Victorine	Slatter, Henry F.	Dec. 31, 1846	Balto.
Compton	Winney	30	Victorine	Slatter, Henry F.	Dec. 31, 1846	Balto.
Coney	John	14	Paoli	Harker, William	Dec. 27, 1845	Balto.
Coney	Lewis	16	Paoli	Harker, William	Dec. 27, 1845	Balto.
Conn	Ellen	24	Harriet Cooper	Webb, W.L.	June 12, 1850	Balto.
Conn	John	26	Harriet Cooper	Webb, W.L.	June 12, 1850	Balto.
Conner	Fanny	17	Tippecanoe	Purvis, James Franklin	Jan. 17, 1842	Balto.
Conner	Henry	24	Union	Slatter, Hope Hull	July 26, 1847	Balto.
Connor	Isador	54	Harriet	Carroll, Charles	Dec. 7, 1836	Balto.
Connor	Violet	9	Kirkwood	Slatter, Hope Hull	Dec. 23, 1843	Balto.
Conoway	Jesse	22	Home	Rodbind, Ebenezer	March 22, 1845	Balto.
Contee	Allen	11	Paoli	Campbell, Bernard M.	Dec. 27, 1845	Balto.
Contee	Dawson	20	Kirkwood	Donovan, Joseph S.	Sept. 28, 1846	Balto.
Contee	Elizabeth	20	Victorine	Rodbind, Ebenezer	May 14, 1845	Balto.
Contee	Harry	24	Hermitage	Williams, Thomas	Oct. 28, 1846	Balto.
Contee	Harry	51	Kirkwood	Rodbind, Ebenezer	Apr. 15, 1845	Balto.
Contee	Jane	18	Ewarkee	Purvis, James Franklin	March 4, 1841	Balto.

Surname	First Name	Age	Ship	O/S	Date	Depart
Contee	John	20	Kirkwood	Rodkind, Ebenezer	Apr. 15, 1845	Balto.
Contee	Lucinda	22	Paoli	Campbell, Bernard M.	Dec. 27, 1845	Balto.
Conway	George	26	John S. Gittings	Campbell, Bernard M.	Nov. 20, 1852	Balto.
Conway	Henry	22	John S. Gittings	Campbell, Bernard M.	Nov. 20, 1852	Balto.
Cook	Ann Maria	20	Paoli	Slatter, Hope Hull	Sept. 9, 1845	Balto.
Cook	Betsey	22	Alfred	Woolfolk, Austin	May 7, 1825	Balto.
Cook	Captain Thomas	30	General Pinckney	Slatter, Hope Hull	Feb. 21, 1846	Balto.
Cook	Caroline	16	Kirkwood	Donovan, Joseph S.	Sept. 28, 1846	Balto.
Cook	Daniel	17	Margaret Hugg	Slatter, Hope Hull	Feb. 8, 1845	Balto.
Cook	Flora	10	Victorine	Rodkind, Ebenezer	Dec. 31, 1846	Balto.
Cook	Harriett	25	Victorine	Slatter, Hope Hull	Sept. 12, 1846	Balto.
Cook	Henry	26	Pioneer	Slatter, Hope Hull	Sept. 15, 1847	Balto.
Cook	Isaac	13	Intelligence	Anderson, David	Dec. 20, 1822	Balto.
Cook	Jane	20	Southerner	Donovan, Joseph S.	Oct. 27, 1849	Balto.
Cook	Jim	23	Irad Ferry	Clendenin, A.	Jan. 21, 1840	Balto.
Cook	Joseph	18	Kirkwood	Donovan, Joseph S.	Apr. 4, 1846	Balto.
Cook	Mary	18	Kirkwood	Williams, Thomas	Apr. 4, 1846	Balto.
Cook	Mat	36	Harriet	Carroll, Charles	Dec. 7, 1836	Balto.
Cook	Sarah	16	Solomon Saltus	Slatter, Hope Hull	Oct. 7, 1839	Balto.
Cooley	Sam	14	Kirkwood	Donovan, Joseph S.	Apr. 15, 1845	Balto.
Coolridge	Sophia	10	Kirkwood	Donovan, Joseph S.	Sept. 28, 1846	Balto.
Coombs	Ann	15	Union	Williams, Thomas	Oct. 9, 1848	Balto.
Coombs	John	17	E.H.Chapin	Donovan, Joseph S.	Dec. 2, 1847	Balto.
Cooper	Ann	25	Catharine	Slatter, Hope Hull	Jan. 24, 1843	Balto.
Cooper	Barbary	15	Kirkwood	Donovan, Joseph S.	Sept. 28, 1846	Balto.
Cooper	Charles	16	Kirkwood	Donovan, Joseph S.	Sept. 28, 1846	Balto.

Surname	First Name	Age	Ship	O/S	Date	Depart
Cooper	Charlot	16	Elizabeth	Donovan, Joseph S.	Jan. 2, 1850	Balto.
Cooper	Colonel	18	Kirkwood	Donovan, Joseph S.	Sept. 28, 1846	Balto.
Cooper	David	24	Lapwing	Woolfolk, Austin	Feb. 15, 1827	Balto.
Cooper	Edward	18	Kirkwood	Donovan, Joseph S.	Sept. 28, 1846	Balto.
Cooper	Edward	8	Victorine	Donovan, Joseph S.	May 22, 1844	Balto.
Cooper	Eliza	23	Kirkwood	Campbell, Bernard M.	March 9, 1847	Balto.
Cooper	Ezekiel	18	Irad Ferry	Slatter, Hope Hull	Dec. 9, 1842	Balto.
Cooper	George	5	Victorine	Donovan, Joseph S.	May 22, 1844	Balto.
Cooper	Henry	28	Ann & Leah	Woolfolk, Austin	Nov.1, 1831	Balto.
Cooper	Hetty	15	Margaret Hugg	Campbell, Bernard M.	Feb. 8, 1845	Balto.
Cooper	Hezekiah	18	Alfred	Stansbury, Hammond N.	Nov. 6, 1824	Balto.
Cooper	Isaac	11	Intelligence	Anderson, David	Dec. 20, 1822	Balto.
Cooper	Jarrott	22	Kirkwood	Campbell, Bernard M.	Apr. 4, 1846	Balto.
Cooper	John	21	Kirkwood	Donovan, Joseph S.	Jan. 4, 1845	Balto.
Cooper	Joseph	14	Kirkwood	Donovan, Joseph S.	Oct. 26, 1847	Balto.
Cooper	Joshua	18	Charles	Campbell, Bernard M.	Dec. 18, 1850	Balto.
Cooper	Josiah	26	Kirkwood	Campbell, Bernard M.	Jan. 4, 1845	Balto.
Cooper	Judy	4 weeks	Victorine	Donovan, Joseph S.	May 22, 1844	Balto.
Cooper	Judy	26	Victorine	Donovan, Joseph S.	May 22, 1844	Balto.
Cooper	Leaher	23	Scotia	Slatter, Hope Hull	Sept. 30, 1843	Balto.
Cooper	Louis	11	John C. Calhoun	Donovan, Joseph S.	Oct. 24, 1850	Balto.
Cooper	Lucretia	20	Hamlet	Stansbury, Hammond N.	Apr. 6, 1824	Balto.
Cooper	Mandy	15	Kirkwood	Donovan, Joseph S.	Sept. 28, 1846	Balto.
Cooper	Mariah	18	Hibernia	Woolfolk, Austin	Dec. 5, 1826	Balto.
Cooper	Martha	16	Isaac Franklin	Kephart, George	Feb. 1, 1839	Balto.
Cooper	Philip	3	Victorine	Donovan, Joseph S.	May 22, 1844	Balto.

Surname	First Name	Age	Ship	O/S	Date	Depart
Cooper	Phoebe	16	Louisa	Campbell, Bernard M.	March 31, 1849	Balto.
Cooper	Rachel	20	General Pinckney	Slatter, Hope Hull	Feb. 21, 1846	Balto.
Cooper	Rachel	18	Lapwing	Woolfolk, Samuel M.	Feb. 15, 1827	Balto.
Cooper	Robert	19	Kirkwood	Donovan, Joseph S.	Oct. 26, 1847	Balto.
Cooper	Sam	19	Brunswick	Woolfolk, Austin	Oct. 11, 1831	Balto.
Cooper	Sam	50	Intelligence	Anderson, David	Dec. 20, 1822	Balto.
Cooper	Sarah	45	Intelligence	Anderson, David	Dec. 20, 1822	Balto.
Cooper	Susan	18	Union	Sheckles, B.O.	Nov. 17, 1849	Balto.
Cooper	Windsor	18	Kirkwood	Donovan, Joseph S.	Dec. 23, 1843	Balto.
Copland	Charles	24	Union	Donovan, Joseph S.	Dec. 16, 1848	Balto.
Copper	James	20	Kirkwood	Donovan, Joseph S.	Jan. 4, 1845	Balto.
Corbet	Gilbert	25	Seaman	Slatter, Hope Hull	March 25, 1839	Balto.
Cord	Aly	35	Isaac Franklin	Slatter, Hope Hull	Sept. 28, 1838	Balto.
Cordelia	Amanda	18	Mary Broughton	Campbell, Bernard M.	Nov. 18, 1851	Balto.
Cork	Amelia	18	Union	Donovan, Joseph S.	May 13, 1848	Balto.
Cork	Elizabeth	18	Isaac Franklin	Slatter, Hope Hull	Sept. 28, 1838	Balto.
Cork	Frisby	14	Uncas	Slatter, Hope Hull	Apr. 3, 1838	Balto.
Cornelius	Margaret	26	Isaac Franklin	Slatter, Hope Hull	Sept. 28, 1838	Balto.
Cornelius	Peter	19	Kirkwood	Donovan, Joseph S.	Apr. 15, 1845	Balto.
Cornell	Joshua	20	States	Woolfolk, Austin	Apr. 14, 1828	Balto.
Cornice	Anne	24	Hibernia	Woolfolk, Austin	Dec. 5, 1826	Balto.
Cornich	David	30	Seaman	Slatter, Shadrack	March 25, 1839	Balto.
Cornish	Benjamin	25	Home	Donovan, Joseph S.	March 22, 1845	Balto.
Cornish	Charles	21	St. Mary	Donovan, Joseph S.	Nov. 29, 1845	Balto.
Cornish	Delia	21	General Pinckney	Slatter, Hope Hull	Jan. 19, 1847	Balto.
Cornish	Dennard	18	Scotia	Harker, William	Sept. 30, 1843	Balto.

Surname	First Name	Age	Ship	O/S	Date	Depart
Cornish	Hall	22	Emilie	Anderson, David	March 27, 1821	Balto.
Cornish	Hannah	32	General Pinckney	Slatter, Hope Hull	Nov. 10, 1845	Balto.
Cornish	Harriet	20	Ann & Leah	Woolfolk, Austin	Nov. 1, 1831	Balto.
Cornish	Henry	18	Julia	Woolfolk, Austin	Feb. 10, 1832	Balto.
Cornish	Henry	30	Porpoise	Purvis, James Franklin	Dec. 11, 1841	Balto.
Cornish	Jane	40	Brunswick	Woolfolk, Austin	Oct. 11, 1831	Balto.
Cornish	John	21	Porpoise	Purvis, James Franklin	Dec. 11, 1841	Balto.
Cornish	Joseph	20	Pioneer	Slatter, Hope Hull	Sept. 15, 1847	Balto.
Cornish	Josiah	22	Catharine	Woolfolk, Austin	March 3, 1829	Balto.
Cornish	Josiah	17	Kirkwood	Slatter, Hope Hull	Apr. 15, 1845	Balto.
Cornish	Mahala	21	Victorine	Slatter, Hope Hull	Sept. 12, 1846	Balto.
Cornish	Margrett	18	Kirkwood	Slatter, Hope Hull	Apr. 15, 1845	Balto.
Cornish	Martha Ann	16	Salvadora	Slatter, Hope Hull	Sept. 28, 1846	Balto.
Cornish	Mary Ann	21	Irad Ferry	Wilson, J.W.	May 6, 1839	Balto.
Cornish	Nancy	23	General Pinckney	Slatter, Hope Hull	Nov. 10, 1845	Balto.
Cornish	Parrish	20	Brunswick	Woolfolk, Austin	Oct. 11, 1831	Balto.
Cornish	Samuel	20	Architect	Slatter, Hope Hull	May 20, 1841	Balto.
Cornish	Samuel	infant	General Pinckney	Slatter, Hope Hull	Jan. 19, 1847	Balto.
Cornish	Sidney	32	Seaman	Slatter, Shadrack	March 25, 1839	Balto.
Cornish	Susannah	18	Kirkwood	Slatter, Hope Hull	Jan. 4, 1845	Balto.
Corsey	Ben	30	Irad Ferry	Clendenin, A.	Jan. 16, 1840	Balto.
Corsey	James	40	Kirkwood	Slatter, Hope Hull	Jan. 4, 1845	Balto.
Corsey	John	30	States	Woolfolk, Austin	Apr. 14, 1828	Balto.
Cossy	Nancy	19	Henry A. Barling	Donovan, Joseph S.	Feb. 24, 1851	Balto.
Cost	Tom	23	Arctic	Woolfolk, Austin	Jan. 24, 1829	Balto.
Costley	John	20	Uncas	Slatter, Hope Hull	Jan. 10, 1838	Balto.

Surname	First Name	Age	Ship	O/S	Date	Depart
Cot	Martha	26	Kirkwood	Slatter, Henry F.	Dec. 10, 1846	Balto.
Cotsman	Lazrus	27	Kirkwood	Slatter, Hope Hull	Oct. 16, 1845	Balto.
Cottman	Friendship	50	Hermitage	Slatter, Hope Hull	Oct. 28, 1846	Balto.
Cottman	John	62	Hermitage	Slatter, Hope Hull	Oct. 28, 1846	Balto.
Couch	Bob	2 mon.	Jefferson	Woolfolk, Austin	Dec. 24, 1827	Balto.
Couller	Richard	21	Hermitage	Donovan, Joseph S.	Oct. 28, 1846	Balto.
Countee	Richard	21	Catharine	Slatter, Hope Hull	Jan. 24, 1843	Balto.
Countee	Walter	20	Solomon Saltus	Slatter, Hope Hull	Oct. 7, 1839	Balto.
Counter	Solomon	16	Lafayette	Woolfolk, Austin	Oct. 18, 1828	Balto.
County	Charles	27	Margaret Hugg	Poindexter, T.B.	Nov. 30, 1844	Balto.
Coursay	Mariah	18	Elizabeth	Campbell, Bernard M.	Jan. 2, 1850	Balto.
Coursey	Adline	17	Louisa	Slatter, Hope Hull	Oct. 11, 1847	Balto.
Coursey	Ann	26	Gannicleatt	Slatter, Hope Hull	Nov. 25, 1840	Balto.
Coursey	Charles	infant	Louisa	Slatter, Hope Hull	Oct. 11, 1847	Balto.
Coursey	Elizabeth	16	Edward Everett	Campbell, Bernard M.	March 10, 1851	Balto.
Coursey	William	24	Solomon Saltus	Slatter, Hope Hull	Oct. 7, 1839	Balto.
Courts	Harry	36	Tweed	Forbes, George	Oct. 20, 1836	Town Creek
Courts	Jack	42	Tweed	Forbes, George	Oct. 20, 1836	Town Creek
Covington	Henry	22	Julia	Woolfolk, Austin	Jan. 8, 1829	Balto.
Coward	Isaac	25	Julia	Woolfolk, Austin	Jan. 8, 1829	Balto.
Coward	Lewis	20	Hermitage	Slatter, Hope Hull	Oct. 28, 1846	Balto.
Cowper	General	33	Kirkwood	Rodbind, Ebenezer	Apr. 15, 1845	Balto.
Cox	Abram	8 mon.	Lady Morroe	Woolfolk, Austin	March 25, 1825	Balto.
Cox	Alfred	infant	Hibernia	Woolfolk, Austin	Dec. 5, 1826	Balto.
Cox	Anthony		Lady Morroe	Woolfolk, Austin	March 25, 1825	Balto.
Cox	Cornelius	26	Seaman	Slatter, Shadrack	March 25, 1839	Balto.

Surname	First Name	Age	Ship	O/S	Date	Depart
Cox	Daniel	13	Lady Monroe	Woolfolk, Austin	March 25, 1825	Balto.
Cox	Frederick	18	Ann & Leah	Woolfolk, Austin	Nov. 1, 1831	Balto.
Cox	Horace	18	Lady Monroe	Woolfolk, Austin	March 25, 1825	Balto.
Cox	Maria	9	Lady Monroe	Woolfolk, Austin	March 25, 1825	Balto.
Cox	Mary	40	Lady Monroe	Woolfolk, Austin	March 25, 1825	Balto.
Cox	Sinah	26	Hibernia	Woolfolk, Austin	Dec. 5, 1826	Balto.
Craft	Thomas	20	Julia	Woolfolk, Austin	Jan. 8, 1829	Balto.
Craig	George	22	Union	Williams, Thomas	Oct. 9, 1848	Balto.
Craig	Isabella	15	Lapwing	Hall, Francis	March 22, 1822	Balto.
Crampton	Henson	38	Southerner	Donovan, Joseph S.	Oct. 27, 1849	Balto.
Crampton	Matilda	20	Southerner	Donovan, Joseph S.	Oct. 27, 1849	Balto.
Craney	Abraham	5	Kirkwood	Slatter, Henry F.	Dec. 10, 1846	Balto.
Craney	William	30	Kirkwood	Slatter, Henry F.	Dec. 10, 1846	Balto.
Crawford	Ambrose	infant	Tippecanoe	Slatter, Hope Hull	Apr. 15, 1844	Balto.
Crawford	Andrew J.	20 mon.	Kirkwood	Rodbind, Ebenezer	Oct. 26, 1847	Balto.
Crawford	Ann	15	Northumberland	Slatter, Hope Hull	Feb. 27, 1843	Balto.
Crawford	Caroline	25	Tippecanoe	Slatter, Hope Hull	Apr. 15, 1844	Balto.
Crawford	Cloe Ann	28	Kirkwood	Rodbind, Ebenezer	Oct. 26, 1847	Balto.
Crawford	Evan	21	Kirkwood	Donovan, Joseph S.	March 23, 1844	Balto.
Crawford	Henry	14	Zoe	Slatter, Hope Hull	Feb. 16, 1847	Balto.
Crawley	Martha	16	Victorine	Campbell, Bernard M.	Dec. 31, 1846	Balto.
Crayton	James	21	Union	Slatter, Hope Hull	July 26, 1847	Balto.
Craze	Lyda	18	Victorine	Donovan, Joseph S.	Sept. 29, 1845	Balto.
Creag	Abraham	22	Colonel Howard	Donovan, Joseph S.	Nov. 21, 1844	Balto.
Creag	John	4 mon.	Colonel Howard	Harker, William	Nov. 21, 1844	Balto.
Creaz	Emily	20	Colonel Howard	Harker, William	Nov. 21, 1844	Balto.

Surname	First Name	Age	Ship	O/S	Date	Depart
Crier	Robert	16	Kirkwood	Campbell, Bernard M.	Nov. 28, 1849	Balto.
Crister	Langford	22	Kirkwood	Donovan, Joseph S.	Sept. 28, 1846	Balto.
Cristy	William	24	Billow	Woolfolk, Austin	Feb. 23, 1828	Balto.
Croeus	Henrietta	15	Henry A. Barling	Campbe l, Bernard M.	Dec. 18, 1851	Balto.
Cromwell	Albert	6	Ewarkee	Slatter, Hope Hull	March 4, 1841	Balto.
Cromwell	Edward	18	Kirkwood	Slatter, Hope Hull	Dec. 23, 1843	Balto.
Cromwell	George	20	Union	Campbell, Bernard M.	Apr. 20, 1850	Balto.
Cromwell	John	21	Billow	Woolfolk, Austin	Feb. 23, 1828	Balto.
Cromwell	Margarett	30	Ewarkee	Slatter, Hope Hull	March 4, 1841	Balto.
Cromwell	Margrett	17	Louisa	Slatter, Hope Hull	Oct. 11, 1847	Balto.
Cromwell	Oliver	20	Southerner	Donovan, Joseph S.	Oct. 27, 1849	Balto.
Cromwell	Rachelain	16	Ewarkee	Slatter, Hope Hull	March 4, 1841	Balto.
Cromwell	Susan	26	Isaac Franklin	Slatter, Hope Hull	Sept. 28, 1838	Balto.
Crone	Lewis	40	P.R. Hazeltine	Campbell, Bernard M.	Nov. 15, 1856	Balto.
Crone	Richard	22	Solomon Saltus	Slatter, Hope Hull	Oct. 7, 1839	Balto.
Crop	Mary	9	Isaac Franklin	Slatter, Hope Hull	Sept. 28, 1838	Balto.
Crosby	William	22	Victorine	Slatter, Hope Hull	Sept. 12, 1846	Balto.
Cross	Joseph	48	Saldana	Harker, William	Feb. 27, 1844	Balto.
Croswell	Sarah	17	Louisa	Slatter, Hope Hull	Oct. 11, 1847	Balto.
Croum	Allen	19	Ann & Leah	Woolfolk, Austin	Nov.1, 1831	Balto.
Crow	Rosana	9	Victorine	Slatter, Hope Hull	March 1, 1845	Balto.
Crowell	Hannah	24	Seaman	Slatter, Shadrack	March 25, 1839	Balto.
Crowley	Jane	15	Union	Sheckles, B.O.	Nov. 17, 1849	Balto.
Crowley	Philip	24	Union	Donovan, Joseph S.	May 13, 1848	Balto.
Cully	Ben	24	Kirkwood	Campbell, Bernard M.	March 9, 1847	Balto.
Cully	Elijah	23	Edward Everett	Campbell, Bernard M.	Oct. 18, 1851	Balto.

Surname	First Name	Age	Ship	O/S	Date	Depart
Cully	John	19	Kirkwood	Campbell, Bernard M.	March 9, 1847	Balto.
Culver	Eliza	10	Hermitage	Slatter, Hope Hull	Oct. 28, 1846	Balto.
Culver	Sharlott	9	Elizabeth	Donovan, Joseph S.	Nov. 18, 1848	Balto.
Cumming	Elizabeth	16	Mary Broughton	Campbell, Bernard M.	Nov. 18, 1851	Balto.
Cummings	James	25	Kirkwood	Donovan, Joseph S.	Oct. 26, 1847	Balto.
Cummings	Thomas	22	Kirkwood	Donovan, Joseph S.	Oct. 26, 1847	Balto.
Cunningham	Samuel	24	Architect	Boggs, William	May 25, 1840	Balto.
Cure	Amey	26	Splendid	Slatter, Hope Hull	Apr. 24, 1841	Balto.
Curley	Jim	22	Lapwing	Woolfolk, Austin	Feb. 15, 1827	Balto.
Curley	Joe	14	Lafayette	Woolfolk, Richard	Oct. 18, 1828	Balto.
Curry	Lucida	16	E.H.Chapin	Donovan, Joseph S.	Dec. 2, 1847	Balto.
Curry	Richard	21	Catharine	Donovan, Joseph S.	Jan. 18, 1845	Balto.
Curry	Tom	25	Budget	Spraggins, Samuel M.	Nov. 27, 1821	Balto.
Curtis	David	19	Saldana	Harker, William	Feb. 27, 1844	Balto.
Curtis	Hannah	20	Nathaniel Hooper	Campbell, Bernard M.	Feb. 12, 1852	Balto.
Curtis	Harriet	21	Lafayette	Woolfolk, Austin	Oct. 22, 1828	Balto.
Curtis	Levi	18	Victorine	Slatter, Hope Hull	March 1, 1845	Balto.
Curtis	Lewis	17	Kirkwood	Donovan, Joseph S.	Oct. 26, 1847	Balto.
Curtis	Lewis	25	Union	Donovan, Joseph S.	May 13, 1848	Balto.
Curtis	Moses	20	Irad Ferry	Slatter, Hope Hull	Dec. 9, 1842	Balto.
Curtis	Sandy	21	Kirkwood	Donovan, Joseph S.	Sept. 28, 1846	Balto.
Curtis	Tim	18	Ann & Leah	Woolfolk, Austin	Nov.1, 1831	Balto.
Curtis	William Henry	17	Gannicleff	Slatter, Hope Hull	Nov. 25, 1840	Balto.
Curvis	William	22	Kirkwood	Campbell, Bernard M.	Oct. 14, 1848	Balto.
Dabner	George	25	Isaac Franklin	Kephart, George	Sept. 28, 1838	Balto.
Dabner	Jerry	23	Isaac Franklin	Kephart, George	Sept. 28, 1838	Balto.

Surname	First Name	Age	Ship	O/S	Date	Depart
Dade	Ariana	8	Tweed	Sothoron, William H.	Oct. 20, 1836	Town Creek
Dade	Hinson	48	Tweed	Sothoron, William H.	Oct. 20, 1836	Town Creek
Dade	Letty	22	Union	Rodbind, Ebenezer	Dec. 16, 1848	Balto.
Dade	Lewis	25	Union	Slatter, Hope Hull	July 26, 1847	Balto.
Dade	Seley	44	Tweed	Sothoron, William H.	Oct. 20, 1836	Town Creek
Daid	Joseph	20	Isaac Franklin	Kephart, George	Sept. 28, 1838	Balto.
Dailey	Winney	20	Union	Donovan, Joseph S.	May 13, 1848	Balto.
Dale	William	24	Victorine	Slatter, Hope Hull	Dec. 17, 1845	Balto.
Dalley	John	19	Elizabeth	Donovan, Joseph S.	Oct. 6, 1849	Balto.
Damps	Ellen	23	Superb	Slatter, Hope Hull	Nov. 1, 1843	Balto.
Daniel	Henry M.	20	Eliza F. Mason	Donovan, Joseph S.	Nov. 13, 1851	Balto.
Daniel		33	Kirkwood	Donovan, Joseph S.	Sept. 28, 1846	Balto.
Dant	Edwin	13	Billow	Woolfolk, Austin	Feb. 23, 1828	Balto.
Dare	Thomas	18	Elizabeth	Campbell, Bernard M.	Nov. 18, 1848	Balto.
Daris	Minty	32	Splendid	Slatter, Hope Hull	Apr. 24, 1841	Balto.
Darkes	Joseph	24	Bostonian	Slatter, Hope Hull	Jan. 18, 1841	Balto.
Darnal	Loyd	infant	Hibernia	Woolfolk, Austin	Dec. 5, 1826	Balto.
Darnal	Phoebe	25	Hibernia	Woolfolk, Austin	Dec. 5, 1826	Balto.
Darrell	James	14	General Pinckney	Slatter, Hope Hull	Jan. 19, 1847	Balto.
Dashield	Polly	20	Seaman	Slatter, Hope Hull	Dec. 19, 1838	Balto.
Dauphin	George	19	Mary Broughton	Campbell, Bernard M.	Nov. 18, 1851	Balto.
Davage	Hetty	15	Irad Ferry	Purvis, James Franklin	Feb. 5, 1842	Balto.
Davidge	Mary	18	Northumberland	Slatter, Hope Hull	Feb. 27, 1843	Balto.
Davidson	Charles	14	Kirkwood	Donovan, Joseph S.	Oct. 26, 1847	Balto.
Davige	Charles	17	Catharine	Donovan, Joseph S.	Jan. 18, 1845	Balto.
Davis	Amos	22	Billow	Woolfolk, Austin	Feb. 23, 1828	Balto.

Surname	First Name	Age	Ship	O/S	Date	Depart
Davis	Archibald	23	Jefferson	Woolfolk, Austin	Dec. 24, 1827	Balto.
Davis	Archy	20	Architect	Slatter, Hope Hull	May 20, 1841	Balto.
Davis	Benjamin	19	Henry A. Barling	Campbell, Bernard M.	Dec. 18, 1851	Balto.
Davis	Bill	24	Hibernia	Woolfolk, Austin	Dec. 5, 1826	Balto.
Davis	Charity	17	General Pinckney	Slatter, Hope Hull	Jan. 19, 1847	Balto.
Davis	Charles	28	Elizabeth	Campbell, Bernard M.	March 21, 1850	Balto.
Davis	Charles	10	Lafayette	Woolfolk, Richard	Oct. 18, 1828	Balto.
Davis	Cheston	21	Elizabeth	Donovan, Joseph S.	March 21, 1850	Balto.
Davis	Clara	24	Phoenix	Slatter, Hope Hull	March 27, 1847	Balto.
Davis	Dianna	19	Kirkwood	Campbell, Bernard M.	Oct. 14, 1848	Balto.
Davis	Edwin	20	Jefferson	Woolfolk, Austin	Dec. 24, 1827	Balto.
Davis	Elijah	18	Irad Ferry	Clendenin, A.	Jan. 16, 1840	Balto.
Davis	Elisa	15	Catharine	Woolfolk, Austin	March 3. 1829	Balto.
Davis	Eliza	16	Eliza F.Mason	Donovan, Joseph S.	Nov. 13, 1851	Balto.
Davis	Eliza	8	Superb	Slatter, Hope Hull	Nov. 1, 1843	Balto.
Davis	Elizebeth	infant	Victorine	Slatter, Hope Hull	Dec. 17, 1845	Balto.
Davis	Ellen	18	Kirkwood	Donovan, Joseph S.	Dec. 10, 1846	Balto.
Davis	Ellen	40	Kirkwood	Slatter, Hope Hull	Jan. 14, 1846	Balto.
Davis	Emaline	22	Victorine	Slatter, Hope Hull	Dec. 17, 1845	Balto.
Davis	Emanuel	21	Union	Sheckles, B.O.	Nov. 17, 1849	Balto.
Davis	Fanney	6	Phoenix	Slatter, Hope Hull	March 27, 1847	Balto.
Davis	Fanny	16	Architect	Donovan, Joseph S.	Apr. 25, 1846	Balto.
Davis	Fanny	10	Topaz	Woolfolk, Austin	Apr. 20, 1829	Balto.
Davis	Frank	17	Union	Donovan, Joseph S.	Dec. 16, 1848	Balto.
Davis	George	19	Victorine	Williams, Thomas	Dec. 20, 1844	Balto.
Davis	Hannah	18	Tippecanoe	Slatter, Hope Hull	Jan. 17, 1842	Balto.

Surname	First Name	Age	Ship	O/S	Date	Depart
Davis	Harriet	17	Isaac Franklin	Kephart, George	Feb. 1, 1839	Balto.
Davis	Harriett	19	General Pinckney	Donovan, Joseph S.	Nov. 10, 1845	Balto.
Davis	Harriett	11	Kirkwood	Donovan, Joseph S.	Oct. 26, 1847	Balto.
Davis	Harriott	16	Billow	Woolfolk, Austin	Feb. 23, 1828	Balto.
Davis	Henrietta	20	Helen A. Miller	Campbell, Bernard M.	Oct. 18, 1852	Balto.
Davis	Henry	17	Ann & Leah	Woolfolk, Austin	Nov. 1, 1831	Balto.
Davis	Henry	40	E.H.Chapin	Slatter, Hope Hull	Nov. 30, 1847	Balto.
Davis	Isaac	15	Billow	Woolfolk, Austin	Feb. 23, 1828	Balto.
Davis	Jackson	20	Elizabeth	Donovan, Joseph S.	March 21, 1850	Balto.
Davis	Jacob	34	Henry A. Barling	Campbell, Bernard M.	Feb. 24, 1851	Balto.
Davis	James	20	Pioneer	Slatter, Hope Hull	Sept. 15, 1847	Balto.
Davis	Jane	14	Union	Campbel, Bernard M.	March 17, 1849	Balto.
Davis	Jane	21	Victorine	Donovan, Joseph S.	Dec. 31, 1846	Balto.
Davis	Jim	17	Delawarian	Campbell, Bernard M.	Dec. 1, 1848	Balto.
Davis	John	18	E.H.Chapin	Donovan Joseph S.	Dec. 2, 1847	Balto.
Davis	John	27	Hope & Hannah	Woolfolk, Austin	March 11, 1829	Balto.
Davis	John	22	Lafayette	Woolfolk, Austin	Oct. 18, 1828	Balto.
Davis	John	17	Leda	Donovan. Joseph S.	May 30, 1846	Balto.
Davis	John	21	States	Woolfolk, Austin	Apr. 14, 1828	Balto.
Davis	John	19	Tippecanoe	Slatter, Hope Hull	Jan. 17, 1842	Balto.
Davis	Kitty	17	Helen A. Miller	Nally, William	Oct. 18, 1852	Balto.
Davis	Leonard	infant	General Finckney	Donovan, Joseph S.	Nov. 10, 1845	Balto.
Davis	Lewis	25	General Finckney	Donovan, Joseph S.	Feb. 21, 1846	Balto.
Davis	Lloyd	18	Scotia	Harker, William	Sept. 30, 1843	Balto.
Davis	Louisa	22	Helen A. Miller	Campbell. Bernard M.	Oct. 18, 1852	Balto.
Davis	Louisa	19	Hermitage	Slatter, Hope Hull	Oct. 28, 1846	Balto.

Surname	First Name	Age	Ship	O/S	Date	Depart
Davis	Maria	24	Margaret Hugg	Campbell, Bernard M.	Nov. 30, 1844	Balto.
Davis	Mary Ann	17	Elizabeth	Rodbind, Ebenezer	Nov. 18, 1848	Balto.
Davis	Matilda	3	Narragansett	Campbell, Bernard M.	Nov. 27, 1850	Balto.
Davis	Millnett Ann	infant	Phoenix	Slatter, Hope Hull	March 27, 1847	Balto.
Davis	Nancy	15	Victorine	Donovan, Joseph S.	Dec. 31, 1846	Balto.
Davis	Ned	40	Architect	Slatter, Hope Hull	May 20, 1841	Balto.
Davis	Peter	20	Catharine	Donovan, Joseph S.	Jan. 18, 1845	Balto.
Davis	Peter	19	Kirkwood	Donovan, Joseph S.	Sept. 28, 1846	Balto.
Davis	Rachael	11	Home	Donovan, Joseph S.	March 22, 1845	Balto.
Davis	Rachael Ann	21	Home	Donovan, Joseph S.	March 22, 1845	Balto.
Davis	Richard	17	Julia	Woolfolk, Austin	Jan. 8, 1829	Balto.
Davis	Rosetta	16	Abbott Lord	Campbell, Bernard M.	April 28, 1852	Balto.
Davis	Rozine	25	Elizabeth	Campbell, Bernard M.	March 21, 1850	Balto.
Davis	Sarah	17	Mary	Harker, William	Feb. 10, 1844	Balto.
Davis	Sarah	22	Sarah Bridge	Campbell, Bernard M.	Feb. 8, 1851	Balto.
Davis	Shadrack	20	Elizabeth	Campbell, Bernard M.	March 21, 1850	Balto.
Davis	Solomon	16	Russell	Slatter, Hope Hull	March 1, 1839	Balto.
Davis	Sophia	24	Kirkwood	Slatter, Hope Hull	Jan. 14, 1846	Balto.
Davis	Spencer	28	Margaret Hugg	Campbell, Bernard M.	Nov. 30, 1844	Balto.
Davis	Susan	24	Narragansett	Campbell, Bernard M.	Nov. 27, 1850	Balto.
Davis	Thomas	20	Architect	Donovan, Joseph S.	Apr. 25, 1846	Balto.
Davis	Thomas	18	Gazelle	Staples, Joseph	Feb.28, 1842	Balto.
Davis	Thomas	21	Kirkwood	Donovan, Joseph S.	March 23, 1844	Balto.
Davis	Virginia	4	Victorine	Slatter, Hope Hull	Dec. 17, 1845	Balto.
Davis	William	22	Clio	Coalman, Henry E.	March 20, 1819	Balto.
Davis	William	17	E.H.Chapin	Slatter, Hope Hull	Nov. 30, 1847	Balto.

Surname	First Name	Age	Ship	O/S	Date	Depart
Davis	William	18	Kirkwood	Donovan, Joseph S.	Oct. 14, 1848	Balto.
Davis	William	17	Kirkwood	Donovan, Joseph S.	Oct. 26, 1847	Balto.
Davis	Winah	16	Edward Everett	Campbell, Bernard M.	March 10, 1851	Balto.
Davis		21	Kirkwood	Donovan, Joseph S.	Dec. 10, 1846	Balto.
Davis		infant	Kirkwood	Campbell, Bernard M.	Oct. 14, 1848	Balto.
Davius	Charlot	18	Union	Sheckles, B.O.	Nov. 17, 1849	Balto.
Davy	Sarah	5	Kirkwood	Donovan, Joseph S.	Oct. 26, 1847	Balto.
Davy		10	Kirkwood	Donovan, Joseph S.	Oct. 26, 1847	Balto.
Davy		32	Kirkwood	Donovan, Joseph S.	Oct. 26, 1847	Balto.
Dawnes	Annice	24	Hermitage	Slatter, Hope Hull	Oct. 28, 1846	Balto.
Dawson	Henny	18	Kirkwood	Slatter, Hope Hull	Oct. 16, 1845	Balto.
Dawson	Jerry	24	Victorine	Donovan, Joseph S.	Dec. 31, 1846	Balto.
Dawson	Nelson	11	Victorine	Donovan, Joseph S.	Dec. 31, 1846	Balto.
Day	Charles	25	Victorine	Donovan, Joseph S.	Sept. 29, 1845	Balto.
Day	Horace	23	Kirkwood	Campbell, Bernard M.	Apr. 4, 1846	Balto.
Day	John	19	Kirkwood	Campbell, Bernard M.	Oct. 14, 1848	Balto.
Day	Lucy	16	Arctic	Woolfolk, Austin	Jan. 24, 1829	Balto.
Day	Lucy Ellen	15	Victorine	Slatter, Hope Hull	March 1, 1845	Balto.
Day	Samuel	25	Paoli	Slatter, Hope Hull	Sept. 9, 1845	Balto.
Dayton	Henrietta	15	Victorine	Slatter, Hope Hull	May 14, 1845	Balto.
Deal	Mary	16	Colonel Howard	Donovan, Joseph S.	Nov. 21, 1844	Balto.
Deal	Peter	29	John C. Calhoun	Donovan, Joseph S.	Oct. 24, 1850	Balto.
Deane	Henry	22	Narragansett	Donovan, Joseph S.	Nov. 27, 1850	Balto.
Decker	Harriett	26	Kirkwood	Slatter, Henry F.	Dec. 10, 1846	Balto.
Deford	Samuel	30	Victorine	Slatter, Hope Hull	May 14, 1845	Balto.
Delany	Eliza	8	Kirkwood	Williams, Thomas	Apr. 4, 1846	Balto.

Surname	First Name	Age	Ship	O/S	Date	Depart
Demby	Edward	23	Kirkwood	Slatter, Hope Hull	Dec. 23, 1843	Balto.
Demby	George	21	Paoli	Slatter, Hope Hull	Sept. 9, 1845	Balto.
Demby	James	25	Hermitage	Slatter, Hope Hull	Oct. 28, 1846	Balto.
Demby	Perry	19	Victorine	Slatter, Hope Hull	Sept. 12, 1846	Balto.
Demby	Phil	21	Hermitage	Slatter, Hope Hull	Oct. 28, 1846	Balto.
Demby	Theodore	26	Victorine	Slatter, Hope Hull	Dec. 17, 1845	Balto.
Dembey	Tench	26	States	Woolfolk, Austin	Apr. 14, 1828	Balto.
Denby	Barney	21	John C. Calhoun	Donovan, Joseph S.	Oct. 24, 1850	Balto.
Denby	John	15	Abbott Lord	Campbell, Bernard M.	April 28, 1852	Balto.
Denby	Jones	23	Irad Ferry	Slatter, Hope Hull	Dec. 9, 1842	Balto.
Denby	Margaret	19	Billow	Woolfolk, Austin	Feb. 23, 1828	Balto.
Denby	Margaret	14	Southerner	Campbell, Bernard M.	Oct. 27, 1849	Balto.
Denby	Ned	41	Lawrence	Salisbury, James	May 6, 1823	Balto.
Denney	Matilda	16	Billow	Woolfolk, Austin	Feb. 23, 1828	Balto.
Denning	Margaret	16	States	Woolfolk, Austin	Nov. 21, 1827	Balto.
Denning	Margrit	8	Architect	Slatter, Hope Hull	May 20, 1841	Balto.
Dennis	Charles	22	Architect	Slatter, Hope Hull	Feb. 13, 1843	Balto.
Dennis	David	23	Emilie	Anderson, David	March 27, 1821	Balto.
Dennis	Hannah	20	Pioneer	Slatter, Hope Hull	Sept. 15, 1847	Balto.
Dennis	James	30	Brunswick	Woolfolk, Austin	Oct. 11, 1831	Balto.
Dennis	Littleton	24	Kirkwood	Slatter, Hope Hull	Oct. 16, 1845	Balto.
Dennis	Moses	25	Kirkwood	Slatter, Henry F.	Dec. 10, 1846	Balto.
Dennis	Pricilla	8	Margaret Forbs	Slatter, Hope Hull	Nov. 28, 1838	Balto.
Dennis		21	Isaac Franklin	Kephart, George	Sept. 28, 1838	Balto.
Denny	James	25	Orbit	Woolfolk, Joseph B.	Apr. 16, 1825	Balto.
Denny	Leah	23	Brunswick	Woolfolk, Austin	Oct. 11, 1831	Balto.

Surname	First Name	Age	Ship	O/S	Date	Depart
Depon	John E.	2	Tweed	Forbes, George	Oct. 20, 1836	Town Creek
Depon	Sylvia	30	Tweed	Forbes, George	Oct. 20, 1836	Town Creek
Derrick	Lucy	21	States	Woolfolk, Austin	Nov. 21, 1827	Balto.
Derrick	Matilda	40	States	Woolfolk, Austin	Nov. 21, 1827	Balto.
Derrick	William	1	States	Woolfolk, Austin	Nov. 21, 1827	Balto.
Derricks	Alfred	22	Nathaniel Hooper	Donovan, Jospeh S.	Feb. 12, 1852	Balto.
Deshield	Robert	21	Tippecanoe	Purvis, James Franklin	Apr. 1, 1841	Balto.
Deston	Jinny	18	Victorine	Harker, William	March 9, 1844	Balto.
Devinsrey	Remilton	20	Victorine	Donovan, Joseph S.	Dec. 17, 1845	Balto.
Deward	Lucy	15	Ewarkee	Purvis, James Franklin	March 4, 1841	Balto.
Diar	George	28	Kirkwood	Slatter, Hope Hull	Jan. 14, 1846	Balto.
Dick	Julia	2	Kirkwood	Slatter, Hope Hull	Jan. 14, 1846	Balto.
Dickens	Mahala	16	Brunswick	Woolfolk, Austin	Oct. 11, 1831	Balto.
Dickeson	Lavinia	18	States	Woolfolk, Austin	Nov. 21, 1827	Balto.
Dickinson	John	28	Alfred	Woolfolk, Austin	May 7, 1825	Balto.
Dickinson	Mazy	18	Seguin	Campbell, Bernard M.	July 12, 1853	Balto.
Dickinson		infant	Seguin	Campbell, Bernard M.	July 12, 1853	Balto.
Dickinson		infant	Seguin	Campbell, Bernard M.	July 12, 1853	Balto.
Dicks	Sarah	17	Kirkwooc	Donovan, Joseph S.	Apr. 4, 1846	Balto.
Dickson	Hariett	18	Elizabeth	Donovan, Joseph S.	March 21, 1850	Balto.
Dickson	Nick	35	Zoe	Slatter, Hope Hull	Feb. 16, 1847	Balto.
Dickson	Wilson	17	Elizabeth	Donovan, Joseph S.	Nov. 18, 1848	Balto.
Diggs	Ann	18	Eliza F. Mason	Donovan, Joseph S.	Nov. 13, 1851	Balto.
Diggs	Anthony	28	Kirkwooc	Slatter, Hope Hull	Oct. 16, 1845	Balto.
Diggs	Bill	16	General Pinckney	Williams, Thomas	Jan. 19, 1847	Balto.
Diggs	Cassy	18	Topaz	Woolfolk, Austin	Apr. 20, 1829	Balto.

Surname	First Name	Age	Ship	O/S	Date	Depart
Diggs	Cathrin	24	Kirkwood	Slatter, Hope Hull	Oct. 16, 1845	Balto.
Diggs	Edward	14	Kirkwood	Donovan, Joseph S.	Dec. 10, 1846	Balto.
Diggs	Eliza	19	Lafayette	Woolfolk, Richard	Oct. 18, 1828	Balto.
Diggs	Gabriel	23	Harriett	Woolfolk, Austin	March 23, 1822	Balto.
Diggs	Gabriel	16	Irad Ferry	Wilson, J.W.	May 6, 1839	Balto.
Diggs	James	6	Kirkwood	Slatter, Hope Hull	Oct. 16, 1845	Balto.
Diggs	Jane	36	Union	Campbell, Bernard M.	Nov. 17, 1849	Balto.
Diggs	John	18	Victorine	Slatter, Hope Hull	Dec. 17, 1845	Balto.
Diggs	Louisa	16	Hermitage	Donovan, Joseph S.	Oct. 28, 1846	Balto.
Diggs	Mariah	15	St. Mary	Donovan, Joseph S.	Nov. 29, 1845	Balto.
Diggs	Miles	21	Phoenix	Slatter, Hope Hull	March 27, 1847	Balto.
Diggs	Peter	38	Margaret Hugg	Campbell, Bernard M.	Nov. 30, 1844	Balto.
Diggs	Peter	23	Union	Rodbind, Ebenezer	Dec. 16, 1848	Balto.
Diggs	Robert	infant	Kirkwood	Slatter, Hope Hull	Oct. 16, 1845	Balto.
Diggs	Sarah	28	John S. Gittings	Campbell, Bernard M.	Nov. 20, 1852	Balto.
Diggs	Suckey	27	Margaret Hugg	Poindexter, T.B.	Nov. 30, 1844	Balto.
Diggs	Thomas	8	Home	Donovan, Joseph S.	March 22, 1845	Balto.
Diggs	William	38	Kirkwood	Donovan, Joseph S.	Nov. 28, 1849	Balto.
Diggs	William	24	Victorine	Slatter, Hope Hull	Sept. 12, 1846	Balto.
Diggs	Willis	26	Margaret Hugg	Poindexter, T.B.	Nov. 30, 1844	Balto.
Diggs		infant	John S. Gittings	Campbell, Bernard M.	Nov. 20, 1852	Balto.
Digs	John	24	Margaret Forbs	Slatter, Hope Hull	Nov. 28, 1838	Balto.
Dimmer	Harriet	27	St. Mary	Williams, Thomas	Nov. 29, 1845	Balto.
Dimmer	Mary A.	infant	St. Mary	Williams, Thomas	Nov. 29, 1845	Balto.
Dines	Alfred	18	Zoe	Slatter, Hope Hull	Feb. 16, 1847	Balto.
Dines	Catherin	9	Kirkwood	Donovan, Joseph S.	Dec. 10, 1846	Balto.

Surname	First Name	Age	Ship	O/S	Date	Depart
Ding	Sarah	26	Kirkwood	Donovan, Joseph S.	March 9, 1847	Balto.
Dinniston	Thomas	25	Intelligence	Anderson David	May 1, 1821	Balto.
Dinson	Maria W.	32	Victorine	Gardiner, Richard S.D.	Dec. 21, 1844	Balto.
Dishroon	Charles	18	Waverly	Donovan, Joseph S.	Apr. 3, 1851	Balto.
Dixon	Anna		St. Mary	Williams, Thomas	Nov. 29, 1845	Balto.
Dixon	Bank	17	Kirkwood	Donovan, Joseph S.	Oct. 26, 1847	Balto.
Dixon	Charity	17	Kirkwood	Donovan, Joseph S.	Dec. 10, 1846	Balto.
Dixon	Daniel	28	Kirkwood	Donovan, Joseph S.	Oct. 26, 1847	Balto.
Dixon	Elizabeth	17	Hibernia	Woolfolk, Austin	Dec. 5, 1826	Balto.
Dixon	Ellen	16	St. Mary	Williams, Thomas	Nov. 29, 1845	Balto.
Dixon	Francis	23	Tippecanoe	Slatter, Hope Hull	Apr. 15, 1844	Balto.
Dixon	John		St. Mary	Williams, Thomas	Nov. 29, 1845	Balto.
Dixon	Macko	19	Elizabeth	Campbell Bernard M.	March 21, 1850	Balto.
Dixon	Margrett	20	Union	Slatter, Hope Hull	July 26, 1847	Balto.
Dixon	Perry	18	Brunswick	Woolfolk, Austin	Oct. 11, 1831	Balto.
Dixon	Samuel	20	Victorine	Donovan, Joseph S.	March 1, 1845	Balto.
Dixon	Thomas	28	Justina	Donovan, Joseph S.	Dec. 2, 1852	Balto.
Dixon	William	26	Kirkwood	Donovan, Joseph S.	Oct. 26, 1847	Balto.
Dock	Kitty	22	Union	Campbell Bernard M.	March 17, 1849	Balto.
Docket	William	20	Superb	Donovan, Joseph S.	Nov. 2, 1843	Balto.
Dockett	Louisa	17	Margaret Hugg	Slatter, Hope Hull	Feb. 8, 1845	Balto.
Dockett	Robert	21	Kirkwood	Campbell Bernard M.	Oct. 14, 1848	Balto.
Dodd	Benjamin	9	Ewarkee	Slatter, Hope Hull	March 4, 1841	Balto.
Dodson	Edmund	21	Victorine	Rodbind, Ebenezer	May 14, 1845	Balto.
Dodson	Henry	22	Superb	Slatter, Hope Hull	Nov. 1, 1843	Balto.
Dogan	Ellen	30	Victorine	Rodbind, Ebenezer	Dec. 31, 1846	Balto.

Surname	First Name	Age	Ship	O/S	Date	Depart
Dogans	Charles	22	St. Mary	Donovan, Joseph S.	Nov. 29, 1845	Balto.
Doggens	Ann Maria	13	Kirkwood	Slatter, Hope Hull	Apr. 15, 1845	Balto.
Doginger	Hester Ann	17	Scotia	Slatter, Hope Hull	Sept. 30, 1843	Balto.
Dolly	Ailsey	30	Charles	Donovan, Joseph S.	Apr. 23, 1851	Balto.
Dolly	Alexander	2	Charles	Donovan, Joseph S.	Apr. 23, 1851	Balto.
Dolly	Charles	35	Charles	Donovan, Joseph S.	Apr. 23, 1851	Balto.
Dolly	Charles Jr.	10	Charles	Donovan, Joseph S.	Apr. 23, 1851	Balto.
Dolly	John	6	Charles	Donovan, Joseph S.	Apr. 23, 1851	Balto.
Dolly	Kitty	infant	Charles	Donovan, Joseph S.	Apr. 23, 1851	Balto.
Dolly	Mary	4	Charles	Donovan, Joseph S.	Apr. 23, 1851	Balto.
Dolly	Sam	8	Charles	Donovan, Joseph S.	Apr. 23, 1851	Balto.
Donahoe	George	9	Lady Monroe	Woolfolk, Austin	March 25, 1825	Balto.
Done	Ann	25	Phoenix	Donovan, Joseph S.	March 27, 1847	Balto.
Donivan	Ann	13	Tippecanoe	Slatter, Hope Hull	Apr. 1, 1841	Balto.
Dooley	Jim	26	Intelligence	Woolfolk, Austin	Apr. 5, 1823	Balto.
Dority	Joseph	25	Victorine	Donovan, Joseph S.	Dec. 17, 1845	Balto.
Dority	Sargent	23	Victorine	Donovan, Joseph S.	Dec. 17, 1845	Balto.
Dorman	John	22	Tippecanoe	Wilson, William N.	May 4, 1842	Balto.
Dorris	Charlotte	25	Catharine	Donovan, Joseph S.	Jan. 18, 1845	Balto.
Dorrity	Eliza	10	Kirkwood	Slatter, Hope Hull	Apr. 15, 1845	Balto.
Dorrity	Jane	18	Kirkwood	Slatter, Hope Hull	Apr. 15, 1845	Balto.
Dorsey	Alexander	28	Home	Donovan, Joseph S.	March 22, 1845	Balto.
Dorsey	Alferd	13	Northumberland	Slatter, Hope Hull	Feb. 27, 1843	Balto.
Dorsey	Ann	18	General Pinckney	Slatter, Hope Hull	Jan. 19, 1847	Balto.
Dorsey	Ann	21	Irad Ferry	Slatter, Hope Hull	Dec. 9, 1842	Balto.
Dorsey	Ann	26	Margaret Hugg	Slatter, Hope Hull	Feb. 8, 1845	Balto.

Surname	First Name	Age	Ship	O/S	Date	Depart
Dorsey	Basil	45	Victorine	Woolfolk, Austin	Sept. 12, 1846	Balto.
Dorsey	Benjamin	23	Kirkwood	Donovan, Joseph S.	Oct. 14, 1848	Balto.
Dorsey	Benjamin	20	Narragansett	Donovan, Joseph S.	Nov. 27, 1850	Balto.
Dorsey	Caroline	15	States	Woolfolk, Austin	Nov. 21, 1827	Balto.
Dorsey	Cassandra	20	Colonel Howard	Harker, William	Nov. 21, 1844	Balto.
Dorsey	Charles	18	Bostonian	Slatter, Hope Hull	Jan. 18, 1841	Balto.
Dorsey	Charlotte	11	Eliza F. Mason	Donovan, Joseph S.	Nov. 13, 1851	Balto.
Dorsey	Charlotte	20	Nathaniel Hooper	Donovan, Jospeh S.	Feb. 12, 1852	Balto.
Dorsey	Clem	10	Victorine	Harker, William	March 9, 1844	Balto.
Dorsey	Coffee	30	Peru	Slatter, Hope Hull	Nov. 16, 1842	Balto.
Dorsey	Cordelia	infant	Margaret Hugg	Slatter, Hope Hull	Feb. 8, 1845	Balto.
Dorsey	Dick	20	Lady Monroe	Woolfolk, Austin	March 25, 1825	Balto.
Dorsey	Elisa	16	Bostonian	Slatter, Hope Hull	Jan. 18, 1841	Balto.
Dorsey	Elizabeth	20	Sarah Bridge	Campbell, Bernard M.	Feb. 8, 1851	Balto.
Dorsey	Frisby	11	Sabine	Donovan, Joseph S.	Feb. 10, 1844	Balto.
Dorsey	George	13	General Finckney	Slatter, Hope Hull	Feb. 21, 1846	Balto.
Dorsey	Gracy	21	Kirkwood	Donovan, Joseph S.	Oct. 16, 1845	Balto.
Dorsey	Hannah	19	General Finckney	Donovan, Joseph S.	Nov. 10, 1845	Balto.
Dorsey	Hannah	18	Harriet	Carroll, Charles	Dec. 7, 1836	Balto.
Dorsey	Harriet	16	Eliza F. Mason	Donovan, Joseph S.	Nov. 13, 1851	Balto.
Dorsey	Harriet	18	Kirkwood	Donovan, Joseph S.	Apr. 4, 1846	Balto.
Dorsey	Henrietta	20	John C. Calhoun	Donovan, Joseph S.	Oct. 24, 1850	Balto.
Dorsey	Henry	14	Cora	Donovan, Jospeh S.	Jan. 21, 1851	Balto.
Dorsey	Henry	28	General Finckney	Slatter, Hope Hull	Jan. 19, 1847	Balto.
Dorsey	Henry	16	Kirkwood	Campbell, Bernard M.	Jan. 14, 1846	Balto.
Dorsey	Henry	21	Victorine	Donovan, Joseph S.	Sept. 29, 1845	Balto.

Surname	First Name	Age	Ship	O/S	Date	Depart
Dorsey	Hester Ann	12 mon.	Colonel Howard	Harker, William	Nov. 21, 1844	Balto.
Dorsey	Horace	17	Henry A. Barling	Campbell, Bernard M.	Dec. 18, 1851	Balto.
Dorsey	Isaac	35	Kirkwood	Donovan, Joseph S.	Dec. 23, 1843	Balto.
Dorsey	Isaac	14	Phoenix	Donovan, Joseph S.	March 27, 1847	Balto.
Dorsey	James	22	Tippecanoe	Slatter, Hope Hull	Dec. 16, 1840	Balto.
Dorsey	Job	21	Kirkwood	Donovan, Joseph S.	Oct. 14, 1848	Balto.
Dorsey	John	28	Helen A. Miller	Campbell, Bernard M.	Oct. 18, 1852	Balto.
Dorsey	John	30	Irad Ferry	Wilson, J.W.	May 6, 1839	Balto.
Dorsey	John	18	Kirkwood	Donovan, Joseph S.	Nov. 28, 1849	Balto.
Dorsey	Joseph	14	Home	Donovan, Joseph S.	March 22, 1845	Balto.
Dorsey	Julia Ann	16	Kirkwood	Donovan, Joseph S.	Oct. 14, 1848	Balto.
Dorsey	Kitty	9	States	Woolfolk, Austin	Nov. 21, 1827	Balto.
Dorsey	Lewis	12	Home	Donovan, Joseph S.	March 22, 1845	Balto.
Dorsey	Louisa	19	Pioneer	Slatter, Hope Hull	Sept. 15, 1847	Balto.
Dorsey	Margrett	22	Pioneer	Slatter, Hope Hull	Sept. 15, 1847	Balto.
Dorsey	Maria	18	Margaret Forbs	Slatter, Hope Hull	Nov. 28, 1838	Balto.
Dorsey	Martha	17	Henry A. Barling	Campbell, Bernard M.	Dec. 18, 1851	Balto.
Dorsey	Mary	18	Home	Slatter, Hope Hull	March 22, 1845	Balto.
Dorsey	Mary	22	Isaac Franklin	Slatter, Hope Hull	Sept. 28, 1838	Balto.
Dorsey	Nicholas	15	Kirkwood	Donovan, Joseph S.	Oct. 14, 1848	Balto.
Dorsey	Nicholas	23	Russell	Slatter, Hope Hull	March 1, 1839	Balto.
Dorsey	Phil	20	John S. Gittings	Campbell, Bernard M.	Nov. 20, 1852	Balto.
Dorsey	Rachael	22	Colonel Howard	Harker, William	Nov. 21, 1844	Balto.
Dorsey	Rachel	16	Helen A. Miller	Campbell, Bernard M.	Oct. 18, 1852	Balto.
Dorsey	Robert	20	Waverly	Donovan, Joseph S.	Apr. 3, 1851	Balto.
Dorsey	Salisbury	20	Hermitage	Slatter, Hope Hull	Oct. 28, 1846	Balto.

Surname	First Name	Age	Ship	O/S	Date	Depart
Dorsey	Sam	22	Porpoise	Purvis, James Franklin	Dec. 11, 1841	Balto.
Dorsey	Sam	20	Union	Williams, Thomas	Oct. 9, 1848	Balto.
Dorsey	Singleton	23	Lafayette	Woolfolk, Austin	Oct. 18, 1828	Balto.
Dorsey	Sophia	24	Eliza F. Mason	Donovan, Joseph S.	Nov. 13, 1851	Balto.
Dorsey	Susanna	15	Southerner	Donovan, Joseph S.	Oct. 27, 1849	Balto.
Dorsey	Thom	54	Harriet	Carroll, Charles	Dec. 7, 1836	Balto.
Dorsey	Thomas	35	Irad Ferry	Clendenin, A.	Jan. 16, 1840	Balto.
Dorsey	Thomas	1	Isaac Franklin	Slatter, Hope Hull	Sept. 28, 1838	Balto.
Dorsey	Thomas	18	Justina	Donovan, Joseph S.	Dec. 2, 1852	Balto.
Dorsey	Thomas	19	Kirkwood	Donovan, Joseph S.	Nov. 28, 1849	Balto.
Dorsey	Thomas	20	Victorine	Williams, Thomas	Dec. 20, 1844	Balto.
Dorsey	Vashti	19	General Pinckney	Slatter, Hope Hull	Feb. 21, 1846	Balto.
Dorsey	Washington	21	Zoe	Williams, Thomas	Feb. 16, 1847	Balto.
Dorsey	William	22	General Pinckney	Slatter, Hope Hull	Nov. 10, 1845	Balto.
Dorsey	William	16	Southerner	Donovan, Joseph S.	Oct. 27, 1849	Balto.
Dorsey	William	13	Topaz	Woolfolk, Austin	Apr. 20, 1829	Balto.
Doster	Edward	21	James Ramsay	Thompson, James	Sept. 30, 1831	Balto.
Douglas	Colbert	19	Louisa	Donovan, Joseph S.	Oct. 9, 1847	Balto.
Douglas	Lucinda	11	Louisa	Donovan, Joseph S.	Oct. 9, 1847	Balto.
Douglas	Mary	24	Mary	Harker, William	Feb. 10, 1844	Balto.
Douglas	Phillis	21	Union	Campbell, Bernard M.	March 17, 1849	Balto.
Douglas	Solomon	27	Caroline	Ferguson, Thomas	March 2, 1821	Balto.
Douglas	William	18	Isaac Franklin	Kephart, George	Feb. 1, 1839	Balto.
Douglas	William	19	Kirkwood	Donovan, Joseph S.	Oct. 26, 1847	Balto.
Douglas	William	24	Scotia	Harker, William	Sept. 30, 1843	Balto.
Douglass	Grace	infant	Victorine	Slatter, Hope Hull	May 14, 1845	Balto.

Surname	First Name	Age	Ship	O/S	Date	Depart
Douglass	John	23	Burlington	Slatter, Hope Hull	Oct. 21, 1842	Balto.
Douglass	John	14	Victorine	Donovan, Joseph S.	Sept. 29, 1845	Balto.
Douglass	Mary	25	Victorine	Slatter, Hope Hull	May 14, 1845	Balto.
Douglass	Matilda	20	Kirkwood	Donovan, Joseph S.	Oct. 26, 1847	Balto.
Douglass	Sarah	13	Kirkwood	Donovan, Joseph S.	Oct. 26, 1847	Balto.
Douglass	Silvey	26	Victorine	Slatter, Hope Hull	Sept. 12, 1846	Balto.
Douglass	William	11	Leda	Nelson, James	Nov. 16, 1848	Balto.
Douglass	William	38	Scotia	Harker, William	Sept. 30, 1843	Balto.
Dove	Basel	15	General Pinckney	Slatter, Hope Hull	Jan. 19, 1847	Balto.
Dove	Osborne	11	General Pinckney	Slatter, Hope Hull	Jan. 19, 1847	Balto.
Dove	William	17	General Pinckney	Slatter, Hope Hull	Jan. 19, 1847	Balto.
Dover	George	10	Zoe	Williams, Thomas	Feb. 16, 1847	Balto.
Dowell	John	16	Ann & Leah	Woolfolk, Austin	Nov.1, 1831	Balto.
Dowell	Peter	18	Kirkwood	Campbell, Bernard M.	Oct. 14, 1848	Balto.
Dowery	Adam	26	Tippecanoe	Slatter, Hope Hull	Apr. 15, 1844	Balto.
Dowlan	Catherin	6	Kirkwood	Slatter, Hope Hull	Jan. 14, 1846	Balto.
Downds	Ebbin	27	Lafayette	Woolfolk, Joseph B.	Oct. 18, 1828	Balto.
Downer	George	26	Union	Slatter, Hope Hull	July 26, 1847	Balto.
Downes	George	11	Narragansett	Donovan, Joseph S.	Nov. 27, 1850	Balto.
Downes	Julia Ann	28	Solomon Saltus	Slatter, Hope Hull	Oct. 7, 1839	Balto.
Downing	Ann	14	Zoe	Slatter, Hope Hull	Feb. 16, 1847	Balto.
Downs	Catherine	17	Edward Everett	Campbell, Bernard M.	March 10, 1851	Balto.
Downs	David	23	States	Woolfolk, Austin	Apr. 14, 1828	Balto.
Downs	Hannah	28	Hibernia	Woolfolk, Austin	Dec. 5, 1826	Balto.
Downs	Harriet	6	Hibernia	Woolfolk, Austin	Dec. 5, 1826	Balto.
Downs	John	6	Hibernia	Woolfolk, Austin	Dec. 5, 1826	Balto.

Surname	First Name	Age	Ship	O/S	Date	Depart
Downs	John	13	Margaret Hugg	Wilson, Thomas C.	Nov. 30, 1844	Balto.
Downs	Maranda	16	Union	Donovan, Joseph S.	May 13, 1848	Balto.
Downs	Phill	8	Hibernia	Woolfolk, Austin	Dec. 5, 1826	Balto.
Downs	Washington	19	Edward Everett	Campbell, Bernard M.	March 10, 1851	Balto.
Doyle	Cyrus	21	States	Woolfolk, Austin	Nov. 21, 1827	Balto.
Doyle	Emanuel	4	London	Hoyle, H.B.	Nov. 5, 1840	Balto.
Draper	York	25	Brunswick	Woolfolk, Austin	Oct. 11, 1831	Balto.
Driver	Caleb	19	Victorine	Gardiner, Richard S.D.	Dec. 21, 1844	Balto.
Driver	David	16	Tweed	Bowling, John D.	Oct. 20, 1836	Town Creek
Driver	Esther	18	Ewarkee	Purvis, James Franklin	March 4, 1841	Balto.
Driver	John	2 mon.	Ewarkee	Purvis, James Franklin	March 4, 1841	Balto.
Ducket	Adolphus	21	Victorine	Donovan, Joseph S.	Sept. 29, 1845	Balto.
Ducket	Charlott	23	Victorine	Rodbind, Ebenezer	Dec. 31, 1846	Balto.
Ducket	James	22	Ewarkee	Slatter, Hope Hull	March 4, 1841	Balto.
Ducket	Mary	18	Sarah Bridge	Campbell, Bernard M.	Feb. 8, 1851	Balto.
Ducket	Patrick	25	Victorine	Rodbind, Ebenezer	Dec. 31, 1846	Balto.
Duckett	Alexander	21	Kirkwood	Donovan, Joseph S.	Apr. 15, 1845	Balto.
Duckett	Henry	25	Elizabeth	Campbell, Bernard M.	March 21, 1850	Balto.
Duckett	Isaac	21	General Pinckney	Donovan, Joseph S.	Nov. 10, 1845	Balto.
Duckett	John	21	Southerner	Donovan, Jospeh S.	Jan. 5, 1852	Balto.
Duckett	John	21	Union	Slatter, Hope Hull	July 26, 1847	Balto.
Duckett	Samuel	23	Paoli	Slatter, Hope Hull	Sept. 9, 1845	Balto.
Duckett	William	21	Southerner	Donovan, Joseph S.	Oct. 27, 1849	Balto.
Duckit	Richard	12	Catharine	Slatter, Hope Hull	Jan. 24, 1843	Balto.
Dudley	Louisa	16	Lafayette	Woolfolk, Austin	Oct. 18, 1828	Balto.
Dudley	Violet	17	Lafayette	Woolfolk, Austin	Oct. 22, 1828	Balto.

Surname	First Name	Age	Ship	O/S	Date	Depart
Duff	Zacaria	30	Victorine	Slatter, Hope Hull	March 14, 1846	Balto.
Duffin	Harriett	23	General Pinckney	Slatter, Hope Hull	Jan. 19, 1847	Balto.
Duffin	Joe	infant	General Pinckney	Slatter, Hope Hull	Jan. 19, 1847	Balto.
Duglass	John	9	Northumberland	Slatter, Hope Hull	Feb. 27, 1843	Balto.
Duglass	Louisa	18	Victorine	Rodbind, Ebenezer	Dec. 31, 1846	Balto.
Dukes	David	23	Kirkwood	Slatter, Hope Hull	Jan. 4, 1845	Balto.
Dukes	William	18	Hermitage	Slatter, Hope Hull	Oct. 28, 1846	Balto.
Dulany	Oscar	25	Henry A. Barling	Campbell, Bernard M.	Feb. 24, 1851	Balto.
Dunbar	Betsey	30	Splendid	Slatter, Hope Hull	Apr. 24, 1841	Balto.
Dunbar	Charles	9	Splendid	Slatter, Hope Hull	Apr. 24, 1841	Balto.
Dunbar	Mary	infant	Splendid	Slatter, Hope Hull	Apr. 24, 1841	Balto.
Dunbar	Richard	7	Splendid	Slatter, Hope Hull	Apr. 24, 1841	Balto.
Dunbar	Stephen	3	Splendid	Slatter, Hope Hull	Apr. 24, 1841	Balto.
Duncan	Elias	23	Narragansett	Donovan, Joseph S.	Nov. 27, 1850	Balto.
Duncan	Lucinda	20	Narragansett	Donovan, Joseph S.	Nov. 27, 1850	Balto.
Dunn	Clarisa	16	Superb	Slatter, Hope Hull	Nov. 1, 1843	Balto.
Dunn	Dave	23	Victorine	Rodbind, Ebenezer	Dec. 31, 1846	Balto.
Dunn	Elizabeth	17	Topaz	Woolfolk, Austin	Apr. 20, 1829	Balto.
Dunn	Lucretia	18	Victorine	Rodbind, Ebenezer	Dec. 31, 1846	Balto.
Duppin	Caesar	28	Jefferson	Woolfolk, Austin	Dec. 24, 1827	Balto.
Durfield	Robert	25	Victorine	Woolfolk, Austin	Sept. 12, 1846	Balto.
Dutch	Rachel	24	Victorine	Rodbind, Ebenezer	March 1, 1845	Balto.
Dutton	Ann	19	Orbit	Woolfolk, Austin	Apr. 16, 1825	Balto.
Dutton	Dennis	3 mon.	Orbit	Woolfolk, Austin	Apr. 16, 1825	Balto.
Dutton	Frank	35	Lafayette	Woolfolk, Austin	Oct. 18, 1828	Balto.
Dutton	Kitty	40	Elizabeth	Donovan, Joseph S.	Nov. 18, 1848	Balto.

Surname	First Name	Age	Ship	O/S	Date	Depart
Dutton	Phoebe	9	Brunswick	Woolfolk, Austin	Oct. 11, 1831	Balto.
Duvall	Lydia Ann	22	Kirkwood	Slatter, Henry F.	Dec. 10, 1846	Balto.
Duvall	Martha	16	E.H.Chapin	Slatter, Hope Hull	Nov. 30, 1847	Balto.
Dye	Martha	16	Helen A. Miller	Campbell, Bernard M.	Oct. 18, 1852	Balto.
Dyer	Betty Ann	25	General Pinckney	Williams, Thomas	Jan. 19, 1847	Balto.
Dyer	Lucy	2	General Pinckney	Williams, Thomas	Jan. 19, 1847	Balto.
Dyer	Martha	19	Hermitage	Williams, Thomas	Oct. 28, 1846	Balto.
Dyer	Mary	3	General Pinckney	Williams, Thomas	Jan. 19, 1847	Balto.
Dyer	William	18	Billow	Woolfolk, Austin	Feb. 23, 1828	Balto.
Dykes	Basil	45	Kirkwood	Campbell, Bernard M.	Apr. 4, 1846	Balto.
Dykes	Ben	30	Lapwing	King, Gideon T.	March 22, 1822	Balto.
Dyson	Ann	18	General Pinckney	Slatter, Hope Hull	Jan. 19, 1847	Balto.
Dyson	Daniel	26	Victorine	Rodbind, Ebenezer	Dec. 31, 1846	Balto.
Dyson	Emily	20	Kirkwood	Slatter, Henry F.	Dec. 10, 1846	Balto.
Dyson	Fanny	15	Tweed	Sothoron, William H.	Oct. 20, 1836	Town Creek
Dyson	Henry	14	Victorine	Donovan, Joseph S.	May 22, 1844	Balto.
Dyson	Lewis	20	General Pinckney	Rodbind, Ebenezer	Feb. 21, 1846	Balto.
Dyson	Samuel	23	Elizabeth	Campbell, Bernard M.	May 12, 1849	Balto.
Dyson	Stephenn	32	Uncas	Slatter, Hope Hull	Jan. 10, 1838	Balto.
Ealter	Jim	22	Cora	Campbell, Bernard M.	Jan. 20, 1851	Balto.
Eans	Oscar	17	Nathaniel Hooper	Donovan, Joseph S.	Feb. 12, 1852	Balto.
Earl	Richard	22	Eliza F.Mason	Donovan, Joseph S.	Nov. 13, 1851	Balto.
Easter	Henry	infant	Kirkwood	Donovan, Joseph S.	Dec. 10, 1846	Balto.
Eatin	Eliza	20	Irad Ferry	Slatter, Hope Hull	Dec. 9, 1842	Balto.
Eatin	Rachel	20	Irad Ferry	Slatter, Hope Hull	Dec. 9, 1842	Balto.
Eaton	Henry	21	Brunswick	Woolfolk, Austin	Oct. 11, 1831	Balto.

Surname	First Name	Age	Ship	O/S	Date	Depart
Eckard	Isaac	23	Helen A. Miller	Campbell, Bernard M.	Oct. 18, 1852	Balto.
Eddison	Charles	20	John C. Calhoun	Donovan, Joseph S.	Oct. 24, 1850	Balto.
Edelin	George	17	Union	Rodbind, Ebenezer	Nov. 17, 1849	Balto.
Edelin	Harriet	25	Eliza	Slatter, Hope Hull	Oct. 9, 1840	Balto.
Edelin	Louisa	17	Zoe	Campbell, Bernard M.	Feb. 16, 1847	Balto.
Edinger	Benjamin	22	General Pinckney	Slatter, Hope Hull	Jan. 19, 1847	Balto.
Edmonds	George	22	Victorine	Slatter, Hope Hull	March 14, 1846	Balto.
Edmonds	Simpson	22	Kirkwood	Slatter, Hope Hull	Jan. 4, 1845	Balto.
Edmonds	Susan	15	Tippecanoe	Slatter, Hope Hull	Jan. 17, 1842	Balto.
Edmons	Willis	22	General Pinckney	Donovan, Joseph S.	Feb. 21, 1846	Balto.
Edmonson	Emly	15	Union	Donovan, Joseph S.	May 13, 1848	Balto.
Edmonson	Ephrim	30	Union	Donovan, Joseph S.	May 13, 1848	Balto.
Edmonson	John	26	Union	Donovan, Joseph S.	May 13, 1848	Balto.
Edmonson	Mary	17	Union	Donovan, Joseph S.	May 13, 1848	Balto.
Edmonson	Richard	24	Union	Donovan, Joseph S.	May 13, 1848	Balto.
Edmonson	Samuel	21	Union	Donovan, Joseph S.	May 13, 1848	Balto.
Edward	Joshua	22	Tippecanoe	Slatter, Hope Hull	Dec. 16, 1840	Balto.
Edward	William	2	Tippecanoe	Slatter, Hope Hull	Apr. 15, 1844	Balto.
Edwards	Celly	15	Glasgow	Slatter, Hope Hull	Oct. 11, 1838	Balto.
Edwards	Charles	14	Irad Ferry	Purvis, James Franklin	Oct. 30, 1841	Balto.
Edwards	Charles	18	Union	Slatter, Hope Hull	July 26, 1847	Balto.
Edwards	Charlott	16	Elizabeth	Donovan, Joseph S.	Nov. 18, 1848	Balto.
Edwards	George Anna	3	Zoe	Slatter, Hope Hull	Feb. 16, 1847	Balto.
Edwards	Jane	14	Victorine	Crow, William	March 14, 1846	Balto.
Edwards	Margaret	18	Billow	Woolfolk, Austin	Feb. 23, 1828	Balto.
Edwards	Matilda	25	Zoe	Slatter, Hope Hull	Feb. 16, 1847	Balto.

Surname	First Name	Age	Ship	O/S	Date	Depart
Edwards	Morgan	18	Elizabeth	Campbell, Bernard M.	Jan. 2, 1850	Balto.
Edwards	Nace	33	Irad Ferry	Wilson, J. W.	May 6, 1839	Balto.
Edwards	Ned	25	General Pinckney	Donovan, Joseph S.	Feb. 21, 1846	Balto.
Edwards	Thomas	17	St. Mary	Williams, Thomas	Nov. 29, 1845	Balto.
Edwards	Thomas	5	Zoe	Slatter, Hope Hull	Feb. 16, 1847	Balto.
Egertin	Mary Ann	16	Tippecance	Slatter, Hope Hull	Apr. 1, 1841	Balto.
Egertin	Sarah	35	Tippecance	Slatter, Hope Hull	Apr. 1, 1841	Balto.
Egerton	Henry	14	Peru	Slatter, Hope Hull	Nov. 16, 1842	Balto.
Egerton	Vincent	8	Peru	Slatter, Hope Hull	Nov. 16, 1842	Balto.
Eggleston	Charles	23	Billow	Woolfolk, Joseph B.	Feb. 23, 1828	Balto.
Egland	Stanley	24	Union	Rodbind, Ebenezer	Dec. 16, 1848	Balto.
Egleton	Barbara	18	Henry A. Barling	Donovan, Joseph S.	Feb. 24, 1851	Balto.
Egleton	Eliza	16	Henry A. Barling	Donovan, Joseph S.	Feb. 24, 1851	Balto.
Eglin	George	24	John S. Gittings	Campbell, Bernard M.	Nov. 20, 1852	Balto.
Elbert	Frank	21	Lapwing	King, Gideon T.	March 22, 1822	Balto.
Elbert	Henry	18	Kirkwood	Donovan, Joseph S.	Oct. 14, 1848	Balto.
Elbert	John	14	Lafayette	Woolfolk, Austin	Oct. 18, 1828	Balto.
Elias	Abram	36	General Pinckney	Slatter, Hope Hull	Nov. 10, 1845	Balto.
Elias	Benjamin	21	Paoli	Slatter, Hope Hull	Sept. 9, 1845	Balto.
Elkin	Marshall	15	Louisa	Campbell Bernard M.	Nov. 5, 1849	Balto.
Elkin	Wilson	25	Louisa	Campbell Bernard M.	Nov. 5, 1849	Balto.
Ellen	Ann	3	Irad Ferry	Clendenir, A.	Jan. 16, 1840	Balto.
Elliason	George	20	Ganniclefft	Slatter, Hope Hull	Nov. 25, 1840	Balto.
Ellin	Barbary	14	Tippecanoe	Slatter, Hope Hull	Jan. 17, 1842	Balto.
Elliot	Debby Ann	14	Kirkwood	Donovan, Joseph S.	March 23, 1844	Balto.
Elliott	Caroline	28	Irad Ferry	Slatter, Hope Hull	Dec. 9, 1842	Balto.

Surname	First Name	Age	Ship	O/S	Date	Depart
Elliott	Elizebeth	20	Kirkwood	Slatter, Hope Hull	Jan. 14, 1846	Balto.
Elliott	Leaher	30	Superb	Slatter, Hope Hull	Nov. 1, 1843	Balto.
Elliott	Maria	15	Zoe	Donovan, Joseph S.	Feb. 16, 1847	Balto.
Elliott	Mary	16	St. Mary	Donovan, Joseph S.	Nov. 29, 1845	Balto.
Elliott	Mary Ann	infant	Kirkwood	Slatter, Hope Hull	Jan. 14, 1846	Balto.
Elliott	Parris	30	Isaac Franklin	Kephart, George	Feb. 1, 1839	Balto.
Elliott	Rhebecca	23	Tippecanoe	Slatter, Hope Hull	Jan. 17, 1842	Balto.
Elliott	Robert	35	Leda	Peacock, William W.	Nov. 15, 1848	Balto.
Ellis	Abram	26	Lafayette	Woolfolk, Richard	Oct. 18, 1828	Balto.
Ellis	Henrietta	18	Solomon Saltus	Slatter, Hope Hull	Oct. 7, 1839	Balto.
Ellis	James	20	Kirkwood	Donovan, Joseph S.	Oct. 14, 1848	Balto.
Ellis	John	18	Palestine	Slatter, Hope Hull	Nov. 16, 1835	Balto.
Emery	Eli	25	Southerner	Campbell, Bernard M.	Jan. 5, 1852	Balto.
Emmerson	John	20	Henry A. Barling	Campbell, Bernard M.	Apr. 19, 1849	Balto.
Emory	Abram	23	Waverly	Harris, Alexander	Apr. 3, 1851	Balto.
Emory	Harriett	17	Union	Slatter, Hope Hull	July 26, 1847	Balto.
Emory	Hester	16	Julia	Woolfolk, Austin	Jan. 8, 1829	Balto.
Emory	Louisa	18	Lafayette	Woolfolk, Joseph B.	Oct. 18, 1828	Balto.
Emory	Perry	19	Kirkwood	Donovan, Joseph S.	Jan. 4, 1845	Balto.
Emory	Richard	25	Burlington	Slatter, Hope Hull	Oct. 21, 1842	Balto.
Emsley	Sarah	38	Victorine	Donovan, Joseph S.	May 22, 1844	Balto.
Encerralls	John	29	Bourne	Sterrett, Harrison	July, 21, 1832	Balto.
Engium	William	15	Glasgow	Slatter, Hope Hull	Oct. 11, 1838	Balto.
Ennis	Henry	19	Kirkwood	Slatter, Hope Hull	Dec. 23, 1843	Balto.
Ennis	Sarah	9	Catharine	Slatter, Hope Hull	Jan. 24, 1843	Balto.
Ennols	Eliza	18	Victorine	Slatter, Hope Hull	Sept. 12, 1846	Balto.

Surname	First Name	Age	Ship	O/S	Date	Depart
Ennols	Elizabeth	18	Salvadora	Slatter, Hope Hull	Sept. 28, 1846	Balto.
Enny	John	22	Ann & Lean	Woolfolk, Austin	Nov. 1, 1831	Balto.
Ensey	Harriett	10	Union	Donovan, Joseph S.	Dec. 16, 1848	Balto.
Ensey	Lucy	15	Union	Donovan, Joseph S.	Dec. 16, 1848	Balto.
Erving	John	25	Mechanic	Woolfolk, Austin	Jan. 1, 1831	Balto.
Erwin	Horace	2	Brunswick	Woolfolk, Austin	Oct. 11, 1831	Balto.
Erwin	Rachel	19	Brunswick	Woolfolk, Austin	Oct. 11, 1831	Balto.
Eskridge	Charles	22	Union	Donovan, Joseph S.	Dec. 16, 1848	Balto.
Esler	Fanny	19	Tangier	Campbell, Bernard M.	Nov. 26, 1853	Balto.
Etchison	Julia	16	Union	Sheckles, B.O.	Nov. 17, 1849	Balto.
Evans	Jane	19	Victorine	Slatter, Hope Hull	March 14, 1846	Balto.
Evans	Matilda	16	Catharine	Slatter, Hope Hull	Jan. 24, 1843	Balto.
Evans	Nathaniel	28	E.H.Chapin	Slatter, Hope Hull	Nov. 30, 1847	Balto.
Evans	Sarah	16	Union	Slatter, Hope Hull	July 26, 1847	Balto.
Evard	Dolly	8	General Pinckney	Slatter, Hope Hull	Jan. 19, 1847	Balto.
Evard	Frank	5	General Pinckney	Slatter, Hope Hull	Jan. 19, 1847	Balto.
Evard	Jane	25	General Pinckney	Slatter, Hope Hull	Jan. 19, 1847	Balto.
Evard	Mary Jane	infant	General Pinckney	Slatter, Hope Hull	Jan. 19, 1847	Balto.
Fails	Jim	23	States	Woolfolk, Joseph B.	Nov. 21, 1827	Balto.
Fairfax	Ceasar	30	Kirkwood	Williams Thomas	Apr. 4, 1846	Balto.
Fairfax	Jacob	17	Union	Williams Thomas	Oct. 9, 1848	Balto.
Fairfax	Lorenzo	20	Elizabeth	Campbell, Bernard M.	March 21, 1850	Balto.
Fairman	Juliana	20	Uncas	Slatter, Hope Hull	Jan. 10, 1838	Balto.
Falford	Rebecca	18	Lady Monroe	Woolfolk, Austin	March 25, 1825	Balto.
Fantelroy	Emily	17	General Finckney	Donovan, Joseph S.	Feb. 21, 1846	Balto.
Fantelroy	Mary	18	General Finckney	Donovan, Joseph S.	Feb. 21, 1846	Balto.

Surname	First Name	Age	Ship	O/S	Date	Depart
Farrow	James	13	Lafayette	Woolfolk, Joseph B.	Oct. 18, 1828	Balto.
Fassitt	Andrew	35	Sherwood	Boyd, P.D.	Nov. 14, 1853	Balto.
Fawkerson	Abraham	17	John C. Calhoun	Donovan, Joseph S.	Oct. 24, 1850	Balto.
Felton	Henderson	13	Seaman	Slatter, Hope Hull	March 25, 1839	Balto.
Fendall	Henry	17	Kirkwood	Williams, Thomas	Apr. 4, 1846	Balto.
Fender	Richard	20	Ewarkee	Slatter, Hope Hull	March 4, 1841	Balto.
Fennick	Lavina	18	Superb	Slatter, Hope Hull	Nov. 1, 1843	Balto.
Ferguson	Henry	40	John S. Gittings	Campbell, Bernard M.	Nov. 20, 1852	Balto.
Ferguson		28	Zoe	Donovan, Joseph S.	Feb. 16, 1847	Balto.
Fidderman	Isaac	22	Seaman	Slatter, Hope Hull	Dec. 19, 1838	Balto.
Fideaen	David	35	Catharine	Donovan, Joseph S.	Jan. 18, 1845	Balto.
Field	Cipio	20	Kirkwood	Donovan, Joseph S.	Apr. 4, 1846	Balto.
Field	James	12	Kirkwood	Donovan, Joseph S.	Sept. 28, 1846	Balto.
Fields	Albert	28	Southerner	Donovan, Joseph S.	Oct. 27, 1849	Balto.
Fields	Fransis	20	Kirkwood	Donovan, Joseph S.	March 9, 1847	Balto.
Fillis	James	9	Clio	Starnsburg, William	March 22, 1819	Balto.
Finch	Reuben	18	Lady Richmond	Woolfolk, Austin	Apr. 30, 1827	Balto.
Finicks	Kitty	10	Nathaniel Hooper	Donovan, Jospeh S.	Feb. 12, 1852	Balto.
Finley	Anne	19	Henry Clay	Woolfolk, Austin	Dec. 4, 1828	Balto.
Finley	Maria J.	19	Henry Clay	Woolfolk, Austin	Dec. 4, 1828	Balto.
Fisburg	Caroline	20	Russell	Slatter, Hope Hull	March 1, 1839	Balto.
Fisher	Ann	40	Lafayette	Woolfolk, Austin	Oct. 22, 1828	Balto.
Fisher	Ben	11	Seaman	Rush, George Jr.	Dec. 16, 1841	Balto.
Fisher	Ben	51	Seaman	Rush, George Jr.	Dec. 16, 1841	Balto.
Fisher	Eliza	15	General Pinckney	Donovan, Joseph S.	Nov. 10, 1845	Balto.
Fisher	Eliza	21	Helen A. Miller	Campbell, Bernard M.	Oct. 18, 1852	Balto.

Surname	First Name	Age	Ship	O/S	Date	Depart
Fisher	Fred	10	Seaman	Rush, George Jr.	Dec. 16, 1841	Balto.
Fisher	Harry	35	Tippecanoe	Purvis, James Franklin	Jan. 17, 1842	Balto.
Fisher	Henry	6	Seaman	Rush, George Jr.	Dec. 16, 1841	Balto.
Fisher	Jane	21	Lafayette	Woolfolk, Austin	Oct. 22, 1828	Balto.
Fisher	Levin	20	Tippecanoe	Slatter, Hope Hull	Jan. 17, 1842	Balto.
Fisher	Libby	14	States	Woolfolk, Austin	Nov. 21, 1827	Balto.
Fisher	Lucy	3	Seaman	Rush, George Jr.	Dec. 16, 1841	Balto.
Fisher	Memry	16	Lafayette	Woolfolk, Austin	Oct. 18, 1828	Balto.
Fisher	Milly	35	Seaman	Rush, George Jr.	Dec. 16, 1841	Balto.
Fisher	Polly	30	Tippecanoe	Purvis, James Franklin	Jan. 17, 1842	Balto.
Fisher	Rebecca	22	Lady Monroe	Woolfolk, Austin	March 25, 1825	Balto.
Fisher	Richard	4	Seaman	Rush, George Jr.	Dec. 16, 1841	Balto.
Fisher	Ruth	13	Russell	Slatter, Hope Hull	March 1, 1839	Balto.
Fisher	Sam	11	Home	Donovan, Joseph S.	March 22, 1845	Balto.
Fisher	Tom	9	Seaman	Rush, George Jr.	Dec. 16, 1841	Balto.
Fisher	William	18	Seaman	Slatter, Hope Hull	Dec. 19, 1838	Balto.
Fisher		10 mon.	Seaman	Rush, George Jr.	Dec. 16, 1841	Balto.
Fitshugh	Joseph	23	Union	Donovan, Joseph S.	Dec. 16, 1848	Balto.
Fitzchur	Susan	18	Union	Slatter, Hope Hull	July 26, 1847	Balto.
Flecher	Betsey	20	Kirkwood	Rodbind, Ebenezer	Apr. 15, 1845	Balto.
Flecher	Frank	19	Kirkwood	Rodbind, Ebenezer	Apr. 15, 1845	Balto.
Fleetwood	Elizabeth	17	Victorine	Donovan, Joseph S.	Dec. 31, 1846	Balto.
Fleetwood	Ellen	14	Hibernia	Woolfolk, Austin	Dec. 5, 1826	Balto.
Fleming	Ann Maria	20	General Pinckney	Slatter, Hope Hull	Nov. 10, 1845	Balto.
Flemming	Harriett	infant	General Pinckney	Slatter, Hope Hull	Nov. 10, 1845	Balto.
Flesbury	William	35	Intelligence	King, Gideon T.	Sept. 18, 1821	Balto.

Surname	First Name	Age	Ship	O/S	Date	Depart
Fletcher	Alfred	23	General Pinckney	Slatter, Hope Hull	Jan. 19, 1847	Balto.
Fletcher	Cecelia	16	Kirkwood	Donovan, Joseph S.	Nov. 28, 1849	Balto.
Fletcher	Edward	20	Catharine	Slatter, Hope Hull	Jan. 24, 1843	Balto.
Fletcher	Emily	17	John S. Gittings	Campbell, Bernard M.	Nov. 20, 1852	Balto.
Fletcher	Frank	17	Kirkwood	Slatter, Hope Hull	Dec. 23, 1843	Balto.
Fletcher	Henry	18	Union	Sheckles, Gannon	March 17, 1849	Balto.
Fletcher	James	13	Union	Sheckles, B.O.	Nov. 17, 1849	Balto.
Fletcher	Rachel	20	Kirkwood	Slatter, Hope Hull	Dec. 23, 1843	Balto.
Fletcher	Rosana	18	Kirkwood	Slatter, Hope Hull	Dec. 23, 1843	Balto.
Fletcher	Stephen	17	Kirkwood	Slatter, Hope Hull	Dec. 23, 1843	Balto.
Flint	Stephen	30	Ewarkee	Slatter, Hope Hull	March 4, 1841	Balto.
Floyd	Alfred	21	Union	Rodbind, Ebenezer	Dec. 16, 1848	Balto.
Floyd	William	25	Lafayette	Woolfolk, Austin	Oct. 18, 1828	Balto.
Foard	Henry	28	Victorine	Donovan, Joseph S.	Sept. 29, 1845	Balto.
Foman	Catherin	18	Victorine	Slatter, Hope Hull	May 14, 1845	Balto.
Foman	William	21	Victorine	Slatter, Hope Hull	May 14, 1845	Balto.
Forbs	Jim	9	Union	Rodbind, Ebenezer	Dec. 16, 1848	Balto.
Force	Cyrus	15	Lady Monroe	Woolfolk, Austin	March 25, 1825	Balto.
Ford	Betsey	12	Kirkwood	Donovan, Joseph S.	Jan. 14, 1846	Balto.
Ford	Charlotte	9	Kirkwood	Williams, Thomas	Apr. 4, 1846	Balto.
Ford	Dallas	26	Victorine	Slatter, Hope Hull	March 1, 1845	Balto.
Ford	Dennis	27	Burlington	Slatter, Hope Hull	Oct. 21, 1842	Balto.
Ford	Eliza	25	Edward Everett	Campbell, Bernard M.	March 10, 1851	Balto.
Ford	Fanny	22	Hermitage	Williams, Thomas	Oct. 28, 1846	Balto.
Ford	Hillary	3	Kirkwood	Donovan, Joseph S.	Oct. 14, 1848	Balto.
Ford	James	16	Elizabeth	Donovan, Joseph S.	Nov. 18, 1848	Balto.

Surname	First Name	Age	Ship	O/S	Date	Depart
Ford	John	24	Kirkwood	Campbell, Bernard M.	Nov. 28, 1849	Balto.
Ford	John	20	Pioneer	Slatter, Hope Hull	Sept. 15, 1847	Balto.
Ford	Mary	23	Kirkwood	Donovan, Joseph S.	Oct. 14, 1848	Balto.
Ford	Washington	infant	Kirkwood	Donovan, Joseph S.	Oct. 14, 1848	Balto.
Ford	Washington	22	Sabine	Donovan, Joseph S.	Feb. 10, 1844	Balto.
Ford	William	30	Kirkwood	Donovan, Joseph S.	Oct. 14, 1848	Balto.
Foreman	Edward	19	Architect	Donovan, Joseph S.	Apr. 25, 1846	Balto.
Foreman	Phillis	19	Lafayette	Woolfolk, Austin	Oct. 18, 1828	Balto.
Foreman	William	25	Brunswick	Woolfolk, Austin	Oct. 11, 1831	Balto.
Forge	Anthony	19	Kirkwood	Donovan, Joseph S.	March 9, 1847	Balto.
Forman	Ellen	25	Tippecanoe	Wilson, William N.	May 4, 1842	Balto.
Forrest	Caroline	18	Superb	Slatter, Hope Hull	Nov. 1, 1843	Balto.
Forrest	Charles	22	Seaman	Slatter, Hope Hull	March 25, 1839	Balto.
Forrest	Joseph	34	Union	Donovan, Joseph S.	May 13, 1848	Balto.
Foskey	Purnell	18	Home	Rodbind, Ebenezer	March 22, 1845	Balto.
Fossett	Isaac	15	Kirkwood	Harker, William	March 23, 1844	Balto.
Foster	David	21	General Pinckney	Donovan, Joseph S.	Feb. 21, 1846	Balto.
Foster	Levin	22	Victorine	Slatter, Hope Hull	Dec. 17, 1845	Balto.
Foster	William	28	Union	Donovan, Joseph S.	Dec. 16, 1848	Balto.
Fouk	Priscilla	18	Mary Broughton	Campbell, Bernard M.	Nov. 18, 1851	Balto.
Fouler	Rachel	3	States	Woolfolk, Austin	Apr. 14, 1828	Balto.
Foulk	Hariet	19	Lafayette	Woolfolk, Austin	Oct. 18, 1828	Balto.
Foulks	Almira	18	Union	Donovan, Joseph S.	May 13, 1848	Balto.
Fountain	Henrietta	26	Kirkwood	Donovan, Joseph S.	Dec. 10, 1846	Balto.
Fountain	Henry	22	E.H.Chapin	Slatter, Hope Hull	Nov. 30, 1847	Balto.
Fountain	Wesley	22	Margaret Hugg	Slatter, Hope Hull	Feb. 8, 1845	Balto.

Surname	First Name	Age	Ship	O/S	Date	Depart
Fourman	Jarritt	8	Victorine	Donovan, Joseph S.	Sept. 29, 1845	Balto.
Fowler	Frederick	28	Helen A. Miller	Campbell, Bernard M.	Oct. 18, 1852	Balto.
Fowler	Gilbert	18	Kirkwood	Campbell, Bernard M.	Oct. 14, 1848	Balto.
Fowler	Jacob	24	Jane Henderson	Campbell, Bernard M.	Nov. 1, 1852	Balto.
Fowler	Uriah	18	John C. Calhoun	Donovan, Joseph S.	Oct. 24, 1850	Balto.
Fox	Dudley	23	Kirkwood	Campbell, Bernard M.	Oct. 14, 1848	Balto.
Fox	George	21	Justina	Donovan, Joseph S.	Dec. 2, 1852	Balto.
Fox	James	18	Edward Everett	Campbell, Bernard M.	March 10, 1851	Balto.
Fox	Peter	20	Victorine	Rodbind, Ebenezer	March 14, 1846	Balto.
France	Leonard	19	John C. Calhoun	Donovan, Joseph S.	Oct. 24, 1850	Balto.
France	Wesley	22	Narragansett	Donovan, Joseph S.	Nov. 27, 1850	Balto.
Frances	Sarah	17	St. Mary	Williams, Thomas	Nov. 29, 1845	Balto.
Francis	Adaline	6	Home	Slatter, Hope Hull	March 22, 1845	Balto.
Francis	Henry	18	John C. Calhoun	Donovan, Joseph S.	Oct. 24, 1850	Balto.
Francis	John	9	Porpoise	Purvis, James Franklin	Dec. 11, 1841	Balto.
Francis	Maryann	28	Catharine	Slatter, Hope Hull	Jan. 24, 1843	Balto.
Francis	Philip		Catharine	Donovan, Joseph S.	Jan. 18, 1845	Balto.
Franklin	Alexander	18	Tweed	Tucker, J.B.	Oct. 20, 1836	Town Creek
Franklin	Ally	24	Charles	Campbell, Bernard M.	Apr. 23, 1851	Balto.
Franklin	Caroline	9	E.H.Chapin	Slatter, Hope Hull	Nov. 30, 1847	Balto.
Franklin	Charles	infant	E.H.Chapin	Slatter, Hope Hull	Nov. 30, 1847	Balto.
Franklin	Daniel	25	Charles	Campbell, Bernard M.	Apr. 23, 1851	Balto.
Franklin	George	3	E.H.Chapin	Slatter, Hope Hull	Nov. 30, 1847	Balto.
Franklin	George	infant	Isaac Franklin	Slatter, Hope Hull	Sept. 28, 1838	Balto.
Franklin	Henry	11	E.H.Chapin	Slatter, Hope Hull	Nov. 30, 1847	Balto.
Franklin	Hester	17	Margaret Hugg	Wilson, Thomas C.	Nov. 30, 1844	Balto.

Surname	First Name	Age	Ship	O/S	Date	Depart
Franklin	Horrace	5	E.H.Chapin	Slatter, Hope Hull	Nov. 30, 1847	Balto.
Franklin	Isaac	8	E.H.Chapin	Slatter, Hope Hull	Nov. 30, 1847	Balto.
Franklin	Leaher	35	E.H.Chapin	Slatter, Hope Hull	Nov. 30, 1847	Balto.
Franklin	Littleton	7	E.H.Chapin	Slatter, Hope Hull	Nov. 30, 1847	Balto.
Franklin	Mary	25	E.H.Chapin	Slatter, Hope Hull	Nov. 30, 1847	Balto.
Franklin	Primus	23	Lafayette	Woolfolk, Austin	Oct. 18, 1828	Balto.
Franklin	Rachel	13	Uncas	Slatter, Hope Hull	Jan. 10, 1838	Balto.
Franklin	Robert	18	E.H.Chapin	Slatter, Hope Hull	Nov. 30, 1847	Balto.
Franklin	Rollin	5	E.H.Chapin	Slatter, Hope Hull	Nov. 30, 1847	Balto.
Franklin	Rufus	10	E.H.Chapin	Slatter, Hope Hull	Nov. 30, 1847	Balto.
Franklin	Sarah	21	E.H.Chapin	Slatter, Hope Hull	Nov. 30, 1847	Balto.
Franklin	Sarah	38	Uncas	Slatter, Hope Hull	Jan. 10, 1838	Balto.
Franklin	Susan	3	E.H.Chapin	Slatter, Hope Hull	Nov. 30, 1847	Balto.
Franklin	Susan	infant	E.H.Chapin	Slatter, Hope Hull	Nov. 30, 1847	Balto.
Franks	Sarah	23	Uncas	Slatter, Hope Hull	Jan. 10, 1838	Balto.
Frasieur	Kitty Ann	19	Catharine	Woolfolk, Austin	March 3, 1829	Balto.
Frasure	Charlotte	16	Solomon Saltus	Slatter, Hope Hull	Oct. 7, 1839	Balto.
Frazier	Gertrude	17	Superb	Slatter, Hope Hull	Nov. 1, 1843	Balto.
Frazier	John	infant	Jefferson	Woolfolk, Joseph B.	Dec. 24, 1827	Balto.
Frazier	Louisa Ann	20	Kirkwood	Donovan, Joseph S.	Jan. 14, 1846	Balto.
Frazier	Martha Jane	17	Henry A. Barling	Campbell, Bernard M.	Feb. 24, 1851	Balto.
Frazier	Nathan	18	Kirkwood	Donovan, Joseph S.	Jan. 14, 1846	Balto.
Frazier	William	18	General Pinckney	Slatter, Hope Hull	Jan. 19, 1847	Balto.
Frederick	Dick	19	Mary Broughton	Campbell, Bernard M.	Nov. 18, 1851	Balto.
		19	Eliza F.Mason	Donovan, Joseph S.	Nov. 13, 1851	Balto.
		26	Tweed	Forbes, George	Oct. 20, 1836	Town Creek

Surname	First Name	Age	Ship	O/S	Date	Depart
Frederick	Harriet	5	Tweed	Forbes, George	Oct. 20, 1836	Town Creek
Frederick	James	24	John S. Gittings	Campbell, Bernard M.	Nov. 20, 1852	Balto.
Frederick	John	11	Henry A. Barling	Donovan, Joseph S.	Dec. 18, 1851	Balto.
Frederick	Juliet	1	Tweed	Forbes, George	Oct. 20, 1836	Town Creek
Frederick	Mary	22	Tweed	Forbes, George	Oct. 20, 1836	Town Creek
Fredericks	Oliver	19	Tippecanoe	Slatter, Hope Hull	Jan. 17, 1842	Balto.
Fredrick	Ann	18	Victorine	Donovan, Joseph S.	Sept. 29, 1845	Balto.
Free	Nelly	15	Lady Monroe	Woolfolk, Austin	March 25, 1825	Balto.
Freeland	John	26	Palestine	Slatter, Hope Hull	Nov. 16, 1835	Balto.
Freeman	Charles	20	Isaac Franklin	Slatter, Hope Hull	Sept. 28, 1838	Balto.
Freeman	Elizabeth	17	Union	Donovan, Joseph S.	Dec. 16, 1848	Balto.
Freeman	Frisby	18	Ann & Leah	Woolfolk, Austin	Nov.1, 1831	Balto.
Freeman	Hillary	19	Kirkwood	Donovan, Joseph S.	Oct. 14, 1848	Balto.
Freeman	Horace	17	Kirkwood	Donovan, Joseph S.	Oct. 14, 1848	Balto.
Freeman	Isaac	17	Julia	Woolfolk, Austin	Jan. 8, 1829	Balto.
Freeman	Joseph	21	Victorine	Donovan, Joseph S.	Sept. 29, 1845	Balto.
Freeman	Minty	16	Elizabeth	Donovan, Joseph S.	Nov. 18, 1848	Balto.
Frellman	Richard	21	Burlington	Slatter, Hope Hull	Oct. 21, 1842	Balto.
French	Benjamin	16	Victorine	Donovan, Joseph S.	Dec. 31, 1846	Balto.
French	Elizabeth	20	Catharine	Slatter, Hope Hull	Jan. 24, 1843	Balto.
French	Francis	20	Catharine	Slatter, Hope Hull	Jan. 24, 1843	Balto.
French	Lewis	21	St. Mary	Donovan, Joseph S.	Nov. 29, 1845	Balto.
French	Moses	25	Catharine	Slatter, Hope Hull	Jan. 24, 1843	Balto.
Frey	Clement	20	Milton	Crawford, William	May 22, 1832	Balto.
Friah	John	35	Justina	Donovan, Joseph S.	Dec. 2, 1852	Balto.
Frisby	Ann	22	Waverly	Campbell, Bernard M.	Apr. 3, 1851	Balto.

Surname	First Name	Age	Ship	O/S	Date	Depart
Frisby	Harriett	14	Harriett	Woolfolk, Austin	March 23, 1822	Balto.
Frisby	Harriett	35	St. Mary	Donovan, Joseph S.	Nov. 29, 1845	Balto.
Frisby	James	17	Margaret Hugg	Slatter, Hope Hull	Feb. 8, 1845	Balto.
Frisby	Juliana	6	Burlington	Slatter, Hope Hull	Oct. 21, 1842	Balto.
Frisby	July ?	30	Burlington	Slatter, Hope Hull	Oct. 21, 1842	Balto.
Frisby	Phillis	17	Brunswick	Woolfolk, Austin	Oct. 11, 1831	Balto.
Frisby	Rebecca	17	Elizabeth	Donovan, Joseph S.	Nov. 18, 1848	Balto.
Frisby	Sarah Ann	17	Kirkwood	Slatter, Hope Hull	Jan. 14, 1846	Balto.
Frisby	Thomas	16	Billow	Woolfolk, Joseph B.	Feb. 23, 1828	Balto.
Frisby	Thomas	2	Burlington	Slatter, Hope Hull	Oct. 21, 1842	Balto.
Frisby	William	10	Kirkwood	Donovan, Joseph S.	Oct. 14, 1848	Balto.
Froker	Philip	37	Kirkwood	Campbell, Bernard M.	Oct. 16, 1845	Balto.
Fry	James	27	Kirkwood	Slatter, Hope Hull	Dec. 23, 1843	Balto.
Fry	John	32	Irad Ferry	Slatter, Hope Hull	Jan. 22, 1840	Balto.
Frye	Robert	22	Elizabeth	Campbell, Walter L.	Oct. 6, 1849	Balto.
Fulton	James	18	Justina	Donovan, Joseph S.	Dec. 2, 1852	Balto.
Furgason	Henry	30	Kirkwood	Donovan, Joseph S.	Oct. 14, 1848	Balto.
Furgerson	Charles	23	Kirkwood	Donovan, Joseph S.	Oct. 26, 1847	Balto.
Furgerson	George	21	Victorine	Rodbind, Ebenezer	Dec. 31, 1846	Balto.
Furgerson	Sam	20	Victorine	Rodbind, Ebenezer	Dec. 31, 1846	Balto.
Furley	Atwell	19	Isaac Franklin	Kephart, George	Feb. 1, 1839	Balto.
Furlong	Singleton	14	Sarah Bridge	Campbell, Bernard M.	Feb. 8, 1851	Balto.
Furlong	Thomas	46	Zoe	Slatter, Hope Hull	Feb. 16, 1847	Balto.
Furlong	Ursley	45	Zoe	Slatter, Hope Hull	Feb. 16, 1847	Balto.
Furnace	Maria	24	Kirkwood	Slatter, Hope Hull	Oct. 16, 1845	Balto.
Furr	Lewis		St. Mary	Williams, Thomas	Nov. 29, 1845	Balto.

Surname	First Name	Age	Ship	O/S	Date	Depart
Gaddes	Thomas	19	Justina	Donovan, Joseph S.	Dec. 2, 1852	Balto.
Gaddis	Mary	17	Hibernia	Woolfolk, Austin	Dec. 5, 1826	Balto.
Gadkim	Faney	18	Julia	Woolfolk, Austin	Jan. 8, 1829	Balto.
Gadsby	Amos	22	Union	Slatter, Hope Hull	July 26, 1847	Balto.
Gadsby	Ann	16	Harriett	Woolfolk, Austin	March 23, 1822	Balto.
Gage	Sam	16	Mary Broughton	Campbell, Bernard M.	Nov. 18, 1851	Balto.
Gaines	Elizabeth	18	Helen A. Miller	Campbell, Bernard M.	Oct. 18, 1852	Balto.
Gains	Maria	14	Kirkwood	Donovan, Joseph S.	Apr. 15, 1845	Balto.
Gaither	Daniel	20	Victorine	Donovan, Joseph S.	May 22, 1844	Balto.
Gaither	John	13	Union	Donovan, Joseph S.	Dec. 16, 1848	Balto.
Gales	Betsey	21	Arctic	Woolfolk, Austin	May 15, 1828	Balto.
Gales	Isaac	21	Lafayette	Woolfolk, Austin	Oct. 18, 1828	Balto.
Gales	Mary Jane	2	Arctic	Woolfolk, Austin	May 15, 1828	Balto.
Gales	Perry	25	Arctic	Woolfolk, Austin	May 15, 1828	Balto.
Gales	Rachel	3	Arctic	Woolfolk, Austin	May 15, 1828	Balto.
Gallanay	Jeffry	17	Salvadora	Slatter, Hope Hull	Sept. 28, 1846	Balto.
Galloway	Allen	22	Victorine	Slatter, Hope Hull	March 1, 1845	Balto.
Galloway	Charles	25	Billow	Woolfolk, Austin	Feb. 23, 1828	Balto.
Galloway	Charles	22	Kirkwood	Slatter, Hope Hull	Jan. 14, 1846	Balto.
Galloway	Charles	20	Pioneer	Slatter, Hope Hull	Sept. 15, 1847	Balto.
Galloway	Edward	19	Elizabeth	Donovan, Joseph S.	May 12, 1849	Balto.
Galloway	Edward	11	Narragansett	Campbell, Bernard M.	Nov. 27, 1850	Balto.
Galloway	Maria	18	Uncas	Slatter, Hope Hull	Jan. 10, 1838	Balto.
Galloway	Mary	22	Billow	Woolfolk, Austin	Feb. 23, 1828	Balto.
Galloway	Mary	40	P. Soule	Gittings, Lambert	Oct. 9, 1845	Balto.
Galloway	Perry	infant	Kirkwood	Donovan, Joseph S.	Sept. 28, 1846	Balto.

Surname	First Name	Age	Ship	O/S	Date	Depart
Galoway	Ben	26	Zoe	Campbell, Bernard M.	Feb. 16, 1847	Balto.
Galoway	Theodore	14	Tippecanoe	Slatter, Hope Hull	Jan. 17, 1842	Balto.
Gambrill	Polly	16	Elizabeth	Donovan, Joseph S.	Jan. 2, 1850	Balto.
Game	John Henry	15	Architect	Purvis, James Franklin	Feb. 3, 1841	Balto.
Gannon	Benjamin	13	General Pinckney	Slatter, Hope Hull	Nov. 10, 1845	Balto.
Gant	Albert	20	Isaac Franklin	Kephart, George	Sept. 28, 1838	Balto.
Gant	Frederick	3	Isaac Franklin	Kephart, George	Sept. 28, 1838	Balto.
Gant	James H.	13	Catharine	Donovan, Joseph S.	Jan. 18, 1845	Balto.
Gant	Jane	17	Margaret Forbs	Slatter, Hope Hull	Nov. 28, 1838	Balto.
Gant	John	27	Henry A. Barling	Donovan, Joseph S.	Dec. 18, 1851	Balto.
Gant	John	25	Margaret Hugg	Campbell, Bernard M.	Nov. 30, 1844	Balto.
Gant	John	17	Union	Donovan, Joseph S.	Dec. 16, 1848	Balto.
Gant	John	18	Union	Campbell, Bernard M.	March 17, 1849	Balto.
Gant	Judy	26	Isaac Franklin	Kephart, George	Sept. 28, 1838	Balto.
Gant	Kitty	5	General Pinckney	Slatter, Hope Hull	Jan. 19, 1847	Balto.
Gant	Margaret	infant	General Pinckney	Slatter, Hope Hull	Jan. 19, 1847	Balto.
Gant	Mary	18	Victorine	Donovan, Joseph S.	Sept. 29, 1845	Balto.
Gant	Washington	5	Isaac Franklin	Kephart, George	Sept. 28, 1838	Balto.
Gant	William	21	Margaret Hugg	Donovan, Joseph S.	Feb. 8, 1845	Balto.
Gant		32	Catharine	Donovan, Joseph S.	Jan. 18, 1845	Balto.
Gantt	Douglass	19	Justina	Donovan, Joseph S.	Dec. 2, 1852	Balto.
Gantt	George	21	Paoli	Slatter, Hope Hull	Sept. 9, 1845	Balto.
Gantt	Henry	21	Paoli	Slatter, Hope Hull	Sept. 9, 1845	Balto.
Gantt	Hillen	16	Zoe	Williams, Thomas	Feb. 16, 1847	Balto.
Gantt	Jane	25	Pioneer	Slatter, Hope Hull	Sept. 15, 1847	Balto.
Gantt	Lamar	20	Scotia	Slatter, Hope Hull	Sept. 30, 1843	Balto.

Surname	First Name	Age	Ship	O/S	Date	Depart
Gantt	Prince	18	Paoli	Slatter, Hope Hull	Sept. 9, 1845	Balto.
Gantz	Harriott	14	Victorine	Donovan, Joseph S.	Sept. 29, 1845	Balto.
Gardener	Henrietta	16	Isaac Franklin	Kephart, George	Sept. 28, 1838	Balto.
Gardiner	Anthony	19	Victorine	Donovan, Joseph S.	Dec. 31, 1846	Balto.
Gardiner	Isaac	22	Waverly	Campbell, Bernard M.	Apr. 3, 1851	Balto.
Gardiner	Lucy	21	Henry A. Barling	Campbell, Bernard M.	Dec. 18, 1851	Balto.
Gardiner	Truman	27	Henry A. Barling	Campbell, Bernard M.	Dec. 18, 1851	Balto.
Gardner	Ann	18	Osprey	Rodbind, Ebenezer	Nov. 11, 1847	Balto.
Gardner	Daniel	7 mon.	Margaret Hugg	Poindexter, T.B.	Nov. 30, 1844	Balto.
Gardner	Eliza	3	Margaret Hugg	Poindexter, T.B.	Nov. 30, 1844	Balto.
Gardner	Lucinda	18	Kirkwood	Slatter, Hope Hull	Jan. 4, 1845	Balto.
Gardner	Luke	23	Russell	Slatter, Hope Hull	March 1, 1839	Balto.
Gardner	Rosetta	20	Margaret Hugg	Poindexter, T.B.	Nov. 30, 1844	Balto.
Garey	William	28	John C. Calhoun	Donovan, Joseph S.	Oct. 24, 1850	Balto.
Garner	Amy	18	Victorine	Rodbind, Ebenezer	May 14, 1845	Balto.
Garner	Hamilton	27	Henry A. Barling	Campbell, Bernard M.	Dec. 18, 1851	Balto.
Garner	Harriot	13	Seaman	Rush, George Jr.	Dec. 16, 1841	Balto.
Garner	James	18	Victorine	Donovan, Joseph S.	Sept. 29, 1845	Balto.
Garner	Magdelana	17	Kirkwood	Rodbind, Ebenezer	Oct. 26, 1847	Balto.
Garner	Sophie	16	Isaac Franklin	Kephart, George	Sept. 28, 1838	Balto.
Garnet	Jane	21	Balloon	Milligan, George	Dec. 17, 1821	Balto.
Garnet	Sam	16	Balloon	Milligan, George	Dec. 17, 1821	Balto.
Garnett	Elsberry	20	Helen A. Miller	Campbell, Bernard M.	Oct. 18, 1852	Balto.
Garret	Henry	44	Franklin	Yeiser, John	Nov. 27, 1819	Balto.
Garrett	Abraham	19	Burlington	Slatter, Hope Hull	Oct. 21, 1842	Balto.
Garrett	Rebecca	16	Henry A. Barling	Donovan, Joseph S.	Feb. 24, 1851	Balto.

Surname	First Name	Age	Ship	O/S	Date	Depart
Garrett	Rebecca	40	Henry A. Barling	Donovan, Joseph S.	Feb. 24, 1851	Balto.
Garrett	Richard	20	Henry A. Barling	Donovan, Joseph S.	Feb. 24, 1851	Balto.
Garrett	Sarah Jean	13	Henry A. Barling	Donovan, Joseph S.	Feb. 24, 1851	Balto.
Garrett	William	22	Superb	Slatter, Hope Hull	Nov. 1, 1843	Balto.
Garrison	John	13	Superb	Slatter, Hope Hull	Nov. 1, 1843	Balto.
Garrott	William	19	John C. Calhoun	Donovan, Joseph S.	Oct. 24, 1850	Balto.
Gary	Cecelia	17	Union	Rodbind, Ebenezer	Nov. 17, 1849	Balto.
Gary	Prince	26	Mary Broughton	Campbell, Bernard M.	Nov. 18, 1851	Balto.
Gasaway	Ned	21	Lafayette	Woolfolk, Austin	Oct. 18, 1828	Balto.
Gasaway	William	24	Lapwing	Woolfolk, Samuel M.	Feb. 15, 1827	Balto.
Gaskin	Tosker	22	St. Mary	Williams, Thomas	Nov. 29, 1845	Balto.
Gassaway	Eba	22	Kirkwood	Slatter, Hope Hull	Oct. 16, 1845	Balto.
Gassaway	Ellen	6	Kirkwood	Slatter, Hope Hull	Oct. 16, 1845	Balto.
Gassaway	Jane	23	Kirkwood	Slatter, Hope Hull	Oct. 16, 1845	Balto.
Gassaway	John	18	Narragansett	Donovan, Joseph S.	Nov. 27, 1850	Balto.
Gassaway	Lewis	22	Kirkwood	Slatter, Hcpe Hull	Oct. 16, 1845	Balto.
Gassaway	Margrett	4	Kirkwood	Slatter, Hcpe Hull	Oct. 16, 1845	Balto.
Gassaway	Maria	24	Kirkwood	Slatter, Hope Hull	Oct. 16, 1845	Balto.
Gassaway	Mariah	15	Eliza	Slatter, Hope Hull	Oct. 9, 1840	Balto.
Gassaway	Nickolas	infant	Kirkwood	Slatter, Hope Hull	Oct. 16, 1845	Balto.
Gassaway	Richard	13	Sarah Bridge	Campbell, Bernard M.	Feb. 8, 1851	Balto.
Gassaway	Robert	24	Sarah Bridge	Campbell, Bernard M.	Feb. 8, 1851	Balto.
Gassaway	Tilman	16	Julia	Woolfolk, Austin	Jan. 8, 1829	Balto.
Gates	Betsey	18	Zoe	Donovan, Joseph S.	Feb. 16, 1847	Balto.
Gates	Harrison	18	Kirkwood	Donovan, Joseph S.	Oct. 26, 1847	Balto.
Gates	Keziah	16	General Pinckney	Donovan, Joseph S.	Feb. 21, 1846	Balto.

Surname	First Name	Age	Ship	O/S	Date	Depart
Gatewood	Henny	infant	Kirkwood	Crow, William	Jan. 14, 1846	Balto.
Gatewood	Priscilla	19	Kirkwood	Crow, William	Jan. 14, 1846	Balto.
Gather	Jack	24	Henry Clay	Woolfolk, Austin	Dec. 4, 1828	Balto.
Gather	Joseph	14	Union	Donovan, Joseph S.	Dec. 16, 1848	Balto.
Gather	Mary	16	Union	Donovan, Joseph S.	Dec. 16, 1848	Balto.
Gathis	Dennis	21	Victorine	Donovan, Joseph S.	Sept. 29, 1845	Balto.
Gattin	Ann	20	Mary	Harker, William	Feb. 10, 1844	Balto.
Gattin	Hetty	18 mon.	Mary	Harker, William	Feb. 10, 1844	Balto.
Gaulph	John	18	Brunswick	Woolfolk, Austin	Oct. 11, 1831	Balto.
Gazaw	Vachel	17	Hibernia	Woolfolk, Austin	Dec. 5, 1826	Balto.
Gear	John	11	Union	Donovan, Joseph S.	March 17, 1849	Balto.
Geddes	Daniel	18	Elizabeth	Campbell, Bernard M.	Nov. 18, 1848	Balto.
Gedes	Moses	20	Kirkwood	Slatter, Hope Hull	Dec. 23, 1843	Balto.
Gent	Harriet	22	Eliza	Slatter, Hope Hull	Oct. 9, 1840	Balto.
Gent		infant	Eliza	Slatter, Hope Hull	Oct. 9, 1840	Balto.
Ghant	Henry	22	Osprey	Tilletson, S.R.	Nov. 11, 1847	Balto.
Gibbs	James	25	Elizabeth	Donovan, Joseph S.	Nov. 18, 1848	Balto.
Gibbs	Maria	16	Hibernia	Woolfolk, Austin	Dec. 5, 1826	Balto.
Gibson	Affy	25	Tippecanoe	Slatter, Hope Hull	Jan. 17, 1842	Balto.
Gibson	Ann	16	Kirkwood	Donovan, Joseph S.	Sept. 28, 1846	Balto.
Gibson	Ben	19	Union	Rodbind, Ebenezer	Dec. 16, 1848	Balto.
Gibson	Betsey	30	Bostonian	Slatter, Hope Hull	Jan. 18, 1841	Balto.
Gibson	Betsey	17	Kirkwood	Donovan, Joseph S.	Jan. 4, 1845	Balto.
Gibson	Caroline	20	E.H.Chapin	Slatter, Hope Hull	Nov. 30, 1847	Balto.
Gibson	Charles	25	Kirkwood	Campbell, Bernard M.	Dec. 10, 1846	Balto.
Gibson	Charles	22	St. Mary	Donovan, Joseph S.	Nov. 29, 1845	Balto.

Surname	First Name	Age	Ship	O/S	Date	Depart
Gibson	Charles	22	Victorine	Campbell, Bernard M.	Dec. 31, 1846	Balto.
Gibson	Clara	infant	E.H.Chapin	Slatter, Hope Hull	Nov. 30, 1847	Balto.
Gibson	Clarissa	23	Hibernia	Woolfolk, Austin	Dec. 5, 1826	Balto.
Gibson	Dealey	3	Bostonian	Slatter, Hope Hull	Jan. 18, 1841	Balto.
Gibson	Edward	23	Architect	Donovan, Joseph S.	Apr. 25, 1846	Balto.
Gibson	Edward	19	Kirkwood	Donovan, Joseph S.	Jan. 4, 1845	Balto.
Gibson	Eliza Ann	17	Kirkwood	Donovan, Joseph S.	Jan. 4, 1845	Balto.
Gibson	Florida	16	Architect	Donovan, Joseph S.	Apr. 25, 1846	Balto.
Gibson	Francis	16	Henry A. Barling	Donovan, Joseph S.	Feb. 24, 1851	Balto.
Gibson	George	19	Billow	Woolfolk, Joseph B.	Feb. 23, 1828	Balto.
Gibson	George	21	Kirkwood	Crow, William	Jan. 14, 1846	Balto.
Gibson	George	16	Kirkwood	Campbell, Bernard M.	Jan. 4, 1845	Balto.
Gibson	Harrison	20	Superb	Slatter, Hope Hull	Nov. 1, 1843	Balto.
Gibson	Harrison	12	Zoe	Slatter, Hope Hull	Feb. 16, 1847	Balto.
Gibson	Henry	4	E.H.Chapin	Slatter, Hope Hull	Nov. 30, 1847	Balto.
Gibson	Henry	28	E.H.Chapin	Slatter, Hope Hull	Nov. 30, 1847	Balto.
Gibson	Henry	10	Henry Clay	Woolfolk, Austin	Dec. 4, 1828	Balto.
Gibson	Henry	40	Isaac Franklin	Slatter, Hope Hull	Sept. 28, 1838	Balto.
Gibson	James	3	Henry Clay	Woolfolk, Austin	Dec. 4, 1828	Balto.
Gibson	James	22	Union	Donovan, Joseph S.	Dec. 16, 1848	Balto.
Gibson	James	24	Victorine	Slatter, Henry F.	Dec. 31, 1846	Balto.
Gibson	Jane	20	Kirkwood	Donovan, Joseph S.	Jan. 4, 1845	Balto.
Gibson	John	20	Seaman	Williamson, G.W.	Dec. 18, 1838	Balto.
Gibson	John	23	Victorine	Slatter, Henry F.	Dec. 31, 1846	Balto.
Gibson	Josiah	30	E.H.Chapin	Donovan, Joseph S.	Dec. 2, 1847	Balto.
Gibson	Kitty	5	Bostonian	Slatter, Hope Hull	Jan. 18, 1841	Balto.

Surname	First Name	Age	Ship	O/S	Date	Depart
Gibson	Lloyd	17	Catharine	Bossiere, Joseph S.	Apr. 1, 1831	Balto.
Gibson	Mary	5	E.H.Chapin	Slatter, Hope Hull	Nov. 30, 1847	Balto.
Gibson	Mary	16	Southerner	Donovan, Joseph S.	Oct. 27, 1849	Balto.
Gibson	Robert	13	Topaz	Woolfolk, Austin	Apr. 20, 1829	Balto.
Gibson	Sam	23	Virginia	Woolfolk, Joseph B.	Dec. 19, 1825	Balto.
Gibson	Sinah	27	Henry Clay	Woolfolk, Austin	Dec. 4, 1828	Balto.
Gibson	Susan	18	Architect	Purvis, James Franklin	Feb. 3, 1841	Balto.
Gibson	Thomas	35	Intelligence	King, Gideon T.	Sept. 18, 1821	Balto.
Gibson	Washington	23	Tippecanoe	Slatter, Hope Hull	Jan. 17, 1842	Balto.
Gibson	Wesley	infant	Hibernia	Woolfolk, Austin	Dec. 5, 1826	Balto.
Gibson	William	19	Kirkwood	Slatter, Hope Hull	Apr. 15, 1845	Balto.
Gibson	William	19	Kirkwood	Crow, William	Jan. 14, 1846	Balto.
Gibson	William	17	Kirkwood	Donovan, Joseph S.	Jan. 4, 1845	Balto.
Gibson	William	21	Kirkwood	Donovan, Joseph S.	Jan. 4, 1845	Balto.
Giddings	Harriett	12	Colonel Howard	Harker, William	Nov. 21, 1844	Balto.
Gilbert	Isaac	18	E.H.Chapin	Slatter, Hope Hull	Nov. 30, 1847	Balto.
Gilbert	James	24	Tippecanoe	Slatter, Hope Hull	Dec. 16, 1840	Balto.
Gilbert	Maria	19	Southerner	Rodbind, Ebenezer	Jan. 21, 1850	Balto.
Giles	Abraham	19	Tippecanoe	Slatter, Hope Hull	Jan. 17, 1842	Balto.
Giles	Daniel	20	Isaac Franklin	Kephart, George	Feb. 1, 1839	Balto.
Giles	Dennis	25	Seaman	Slatter, Shadrack	March 25, 1839	Balto.
Giles	George	20	Victorine	Woolfolk, Austin	Sept. 12, 1846	Balto.
Giles	Sarah Ann	20	Superb	Slatter, Hope Hull	Nov. 1, 1843	Balto.
Giles	William	25	Home	Donovan, Joseph S.	March 22, 1845	Balto.
Gilham	Elizabeth	21	Isaac Franklin	Kephart, George	Sept. 28, 1838	Balto.
Gillis	James	25	Kirkwood	Donovan, Joseph S.	Jan. 4, 1845	Balto.

Surname	First Name	Age	Ship	O/S	Date	Depart
Gilman	Maria	23	Isaac Franklin	Slatter, Hope Hull	Sept. 28, 1838	Balto.
Gilpin	Alexander	35	Hibernia	Woolfolk, Austin	Dec. 5, 1826	Balto.
Gily	James	23	Jasper	Woolfolk, Austin	Apr. 7, 1827	Balto.
Gipson	Alisa	21	Irad Ferry	Wilson, J.W.	May 6, 1839	Balto.
Gladden	Maria	20	Home	Hollins, George V.	March 19, 1845	Balto.
Glee	Daniel	23	E.H.Chapin	Slatter, Hope Hull	Nov. 30, 1847	Balto.
Glee	Henry	infant	E.H.Chapin	Slatter, Hope Hull	Nov. 30, 1847	Balto.
Glee	Louisa	20	E.H.Chapin	Slatter, Hope Hull	Nov. 30, 1847	Balto.
Gleeves	Adeline	7	Kirkwood	Donovan, Joseph S.	Jan. 4, 1845	Balto.
Gleeves	Ann	15	Kirkwood	Donovan, Joseph S.	Jan. 4, 1845	Balto.
Gleeves	Betsey	17	Kirkwood	Donovan, Joseph S.	Jan. 4, 1845	Balto.
Gleeves	Emey	8	Kirkwood	Donovan, Joseph S.	Jan. 4, 1845	Balto.
Gleeves	Henry	infant	Kirkwood	Donovan, Joseph S.	Jan. 4, 1845	Balto.
Gleeves	Marena	16	Kirkwood	Donovan, Joseph S.	Jan. 4, 1845	Balto.
Gleeves	Patty	18	Kirkwood	Donovan, Joseph S.	Jan. 4, 1845	Balto.
Gleeves	Thomas	20	Kirkwood	Donovan, Joseph S.	Jan. 4, 1845	Balto.
Glover	Anthony	23	Seaman	Slatter, Hope Hull	March 25, 1839	Balto.
Glover	Henry	22	Seaman	Slatter, Hope Hull	March 25, 1839	Balto.
Glover	Jenny	22	Seaman	Slatter, Hope Hull	March 25, 1839	Balto.
Glover	Judy	15	Seaman	Slatter, Hope Hull	March 25, 1839	Balto.
Glover	Mary	15	Ewarkee	Purvis, James Franklin	March 4, 1841	Balto.
Glover	Matilda	16	Seaman	Slatter, Hope Hull	March 25, 1839	Balto.
Glover	Ron	16	Seaman	Slatter, Hope Hull	March 25, 1839	Balto.
Godfry	Louisa	4	Jefferson	Woolfolk, Austin	Dec. 24, 1827	Balto.
Goff	Samuel	25	Eliza F.Mason	Donovan, Joseph S.	Nov. 13, 1851	Balto.
Goff	Sarah Ann	26	Salvadora	Slatter, Hope Hull	Sept. 28, 1846	Balto.

Surname	First Name	Age	Ship	O/S	Date	Depart
Gold	Frisby	17	Lady Monroe	Woolfolk, Austin	March 25, 1825	Balto.
Gold	Josiah	21	Superb	Donovan, Joseph S.	Nov. 2, 1843	Balto.
Golden	Asbury	17	Hibernia	Woolfolk, Austin	Dec. 5, 1826	Balto.
Golden	Ned	25	Pilgrim	Beal Ranndall	Dec. 4, 1837	Balto.
Goldsborough	Ann	11	Billow	Woolfolk, Joseph B.	Feb. 23, 1828	Balto.
Goldsborough	Daniel	18	Superb	Slatter, Hope Hull	Nov. 1, 1843	Balto.
Goldsborough	John	24	Union	Campbell, Bernard M.	Oct. 9, 1848	Balto.
Goldsborough	Kitty	18	Billow	Woolfolk, Joseph B.	Feb. 23, 1828	Balto.
Goldsborough		infant	Billow	Woolfolk, Joseph B.	Feb. 23, 1828	Balto.
Goldsbury	Lewis	16	Henry A. Barling	Campbell, Bernard M.	Feb. 24, 1851	Balto.
Gooby	Priscilla	18	Hibernia	Woolfolk, Austin	Dec. 5, 1826	Balto.
Good	Ann	8	States	Woolfolk, Austin	Apr. 14, 1828	Balto.
Goodhand	Arthur	8	Lafayette	Woolfolk, Austin	Oct. 18, 1828	Balto.
Goodhand	Author	21	Scotia	Slatter, Hope Hull	Sept. 30, 1843	Balto.
Gooding	Jim	14	Lady Monroe	Woolfolk, Austin	Sept. 29, 1825	Balto.
Goodins	Green	15	John C. Calhoun	Donovan, Joseph S.	Oct. 24, 1850	Balto.
Goodrick	Ellen	15	Union	Williams, Thomas	Oct. 9, 1848	Balto.
Goodridge	Charles	19	Union	Sheckles, Gannon	March 17, 1849	Balto.
Goodwin	Caleb	22	Hibernia	Woolfolk, Austin	Dec. 5, 1826	Balto.
Gordan	Emily Ann	15	Tippecanoe	Slatter, Hope Hull	Jan. 17, 1842	Balto.
Gordon	Charles	22	Kirkwood	Slatter, Hope Hull	Apr. 15, 1845	Balto.
Gordon	Clement	39	Victorine	Donovan, Joseph S.	May 22, 1844	Balto.
Gordon	Edward	9	Kirkwood	Slatter, Hope Hull	Dec. 23, 1843	Balto.
Gordon	Edward	25	Kirkwood	Donovan, Joseph S.	Jan. 4, 1845	Balto.
Gordon	Eliza	20	Solomon Saltus	Slatter, Hope Hull	Oct. 7, 1839	Balto.
Gordon	Fredrick	22	Union	Williams, Thomas	Oct. 9, 1848	Balto.

Surname	First Name	Age	Ship	O/S	Date	Depart
Gordon	George	16	Union	Rodbind, Ebenezer	Dec. 16, 1848	Balto.
Gordon	Henry	22	Union	Williams, Thomas	Oct. 9, 1848	Balto.
Gordon	Levy	9	Bostonian	Slatter, Hope Hull	Jan. 18, 1841	Balto.
Gordon	Louisa	14	Victorine	Rodbind, Ebenezer	March 1, 1845	Balto.
Gordon	Lucretia	16	Kirkwood	Donovan Joseph S.	Jan. 4, 1845	Balto.
Gordon	Martha	18	Jefferson	Woolfolk, Joseph B.	Dec. 24, 1827	Balto.
Gordon	Matilda	20	Victorine	Slatter, Hope Hull	Dec. 17, 1845	Balto.
Gordon	Mosses	23	Kirkwood	Donovan Joseph S.	Oct. 26, 1847	Balto.
Gordon	Rachel	26	Victorine	Williams, Thomas	Dec. 20, 1844	Balto.
Gordon	Thornton	26	Zoe	Williams, Thomas	Feb. 16, 1847	Balto.
Gordy	John	22	Pioneer	Stuart, William R.	July 20, 1848	Balto.
Gore	Daniel	20	Kirkwood	Donovan, Joseph S.	Sept. 28, 1846	Balto.
Gorman	David	21	Louisa	Campbell, Bernard M.	Nov. 5, 1849	Balto.
Gorsuch	Sophia	14	Margaret Forbs	Slatter, Hope Hull	Nov. 28, 1838	Balto.
Gouch	Presley	20	Southerner	Rodbind, Ebenezer	Jan. 21, 1850	Balto.
Gough	Joe	28	Mary	Woolfolk, Austin	Oct. 7, 1843	Balto.
Gough	Mariah	15	Sabine	Donovan, Joseph S.	Feb. 10, 1844	Balto.
Gough	Tracy	50	Mary	Woolfolk, Austin	Oct. 7, 1843	Balto.
Gould	Henry	11	Kirkwood	Campbell, Bernard M.	March 23, 1844	Balto.
Gould	Jacob	20	States	Woolfolk, Joseph B.	Nov. 21, 1827	Balto.
Gould	Martha	11	Salvadora	Slatter, Hope Hull	Sept. 28, 1846	Balto.
Gould	Samuel	22	Kirkwood	Slatter, Hope Hull	Jan. 14, 1846	Balto.
Gover	George	20	Kirkwood	Donovan, Joseph S.	Oct. 26, 1847	Balto.
Grace	Joseph	21	Intelligence	Woolfolk, Austin	Apr. 5, 1823	Balto.
Grace	Ned	25	Lapwing	Anderson, David	March 22, 1822	Balto.
Grace	Timison	16	Virginia	Woolfolk, Joseph B.	Dec. 19, 1825	Balto.

Surname	First Name	Age	Ship	O/S	Date	Depart
Gracy	Siah	8	Lafayette	Woolfolk, Richard	Oct. 18, 1828	Balto.
Grady	Mary J.	17	Victorine	Rodbind, Ebenezer	Dec. 31, 1846	Balto.
Grady	Robert	20	E.H.Chapin	Slatter, Hope Hull	Nov. 30, 1847	Balto.
Graham	Ellener	16	Kirkwood	Rodbind, Ebenezer	Oct. 26, 1847	Balto.
Graham	Henrietta	18	General Pinckney	Donovan, Joseph S.	Nov. 10, 1845	Balto.
Graham	James	28	Billow	Woolfolk, Austin	Feb. 23, 1828	Balto.
Graham	Jerry	33	Union	Williams, Thomas	Oct. 9, 1848	Balto.
Graham	John	19	General Pinckney	Slatter, Hope Hull	Nov. 10, 1845	Balto.
Graham	William	35	Kirkwood	Slatter, Hope Hull	Dec. 23, 1843	Balto.
Granam	Nancy	16	John C. Calhoun	Donovan, Joseph S.	Oct. 24, 1850	Balto.
Graner	Andrew	20	Henry Clay	Woolfolk, Austin	Dec. 4, 1828	Balto.
Granger	John	24	Scotia	Slatter, Hope Hull	Sept. 30, 1843	Balto.
Grant	Ellen	19	Kirkwood	Donovan, Joseph S.	Dec. 10, 1846	Balto.
Grantt	George	22	Kirkwood	Slatter, Hope Hull	Oct. 16, 1845	Balto.
Graves	Manuel	19	Kirkwood	Slatter, Hope Hull	Jan. 14, 1846	Balto.
Graves	Sarah	28	Victorine	Slatter, Hope Hull	Dec. 17, 1845	Balto.
Graves	Thomas	25	Narragansett	Forbes, George	Oct. 20, 1836	Town Creek
Gray	Albert	18	Narragansett	Donovan, Joseph S.	Nov. 27, 1850	Balto.
Gray	Anne	11	Topaz	Woolfolk, Austin	Apr. 20, 1829	Balto.
Gray	Augustus	25	Kirkwood	Campbell, Bernard M.	Nov. 28, 1849	Balto.
Gray	Ben	21	Architect	Frisby F. Chew	May 2, 1838	Balto.
Gray	Charles	13	Lady Monroe	Woolfolk, Austin	March 25, 1825	Balto.
Gray	Elisa	10	Lady Monroe	Woolfolk, Austin	March 25, 1825	Balto.
Gray	Emily	18	Kirkwood	Campbell, Bernard M.	Nov. 28, 1849	Balto.
Gray	Fanny	17	Helen A. Miller	Campbell, Bernard M.	Oct. 18, 1852	Balto.
Gray	Fanny	19	Union	Rodbind, Ebenezer	Dec. 16, 1848	Balto.

Surname	First Name	Age	Ship	O/S	Date	Depart
Gray	George	20	Paoli	Slatter, Hope Hull	Sept. 9, 1845	Balto.
Gray	Hariet	16	Kirkwood	Donovan, Joseph S.	Dec. 23, 1843	Balto.
Gray	Henry	24	Elizabeth	Campbell, Bernard M.	Nov. 18, 1848	Balto.
Gray	Henry	18	Jasper	Woolfolk, Austin	Apr. 7, 1827	Balto.
Gray	Henry	24	Paoli	Harker, William	Dec. 27, 1845	Balto.
Gray	Jacob	24	Kirkwood	Campbell, Bernard M.	March 23, 1844	Balto.
Gray	James	22	Victorine	Donovan, Joseph S.	Sept. 29, 1845	Balto.
Gray	Jane	2	Tweed	Tucker, I.B.	Oct. 20, 1836	Town Creek
Gray	John	38	Elizabeth	Donovan, Joseph S.	Jan. 2, 1850	Balto.
Gray	John	17	Margaret Hugg	Campbell, Bernard M.	Feb. 8, 1845	Balto.
Gray	John	30	Palestine	Slatter, Hope Hull	Nov. 16, 1835	Balto.
Gray	Juenta	6	Jasper	Woolfolk, Austin	Apr. 7, 1827	Balto.
Gray	Louisa	24	Paoli	Slatter, Hope Hull	Sept. 9, 1845	Balto.
Gray	Lucy	9	Lady Mcnroe	Woolfolk, Austin	March 25, 1825	Balto.
Gray	Mary	16	Union	Donovan, Joseph S.	Dec. 16, 1848	Balto.
Gray	Mary Letty	18	Colonel Howard	Harker, William	Nov. 21, 1844	Balto.
Gray	Milly	25	Jasper	Woolfolk, Austin	Apr. 7, 1827	Balto.
Gray	Perry	12 mon.	Jasper	Woolfolk, Austin	Apr. 7, 1827	Balto.
Gray	Rebeca	13	Northumberland	Slatter, Hope Hull	Feb. 27, 1843	Balto.
Gray	Richard	24	Southerner	Campbell, Bernard M.	Jan. 5, 1852	Balto.
Gray	Sam	20	Isaac Franklin	Kephart, George	Feb. 1, 1839	Balto.
Gray	Samuel	25	Kirkwood	Campbell, Bernard M.	Dec. 10, 1846	Balto.
Gray	Sandy	28	Brunswick	Woolfolk, Austin	Oct. 11, 1831	Balto.
Gray	Sarah	20	Kirkwood	Donovan, Joseph S.	Oct. 26, 1847	Balto.
Gray	Solomon	15	Zoe	Williams, Thomas	Feb. 16, 1847	Balto.
Grayson	Eliza	14	Isaac Franklin	Kephart, George	Sept. 28, 1838	Balto.

Surname	First Name	Age	Ship	O/S	Date	Depart
Green	Abraham	26	Tippecanoe	Purvis, James Franklin	Jan. 17, 1842	Balto.
Green	Ann	10	Jefferson	Woolfolk, Austin	Dec. 24, 1827	Balto.
Green	Benjamin	23	Kirkwood	Donovan, Joseph S.	Sept. 28, 1846	Balto.
Green	Betsey	45	Southerner	Campbell, Bernard M.	Jan. 5, 1852	Balto.
Green	Caroline	21	Kirkwood	Slatter, Hope Hull	Oct. 16, 1845	Balto.
Green	Charles	14	Elizabeth	Donovan, Joseph S.	March 21, 1850	Balto.
Green	Charles	17	Phoenix	Rodbind, Ebenezer	March 27, 1847	Balto.
Green	Charlotte	14	Hope & Hannah	Woolfolk, Austin	March 11, 1829	Balto.
Green	Charlotte	17	Margaret Hugg	Donovan, Joseph S.	Feb. 8, 1845	Balto.
Green	Cloe	42	Tweed	Forbes, George	Oct. 20, 1836	Town Creek
Green	David	18	Kirkwood	Donovan, Joseph S.	Sept. 28, 1846	Balto.
Green	Eliza	14	General Pinckney	Williams, Thomas	Jan. 19, 1847	Balto.
Green	Elizabeth	18	Union	Campbell, Bernard M.	Apr. 20, 1850	Balto.
Green	Elizebeth	15	Kirkwood	Slatter, Hope Hull	Apr. 15, 1845	Balto.
Green	Ellen	16	Victorine	Slatter, Hope Hull	Dec. 17, 1845	Balto.
Green	Ellen	25	Victorine	Slatter, Hope Hull	Sept. 12, 1846	Balto.
Green	Francis	16	Seaman	Slatter, Shadrack	March 25, 1839	Balto.
Green	Granderson	12	General Pinckney	Williams, Thomas	Jan. 19, 1847	Balto.
Green	Hamilton	16	Victorine	Williams, Thomas	Dec. 20, 1844	Balto.
Green	Harriett	infant	Kirkwood	Slatter, Hope Hull	Oct. 16, 1845	Balto.
Green	Harriett	17	Pioneer	Slatter, Hope Hull	Sept. 15, 1847	Balto.
Green	Henrietta	16	Margaret Hugg	Donovan, Joseph S.	Feb. 8, 1845	Balto.
Green	Jackson	2 mon.	Arctic	Woolfolk, Austin	Jan. 24, 1829	Balto.
Green	James	12	Hibernia	Woolfolk, Austin	Dec. 5, 1826	Balto.
Green	Jefferson	36	Burlington	Slatter, Hope Hull	Oct. 21, 1842	Balto.
Green	Jelsin	20	Irad Ferry	Slatter, Hope Hull	Dec. 9, 1842	Balto.

Surname	First Name	Age	Ship	O/S	Date	Depart
Green	Jerry	30	Helen A. Miller	Campbell, Bernard M.	Oct. 18, 1852	Balto.
Green	Jesse	2 mon.	Arctic	Woolfolk, Austin	Jan. 24, 1829	Balto.
Green	John	40	Henry A. Barling	Marriott, William H.	Oct. 28, 1848	Balto.
Green	John	17	Mary	Short, Hugh	Feb. 9, 1844	Balto.
Green	John	19	States	Woolfolk, Austin	Nov. 21, 1827	Balto.
Green	Joseph	17	Union	Campbell, Bernard M.	Apr. 20, 1850	Balto.
Green	Kelly	9	States	Woolfolk, Austin	Apr. 14, 1828	Balto.
Green	Kitty	17	Victorine	Rodbind, Ebenezer	March 1, 1845	Balto.
Green	Leonard	26	Nancy W. Stevens	Harker, James	Oct. 25, 1843	Balto.
Green	Lewis	23	Kirkwood	Rodbind, Ebenezer	Oct. 26, 1847	Balto.
Green	Lydia	38	Uncas	Slatter, Hope Hull	Apr. 3, 1838	Balto.
Green	Maria	14	General Pinckney	Slatter, Hope Hull	Nov. 10, 1845	Balto.
Green	Maria	26	Victorine	Slatter, Hope Hull	March 14, 1846	Balto.
Green	Martha	infant	Victorine	Rodbind, Ebenezer	March 1, 1845	Balto.
Green	Mary	20	General Pinckney	Slatter, Hope Hull	Nov. 10, 1845	Balto.
Green	Mary	16	States	Woolfolk, Austin	Nov. 21, 1827	Balto.
Green	Mary Ann	19	Kirkwood	Slatter, Hope Hull	Oct. 16, 1845	Balto.
Green	Moses	12	Hibernia	Woolfolk, Austin	Dec. 5, 1826	Balto.
Green	Owen	19	Victorine	Slatter, Hope Hull	Sept. 12, 1846	Balto.
Green	Patrick	22	Irad Ferry	Clendenin, A.	Jan. 16, 1840	Balto.
Green	Paula	infant	Victorine	Donovan, Joseph S.	May 14, 1845	Balto.
Green	Philip	21	Uncas	Slatter, Hope Hull	Jan. 10, 1838	Balto.
Green	Rachel	2 mon.	Arctic	Woolfolk, Austin	Jan. 24, 1829	Balto.
Green	Richard	20	Margaret Hugg	Campbell, Bernard M.	Nov. 30, 1844	Balto.
Green	Sally	22	Arctic	Woolfolk, Austin	Jan. 24, 1829	Balto.
Green	Samuel	20	John C. Calhoun	Donovan, Joseph S.	Oct. 24, 1850	Balto.

Surname	First Name	Age	Ship	O/S	Date	Depart
Green	Sarah	16	Victorine	Donovan, Joseph S.	May 14, 1845	Balto.
Green	Sarah Ann	17	Superb	Slatter, Hope Hull	Nov. 1, 1843	Balto.
Green	Susan	20	Catharine	Donovan, Joseph S.	Jan. 18, 1845	Balto.
Green	Susan	20	Kirkwood	Rodbind, Ebenezer	Apr. 15, 1845	Balto.
Green	Vass	20	Mary	Purvis, James Franklin	Feb. 8, 1841	Balto.
Green	Viney	19	General Pinckney	Slatter, Hope Hull	Jan. 19, 1847	Balto.
Green	Warner	21	Julia	Woolfolk, Austin	Jan. 8, 1829	Balto.
Green	Wesley	21	Kirkwood	Donovan, Joseph S.	Dec. 10, 1846	Balto.
Green	William	15	Superb	Slatter, Hope Hull	Nov. 1, 1843	Balto.
Greene	Charles	22	General Pinckney	Campbell, Bernard M.	Jan. 19, 1847	Balto.
Greene	Ruth Ellen	14	Solomon Saltus	Slatter, Hope Hull	Oct. 7, 1839	Balto.
Greenfield	Aaron	24	Kirkwood	Donovan, Joseph S.	Apr. 15, 1845	Balto.
Greenfield	Charles	21	Hermitage	Donovan, Joseph S.	Oct. 28, 1846	Balto.
Greenfield	Ellen	16	Scotia	Slatter, Hope Hull	Sept. 30, 1843	Balto.
Greenfield	Jake	4	Tweed	Sothoron, William H.	Oct. 20, 1836	Town Creek
Greenfield	Matilda	40	Tweed	Sothoron, William H.	Oct. 20, 1836	Town Creek
Greenfield	Ritter	9	Tweed	Sothoron, William H.	Oct. 20, 1836	Town Creek
Greenfield	Samuel	19	Hermitage	Donovan, Joseph S.	Oct. 28, 1846	Balto.
Greenfield	Walter	18	Union	Rodbind, Ebenezer	Nov. 17, 1849	Balto.
Greenleaf	William	25	Kirkwood	Donovan, Joseph S.	Oct. 26, 1847	Balto.
Greenwood	John	3	Kirkwood	Donovan, Joseph S.	Jan. 4, 1845	Balto.
Greenwood	Mable	22	Kirkwood	Donovan, Joseph S.	Jan. 4, 1845	Balto.
Greenwood	Mary	24	Kirkwood	Donovan, Joseph S.	Jan. 4, 1845	Balto.
Greenwood	Rachel	infant	Kirkwood	Donovan, Joseph S.	Jan. 4, 1845	Balto.
Grey	David	18	Southerner	Donovan, Joseph S.	Oct. 27, 1849	Balto.
Grice	Moses	26	Lapwing	Woolfolk, Joseph B.	Feb. 15, 1827	Balto.

Surname	First Name	Age	Ship	O/S	Date	Depart
Gross	Henry	20	Helen A. Miller	Campbell, Bernard M.	Oct. 18, 1852	Balto.
Gross	Isaac	6	Arctic	Woolfolk, Austin	May 15, 1828	Balto.
Gross	Jacob	19	Pioneer	Slatter, Hope Hull	Sept. 15, 1847	Balto.
Gross	James	17	Kirkwood	Donovan, Joseph S.	Oct. 26, 1847	Balto.
Gross	John	19	Architect	Donovan, Joseph S.	Apr. 25, 1846	Balto.
Gross	John	infant	Salvadora	Slatter, Hope Hull	Sept. 28, 1846	Balto.
Gross	Judy	40	Arctic	Woolfolk, Austin	May 15, 1828	Balto.
Gross	Juliann	17	Billow	Woolfolk, Joseph B.	Feb. 23, 1828	Balto.
Gross	July?	38	Kirkwood	Slatter, Hope Hull	Apr. 15, 1845	Balto.
Gross	Kitty	24	Salvadora	Slatter, Hope Hull	Sept. 28, 1846	Balto.
Gross	Levi	22	Kirkwood	Donovan, Joseph S.	March 9, 1847	Balto.
Gross	Margrett	4	Kirkwood	Slatter, Hope Hull	Apr. 15, 1845	Balto.
Gross	Mary	14	Victorine	Rodbind, Ebenezer	Dec. 31, 1846	Balto.
Gross	Nace	22	Eliza F.Mason	Donovan, Joseph S.	Nov. 13, 1851	Balto.
Gross	Perry	18	Elizabeth	Donovan, Joseph S.	Nov. 18, 1848	Balto.
Gross	Perry	23	Union	Donovan, Joseph S.	May 13, 1848	Balto.
Gross	Peter	20	Phoenix	Rodbind, Ebenezer	March 27, 1847	Balto.
Gross	Richard	19	Victorine	Rodbind, Ebenezer	Dec. 31, 1846	Balto.
Gross	Samuel	7	Elizabeth	Campbell, Bernard M.	Nov. 18, 1848	Balto.
Gross	Sarah	18	Helen A. Miller	Campbell, Bernard M.	Oct. 18, 1852	Balto.
Gross	Thomas	35	Victorine	Donovan, Joseph S.	May 14, 1845	Balto.
Gross	Tom	14	Arctic	Woolfolk, Austin	May 15, 1828	Balto.
Gross	Tower	19	Arctic	Woolfolk, Austin	May 15, 1828	Balto.
Gross	William	8	Arctic	Woolfolk, Austin	May 15, 1828	Balto.
Gross	William	40	Kirkwood	Donovan, Joseph S.	Oct. 26, 1847	Balto.
Gross	William	21	Victorine	Slatter, Hope Hull	Dec. 17, 1845	Balto.

Surname	First Name	Age	Ship	O/S	Date	Depart
Gross		20	Kirkwood	Donovan, Joseph S.	Oct. 26, 1847	Balto.
Gunby	Noah	23	Kirkwood	Donovan, Joseph S.	Oct. 26, 1847	Balto.
Gustin	John	20	Seaman	Slatter, Shadrack	March 25, 1839	Balto.
Gustis	Rachel	24	Billow	Woolfolk, Joseph B.	Feb. 23, 1828	Balto.
Gustus	Daniel	22	Solomon Saltus	Harker, William	March 18, 1842	Balto.
Gustus	Jacob	34	Lafayette	Woolfolk, Austin	Oct. 18, 1828	Balto.
Gustus	Rachel	20	Lafayette	Woolfolk, Richard	Oct. 18, 1828	Balto.
Guthridge	William	14	General Pinckney	Donovan, Joseph S.	Feb. 21, 1846	Balto.
Gutridge	John	24	Elizabeth	Donovan, Joseph S.	Nov. 18, 1848	Balto.
Guy	Ann	19	Henry Clay	Woolfolk, Austin	Dec. 4, 1828	Balto.
Guy	George	infant	Henry Clay	Woolfolk, Austin	Dec. 4, 1828	Balto.
Guy	Roxana	4	Henry Clay	Woolfolk, Austin	Dec. 4, 1828	Balto.
Guyton	Emaline	15	Architect	Slatter, Hope Hull	Feb. 16, 1843	Balto.
Gwin	Mary	20	Uncas	Slatter, Hope Hull	Jan. 10, 1838	Balto.
Hachet	William	25	States	Woolfolk, Austin	Nov. 26, 1825	Balto.
Hacket	Kitty	17	Lafayette	Woolfolk, Austin	Oct. 18, 1828	Balto.
Hacket	Margaret	9 mon.	Lafayette	Woolfolk, Austin	Oct. 18, 1828	Balto.
Hacket	Melvin	9	States	Woolfolk, Austin	Apr. 14, 1828	Balto.
Hackett	Harriett	18	Paoli	Slatter, Hope Hull	Sept. 9, 1845	Balto.
Hackett	Henny	24	Intelligence	King, Gideon T.	Sept. 18, 1821	Balto.
Hackett	Sarah	20	Kirkwood	Campbell, Bernard M.	March 23, 1844	Balto.
Hackot	Perry	20	Harriett	Woolfolk, Austin	March 23, 1822	Balto.
Hadkim	Jones	19	Julia	Woolfolk, Austin	Jan. 8, 1829	Balto.
Hagan	Corrick	18	Victorine	Donovan, Joseph S.	May 14, 1845	Balto.
Hagan	Fillis	infant	Victorine	Donovan, Joseph S.	May 14, 1845	Balto.
Hail	Charlotte	infant	Burlington	Slatter, Hope Hull	Oct. 21, 1842	Balto.

Surname	First Name	Age	Ship	O/S	Date	Depart
Hail	Lindy	17	Burlington	Slatter, Hope Hull	Oct. 21, 1842	Balto.
Haley	Caroline	6	Victorine	Slatter, Hope Hull	Dec. 17, 1845	Balto.
Haley	Celia	28	Victorine	Slatter, Hope Hull	Dec. 17, 1845	Balto.
Haley	Ellen	11	Victorine	Slatter, Hope Hull	Dec. 17, 1845	Balto.
Haley	John	3	Victorine	Slatter, Hope Hull	Dec. 17, 1845	Balto.
Haley	Julia	13	Victorine	Slatter, Hope Hull	Dec. 17, 1845	Balto.
Haley	Julianna	18	Kirkwood	Slatter, Hope Hull	Apr. 4, 1846	Balto.
Haley	Larry	38	Victorine	Slatter, Hope Hull	Dec. 17, 1845	Balto.
Haley	Lewis	6	Victorine	Slatter, Hope Hull	Dec. 17, 1845	Balto.
Haley	Manuel	9	Victorine	Slatter, Hope Hull	Dec. 17, 1845	Balto.
Haley	Marcilina	13	Victorine	Slatter, Hope Hull	Dec. 17, 1845	Balto.
Haley	Martha	infant	Victorine	Slatter, Hope Hull	Dec. 17, 1845	Balto.
Haley	Mary	infant	Victorine	Slatter, Hope Hull	Dec. 17, 1845	Balto.
Haley	Mary	5	Victorine	Slatter, Hope Hull	Dec. 17, 1845	Balto.
Haley	Nace	34	Victorine	Slatter, Hope Hull	Dec. 17, 1845	Balto.
Haley	Sarah	38	Victorine	Slatter, Hope Hull	Dec. 17, 1845	Balto.
Haley	Virginia	9	Victorine	Slatter, Hope Hull	Dec. 17, 1845	Balto.
Hall	Abraham	24	Eliza F.Mason	Donovan, Joseph S.	Nov. 13, 1851	Balto.
Hall	Adeline	17	Irad Ferry	Wilson, J.W. .	May 6, 1839	Balto.
Hall	Ann	20	Hibernia	Woolfolk, Austin	Dec. 5, 1826	Balto.
Hall	Ann	24	Kirkwood	Slatter, Hope Hull	Oct. 16, 1845	Balto.
Hall	Ben	20	Lady Monroe	Woolfolk, Austin	Sept. 29, 1825	Balto.
Hall	Caroline	17	Isaac Franklin	Kephart, George	Feb. 1, 1839	Balto.
Hall	Catherin	22	Home	Slatter, Hope Hull	March 22, 1845	Balto.
Hall	Charity	16	Victorine	Williams, Thomas	Dec. 20, 1844	Balto.
Hall	Charles	25	Pharsalia	Henderson, G.R.	Jan. 6, 1855	Balto.

Surname	First Name	Age	Ship	O/S	Date	Depart
Hall	Columbus	16	Isaac Franklin	Kephart, George	Feb. 1, 1839	Balto.
Hall	Cornelius	23	Ann & Leah	Woolfolk, Austin	Nov.1, 1831	Balto.
Hall	Duke	22	Leda	Donovan, Joseph S.	May 30, 1846	Balto.
Hall	Elias	25	Peru	Slatter, Hope Hull	Nov. 16, 1842	Balto.
Hall	Elisa	15	Russell	Slatter, Hope Hull	March 1, 1839	Balto.
Hall	Eliza	16	Kirkwood	Slatter, Hope Hull	Dec. 23, 1843	Balto.
Hall	Eliza	20	Union	Slatter, Hope Hull	July 26, 1847	Balto.
Hall	Gassaway	23	Charles	Donovan, Joseph S.	Apr. 23, 1851	Balto.
Hall	George	27	Kirkwood	Slatter, Hope Hull	Apr. 15, 1845	Balto.
Hall	George	17	States	Woolfolk, Austin	Nov. 21, 1827	Balto.
Hall	George	21	Victorine	Slatter, Henry F.	Dec. 31, 1846	Balto.
Hall	George Lewis	22	Victorine	Slatter, Henry F.	Dec. 31, 1846	Balto.
Hall	Harriet	16	Ewarkee	Purvis, James Franklin	March 4, 1841	Balto.
Hall	Harriett Ann	14	Scotia	Slatter, Hope Hull	Sept. 30, 1843	Balto.
Hall	Harry	32	Lafayette	Woolfolk, Austin	Oct. 18, 1828	Balto.
Hall	Henrietta	16	Victorine	Slatter, Henry F.	Dec. 31, 1846	Balto.
Hall	Henry	38	Kirkwood	Donovan, Joseph S.	Dec. 10, 1846	Balto.
Hall	Henry	15	Kirkwood	Donovan, Joseph S.	Dec. 23, 1843	Balto.
Hall	Henry	18	Phoenix	Slatter, Hope Hull	March 27, 1847	Balto.
Hall	Henry	20	Tippecanoe	Slatter, Hope Hull	Apr. 1, 1841	Balto.
Hall	Horace	30	Elizabeth	Donovan, Joseph S.	Jan. 2, 1850	Balto.
Hall	Isaac	25	Lawrence	Woolfolk, Austin	May 9, 1823	Balto.
Hall	Isaac	17	Victorine	Slatter, Henry F.	May 14, 1845	Balto.
Hall	James	25	Superb	Anderson, David	Apr. 6, 1819	Balto.
Hall	James	20	Victorine	Slatter, Henry F.	Dec. 31, 1846	Balto.
Hall	Jane	30	Kirkwood	Slatter, Hope Hull	Dec. 23, 1843	Balto.

Surname	First Name	Age	Ship	O/S	Date	Depart
Hall	Jerri	14	Waverly	Weems, Martha	Apr. 3, 1851	Balto.
Hall	Jesse	24	Scotia	Slatter, Hope Hull	Sept. 30, 1843	Balto.
Hall	John	20	Salvadora	Slatter, Hope Hull	Sept. 28, 1846	Balto.
Hall	John	4 mon.	Victorine	Williams, Thomas	Dec. 20, 1844	Balto.
Hall	July Ann	18	Victorine	Slatter, Hope Hull	March 1, 1845	Balto.
Hall	Kitty	48	Victorine	Williams, Thomas	Dec. 20, 1844	Balto.
Hall	Leathy	19	Victorine	Donovan, Joseph S.	May 22, 1844	Balto.
Hall	Letty	18	Zoe	Slatter, Hope Hull	Feb. 16, 1847	Balto.
Hall	Loyd	19	States	Woolfolk, Austin	Nov. 21, 1827	Balto.
Hall	Maria	19	Delawarian	Campbell, Bernard M.	Dec. 1, 1848	Balto.
Hall	Mary	7	Kirkwood	Slatter, Hope Hull	Oct. 16, 1845	Balto.
Hall	Mary Jane	2	Kirkwood	Slatter, Hope Hull	Dec. 23, 1843	Balto.
Hall	Milly	19	Victorine	Williams, Thomas	Dec. 20, 1844	Balto.
Hall	Morris	23	Home	Donovan, Joseph S.	March 22, 1845	Balto.
Hall	Polly	13	Kirkwood	Donovan, Joseph S.	March 9, 1847	Balto.
Hall	Rachel	21	Jefferson	Woolfolk, Austin	Dec. 24, 1827	Balto.
Hall	Rebecca	17	Southerner	Donovan, Jospeh S.	Jan. 5, 1852	Balto.
Hall	Richard	17	Union	Sheckles, Gannon	March 17, 1849	Balto.
Hall	Sally	11	Victorine	Williams, Thomas	Dec. 20, 1844	Balto.
Hall	Sam	29	Gulnare	Kelso, George G.	Nov. 3, 1830	Balto.
Hall	Susan	infant	Kirkwood	Slatter, Hope Hull	Oct. 16, 1845	Balto.
Hall	Sylvester	45	Victorine	Williams, Thomas	Dec. 20, 1844	Balto.
Hall	Thomas	19	Isaac Franklin	Kephart, George	Feb. 1, 1839	Balto.
Hall	Washington	22	Peru	Slatter, Hope Hull	Nov. 16, 1842	Balto.
Hall	William	24	Elizabeth	Campbell, Bernard M.	Jan. 2, 1850	Balto.
Hall	William	17	Hermitage	Donovan, Joseph S.	Oct. 28, 1846	Balto.

Surname	First Name	Age	Ship	O/S	Date	Depart
Hall	William	4	Kirkwood	Slatter, Hope Hull	Dec. 23, 1843	Balto.
Hall	William	18	Salvadora	Slatter, Hope Hull	Sept. 28, 1846	Balto.
Haller	Clarecy	26	Ewarkee	Slatter, Hope Hull	March 4, 1841	Balto.
Haller	Randolph	infant	Ewarkee	Slatter, Hope Hull	March 4, 1841	Balto.
Hallinswadt	Jacob	17	Kirkwood	Donovan, Joseph S.	Oct. 26, 1847	Balto.
Hallot	Rachel	15	Lafayette	Woolfolk, Richard	Oct. 18, 1828	Balto.
Haloday	William	55	Architect	Crow, William	Feb. 3, 1841	Balto.
Haman	Amey	29	Henry Clay	Woolfolk, Austin	Dec. 4, 1828	Balto.
Haman	Ball	18 mon.	Henry Clay	Woolfolk, Austin	Dec. 4, 1828	Balto.
Haman	Hetty	7	Henry Clay	Woolfolk, Austin	Dec. 4, 1828	Balto.
Haman	John	4	Henry Clay	Woolfolk, Austin	Dec. 4, 1828	Balto.
Hambleton	Eli	12	Kirkwood	Slatter, Hope Hull	Dec. 23, 1843	Balto.
Hambleton	Frisby	30	Palestine	Slatter, Hope Hull	Nov. 16, 1835	Balto.
Hambleton	Matilda	16	Victorine	Slatter, Hope Hull	March 1, 1845	Balto.
Hamblin	Ned	25	General Pinckney	Slatter, Hope Hull	Jan. 19, 1847	Balto.
Hamilton	Alexander	35	Isaac Franklin	Slatter, Hope Hull	Sept. 28, 1838	Balto.
Hamilton	Caroline	13	Victorine	Donovan, Joseph S.	March 1, 1845	Balto.
Hamilton	Daniel	17	Zoe	Slatter, Hope Hull	Feb. 16, 1847	Balto.
Hamilton	George	21	Kirkwood	Rodbind, Ebenezer	Apr. 15, 1845	Balto.
Hamilton	John	28	Louisa	Campbell, Bernard M.	Nov. 5, 1849	Balto.
Hammond	Anne	22	Union	Sheckles, B.O.	Nov. 17, 1849	Balto.
Hammond	Charles	infant	P. Soule	Elder, Joseph E.	Oct. 10, 1845	Balto.
Hammond	Dick	9	Lapwing	Woolfolk, Austin	Feb. 15, 1827	Balto.
Hammond	Ellenora	14	Home	Slatter, Hope Hull	March 22, 1845	Balto.
Hammond	Isaac	26	Billow	Woolfolk, Austin	Feb. 23, 1828	Balto.
Hammond	Jacob	20	Lafayette	Woolfolk, Austin	Oct. 18, 1828	Balto.

Surname	First Name	Age	Ship	O/S	Date	Depart
Hammond	Jerry	22	Kirkwood	Donovan, Joseph S.	Oct. 26, 1847	Balto.
Hammond	Julian	16	Southerner	Donovan, Joseph S.	Oct. 27, 1849	Balto.
Hammond	Margaret	25	States	Woolfolk, Austin	Nov. 21, 1827	Balto.
Hammond	Maria		Victorine	Donovan, Joseph S.	Sept. 29, 1845	Balto.
Hammond	R.		Jefferson	Woolfolk, Austin	Dec. 24, 1827	Balto.
Hammond	Rachel	9	Ann & Leah	Woolfolk, Austin	Nov.1, 1831	Balto.
Hammond	Rachel	30	P. Soule	Elder, Joseph E.	Oct. 10, 1845	Balto.
Hammond	Richard	20	Union	Sheckles, B.O.	Nov. 17, 1849	Balto.
Hammond	Samuel	3	P. Soule	Elder, Joseph E.	Oct. 10, 1845	Balto.
Hammond	Sarah	32	Kirkwood	Slatter, Hope Hull	Jan. 4, 1845	Balto.
Hammond	Susannah	5	P. Soule	Elder, Joseph E.	Oct. 10, 1845	Balto.
Hammond	Vachel	40	P. Soule	Elder, Joseph E.	Oct. 10, 1845	Balto.
Hanay	Aleck	22	Kirkwood	Campbell, Bernard M.	Oct. 14, 1848	Balto.
Hancock	Tom	9	Lafayette	Woolfolk, Austin	Oct. 18, 1828	Balto.
Hancy	Robert	22	Isaac Franklin	Kephart, George	Feb. 1, 1839	Balto.
Handy	Benjamin	20	Jefferson	Woolfolk, Joseph B.	Dec. 24, 1827	Balto.
Handy	Eliza	20	Kirkwood	Slatter, Hope Hull	Jan. 14, 1846	Balto.
Handy	George	22	Kirkwood	Donovan, Joseph S.	Nov. 28, 1849	Balto.
Handy	Harriet	17	Topaz	Woolfolk, Austin	Apr. 20, 1829	Balto.
Handy	Hetty	17	Seaman	Handy, L.D.	Nov. 26, 1839	Balto.
Handy	John	17	Kirkwood	Donovan, Joseph S.	Sept. 28, 1846	Balto.
Handy	Josiah	40	Kirkwood	Campbell, Bernard M.	Nov. 28, 1849	Balto.
Handy	Macorial	18	Kirkwood	Donovan, Joseph S.	Nov. 28, 1849	Balto.
Handy	Perry	22	Elizabeth	Donovan, Joseph S.	Jan. 2, 1850	Balto.
Handy	Robert	28	Pioneer	Slatter, Hope Hull	Sept. 15, 1847	Balto.
Handy	Thomas	14	Kirkwood	Donovan, Joseph S.	Oct. 26, 1847	Balto.

Surname	First Name	Age	Ship	O/S	Date	Depart
Handy	Thomas	18	Kirkwood	Donovan, Joseph S.	Sept. 28, 1846	Balto.
Hanes	Elizabeth	20	Hermitage	Slatter, Hope Hull	Oct. 28, 1846	Balto.
Hanis	Charles	35	Nancy W. Stevens	Rodbind, Ebenezer	Feb. 18, 1845	Balto.
Hankins	Isaac	19	Ganniclefft	Slatter, Hope Hull	Nov. 25, 1840	Balto.
Hanson	Elisa	16	Catharine	Woolfolk, Austin	March 3. 1829	Balto.
Hanson	Eliza	24	Kirkwood	Campbell, Bernard M.	Oct. 14, 1848	Balto.
Hanson	Jane	17	Glasgow	Slatter, Hope Hull	Oct. 11, 1838	Balto.
Hanson	John	17	Kirkwood	Slatter, Henry F.	Dec. 10, 1846	Balto.
Hanson	John	30	Louisa	Campbell, Bernard M.	March 31, 1849	Balto.
Hanson	Mary	18	Henry A. Barling	Campbell, Bernard M.	Dec. 18, 1851	Balto.
Hanson	Perry	21	Kirkwood	Donovan, Joseph S.	Oct. 14, 1848	Balto.
Hanson	William	21	Scotia	Slatter, Hope Hull	Sept. 30, 1843	Balto.
Hanson	infant		Henry A. Barling	Campbell, Bernard M.	Dec. 18, 1851	Balto.
Hanson	infant		Kirkwood	Campbell, Bernard M.	Oct. 14, 1848	Balto.
Hardcastle	George	21	John C. Calhoun	Donovan, Joseph S.	Oct. 24, 1850	Balto.
Hardcastle	William	15	Billow	Woolfolk, Joseph B.	Feb. 23, 1828	Balto.
Hardcastle	William	23	States	Woolfolk, Austin	Nov. 21, 1827	Balto.
Harden	Jane	13	Topaz	Woolfolk, Austin	Apr. 20, 1829	Balto.
Harden	Jarratt	11	Jefferson	Woolfolk, Austin	Dec. 24, 1827	Balto.
Harden	Joshua	19	States	Woolfolk, Austin	Nov. 21, 1827	Balto.
Harden	Nickolas	28	Victorine	Slatter, Hope Hull	May 14, 1845	Balto.
Hardgrave	John	27	Kirkwood	Donovan, Joseph S.	Oct. 26, 1847	Balto.
Hardin	John	20	Zoe	Campbell, Bernard M.	Feb. 16, 1847	Balto.
Hardy	Alfred	23	Union	Donovan, Joseph S.	Dec. 16, 1848	Balto.
Hardy	Catharine	16	Kirkwood	Donovan, Joseph S.	Oct. 26, 1847	Balto.
Hardy	Henry	22	Eliza F.Mason	Donovan, Joseph S.	Nov. 13, 1851	Balto.

Surname	First Name	Age	Ship	O/S	Date	Depart
Hare	Charles	33	Missouri	Gilmore, John	March 1, 1819	Balto.
Harker	Benjamin	18	Lady Monroe	Woolfolk, Austin	March 25, 1825	Balto.
Harker	Mary	14	Victorine	Slatter, Hope Hull	March 1, 1845	Balto.
Harmon	George	17	Union	Donovan, Joseph S.	Dec. 16, 1848	Balto.
Harmon	Samuel	31	Lafayette	Woolfolk, Austin	Oct. 18, 1828	Balto.
Harness	Abraam	15	Edward Everett	Campbell, Bernard M.	March 10, 1851	Balto.
Harness	Adam	18	Edward Everett	Campbell, Bernard M.	March 10, 1851	Balto.
Harness	Esau	15	Edward Everett	Campbell, Bernard M.	March 10, 1851	Balto.
Harness	Peggy	18	Edward Everett	Campbell, Bernard M.	March 10, 1851	Balto.
Harper	Dennis	16	Osprey	Rodbind, Ebenezer	Nov. 11, 1847	Balto.
Harper	Henry	17	Kirkwood	Donovan, Joseph S.	Sept. 28, 1846	Balto.
Harper	Joseph	18	Paoli	Slatter, Hope Hull	Sept. 9, 1845	Balto.
Harper	Mary Jane	15	Home	Rodbind, Ebenezer	March 22, 1845	Balto.
Harriday	Nace	24	Splendid	Slatter, Hope Hull	Apr. 24, 1841	Balto.
Harriett	Ellen	6	Kirkwood	Slatter, Hope Hull	Oct. 16, 1845	Balto.
Harriett	Maria	18	Victorine	Donovan, Joseph S.	Sept. 29, 1845	Balto.
Harris	Adaline	17	Victorine	Donovan, Joseph S.	Sept. 29, 1845	Balto.
Harris	Adam	11	Topaz	Woolfolk, Austin	Apr. 20, 1829	Balto.
Harris	Anderson	17	Isaac Franklin	Kephart, George	Sept. 28, 1838	Balto.
Harris	Ann		Louisa	Donovan, Joseph S.	Oct. 9, 1847	Balto.
Harris	Ann Maria	28	Tweed	Sothoron, William H.	Oct. 20, 1836	Town Creek
Harris	Arimintia	32	Catharine	Slatter, Hope Hull	Jan. 24, 1843	Balto.
Harris	Caroline	16	Victorine	Donovan, Joseph S.	March 1, 1845	Balto.
Harris	Celia	19	Kirkwood	Campbell, Bernard M.	Oct. 14, 1848	Balto.
Harris	Charles	42	Elizabeth	Donovan, Joseph S.	Jan. 2, 1850	Balto.
Harris	Charles	30	Isaac Franklin	Kephart, George	Feb. 1, 1839	Balto.

Surname	First Name	Age	Ship	O/S	Date	Depart
Harris	Charles		Louisa	Donovan, Joseph S.	Oct. 9, 1847	Balto.
Harris	Cornelia	11	Isaac Franklin	Kephart, George	Sept. 28, 1838	Balto.
Harris	Dionna	25	Victorine	Donovan, Joseph S.	Sept. 29, 1845	Balto.
Harris	Dolly	40	Tippecanoe	Gray, A.	Jan. 15, 1842	Balto.
Harris	Elisha	18	Jefferson	Woolfolk, Austin	Dec. 24, 1827	Balto.
Harris	Elizabeth	10	Victorine	Donovan, Joseph S.	Dec. 31, 1846	Balto.
Harris	Emanuel	17	Kirkwood	Campbell, Bernard M.	Oct. 14, 1848	Balto.
Harris	Emma	16	Kirkwood	Slatter, Hope Hull	Oct. 16, 1845	Balto.
Harris	Ephraim	22	Lady Monroe	Woolfolk, Austin	March 25, 1825	Balto.
Harris	George	19	Isaac Franklin	Kephart, George	Sept. 28, 1838	Balto.
Harris	Georgie	43	Isaac Franklin	Kephart, George	Sept. 28, 1838	Balto.
Harris	Hannah	20	Narragansett	Donovan, Joseph S.	Nov. 27, 1850	Balto.
Harris	Harriet	17	General Pinckney	Campbell, Bernard M.	Jan. 19, 1847	Balto.
Harris	Harry	20	General Pinckney	Rodbind, Ebenezer	Feb. 21, 1846	Balto.
Harris	Henny	16	Clio	Anderson, David	March 20, 1819	Balto.
Harris	Henry	30	E.H.Chapin	Slatter, Hope Hull	Nov. 30, 1847	Balto.
Harris	Henry	25	Tippecanoe	Harker, William	Apr. 15, 1844	Balto.
Harris	Hester Ann	19	Scotia	Slatter, Hope Hull	Sept. 30, 1843	Balto.
Harris	Isabella	18	Solomon Saltus	Slatter, Hope Hull	Oct. 7, 1839	Balto.
Harris	James	22	Solomon Saltus	Slatter, Hope Hull	Oct. 7, 1839	Balto.
Harris	James	20	Victorine	Slatter, Hope Hull	Sept. 12, 1846	Balto.
Harris	Jim	20	Hibernia	Woolfolk, Austin	Dec. 5, 1826	Balto.
Harris	Jim	19	Lapwing	Woolfolk, Austin	Feb. 15, 1827	Balto.
Harris	John	15	Charles	Campbell, Bernard M.	Apr. 23, 1851	Balto.
Harris	John	18	John C. Calhoun	Donovan, Joseph S.	Oct. 24, 1850	Balto.
Harris	John	20	Kirkwood	Campbell, Bernard M.	Oct. 14, 1848	Balto.

Surname	First Name	Age	Ship	O/S	Date	Depart
Harris	John	31	Lafayette	Woolfolk, Austin	Oct. 18, 1828	Balto.
Harris	John W.	20	Victorine	Donovan, Joseph S.	May 22, 1844	Balto.
Harris	Joseph	16	Victorine	Donovan, Joseph S.	Sept. 29, 1845	Balto.
Harris	Judy	10	States	Woolfolk, Austin	Apr. 14, 1828	Balto.
Harris	Lavania	24	Scotia	Slatter, Hope Hull	Sept. 30, 1843	Balto.
Harris	Levin	30	Isaac Franklin	Slatter, Hope Hull	Sept. 28, 1838	Balto.
Harris	Luther	23	E.H. Chapin	Campbell, Walter L.	June 7, 1848	Balto.
Harris	Malissa	18	Architect	Slatter, Hope Hull	May 20, 1841	Balto.
Harris	Maria	11	Victorine	Donovan, Joseph S.	Sept. 29, 1845	Balto.
Harris	Mariah	20	Victorine	Donovan, Joseph S.	May 22, 1844	Balto.
Harris	Mary	12	Hibernia	Woolfolk, Austin	Dec. 5, 1826	Balto.
Harris	Mary	25	Seguin	Campbell, Bernard M.	July 12, 1853	Balto.
Harris	Mary Jane	20	Home	Slatter, Hope Hull	March 22, 1845	Balto.
Harris	Moses	22	Lady Monroe	Woolfolk, Austin	March 25, 1825	Balto.
Harris	Nancy	42	Isaac Franklin	Kephart, George	Sept. 28, 1838	Balto.
Harris	Nathan	11	Kirkwood	Campbell, Bernard M.	Jan. 14, 1846	Balto.
Harris	Nelson	21	Southerner	Donovan, Joseph S.	Oct. 27, 1849	Balto.
Harris	Priscilla	14	Isaac Franklin	Kephart, George	Sept. 28, 1838	Balto.
Harris	Rachel	18	Victorine	Slatter, Hope Hull	Sept. 12, 1846	Balto.
Harris	Richard	22	Solomon Saltus	Slatter, Hope Hull	Oct. 7, 1839	Balto.
Harris	Richard	9	Victorine	Donovan, Joseph S.	Sept. 29, 1845	Balto.
Harris	Robert	20	Union	Rodbind, Ebenezer	Nov. 17, 1849	Balto.
Harris	Samuel	23	Lafayette	Woolfolk, Austin	Oct. 18, 1828	Balto.
Harris	Si	47	Isaac Franklin	Kephart, George	Sept. 28, 1838	Balto.
Harris	Sylla	35	Kirkwood	Campbell, Bernard M.	Jan. 14, 1846	Balto.
Harris	Vickey	19	Tweed	Sothoron, William H.	Oct. 20, 1836	Town Creek

Surname	First Name	Age	Ship	O/S	Date	Depart
Harris	William	19	Hermitage	Donovan, Joseph S.	Oct. 28, 1846	Balto.
Harris	William	20	Narragansett	Donovan, Joseph S.	Nov. 27, 1850	Balto.
Harris	William	23	Tweed	Sothoron, William H.	Oct. 20, 1836	Town Creek
Harris	William H.	21	Victorine	Rodbind, Ebenezer	Dec. 31, 1846	Balto.
Harris		18	Lafayette	Woolfolk, Richard	Oct. 18, 1828	Balto.
Harris			Lafayette	Woolfolk, Richard	Oct. 18, 1828	Balto.
Harris		10	Victorine	Donovan, Joseph S.	Sept. 29, 1845	Balto.
Harrison	Alice	23	Louisa	Ellicott, P.T.	March 31, 1849	Balto.
Harrison	Andrew	18	Kirkwood	Slatter, Hope Hull	Oct. 16, 1845	Balto.
Harrison	Dennis	14	Elizabeth	Donovan, Joseph S.	March 21, 1850	Balto.
Harrison	Elisabeth	30	Kirkwood	Donovan, Joseph S.	Dec. 10, 1846	Balto.
Harrison	Eliza	25	Tippecanoe	Slatter, Hope Hull	Apr. 15, 1844	Balto.
Harrison	George	7	Louisa	Ellicott, P.T.	March 31, 1849	Balto.
Harrison	Harriet	8	Brunswick	Woolfolk, Austin	Oct. 11, 1831	Balto.
Harrison	Henry	22	Kirkwood	Donovan, Joseph S.	Oct. 26, 1847	Balto.
Harrison	Henry	19	Sarah Bridge	Campbell, Bernard M.	Feb. 8, 1851	Balto.
Harrison	John	23	Union	Sheckles, B.O.	Nov. 17, 1849	Balto.
Harrison	Josephine	14	Superb	Slatter, Hope Hull	Nov. 1, 1843	Balto.
Harrison	Margaret	16	Eliza	Slatter, Hope Hull	Oct. 9, 1840	Balto.
Harrison	Mary Jane	13	Superb	Slatter, Hope Hull	Nov. 1, 1843	Balto.
Harrison	Mathew	infant	Kirkwood	Donovan, Joseph S.	Dec. 10, 1846	Balto.
Harrison	Rosetta	18	Tippecanoe	Harker, William	Apr. 15, 1844	Balto.
Harrison	Samuel	12	Billow	Woolfolk, Joseph B.	Feb. 23, 1828	Balto.
Harrison		infant	Louisa	Ellicott, P.T.	March 31, 1849	Balto.
Harriss	Casset	15	Union	Slatter, Hope Hull	July 26, 1847	Balto.
Harriss	Hannah	21	Union	Slatter, Hope Hull	July 26, 1847	Balto.

Surname	First Name	Age	Ship	O/S	Date	Depart
Harriss	Maria	infant	Union	Slatter, Hope Hull	July 26, 1847	Balto.
Harriss	Minty	17	Union	Slatter, Hope Hull	July 26, 1847	Balto.
Harrod	Eliza	18	Kirkwood	Donovan, Joseph S.	Sept. 28, 1846	Balto.
Harrod	Ellen	17	Brunswick	Woolfolk, Austin	Oct. 11, 1831	Balto.
Harrod	Filly	15	States	Woolfolk, Austin	Nov. 21, 1827	Balto.
Harrod	Joe	36	Topaz	Woolfolk, Austin	Apr. 20, 1829	Balto.
Harrod	Lemuel	30	Union	Campbell, Bernard M.	Dec. 16, 1848	Balto.
Harrod	Major	27	Billow	Woolfolk, Austin	Feb. 23, 1828	Balto.
Harrod	Rachel	17	Billow	Woolfolk, Austin	Feb. 23, 1828	Balto.
Harrod	Thomas	26	States	Woolfolk, Austin	Apr. 14, 1828	Balto.
Hart	George	21	Kirkwood	Donovan, Joseph S.	Oct. 16, 1845	Balto.
Hart	Henry	22	General Pinckney	Donovan, Joseph S.	Nov. 10, 1845	Balto.
Hart	Mary	54	Harriet	Carroll, Charles	Dec. 7, 1836	Balto.
Hart	Rachel	32	Kirkwood	Slatter, Hope Hull	Dec. 23, 1843	Balto.
Harvey	Fanny	20	Irad Ferry	Wilson, J.W.	May 6, 1839	Balto.
Harvey	Moses	26	Lady Monroe	Woolfolk, Austin	March 25, 1825	Balto.
Hasaway	Martha	15	Southerner	Donovan, Joseph S.	Oct. 27, 1849	Balto.
Haskins	Frederick	31	Louisa	Donovan, Joseph S.	Oct. 9, 1847	Balto.
Haskins	James	21	Union	Sheckles. B.O.	Nov. 17, 1849	Balto.
Haskins	Mary	16	Victorine	Donovan, Joseph S.	May 22, 1844	Balto.
Hastey	Joab	20	Lafayette	Harker, William	March 25, 1843	Balto.
Hasty	Richard	25	Helen A. Miller	Campbell, Bernard M.	Oct. 18, 1852	Balto.
Hatcher	Bill	16	St. Mary	Williams, Thomas	Nov. 29, 1845	Balto.
Hathman	Charles	25	Pioneer	Slatter, Hope Hull	Sept. 15, 1847	Balto.
Hatter	Harriett	33	Elizabeth	Donovan, Joseph S.	Nov. 18, 1848	Balto.
Hatter	James	21	Union	Donovan, Joseph S.	Dec. 16, 1848	Balto.

Surname	First Name	Age	Ship	O/S	Date	Depart
Haven	Tom	38	Liberator	Woolfolk, Austin	Nov. 12, 1828	Balto.
Hawkins	Alexander	18	Victorine	Donovan, Joseph S.	Dec. 31, 1846	Balto.
Hawkins	Allen	25	Union	Williams, Thomas	Oct. 9, 1848	Balto.
Hawkins	Ann	25	Kirkwood	Slatter, Hope Hull	Oct. 16, 1845	Balto.
Hawkins	Ann Maria	17	Scotia	Slatter, Hope Hull	Sept. 30, 1843	Balto.
Hawkins	Cato	38	Victorine	Slatter, Hope Hull	Dec. 17, 1845	Balto.
Hawkins	Charlott	18	Victorine	Rodbind, Ebenezer	March 1, 1845	Balto.
Hawkins	Clarrisa	16	Kirkwood	Slatter, Hope Hull	Oct. 16, 1845	Balto.
Hawkins	Cornelia	22	Victorine	Donovan, Joseph S.	May 22, 1844	Balto.
Hawkins	Daniel	18	Strafford	Harker, William	Nov. 22, 1843	Balto.
Hawkins	David	22	Scotia	Harker, William	Sept. 30, 1843	Balto.
Hawkins	Dennis	25	John S. Gittings	Campbell, Bernard M.	Nov. 20, 1852	Balto.
Hawkins	Edward	18	Kirkwood	Donovan, Joseph S.	Sept. 28, 1846	Balto.
Hawkins	Edward	25	Scotia	Harker, William	Sept. 30, 1843	Balto.
Hawkins	Elizabeth	15	Isaac Franklin	Kephart, George	Sept. 28, 1838	Balto.
Hawkins	Elizabeth	16	Union	Rodbind, Ebenezer	Nov. 17, 1849	Balto.
Hawkins	Ellen	18	Victorine	Slatter, Hope Hull	Dec. 17, 1845	Balto.
Hawkins	Emeline	21	Isaac Franklin	Kephart, George	Sept. 28, 1838	Balto.
Hawkins	Emily	12	Victorine	Rodbind, Ebenezer	March 1, 1845	Balto.
Hawkins	Fenetta	17	Mary Broughton	Campbell, Bernard M.	Nov. 18, 1851	Balto.
Hawkins	Flora	24	Bostonian	Slatter, Hope Hull	Jan. 18, 1841	Balto.
Hawkins	Frank	21	Victorine	Rodbind, Ebenezer	Dec. 31, 1846	Balto.
Hawkins	George	22	Kirkwood	Slatter, Hope Hull	Apr. 15, 1845	Balto.
Hawkins	Hannah	17	Victorine	Rodbind, Ebenezer	March 1, 1845	Balto.
Hawkins	Henry	20	Helen A. Miller	Campbell, Bernard M.	Oct. 18, 1852	Balto.
Hawkins	Henry	17	Henry A. Barling	Donovan, Joseph S.	Feb. 24, 1851	Balto.

Surname	First Name	Age	Ship	O/S	Date	Depart
Hawkins	Henry	22	Kirkwood	Slatter, Hope Hull	Jan. 4, 1845	Balto.
Hawkins	Hillory	infant	General Pinckney	Slatter, Hope Hull	Feb. 21, 1846	Balto.
Hawkins	Isaac	30	Kirkwood	Slatter, Hope Hull	Dec. 23, 1843	Balto.
Hawkins	Isaac	22	Union	Williams, Thomas	Oct. 9, 1848	Balto.
Hawkins	James	19	Kirkwood	Donovan, Joseph S.	Sept. 28, 1846	Balto.
Hawkins	Jane	20	General Pinckney	Slatter, Hope Hull	Feb. 21, 1846	Balto.
Hawkins	John	26	Henry A. Barling	Campbell, Bernard M.	Dec. 18, 1851	Balto.
Hawkins	John	25	Lafayette	Woolfolk, Richard	Oct. 18, 1828	Balto.
hawkins	John	21	Victorine	Slatter, Hope Hull	March 14, 1846	Balto.
Hawkins	Julia	18	Elizabeth	Campbell, Bernard M.	March 21, 1850	Balto.
Hawkins	Kitty	17	Kirkwood	Donovan, Joseph S.	Sept. 28, 1846	Balto.
Hawkins	Lewis	14	Kirkwood	Campbell, Bernard M.	Jan. 14, 1846	Balto.
Hawkins	Linda	17	Victorine	Rodbind, Ebenezer	May 14, 1845	Balto.
Hawkins	Luke	26	Southerner	Donovan, Joseph S.	Oct. 27, 1849	Balto.
Hawkins	Margery	26	Kirkwood	Slatter, Hope Hull	Dec. 23, 1843	Balto.
Hawkins	Maria	14	Brunswick	Woolfolk, Austin	Oct. 11, 1831	Balto.
Hawkins	Martha Ann	23	Kirkwood	Slatter, Hope Hull	Jan. 4, 1845	Balto.
Hawkins	Mary	20	Hermitage	Williams, Thomas	Oct. 28, 1846	Balto.
Hawkins	Mary	15	Kirkwood	Donovan, Joseph S.	Sept. 28, 1846	Balto.
Hawkins	Mary	24	Paoli	Slatter, Hope Hull	Sept. 9, 1845	Balto.
Hawkins	Oston	18	Henry A. Barling	Campbell, Bernard M.	Feb. 24, 1851	Balto.
Hawkins	Sally	infant	Victorine	Slatter, Hope Hull	Dec. 17, 1845	Balto.
Hawkins	Sam	20	Elizabeth	Campbell, Bernard M.	March 21, 1850	Balto.
Hawkins	Sandy	21	Helen A. Miller	Campbell, Bernard M.	Oct. 18, 1852	Balto.
Hawkins	Sarah	20	Henry A. Barling	Campbell, Bernard M.	Dec. 18, 1851	Balto.
Hawkins	Sarah	15	St. Mary	Donovan, Joseph S.	Nov. 29, 1845	Balto.

Surname	First Name	Age	Ship	O/S	Date	Depart
Hawkins	Sarah Ann	22	Salvadora	Slatter, Hope Hull	Sept. 28, 1846	Balto.
Hawkins	Sophia	17	Southerner	Donovan, Jospeh S.	Jan. 5, 1852	Balto.
Hawkins	Susan	5	General Pinckney	Williams, Thomas	Jan. 19, 1847	Balto.
Hawkins	Syntha	22	Kirkwood	Slatter, Hope Hull	Apr. 15, 1845	Balto.
Hawkins	William	25	John S. Gittings	Campbell, Bernard M.	Nov. 20, 1852	Balto.
Hawkins	William	19	Union	Rodbind, Ebenezer	Nov. 17, 1849	Balto.
Hawkins		infant	Henry A. Barling	Campbell, Bernard M.	Dec. 18, 1851	Balto.
Hawley	James	29	Scotia	Slatter, Hope Hull	Sept. 30, 1843	Balto.
Hayden	George	15	Hermitage	Donovan, Joseph S.	Oct. 28, 1846	Balto.
Hayden	Mary	20	Pioneer	Slatter, Hope Hull	Sept. 15, 1847	Balto.
Hayes	Rebecca	35	Hermitage	Slatter, Hope Hull	Oct. 28, 1846	Balto.
Haynes	Benjamin	30	Margaret Hugg	Slatter, Hope Hull	Feb. 8, 1845	Balto.
Haynes	Harriett	16	Margaret Hugg	Slatter, Hope Hull	Feb. 8, 1845	Balto.
Haynes	Madison	24	Elizabeth	Campbell, Bernard M.	Nov. 18, 1848	Balto.
Hays	Fanny	30	Tippecanoe	Slatter, Hope Hull	Dec. 16, 1840	Balto.
Hays	Mary	16	Abbott Lord	Campbell, Bernard M.	April 28, 1852	Balto.
Haysty	Arthur	25	Irad Ferry	Wilson, J.W.	May 6, 1839	Balto.
Hayward	Catherine	18	Architect	Slatter, Hope Hull	Feb. 13, 1843	Balto.
Hayward	Eba	infant	Architect	Slatter, Hope Hull	Feb. 13, 1843	Balto.
Hayward	Ebin	18	Architect	Slatter, Hope Hull	Feb. 13, 1843	Balto.
Hayward	Henrietta	38	Architect	Slatter, Hope Hull	Feb. 13, 1843	Balto.
Hayward	James	9	Architect	Slatter, Hope Hull	Feb. 13, 1843	Balto.
Hayward	Samuel	22	Scotia	Slatter, Hope Hull	Sept. 30, 1843	Balto.
Haywood	Isaac	19	Kirkwood	Campbell, Bernard M.	Oct. 14, 1848	Balto.
Haywood	James	20	Eliza F.Mason	Donovan, Joseph S.	Nov. 13, 1851	Balto.
Haywood	William	21	John C. Calhoun	Donovan, Joseph S.	Oct. 24, 1850	Balto.

Surname	First Name	Age	Ship	O/S	Date	Depart
Hazard	Rachel	21	Isaac Franklin	Slatter, Hope Hull	Sept. 28, 1838	Balto.
Hazlett	Winder	23	Kirkwood	Campbell, Bernard M.	March 23, 1844	Balto.
Heagan	Jerry	21	Pioneer	Slatter, Hope Hull	Sept. 15, 1847	Balto.
Healey	Hannah	16	Catharine	Slatter, Hope Hull	Jan. 24, 1843	Balto.
Heard	Michael	19	Union	Campbell, Bernard M.	Dec. 16, 1848	Balto.
Heath	Bill	22	Henry Clay	Woolfolk, Austin	Dec. 4, 1828	Balto.
Heath	Margaret	17	Henry Clay	Woolfolk, Austin	Dec. 4, 1828	Balto.
Hebbern	John	22	Victorine	Slatter, Hope Hull	March 9, 1844	Balto.
Hellems	Reuben	21	General Pinckney	Slatter, Hope Hull	Nov. 10, 1845	Balto.
Helmons	Mary	18	Kirkwood	Donovan, Joseph S.	Sept. 28, 1846	Balto.
Helmsley	John	21	Helen A. Miller	Campbell, Bernard M.	Oct. 18, 1852	Balto.
Hemmings	Martha	12	Ewarkee	Purvis, James Franklin	March 4, 1841	Balto.
Hemsley	George	18	Victorine	Donovan, Joseph S.	Sept. 29, 1845	Balto.
Hemsley	Jacob	17	Lady Monroe	Woolfolk, Austin	March 25, 1825	Balto.
Hemsley	James	22	Kirkwood	Donovar, Joseph S.	Apr. 15, 1845	Balto.
Hemsley	Prescilla	15	Southerner	Donovan, Jospeh S.	Jan. 5, 1852	Balto.
Henderson	Edward	20	Pioneer	Stuart, William R.	July 20, 1848	Balto.
Henderson	George	25	Catharine	Woolfolk, Austin	March 3, 1829	Balto.
Henderson	Hannah	24	General Pinckney	Slatter, Hope Hull	Feb. 21, 1846	Balto.
Henderson	Horrace	infant	General Pinckney	Slatter, Hope Hull	Feb. 21, 1846	Balto.
Henderson	Marthy	15	E.H.Chapin	Donovan, Joseph S.	Dec. 2, 1847	Balto.
Henderson	Mary Jane	18	Isaac Franklin	Kephart, George	Sept. 28, 1838	Balto.
Henderson	Otho	16	States	Woolfolk, Austin	Apr. 14, 1828	Balto.
Henderson	Ranson	21	Eliza F.Mason	Donovan, Joseph S.	Nov. 13, 1851	Balto.
Henderson	Richard	23	Nathaniel Hooper	Campbell, Bernard M.	Feb. 12, 1852	Balto.
Henderson	Rosetta	15	Billow	Woolfolk, Austin	Feb. 23, 1828	Balto.

Surname	First Name	Age	Ship	O/S	Date	Depart
Henning	Emeline	9	Margaret Hugg	Harker, William	Feb. 8, 1845	Balto.
Henry	Abraham	40	Burlington	Slatter, Hope Hull	Oct. 21, 1842	Balto.
Henry	Basil	15	Sabine	Donovan, Joseph S.	Feb. 10, 1844	Balto.
Henry	Charles	15	John S. Gittings	Campbell, Bernard M.	Nov. 20, 1852	Balto.
Henry	Charles	3	Kirkwood	Slatter, Henry F.	Dec. 10, 1846	Balto.
Henry	Charles	11	Kirkwood	Donovan, Joseph S.	March 23, 1844	Balto.
Henry	Cloe	22	Victorine	Slatter, Hope Hull	May 14, 1845	Balto.
Henry	David	11	Margaret Forbs	Slatter, Hope Hull	Nov. 28, 1838	Balto.
Henry	Dennis	22	Kirkwood	Donovan, Joseph S.	Oct. 14, 1848	Balto.
Henry	Elizebeth	16	Kirkwood	Slatter, Hope Hull	Apr. 15, 1845	Balto.
Henry	George	22	Victorine	Donovan, Joseph S.	Dec. 31, 1846	Balto.
Henry	George	infant	Victorine	Slatter, Henry F.	Dec. 31, 1846	Balto.
Henry	James	11	General Pinckney	Slatter, Hope Hull	Jan. 19, 1847	Balto.
Henry	James	infant	Kirkwood	Slatter, Hope Hull	Apr. 15, 1845	Balto.
Henry	Jane	17	Kirkwood	Slatter, Hope Hull	Apr. 15, 1845	Balto.
Henry	John	17	General Pinckney	Slatter, Hope Hull	Jan. 19, 1847	Balto.
Henry	John	19	Kirkwood	Donovan, Joseph S.	Apr. 15, 1845	Balto.
Henry	John	10	Kirkwood	Donovan, Joseph S.	Oct. 26, 1847	Balto.
Henry	John	20	Margaret Forbs	Slatter, Hope Hull	Nov. 28, 1838	Balto.
Henry	John	18	Mary Broughton	Campbell, Bernard M.	Nov. 18, 1851	Balto.
Henry	Joseph	18	Kirkwood	Campbell, Bernard M.	Apr. 15, 1845	Balto.
Henry	Levin	17	Southerner	Donovan, Jospeh S.	Jan. 5, 1852	Balto.
Henry	Robert	11	General Pinckney	Slatter, Hope Hull	Jan. 19, 1847	Balto.
Henry	Sonia	22	Northumberland	Slatter, Hope Hull	Feb. 27, 1843	Balto.
Henry	William	3	Kirkwood	Slatter, Henry F.	Dec. 10, 1846	Balto.
Henry	William	13	Shamrock	Guyton, Elisha	March 13, 1840	Balto.

Surname	First Name	Age	Ship	O/S	Date	Depart
Henry	William	18	Tippecanoe	Slatter, Hope Hull	Jan. 17, 1842	Balto.
Henson	David	17	Colonel Howard	Harker, William	Nov. 21, 1844	Balto.
Henson	David	20	Jefferson	Woolfolk, Austin	Dec. 24, 1827	Balto.
Henson	Edward	25	Louisa	Campbell, Bernard M.	Nov. 5, 1849	Balto.
Henson	Elizabeth	18	Southerner	Donovan, Joseph S.	Oct. 27, 1849	Balto.
Henson	Emeline	11	Victorine	Donovan, Joseph S.	May 14, 1845	Balto.
Henson	Gabriel	17	General Pinckney	Williams, Thomas	Jan. 19, 1847	Balto.
Henson	Hannah	20	Jefferson	Woolfolk, Austin	Dec. 24, 1827	Balto.
Henson	Harry	30	Mars	Woolfolk, Austin	Oct. 30, 1824	Balto.
Henson	Henry	18	Union	Campbell, Bernard M.	Oct. 9, 1848	Balto.
Henson	Isaac	7	Liberator	Woolfolk, Austin	Nov. 12, 1828	Balto.
Henson	James	21	Victorine	Donovan, Joseph S.	May 14, 1845	Balto.
Henson	Jane	35	General Pinckney	Donovan, Joseph S.	Feb. 21, 1846	Balto.
Henson	John	20	Union	Donovan, Joseph S.	March 17, 1849	Balto.
Henson	Matilda	20	Southerner	Rodbind, Ebenezer	Jan. 21, 1850	Balto.
Henson	Noah	22	E.H.Chapin	Donovan, Joseph S.	Dec. 2, 1847	Balto.
Henson	Perry	25	E.H.Chapin	Donovan, Joseph S.	Dec. 2, 1847	Balto.
Henson	Richard	13	General Pinckney	Slatter, Hope Hull	Jan. 19, 1847	Balto.
Henson	Richard	26	Lafayette	Woolfolk, Austin	Oct. 18, 1828	Balto.
Henson	Sandy	25	Elizabeth	Donovan, Joseph S.	Nov. 18, 1848	Balto.
Hepbern	Harrod	22	Lafayette	Harker, William	March 25, 1843	Balto.
Herod	King	20	Mary Broughton	Campbell, Bernard M.	Nov. 18, 1851	Balto.
Heywood	Henry	21	Tippecanoe	Harker, William	Apr. 15, 1844	Balto.
Hick	Jane	18	Kirkwood	Campbell, Bernard M.	Apr. 4, 1846	Balto.
Hickman	General	40	Kirkwood	Donovan, Joseph S.	Oct. 26, 1847	Balto.
Hicks	Agnus	34	Elizabeth	Donovan, Joseph S.	Jan. 2, 1850	Balto.

Surname	First Name	Age	Ship	O/S	Date	Depart
Hicks	Andrew	22	Narragansett	Donovan, Joseph S.	Nov. 27, 1850	Balto.
Hicks	Dorra	22	Pioneer	Slatter, Hope Hull	Sept. 15, 1847	Balto.
Hicks	Hannah	infant	Elizabeth	Donovan, Joseph S.	Jan. 2, 1850	Balto.
Hicks	Harriet	20	General Pinckney	Campbell, Bernard M.	Jan. 19, 1847	Balto.
Hicks	John	18	Ann & Leah	Woolfolk, Austin	Nov.1, 1831	Balto.
Higgins	Arianna	19	Architect	Slatter, Hope Hull	Feb. 16, 1843	Balto.
Higgins	Jerry	22	Pioneer	Slatter, Hope Hull	Sept. 15, 1847	Balto.
Higgins	Thomas	10	Victorine	Rodbind, Ebenezer	Dec. 31, 1846	Balto.
High	Peter	28	Brunswick	Woolfolk, Austin	Oct. 11, 1831	Balto.
Highland	Eliza	24	Kirkwood	Donovan, Joseph S.	Nov. 28, 1849	Balto.
Highland	Sewell	24	Southerner	Donovan, Joseph S.	Oct. 27, 1849	Balto.
Hile	Harry	19	Nancy W.Stevens	Harker, James	Oct. 25, 1843	Balto.
Hill	Abram	20	Lafayette	Woolfolk, Austin	Oct. 18, 1828	Balto.
Hill	Ann R.	infant	Kirkwood	Slatter, Hope Hull	Dec. 23, 1843	Balto.
Hill	Caleb	22	Kirkwood	Slatter, Hope Hull	Oct. 16, 1845	Balto.
Hill	Charlotte	16	Abbott Lord	Campbell, Bernard M.	April 28, 1852	Balto.
Hill	Clarissa	20	Lafayette	Woolfolk, Austin	Oct. 18, 1828	Balto.
Hill	Ellen	22	Julia	Woolfolk, Austin	Jan. 8, 1829	Balto.
Hill	Ellen	13	Kirkwood	Williams, Thomas	Apr. 4, 1846	Balto.
Hill	Ennels	8	Solomon Saltus	Slatter, Hope Hull	Oct. 7, 1839	Balto.
Hill	Fanny	16	Salvadora	Slatter, Hope Hull	Sept. 28, 1846	Balto.
Hill	George	21	John C. Calhoun	Donovan, Joseph S.	Oct. 24, 1850	Balto.
Hill	Henny	35	Solomon Saltus	Slatter, Hope Hull	Oct. 7, 1839	Balto.
Hill	Isabella	11	Splendid	Slatter, Hope Hull	Apr. 24, 1841	Balto.
Hill	Jane	20	Kirkwood	Donovan, Joseph S.	March 9, 1847	Balto.
Hill	Kitty	17	Splendid	Slatter, Hope Hull	Apr. 24, 1841	Balto.

Surname	First Name	Age	Ship	O/S	Date	Depart
Hill	Leathy	32	Splendid	Slatter, Hope Hull	Apr. 24, 1841	Balto.
Hill	Maria	16	Kirkwood	Donovan, Joseph S.	March 9, 1847	Balto.
Hill	Martha	15	Splendid	Slatter, Hope Hull	Apr. 24, 1841	Balto.
Hill	Ned	7	Solomon Saltus	Slatter, Hope Hull	Oct. 7, 1839	Balto.
Hill	Philip	13	Brunswck	Woolfolk, Austin	Oct. 11, 1831	Balto.
Hill	Rebecca	23	Kirkwood	Slatter, Hope Hull	Dec. 23, 1843	Balto.
Hill	Rose	16	Union	Donovan, Joseph S.	March 17, 1849	Balto.
Hill	Signet	35	Signet	Woolfolk, Austin	Nov. 12, 1831	Balto.
Hilland	Ned	29	Julia	Woolfolk, Austin	Jan. 8, 1829	Balto.
Hilliard	Samuel	23	Russell	Slatter, Hope Hull	March 1, 1839	Balto.
Hillory	Lewis	33	Tippecanoe	Slatter, Hope Hull	Jan. 17, 1842	Balto.
Hills	Harriot	infant	Billow	Woolfolk, Austin	Feb. 23, 1828	Balto.
Hills	Mary	24	Billow	Woolfolk, Austin	Feb. 23, 1828	Balto.
Hillyard	Mahala	19	Victorine	Slatter, Hope Hull	Sept. 12, 1846	Balto.
Hilman	Ann	17	Victorine	Donovan, Joseph S.	Sept. 29, 1845	Balto.
Hilman	Harriet	18	Isaac Franklin	Slatter, Hope Hull	Sept. 28, 1838	Balto.
Hines	Joshua	9	Lady Monroe	Woolfolk, Austin	March 25, 1825	Balto.
Hines	Perry	23	Burlington	Slatter, Hope Hull	Oct. 21, 1842	Balto.
Hinson	Bertha	2	Victorine	Slatter, Hope Hull	March 14, 1846	Balto.
Hinson	Caroline	18	Scotia	Slatter, Hope Hull	Sept. 30, 1843	Balto.
Hinson	Charity	18	Hermitage	Slatter, Hope Hull	Oct. 28, 1846	Balto.
Hinson	Charles	20	Victorine	Slatter, Hope Hull	May 14, 1845	Balto.
Hinson	Chris	18 mon.	Victorine	Campbell, Bernard M.	March 1, 1845	Balto.
Hinson	Cleann	15	General Pinckney	Williams, Thomas	Jan. 19, 1847	Balto.
Hinson	Dennis	18	Sabine	Donovan, Joseph S.	Feb. 10, 1844	Balto.
Hinson	Edmond	18	Kirkwood	Donovan, Joseph S.	Sept. 28, 1846	Balto.

Surname	First Name	Age	Ship	O/S	Date	Depart
Hinson	Edward	20	Burlington	Slatter, Hope Hull	Oct. 21, 1842	Balto.
Hinson	Emaly	18	Scotia	Slatter, Hope Hull	Sept. 30, 1843	Balto.
Hinson	Emily	15	Home	Campbell, Bernard M.	March 22, 1845	Balto.
Hinson	Flarilla	18	Victorine	Donovan, Joseph S.	May 14, 1845	Balto.
Hinson	Henrietta	13	Superb	Slatter, Hope Hull	Nov. 1, 1843	Balto.
Hinson	Kitty	26	Victorine	Slatter, Hope Hull	March 14, 1846	Balto.
Hinson	Louisa	11	Victorine	Slatter, Henry F.	Dec. 31, 1846	Balto.
Hinson	Margarett	18	Tippecanoe	Purvis, James Franklin	Apr. 1, 1841	Balto.
Hinson	Mariah	12	Elizabeth	Campbell, Bernard M.	Nov. 18, 1848	Balto.
Hinson	Pere	19	Hermitage	Donovan, Joseph S.	Oct. 28, 1846	Balto.
Hinson	Robert	17	Helen A. Miller	Campbell, Bernard M.	Oct. 18, 1852	Balto.
Hinson	Sarah	16	Elizabeth	Donovan, Joseph S.	Jan. 2, 1850	Balto.
Hinson	Sarah	13	P.R. Hazeltine	Campbell, Bernard M.	Nov. 15, 1856	Balto.
Hinson	Sarah	infant	Victorine	Slatter, Hope Hull	March 14, 1846	Balto.
Hinson	Sarah Anne	infant	Victorine	Donovan, Joseph S.	May 14, 1845	Balto.
Hinton	Francis	17	Margaret Hugg	Wilson, Thomas C.	Nov. 30, 1844	Balto.
Hintz	James	1	Irad Ferry	Purvis, James Franklin	Feb. 5, 1842	Balto.
Hitch	Mathias	24	Narragansett	Donovan, Joseph S.	Nov. 27, 1850	Balto.
Hittle	Romeo	23	Irad Ferry	Slatter, Hope Hull	Dec. 9, 1842	Balto.
Hittle	Romeo	26	Seaman	Rush, George Jr.	Dec. 16, 1841	Balto.
Hobbs	Caleb	20	Solomon Saltus	Slatter, Hope Hull	Oct. 7, 1839	Balto.
Hobbs	George	28	Hope & Hannah	Woolfolk, Austin	March 11, 1829	Balto.
Hobbs	Luther	12	Irad Ferry	Wilson, J.W.	May 6, 1839	Balto.
Hobbs	Mahaley	15	Seaman	Slatter, Shadrack	March 25, 1839	Balto.
Hobbs	Mary	15	Seaman	Slatter, Shadrack	March 25, 1839	Balto.
Hobel	Edward	22	Union	Rodbind, Ebenezer	Dec. 16, 1848	Balto.

Surname	First Name	Age	Ship	O/S	Date	Depart
Hockings	Perry	28	Paoli	Slatter, Hope Hull	Sept. 9, 1845	Balto.
Hodge	Charles	20	Union	Campbell, Bernard M.	Nov. 17, 1849	Balto.
Hodge	Mary	18	Victorine	Donovan, Joseph S.	March 14, 1846	Balto.
Hodge	Stephen	19	Union	Campbell, Bernard M.	Nov. 17, 1849	Balto.
Hodge	Thomas	17	Union	Campbell, Bernard M.	Nov. 17, 1849	Balto.
Hodge	William	22	Union	Campbell, Bernard M.	Nov. 17, 1849	Balto.
Hodgers	Alice	infant	Superb	Slatter, Hope Hull	Nov. 1, 1843	Balto.
Hodgers	Pricilla	18	Superb	Slatter, Hope Hull	Nov. 1, 1843	Balto.
Hodges	Cornelia	24	Zoe	Slatter, Hope Hull	Feb. 16, 1847	Balto.
Hodges	Joseph	22	Victorine	Slatter, Hope Hull	Sept. 12, 1846	Balto.
Hodges	Zedekiah	infant	Zoe	Slatter, Hope Hull	Feb. 16, 1847	Balto.
Hogan	Catherin	4	Home	Slatter, Hope Hull	March 22, 1845	Balto.
Hogan	Charlotte	26	Home	Slatter, Hope Hull	March 22, 1845	Balto.
Hogans	Bill	20	Balloon	Milligan, George	Dec. 17, 1821	Balto.
Holand	Alexander	21	States	Woolfolk, Austin	Apr. 14, 1828	Balto.
Hollady	Henry	25	Superb	Slatter, Hope Hull	Nov. 1, 1843	Balto.
Hollam	Heny	40	Kirkwood	Slatter, Hope Hull	Dec. 23, 1843	Balto.
Holland	Andrew	20	Elizabeth	Campbell, Bernard M.	March 21, 1850	Balto.
Holland	Ann	32	Hermitage	Slatter, Hope Hull	Oct. 28, 1846	Balto.
Holland	Anthony	35	Liberator	Woolfolk, Austin	Nov. 12, 1828	Balto.
Holland	Caroline	20	Phoenix	Slatter, Hope Hull	March 27, 1847	Balto.
Holland	Catherine	16	Abbott Lord	Campbell, Bernard M.	April 28, 1852	Balto.
Holland	Daniel	17	Victorine	Slatter, Hope Hull	Dec. 17, 1845	Balto.
Holland	David	21	Victorine	Slatter, Hope Hull	Sept. 12, 1846	Balto.
Holland	Fanny	21	Russell	Slatter, Hope Hull	March 1, 1839	Balto.
Holland	George	4	Narragansett	Campbell, Bernard M.	Nov. 27, 1850	Balto.

Surname	First Name	Age	Ship	O/S	Date	Depart
Holland	Henrietta	16	Hermitage	Slatter, Hope Hull	Oct. 28, 1846	Balto.
Holland	Henry	20	General Pinckney	Campbell, Bernard M.	Jan. 19, 1847	Balto.
Holland	Henry	19	Phoenix	Slatter, Hope Hull	March 27, 1847	Balto.
Holland	Lloyd	21	Phoenix	Slatter, Hope Hull	March 27, 1847	Balto.
Holland	Mariah	24	Narragansett	Campbell, Bernard M.	Nov. 27, 1850	Balto.
Holland	Nelson	21	Kirkwood	Donovan, Joseph S.	Jan. 4, 1845	Balto.
Holland	Reason	7	Narragansett	Campbell, Bernard M.	Nov. 27, 1850	Balto.
Holland	Rebecca	16	Narragansett	Donovan, Joseph S.	Nov. 27, 1850	Balto.
Holland	Sarah	6	Hermitage	Slatter, Hope Hull	Oct. 28, 1846	Balto.
Holland	Susan	5	Narragansett	Campbell, Bernard M.	Nov. 27, 1850	Balto.
Holland	Violetta	17	General Pinckney	Slatter, Hope Hull	Nov. 10, 1845	Balto.
Holland	Wesley	35	Victorine	Slatter, Hope Hull	Sept. 12, 1846	Balto.
Holland	William	24	Ewarkee	Slatter, Hope Hull	March 4, 1841	Balto.
Holland	William	24	Ewarkee	Slatter, Hope Hull	March 4, 1841	Balto.
Holland	William	23	Victorine	Slatter, Hope Hull	Dec. 17, 1845	Balto.
Hollday	Sophia	13	Orbit	Woolfolk, Austin	Apr. 16, 1825	Balto.
Holldiay	John	21	Tippecanoe	Slatter, Hope Hull	Apr. 1, 1841	Balto.
Holley	Harriett	17	Victorine	Slatter, Hope Hull	Sept. 12, 1846	Balto.
Hollick	Dennis	26	Tippecanoe	Slatter, Hope Hull	Jan. 17, 1842	Balto.
Holliday	George	18	States	Woolfolk, Jospeh B.	March 10, 1826	Balto.
Holliday	Samuel	22	Northumberland	Slatter, Hope Hull	Feb. 27, 1843	Balto.
Holliday	William	24	Victorine	Slatter, Hope Hull	Sept. 12, 1846	Balto.
Hollingsworth	Sam	20	Julia	Woolfolk, Austin	Jan. 8, 1829	Balto.
Hollins	Hannah	25	Decatur	Stansburg, Tobias E.	Oct. 24, 1819	Balto.
Hollins	Mary Ann	14	Margaret Hugg	Wilson, Thomas C.	Nov. 30, 1844	Balto.
Hollis	Ann	18	Uncas	Slatter, Hope Hull	Jan. 10, 1838	Balto.

Surname	First Name	Age	Ship	O/S	Date	Depart
Hollis	Caroline	18	Ewarkee	Slatter, Hope Hull	March 4, 1841	Balto.
Holliston	Betsey	23	Ann & Leah	Woolfolk, Austin	Nov. 1, 1831	Balto.
Hollman	Eliza	13	Union	Sheckles, Gannon	March 17, 1849	Balto.
Holloway	Nelson	30	Pioneer	Stuart, William R.	July 20, 1848	Balto.
Holly	Cambridge	18	Tippecanoe	Staples, Joshua	Jan. 17, 1842	Balto.
Holly	Henry	18	Louisa	Campbell, Bernard M.	March 31, 1849	Balto.
Holly	Isaac	17	Isaac Franklin	Slatter, Hope Hull	Sept. 28, 1838	Balto.
Holly	Joe	12	Helen A. Miller	Maddox, G.F.	Oct. 18, 1852	Balto.
Holly	Joseph	21	Kirkwood	Donovan, Joseph S.	Nov. 28, 1849	Balto.
Holly	Mary	18	Isaac Franklin	Kephart, George	Sept. 28, 1838	Balto.
Holmes	Betty	24	Union	Campbell, Bernard M.	Nov. 17, 1849	Balto.
Holmes	Daniel	16	John S. Gittings	Campbell, Bernard M.	Nov. 20, 1852	Balto.
Holmes	Henry	20	Paoli	Slatter, Hope Hull	Sept. 9, 1845	Balto.
Holmes		infant	Union	Campbell, Bernard M.	Nov. 17, 1849	Balto.
Holton	Katy	25	Intelligence	De Mapiere, Victor	Apr. 30, 1821	Balto.
Homan	Phillip	20	Union	Slatter, Hope Hull	July 26, 1847	Balto.
Homes	Catharine	20	Southerner	Rodbind, Ebenezer	Jan. 21, 1850	Balto.
Honest	Ann	18	Ewarkee	Purvis, James Franklin	March 4, 1841	Balto.
Honest	Melvina	16	Ewarkee	Purvis, James Franklin	March 4, 1841	Balto.
Honey	Fanny	20	Isaac Franklin	Kephart, George	Sept. 28, 1838	Balto.
Hood	Daniel	21	Victorine	Slatter, Hope Hull	Dec. 17, 1845	Balto.
Hook	Nathan	21	Liberator	Woolfolk, Austin	Nov. 12, 1828	Balto.
Hooks	Sandy	12	Solomon Saltus	Slatter, Hope Hull	Oct. 7, 1839	Balto.
Hooper	Ann	16	Alfred	Woolfolk, Austin	May 7, 1825	Balto.
Hooper	Anthony	24	Kirkwood	Donovan, Joseph S.	Sept. 28, 1846	Balto.
Hooper	Charles	6	Elizabeth	Rodbind, Ebenezer	Nov. 18, 1848	Balto.

Surname	First Name	Age	Ship	O/S	Date	Depart
Hooper	Eliza	22	Kirkwood	Slatter, Hope Hull	Oct. 16, 1845	Balto.
Hooper	W.	30	Tippecanoe	Harker, William	Dec. 16, 1840	Balto.
Hooper	William	30	Henry A. Barling	Donovan, Joseph S.	May 17, 1851	Balto.
Hopeful	Harriet	14	Lady Richmond	Woolfolk, Austin	Apr. 30, 1827	Balto.
Hopefull	Harry	24	Lapwing	Woolfolk, Austin	Feb. 15, 1827	Balto.
Hopewell	Ann	12	Kirkwood	Donovan, Joseph S.	Oct. 26, 1847	Balto.
Hopewell	Chance	28	Cora	Campbell, Bernard M.	Jan. 20, 1851	Balto.
Hopewell	Emeline	16	Victorine	Donovan, Joseph S.	Sept. 29, 1845	Balto.
Hopewell	Levenia	20	Kirkwood	Slatter, Hope Hull	Jan. 4, 1845	Balto.
Hopkins	Alfred	17	Kirkwood	Donovan, Joseph S.	Oct. 14, 1848	Balto.
Hopkins	Catherine	18	Burlington	Slatter, Hope Hull	Oct. 21, 1842	Balto.
Hopkins	Charles	25	Intelligence	King, Gideon T.	Sept. 18, 1821	Balto.
Hopkins	Emaly	17	Superb	Slatter, Hope Hull	Nov. 1, 1843	Balto.
Hopkins	Essex		Arctic	Thompson, Henry	Oct. 5, 1827	Balto.
Hopkins	Henry	18	Burlington	Slatter, Hope Hull	Oct. 21, 1842	Balto.
Hopkins	Jane	18	Superb	Donovan, Joseph S.	Nov. 2, 1843	Balto.
Hopkins	Perry	19	Eliza F.Mason	Donovan, Joseph S.	Nov. 13, 1851	Balto.
Hopp	Daniel	26	Kirkwood	Slatter, Hope Hull	Apr. 15, 1845	Balto.
Hopp	David	27	Kirkwood	Slatter, Hope Hull	Apr. 15, 1845	Balto.
Hopp	Harriett	26	Kirkwood	Slatter, Hope Hull	Apr. 15, 1845	Balto.
Hopp	Nathan	25	Kirkwood	Slatter, Hope Hull	Apr. 15, 1845	Balto.
Hopp	Thomas	4	Kirkwood	Slatter, Hope Hull	Apr. 15, 1845	Balto.
Hopp	Washington	8	Kirkwood	Slatter, Hope Hull	Apr. 15, 1845	Balto.
Horace	Thomas	22	Lafayette	Woolfolk, Austin	Oct. 18, 1828	Balto.
Horsand	James	17	Uncas	Slatter, Hope Hull	Apr. 3, 1838	Balto.
Horsey	Sarah	17	Victorine	Slatter, Hope Hull	May 14, 1845	Balto.

Surname	First Name	Age	Ship	O/S	Date	Depart
Howard	Ambrose	infant	Zoe	Slatter, Hope Hull	Feb. 16, 1847	Balto.
Howard	Brice	18	Elizabeth	Donovan, Joseph S.	Nov. 18, 1848	Balto.
Howard	Brice	15	Tippecanoe	Slatter, Hope Hull	Jan. 17, 1842	Balto.
Howard	Charity	13	Brunswick	Woolfolk, Austin	Oct. 11, 1831	Balto.
Howard	Charles	6	Brunswick	Woolfolk, Austin	Oct. 11, 1831	Balto.
Howard	Charles Henry	11	Ewarkee	Purvis, James Franklin	March 4, 1841	Balto.
Howard	Charlotte	18	Kirkwood	Slatter, Hope Hull	Jan. 4, 1845	Balto.
Howard	Eliza	19	Louisa	Slatter, Hope Hull	Oct. 11, 1847	Balto.
Howard	Elizabeth	16	Kirkwood	Donovan, Joseph S.	Oct. 14, 1848	Balto.
Howard	Emeline	25	Brunswick	Woolfolk, Austin	Oct. 11, 1831	Balto.
Howard	Frances	20	Zoe	Slatter, Hope Hull	Feb. 16, 1847	Balto.
Howard	George	4	Brunswick	Woolfolk, Austin	Oct. 11, 1831	Balto.
Howard	Henry	18	Ganniclefft	Slatter, Hope Hull	Nov. 25, 1840	Balto.
Howard	Jane	17	Home	Donovan, Joseph S.	March 22, 1845	Balto.
Howard	John	24	Kirkwood	Campbell, Bernard M.	Dec. 10, 1846	Balto.
Howard	John	17	Victorine	Donovan, Joseph S.	Dec. 31, 1846	Balto.
Howard	Lewis	3	Zoe	Slatter, Hope Hull	Feb. 16, 1847	Balto.
Howard	Mary	17	States	Woolfolk, Austin	Nov. 21, 1827	Balto.
Howard	Mary Ann	16	States	Woolfolk, Austin	Nov. 21, 1827	Balto.
Howard	Nace	10	Ewarkee	Purvis, James Franklin	March 4, 1841	Balto.
Howard	Rebecca	18	Lafayette	Woolfolk, Austin	Oct. 22, 1828	Balto.
Howard	Sophia	20	Helen A. Miller	Campbell, Bernard M.	Oct. 18, 1852	Balto.
Howard	William	19	John C. Calhoun	Donovan, Joseph S.	Oct. 24, 1850	Balto.
Howard	William	17	Union	Donovan, Joseph S.	Dec. 16, 1848	Balto.
Howard	William Lewis	20	Tippecance	Slatter, Hope Hull	Jan. 17, 1842	Balto.
Howe	Ann	17	Northumberland	Slatter, Hope Hull	Feb. 27, 1843	Balto.

Surname	First Name	Age	Ship	O/S	Date	Depart
Hubbard	Phil	20	Henry A. Barling	Donovan, Joseph S.	Feb. 24, 1851	Balto.
Huddleson	Betty Jane	14	Kirkwood	Donovan, Joseph S.	March 23, 1844	Balto.
Hudson	Rachel	18	Lafayette	Woolfolk, Joseph B.	Oct. 18, 1828	Balto.
Hughes	Alvina	19	Paoli	Slatter, Hope Hull	Sept. 9, 1845	Balto.
Hughes	Harry	28	Lafayette	Woolfolk, Joseph B.	Oct. 18, 1828	Balto.
Hughes	Patty	21	Kirkwood	Slatter, Hope Hull	Oct. 16, 1845	Balto.
Hughes	Susan	18	Victorine	Slatter, Hope Hull	May 14, 1845	Balto.
Hughes	Vickey	15	Union	Rodbind, Ebenezer	Nov. 17, 1849	Balto.
Hughs	Catharine	19	Kirkwood	Donovan, Joseph S.	Oct. 26, 1847	Balto.
Hughs	James	19	Kirkwood	Donovan, Joseph S.	Oct. 26, 1847	Balto.
Hughs	Singelton	20	Kirkwood	Donovan, Joseph S.	Oct. 14, 1848	Balto.
Hughson	Henrietta	12	Kirkwood	Campbell, Bernard M.	Oct. 14, 1848	Balto.
Hughsten	Arthur	4	Ewarkee	Slatter, Hope Hull	March 4, 1841	Balto.
Hughsten	Cornelius	6	Ewarkee	Slatter, Hope Hull	March 4, 1841	Balto.
Hughsten	Indianna	infant	Ewarkee	Slatter, Hope Hull	March 4, 1841	Balto.
Hughsten	Rachel	30	Ewarkee	Slatter, Hope Hull	March 4, 1841	Balto.
Hughsten	Randolph	8	Ewarkee	Slatter, Hope Hull	March 4, 1841	Balto.
Hull	Abraham	21	Narragansett	Donovan, Joseph S.	Nov. 27, 1850	Balto.
Humphreys	Sarah	22	Nathaniel Hooper	Campbell, Bernard M.	Feb. 12, 1852	Balto.
Humphries	Betsey	20	Kirkwood	Donovan, Joseph S.	Sept. 28, 1846	Balto.
Hungerford	Milly	19	States	Woolfolk, Austin	Nov. 21, 1827	Balto.
Hunt	Benjamin	25	Lapwing	Woolfolk, Austin	Feb. 15, 1827	Balto.
Hunt	Jane	17	States	Woolfolk, Austin	Nov. 21, 1827	Balto.
Hunter	Daniel	30	Victorine	Slatter, Hope Hull	Dec. 17, 1845	Balto.
Hunter	Henry	20	Southerner	Donovan, Joseph S.	Oct. 27, 1849	Balto.
Hunter	James	26	Kirkwood	Donovan, Joseph S.	Oct. 26, 1847	Balto.

Surname	First Name	Age	Ship	O/S	Date	Depart
Hunter	Jane	11	Kirkwood	Donovan, Joseph S.	Sept. 28, 1846	Balto.
Hurbald	David	22	Union	Williams, Thomas	Oct. 9, 1848	Balto.
Huston	Levin	20	Elizabeth	Donovan, Joseph S.	May 12, 1849	Balto.
Huston	Mariah	18	Eliza	Slatter, Hope Hull	Oct. 9, 1840	Balto.
Huston	Rose	18	Louisa	Donovan, Joseph S.	Oct. 9, 1847	Balto.
Hutchenson	Jacob	23	Union	Donovan, Joseph S.	Dec. 16, 1848	Balto.
Hutchins	Hannah	11	Victorine	Donovan, Joseph S.	May 22, 1844	Balto.
Hutchins	Henry	24	Billow	Woolfolk, Joseph B.	Feb. 23, 1828	Balto.
Hutchins	Hiram	17	Elizabeth	Campbell, Bernard M.	Jan. 2, 1850	Balto.
Hutchins	Lewis	21	Kirkwood	Donovan, Joseph S.	March 23, 1844	Balto.
Hutchins	Rachel	15	Kirkwood	Campbell, Bernard M.	March 23, 1844	Balto.
Hutchins	Sarah	20	Supert	Slatter, Hope Hull	Nov. 1, 1843	Balto.
Hutchins	William	21	Ganniclefft	Slatter, Hope Hull	Nov. 25, 1840	Balto.
Hutchison	Maria	16	Kirkwood	Donovan, Joseph S.	March 23, 1844	Balto.
Hutson	Alexena	20	Kirkwood	Donovan, Joseph S.	Nov. 28, 1849	Balto.
Hutson	Juliana	25	Salvadora	Slatter, Hope Hull	Sept. 28, 1846	Balto.
Hutton	Mary	25	Mary Broughton	Campbell, Bernard M.	Nov. 18, 1851	Balto.
Hutton	Richard	26	Mary Broughton	Campbell, Bernard M.	Nov. 18, 1851	Balto.
Hyatt	Beckey	14	Victorine	Rodbind, Ebenezer	Dec. 31, 1846	Balto.
Hyland	Henry	22	Phoenix	Donovan, Joseph S.	March 27, 1847	Balto.
Hymes	Rachel	16	Missouri	Gilmore, John	March 1, 1819	Balto.
Iggius	Harriet	17	Mary Broughton	Campbell, Bernard M.	Nov. 18, 1851	Balto.
Ingram	Sophia	25	Elizabeth	Campbell, Bernard M.	Nov. 18, 1848	Balto.
Innes	Solomon	30	Lafayette	Woolfolk, Joseph B.	Oct. 18, 1828	Balto.
Irving	Samuel	20	Elizabeth	Campbell, Bernard M.	Nov. 18, 1848	Balto.
Israel	Henry	20	Union	Campbell, Bernard M.	Dec. 16, 1848	Balto.

Surname	First Name	Age	Ship	O/S	Date	Depart
Iverson	Vina	16	Tangier	Campbell, Bernard M.	Nov. 26, 1853	Balto.
Jackson	Alfred	20	Louisa	Slatter, Hope Hull	Oct. 11, 1847	Balto.
Jackson	Andrew	16	E.H.Chapin	Donovan, Joseph S.	Dec. 2, 1847	Balto.
Jackson	Andrew	10	Ewarkee	Purvis, James Franklin	March 4, 1841	Balto.
Jackson	Andrew	12	Porpoise	Purvis, James Franklin	Dec. 11, 1841	Balto.
Jackson	Andrew	22	Southerner	Donovan, Joseph S.	Jan. 5, 1852	Balto.
Jackson	Angelina	21	Mary	Maganor, Jane	Nov. 7, 1839	Balto.
Jackson	Angeline	18	General Pinckney	Donovan, Joseph S.	Nov. 10, 1845	Balto.
Jackson	Ann Maria	19	Superb	Slatter, Hope Hull	Nov. 1, 1843	Balto.
Jackson	Archabal	19	Southerner	Donovan, Joseph S.	Oct. 27, 1849	Balto.
Jackson	Arianna	infant	Louisa	Slatter, Hope Hull	Oct. 11, 1847	Balto.
Jackson	Barbara	16	Northumberland	Donovan, Joseph S.	Feb. 27, 1843	Balto.
Jackson	Ben	13	Kirkwood	Donovan, Joseph S.	March 23, 1844	Balto.
Jackson	Butler	20	Phoenix	Rodbind, Ebenezer	March 27, 1847	Balto.
Jackson	Caroline	18	Victorine	Slatter, Hope Hull	Dec. 17, 1845	Balto.
Jackson	Catherine	16	General Pinckney	Donovan, Joseph S.	Nov. 10, 1845	Balto.
Jackson	Charles	9	Northumberland	Slatter, Hope Hull	Feb. 27, 1843	Balto.
Jackson	Charles	20	Union	Donovan, Joseph S.	May 13, 1848	Balto.
Jackson	Charles	18	Victorine	Rodbind, Ebenezer	Dec. 31, 1846	Balto.
Jackson	Chloe	13	Kirkwood	Donovan, Joseph S.	March 23, 1844	Balto.
Jackson	Clare	23	Elizabeth	Donovan, Joseph S.	Nov. 18, 1848	Balto.
Jackson	Cornelius	20	Justina	Donovan, Joseph S.	Dec. 2, 1852	Balto.
Jackson	Crissy	20	Isaac Franklin	Kephart, George	Sept. 28, 1838	Balto.
Jackson	David	22	Helen A. Miller	Campbell, Bernard M.	Oct. 18, 1852	Balto.
Jackson	David	21	Kirkwood	Donovan, Joseph S.	Apr. 15, 1845	Balto.
Jackson	David	7	Pioneer	Slatter, Hope Hull	Sept. 15, 1847	Balto.

Surname	First Name	Age	Ship	O/S	Date	Depart
Jackson	Deby	17	Kirkwood	Slatter, Hope Hull	Dec. 23, 1843	Balto.
Jackson	Delila	14	Victorine	Rodhind, Ebenezer	Dec. 31, 1846	Balto.
Jackson	Eda	15	Victorine	Slatter, Hope Hull	March 1, 1845	Balto.
Jackson	Edward	20	Jane Henderson	Campbell, Bernard M.	Nov. 1, 1852	Balto.
Jackson	Edward	16	Northumberland	Slatter, Hope Hull	Feb. 27, 1843	Balto.
Jackson	Elijah	20	Lady Monroe	Woo folk, Austin	March 25, 1825	Balto.
Jackson	Eliza	25	General Pinckney	Slatter, Hope Hull	Jan. 19, 1847	Balto.
Jackson	Eliza	4	Isaac Franklin	Kephart, George	Sept. 28, 1838	Balto.
Jackson	Eliza	23	Narragansett	Campbell, Bernard M.	Nov. 27, 1850	Balto.
Jackson	Eliza	23	Pioneer	Slatter, Hope Hull	Sept. 15, 1847	Balto.
Jackson	Elizabeth	17	Isaac Franklin	Kephart, George	Sept. 28, 1838	Balto.
Jackson	Ellen	25	General Pinckney	Slatter, Hope Hull	Jan. 19, 1847	Balto.
Jackson	Emly	10	Union	Donovan, Joseph S.	March 17, 1849	Balto.
Jackson	Ephraim	28	Pioneer	Stuart, William R.	July 20, 1848	Balto.
Jackson	Eveline	16	Southerner	Campbell, Bernard M.	Jan. 5, 1852	Balto.
Jackson	Frank	19	Kirkwood	Slatter, Hope Hull	Dec. 23, 1843	Balto.
Jackson	George	12	Napier	Hammond. T.G.	Nov. 3, 1842	Balto.
Jackson	Harriett	19	Kirkwood	Slatter, Hope Hull	Oct. 16, 1845	Balto.
Jackson	Harriett	4	Pioneer	Slatter, Hope Hull	Sept. 15, 1847	Balto.
Jackson	Harry	15	Lady Mcnroe	Woolfolk, Austin	March 25, 1825	Balto.
Jackson	Henney	18	Louisa	Slatter, Hope Hull	Oct. 11, 1847	Balto.
Jackson	Henrietta	25	Jefferson	Woolfolk. Austin	Dec. 24, 1827	Balto.
Jackson	Henry	24	Elizabeth	Campbell Bernard M.	March 21, 1850	Balto.
Jackson	Henry	26	General Pinckney	Slatter, Hope Hull	Jan. 19, 1847	Balto.
Jackson	Henry	20	John C. Calhoun	Donovan, Joseph S.	Oct. 24, 1850	Balto.
Jackson	Henry	25	Solomon Saltus	Slatter, Hope Hull	Oct. 7, 1839	Balto.

Surname	First Name	Age	Ship	O/S	Date	Depart
Jackson	Henry	13	Southerner	Donovan, Joseph S.	Oct. 27, 1849	Balto.
Jackson	Henry	14	Union	Donovan, Joseph S.	Dec. 16, 1848	Balto.
Jackson	Jack	25	Kirkwood	Donovan, Joseph S.	Oct. 16, 1845	Balto.
Jackson	James	12	Elizabeth	Donovan, Joseph S.	Nov. 18, 1848	Balto.
Jackson	James	10	Northumberland	Slatter, Hope Hull	Feb. 27, 1843	Balto.
Jackson	James	32	Orbit	Woolfolk, Austin	Apr. 16, 1825	Balto.
Jackson	James	27	Orbit	Woolfolk, Joseph B.	Apr. 16, 1825	Balto.
Jackson	James	20	Union	Rodbind, Ebenezer	Nov. 17, 1849	Balto.
Jackson	Jesse	30	Ewarkee	Slatter, Hope Hull	March 4, 1841	Balto.
Jackson	Joe	12	Peru	Slatter, Hope Hull	Nov. 16, 1842	Balto.
Jackson	John	infant	General Pinckney	Slatter, Hope Hull	Jan. 19, 1847	Balto.
Jackson	John	26	Helen A. Miller	Campbell, Bernard M.	Oct. 18, 1852	Balto.
Jackson	John	18	Henry A. Barling	Campbell, Bernard M.	Feb. 24, 1851	Balto.
Jackson	John	4	Narragansett	Campbell, Bernard M.	Nov. 27, 1850	Balto.
Jackson	John	20	Nathaniel Hooper	Donovan, Joseph S.	Feb. 12, 1852	Balto.
Jackson	John	7	Peru	Slatter, Hope Hull	Nov. 16, 1842	Balto.
Jackson	John	16	Southerner	Campbell, Bernard M.	Jan. 5, 1852	Balto.
Jackson	John	16	Zoe	Slatter, Hope Hull	Feb. 16, 1847	Balto.
Jackson	Jonathan	20	Home	Donovan, Joseph S.	March 22, 1845	Balto.
Jackson	Joseph	18	Union	Donovan, Joseph S.	Dec. 16, 1848	Balto.
Jackson	Kell	13	Brunswick	Woolfolk, Austin	Oct. 11, 1831	Balto.
Jackson	Keziah	22	Uncas	Slatter, Hope Hull	Jan. 10, 1838	Balto.
Jackson	Lemeul	18	Union	Campbell, Bernard M.	March 17, 1849	Balto.
Jackson	Levi	22	Victorine	Rodbind, Ebenezer	Dec. 31, 1846	Balto.
Jackson	Lewis	22	Ewarkee	Purvis, James Franklin	March 4, 1841	Balto.
Jackson	Lewis	20	Superb	Slatter, Hope Hull	Nov. 1, 1843	Balto.

Surname	First Name	Age	Ship	O/S	Date	Depart
Jackson	Lewis	22	Victorine	Rodbind, Ebenezer	Dec. 31, 1846	Balto.
Jackson	Loyd	21	Leda	Donovan, Joseph S.	May 30, 1846	Balto.
Jackson	Lucy	20	Louisa	Slatter, Hope Hull	Oct. 11, 1847	Balto.
Jackson	Madison	23	Victorine	Slatter, Hope Hull	Sept. 12, 1846	Balto.
Jackson	Marcia	21	Billow	Woolfolk, Joseph B.	Feb. 23, 1828	Balto.
Jackson	Margaret	6 mon.	Isaac Franklin	Kephart, George	Sept. 28, 1838	Balto.
Jackson	Margrey	14	Victorine	Rodbind, Ebenezer	March 1, 1845	Balto.
Jackson	Maria	20	Jasper	Woolfolk, Austin	Apr. 7, 1827	Balto.
Jackson	Maria	14	Louisa	Slatter, Hope Hull	Oct. 11, 1847	Balto.
Jackson	Maria	19	Margaret Hugg	Slatter, Hope Hull	Feb. 8, 1845	Balto.
Jackson	Mariah	15	Kirkwood	Donovan, Joseph S.	Oct. 26, 1847	Balto.
Jackson	Mariah	21	Victorine	Donovan, Joseph S.	May 22, 1844	Balto.
Jackson	Marshall	14	General Pinckney	Donovan, Joseph S.	Nov. 10, 1845	Balto.
Jackson	Mary	3	Elizabeth	Donovan, Joseph S.	Nov. 18, 1848	Balto.
Jackson	Mary	18	Frances Amy	Donovan, Joseph S.	Jan. 20, 1847	Balto.
Jackson	Mary	19	Hermitage	Williams, Thomas	Oct. 28, 1846	Balto.
Jackson	Mary	infant	Southerner	Donovan, Jospeh S.	Jan. 5, 1852	Balto.
Jackson	Mary A.	40	Victorine	Rodbind, Ebenezer	Dec. 31, 1846	Balto.
Jackson	Middleton	4	Billow	Woolfolk, Joseph B.	Feb. 23, 1828	Balto.
Jackson	Nancy	14	Margaret Hugg	Campbell, Bernard M.	Nov. 30, 1844	Balto.
Jackson	Nathan	21	Bostonian	Slatter, Hope Hull	Jan. 18, 1841	Balto.
Jackson	Ned	30	Helen A. Miller	Campbell, Bernard M.	Oct. 18, 1852	Balto.
Jackson	Oliver	25	Ann & Leah	Woolfolk, Austin	Nov.1, 1831	Balto.
Jackson	Perry	20	Lady Monroe	Woolfolk, Austin	Sept. 29, 1825	Balto.
Jackson	Peter	23	Mary Broughton	Campbell, Bernard M.	Nov. 18, 1851	Balto.
Jackson	Philip	16	Victorine	Rodbind, Ebenezer	Dec. 31, 1846	Balto.

Surname	First Name	Age	Ship	O/S	Date	Depart
Jackson	Priscilla	25	Salvadora	Slatter, Hope Hull	Sept. 28, 1846	Balto.
Jackson	Robert	18	Ganniclefft	Slatter, Hope Hull	Nov. 25, 1840	Balto.
Jackson	Robert	28	Kirkwood	Rodbind, Ebenezer	Apr. 15, 1845	Balto.
Jackson	Rose	22	States	Woolfolk, Austin	Nov. 21, 1827	Balto.
Jackson	Rose	16	Tippecanoe	Staples, Joshua	Jan. 17, 1842	Balto.
Jackson	Sam	50	Isaac Franklin	Kephart, George	Feb. 1, 1839	Balto.
Jackson	Samuel	11	Catharine	Donovan, Joseph S.	Jan. 18, 1845	Balto.
Jackson	Samuel	20	Kirkwood	Donovan, Joseph S.	Dec. 10, 1846	Balto.
Jackson	Samuel	18	Victorine	Donovan, Joseph S.	Sept. 29, 1845	Balto.
Jackson	Sandy	22	Louisa	Campbell, Bernard M.	May 18, 1846	Balto.
Jackson	Sophia	4	Louisa	Slatter, Hope Hull	Oct. 11, 1847	Balto.
Jackson	Srarah	17	Kirkwood	Williams, Thomas	Apr. 4, 1846	Balto.
Jackson	Stephen	21	Lafayette	Woolfolk, Austin	Oct. 18, 1828	Balto.
Jackson	Thomas	18	Charles	Donovan, Joseph S.	Apr. 23, 1851	Balto.
Jackson	Thomas	15	Kirkwood	Donovan, Joseph S.	Dec. 10, 1846	Balto.
Jackson	Thomas	16	Kirkwood	Campbell, Bernard M.	March 9, 1847	Balto.
Jackson	Thomas	24	Sarah Bridge	Campbell, Bernard M.	Feb. 8, 1851	Balto.
Jackson	Thomas	20	Victorine	Donovan, Joseph S.	March 14, 1846	Balto.
Jackson	Washington	14	Ann & Leah	Woolfolk, Austin	Nov.1, 1831	Balto.
Jackson	William	20	Nancy W. Stevens	Rodbind, Ebenezer	Feb. 18, 1845	Balto.
Jackson	William	9	Peru	Slatter, Hope Hull	Nov. 16, 1842	Balto.
Jackson	William	31	States	Woolfolk, Austin	Nov. 21, 1827	Balto.
Jackson	William	17	Union	Campbell, Bernard M.	Dec. 16, 1848	Balto.
Jackson	Wotter	21	Isaac Franklin	Kephart, George	Sept. 28, 1838	Balto.
Jackson			Frances Amy	Donovan, Joseph S.	Jan. 20, 1847	Balto.
Jackson		19	Lafayette	Woolfolk, Richard	Oct. 18, 1828	Balto.

Surname	First Name	Age	Ship	O/S	Date	Depart
Jackson		infant	Phoenix	Donovan, Joseph S.	March 27, 1847	Balto.
Jacobs	Amelia	22	Lafayette	Harker, William	March 25, 1843	Balto.
Jacobs	Henry	11	Superb	Slatter, Hope Hull	Nov. 1, 1843	Balto.
Jacobs	Hiram	19	Ewarkee	Purvis, James Franklin	March 4, 1841	Balto.
Jacobs	Linbly	8	Home	Donovan, Joseph S.	March 22, 1845	Balto.
Jacobs	Mary Jane	4	Lafayette	Harker, William	March 25, 1843	Balto.
Jacobs	Rebecca	12 mon.	Lafayette	Harker, William	March 25, 1843	Balto.
James	Barbara	20	Northumberland	Slatter, Hope Hull	Feb. 27, 1843	Balto.
James	Ben	18	Brunswick	Woolfolk, Austin	Oct. 11, 1831	Balto.
James	Caroline	26	Victorine	Slatter, Hope Hull	March 9, 1844	Balto.
James	Daniel	20	Helen A. Miller	Campbell, Bernard M.	Oct. 18, 1852	Balto.
James	Elizabeth	20	Pioneer	Slatter, Hope Hull	Sept. 15, 1847	Balto.
James	Francis	21	Tippecanoe	Slatter, Hope Hull	Apr. 1, 1841	Balto.
James	Francis	infant	Victorine	Donovan, Joseph S.	May 14, 1845	Balto.
James	George	20	Kirkwood	Donovan, Joseph S.	Oct. 14, 1848	Balto.
James	James Henry	infant	Victorine	Slatter, Hope Hull	March 9, 1844	Balto.
James	Josiah	19	Victorine	Donovar, Joseph S.	May 14, 1845	Balto.
James	Ladd	22	Ann & Leah	Woolfolk, Austin	Nov.1, 1831	Balto.
James	Levia	16	Superb	Slatter, Hope Hull	Nov. 1, 1843	Balto.
Jameson	Asbury	25	Kirkwood	Slatter, Hope Hull	Dec. 23, 1843	Balto.
Jamison	James	22	John C. Calhoun	Donovan, Joseph S.	Oct. 24, 1850	Balto.
Jane	Eliza	5	Margaret Hugg	Campbell, Bernard M.	Nov. 30, 1844	Balto.
Jane	Hester	10	Margaret Hugg	Campbell, Bernard M.	Nov. 30, 1844	Balto.
Janes	Harriett	3	Alfred	Woolfolk, Austin	May 7, 1825	Balto.
Janifer	Colonel	39	General Pinckney	Slatter, Hope Hull	Jan. 19, 1847	Balto.
Janus	Liddy	18	Tippecanoe	Slatter, Hope Hull	Jan. 17, 1842	Balto.

Surname	First Name	Age	Ship	O/S	Date	Depart
Jarett	Randall	22	Louisa	Campbell, Bernard M.	Nov. 5, 1849	Balto.
Jarvis	Curry	20	Ewarkee	Purvis, James Franklin	March 4, 1841	Balto.
Jason	John	13	Billow	Woolfolk, Austin	Feb. 23, 1828	Balto.
Jason	Lewis	20	Union	Donovan, Joseph S.	May 13, 1848	Balto.
Jeams	Henry	24	Kirkwood	Rodbind, Ebenezer	Apr. 15, 1845	Balto.
Jefferson	Charles	38	Arctic	Smith, Leonard J.	Jan. 29, 1828	St. Mary's
Jefferson	Henny	3	Brunswick	Woolfolk, Austin	Oct. 11, 1831	Balto.
Jefferson	Thomas	45	Brandywine	Campbell, Bernard M.	Oct. 15, 1852	Balto.
Jefferson	Thomas	21	Margaret Forbs	Slatter, Hope Hull	Nov. 28, 1838	Balto.
Jefferson	Thomas	28	Solomon Saltus	Slatter, Hope Hull	Oct. 7, 1839	Balto.
Jefferson	Thomas	35	Strafford	Harker, William	Nov. 22, 1843	Balto.
Jefferson	Washington	16	Margaret Hugg	Slatter, Hope Hull	Feb. 8, 1845	Balto.
Jefferson	William	14	Irad Ferry	Purvis, James Franklin	Feb. 5, 1842	Balto.
Jeffrey	John	24	Victorine	Slatter, Hope Hull	March 9, 1844	Balto.
Jeffry	Josana	21	John C. Calhoun	Donovan, Joseph S.	Oct. 24, 1850	Balto.
Jeffry	William	23	John C. Calhoun	Donovan, Joseph S.	Oct. 24, 1850	Balto.
Jemison	Abraham	23	Architect	Donovan, Joseph S.	Apr. 25, 1846	Balto.
Jenifer	Edward	20	General Pinckney	Campbell, Bernard M.	Jan. 19, 1847	Balto.
Jenifer	James	25	Isaac Franklin	Slatter, Hope Hull	Sept. 28, 1838	Balto.
Jenifer	John	20	John C. Calhoun	Donovan, Joseph S.	Oct. 24, 1850	Balto.
Jenifer	John	10	Mary	Harker, William	Feb. 10, 1844	Balto.
Jenifer	John	15	Victorine	Harker, William	March 9, 1844	Balto.
Jenifer	Sally	18	Henry A. Barling	Campbell, Walter L.	Oct. 28, 1848	Balto.
Jenkins	Adeline	19	Kirkwood	Donovan, Joseph S.	Nov. 28, 1849	Balto.
Jenkins	Ann	28	Burlington	Slatter, Hope Hull	Oct. 21, 1842	Balto.
Jenkins	Ann	32	Burlington	Slatter, Hope Hull	Oct. 21, 1842	Balto.

Surname	First Name	Age	Ship	O/S	Date	Depart
Jenkins	Ann	18	Tweed	Tucker, J.B.	Oct. 20, 1836	Town Creek
Jenkins	Armstead	18	Kirkwood	Donovan, Joseph S.	March 9, 1847	Balto.
Jenkins	Elizabeth	16	Kirkwood	Donovan, Joseph S.	Nov. 28, 1849	Balto.
Jenkins	George	16	Isaac Franklin	Slatter, Hope Hull	Sept. 28, 1838	Balto.
Jenkins	George	21	Kirkwood	Donovan, Joseph S.	March 9, 1847	Balto.
Jenkins	George	19	Victorine	Donovan, Joseph S.	Dec. 31, 1846	Balto.
Jenkins	Jacob	21	Victorine	Donovan, Joseph S.	May 22, 1844	Balto.
Jenkins	John	23	Southerner	Donovan, Joseph S.	Oct. 27, 1849	Balto.
Jenkins	Joseph	20	Orbit	Woolfolk, Austin	Apr. 16, 1825	Balto.
Jenkins	Joshua	22	Superb	Anderson, David	Apr. 6, 1819	Balto.
Jenkins	Mary	15	Elizabeth	Campbell, Bernard M.	Jan. 2, 1850	Balto.
Jenkins	Mary	19	Tweed	Tucker, J.B.	Oct. 20, 1836	Town Creek
Jenkins	Simon	23	Brunswick	Woolfolk, Austin	Oct. 11, 1831	Balto.
Jenkins	Thomas	12	Victorine	Campbell, Bernard M.	Dec. 31, 1846	Balto.
Jenkins	Vincent	21	States	Woolfolk, Austin	Nov. 21, 1827	Balto.
Jenkins	William	18	Union	Campbell, Bernard M.	Dec. 16, 1848	Balto.
Jennings	Betsey	15	Jefferson	Woolfolk, Austin	Dec. 24, 1827	Balto.
Jennings	Mary	15	Kirkwood	Donovan, Joseph S.	Dec. 10, 1846	Balto.
Jenus	Christina	24	Kirkwood	Donovan, Joseph S.	Jan. 4, 1845	Balto.
Jenus	William	25	Kirkwood	Donovan, Joseph S.	Jan. 4, 1845	Balto.
Jessop	Harriet	16	Kirkwood	Donovan, Joseph S.	Jan. 4, 1845	Balto.
Jett	Winney	30	General Pinckney	Rodbind, Ebenezer	Feb. 21, 1846	Balto.
Jiams	Lucius	26	Seaman	Slatter, Hope Hull	Dec. 19, 1838	Balto.
Jiles	Henson	20	Isaac Franklin	Slatter, Hope Hull	Sept. 28, 1838	Balto.
Jiles	Susan	16	Union	Campbell, Bernard M.	March 17, 1849	Balto.
Joans	Isaac	30	Architect	Slatter, Hope Hull	May 20, 1841	Balto.

Surname	First Name	Age	Ship	O/S	Date	Depart
Jobs	Mariah	17	Kirkwood	Donovan, Joseph S.	Oct. 14, 1848	Balto.
Johns	Cassy	24	Brunswick	Woolfolk, Austin	Oct. 11, 1831	Balto.
Johns	Charles	21	Tippecanoe	Slatter, Hope Hull	Apr. 1, 1841	Balto.
Johns	Edward	26	Elizabeth	Campbell, Bernard M.	Jan. 2, 1850	Balto.
Johns	Ennolds	24	Brunswick	Woolfolk, Austin	Oct. 11, 1831	Balto.
Johns	Henry	24	Scotia	Harker, William	Sept. 30, 1843	Balto.
Johns	Hercules	5	Decatur	Stansburg, Tobias E.	Oct. 24, 1819	Balto.
Johns	Jack	30	Isaac Franklin	Slatter, Hope Hull	Sept. 28, 1838	Balto.
Johns	Jacob	19	Liberator	Woolfolk, Austin	Nov. 12, 1828	Balto.
Johns	Louisa	20	Decatur	Stansburg, Tobias E.	Oct. 24, 1819	Balto.
Johns	Matilda	16	Brunswick	Woolfolk, Austin	Oct. 11, 1831	Balto.
Johns	Sarah	18	Eliza	Slatter, Hope Hull	Oct. 9, 1840	Balto.
Johns	William	19	Tippecanoe	Slatter, Hope Hull	Apr. 1, 1841	Balto.
Johnson	Abigail	16	Victorine	Donovan, Joseph S.	Oct. 25, 1844	Balto.
Johnson	Abraham	25	America	Lewing, Clinton	Sept. 23, 1852	Balto.
Johnson	Abraham	12	Superb	Woolfolk, Austin	Apr. 6, 1819	Balto.
Johnson	Alexander	infant	Kirkwood	Donovan, Joseph S.	Jan. 4, 1845	Balto.
Johnson	Alice	16	Salvadora	Slatter, Hope Hull	Sept. 28, 1846	Balto.
Johnson	Alvina	9	Kirkwood	Donovan, Joseph S.	Oct. 14, 1848	Balto.
Johnson	Amanda	20	Margaret Hugg	Harker, William	Feb. 8, 1845	Balto.
Johnson	Amanda	16	Solomon Saltus	Slatter, Hope Hull	Oct. 7, 1839	Balto.
Johnson	Amos	26	Harriett	Murdock, William	March 4, 1823	Balto.
Johnson	Andrew	15	Irad Ferry	Slatter, Hope Hull	Dec. 9, 1842	Balto.
Johnson	Ann	18	Bostonian	Slatter, Hope Hull	Jan. 18, 1841	Balto.
Johnson	Ann	19	Henry A. Barling	Campbell, Walter L.	Oct. 28, 1848	Balto.
Johnson	Ann	17	Isaac Franklin	Slatter, Hope Hull	Sept. 28, 1838	Balto.

Surname	First Name	Age	Ship	O/S	Date	Depart
Johnson	Ann	28	Jane Henderson	Campbell, Bernard M.	Nov. 1, 1852	Balto.
Johnson	Barney	24	Paol	Slatter, Hope Hull	Sept. 9, 1845	Balto.
Johnson	Becky	20	Irad Ferry	Wilson, J.W.	May 6, 1839	Balto.
Johnson	Belsa	14	Kirkwood	Donovan, Joseph S.	Oct. 14, 1848	Balto.
Johnson	Benjamin	21	Phoenix	Donovan, Joseph S.	March 27, 1847	Balto.
Johnson	Benjamin	10	Southerner	Donovan, Joseph S.	Oct. 27, 1849	Balto.
Johnson	Benjamin	18	Waverly	Campbell, Bernard M.	Apr. 3, 1851	Balto.
Johnson	Betsey	11	Ann & Leah	Woolfolk, Austin	Nov.1, 1831	Balto.
Johnson	Betty	20	Julia	Woolfolk, Austin	Jan. 8, 1829	Balto.
Johnson	Burgess	infant	Victorine	Rodbird, Ebenezer	May 14, 1845	Balto.
Johnson	Caleb	17	Lady Richmond	Woolfolk, Austin	Apr. 30, 1827	Balto.
Johnson	Caroline	16	Glasgow	Slatter, Hope Hull	Oct. 11, 1838	Balto.
Johnson	Caroline	16	Margaret Hugg	Donovan, Joseph S.	Feb. 8, 1845	Balto.
Johnson	Cassey	18	Kirkwood	Donovan, Joseph S.	Oct. 26, 1847	Balto.
Johnson	Catharine	18	Orbit	Woolfolk, Austin	Apr. 16, 1825	Balto.
Johnson	Catherine	21	Superb	Slatter, Hope Hull	Nov. 1, 1843	Balto.
Johnson	Cecilia	12	Uncas	Slatter, Hope Hull	Jan. 10, 1838	Balto.
Johnson	Charles	28	Billow	Woolfolk, Austin	Feb. 23, 1828	Balto.
Johnson	Charles	18	Julia	Woolfolk, Austin	Jan. 8, 1829	Balto.
Johnson	Charles	20	Kirkwood	Slatter, Hope Hull	Oct. 16, 1845	Balto.
Johnson	Charles	18	Kirkwood	Donovan, Joseph S.	Oct. 26, 1847	Balto.
Johnson	Charles	18	Victorine	Slatter, Hope Hull	Dec. 17, 1845	Balto.
Johnson	Charles	18	Waverly	Campbell, Bernard M.	Apr. 3, 1851	Balto.
Johnson	Charlotte	19	Julia	Woolfolk, Austin	Jan. 8, 1829	Balto.
Johnson	Charlotte		Kirkwood	Donovan, Joseph S.	Sept. 28, 1846	Balto.
Johnson	Clara	infant	Union	Sheckles, B.O.	Nov. 17, 1849	Balto.

Surname	First Name	Age	Ship	O/S	Date	Depart
Johnson	Crissa	25	Charles	Campbell, Bernard M.	Dec. 18, 1850	Balto.
Johnson	Curtis	40	Elizabeth	Donovan, Joseph S.	Oct. 6, 1849	Balto.
Johnson	Daniel	25	Jefferson	Woolfolk, Austin	Dec. 24, 1827	Balto.
Johnson	David	18	General Pinckney	Slatter, Hope Hull	Jan. 19, 1847	Balto.
Johnson	David	12 mon.	Kirkwood	Crow, William	March 23, 1844	Balto.
Johnson	David	32	Victorine	Slatter, Hope Hull	March 1, 1845	Balto.
Johnson	Delia	15	Home	Rodbind, Ebenezer	March 22, 1845	Balto.
Johnson	Delila	21	Zoe	Slatter, Hope Hull	Feb. 16, 1847	Balto.
Johnson	Dennis	21	Kirkwood	Donovan, Joseph S.	March 23, 1844	Balto.
Johnson	Dianna	20	Kirkwood	Donovan, Joseph S.	Oct. 14, 1848	Balto.
Johnson	Edward	16	Brunswick	Woolfolk, Austin	Oct. 11, 1831	Balto.
Johnson	Edward	20	Catharine	Slatter, Hope Hull	Jan. 24, 1843	Balto.
Johnson	Edward	26	Victorine	Slatter, Hope Hull	Sept. 12, 1846	Balto.
Johnson	Elijah	19	Seaman	Slatter, Shadrack	March 25, 1839	Balto.
Johnson	Eliza	16	Frances Amy	Donovan, Joseph S.	Jan. 20, 1847	Balto.
Johnson	Eliza	16	Kirkwood	Donovan, Joseph S.	Dec. 23, 1843	Balto.
Johnson	Eliza Ann	17	Tippecanoe	Purvis, James Franklin	Jan. 17, 1842	Balto.
Johnson	Eliza Jane	16	Superb	Slatter, Hope Hull	Nov. 1, 1843	Balto.
Johnson	Elizabeth	16	Kirkwood	Campbell, Bernard M.	March 9, 1847	Balto.
Johnson	Elizabeth	16	Margaret Hugg	Donovan, Joseph S.	Feb. 8, 1845	Balto.
Johnson	Elizabeth	18	Seaman	Slatter, Shadrack	March 25, 1839	Balto.
Johnson	Elizabeth	15	Union	Rodbind, Ebenezer	Dec. 16, 1848	Balto.
Johnson	Elizabeth	infant	Victorine	Slatter, Hope Hull	March 9, 1844	Balto.
Johnson	Ellen	17	Kirkwood	Donovan, Joseph S.	Dec. 10, 1846	Balto.
Johnson	Ellen	18	Tippecanoe	Slatter, Hope Hull	Jan. 17, 1842	Balto.
Johnson	Ellen	2	Victorine	Slatter, Hope Hull	March 9, 1844	Balto.

Surname	First Name	Age	Ship	O/S	Date	Depart
Johnson	Ellin	8	Kirkwood	Donovan, Joseph S.	Oct. 14, 1848	Balto.
Johnson	Emmit	26	Northumberland	Slatter, Hope Hull	Feb. 27, 1843	Balto.
Johnson	Ezekiel	19	Henry A. Barling	Donovan, Joseph S.	Feb. 24, 1851	Balto.
Johnson	Fanny	9	Hibernia	Woolfolk, Austin	Dec. 5, 1826	Balto.
Johnson	Fanny	14	Victorine	Rodbird, Ebenezer	March 14, 1846	Balto.
Johnson	Fillis	35	Victorine	Slatter, Hope Hull	March 9, 1844	Balto.
Johnson	Flavilla	17	Pioneer	Slatter, Hope Hull	Sept. 15, 1847	Balto.
Johnson	Frank	19	Ann & Leah	Woolfolk, Austin	Nov. 1, 1831	Balto.
Johnson	Frederick	14	John C. Calhoun	Donovan, Joseph S.	Oct. 24, 1850	Balto.
Johnson	George	20	Architect	Campbell, Bernard M.	Apr. 25, 1846	Balto.
Johnson	George	20	Ewarkee	Slatter, Hope Hull	March 4, 1841	Balto.
Johnson	George	19	Gazelle	Staples, Joseph	Feb. 28, 1842	Balto.
Johnson	George	19	Kirkwood	Slatter, Hope Hull	Dec. 23, 1843	Balto.
Johnson	George	14	Kirkwood	Campbell, Bernard M.	Jan. 4, 1845	Balto.
Johnson	George	21	Kirkwood	Donovan, Joseph S.	Sept. 28, 1846	Balto.
Johnson	George	20	Mars	Woolfolk, Austin	Oct. 30, 1824	Balto.
Johnson	George	18	Sultana	Kelso, George G.	Oct. 31, 1827	Balto.
Johnson	George	14	Superb	Slatter, Hope Hull	Nov. 1, 1843	Balto.
Johnson	George Thomas	15	Manchester	Elder, B.T.	June 14, 1848	Balto.
Johnson	Gracy	20	Ann & Leah	Woolfolk, Austin	Nov. 1, 1831	Balto.
Johnson	Gracy	24	Cora	Campbell, Bernard M.	Jan. 20, 1851	Balto.
Johnson	Grafton	20	Southerner	Donovan, Joseph S.	Oct. 27, 1849	Balto.
Johnson	Hannah	19	Kirkwood	Crow, William	March 23, 1844	Balto.
Johnson	Hannah	15	Paoli	Slatter, Hope Hull	Sept. 9, 1845	Balto.
Johnson	Harriet	infant	Kirkwood	Campbell, Bernard M.	Dec. 10, 1846	Balto.
Johnson	Harriett	16	Betsey	Woolfolk, Austin	Apr. 29, 1828	Balto.

Surname	First Name	Age	Ship	O/S	Date	Depart
Johnson	Harriett	20	Kirkwood	Donovan, Joseph S.	Dec. 10, 1846	Balto.
Johnson	Harriett	11	Kirkwood	Donovan, Joseph S.	Oct. 14, 1848	Balto.
Johnson	Harriott	22	Catharine	Slatter, Hope Hull	Jan. 24, 1843	Balto.
Johnson	Harry	37	Harriett	Greendy, Thomas B.	March 6, 1823	Balto.
Johnson	Harry	35	Victorine	Rodbind, Ebenezer	March 1, 1845	Balto.
Johnson	Henaritta	16	Victorine	Donovan, Joseph S.	Sept. 29, 1845	Balto.
Johnson	Henney	15	Jefferson	Woolfolk, Austin	Dec. 24, 1827	Balto.
Johnson	Henrietta	10	Kirkwood	Campbell, Bernard M.	Apr. 15, 1845	Balto.
Johnson	Henry	3	Jefferson	Woolfolk, Joseph B.	Dec. 24, 1827	Balto.
Johnson	Henry	24	John C. Calhoun	Donovan, Joseph S.	Oct. 24, 1850	Balto.
Johnson	Henry	13	Kirkwood	Slatter, Hope Hull	Apr. 15, 1845	Balto.
Johnson	Henry	17	Kirkwood	Campbell, Bernard M.	Jan. 14, 1846	Balto.
Johnson	Henry	6	Kirkwood	Donovan, Joseph S.	Oct. 14, 1848	Balto.
Johnson	Henry	17	Seaman	Slatter, Shadrack	March 25, 1839	Balto.
Johnson	Henry	28	States	Woolfolk, Austin	Apr. 14, 1828	Balto.
Johnson	Henry	21	Victorine	Slatter, Hope Hull	Sept. 12, 1846	Balto.
Johnson	Henry (Jr.)	17	Victorine	Slatter, Hope Hull	Sept. 12, 1846	Balto.
Johnson	Henson	18	Kirkwood	Donovan, Joseph S.	Apr. 15, 1845	Balto.
Johnson	Hester	16	Nathaniel Hooper	Campbell, Bernard M.	Feb. 12, 1852	Balto.
Johnson	Hiram	21	Kirkwood	Donovan, Joseph S.	Oct. 14, 1848	Balto.
Johnson	Horace	10	Ewarkee	Purvis, James Franklin	March 4, 1841	Balto.
Johnson	Isaac	25	Margaret Hugg	Donovan, Joseph S.	Feb. 8, 1845	Balto.
Johnson	Isaac	25	Superb	Slatter, Hope Hull	Nov. 1, 1843	Balto.
Johnson	Isabella	22	Kirkwood	Slatter, Hope Hull	Jan. 4, 1845	Balto.
Johnson	Israel	20	Kirkwood	Donovan, Joseph S.	Oct. 14, 1848	Balto.
Johnson	Jackson	20	Southerner	Rodbind, Ebenezer	Jan. 21, 1850	Balto.

Surname	First Name	Age	Ship	O/S	Date	Depart
Johnson	Jacob	21	Lady Monroe	Woolfolk, Austin	March 25, 1825	Balto.
Johnson	James	23	Clio	Anderson, David	March 20, 1819	Balto.
Johnson	James	29	Henry A. Barling	Donovan, Joseph S.	Feb. 24, 1851	Balto.
Johnson	James	25	Hibernia	Woolfolk, Austin	Dec. 5, 1826	Balto.
Johnson	James	infant	Kirkwood	Donovan, Joseph S.	Oct. 14, 1848	Balto.
Johnson	James	26	Victorine	Slatter, Hope Hull	March 9, 1844	Balto.
Johnson	Jane	22	Kirkwood	Campbell, Bernard M.	Dec. 10, 1846	Balto.
Johnson	Jane	15	Kirkwood	Campbell, Bernard M.	March 9, 1847	Balto.
Johnson	Jane	20	Union	Sheckles, B.O.	Nov. 17, 1849	Balto.
Johnson	Jarrett	24	Southerner	Campbell, Bernard M.	Jan. 5, 1852	Balto.
Johnson	Jarvis	21	Isaac Franklin	Kephart, George	Sept. 28, 1838	Balto.
Johnson	Jeffrey	26	Jane Henderson	Campbell, Bernard M.	Nov. 1, 1852	Balto.
Johnson	Jerry	23	Brunswick	Woolfolk, Austin	Oct. 11, 1831	Balto.
Johnson	Jesse	18	Kirkwood	Campbell, Bernard M.	Nov. 28, 1849	Balto.
Johnson	Jim	22	Kirkwood	Rodbind, Ebenezer	Oct. 26, 1847	Balto.
Johnson	Jim	18	Mary Broughton	Campbell, Bernard M.	Nov. 18, 1851	Balto.
Johnson	Jim	10	Pioneer	Slatter, Hope Hull	Sept. 15, 1847	Balto.
Johnson	Jim	22	States	Woolfolk, Joseph B.	Nov. 21, 1827	Balto.
Johnson	John	23	Architect	Donovan, Joseph S.	Apr. 25, 1846	Balto.
Johnson	John	22	Burlington	Slatter, Hope Hull	Oct. 21, 1842	Balto.
Johnson	John	21	Emilie	Anderson, David	March 27, 1821	Balto.
Johnson	John	28	Hercules	Kennedy, William	July 14, 1832	Balto.
Johnson	John	21	Isaac Franklin	Slatter, Hope Hull	Sept. 28, 1838	Balto.
Johnson	John	40	Jefferson	Woolfolk, Joseph B.	Dec. 24, 1827	Balto.
Johnson	John	21	Justina	Donovan, Joseph S.	Dec. 2, 1852	Balto.
Johnson	John	20	Mary	Purvis, Isaac	March 2, 1840	Balto.

Surname	First Name	Age	Ship	O/S	Date	Depart
Johnson	John	23	St. Mary	Donovan, Joseph S.	Nov. 29, 1845	Balto.
Johnson	John	26	Superb	Slatter, Hope Hull	Nov. 1, 1843	Balto.
Johnson	John	28	Superb	Donovan, Joseph S.	Nov. 2, 1843	Balto.
Johnson	John	22	Tippecanoe	Slatter, Hope Hull	Apr. 1, 1841	Balto.
Johnson	John	3 mon.	Virginia	Woolfolk, Joseph B.	Dec. 19, 1825	Balto.
Johnson	John	20	Zoe	Williams, Thomas	Feb. 16, 1847	Balto.
Johnson	John M.	25	Zoe	Williams, Thomas	Feb. 16, 1847	Balto.
Johnson	Joseph	21	Kirkwood	Crow, William	March 23, 1844	Balto.
Johnson	Joseph		Phoenix	Donovan, Joseph S.	March 27, 1847	Balto.
Johnson	Joseph	22	Scotia	Harker, William	Sept. 30, 1843	Balto.
Johnson	Joseph	21	Victorine	Donovan, Joseph S.	Sept. 29, 1845	Balto.
Johnson	Julia	14	Isaac Franklin	Slatter, Hope Hull	Sept. 28, 1838	Balto.
Johnson	Juliana	11	Kirkwood	Donovan, Joseph S.	Oct. 26, 1847	Balto.
Johnson	Karet	16	Russell	Slatter, Hope Hull	March 1, 1839	Balto.
Johnson	Kathy	35	Bostonian	Slatter, Hope Hull	Jan. 18, 1841	Balto.
Johnson	Kitty	16	Brunswick	Woolfolk, Austin	Oct. 11, 1831	Balto.
Johnson	Kitty	16	Home	Rodbind, Ebenezer	March 22, 1845	Balto.
Johnson	Laura	9	Tweed	Forbes, George	Oct. 20, 1836	Town Creek
Johnson	Leah	20	Lafayette	Woolfolk, Austin	Oct. 18, 1828	Balto.
Johnson	Lenard	23	Victorine	Donovan, Joseph S.	March 14, 1846	Balto.
Johnson	Levin	23	Lafayette	Woolfolk, Austin	Oct. 18, 1828	Balto.
Johnson	Lewis	25	Isaac Franklin	Kephart, George	Feb. 1, 1839	Balto.
Johnson	Lewis	17	Isaac Franklin	Slatter, Hope Hull	Sept. 28, 1838	Balto.
Johnson	Lewis	21	Mary	Purvis, James Franklin	Feb. 8, 1841	Balto.
Johnson	Lewis	30	St. Mary	Williams, Thomas	Nov. 29, 1845	Balto.
Johnson	Louisa	16	Abbott Lord	Campbell, Bernard M.	April 28, 1852	Balto.

Surname	First Name	Age	Ship	O/S	Date	Depart
Johnson	Louisa	17	Lapwing	Woolfolk, Samuel M.	Feb. 15, 1827	Balto.
Johnson	Louisa	21	Victorine	Slatter, Hope Hull	March 9, 1844	Balto.
Johnson	Lucretia	17	Narragansett	Donovan, Joseph S.	Nov. 27, 1850	Balto.
Johnson	Mahaly	25	Solomon Saltus	Slatter, Hope Hull	Oct. 7, 1839	Balto.
Johnson	Maranda	21	Kirkwood	Slatter, Hope Hull	Oct. 16, 1845	Balto.
Johnson	Margaret	16	Kirkwood	Donovan, Joseph S.	Nov. 28, 1849	Balto.
Johnson	Margaret	20	Margaret Forbs	Slatter, Hope Hull	Nov. 28, 1838	Balto.
Johnson	Margarett	25	Southerner	Donovan, Jospeh S.	Jan. 5, 1852	Balto.
Johnson	Maria	1	Catharine	Slatter, Hope Hull	Jan. 24, 1843	Balto.
Johnson	Maria	1	Lafayette	Woolfolk, Austin	Oct. 18, 1828	Balto.
Johnson	Maria	11	Phoenix	Donovan, Joseph S.	March 27, 1847	Balto.
Johnson	Mariah	20	Narragansett	Donovan, Joseph S.	Nov. 27, 1850	Balto.
Johnson	Mariah	20	Seguin	Campbell, Bernard M.	July 12, 1853	Balto.
Johnson	Mariah	13	Victorine	Donovan, Joseph S.	March 14, 1846	Balto.
Johnson	Mary	19	Ann & Leah	Woolfolk, Austin	Nov. 1, 1831	Balto.
Johnson	Mary	16	Architect	Campbell, Bernard M.	Apr. 25, 1846	Balto.
Johnson	Mary	22	Eliza	Slatter, Hope Hull	Oct. 9, 1840	Balto.
Johnson	Mary	17	Hibernia	Woolfolk, Austin	Dec. 5, 1826	Balto.
Johnson	Mary	17	Jane Henderson	Campbell, Bernard M.	Nov. 1, 1852	Balto.
Johnson	Mary	40	Jefferson	Woolfolk, Joseph B.	Dec. 24, 1827	Balto.
Johnson	Mary	30	Kirkwood	Slatter, Hope Hull	Apr. 15, 1845	Balto.
Johnson	Mary	15	Kirkwood	Donovan, Joseph S.	Dec. 10, 1846	Balto.
Johnson	Mary	17	Mars	Woolfolk, Austin	Oct. 30, 1824	Balto.
Johnson	Mary	14	Phoenix	Donovan, Joseph S.	March 27, 1847	Balto.
Johnson	Mary	18	Tippecanoe	Slatter, Hope Hull	Dec. 16, 1840	Balto.
Johnson	Mary	9	Victorine	Harker, William	March 9, 1844	Balto.

Surname	First Name	Age	Ship	O/S	Date	Depart
Johnson	Mary	19	Victorine	Rodbind, Ebenezer	May 14, 1845	Balto.
Johnson	Mary	18	W.H.D.C.Wright	Slatter, Hope Hull	Nov. 7, 1847	Balto.
Johnson	Mary Ann	18	Hermitage	Slatter, Hope Hull	Oct. 28, 1846	Balto.
Johnson	Mary Clare	17	Kirkwood	Donovan, Joseph S.	March 23, 1844	Balto.
Johnson	Mary Elizabeth	20	Kirkwood	Slatter, Hope Hull	Jan. 4, 1845	Balto.
Johnson	Mary Jane	13	Manchester	Elder, B.T.	June 14, 1848	Balto.
Johnson	Matilda	18	Ann & Leah	Woolfolk, Austin	Nov.1, 1831	Balto.
Johnson	Matilda	16	Kirkwood	Slatter, Hope Hull	Dec. 23, 1843	Balto.
Johnson	Matty	26	Tangier	Campbell, Bernard M.	Nov. 26, 1853	Balto.
Johnson	Milly	12	Ann & Leah	Woolfolk, Austin	Nov.1, 1831	Balto.
Johnson	Milly	9	Salvadora	Slatter, Hope Hull	Sept. 28, 1846	Balto.
Johnson	Minta	7	Isaac Franklin	Slatter, Hope Hull	Sept. 28, 1838	Balto.
Johnson	Minty	19	Helen A. Miller	Campbell, Bernard M.	Oct. 18, 1852	Balto.
Johnson	Moses	24	John C. Calhoun	Donovan, Joseph S.	Oct. 24, 1850	Balto.
Johnson	Nace	17	Kirkwood	Donovan, Joseph S.	Oct. 14, 1848	Balto.
Johnson	Nacky	17	Virginia	Woolfolk, Joseph B.	Dec. 19, 1825	Balto.
Johnson	Nancy	8	Ann & Leah	Woolfolk, Austin	Nov.1, 1831	Balto.
Johnson	Nathaniel	26	Ewarkee	Purvis, James Franklin	March 4, 1841	Balto.
Johnson	Ned	17	Kirkwood	Campbell, Bernard M.	March 9, 1847	Balto.
Johnson	Nickolas	20	Brunswick	Woolfolk, Austin	Oct. 11, 1831	Balto.
Johnson	Noah	28	Kirkwood	Campbell, Bernard M.	Oct. 14, 1848	Balto.
Johnson	Oliver	14	Kirkwood	Slatter, Hope Hull	Dec. 23, 1843	Balto.
Johnson	Perry	18	Brunswick	Woolfolk, Austin	Oct. 11, 1831	Balto.
Johnson	Perry	24	Ewarkee	Purvis, James Franklin	March 4, 1841	Balto.
Johnson	Perry	22	General Pinckney	Slatter, Hope Hull	Jan. 19, 1847	Balto.
Johnson	Perry	24	Tippecanoe	Purvis, James Franklin	Apr. 1, 1841	Balto.

Surname	First Name	Age	Ship	O/S	Date	Depart
Johnson	Peter	21	Topaz	Woolfolk, Austin	Apr. 20, 1829	Balto.
Johnson	Phil	18	Burlington	Slatter, Hope Hull	Oct. 21, 1842	Balto.
Johnson	Phoebe	19	Hiberria	Woolfolk, Austin	Dec. 5, 1826	Balto.
Johnson	Polly	9	Glasgow	Slatter, Hope Hull	Oct. 11, 1838	Balto.
Johnson	Pompey	2	Saldana	Harker, William	Feb. 27, 1844	Balto.
Johnson	Rachael	16	Louisa	Campbell, Bernard M.	Nov. 5, 1849	Balto.
Johnson	Rachel	20	Kirkwood	Campbell, Bernard M.	March 23, 1844	Balto.
Johnson	Reason	27	Ewarkee	Slatter, Hope Hull	March 4, 1841	Balto.
Johnson	Reason	24	Union	Campbell, Bernard M.	Nov. 17, 1849	Balto.
Johnson	Rebecca	48	Narragansett	Campbell, Bernard M.	Nov. 27, 1850	Balto.
Johnson	Rebecca	30	Scotia	Slatter, Hope Hull	Sept. 30, 1843	Balto.
Johnson	Richard	32	Porpoise	Purvis, James Franklin	Dec. 11, 1841	Balto.
Johnson	Richard	22	St. Mary	Donovan, Joseph S.	Nov. 29, 1845	Balto.
Johnson	Richard	17	Superb	Slatter, Hope Hull	Nov. 1, 1843	Balto.
Johnson	Robert	19	Hermitage	Slatter, Hope Hull	Oct. 28, 1846	Balto.
Johnson	Robert	21	Superb	Donovan, Joseph S.	Nov. 2, 1843	Balto.
Johnson	Rose E.	6	Tweed	Forbes, George	Oct. 20, 1836	Town Creek
Johnson	Rosetta	infant	Kirkwood	Slatter, Hope Hull	Jan. 4, 1845	Balto.
Johnson	Rosetta	19	States	Woolfolk, Austin	Nov. 21, 1827	Balto.
Johnson	Rosetta	9	Victorine	Slatter, Hope Hull	March 9, 1844	Balto.
Johnson	Ruben	18	Kirkwood	Donovan, Joseph S.	March 9, 1847	Balto.
Johnson	Ruth	10	General Pinckney	Slatter, Hope Hull	Nov. 10, 1845	Balto.
Johnson	Samuel	17	Billow	Woolfolk, Austin	Feb. 23, 1828	Balto.
Johnson	Samuel	24	General Pinckney	Slatter, Hope Hull	Jan. 19, 1847	Balto.
Johnson	Samuel	22	Kirkwood	Denning, John N.	Jan. 14, 1846	Balto.
Johnson	Samuel	16	Phoenix	Donovan, Joseph S.	March 27, 1847	Balto.

Surname	First Name	Age	Ship	O/S	Date	Depart
Johnson	Samuel	26	Pioneer	Slatter, Hope Hull	Sept. 15, 1847	Balto.
Johnson	Samuel	19	Solomon Saltus	Slatter, Hope Hull	Oct. 7, 1839	Balto.
Johnson	Samuel	21	Victorine	Donovan, Joseph S.	Dec. 31, 1846	Balto.
Johnson	Samuel	30	Victorine	Slatter, Hope Hull	Sept. 12, 1846	Balto.
Johnson	Samuel	35	Victorine	Donovan, Joseph S.	Sept. 29, 1845	Balto.
Johnson	Sandy	18	Kirkwood	Donovan, Joseph S.	Dec. 23, 1843	Balto.
Johnson	Sarah	10	E.H.Chapin	Slatter, Hope Hull	Nov. 30, 1847	Balto.
Johnson	Sarah	19	Henry Clay	Woolfolk, Austin	Dec. 4, 1828	Balto.
Johnson	Sarah	40	Home	Slatter, Hope Hull	March 22, 1845	Balto.
Johnson	Sarah	15	Scotia	Slatter, Hope Hull	Sept. 30, 1843	Balto.
Johnson	Sarah	17	Victorine	Rodbind, Ebenezer	March 14, 1846	Balto.
Johnson	Sarah A.	16	Kirkwood	Slatter, Hope Hull	Dec. 23, 1843	Balto.
Johnson	Sarah Ann	16	Tippecanoe	Slatter, Hope Hull	Apr. 1, 1841	Balto.
Johnson	Sarah Ann	21	Victorine	Rodbind, Ebenezer	Dec. 31, 1846	Balto.
Johnson	Serena	28	Saldana	Harker, William	Feb. 27, 1844	Balto.
Johnson	Sevilla	15	Isaac Franklin	Slatter, Hope Hull	Sept. 28, 1838	Balto.
Johnson	Shadrack	23	Kirkwood	Donovan, Joseph S.	Sept. 28, 1846	Balto.
Johnson	Solomon	18	Jefferson	Woolfolk, Austin	Dec. 24, 1827	Balto.
Johnson	Solomon	22	Scotia	Slatter, Hope Hull	Sept. 30, 1843	Balto.
Johnson	Sophia	15	Tweed	Forbes, George	Oct. 20, 1836	Town Creek
Johnson	Sophy	9	Jefferson	Woolfolk, Joseph B.	Dec. 24, 1827	Balto.
Johnson	Stephen	35	Kirkwood	Donovan, Joseph S.	Jan. 4, 1845	Balto.
Johnson	Stephen	20	P.R. Hazeltine	Campbell, Bernard M.	Nov. 15, 1856	Balto.
Johnson	Stephen	21	Uncas	Slatter, Hope Hull	Jan. 10, 1838	Balto.
Johnson	Susan	25	Isaac Franklin	Slatter, Hope Hull	Sept. 28, 1838	Balto.
Johnson	Susan	infant	Superb	Slatter, Hope Hull	Nov. 1, 1843	Balto.

Surname	First Name	Age	Ship	O/S	Date	Depart
Johnson	Susan	13	Victorine	Slatter, Hope Hull	March 9, 1844	Balto.
Johnson	Susanna	32	Kirkwood	Donovan, Joseph S.	Oct. 14, 1848	Balto.
Johnson	Susanna	16	Zoe	Slatter, Hope Hull	Feb. 16, 1847	Balto.
Johnson	Thomas	24	Brunswick	Woolfolk, Austin	Oct. 11, 1831	Balto.
Johnson	Thomas	30	General Pinckney	Donovan, Joseph S.	Feb. 21, 1846	Balto.
Johnson	Thomas	19	Hibernia	Woolfolk, Austin	Dec. 5, 1826	Balto.
Johnson	Tom	22	States	Woolfolk, Austin	Nov. 21, 1827	Balto.
Johnson	Varnell	22	Hibernia	Woolfolk, Austin	Dec. 5, 1826	Balto.
Johnson	Virginia	15	Kirkwood	Donovan, Joseph S.	Oct. 14, 1848	Balto.
Johnson	Wesly	18	Henry A. Barling	Campbell, Bernard M.	Dec. 18, 1851	Balto.
Johnson	William	18	Billow	Woolfolk, Austin	Feb. 23, 1828	Balto.
Johnson	William	30	Eliza F. Mason	Donovan, Joseph S.	Nov. 13, 1851	Balto.
Johnson	William	18	Home	Slatter, Hope Hull	March 22, 1845	Balto.
Johnson	William	25	Justina	Donovan, Joseph S.	Dec. 2, 1852	Balto.
Johnson	William	20	Kirkwood	Donovan, Joseph S.	Dec. 23, 1843	Balto.
Johnson	William	20	Kirkwood	Donovan, Joseph S.	Jan. 4, 1845	Balto.
Johnson	William	20	Kirkwood	Donovan, Joseph S.	Oct. 14, 1848	Balto.
Johnson	William	20	Margaret Hugg	Slatter, Hope Hull	Feb. 8, 1845	Balto.
Johnson	William	23	Topaz	Woolfolk, Austin	Apr. 20, 1829	Balto.
Johnson	William	18	Zoe	Slatter, Hope Hull	Feb. 16, 1847	Balto.
Johnson	Zedock	22	Tippecanoe	Slatter, Hope Hull	Apr. 15, 1844	Balto.
Johnson		10	Charles Henry	Burgess, F.B.F	Dec. 9, 1839	Balto.
Johnson		infant	Cora	Campbell, Bernard M.	Jan. 20, 1851	Balto.
Johnson		23	Lafayette	Woolfolk, Austin	Oct. 18, 1828	Balto.
Johnson		5	Signet	Woolfolk, Austin	Nov. 12, 1831	Balto.
Johnston	Abraham	18	Irad Ferry	Wilson, J.W.	May 6, 1839	Balto.

Surname	First Name	Age	Ship	O/S	Date	Depart
Johnston	Abram	18	Kirkwood	Campbell, Bernard M.	Oct. 14, 1848	Balto.
Johnston	Alfred	22	Paoli	Campbell, Bernard M.	Dec. 27, 1845	Balto.
Johnston	Ann	10	Elizabeth	Donovan, Joseph S.	Jan. 2, 1850	Balto.
Johnston	Caroline	30	Elizabeth	Donovan, Joseph S.	Jan. 2, 1850	Balto.
Johnston	Charles	25	Kirkwood	Campbell, Bernard M.	Oct. 14, 1848	Balto.
Johnston	Charles	15	Margaret Hugg	Campbell, Bernard M.	Nov. 30, 1844	Balto.
Johnston	Daniel	18	Elizabeth	Donovan, Joseph S.	Nov. 18, 1848	Balto.
Johnston	Elizabeth	20	Victorine	Harker, William	March 14, 1846	Balto.
Johnston	Fanny	17	Southerner	Campbell, Bernard M.	Jan. 5, 1852	Balto.
Johnston	Henry	infant	Elizabeth	Donovan, Joseph S.	Nov. 18, 1848	Balto.
Johnston	John	22	Kirkwood	Campbell, Bernard M.	Oct. 14, 1848	Balto.
Johnston	Martha		Louisa	Donovan, Joseph S.	Oct. 9, 1847	Balto.
Johnston	Mary	11	Paoli	Campbell, Bernard M.	Dec. 27, 1845	Balto.
Johnston	Nace	17	Union	Sheckles, Gannon	March 17, 1849	Balto.
Johnston	Perry	19	Eliza F. Mason	Donovan, Joseph S.	Nov. 13, 1851	Balto.
Johnston	Richard	21	Elizabeth	Donovan, Joseph S.	Nov. 18, 1848	Balto.
Johnston	Robert	24	Margaret Hugg	Poindexter, T.B.	Nov. 30, 1844	Balto.
Johnston	Sarah	18	Elizabeth	Donovan, Joseph S.	Nov. 18, 1848	Balto.
Johnston	Thomas	20	Elizabeth	Donovan, Joseph S.	Nov. 18, 1848	Balto.
Johnston	William	20	Kirkwood	Campbell, Bernard M.	Oct. 14, 1848	Balto.
Joins	Ben	3	Ann & Leah	Woolfolk, Austin	Nov.1, 1831	Balto.
Jones	Abraham	infant	Kirkwood	Donovan, Joseph S.	Nov. 28, 1849	Balto.
Jones	Ailsey	19	Ganniclefft	Slatter, Hope Hull	Nov. 25, 1840	Balto.
Jones	Alexander	infant	Union	Slatter, Hope Hull	July 26, 1847	Balto.
Jones	Alfred	19	Leda	Donovan, Joseph S.	May 30, 1846	Balto.
Jones	Alfred	18	Southerner	Rodbind, Ebenezer	Jan. 21, 1850	Balto.

Surname	First Name	Age	Ship	O/S	Date	Depart
Jones	Amelia	infant	Kirkwood	Donovan, Joseph S.	Apr. 15, 1845	Balto.
Jones	Andrew	2	Irad Ferry	Slatter, Hope Hull	Dec. 9, 1842	Balto.
Jones	Ann	21	Elizabeth	Campbell, Bernard M.	Nov. 18, 1848	Balto.
Jones	Ann	14	Lafayette	Woolfolk, Joseph B.	Oct. 18, 1828	Balto.
Jones	Ann	16	Louisa	Donovan, Joseph S.	Oct. 9, 1847	Balto.
Jones	Aveline	4	General Finckney	Campbell, Bernard M.	Jan. 19, 1847	Balto.
Jones	Barbara	13	Kirkwood	Slatter, Hope Hull	Oct. 16, 1845	Balto.
Jones	Benjamin	6	Irad Ferry	Slatter, Hope Hull	Dec. 9, 1842	Balto.
Jones	Benjamin	16	Seaman	Freeman, Theophilus	March 25, 1839	Balto.
Jones	Bozetta	19	Uncas	Slatter, Hope Hull	Jan. 10, 1838	Balto.
Jones	Briggett	32	Victorine	Slatter, Hope Hull	Dec. 17, 1845	Balto.
Jones	Clarrasa	infant	Tippecanoe	Slatter, Hope Hull	Apr. 15, 1844	Balto.
Jones	David	26	Ewarkee	Slatter, Hope Hull	March 4, 1841	Balto.
Jones	David	19	Kirkwood	Slatter, Hope Hull	Apr. 4, 1846	Balto.
Jones	David	18	Louisa	Campbell, Bernard M.	Nov. 5, 1849	Balto.
Jones	Edward	20	Kirkwood	Williams, William H.	Jan. 14, 1846	Balto.
Jones	Edwin	23	Home	Slatter, Hope Hull	March 22, 1845	Balto.
Jones	Eliza	18	General Pinckney	Slatter, Hope Hull	Jan. 19, 1847	Balto.
Jones	Eliza	18	Union	Slatter, Hope Hull	July 26, 1847	Balto.
Jones	Eliza	16	Union	Campbell, Bernard M.	Nov. 17, 1849	Balto.
Jones	Elizabeth	22	Kirkwood	Donovan, Joseph S.	Nov. 28, 1849	Balto.
Jones	Elizabeth	24	Kirkwood	Donovan, Joseph S.	Oct. 26, 1847	Balto.
Jones	Elizabeth	3	Lafayette	Woolfolk, Joseph B.	Oct. 18, 1828	Balto.
Jones	Ellen	infant	Elizabeth	Rodbind, Ebenezer	Nov. 18, 1848	Balto.
Jones	Ellen	24	Victorine	Slatter, Hope Hull	Sept. 12, 1846	Balto.
Jones	Ellin	21	Irad Ferry	Slatter, Hope Hull	Dec. 9, 1842	Balto.

Surname	First Name	Age	Ship	O/S	Date	Depart
Jones	Emeline	20	Union	Campbell, Bernard M.	Dec. 16, 1848	Balto.
Jones	Emily	10	Russell	Slatter, Hope Hull	March 1, 1839	Balto.
Jones	Emory	14	Victorine	Donovan, Joseph S.	Sept. 29, 1845	Balto.
Jones	Fanny	23	Irad Ferry	Slatter, Hope Hull	Dec. 9, 1842	Balto.
Jones	Frisby	20	Elizabeth	Campbell, Bernard M.	Nov. 18, 1848	Balto.
Jones	Grace	30	Irad Ferry	Clendenin, A.	Jan. 16, 1840	Balto.
Jones	Harriet	14	Edward Everett	Cook, William	Dec. 4, 1856	Balto.
Jones	Harriet	20	Union	Donovan, Joseph S.	Dec. 16, 1848	Balto.
Jones	Henry	19	General Pinckney	Donovan, Joseph S.	Nov. 10, 1845	Balto.
Jones	Henry	23	General Pinckney	Slatter, Hope Hull	Nov. 10, 1845	Balto.
Jones	Henry	3	Lady Monroe	Woolfolk, Austin	March 25, 1825	Balto.
Jones	Henry	21	Victorine	Rodbind, Ebenezer	Dec. 31, 1846	Balto.
Jones	Henry	17	Victorine	Harker, William	March 14, 1846	Balto.
Jones	Hester Ann	17	General Pinckney	Slatter, Hope Hull	Jan. 19, 1847	Balto.
Jones	Hillery	30	Superb	Donovan, Joseph S.	Nov. 2, 1843	Balto.
Jones	Horrace	16	Irad Ferry	Purvis, James Franklin	Feb. 5, 1842	Balto.
Jones	Howard	11	Pioneer	Stuart, William R.	July 20, 1848	Balto.
Jones	Isarael	18	Pioneer	Slatter, Hope Hull	Sept. 15, 1847	Balto.
Jones	Jacob	11	Victorine	Rodbind, Ebenezer	Dec. 31, 1846	Balto.
Jones	James	22	Ann & Leah	Woolfolk, Austin	Nov. 1, 1831	Balto.
Jones	James	13	Charles	Campbell, Bernard M.	Dec. 18, 1850	Balto.
Jones	James	20	Ganniclefft	Slatter, Hope Hull	Nov. 25, 1840	Balto.
Jones	James	25	Hermitage	Slatter, Hope Hull	Oct. 28, 1846	Balto.
Jones	Jane	18	Superb	Donovan, Joseph S.	Nov. 2, 1843	Balto.
Jones	Jim	19	Kirkwood	Rodbind, Ebenezer	Oct. 26, 1847	Balto.
Jones	John	22	E.H. Chapin	Campbell, Walter L.	June 7, 1848	Balto.

Surname	First Name	Age	Ship	O/S	Date	Depart
Jones	John	infant	General Pinckney	Campbell, Bernard M.	Jan. 19, 1847	Balto.
Jones	John	13	General Pinckney	Campbell, Bernard M.	Jan. 19, 1847	Balto.
Jones	John	20	Helen A. Miller	Campbell, Bernard M.	Oct. 18, 1852	Balto.
Jones	John	25	Irad Ferry	Slatter, Hope Hull	Dec. 9, 1842	Balto.
Jones	John	28	Kirkwood	Campbell, Bernard M.	Apr. 15, 1845	Balto.
Jones	John	22	Kirkwood	Slatter, Hope Hull	Jan. 14, 1846	Balto.
Jones	John	18	Louisa	Campbell, Bernard M.	March 31, 1849	Balto.
Jones	John	17	Phoenix	Donovan, Joseph S.	March 27, 1847	Balto.
Jones	John	6	Salvadora	Slatter, Hope Hull	Sept. 28, 1846	Balto.
Jones	John	50	Tippecanoe	Slatter, Hope Hull	Apr. 15, 1844	Balto.
Jones	John	16	Tippecanoe	Slatter, Hope Hull	Jan. 17, 1842	Balto.
Jones	Joseph	8	General Pinckney	Campbell, Bernard M.	Jan. 19, 1847	Balto.
Jones	Joseph	28	Kirkwood	Slatter, Hope Hull	Jan. 14, 1846	Balto.
Jones	Joseph	15	Superb	Slatter, Hope Hull	Nov. 1, 1843	Balto.
Jones	Joshua	14	Kirkwood	Donovan, Joseph S.	Sept. 28, 1846	Balto.
Jones	Julia Ann	10	Kirkwood	Donovan, Joseph S.	Apr. 15, 1845	Balto.
Jones	Ketty	12	Clio	Starnsburg, William	March 22, 1819	Balto.
Jones	Kitty	16	Jasper	Woolfolk, Austin	Apr. 7, 1827	Balto.
Jones	Leah	25	Lafayette	Woolfolk, Joseph B.	Oct. 18, 1828	Balto.
Jones	Lephry	32	General Pinckney	Campbell, Bernard M.	Jan. 19, 1847	Balto.
Jones	Lewis	23	Charles	Donovan, Joseph S.	Apr. 23, 1851	Balto.
Jones	Lewis	19	Kirkwood	Donovan, Joseph S.	Oct. 26, 1847	Balto.
Jones	Louisa	40	Tippecanoe	Slatter, Hope Hull	Apr. 15, 1844	Balto.
Jones	Margaret	19	Lady Monroe	Woolfolk, Austin	March 25, 1825	Balto.
Jones	Maria	25	Hermitage	Slatter, Hope Hull	Oct. 28, 1846	Balto.
Jones	Martha	17	Victorine	Rodbind, Ebenezer	March 14, 1846	Balto.

Surname	First Name	Age	Ship	O/S	Date	Depart
Jones	Mary	22	General Pinckney	Campbell, Bernard M.	Jan. 19, 1847	Balto.
Jones	Mary	18	Helen A. Miller	Campbell, Bernard M.	Oct. 18, 1852	Balto.
Jones	Mary	2	Irad Ferry	Slatter, Hope Hull	Dec. 9, 1842	Balto.
Jones	Mary	18	Irad Ferry	Slatter, Hope Hull	Jan. 22, 1840	Balto.
Jones	Mary	13	Union	Sheckles, Gannon	March 17, 1849	Balto.
Jones	Mary Ellen	17	Ewarkee	Slatter, Hope Hull	March 4, 1841	Balto.
Jones	Mary Jones	3	Hermitage	Slatter, Hope Hull	Oct. 28, 1846	Balto.
Jones	Matilda	17	Kirkwood	Donovan, Joseph S.	Dec. 10, 1846	Balto.
Jones	Matilda	22	Splendid	Slatter, Hope Hull	Apr. 24, 1841	Balto.
Jones	Michael	29	Harriet	Carroll, Charles	Dec. 7, 1836	Balto.
Jones	Moses	18	Southerner	Donovan, Joseph S.	Jan. 21, 1850	Balto.
Jones	Nancy	12	Burlington	Slatter, Hope Hull	Oct. 21, 1842	Balto.
Jones	Nathan	21	Catharine	Donovan, Joseph S.	Jan. 18, 1845	Balto.
Jones	Ned	9	States	Woolfolk, Austin	Apr. 14, 1828	Balto.
Jones	Nelly	16	General Pinckney	Campbell, Bernard M.	Jan. 19, 1847	Balto.
Jones	Nelly	17	Kirkwood	Donovan, Joseph S.	Apr. 15, 1845	Balto.
Jones	Noble	15	Kirkwood	Campbell, Bernard M.	March 9, 1847	Balto.
Jones	Oliver	16	Helen A. Miller	Campbell, Bernard M.	Oct. 18, 1852	Balto.
Jones	Oliver	18	Julia	Woolfolk, Austin	Jan. 8, 1829	Balto.
Jones	Oliver	21	Kirkwood	Donovan, Joseph S.	Oct. 26, 1847	Balto.
Jones	Olivia	6	General Pinckney	Campbell, Bernard M.	Jan. 19, 1847	Balto.
Jones	Peter	8	Lafayette	Woolfolk, Joseph B.	Oct. 18, 1828	Balto.
Jones	Peter	17	Southerner	Donovan, Joseph S.	Oct. 27, 1849	Balto.
Jones	Priscilla	18	Victorine	Slatter, Henry F.	Dec. 31, 1846	Balto.
Jones	Rachael	10	Tippecanoe	Zacharie, James W.	Dec. 15, 1840	Balto.
Jones	Rachel	13	Topaz	Woolfolk, Austin	Apr. 20, 1829	Balto.

Surname	First Name	Age	Ship	O/S	Date	Depart
Jones	Rachel	24	Union	Slatter, Hope Hull	July 26, 1847	Balto.
Jones	Rebecca	4	Lafayette	Woolfolk, Joseph B.	Oct. 18, 1828	Balto.
Jones	Revel	45	Waverly	Campbell, Bernard M.	Apr. 3, 1851	Balto.
Jones	Ruthy	infant	Splendid	Slatter, Hope Hull	Apr. 24, 1841	Balto.
Jones	Sam	42	General Pinckney	Campbell, Bernard M.	Jan. 19, 1847	Balto.
Jones	Sam	20	Isaac Franklin	Kephart, George	Feb. 1, 1839	Balto.
Jones	Sam	25	Union	Rodbind, Ebenezer	Dec. 16, 1848	Balto.
Jones	Sam Patch	10	General Pinckney	Campbell, Bernard M.	Jan. 19, 1847	Balto.
Jones	Samuel	21	Hermitage	Slatter, Hope Hull	Oct. 28, 1846	Balto.
Jones	Samuel	20	Jefferson	Woolfolk, Austin	Dec. 24, 1827	Balto.
Jones	Sarah	5	Hermitage	Slatter, Hope Hull	Oct. 28, 1846	Balto.
Jones	Sarah	16	Southerner	Donovan, Joseph S.	Jan. 5, 1852	Balto.
Jones	Sarah	infant	Union	Slatter, Hope Hull	July 26, 1847	Balto.
Jones	Sophiah	16	Kirkwood	Donovan, Joseph S.	Nov. 28, 1849	Balto.
Jones	Stephen	24	Jasper	Woolfolk, Austin	Apr. 7, 1827	Balto.
Jones	Susan	19	General Pinckney	Campbell, Bernard M.	Jan. 19, 1847	Balto.
Jones	Susan	17	Solomon Saltus	Slatter, Hope Hull	Oct. 7, 1839	Balto.
Jones	Susan	8	Tippecanoe	Slatter, Hope Hull	Apr. 15, 1844	Balto.
Jones	Thomas	20	Hermitage	Slatter, Hope Hull	Oct. 28, 1846	Balto.
Jones	Toby	14	Kirkwood	Donovan, Joseph S.	Dec. 10, 1846	Balto.
Jones	Warner	24	Union	Slatter, Hope Hull	July 26, 1847	Balto.
Jones	Washington	19	Jasper	Woolfolk, Austin	Apr. 7, 1827	Balto.
Jones	Wesley	14	Kirkwood	Slatter, Hope Hull	Dec. 23, 1843	Balto.
Jones	William	24	Clio	Coleman, Daniel J.	March 20, 1819	Balto.
Jones	William	25	Elizabeth	Campbell, Bernard M.	March 21, 1850	Balto.
Jones	William	21	Hermitage	Donovan, Joseph S.	Oct. 28, 1846	Balto.

Surname	First Name	Age	Ship	O/S	Date	Depart
Jones	William	23	Hermitage	Slatter, Hope Hull	Oct. 28, 1846	Balto.
Jones	William	20	Sarah Bridge	Campbell, Bernard M.	Feb. 8, 1851	Balto.
Jones	William	24	Solomon Saltus	Slatter, Hope Hull	Oct. 7, 1839	Balto.
Jones	William	19	Superb	Anderson, David	Apr. 6, 1819	Balto.
Jones	William	19	Superb	Slatter, Hope Hull	Nov. 1, 1843	Balto.
Jones	William	24	Union	Campbell, Bernard M.	Apr. 20, 1850	Balto.
Jones		40	Brunswick	Woolfolk, Austin	Oct. 11, 1831	Balto.
Jones		infant	Elizabeth	Campbell, Bernard M.	Nov. 18, 1848	Balto.
Jones		infant	Union	Campbell, Bernard M.	Dec. 16, 1848	Balto.
Jonson	Henry	25	Union	Slatter, Hope Hull	July 26, 1847	Balto.
Jonson	Jim	29	Hibernia	Woolfolk, Austin	Dec. 5, 1826	Balto.
Jordan	Albert	21	Elizabeth	Donovan, Joseph S.	Jan. 2, 1850	Balto.
Jordan	Ann	24	Kirkwood	Donovan, Joseph S.	Apr. 15, 1845	Balto.
Jordan	Eli	18	Waverly	Donovan, Joseph S.	Apr. 3, 1851	Balto.
Jordan	Fleming	21	Isaac Franklin	Kephart, George	Feb. 1, 1839	Balto.
Jordan	Louisa	3	Kirkwood	Donovan, Joseph S.	Apr. 15, 1845	Balto.
Jordan	Mordica	16	Home	Slatter, Hope Hull	March 22, 1845	Balto.
Jordon	Elizebeth	24	Kirkwood	Slatter, Hope Hull	Apr. 15, 1845	Balto.
Jordon	Hinson	5	Kirkwood	Slatter, Hope Hull	Apr. 15, 1845	Balto.
Jordon	Maria	7	Kirkwood	Slatter, Hope Hull	Apr. 15, 1845	Balto.
Jordon	Wesley	infant	Kirkwood	Slatter, Hope Hull	Apr. 15, 1845	Balto.
Jordon	William	25	Kirkwood	Slatter, Hope Hull	Apr. 15, 1845	Balto.
Journey	Thomas	11	Kirkwood	Donovan, Joseph S.	Sept. 28, 1846	Balto.
Joyce	Hillery	18	General Pinckney	Donovan, Joseph S.	Nov. 10, 1845	Balto.
Joyce	Nancy	19	Strafford	Harker, William	Nov. 22, 1843	Balto.
Jude	Elen	26	Isaac Franklin	Slatter, Hope Hull	Sept. 28, 1838	Balto.

Surname	First Name	Age	Ship	O/S	Date	Depart
Judson	Letty	19	Abbott Lord	Campbell, Bernard M.	April 28, 1852	Balto.
Juniper	Tom	19	Ann & Leah	Woolfolk, Austin	Nov. 1, 1831	Balto.
Jurden	Richard	16	Searran	Slatter, Shadrack	March 25, 1839	Balto.
Justin	Mahalia	21	Billow	Woolfolk, Joseph B.	Feb. 23, 1828	Balto.
Justin		infant	Billow	Woolfolk, Joseph B.	Feb. 23, 1828	Balto.
Juvens	Maria	5 mon.	Ann & Leah	Woolfolk, Austin	Nov. 1, 1831	Balto.
Juvens	Mary	20	Ann & Leah	Woolfolk, Austin	Nov. 1, 1831	Balto.
Juxuat	John	32	General Pinckney	Campbell, Bernard M.	Jan. 19, 1847	Balto.
Kain	Lloyd	24	Victorine	Slatter, Hope Hull	March 9, 1844	Balto.
Kane	Elizabeth	17	Elizabeth	Campbell, Bernard M.	March 21, 1850	Balto.
Kane	Levin	24	Victorine	Slatter, Hope Hull	Sept. 12, 1846	Balto.
Kane	Mary Ann	17	Kirkwood	Campbell, Bernard M.	Oct. 14, 1848	Balto.
Kane	William	25	Southerner	Campbell, Bernard M.	Oct. 27, 1849	Balto.
Kanty	Peter	30	Kirkwood	Slatter, Hope Hull	Dec. 23, 1843	Balto.
Kasie	Charles	18	Seaman	Purvis, James Franklin	Apr. 8, 1842	Balto.
Keartenan	George	24	Scotia	Harker, William	Sept. 30, 1843	Balto.
Keath	William	20	Kirkwood	Donovan, Joseph S.	Sept. 28, 1846	Balto.
Keith	John	24	Architect	Campbell, Bernard M.	Apr. 25, 1846	Balto.
Kell	Henry	15	Victorine	Slatter, Hope Hull	May 14, 1845	Balto.
Kell	Margritt	28	Kirkwood	Slatter, Hope Hull	Oct. 16, 1845	Balto.
Kell	William	19	Harriett	Woolfolk, Austin	March 23, 1822	Balto.
Kelley	Laura	16	Victorine	Slatter, Henry F.	Dec. 31, 1846	Balto.
Kelly	James	18	Jefferson	Woolfolk, Austin	Dec. 24, 1827	Balto.
Kelly	Maria	16	Lapwing	Woolfolk, Austin	Feb. 15, 1827	Balto.
Kelly	Mary	26	Burlington	Slatter, Hope Hull	Oct. 21, 1842	Balto.
Kelly	Mary	16	Superb	Slatter, Hope Hull	Nov. 1, 1843	Balto.

Surname	First Name	Age	Ship	O/S	Date	Depart
Kelsey	Bill	18	Lafayette	Woolfolk, Joseph B.	Oct. 18, 1828	Balto.
Kemp	Ceasar	22	Seaman	Slatter, Hope Hull	March 25, 1839	Balto.
Kemp	Elizabeth	20	Solomon Saltus	Slatter, Hope Hull	Oct. 7, 1839	Balto.
Kemp	Garrison	7	Lafayette	Woolfolk, Austin	Oct. 18, 1828	Balto.
Ken	Edward	25	Glasgow	Slatter, Hope Hull	Oct. 11, 1838	Balto.
Kennard	George	19	Isaac Franklin	Slatter, Hope Hull	Sept. 28, 1838	Balto.
Kennard	Henry	25	Superb	Slatter, Hope Hull	Nov. 1, 1843	Balto.
Kennard	Isaac	22	Architect	Campbell, Bernard M.	Apr. 25, 1846	Balto.
Kennard	James	14	Elizabeth	Chaplain, J. Bond	Nov. 18, 1848	Balto.
Kennard	Richard	17	Isaac Franklin	Slatter, Hope Hull	Sept. 28, 1838	Balto.
Kennard	Richard	19	Splendid	Slatter, Hope Hull	Apr. 24, 1841	Balto.
Kent	Edward	18	Seaman	Slatter, Shadrack	March 25, 1839	Balto.
Kent	Elizabeth	19	Seaman	Slatter, Shadrack	March 25, 1839	Balto.
Kent	Nancy	13	General Pinckney	Slatter, Hope Hull	Jan. 19, 1847	Balto.
Kent	Rachael	30	Union	Campbell, Bernard M.	Dec. 16, 1848	Balto.
Kent	Thomas	17	Salvadora	Slatter, Hope Hull	Sept. 28, 1846	Balto.
Kerr	Henny	8	Hermitage	Slatter, Hope Hull	Oct. 28, 1846	Balto.
Kerr	William	18	Lafayette	Woolfolk, Richard	Oct. 18, 1828	Balto.
Key	Edward	19	Southerner	Campbell, Bernard M.	Oct. 27, 1849	Balto.
Key	Jake	17	Victorine	Donovan, Joseph S.	Dec. 31, 1846	Balto.
Key	Lewis	19	Abbott Lord	Campbell, Bernard M.	April 28, 1852	Balto.
Key		21	Victorine	Donovan, Joseph S.	Sept. 29, 1845	Balto.
Keyes	Latitia	18	Salvadora	Slatter, Hope Hull	Sept. 28, 1846	Balto.
Keyes	Uriah	22	Victorine	Slatter, Henry F.	Dec. 31, 1846	Balto.
Keys	Lewis	11	Lawrence	Woolfolk, Austin	May 9, 1823	Balto.
Keys	Thomas	22	Kirkwood	Slatter, Hope Hull	Oct. 16, 1845	Balto.

Surname	First Name	Age	Ship	O/S	Date	Depart
Kian	George	20	Architect	Harker, William	Feb. 15, 1840	Balto.
Kilson	Eliza	20	Paoli	Slatter, Hope Hull	Sept. 9, 1845	Balto.
Kimble	Mary	16	Searan	Slatter, Hope Hull	March 25, 1839	Balto.
King	Alfred	22	Isaac Franklin	Kephart, George	Feb. 1, 1839	Balto.
King	Barnett	23	Superb	Slatter, Hope Hull	Nov. 1, 1843	Balto.
King	Benjamin	17	Union	Campbell, Bernard M.	March 17, 1849	Balto.
King	Charles	21	Kirkwood	Donovan, Joseph S.	Apr. 4, 1846	Balto.
King	Charles	15	Victorine	Rodbird, Ebenezer	March 14, 1846	Balto.
King	Henry	21	Louisa	Donovan, Joseph S.	Oct. 9, 1847	Balto.
King	Jane	16	Lafayette	Woolfolk, Austin	Oct. 18, 1828	Balto.
King	John	16	Home	Slatter, Hope Hull	March 22, 1845	Balto.
King	Martha	17	Elizabeth	Donovan, Joseph S.	Jan. 2, 1850	Balto.
King	Mike	30	Irad Ferry	Slatter, Hope Hull	Jan. 22, 1840	Balto.
King	Philip	22	Gannicefft	Slatter, Hope Hull	Nov. 25, 1840	Balto.
King	Prescilla	14	Nathaniel Hooper	Donovan, Jospeh S.	Feb. 12, 1852	Balto.
King	Reason	28	Isaac Franklin	Kephart, George	Sept. 28, 1838	Balto.
King	William	17	Clio	Starnsburg, William	March 22, 1819	Balto.
King	Winsor	22	Kirkwood	Rodbinc, Ebenezer	Oct. 26, 1847	Balto.
Kinner	Evelin	20	Kirkwood	Slatter, Hope Hull	Dec. 23, 1843	Balto.
Kinner	Henry	18	General Pinckney	Donovan, Joseph S.	Nov. 10, 1845	Balto.
Kinsey	John	11	Colonel Howard	Harker, William	Nov. 21, 1844	Balto.
Kirby	Henrietta	18	Porpoise	Purvis, James Franklin	Dec. 11, 1841	Balto.
Kittel	Peter	27	Victorine	Donovan, Joseph S.	Sept. 29, 1845	Balto.
Knight	Alford	20	Abbott Lord	Campbell, Bernard M.	April 28, 1852	Balto.
Knight	Elen	30	Isaac Franklin	Slatter, Hope Hull	Sept. 28, 1838	Balto.
Knight	Peter	25	Liberator	Woolfolk, Austin	Nov. 12, 1828	Balto.

Surname	First Name	Age	Ship	O/S	Date	Depart
Knoll	Ignatius	38	Tweed	Forbes, George	Oct. 20, 1836	Town Creek
Knox	Miles	40	Tangier	Campbell, Bernard M.	Nov. 26, 1853	Balto.
Krawford	Charles	23	Lady Monroe	Woolfolk, Austin	March 25, 1825	Balto.
Lacey	Peter	18	Lafayette	Woolfolk, Richard	Oct. 18, 1828	Balto.
Lacy	Charles	22	Southerner	Campbell, Bernard M.	Oct. 27, 1849	Balto.
Lacy	Littleton	26	Henry A. Barling	Campbell, Bernard M.	Feb. 24, 1851	Balto.
Lagger	Daniel	50	Solomon Saltus	Slatter, Hope Hull	Oct. 7, 1839	Balto.
Lagger	Eliza	30	Solomon Saltus	Slatter, Hope Hull	Oct. 7, 1839	Balto.
Lagger		infant	Solomon Saltus	Slatter, Hope Hull	Oct. 7, 1839	Balto.
Lamar	George	25	Kirkwood	Donovan, Joseph S.	Oct. 14, 1848	Balto.
Lambdin	John	19	Kirkwood	Campbell, Bernard M.	March 9, 1847	Balto.
Lancaster	Ben	20	Abbott Lord	Campbell, Bernard M.	April 28, 1852	Balto.
Lancaster	Ellen	17	Tippecanoe	Staples, Joshua	Jan. 17, 1842	Balto.
Lancaster	Harriet	20	Isaac Franklin	Kephart, George	Sept. 28, 1838	Balto.
Lancaster	James	36	Tweed	Bowling, John D.	Oct. 20, 1836	Town Creek
Lancaster	John	28	General Pinckney	Slatter, Hope Hull	Jan. 19, 1847	Balto.
Lancaster	Minty	35	Tweed	Bowling, John D.	Oct. 20, 1836	Town Creek
Lancaster	Peres	5	Tweed	Bowling, John D.	Oct. 20, 1836	Town Creek
Lancaster	Treacy	25	General Pinckney	Slatter, Hope Hull	Jan. 19, 1847	Balto.
Lancaster		3	Tweed	Bowling, John D.	Oct. 20, 1836	Town Creek
Lancaster		14	Tweed	Bowling, John D.	Oct. 20, 1836	Town Creek
Lance	Julia	23	Henry A. Barling	Campbell, Bernard M.	Dec. 18, 1851	Balto.
Lance	Lucinda	20	Henry A. Barling	Campbell, Bernard M.	Dec. 18, 1851	Balto.
Lands	John	16	Solomon Saltus	Slatter, Hope Hull	Oct. 7, 1839	Balto.
Lane	Daniel	25	Hermitage	Williams, Thomas	Oct. 28, 1846	Balto.
Lane	George	9	Solomon Saltus	Slatter, Hope Hull	Oct. 7, 1839	Balto.

Surname	First Name	Age	Ship	O/S	Date	Depart
Lane	Harriett Ann	15	Solomon Saltus	Slatter, Hope Hull	Oct. 7, 1839	Balto.
Lane	Henry	43	Scotia	Slatter, Hope Hull	Sept. 30, 1843	Balto.
Lane	Juliet	20	Solomon Saltus	Slatter, Hope Hull	Oct. 7, 1839	Balto.
Lane	Mary	24	Solomon Saltus	Slatter, Hope Hull	Oct. 7, 1839	Balto.
Lane	Thomas	24	Victorine	Slatter, Hope Hull	Sept. 12, 1846	Balto.
Lane	William	11	Phoenix	Slatter, Hope Hull	March 27, 1847	Balto.
Lane		infant	Solomon Saltus	Slatter, Hope Hull	Oct. 7, 1839	Balto.
Lane		infant	Solomon Saltus	Slatter Hope Hull	Oct. 7, 1839	Balto.
Langley	Louisa	10	Hermitage	Slatter. Hope Hull	Oct. 28, 1846	Balto.
Langly	Isaac	25	Sarah Bridge	Campbell, Bernard M.	Feb. 8, 1851	Balto.
Langsten	Henry	21	Lafayette	Harker, William	March 25, 1843	Balto.
Lanidan	Sarah	16	Isaac Franklin	Kephart, George	Sept. 28, 1838	Balto.
Lankford	Francis	20	Cora	Campbell, Bernard M.	Jan. 20, 1851	Balto.
Lansdale	Hilton	30	Union	Donovan, Joseph S.	Dec. 16, 1848	Balto.
Lansdale	William	22	Waverly	Donovan, Joseph S.	Apr. 3, 1851	Balto.
Larkins	Wilber	17	Victorine	Donovan, Joseph S.	Dec. 31, 1846	Balto.
Laskins	Mary Ann	16	Kirkwood	Slatter, Hope Hull	Oct. 16, 1845	Balto.
Lasty	Davis		Intelligence	De Mapiere, Victor	Apr. 30, 1821	Balto.
Lathrum	Edmund	21	Phoenix	Slatter, Hope Hull	March 27, 1847	Balto.
Laws	Cornelius	23	Louisa	Campbell, Bernard M.	Nov. 5, 1849	Balto.
Lawson	Hannah	36	Tippecanoe	Bangs, Theopilus	Apr. 15, 1844	Balto.
Lawson	Judy	22	Hermitage	Williams, Thomas	Oct. 28, 1846	Balto.
Lawson	Washington	21	Helen A. Miller	Campbell, Bernard M.	Oct. 18, 1852	Balto.
Lawson	William	17	Helen A. Miller	Campbell Bernard M.	Oct. 18, 1852	Balto.
Lazenberry	Emila	25	Kirkwood	Rodbind, Ebenezer	Oct. 26, 1847	Balto.
Leach	Hannah	40	Scotia	Slatter, Hope Hull	Sept. 30, 1843	Balto.

Surname	First Name	Age	Ship	O/S	Date	Depart
Leakins	Lewis	20	Southerner	Campbell, Bernard M.	Jan. 20, 1850	Balto.
Learned	Easter	28	Burlington	Slatter, Hope Hull	Oct. 21, 1842	Balto.
Lee	Abraham	32	Southerner	Campbell, Bernard M.	Jan. 5, 1852	Balto.
Lee	Abraham	21	Tippecanoe	Harker, William	Dec. 16, 1840	Balto.
Lee	Abram	22	Paoli	Slatter, Hope Hull	Sept. 9, 1845	Balto.
Lee	Albert	17	Victorine	Donovan, Joseph S.	Sept. 29, 1845	Balto.
Lee	Ann	38	E.H.Chapin	Donovan, Joseph S.	Dec. 2, 1847	Balto.
Lee	Basil	21	Narragansett	Donovan, Joseph S.	Nov. 27, 1850	Balto.
Lee	Caria	16	Victorine	Harker, William	March 9, 1844	Balto.
Lee	Caroline	15	Hibernia	Woolfolk, Austin	Dec. 5, 1826	Balto.
Lee	Cassey	30	Irad Ferry	Clendenin, A.	Jan. 16, 1840	Balto.
Lee	Charles	19	John S. Gittings	Campbell, Bernard M.	Nov. 20, 1852	Balto.
Lee	Charles Henry	2	Kirkwood	Slatter, Hope Hull	Jan. 4, 1845	Balto.
Lee	Christian	30	Pioneer	Slatter, Hope Hull	Sept. 15, 1847	Balto.
Lee	Edward	12	Scotia	Slatter, Hope Hull	Sept. 30, 1843	Balto.
Lee	Eliza	32	Victorine	Donovan, Joseph S.	May 22, 1844	Balto.
Lee	Eliza	18	Zoe	Slatter, Hope Hull	Feb. 16, 1847	Balto.
Lee	Ely	18	Brunswick	Woolfolk, Austin	Oct. 11, 1831	Balto.
Lee	Emaly	20	Hermitage	Donovan, Joseph S.	Oct. 28, 1846	Balto.
Lee	Emory	22	John C. Calhoun	Donovan, Joseph S.	Oct. 24, 1850	Balto.
Lee	Gabriel	25	Home	Slatter, Hope Hull	March 22, 1845	Balto.
Lee	George	27	Henry A. Barling	Donovan, Joseph S.	Feb. 24, 1851	Balto.
Lee	George	18	John C. Calhoun	Donovan, Joseph S.	Oct. 24, 1850	Balto.
Lee	Harriett	18	Paoli	Slatter, Hope Hull	Sept. 9, 1845	Balto.
Lee	Harriett	5	Tippecanoe	Slatter, Hope Hull	Apr. 15, 1844	Balto.
Lee	Henry	22	Narragansett	Donovan, Joseph S.	Nov. 27, 1850	Balto.

Surname	First Name	Age	Ship	O/S	Date	Depart
Lee	Henry	infant	Tippecanoe	Slatter, Hope Hull	Apr. 15, 1844	Balto.
Lee	Henry	32	Tippecanoe	Slatter, Hope Hull	Apr. 15, 1844	Balto.
Lee	Henry	20	Waverly	Donovan, Joseph S.	Apr. 3, 1851	Balto.
Lee	Henson	20	Eliza F. Mason	Donovan, Joseph S.	Nov. 13, 1851	Balto.
Lee	Herbert	23	General Pinckney	Donovan, Joseph S.	Feb. 21, 1846	Balto.
Lee	Jacob	18	Paoli	Slatter, Hope Hull	Sept. 9, 1845	Balto.
Lee	James	17	Kirkwood	Campbell, Bernard M.	Oct. 14, 1848	Balto.
Lee	Jane	14	Home	Rodbind, Ebenezer	March 22, 1845	Balto.
Lee	Jane	30	Kirkwood	Slatter Hope Hull	Jan. 4, 1845	Balto.
Lee	John	20	Kirkwood	Rodbind, Ebenezer	Apr. 15, 1845	Balto.
Lee	John	19	Lafayette	Woolfolk, Austin	Oct. 18, 1828	Balto.
Lee	John	12	Tippecanoe	Slatter, Hope Hull	Apr. 15, 1844	Balto.
Lee	Kane	22	Gannidefft	Slatter, Hope Hull	Nov. 25, 1840	Balto.
Lee	Kitty	18	Lady Monroe	Woolfolk, Austin	March 25, 1825	Balto.
Lee	Levinia	11	Sabine	Donovan, Joseph S.	Feb. 10, 1844	Balto.
Lee	Lucy	40	Tippecanoe	Slatter, Hope Hull	Apr. 15, 1844	Balto.
Lee	Maria	26	Isaac Franklin	Slatter, Hope Hull	Sept. 28, 1838	Balto.
Lee	Maria	18	Union	Slatter, Hope Hull	July 26, 1847	Balto.
Lee	Martha	infant	Hermitage	Donovan, Joseph S.	Oct. 28, 1846	Balto.
Lee	Mary	16	Home	Rodbind Ebenezer	March 22, 1845	Balto.
Lee	Milly	15	Irad Ferry	Clendenin, A.	Jan. 16, 1840	Balto.
Lee	Milly	20	Scotia	Slatter, Hope Hull	Sept. 30, 1843	Balto.
Lee	Rachel	16	Victorine	Rodbind, Ebenezer	May 14, 1845	Balto.
Lee	Richard	22	John C. Calhoun	Donovan, Joseph S.	Oct. 24, 1850	Balto.
Lee	Samuel	23	Lapwing	Woolfolk, Samuel M.	Feb. 15, 1827	Balto.
Lee	Sarah	19	Union	Slatter, Hope Hull	July 26, 1847	Balto.

Surname	First Name	Age	Ship	O/S	Date	Depart
Lee	Stephen	33	Irad Ferry	Clendenin, A.	Jan. 16, 1840	Balto.
Lee	Thomas	17	Margaret Hugg	Poindexter, T.B.	Nov. 30, 1844	Balto.
Lee	Thomas	60	Tweed	Tucker, J.B.	Oct. 20, 1836	Town Creek
Lee	William	19	Ann & Leah	Woolfolk, Austin	Nov.1, 1831	Balto.
Lee	William	30	Kirkwood	Slatter, Hope Hull	Oct. 16, 1845	Balto.
Lee	William	8	Tippecanoe	Slatter, Hope Hull	Apr. 15, 1844	Balto.
Legton	Clementine	19	States	Woolfolk, Austin	Nov. 26, 1825	Balto.
Lelman	Catherine	17	Kirkwood	Campbell, Bernard M.	Nov. 28, 1849	Balto.
Lemmon	Charles	14	John S. Gittings	Campbell, Bernard M.	Nov. 20, 1852	Balto.
Lemmon	Frederick	22	Henry Clay	Woolfolk, Austin	Dec. 4, 1828	Balto.
Lemmon	James	16	John S. Gittings	Campbell, Bernard M.	Nov. 20, 1852	Balto.
Lemmon	James	32	Kirkwood	Slatter, Hope Hull	Apr. 15, 1845	Balto.
Lemmon	Primas	35	Strafford	Harker, William	Nov. 22, 1843	Balto.
Lemmon	Samuel	15	John S. Gittings	Campbell, Bernard M.	Nov. 20, 1852	Balto.
Leonard	Amelia	30	Union	Campbell, Bernard M.	Dec. 16, 1848	Balto.
Leonard	Fanny	13	Union	Campbell, Bernard M.	Dec. 16, 1848	Balto.
Leonard	Frank	6	Union	Campbell, Bernard M.	Dec. 16, 1848	Balto.
Leonard	Jim	4	Union	Campbell, Bernard M.	Dec. 16, 1848	Balto.
Leonard	Jim	50	Union	Campbell, Bernard M.	Dec. 16, 1848	Balto.
Leonard	Sally	10	Union	Campbell, Bernard M.	Dec. 16, 1848	Balto.
Lewellen	Sandy	13	General Pinckney	Slatter, Hope Hull	Jan. 19, 1847	Balto.
Lewis	Andrew	20	Nathaniel Hooper	Campbell, Bernard M.	Feb. 12, 1852	Balto.
Lewis	Archibald	23	Tippecanoe	Harker, William	Apr. 15, 1844	Balto.
Lewis	Betsy	14	Kirkwood	Slatter, Hope Hull	Apr. 15, 1845	Balto.
Lewis	Bill	18	Ewarkee	Purvis, James Franklin	March 4, 1841	Balto.
Lewis	Cassa Ann	22	Superb	Slatter, Hope Hull	Nov. 1, 1843	Balto.

Surname	First Name	Age	Ship	O/S	Date	Depart
Lewis	Charles	18	P.R. Hazeltine	Campbell, Bernard M.	Nov. 15, 1856	Balto.
Lewis	Charlie	17	Pioneer	Stuart, William R.	July 20, 1848	Balto.
Lewis	David	18	Victcrine	Donovan, Joseph S.	Dec. 17, 1845	Balto.
Lewis	Dorsey	21	Kirkwood	Donovan, Joseph S.	Oct. 26, 1847	Balto.
Lewis	Eliza	16	St. Mary	Donovan, Joseph S.	Nov. 29, 1845	Balto.
Lewis	Essep	23	Brunswick	Woolfolk, Austin	Oct. 11, 1831	Balto.
Lewis	Fanny	50	Kirkwood	Myers, Thomas J.	Nov. 27, 1849	Balto.
Lewis	George	39	Victorine	Slatter, Henry F.	Dec. 31, 1846	Balto.
Lewis	Harriet	18	Kirkwood	Donovan, Joseph S.	Apr. 15, 1845	Balto.
Lewis	Hetty	17	Hiberria	Woolfolk, Austin	Dec. 5, 1826	Balto.
Lewis	Horace	12	Tippecanoe	Purvis, James Franklin	Jan. 17, 1842	Balto.
Lewis	Isaac	50	Kirkwood	Myers, Thomas J.	Nov. 27, 1849	Balto.
Lewis	Isaac	35	Tippecanoe	Purvis, James Franklin	Jan. 17, 1842	Balto.
Lewis	Jane	20	Hermitage	Slatter, Hope Hull	Oct. 28, 1846	Balto.
Lewis	Jane	16	Solomon Saltus	Slatter, Hope Hull	Oct. 7, 1839	Balto.
Lewis	Jaron	40	Union	Campbell, Bernard M.	Oct. 9, 1848	Balto.
Lewis	John	17	Isaac Franklin	Kephart, George	Feb. 1, 1839	Balto.
Lewis	Joshua	23	Jasper	Woolfolk, Austin	Apr. 7, 1827	Balto.
Lewis	Margaret	8	Glasgow	Slatter, Hope Hull	Oct. 11, 1838	Balto.
Lewis	Mary	22	Brunswick	Woolfolk, Austin	Oct. 11, 1831	Balto.
Lewis	Rachel	27	Kirkwood	Donovar, Joseph S.	Dec. 10, 1846	Balto.
Lewis	Sarah	2	Brunswick	Woolfoll, Austin	Oct. 11, 1831	Balto.
Lewis	Sarah	9	Kirkwool	Slatter, Hope Hull	Apr. 15, 1845	Balto.
Lewis	Sarah	16	Zoe	Donovan Joseph S.	Feb. 16, 1847	Balto.
Lewis	Washington	10	Lafayette	Woolfolk, Austin	Oct. 18, 1828	Balto.
Lewis	William	12	Isaac Franklin	Kephart, George	Feb. 1, 1839	Balto.

Surname	First Name	Age	Ship	O/S	Date	Depart
Lewis	William	11	Kirkwood	Donovan, Joseph S.	Oct. 26, 1847	Balto.
Lias	Emory	17	Hibernia	Woolfolk, Austin	Dec. 5, 1826	Balto.
Ligget	Harriet	19	Lady Monroe	Woolfolk, Austin	March 25, 1825	Balto.
Ligon	Bill	18	Hibernia	Woolfolk, Austin	Dec. 5, 1826	Balto.
Liles	Clem	22	Kirkwood	Rodbind, Ebenezer	Apr. 15, 1845	Balto.
Liles	Lewis	22	Kirkwood	Rodbind, Ebenezer	Apr. 15, 1845	Balto.
Limber	Rachel	26	Superb	Slatter, Hope Hull	Nov. 1, 1843	Balto.
Limberry	Ellen	22	Burlington	Slatter, Hope Hull	Oct. 21, 1842	Balto.
Linch	Debby	16	Catharine	Woolfolk, Austin	March 3. 1829	Balto.
Lindsay	Elizebeth	25	Pioneer	Slatter, Hope Hull	Sept. 15, 1847	Balto.
Lindsay	James	25	Nathaniel Hooper	Campbell, Bernard M.	Feb. 12, 1852	Balto.
Lindy	Bob	15	States	Tillotson, Giles	Nov. 22, 1827	Balto.
Lingam	Louisa	18	Margaret Hugg	Slatter, Hope Hull	Feb. 8, 1845	Balto.
Lingham	Eliza	18	Solomon Saltus	Slatter, Hope Hull	Oct. 7, 1839	Balto.
Lingum	Abraham	26	Kirkwood	Donovan, Joseph S.	Oct. 26, 1847	Balto.
Linkius	Charles	22	Victorine	Donovan, Joseph S.	Dec. 17, 1845	Balto.
Linsey	Frank	21	Tippecanoe	Purvis, James Franklin	Apr. 1, 1841	Balto.
Linton	Ann	13	Burlington	Slatter, Hope Hull	Oct. 21, 1842	Balto.
Lipiers	Jacob	21	Phoenix	Slatter, Hope Hull	March 27, 1847	Balto.
List	Sarah	16	Julia	Woolfolk, Austin	Jan. 8, 1829	Balto.
Little	James	27	Kirkwood	Donovan, Joseph S.	Oct. 26, 1847	Balto.
Little	John	25	Kirkwood	Donovan, Joseph S.	Oct. 26, 1847	Balto.
Littleton	Gandy	24	Kirkwood	Donovan, Joseph S.	Oct. 14, 1848	Balto.
Lively	Margaret	18	Elizabeth	Campbell, Bernard M.	Nov. 18, 1848	Balto.
Lively	Nicolas	24	Southerner	Campbell, Bernard M.	Jan. 5, 1852	Balto.
Lives	Joseph	21	Glasgow	Slatter, Hope Hull	Oct. 11, 1838	Balto.

Surname	First Name	Age	Ship	O/S	Date	Depart
Livres	Bennett	23	Louisa	Slatter, Hope Hull	Oct. 11, 1847	Balto.
Lloyd	Joseph	18	Eliza F Mason	Donovan, Joseph S.	Nov. 13, 1851	Balto.
Lloyd	Mary Ann	11	Kirkwood	Campbell, Bernard M.	Oct. 14, 1848	Balto.
Locke	Benjamin	20	Paoli	Slatter, Hope Hull	Sept. 9, 1845	Balto.
Lockerman	Leah	17	Kirkwood	Slatter, Henry F.	Dec. 10, 1846	Balto.
Lockerman	Sharlet	11	Kirkwood	Slatter, Henry F.	Dec. 10, 1846	Balto.
Lockwood	Henry	24	Kirkwood	Donovan, Joseph S.	Sept. 28, 1846	Balto.
Logan	Jeff	22	Hermitage	Williams, Thomas	Oct. 28, 1846	Balto.
Logan	Tom	45	Home	Rodbind, Ebenezer	March 22, 1845	Balto.
Lomax	Sam	21	Union	Rodbind, Ebenezer	Dec. 16, 1848	Balto.
Lomax	Thadeus	22	Union	Donovan, Joseph S.	Dec. 16, 1848	Balto.
Lomen	George	21	Kirkwood	Donovan, Joseph S.	Jan. 14, 1846	Balto.
London	Eliza	20	Kirkwood	Campbell, Bernard M.	Oct. 14, 1848	Balto.
London	Sophia	18	Kirkwood	Campbell, Bernard M.	Oct. 14, 1848	Balto.
Loney	Robert	20	Louisa	Slatter, Hope Hull	Oct. 11, 1847	Balto.
Long	Charles	20	John C. Calhoun	Donovan, Joseph S.	Oct. 24, 1850	Balto.
Long	Charles	20	John C. Calhoun	Donovan, Joseph S.	Oct. 24, 1850	Balto.
Long	Eliza	16	Southerner	Donovan, Jospeh S.	Jan. 5, 1852	Balto.
Long	Jane	13	Southerner	Donovan, Jospeh S.	Jan. 5, 1852	Balto.
Long	Jim	17	Balloon	Milligan, George	Dec. 17, 1821	Balto.
Long	Keziah	17	Narragansett	Donovan, Joseph S.	Nov. 27, 1850	Balto.
Longer	Peach	25	Tippecanoe	Harker, William	Apr. 15, 1844	Balto.
Lore	Smith	20	Irad Ferry	Slatter, Hope Hull	Dec. 9, 1842	Balto.
Loud?	Adaline	18	Tippecanoe	Burke, J.W.	Sept. 17, 1844	Balto.
Louden	Jasper	40	Colonel Howard	Harker, William	Nov. 21, 1844	Balto.
Louder	Lucinda	18	General Finckney	Rodbind, Ebenezer	Feb. 21, 1846	Balto.

Surname	First Name	Age	Ship	O/S	Date	Depart
Louis	Martha Jane	18	Kirkwood	Slatter, Hope Hull	Dec. 23, 1843	Balto.
Louis	Nathan	21	Kirkwood	Donovan, Joseph S.	Oct. 14, 1848	Balto.
Louis	Richmond	29	Pioneer	Stuart, William R.	July 20, 1848	Balto.
Louther	Sandy	21	Scotia	Slatter, Hope Hull	Sept. 30, 1843	Balto.
Love	Margaret	25	Isaac Franklin	Slatter, Hope Hull	Sept. 28, 1838	Balto.
Lovedy	Nancy	30	Nathaniel Hooper	Campbell, Bernard M.	Feb. 12, 1852	Balto.
Lovett	Henry	12	Mary	Woolfolk, Austin	Oct. 7, 1843	Balto.
Lowe	Lucy	22	Kirkwood	Rodbind, Ebenezer	Oct. 26, 1847	Balto.
Lowers	William	14	Phoenix	Donovan, Joseph S.	March 27, 1847	Balto.
Lowery	Timothy	24	Lapwing	Woolfolk, Joseph B.	Feb. 15, 1827	Balto.
Lowns	Mariah	20	Porpoise	Purvis, James Franklin	Dec. 11, 1841	Balto.
Lowry	George	20	Lady Monroe	Woolfolk, Austin	March 25, 1825	Balto.
Lowry	Milley	25	Tippecanoe	Purvis, James Franklin	Jan. 17, 1842	Balto.
Loyd	Lee	20	John C. Calhoun	Donovan, Joseph S.	Oct. 24, 1850	Balto.
Loyd	Peter	12	Peru	Slatter, Hope Hull	Nov. 16, 1842	Balto.
Loyd	William	17	Union	Donovan, Joseph S.	Dec. 16, 1848	Balto.
Loydd	Martha	10	Victorine	Rodbind, Ebenezer	March 1, 1845	Balto.
Loyer	Henry	18	W.H.D.C.Wright	Slatter, Hope Hull	Nov. 7, 1847	Balto.
Lucas	Henry	19	Elizabeth	Donovan, Joseph S.	Nov. 18, 1848	Balto.
Lucas	Letey	40	St. Mary	Donovan, Joseph S.	Nov. 29, 1845	Balto.
Lucas	Lewis	35	John S. Gittings	Campbell, Bernard M.	Nov. 20, 1852	Balto.
Luckett	George	20	Scotia	Harker, William	Sept. 30, 1843	Balto.
Luckett	Jane	9	Elizabeth	Donovan, Joseph S.	Nov. 18, 1848	Balto.
Lumkin	Jose	25	Isaac Franklin	Kephart, George	Sept. 28, 1838	Balto.
Lute	Sarah	10	Elizabeth	Donovan, Joseph S.	Jan. 2, 1850	Balto.
Lyle	Delilah	18	Elizabeth	Donovan, Joseph S.	March 21, 1850	Balto.

Surname	First Name	Age	Ship	O/S	Date	Depart
Lyles	Cyrus	20	John C. Calhoun	Donovan, Joseph S.	Oct. 24, 1850	Balto.
Lyles	Dennis	25	Solomon Saltus	Slatter, Hope Hull	Oct. 7, 1839	Balto.
Lyles	George	20	Union	Campbell, Bernard M.	Dec. 16, 1848	Balto.
Lyles	John	18	Southerner	Campbell, Bernard M.	Oct. 27, 1849	Balto.
Lyles	Lee	30	General Pinckney	Campbell, Bernard M.	Jan. 19, 1847	Balto.
Lyles	Mary	20	General Pinckney	Campbell, Bernard M.	Jan. 19, 1847	Balto.
Lyles	Moses	22	John C. Calhoun	Donovan, Joseph S.	Oct. 24, 1850	Balto.
Lyles	Robert	35	Union	Sheckle=, B.O.	Nov. 17, 1849	Balto.
Lyles	Sarah	16	Kirkwood	Donovan, Joseph S.	Oct. 26, 1847	Balto.
Lynch	Ann	16	Isaac Franklin	Slatter, Hope Hull	Sept. 28, 1838	Balto.
Lynch	Zachariah	18	Elizabeth	Donovan, Joseph S.	May 12, 1849	Balto.
Lyons	Betsy	16	Lafayette	Woolfolk, Austin	Oct. 18, 1828	Balto.
Lyons	Priscilla	15	Victorine	Rodbind, Ebenezer	Dec. 31, 1846	Balto.
Macall	Charles	22	Ann & Leah	Woolfolk, Austin	Nov.1, 1831	Balto.
MacDaniel	Hinson	16	Irad Ferry	Purvis, James Franklin	Feb. 5, 1842	Balto.
Macer	Adam	28	Kirkwood	Campbell, Bernard M.	March 23, 1844	Balto.
Mack	Anthony	17	Irad Ferry	Purvis, James Franklin	Feb. 5, 1842	Balto.
Mack	Lewis	18	Kirkwood	Donovan, Joseph S.	Oct. 26, 1847	Balto.
Mackell	John	21	Kirkwood	Donovan, Joseph S.	Dec. 23, 1843	Balto.
Mackey	Fanny	20	Architec=	Harker, William	Feb. 16, 1843	Balto.
Mackey	Horace	12	Brunswick	Woolfolk, Austin	Oct. 11, 1831	Balto.
Mackey	Louisa	10	Kirkwood	Donovan, Joseph S.	Apr. 15, 1845	Balto.
Mackey	Milly	14	Brunswick	Woolfolk, Austin	Oct. 11, 1831	Balto.
Macklin	Mary	17	General Pinckney	Slatter, Hope Hull	Jan. 19, 1847	Balto.
Macorm	Lucy	17	Henry A. Barling	Donovan Joseph S.	Feb. 24, 1851	Balto.
Macullough	William	20	Sabine	Donovan Joseph S.	Feb. 10, 1844	Balto.

Surname	First Name	Age	Ship	O/S	Date	Depart
Madden	Harriett	18	Salvadora	Slatter, Hope Hull	Sept. 28, 1846	Balto.
Madden	Loyd	9	Lafayette	Woolfolk, Austin	Oct. 18, 1828	Balto.
Maddin	Allin	24	Bostonian	Slatter, Hope Hull	Jan. 18, 1841	Balto.
Madison	James	22	Victorine	Slatter, Hope Hull	March 9, 1844	Balto.
Magruder	Catharine	4	E.H.Chapin	Slatter, Hope Hull	Nov. 30, 1847	Balto.
Magruder	Nelson	25	E.H.Chapin	Slatter, Hope Hull	Nov. 30, 1847	Balto.
Magruder	Sam	22	Southerner	Rodbind, Ebenezer	Jan. 21, 1850	Balto.
Magruder	Sarah	7	E.H.Chapin	Slatter, Hope Hull	Nov. 30, 1847	Balto.
Magruder	William	45	Kirkwood	Slatter, Hope Hull	Dec. 23, 1843	Balto.
Mahord	Mary	19	Porpoise	Purvis, James Franklin	Dec. 11, 1841	Balto.
Majors	Horace	24	Kirkwood	Donovan, Joseph S.	Oct. 14, 1848	Balto.
Maker	Mary Jane	17	Scotia	Slatter, Hope Hull	Sept. 30, 1843	Balto.
Mamard	Mary	16	Union	Slatter, Hope Hull	July 26, 1847	Balto.
Mandle	Jatsan	20	General Pinckney	Slatter, Hope Hull	Jan. 19, 1847	Balto.
Mandue	Humphry	21	Kirkwood	Rodbind, Ebenezer	Apr. 15, 1845	Balto.
Manfred	William	25	Victorine	Donovan, Joseph S.	Sept. 29, 1845	Balto.
Manly	Thomas	22	Kirkwood	Donovan, Joseph S.	Oct. 26, 1847	Balto.
Manners	Lloyd	28	Burlington	Slatter, Hope Hull	Oct. 21, 1842	Balto.
Manuel	John	20	Isaac Franklin	Kephart, George	Feb. 1, 1839	Balto.
Many	Moses	23	Isaac Franklin	Slatter, Hope Hull	Sept. 28, 1838	Balto.
Marcella	Hannah	16	Elizabeth	Donovan, Joseph S.	Nov. 18, 1848	Balto.
Marcellas	John	11	Union	Donovan, Joseph S.	Dec. 16, 1848	Balto.
Marchand	Philip	18	States	Woolfolk, Austin	Nov. 21, 1827	Balto.
Marker	George	22	Southerner	Donovan, Joseph S.	Oct. 27, 1849	Balto.
Marling	John	21	Solomon Saltus	Slatter, Hope Hull	Oct. 7, 1839	Balto.
Marlow	Patrick	25	Elizabeth	Rodbind, Ebenezer	Nov. 18, 1848	Balto.

Surname	First Name	Age	Ship	O/S	Date	Depart
Marrell	Henry	20	Searran	Slatter, Hope Hull	Dec. 19, 1838	Balto.
Marriott	Tilghman	22	Henry A. Barling	Campbell, Bernard M.	Apr. 19, 1849	Balto.
Marsh	Harriet	11	States	Woolfolk, Austin	Nov. 21, 1827	Balto.
Marshal	Sandy	19	Kirkwood	Campbell, Bernard M.	Jan. 4, 1845	Balto.
Marshall	Andrew	23	Kirkwood	Slatter, Hope Hull	Oct. 16, 1845	Balto.
Marshall	Chief Justice	11	Kirkwood	Slatter, Hope Hull	Oct. 16, 1845	Balto.
Marshall	Elizabeth	15	Henry A. Barling	Campbell, Bernard M.	Feb. 24, 1851	Balto.
Marshall	Elizebeth	19	Victorine	Slatter, Hope Hull	Dec. 17, 1845	Balto.
Marshall	George	infant	Victorine	Slatter, Hope Hull	Dec. 17, 1845	Balto.
Marshall	Henny	16	Victorine	Slatter Hope Hull	Dec. 17, 1845	Balto.
Marshall	Hinson	26	Henry A. Barling	Campbell, Bernard M.	Dec. 18, 1851	Balto.
Marshall	James	18	Seaman	Slatter, Hope Hull	Dec. 19, 1838	Balto.
Marshall	Jim	36	Intelligence	Griffith, Capt. David	Sept. 18, 1821	Balto.
Marshall	Jim	21	Victorine	Slatter, Hope Hull	Dec. 17, 1845	Balto.
Marshall	Joseph	30	Southerner	Donovan, Joseph S.	Jan. 21, 1850	Balto.
Marshall	Josiah	13	Victorine	Slatter, Hope Hull	Dec. 17, 1845	Balto.
Marshall	Kendal	51	Victorine	Slatter, Hope Hull	Dec. 17, 1845	Balto.
Marshall	Leah	10	Victorine	Slatter, Hope Hull	Dec. 17, 1845	Balto.
Marshall	Lucy	16	Tweed	Sothoron, William H.	Oct. 20, 1836	Town Creek
Marshall	Madison	24	Union	Donovan, Joseph S.	May 13, 1848	Balto.
Marshall	Mariah Ann	15	Kirkwood	Donovan, Joseph S.	Apr. 15, 1845	Balto.
Marshall	Mary	25	Southerner	Donovan, Joseph S.	Jan. 21, 1850	Balto.
Marshall	Mathias	27	Union	Donovan, Joseph S.	May 13, 1848	Balto.
Marshall	Matilda	17	St. Mary	Donovan, Joseph S.	Nov. 29, 1845	Balto.
Marshall	Milby	23	Victorine	Slatter, Hope Hull	Dec. 17, 1845	Balto.
Martin	Charles	14	Lafayette	Woolfolk, Joseph B.	Oct. 18, 1828	Balto.

Surname	First Name	Age	Ship	O/S	Date	Depart
Martin	Charlotte	15	Lafayette	Woolfolk, Austin	Oct. 18, 1828	Balto.
Martin	Charlotte	27	Southerner	Donovan, Jospeh S.	Jan. 5, 1852	Balto.
Martin	Francis	infant	Home	Slatter, Hope Hull	March 22, 1845	Balto.
Martin	Harriett Ann	18	Home	Slatter, Hope Hull	March 22, 1845	Balto.
Martin	Isaac	32	States	Woolfolk, Austin	Apr. 14, 1828	Balto.
Martin	Mariah	20	Eliza	Slatter, Hope Hull	Oct. 9, 1840	Balto.
Martin	Moses	13	Victorine	Donovan, Joseph S.	Sept. 29, 1845	Balto.
Martin	Ruben	28	Eliza F.Mason	Donovan, Joseph S.	Nov. 13, 1851	Balto.
Mary	Branson	45	Elizabeth	Donovan, Joseph S.	Oct. 6, 1849	Balto.
Maryland	Henrietta	17	Charles	Campbell, Bernard M.	Dec. 18, 1850	Balto.
Mason	Alfred	21	Catharine	Donovan, Joseph S.	Jan. 18, 1845	Balto.
Mason	George	21	Home	Rodbind, Ebenezer	March 22, 1845	Balto.
Mason	George	22	Kirkwood	Rodbind, Ebenezer	Oct. 26, 1847	Balto.
Mason	George	28	St. Mary	Williams, Thomas	Nov. 29, 1845	Balto.
Mason	Henney	16	Victorine	Rodbind, Ebenezer	March 1, 1845	Balto.
Mason	Isaac	15	Kirkwood	Crow, William	March 23, 1844	Balto.
Mason	John	17	Kirkwood	Slatter, Hope Hull	Oct. 16, 1845	Balto.
Mason	Margret	25	Victorine	Rodbind, Ebenezer	May 14, 1845	Balto.
Mason	Margrett	infant	Victorine	Rodbind, Ebenezer	March 1, 1845	Balto.
Mason	Margrett	12	Victorine	Slatter, Hope Hull	May 14, 1845	Balto.
Mason	Mary	18	Sabine	Donovan, Joseph S.	Feb. 10, 1844	Balto.
Mason	Milly	17	Superb	Donovan, Joseph S.	Nov. 2, 1843	Balto.
Mason	Perry	22	Isaac Franklin	Kephart, George	Sept. 28, 1838	Balto.
Mason	Richard	20	Delawarian	Campbell, Bernard M.	Dec. 1, 1848	Balto.
Mason	Senna	19	Victorine	Rodbind, Ebenezer	March 1, 1845	Balto.
Mason	Tom	25	Isaac Franklin	Kephart, George	Feb. 1, 1839	Balto.

Surname	First Name	Age	Ship	O/S	Date	Depart
Mason	William	20	Kirkwood	Rodband, Ebenezer	Oct. 26, 1847	Balto.
Massey	Eleusia	16	Billow	Woolfolk, Austin	Feb. 23, 1828	Balto.
Massey	John	23	Wavely	Donovan, Joseph S.	Apr. 3, 1851	Balto.
Massy		21	Kirkwood	Donovan, Joseph S.	Oct. 26, 1847	Balto.
Masy	Charles	20	Russel	Slatter, Hope Hull	March 1, 1839	Balto.
Mathelda	Hetty	16	Victorine	Donovan, Joseph S.	May 22, 1844	Balto.
Mathers	Rind	23	Burlington	Slatter Hope Hull	Oct. 21, 1842	Balto.
Mathews	Amos	14	Victorine	Slatter, Hope Hull	March 9, 1844	Balto.
Mathews	Columbus	14	Union	Donovan, Joseph S.	May 13, 1848	Balto.
Mathews	Elisa Ann	20	Ewarkee	Slatter, Hope Hull	March 4, 1841	Balto.
Mathews	Frank	19	Paoli	Slatter, Hope Hull	Sept. 9, 1845	Balto.
Mathews	Frederick	19	Superb	Slatter, Hope Hull	Nov. 1, 1843	Balto.
Mathews	George	17	Intelligence	De Mapiere, Victor	Apr. 30, 1821	Balto.
Mathews	Hariet	19	Harriett	Woolfolk, Austin	March 23, 1822	Balto.
Mathews	Hester	infant	Victorine	Slatter, Hope Hull	Dec. 17, 1845	Balto.
Mathews	Isaac	16	Home	Slatter, Hope Hull	March 22, 1845	Balto.
Mathews	Lanoy	15	General Pinckney	Williams, Thomas	Jan. 19, 1847	Balto.
Mathews	Mary	30	Victorine	Slatter, Hope Hull	Dec. 17, 1845	Balto.
Mathews	Nicholas	20	Scotia	Slatter, Hope Hull	Sept. 30, 1843	Balto.
Mathews	Peter	25	Victorine	Donovan, Joseph S.	May 22, 1844	Balto.
Mathews	Richard	23	Victorine	Donovan, Joseph S.	May 14, 1845	Balto.
Mathews	Sophia	24	Victorine	Donovan, Joseph S.	May 22, 1844	Balto.
Mathews	Thomas	infant	Henry A Barling	Donovan, Joseph S.	Feb. 24, 1851	Balto.
Mathews	William H.	3 mon.	Victorine	Donovan, Joseph S.	May 22, 1844	Balto.
Matny	Robert	25	Paoli	Slatter, Hope Hull	Sept. 9, 1845	Balto.
Matthews	Abraham	28	Billow	Woolfolk, Austin	Feb. 23, 1828	Balto.

Surname	First Name	Age	Ship	O/S	Date	Depart
Matthews	Charles	23	Saldana	Harker, William	Feb. 27, 1844	Balto.
Matthews	Charlotte	15	Catharine	Donovan, Joseph S.	Jan. 18, 1845	Balto.
Matthews	Charlotte	18	Kirkwood	Donovan, Joseph S.	March 9, 1847	Balto.
Matthews	Elisa	15	Russell	Slatter, Hope Hull	March 1, 1839	Balto.
Matthews	Eliza	10	Zoe	Williams, Thomas	Feb. 16, 1847	Balto.
Matthews	Eliza Jane		Kirkwood	Harker, William	Apr. 4, 1846	Balto.
Matthews	Elizabeth	16	Seaman	Hooper, John P.	Apr. 8, 1842	Balto.
Matthews	Ezekiel	35	Pioneer	Stuart, William R.	July 20, 1848	Balto.
Matthews	Frederick	20	Catharine	Donovan, Joseph S.	Jan. 18, 1845	Balto.
Matthews	Henry	34	Kirkwood	Campbell, Bernard M.	Oct. 14, 1848	Balto.
Matthews	Henry	20	Lapwing	Spraggins, Samuel M.	March 22, 1822	Balto.
Matthews	Jarrett	20	Lapwing	Woolfolk, Samuel M.	Feb. 15, 1827	Balto.
Matthews	Jerry	28	Southerner	Campbell, Bernard M.	Jan. 5, 1852	Balto.
Matthews	Kitty	18	Zoe	Slatter, Hope Hull	Feb. 16, 1847	Balto.
Matthews	Mary	18	Kirkwood	Harker, William	Apr. 4, 1846	Balto.
Matthews	Mary	18	Mary Broughton	Campbell, Bernard M.	Nov. 18, 1851	Balto.
Matthews	Mellany	22	Kirkwood	Campbell, Bernard M.	Oct. 14, 1848	Balto.
Matthews	Pius	19	General Pinckney	Slatter, Hope Hull	Jan. 19, 1847	Balto.
Matthews	Richard	20	Hibernia	Woolfolk, Austin	Dec. 5, 1826	Balto.
Matthews	Sophia	18	Kirkwood	Campbell, Bernard M.	Apr. 4, 1846	Balto.
Matthews	William	18	Phoenix	Slatter, Hope Hull	March 27, 1847	Balto.
Mattingly	Kitty	18	Tweed	Tucker, J.B.	Oct. 20, 1836	Town Creek
Mattingly	Mary	9	Tweed	Tucker, J.B.	Oct. 20, 1836	Town Creek
Maxfield	Henry	22	Superb	Slatter, Hope Hull	Nov. 1, 1843	Balto.
Maxwell	Alexis	30	Abbott Lord	Jenkins, James	Oct. 4, 1851	Balto.
Maynard	Everett	20	John C. Calhoun	Donovan, Joseph S.	Oct. 24, 1850	Balto.

Surname	First Name	Age	Ship	O/S	Date	Depart
Maynard	John	25	Henry A. Barling	Donovan, Joseph S.	Dec. 18, 1851	Balto.
Mc Aldry	Alfred	11	Victorine	Slatter, Henry F.	Dec. 31, 1846	Balto.
McAldry	Adaline	9	Victorine	Slatter, Henry F.	Dec. 31, 1846	Balto.
McAldry	Mary	17	Victorine	Slatter, Henry F.	Dec. 31, 1846	Balto.
McConnick	Hannah	18	Kirkwood	Donovan, Joseph S.	Jan. 4, 1845	Balto.
McCormick	Nathan	16	Ann & Leah	Woolfolk, Austin	Nov. 1, 1831	Balto.
McCoy	Ann	35	Margaret Hugg	Campbell, Bernard M.	Feb. 8, 1845	Balto.
McCoy	Charlotte	20	Henry Clay	Woolfolk, Austin	Dec. 4, 1828	Balto.
McCoy	John	5	Margaret Hugg	Campbell, Bernard M.	Feb. 8, 1845	Balto.
McCoy	Peter	8	Margaret Hugg	Campbell, Bernard M.	Feb. 8, 1845	Balto.
McCubbin	Lloyd	20	Eliza F. Mason	Donovan, Joseph S.	Nov. 13, 1851	Balto.
McDaniel	Alexander	23	Lafayette	Woolfolk, Austin	Oct. 18, 1828	Balto.
McDonnough	Jane	14	States	Woolfolk, Austin	Nov. 21, 1827	Balto.
McFerson	Elizabeth	11	Saldana	Harker, William	Feb. 27, 1844	Balto.
McGruder	Harriett	22	Elizabeth	Donovan, Joseph S.	Nov. 18, 1848	Balto.
McIntire	John	22	Burlington	Slatter, Hope Hull	Oct. 21, 1842	Balto.
McKall	Ann	22	Union	Campbell, Bernard M.	Oct. 9, 1848	Balto.
McKall	Harriet	25	Elizabeth	Campbell, Bernard M.	Nov. 18, 1848	Balto.
McKall	Harriet	20	Union	Campbell, Bernard M.	Oct. 9, 1848	Balto.
McKall	Hessey	10	Delawarian	Campbell, Bernard M.	Dec. 1, 1848	Balto.
McKall	Kitty	3	Elizabeth	Campbell, Bernard M.	Nov. 18, 1848	Balto.
McKall	Lizzie	18	Union	Campbell, Bernard M.	Oct. 9, 1848	Balto.
McKall	Robert	12	Delawarian	Campbel, Bernard M.	Dec. 1, 1848	Balto.
McLane	David	21	Henry A. Barling	Donovar, Joseph S.	Feb. 24, 1851	Balto.
McLaster	Hester	10	Ann & Leah	Woolfolk, Austin	Nov. 1, 1831	Balto.
McLean	William	32	Isaac Franklin	Kephart, George	Sept. 28, 1838	Balto.

Surname	First Name	Age	Ship	O/S	Date	Depart
McPherson	Austin	24	Isaac Franklin	Kephart, George	Feb. 1, 1839	Balto.
McPherson	Jerry	18	Kirkwood	Donovan, Joseph S.	Oct. 14, 1848	Balto.
McQuay	Daniel	20	Lafayette	Woolfolk, Austin	Oct. 18, 1828	Balto.
Meads	Henrietta	20	Eliza F.Mason	Donovan, Joseph S.	Nov. 13, 1851	Balto.
Meads	Sophia	18	Abbott Lord	Campbell, Bernard M.	April 28, 1852	Balto.
Meads	William	18	Kirkwood	Denning, John N.	Jan. 14, 1846	Balto.
Mean	Henry	23	Isaac Franklin	Kephart, George	Sept. 28, 1838	Balto.
Mears	Henry	23	Tippecanoe	Slatter, Hope Hull	Apr. 15, 1844	Balto.
Medars	Joseph	23	Pioneer	Stuart, William R.	July 20, 1848	Balto.
Medley	Amy	25	Kirkwood	Rodbind, Ebenezer	Apr. 15, 1845	Balto.
Medley	Ragas	22	Helen A. Miller	Campbell, Bernard M.	Oct. 18, 1852	Balto.
Medley	Sam	25	Kirkwood	Rodbind, Ebenezer	Apr. 15, 1845	Balto.
Meekins	Ann	20	Irad Ferry	Clendenin, A.	Jan. 16, 1840	Balto.
Mellon	George	35	Kirkwood	Slatter, Hope Hull	Oct. 16, 1845	Balto.
Mercer	Henry	20	Solomon Saltus	Slatter, Hope Hull	Oct. 7, 1839	Balto.
Mercer	Margaret Ann	17	Solomon Saltus	Slatter, Hope Hull	Oct. 7, 1839	Balto.
Mercer	Samuel	19	Margaret Hugg	Campbell, Bernard M.	Feb. 8, 1845	Balto.
Mercer	Sarah Ann	21	Solomon Saltus	Slatter, Hope Hull	Oct. 7, 1839	Balto.
Merrick	Edmond	14	E.H.Chapin	Slatter, Hope Hull	Nov. 30, 1847	Balto.
Merrick	Louisa	17	E.H.Chapin	Slatter, Hope Hull	Nov. 30, 1847	Balto.
Merrity	John	18	Victorine	Rodbind, Ebenezer	March 14, 1846	Balto.
Merryman		22	Louisa	Campbell, Bernard M.	May 18, 1846	Balto.
Miars	James	25	Victorine	Slatter, Hope Hull	March 1, 1845	Balto.
Miars	John	infant	General Pinckney	Slatter, Hope Hull	Feb. 21, 1846	Balto.
Miars	Maria	18	General Pinckney	Slatter, Hope Hull	Feb. 21, 1846	Balto.
Michael	Woodmet	16	Jefferson	Woolfolk, Austin	Dec. 24, 1827	Balto.

Surname	First Name	Age	Ship	O/S	Date	Depart
Middleton	Allcinda	19	Louisa	Donovan, Joseph S.	Oct. 9, 1847	Balto.
Middleton	Benjamin	43	Louisa	Donovan, Joseph S.	Oct. 9, 1847	Balto.
Middleton	Benjamin (Jr.)	11	Louisa	Donovan, Joseph S.	Oct. 9, 1847	Balto.
Middleton	Bushrod	8	Louisa	Donovan, Joseph S.	Oct. 9, 1847	Balto.
Middleton	Floyd	19	Billow	Woolfolk, Austin	Feb. 23, 1828	Balto.
Middleton	Harrison	17	Louisa	Donovan, Joseph S.	Oct. 9, 1847	Balto.
Middleton	Mary Ann	13	Louisa	Donovan, Joseph S.	Oct. 9, 1847	Balto.
Middleton	Sally	13	Louisa	Donovan, Joseph S.	Oct. 9, 1847	Balto.
Middleton	Sam	9	Louisa	Donovan, Joseph S.	Oct. 9, 1847	Balto.
Middleton	William	23	Margaret Hugg	Slatter, Hope Hull	Feb. 8, 1845	Balto.
Midelton	Lewis	22	Union	Williams, Thomas	Oct. 9, 1848	Balto.
Midelton	Milly	17	Union	Williams, Thomas	Oct. 9, 1848	Balto.
Milbourn	George	22	Scotia	Slatter, Hope Hull	Sept. 30, 1843	Balto.
Milbourn	Levi	24	Brunswick	Woolfolk, Austin	Oct. 11, 1831	Balto.
Milburn	Sarah	20	Victorine	Donovan, Joseph S.	Dec. 31, 1846	Balto.
Milckard	Sarah	19	Kirkwood	Donovan, Joseph S.	Oct. 26, 1847	Balto.
Miles	Alexious	19	Tweed	Sothoror, William H.	Oct. 20, 1836	Town Creek
Miles	Alfred	8	Victorine	Rodbind, Ebenezer	Dec. 31, 1846	Balto.
Miles	Catherine	9 mon.	Isaac Franklin	Kephart, George	Sept. 28, 1838	Balto.
Miles	Charles	15	John C. Calhoun	Donovan, Joseph S.	Oct. 24, 1850	Balto.
Miles	Eliza Jane	18	Victorine	Slatter, Henry F.	Dec. 31, 1846	Balto.
Miles	Henry	24	Helen A. Miller	Campbel , Bernard M.	Oct. 18, 1852	Balto.
Miles	Hester	35	Osprey	Rodbind, Ebenezer	Nov. 11, 1847	Balto.
Miles	Minor	19	Kirkwood	Donovan. Joseph S.	Oct. 26, 1847	Balto.
Miles	Rachael	16	Louisa	Campbell, Bernard M.	Nov. 5, 1849	Balto.
Miles	Washington	17	Tweed	Bowling, John D.	Oct. 20, 1836	Town Creek

Surname	First Name	Age	Ship	O/S	Date	Depart
Millad	Jane	16	Tippecanoe	Slatter, Hope Hull	Jan. 17, 1842	Balto.
Millar	Henry	22	Hibernia	Woolfolk, Austin	Dec. 5, 1826	Balto.
Millar	Philip	20	Hibernia	Woolfolk, Austin	Dec. 5, 1826	Balto.
Millard	Mary	18	Louisa	Campbell, Bernard M.	March 31, 1849	Balto.
Miller	Ann Maria	4	Jefferson	Woolfolk, Austin	Dec. 24, 1827	Balto.
Miller	Benjamin	16	Victorine	Donovan, Joseph S.	Sept. 29, 1845	Balto.
Miller	Cassy	19	Hermitage	Williams, Thomas	Oct. 28, 1846	Balto.
Miller	Charity	17	Jefferson	Woolfolk, Austin	Dec. 24, 1827	Balto.
Miller	Charles	17	Southerner	Donovan, Joseph S.	Oct. 27, 1849	Balto.
Miller	David	22	Lafayette	Woolfolk, Austin	Oct. 18, 1828	Balto.
Miller	Dick	18	Hibernia	Chabert, Leon	Dec. 5, 1826	Balto.
Miller	Ellin	16	Victorine	Donovan, Joseph S.	Sept. 29, 1845	Balto.
Miller	Emiline	20	Architect	Harker, William	Feb. 16, 1843	Balto.
Miller	Francis	8	Union	Slatter, Hope Hull	July 26, 1847	Balto.
Miller	George	30	Henry A. Barling	Campbell, Bernard M.	Dec. 18, 1851	Balto.
Miller	Henny	19	Lady Monroe	Woolfolk, Austin	March 25, 1825	Balto.
Miller	Henry	21	Hibernia	Woolfolk, Austin	Dec. 5, 1826	Balto.
Miller	Houston	infant	Hermitage	Donovan, Joseph S.	Oct. 28, 1846	Balto.
Miller	Isaac	10	Russell	Slatter, Hope Hull	March 1, 1839	Balto.
Miller	James	24	Lafayette	Woolfolk, Austin	Oct. 18, 1828	Balto.
Miller	John	22	Architect	Harker, William	Feb. 16, 1843	Balto.
Miller	John	10	Union	Slatter, Hope Hull	July 26, 1847	Balto.
Miller	John	28	Union	Slatter, Hope Hull	July 26, 1847	Balto.
Miller	Joseph	20	Margaret Hugg	Poindexter, T.B.	Nov. 30, 1844	Balto.
Miller	Mary	17	Billow	Woolfolk, Austin	Feb. 23, 1828	Balto.
Miller	Mary E.	14	Kirkwood	Slatter, Hope Hull	Apr. 15, 1845	Balto.

Surname	First Name	Age	Ship	O/S	Date	Depart
Miller	Milly	19	Louisa	Slatter, Hope Hull	Oct. 11, 1847	Balto.
Miller	Nancy	21	Hermitage	Donovan, Joseph S.	Oct. 28, 1846	Balto.
Miller	Nancy	16	Kirkwood	Crow, William	Jan. 14, 1846	Balto.
Miller	Nathan	23	Jasper	Woolfolk, Austin	Apr. 7, 1827	Balto.
Miller	Rear	20	Margaret Hugg	Poindexter, T.B.	Nov. 30, 1844	Balto.
Miller	Remus	23	Kirkwood	Slatter, Hope Hull	Jan. 4, 1845	Balto.
Miller	Riley	18	Henry A. Barling	Campbell, Bernard M.	Dec. 18, 1851	Balto.
Miller	Sarah	16	Kirkwood	Donovan, Joseph S.	Apr. 15, 1845	Balto.
Miller	Sarah	25	Union	Slatter, Hope Hull	July 26, 1847	Balto.
Miller	Sylvester	25	Home	Slatter, Hope Hull	March 22, 1845	Balto.
Miller	William	28	Kirkwood	Donovan, Joseph S.	Dec. 23, 1843	Balto.
Mills	Joseph	25	Union	Williams, Thomas	Oct. 9, 1848	Balto.
Mills	Maria	18	Liberator	Woolfolk, Austin	Nov. 12, 1828	Balto.
Mills	Patty	11	Catharine	Donovan, Joseph S.	Jan. 18, 1845	Balto.
Millstead	Alonzo	23	Union	Donovan, Joseph S.	May 13, 1848	Balto.
Mima	Lilly	infant	Leda	Nelson, James	Nov. 16, 1848	Balto.
Mincer	Benjamin	24	Jasper	Woolfolk, Austin	Apr. 7, 1827	Balto.
Miner	Milly	16	Lafayette	Woolfolk, Richard	Oct. 18, 1828	Balto.
Mines	Ben	22	Kirkwood	Rodbind, Ebenezer	Oct. 26, 1847	Balto.
Miscer	Samuel	24	Irad Ferry	Slatter, Hope Hull	Dec. 9, 1842	Balto.
Mitchel	Perry	17	Julia	Woolfolk, Austin	Jan. 8, 1829	Balto.
Mitchell	Abram	7 weeks	Lady Monroe	Woolfolk, Austin	March 25, 1825	Balto.
Mitchell	Ann	16	Tweed	Sothoron, William H.	Oct. 20, 1836	Town Creek
Mitchell	Charlotte	19	Solomon Saltus	Slatter, Hope Hull	Oct. 7, 1839	Balto.
Mitchell	Daniel	33	Elizabeth	Campbell, Walter L.	Oct. 6, 1849	Balto.
Mitchell	Daniel	15	Isaac Franklin	Slatter, Hope Hull	Sept. 28, 1838	Balto.

Surname	First Name	Age	Ship	O/S	Date	Depart
Mitchell	Fanny	18	Lapwing	Woolfolk, Austin	Feb. 15, 1827	Balto.
Mitchell	George	35	Tweed	Sothoron, William H.	Oct. 20, 1836	Town Creek
Mitchell	Grace	16	Southerner	Campbell, Bernard M.	Jan. 5, 1852	Balto.
Mitchell	Henry	16	Tweed	Sothoron, William H.	Oct. 20, 1836	Town Creek
Mitchell	Isaiah	20	Elizabeth	Donovan, Joseph S.	Nov. 18, 1848	Balto.
Mitchell	Jasper	19	Helen A. Miller	Campbell, Bernard M.	Oct. 18, 1852	Balto.
Mitchell	John	17	Elizabeth	Donovan, Joseph S.	Nov. 18, 1848	Balto.
Mitchell	John	13	Margaret Hugg	Campbell, Bernard M.	Nov. 30, 1844	Balto.
Mitchell	Lucinda	17	Union	Williams, Thomas	Oct. 9, 1848	Balto.
Mitchell	Mary	18	Lady Monroe	Woolfolk, Austin	March 25, 1825	Balto.
Mitchell	Nathan	23	Waverly	Campbell, Bernard M.	Apr. 3, 1851	Balto.
Mitchell	Robert	25	Jefferson	Woolfolk, Joseph B.	Dec. 24, 1827	Balto.
Mitchell	Stephen	26	Seaman	Slatter, Shadrack	March 25, 1839	Balto.
Mitchell	Will	20	Intelligence	King, Gideon T.	Sept. 18, 1821	Balto.
Mitchell	William	22	Sabine	Donovan, Joseph S.	Feb. 10, 1844	Balto.
Mitchell	William	22	Superb	Carrere, John	Apr. 6, 1819	Balto.
Mitchell	William	18	Triton	Anderson, David	Dec. 21, 1819	Balto.
Moales	David	15	Scotia	Slatter, Hope Hull	Sept. 30, 1843	Balto.
Moles	David	13	Irad Ferry	Slatter, Hope Hull	Dec. 9, 1842	Balto.
Mollison	Abraham	33	Tweed	Sothoron, William H.	Oct. 20, 1836	Town Creek
Mollison	Charles	13	Tweed	Sothoron, William H.	Oct. 20, 1836	Town Creek
Mollison	Chloe	7	Tweed	Sothoron, William H.	Oct. 20, 1836	Town Creek
Mollison	Peggy	36	Tweed	Sothoron, William H.	Oct. 20, 1836	Town Creek
Mollison	Robert	9	Tweed	Sothoron, William H.	Oct. 20, 1836	Town Creek
Mollison	Vickey	15	Tweed	Sothoron, William H.	Oct. 20, 1836	Town Creek
Mollison	William	17	Tweed	Sothoron, William H.	Oct. 20, 1836	Town Creek

Surname	First Name	Age	Ship	O/S	Date	Depart
Molton	Hanibal	30	Isaac Franklin	Slatter, Hope Hull	Sept. 28, 1838	Balto.
Money	Abraham	21	Kirkwood	Donovan, Joseph S.	Jan. 4, 1845	Balto.
Monley	Joseph	24	Lapwing	Woolfolk, Samuel M.	Feb. 15, 1827	Balto.
Monroe	James	30	Lapwing	Spraggins, Samuel M.	March 22, 1822	Balto.
Monroe	Lewis	21	Kirkwood	Rodbird, Ebenezer	Oct. 26, 1847	Balto.
Montgomery	Henry	22	Elizabeth	Campbell, Bernard M.	Nov. 18, 1848	Balto.
Montgomery	John		Kirkwood	Donovan, Joseph S.	March 9, 1847	Balto.
Montgomery	Joseph	20	Paoli	Slatter, Hope Hull	Sept. 9, 1845	Balto.
Montgomery	Mariah	23	Edward Everett	Campbell, Bernard M.	March 10, 1851	Balto.
Montgomery	Milby	28	Paoli	Slatter, Hope Hull	Sept. 9, 1845	Balto.
Montgomery	Patty	19	Kirkwood	Crow, William	March 23, 1844	Balto.
Montgomery	Somerville	31	Zoe	Donovan, Joseph S.	Feb. 16, 1847	Balto.
Mony	Mary	15	Billow	Woolfolk, Joseph B.	Feb. 23, 1828	Balto.
Moody	Charles	35	Lawrence	Woolfolk, Austin	May 9, 1823	Balto.
Moody	Charles	35	Supert	Anderson, David	Apr. 6, 1819	Balto.
Moody	Charles	30	Triton	Anderson, David	Dec. 20, 1819	Balto.
Moody	Fanny	18	Lapwing	Woolfolk, Austin	Feb. 15, 1827	Balto.
Moody	Henry	16	Jefferson	Woolfolk, Austin	Dec. 24, 1827	Balto.
Moody	Thomas	21	Seaman	Slatter, Shadrack	March 25, 1839	Balto.
Moor	John William	11	Tippecanoe	Slatter, Hope Hull	Apr. 15, 1844	Balto.
Moordock	Stephen	25	Kirkwood	Slatter, Hope Hull	Jan. 14, 1846	Balto.
Moore	Ann	17	Ann & Leah	Woolfolk, Austin	Nov. 1, 1831	Balto.
Moore	Ann	13	Kirkwood	Donovan, Joseph S.	Oct. 26, 1847	Balto.
Moore	Armstead	5	Catharine	Donovan, Joseph S.	Jan. 18, 1845	Balto.
Moore	Charles	13	Kirkwood	Crow, William	March 23, 1844	Balto.
Moore	Dacy	22	Catharine	Donovan, Joseph S.	Jan. 18, 1845	Balto.

Surname	First Name	Age	Ship	O/S	Date	Depart
Moore	Daniel	9	Lafayette	Woolfolk, Joseph B.	Oct. 18, 1828	Balto.
Moore	Dennis	2 mon.	Ann & Leah	Woolfolk, Austin	Nov.1, 1831	Balto.
Moore	Dick	8	Lafayette	Woolfolk, Joseph B.	Oct. 18, 1828	Balto.
Moore	Driver	21	Seaman	Slatter, Hope Hull	March 25, 1839	Balto.
Moore	Emily	16	Arctic	Woolfolk, Austin	Jan. 24, 1829	Balto.
Moore	Henrietta	23	Victorine	Slatter, Henry F.	Dec. 31, 1846	Balto.
Moore	Henry	19	Architect	Crow, William	Feb. 3, 1841	Balto.
Moore	Isarel	23	Kirkwood	Donovan, Joseph S.	Oct. 26, 1847	Balto.
Moore	James	18	Cora	Donovan, Jospeh S.	Jan. 21, 1851	Balto.
Moore	Jim	18	Sarah Bridge	Campbell, Bernard M.	Feb. 8, 1851	Balto.
Moore	Joseph	15	Nathaniel Hooper	Campbell, Bernard M.	Feb. 12, 1852	Balto.
Moore	Julia Ann	15	Kirkwood	Donovan, Joseph S.	Jan. 4, 1845	Balto.
Moore	Lewis	17	Elizabeth	Campbell, Bernard M.	March 21, 1850	Balto.
Moore	Louisa	15	Kirkwood	Crow, William	Jan. 14, 1846	Balto.
Moore	Lucy	27	Lafayette	Woolfolk, Joseph B.	Oct. 18, 1828	Balto.
Moore	Maria	22	Victorine	Slatter, Hope Hull	Sept. 12, 1846	Balto.
Moore	Mark	23	Seaman	Slatter, Hope Hull	March 25, 1839	Balto.
Moore	Mary	infant	Catharine	Donovan, Joseph S.	Jan. 18, 1845	Balto.
Moore	Mary	16	Isaac Franklin	Kephart, George	Feb. 1, 1839	Balto.
Moore	Mary	18	Mars	Woolfolk, Austin	Oct. 30, 1824	Balto.
Moore	Milly	18	Helen A. Miller	Campbell, Bernard M.	Oct. 18, 1852	Balto.
Moore	Ned	11	Lafayette	Woolfolk, Joseph B.	Oct. 18, 1828	Balto.
Moore	Shirly	22	Margaret Hugg	Wilson, Thomas C.	Nov. 30, 1844	Balto.
Moore	Stephen	20	States	Woolfolk, Austin	Nov. 21, 1827	Balto.
Moore	Thomas	16	Nathaniel Hooper	Campbell, Bernard M.	Feb. 12, 1852	Balto.
Moore	Washington	19	Elizabeth	Donovan, Joseph S.	March 21, 1850	Balto.

Surname	First Name	Age	Ship	O/S	Date	Depart
Moore	Washington	35	Kirkwood	Donovan, Joseph S.	March 23, 1844	Balto.
Moore	William	18	General Pinckney	Slatter, Hope Hull	Feb. 21, 1846	Balto.
Moore	Wilson	16	General Pinckney	Slatter, Hope Hull	Feb. 21, 1846	Balto.
Morgan	James	20	Kirkwood	Harker, William	Apr. 4, 1846	Balto.
Morgan	Jane	22	Kirkwood	Harker, William	Apr. 4, 1846	Balto.
Morgan	John	4	Kirkwood	Harker, William	Apr. 4, 1846	Balto.
Morgan	Joseph	24	Home	Donovan, Joseph S.	March 22, 1845	Balto.
Morgan	William	infant	Kirkwood	Harker, William	Apr. 4, 1846	Balto.
Morgan	Willis	24	Kirkwood	Crow, William	March 23, 1844	Balto.
Morris	Alexina	6	Kirkwood	Donovan, Joseph S.	Apr. 15, 1845	Balto.
Morris	Charles	21	Salvadora	Slatter, Hope Hull	Sept. 28, 1846	Balto.
Morris	Charlotte	25	Isaac Franklin	Slatter, Hope Hull	Sept. 28, 1838	Balto.
Morris	Gusty	infant	Kirkwood	Donovan, Joseph S.	Apr. 15, 1845	Balto.
Morris	Jane	17	Tangier	Campbell, Bernard M.	Nov. 26, 1853	Balto.
Morris	John	19	Victorine	Slatter, Henry F.	Dec. 31, 1846	Balto.
Morris	Louisa F.	20	Glasgow	Slatter Hope Hull	Oct. 11, 1838	Balto.
Morris	Mariah	22	Kirkwood	Donovan, Joseph S.	Apr. 15, 1845	Balto.
Morris	Mary	15	Zoe	Campbell, Bernard M.	Feb. 16, 1847	Balto.
Morris	Nancy	2	Isaac Franklin	Slatter, Hope Hull	Sept. 28, 1838	Balto.
Morris	Nancy	26	Paoli	Slatter, Hope Hull	Sept. 9, 1845	Balto.
Morris	Robert	22	Julia	Woolfolk, Austin	Feb. 10, 1832	Balto.
Morris	William	23	Kirkwood	Donovan, Joseph S.	Apr. 15, 1845	Balto.
Morris		infant	Paoli	Donovan, Joseph S.	Sept. 9, 1845	Balto.
Morrison	Edward	15	Kirkwood	Donovan, Joseph S.	Oct. 14, 1848	Balto.
Morrison	Frank	16	Tweed	Bowling, John D.	Oct. 20, 1836	Town Creek
Morrison	Maria	16	Tippecanoe	Slatter, Hope Hull	Jan. 17, 1842	Balto.

Surname	First Name	Age	Ship	O/S	Date	Depart
Morrison	Nathaniel	20	Kirkwood	Donovan, Joseph S.	Oct. 26, 1847	Balto.
Morsell	Mary	11	Charles	Campbell, Bernard M.	Dec. 18, 1850	Balto.
Morton	Charlotte	17	Hibernia	Woolfolk, Austin	Dec. 5, 1826	Balto.
Morton	James	26	Hibernia	Woolfolk, Austin	Dec. 5, 1826	Balto.
Morton	Mary Jane	10	Ann & Leah	Woolfolk, Austin	Nov. 1, 1831	Balto.
Morton	Nathaniel	24	Tippecanoe	Chenowith, J.W.	Jan. 18, 1842	Balto.
Moseby	Ann	3	Kirkwood	Donovan, Joseph S.	Oct. 26, 1847	Balto.
Moseby	Susan	21	Kirkwood	Donovan, Joseph S.	Oct. 26, 1847	Balto.
Moseley	Henry	26	Home	Rodbind, Ebenezer	March 22, 1845	Balto.
Moten	Berkley	35	Kirkwood	Slatter, Hope Hull	Dec. 23, 1843	Balto.
Motter	Harry	20	Mars	Woolfolk, Joseph B.	Oct. 30, 1824	Balto.
Motts	Urias	21	Kirkwood	Donovan, Joseph S.	March 23, 1844	Balto.
Moulton	John	20	Sarah Bridge	Campbell, Bernard M.	Feb. 8, 1851	Balto.
Mouton	Crawford	9	Solomon Saltus	Slatter, Hope Hull	Oct. 7, 1839	Balto.
Mudd	Lucy	40	Tweed	Tucker, J.B.	Oct. 20, 1836	Town Creek
Mulberry	Peter	21	Brunswick	Woolfolk, Austin	Oct. 11, 1831	Balto.
Munroe	George	21	Sarah Bridge	Campbell, Bernard M.	Feb. 8, 1851	Balto.
Mures	Anne	21	Susan Miller	Woolfolk, Richard T.	Oct. 25, 1822	Balto.
Murphy	Phillis	19	Lafayette	Woolfolk, Austin	Oct. 18, 1828	Balto.
Murray	Abram	21	Hibernia	Woolfolk, Austin	Dec. 5, 1826	Balto.
Murray	Alford	25	Jane Henderson	Campbell, Bernard M.	Nov. 1, 1852	Balto.
Murray	Ann	18	Seaman	Slatter, Shadrack	March 25, 1839	Balto.
Murray	Caleb	29	Kirkwood	Donovan, Joseph S.	Nov. 28, 1849	Balto.
Murray	Charles	40	Seaman	Freeman, Theophilus	March 25, 1839	Balto.
Murray	George	21	Lafayette	Woolfolk, Austin	Oct. 22, 1828	Balto.
Murray	Jams	18	Seaman	Slatter, Hope Hull	Dec. 19, 1838	Balto.

Surname	First Name	Age	Ship	O/S	Date	Depart
Murray	Joseph	26	Victorine	Slatter, Hope Hull	Sept. 12, 1846	Balto.
Murray	Maria	32	Kirkwood	Doncvan, Joseph S.	March 23, 1844	Balto.
Murray	Sarah	16	States	Woolfolk, Austin	Apr. 14, 1828	Balto.
Murry	Alexander	20	Margaret Hugg	Donovan, Joseph S.	Feb. 8, 1845	Balto.
Murry	Daniel	23	Kirkwood	Donovan, Joseph S.	Oct. 14, 1848	Balto.
Murry	Emeline	19	Brunswick	Woolfolk, Austin	Oct. 11, 1831	Balto.
Murry	Hannah	20	General Pinckney	Donovan, Joseph S.	Nov. 10, 1845	Balto.
Murry	Harry	27	Lady Monroe	Woolfolk, Austin	March 25, 1825	Balto.
Murry	Henry	21	Bostonian	Slatter, Hope Hull	Jan. 18, 1841	Balto.
Murry	James	18	Lady Monroe	Woolfolk, Austin	March 25, 1825	Balto.
Murry	Mmandia	18	General Pinckney	Rodbind, Ebenezer	Feb. 21, 1846	Balto.
Murry	Robert	22	Victorine	Donovan, Joseph S.	Dec. 31, 1846	Balto.
Muse	Richard	17	Kirkwood	Crow, William	Jan. 14, 1846	Balto.
Myars	Eliza	25	Victorine	Slatter, Hope Hull	March 9, 1844	Balto.
Myars	Henry	22	Scotia	Slatter, Hope Hull	Sept. 30, 1843	Balto.
Myers	Abraham	22	Tippecanoe	Slatter, Hope Hull	Jan. 17, 1842	Balto.
Myers	Abraham	9	Victorine	Donovan, Joseph S.	Sept. 29, 1845	Balto.
Myers	Caroline	16	Architect	Slatter, Hope Hull	May 20, 1841	Balto.
Myers	Daniel	21	St. Mary	Donovan, Joseph S.	Nov. 29, 1845	Balto.
Myers	David	20	Catharine	Donovan, Joseph S.	Jan. 18, 1845	Balto.
Myers	David	22	St. Mary	Donovan, Joseph S.	Nov. 29, 1845	Balto.
Myers	Edward	26	Margaret Forbs	Slatter, Hope Hull	Nov. 28, 1838	Balto.
Myers	Eliza	17	Louisa	Slatter, Hope Hull	Oct. 11, 1847	Balto.
Myers	Ellen	18	Kirkwood	Slatter, Hope Hull	Apr. 4, 1846	Balto.
Myers	Hannah	18	Bostonian	Slatter, Hope Hull	Jan. 18, 1841	Balto.
Myers	Henry	20	Helen A. Miller	Campbel l, Bernard M.	Oct. 18, 1852	Balto.

Surname	First Name	Age	Ship	O/S	Date	Depart
Myers	Henry	23	Kirkwood	Donovan, Joseph S.	Oct. 26, 1847	Balto.
Myers	James	20	St. Mary	Donovan, Joseph S.	Nov. 29, 1845	Balto.
Myers	John	15	Jasper	Woolfolk, Austin	Apr. 7, 1827	Balto.
Myers	John	23	Uncas	Slatter, Hope Hull	Jan. 10, 1838	Balto.
Myers	Lewis	5 mon.	Brunswick	Woolfolk, Austin	Oct. 11, 1831	Balto.
Myers	Lewis	19	Edward Everett	Campbell, Bernard M.	March 10, 1851	Balto.
Myers	Milly	35	Victorine	Donovan, Joseph S.	Sept. 29, 1845	Balto.
Myers	Nancy	21	Jefferson	Woolfolk, Austin	Dec. 24, 1827	Balto.
Myers	Nancy	16	St. Mary	Donovan, Joseph S.	Nov. 29, 1845	Balto.
Myers	Sarah	25	Hermitage	Slatter, Hope Hull	Oct. 28, 1846	Balto.
Myers	Sophy	8	Victorine	Donovan, Joseph S.	Sept. 29, 1845	Balto.
Myers	Susan	18	Brunswick	Woolfolk, Austin	Oct. 11, 1831	Balto.
Myers	William	19	Sabine	Donovan, Joseph S.	Feb. 10, 1844	Balto.
Nailer	Thomas	20	Henry A. Barling	Campbell, Bernard M.	Apr. 19, 1849	Balto.
Nailor	Benjamin	45	Home	Slatter, Hope Hull	March 22, 1845	Balto.
Nailor	Margrett	13	Kirkwood	Slatter, Hope Hull	Apr. 15, 1845	Balto.
Napper	Joseph	21	Kirkwood	Donovan, Joseph S.	Oct. 26, 1847	Balto.
Napper	Milly	18	Kirkwood	Donovan, Joseph S.	Oct. 26, 1847	Balto.
Napper	William	24	Kirkwood	Donovan, Joseph S.	Oct. 26, 1847	Balto.
Nash	Kitty	18	Victorine	Donovan, Joseph S.	Sept. 29, 1845	Balto.
Nash	Samuel	24	Lafayette	Woolfolk, Austin	Oct. 18, 1828	Balto.
Naylor	Benjamin	19	Russell	Slatter, Hope Hull	March 1, 1839	Balto.
Naylor	Jane	10	Narragansett	Donovan, Joseph S.	Nov. 27, 1850	Balto.
Neal	Bazzell	15	E.H.Chapin	Slatter, Hope Hull	Nov. 30, 1847	Balto.
Neal	Cecelia	22	Kirkwood	Slatter, Hope Hull	Dec. 23, 1843	Balto.
Neal	Eliza	24	Kirkwood	Rodbind, Ebenezer	Oct. 26, 1847	Balto.

Surname	First Name	Age	Ship	O/S	Date	Depart
Neal	Henry	26	Kirkwood	Rodlind, Ebenezer	Oct. 26, 1847	Balto.
Neal	Joseph	21	Superb	Slatter, Hope Hull	Nov. 1, 1843	Balto.
Neal	Nathan	20	Kirkwood	Donovan, Joseph S.	Jan. 4, 1845	Balto.
Neal	Nathan	23	Louisa	Campbell, Bernard M.	May 18, 1846	Balto.
Neal	Uriah	22	Victorine	Donovan, Joseph S.	Dec. 31, 1846	Balto.
Neale	Andrew	8	Tweed	Forbes, George	Oct. 20, 1836	Town Creek
Neale	Julius	8	Tweed	Forbes, George	Oct. 20, 1836	Town Creek
Neale	Lucinda	15	Tweed	Forbes, George	Oct. 20, 1836	Town Creek
Neall	Henry	18	Victorine	Slatter, Henry F.	Dec. 31, 1846	Balto.
Needhams	Jane	14	Elizabeth	Donovan, Joseph S.	Nov. 18, 1848	Balto.
Neil	Washington	20	Delawarian	Campbell, Bernard M.	Dec. 1, 1848	Balto.
Nelson	Cornelia	24	Isaac Franklin	Slatter Hope Hull	Sept. 28, 1838	Balto.
Nelson	Edward	infant	Home	Slatter Hope Hull	March 22, 1845	Balto.
Nelson	Edward	22	Kirkwood	Campbell, Bernard M.	Nov. 28, 1849	Balto.
Nelson	Eliza	11	Kirkwood	Donovan, Joseph S.	Nov. 28, 1849	Balto.
Nelson	George	8	Elizabeth	Donovan, Joseph S.	Nov. 18, 1848	Balto.
Nelson	George	22	Victorine	Slatter, Hope Hull	Sept. 12, 1846	Balto.
Nelson	Henry	17	Kirkwood	Donovan, Joseph S.	Nov. 28, 1849	Balto.
Nelson	Henry	20	Kirkwood	Donovan, Joseph S.	Oct. 26, 1847	Balto.
Nelson	Hinson	21	Margaret Hugg	Donovan, Joseph S.	Feb. 8, 1845	Balto.
Nelson	Isaac	18	States	Woolfolk, Austin	Apr. 14, 1828	Balto.
Nelson	John	21	Kirkwood	Slatter, Hope Hull	Oct. 16, 1845	Balto.
Nelson	Lilly	19	Kirkwood	Donovan, Joseph S.	Oct. 26, 1847	Balto.
Nelson	Maria	20	Seaman	Slatter, Hope Hull	Dec. 19, 1838	Balto.
Nelson	Mary	16	Kirkwood	Donovan, Joseph S.	Apr. 4, 1846	Balto.
Nevill			Zoe	Donovan, Joseph S.	Feb. 16, 1847	Balto.

Surname	First Name	Age	Ship	O/S	Date	Depart
Newby	Joshua	18	Kirkwood	Donovan, Joseph S.	Apr. 15, 1845	Balto.
Newman	Ellen	26	Hibernia	Woolfolk, Austin	Dec. 5, 1826	Balto.
Newman	George	20	Union	Campbell, Bernard M.	Apr. 20, 1850	Balto.
Newman	Jacob	23	Union	Campbell, Bernard M.	Nov. 17, 1849	Balto.
Newman		17	Lady Monroe	Woolfolk, Austin	March 25, 1825	Balto.
Newton	Clarissa	2	Catharine	Slatter, Hope Hull	Jan. 24, 1843	Balto.
Newton	Henry	25	Hermitage	Williams, Thomas	Oct. 28, 1846	Balto.
Newton	John	26	Catharine	Slatter, Hope Hull	Jan. 24, 1843	Balto.
Nichelson	Sempson	25	Intelligence	De Mapiere, Victor	Apr. 30, 1821	Balto.
Nicholas	James	19	States	Woolfolk, Joseph B.	Nov. 21, 1827	Balto.
Nicholds	Henson	21	Colonel Howard	Donovan, Joseph S.	Nov. 21, 1844	Balto.
Nicholds	Levi	24	Colonel Howard	Donovan, Joseph S.	Nov. 21, 1844	Balto.
Nichols	Elisa	7	Lady Monroe	Woolfolk, Austin	March 25, 1825	Balto.
Nichols	Margaret	23	Victorine	Slatter, Hope Hull	Sept. 12, 1846	Balto.
Nichols	Sarah	23	Lady Monroe	Woolfolk, Austin	March 25, 1825	Balto.
Nichols	William	22	Union	Rodbind, Ebenezer	Nov. 17, 1849	Balto.
Nichols		6 mon.	Lady Monroe	Woolfolk, Austin	March 25, 1825	Balto.
Nicholson	Eliza	18	Architect	Rodbind, Ebenezer	Feb. 12, 1840	Balto.
Nicholson	Emeline	9	States	Woolfolk, Austin	Apr. 14, 1828	Balto.
Nicholson	Emeline	18	Victorine	Donovan, Joseph S.	Oct. 25, 1844	Balto.
Nicholson	Jim	20	Jefferson	Woolfolk, Austin	Dec. 24, 1827	Balto.
Nickols	Moses	26	Kirkwood	Slatter, Hope Hull	Oct. 16, 1845	Balto.
Nickolson	George	infant	Victorine	Slatter, Hope Hull	March 9, 1844	Balto.
Nickolson	Milly	26	Victorine	Slatter, Hope Hull	March 9, 1844	Balto.
Nicolas	Charlotte	18	Billow	Woolfolk, Austin	Feb. 23, 1828	Balto.
Nicols	Nancy	17	Hibernia	Woolfolk, Austin	Dec. 5, 1826	Balto.

Surname	First Name	Age	Ship	O/S	Date	Depart
Nicols	William	22	Garniclefft	Slatter, Hope Hull	Nov. 25, 1840	Balto.
Niel	Catharine	10	Eliza F. Mason	Donovan, Joseph S.	Nov. 13, 1851	Balto.
Night	Kate	40	Russell	Slatter, Hope Hull	March 1, 1839	Balto.
Nilmol		infant	Patrick Henry	Campbell, Bernard M.	June 1, 1853	Balto.
Nilmoly	Charles	10	Patrick Henry	Campbell, Bernard M.	June 1, 1853	Balto.
Nilmoly	Emily	5	Patrick Henry	Campbell, Bernard M.	June 1, 1853	Balto.
Nilmoly	Lila	30	Patrick Henry	Campbell, Bernard M.	June 1, 1853	Balto.
Nilmoly	William	32	Patrick Henry	Campbell, Bernard M.	June 1, 1853	Balto.
Noble		17	Lafayette	Woolfolk, Richard	Oct. 18, 1828	Balto.
Noon	Samuel	17	General Pinckney	Slatter, Hope Hull	Feb. 21, 1846	Balto.
Norman	Gerry	9	Signet	Woolfolk, Austin	Nov. 12, 1831	Balto.
Norman	Harriet	22	Signet	Woolfolk, Austin	Nov. 12, 1831	Balto.
Norman	James	28	Waverly	Donovan, Joseph S.	Apr. 3, 1851	Balto.
Norman	William	9 mon.	Signet	Woolfolk, Austin	Nov. 12, 1831	Balto.
Norris	Airy	18	Kirkwood	Donovan, Joseph S.	Oct. 14, 1848	Balto.
Norris	Elizabeth	19	Kirkwood	Donovan, Joseph S.	Oct. 14, 1848	Balto.
Norris	Gracy	21	Lady Monroe	Woolfolk, Austin	March 25, 1825	Balto.
Norris	Henny	18	Victorine	Slatter, Hope Hull	March 9, 1844	Balto.
Norris	Rachel	18	Kirkwood	Slatter, Hope Hull	Dec. 23, 1843	Balto.
Norris	Samuel	15	St. Mary	Donovan, Joseph S.	Nov. 29, 1845	Balto.
Norris	William	22	Kirkwood	Campbell, Bernard M.	March 9, 1847	Balto.
Nugent	Henry	4	Kirkwood	Slatter, Hope Hull	Jan. 14, 1846	Balto.
Nugent	Selina	40	Kirkwood	Slatter, Hope Hull	Jan. 14, 1846	Balto.
Nugent		28	Eliza F. Mason	Donovan, Joseph S.	Nov. 13, 1851	Balto.
Numan	Rachel	17	Lady Monroe	Woolfolk, Austin	March 25, 1825	Balto.
Nutter	Samson	35	Narragansett	Martinet, Jefferson	Nov. 27, 1850	Balto.

Surname	First Name	Age	Ship	O/S	Date	Depart
Office	Harriett	16	Kirkwood	Donovan, Joseph S.	Sept. 28, 1846	Balto.
Ogden	Ann Marie	35	Irad Ferry	Wilson, J.W.	May 6, 1839	Balto.
Ogle	David	28	Gannicleftt	Slatter, Hope Hull	Nov. 25, 1840	Balto.
Ogle	Dennis	14	Victorine	Slatter, Hope Hull	May 14, 1845	Balto.
Ogle	Manuel	15	Victorine	Slatter, Hope Hull	May 14, 1845	Balto.
Olliver	Rebecca	12	Home	Slatter, Hope Hull	March 22, 1845	Balto.
Olliver	Thomas	16	Kirkwood	Donovan, Joseph S.	Oct. 14, 1848	Balto.
Oneal	Martha Ann	16	P.R. Hazeltine	Campbell, Bernard M.	Nov. 15, 1856	Balto.
Oner	Mary Jane	12	Elizabeth	Donovan, Joseph S.	Jan. 2, 1850	Balto.
Orms	James	23	Victorine	Donovan, Joseph S.	Sept. 29, 1845	Balto.
Orrick	Lewis	18	Louisa	Slatter, Hope Hull	Oct. 11, 1847	Balto.
Orsberry	Emanuel	26	St. Mary	Williams, Thomas	Nov. 29, 1845	Balto.
Osborn	Caroline	22	Uncas	Slatter, Hope Hull	Jan. 10, 1838	Balto.
Osborn	Heaton	16	Kirkwood	Crow, William	March 23, 1844	Balto.
Osbourn	Archer	23	Gannicleftt	Slatter, Hope Hull	Nov. 25, 1840	Balto.
Osbourn	Wesley	24	Kirkwood	Donovan, Joseph S.	Dec. 10, 1846	Balto.
Osbourne	Jane Ann	10	Solomon Saltus	Slatter, Hope Hull	Oct. 7, 1839	Balto.
Osbourne	Mary Ann	17	Solomon Saltus	Slatter, Hope Hull	Oct. 7, 1839	Balto.
Osburn	Levi	11	Kirkwood	Donovan, Joseph S.	Apr. 15, 1845	Balto.
Osburn	Nelson	18	Justina	Donovan, Joseph S.	Dec. 2, 1852	Balto.
Osburn	William	18	Home	Donovan, Joseph S.	March 22, 1845	Balto.
Overley	Henry	24	Scotia	Harker, William	Sept. 30, 1843	Balto.
Overly	Matilda	21	Scotia	Harker, William	Sept. 30, 1843	Balto.
Overly		12 mon.	Scotia	Harker, William	Sept. 30, 1843	Balto.
Owen	Nicholas	9	Northumberland	Slatter, Hope Hull	Feb. 27, 1843	Balto.
Owen	Zacariah	16	Kirkwood	Donovan, Joseph S.	March 9, 1847	Balto.

Surname	First Name	Age	Ship	O/S	Date	Depart
Owens	Eliza	20	Signet	Woolfolk, Austin	Nov. 12, 1831	Balto.
Owens	Emeline	3 mon.	Signet	Woolfolk, Austin	Nov. 12, 1831	Balto.
Owens	John	24	Signet	Woolfolk, Austin	Nov. 12, 1831	Balto.
Owin	Betsy	25	Northumberland	Slatter, Hope Hull	Feb. 27, 1843	Balto.
Owings	Jack	18	Jasper	Woolfolk, Austin	Apr. 7, 1827	Balto.
Owings	William	21	Irad Ferry	Slatter Hope Hull	Dec. 9, 1842	Balto.
Paca	Hariett	22	Kirkwood	Donovan, Joseph S.	Nov. 28, 1849	Balto.
Paca	James	29	States	Woolfolk, Austin	Apr. 14, 1828	Balto.
Pacolet	Austin	24	Hibernia	Woolfolk, Austin	Dec. 5, 1826	Balto.
Page	Frederick	22	Kirkwood	Donovan, Joseph S.	Oct. 26, 1847	Balto.
Page	John	22	Southerner	Donovan, Jospeh S.	Jan. 5, 1852	Balto.
Page	Joseph	30	Kirkwood	Crow, William	Jan. 14, 1846	Balto.
Page	Julia	16	E.H.Chapin	Donovan, Joseph S.	Dec. 2, 1847	Balto.
Page	Lemeul	20	Elizabeth	Campbell, Walter L.	Oct. 6, 1849	Balto.
Page	Lucy	20	States	Mortor, George C.	Nov. 26, 1825	Balto.
Page	Lucy Jane	19	Ewarkee	Purvis, James Franklin	March 4, 1841	Balto.
Page	Margaret Ann	infant	States	Mortor, George C.	Nov. 26, 1825	Balto.
Page	Pattey	24	Margaret Hugg	Poindexter, T.B.	Nov. 30, 1844	Balto.
Page	Peter	18	Peru	Slatter, Hope Hull	Nov. 16, 1842	Balto.
Page		17	Kirkwood	Donovan, Joseph S.	Dec. 10, 1846	Balto.
Pain	Martin	12	Lafayette	Woolfolk, Joseph B.	Oct. 18, 1828	Balto.
Pain	Warren	21	Architect	Slatter, Hope Hull	Feb. 16, 1843	Balto.
Paine	Scott	16	Isaac Franklin	Slatter, Hope Hull	Sept. 28, 1838	Balto.
Palm	Israel	22	Home	Donovan, Joseph S.	March 22, 1845	Balto.
Palmer	Samuel	23	Lapwing	Woolfolk, Samuel M.	Feb. 15, 1827	Balto.
Palmer	William	20	Ann & Leah	Woolfolk, Austin	Nov. 1, 1831	Balto.

Surname	First Name	Age	Ship	O/S	Date	Depart
Pane	Harriet	18	Louisa	Donovan, Joseph S.	Oct. 9, 1847	Balto.
Pane	John	25	Paoli	Slatter, Hope Hull	Sept. 9, 1845	Balto.
Parker	Anna	9	Salvadora	Slatter, Hope Hull	Sept. 28, 1846	Balto.
Parker	Cephus	45	Glasgow	Slatter, Hope Hull	Oct. 11, 1838	Balto.
Parker	Comfort	19	Victorine	Slatter, Hope Hull	Sept. 12, 1846	Balto.
Parker	David	19	Union	Campbell, Bernard M.	Nov. 17, 1849	Balto.
Parker	Edward	17	Kirkwood	Campbell, Bernard M.	Dec. 10, 1846	Balto.
Parker	Eliza	19	Kirkwood	Rodbind, Ebenezer	Oct. 26, 1847	Balto.
Parker	Eliza	30	Pioneer	Stuart, William R.	July 20, 1848	Balto.
Parker	Emaline	18	Scotia	Slatter, Hope Hull	Sept. 30, 1843	Balto.
Parker	Grandison	25	General Pinckney	Slatter, Hope Hull	Jan. 19, 1847	Balto.
Parker	Grandison	28	Union	Slatter, Hope Hull	July 26, 1847	Balto.
Parker	Henry	9	Irad Ferry	Slatter, Hope Hull	Jan. 22, 1840	Balto.
Parker	Henry	10	Justina	Donovan, Joseph S.	Dec. 2, 1852	Balto.
Parker	Isaih	18	Pioneer	Slatter, Hope Hull	Sept. 15, 1847	Balto.
Parker	Jacob	25	Isaac Franklin	Slatter, Hope Hull	Sept. 28, 1838	Balto.
Parker	Jacob	25	Victorine	Slatter, Hope Hull	May 14, 1845	Balto.
Parker	Jane	16	Kirkwood	Donovan, Joseph S.	Sept. 28, 1846	Balto.
Parker	John	24	John C. Calhoun	Donovan, Joseph S.	Oct. 24, 1850	Balto.
Parker	John	20	Russell	Woolfolk, Austin	Feb. 27, 1839	Balto.
Parker	John	10	Victorine	Gardiner, Richard S.D.	Dec. 21, 1844	Balto.
Parker	Julia	17	General Pinckney	Donovan, Joseph S.	Feb. 21, 1846	Balto.
Parker	Kitty	16	Victorine	Slatter, Hope Hull	March 14, 1846	Balto.
Parker	Leaher Jane	19	Victorine	Donovan, Joseph S.	May 22, 1844	Balto.
Parker	Louisa	20	Union	Campbell, Bernard M.	Dec. 16, 1848	Balto.
Parker	Marcus	16	Tippecanoe	Slatter, Hope Hull	Jan. 17, 1842	Balto.

Surname	First Name	Age	Ship	O/S	Date	Depart
Parker	Mary	25	Lafayette	Woolfolk, Joseph B.	Oct. 18, 1828	Balto.
Parker	Milly	11	Catharine	Donovan, Joseph S.	Jan. 18, 1845	Balto.
Parker	Nelly	28	Delawarian	Campbell, Bernard M.	Dec. 1, 1848	Balto.
Parker	Reuben	14	Victorine	Rodbird, Ebenezer	May 14, 1845	Balto.
Parker	Rosetta	16	Victorine	Donovan, Joseph S.	May 22, 1844	Balto.
Parker	Sarah	16	Victorine	Donovan, Joseph S.	May 14, 1845	Balto.
Parker	Solomon	25	Helen A. Miller	Campbell, Bernard M.	Oct. 18, 1852	Balto.
Parker	Sophia	14	Victorine	Rodbird, Ebenezer	March 14, 1846	Balto.
Parker	Thornton	33	Tippecanoe	Purvis James Franklin	Jan. 17, 1842	Balto.
Parker	William	20	General Pinckney	Donovan, Joseph S.	Feb. 21, 1846	Balto.
Parker	William	22	Glasgow	Slatter Hope Hull	Oct. 11, 1838	Balto.
Parker		infant	Union	Campbell, Bernard M.	Dec. 16, 1848	Balto.
Parks	Anthony	24	Union	Campbell, Bernard M.	Apr. 20, 1850	Balto.
Parlliss	Daniel	22	Phoenix	Donovan, Joseph S.	March 27, 1847	Balto.
Parran	Alexander	infant	Kirkwood	Campbell, Bernard M.	Dec. 10, 1846	Balto.
Parran	Jacob	23	Kirkwood	Campbell, Bernard M.	Dec. 10, 1846	Balto.
Parran	Mary	20	Kirkwood	Campbell, Bernard M.	Dec. 10, 1846	Balto.
Parraway	Robert	10	Jefferson	Woolfolk, Austin	Dec. 24, 1827	Balto.
Parrin	John	19	Union	Sheckles, B.O.	Nov. 17, 1849	Balto.
Parris	Thomas	11	Justina	Donovan, Joseph S.	Dec. 2, 1852	Balto.
Parsons	Alexander	10	Eliza F.Mason	Donovan, Joseph S.	Nov. 13, 1851	Balto.
Parsons	Alfred	11	Eliza F.Mason	Donovan, Joseph S.	Nov. 13, 1851	Balto.
Parsons	Milkey	18	Architect	Harker, William	Feb. 16, 1843	Balto.
Partisan	Henry	18	Lafayette	Woolfolk, Joseph B.	Oct. 18, 1828	Balto.
Parwell	Nelson	34	Kirkwood	Donovan, Joseph S.	Nov. 28, 1849	Balto.
Paten	Tounsen	20	Justina	Donoven, Joseph S.	Dec. 2, 1852	Balto.

Surname	First Name	Age	Ship	O/S	Date	Depart
Patrick	Violet	23	Isaac Franklin	Slatter, Hope Hull	Sept. 28, 1838	Balto.
Patterson	George	12	Brunswick	Woolfolk, Austin	Oct. 11, 1831	Balto.
Patterson	George	21	Catharine	Donovan, Joseph S.	Jan. 18, 1845	Balto.
Patterson	Hamlet	22	States	Woolfolk, Austin	Nov. 21, 1827	Balto.
Patterson	Harriet	15	Henry A. Barling	Campbell, Bernard M.	Apr. 19, 1849	Balto.
Patterson	Henry	18	Splendid	Slatter, Hope Hull	Apr. 24, 1841	Balto.
Patterson	Henry	19	States	Woolfolk, Austin	Nov. 21, 1827	Balto.
Patterson	James	26	Kirkwood	Slatter, Hope Hull	Apr. 15, 1845	Balto.
Patterson	Mary	12	States	Woolfolk, Austin	Apr. 14, 1828	Balto.
Patterson	Pricilla	18	Union	Slatter, Hope Hull	July 26, 1847	Balto.
Patterson	William	24	Union	Donovan, Joseph S.	Dec. 16, 1848	Balto.
Paul	Henry	23	Union	Campbell, Bernard M.	Dec. 16, 1848	Balto.
Paul	James	27	Harriett	Ducatel, J.T.	March 7, 1823	Balto.
Payne	Ann	20	Helen A. Miller	Campbell, Bernard M.	Oct. 18, 1852	Balto.
Payne	Hester	40	Colonel Howard	Harker, William	Nov. 21, 1844	Balto.
Payne	James		Eliza F.Mason	Donovan, Joseph S.	Nov. 13, 1851	Balto.
Payne	Maria	48	St. Mary	Williams, Thomas	Nov. 29, 1845	Balto.
Payne	Susam	14	Home	Donovan, Joseph S.	March 22, 1845	Balto.
Payton	John	19	Elizabeth	Donovan, Joseph S.	Jan. 2, 1850	Balto.
Payton	Strather	11	Zoe	Slatter, Hope Hull	Feb. 16, 1847	Balto.
Payton	Willis	19	Tippecanoe	Purvis, James Franklin	Jan. 17, 1842	Balto.
Peaken	Humphrey	15	Victorine	Slatter, Henry F.	Dec. 31, 1846	Balto.
Peaker	Charlotte	16	Virginia	Woolfolk, Joseph B.	Dec. 19, 1825	Balto.
Peaker	Daniel	21	Virginia	Woolfolk, Joseph B.	Dec. 19, 1825	Balto.
Peaker	Jesse	22	Paoli	Slatter, Hope Hull	Sept. 9, 1845	Balto.
Pearce	Corilla	24	Elizabeth	Donovan, Joseph S.	March 21, 1850	Balto.

Surname	First Name	Age	Ship	O/S	Date	Depart
Pearce	Precila	10	Elizabeth	Donovan, Joseph S.	March 21, 1850	Balto.
Pearce	Samuel	21	Elizabeth	Donovan, Joseph S.	March 21, 1850	Balto.
Pearce	Tom	24	Elizabeth	Campbell, Bernard M.	March 21, 1850	Balto.
Pearsall	Giles	24	Victorine	Donovan, Joseph S.	Sept. 29, 1845	Balto.
Pearson	Charles	infant	Kirkwood	Donovan, Joseph S.	Dec. 10, 1846	Balto.
Pearson	Ellen	20	Kirkwood	Donovan, Joseph S.	Dec. 10, 1846	Balto.
Pearson	Sarah	22	Hermiage	Berry, Charles H.	Oct. 28, 1846	Balto.
Peck	Thomas	21	Elizabeth	Donovan, Joseph S.	Jan. 2, 1850	Balto.
Pelly	Alfred	22	Seaman	Slatter Hope Hull	Dec. 19, 1838	Balto.
Pelters	Debby	9	Glasgow	Slatter Hope Hull	Oct. 11, 1838	Balto.
Pelton	Charity	22	Victorine	Donovan, Joseph S.	May 22, 1844	Balto.
Pelton	Louisa	4	Victorine	Donovan, Joseph S.	May 22, 1844	Balto.
Pelton	Mary J.	10	Sabine	Donovan, Joseph S.	Feb. 10, 1844	Balto.
Pelton	Nehemiah	1	Victorine	Donovan, Joseph S.	May 22, 1844	Balto.
Pen	Susan	16	Kirkwood	Donovan, Joseph S.	Dec. 10, 1846	Balto.
Pendleton	Alfred	13	Tippecanoe	Slatter, Hope Hull	Jan. 17, 1842	Balto.
Penn	Cloe	19	Henry A. Barling	Campbell, Bernard M.	Dec. 18, 1851	Balto.
Penn	Dennis	25	Elizabeth	Campbell, Bernard M.	Nov. 18, 1848	Balto.
Penn	Henry	14	Edward Everett	Campbell, Bernard M.	March 10, 1851	Balto.
Penn		infant	Henry A. Barling	Campbell, Bernard M.	Dec. 18, 1851	Balto.
Pennington	Charles	23	Kirkwood	Donovan, Joseph S.	Oct. 26, 1847	Balto.
Pennington	Mariah	16	Kirkwood	Donovan, Joseph S.	Jan. 4, 1845	Balto.
Pere	Charles	9	Victorine	Donovan, Joseph S.	Dec. 31, 1846	Balto.
Perkins	Aquilla	17	Kirkwood	Campbell, Bernard M.	March 9, 1847	Balto.
Perkins	Harrietta	18	Seaman	Slatter, Hope Hull	Dec. 19, 1838	Balto.
Perkins	Moses	11	Hibernia	Woolfolk, Austin	Dec. 5, 1826	Balto.

Surname	First Name	Age	Ship	O/S	Date	Depart
Perkins	Pere	23	Russell	Slatter, Hope Hull	March 1, 1839	Balto.
Perkins	Thomas	17	Salvadora	Slatter, Hope Hull	Sept. 28, 1846	Balto.
Permilia	Jane	3	Victorine	Campbell, Bernard M.	Dec. 31, 1846	Balto.
Perry	Allen	15	Kirkwood	Slatter, Hope Hull	Oct. 16, 1845	Balto.
Perry	Dawson	20	Kirkwood	Donovan, Joseph S.	Oct. 26, 1847	Balto.
Perry	Joseph	22	General Pinckney	Donovan, Joseph S.	Feb. 21, 1846	Balto.
Perry	Richard	30	Zoe	Williams, Thomas	Feb. 16, 1847	Balto.
Perry	Sidney	12	Zoe	Slatter, Hope Hull	Feb. 16, 1847	Balto.
Perry	Tom	23	Jefferson	Woolfolk, Austin	Dec. 24, 1827	Balto.
Perry	Washington	21	Southerner	Donovan, Jospeh S.	Jan. 5, 1852	Balto.
Perry	William	17	Henry A. Barling	Donovan, Joseph S.	Dec. 18, 1851	Balto.
Perry	William	21	Kirkwood	Donovan, Joseph S.	Oct. 16, 1845	Balto.
Perryman	Priscilla	25	Jasper	Woolfolk, Austin	Apr. 7, 1827	Balto.
Peters	Bushrod	18	Justina	Donovan, Joseph S.	Dec. 2, 1852	Balto.
Peters	Harriet	13	Brunswick	Woolfolk, Austin	Oct. 11, 1831	Balto.
Peters	James	28	E.H. Chapin	Campbell, Walter L.	June 7, 1848	Balto.
Peters	James	23	Union	Donovan, Joseph S.	May 13, 1848	Balto.
Peters	Joe	25	Isaac Franklin	Kephart, George	Feb. 1, 1839	Balto.
Peters	Mariah	20	Louisa	Campbell, Bernard M.	Nov. 5, 1849	Balto.
Peters	Pinckney	27	Solomon Saltus	Slatter, Hope Hull	Oct. 7, 1839	Balto.
Peters	Susan	18	Louisa	Campbell, Bernard M.	Nov. 5, 1849	Balto.
Peterson	Eveline	22	Henry A. Barling	Campbell, Bernard M.	Dec. 18, 1851	Balto.
Peterson	Harry	20	Kirkwood	Donovan, Joseph S.	Jan. 14, 1846	Balto.
Peterson	Isaac	25	Catharine	Donovan, Joseph S.	Jan. 18, 1845	Balto.
Peterson	Jane	6 mon.	Signet	Woolfolk, Austin	Nov. 17, 1831	Balto.
Peterson	Minty	22	Signet	Woolfolk, Austin	Nov. 17, 1831	Balto.

Surname	First Name	Age	Ship	O/S	Date	Depart
Peterson	Samuel	20	Lafayette	Woolfolk, Austin	Oct. 18, 1828	Balto.
Peyton	Benjamin	20	Gazelle	Staples, Joseph	Feb.28, 1842	Balto.
Phelps	Richard	24	General Pinckney	Slatter, Hope Hull	Feb. 21, 1846	Balto.
Phenix	Emeline	10	General Pinckney	Williams, Thomas	Jan. 19, 1847	Balto.
Philips	Hester	40	Margaret Hugg	Campbell, Bernard M.	Nov. 30, 1844	Balto.
Phillips	Solomon	34	Liberator	Woolfolk, Austin	Nov. 12, 1828	Balto.
Phillips	Toby	18	Scotia	Slatter, Hope Hull	Sept. 30, 1843	Balto.
Phillops	Isaac	22	Catharine	Slatter, Hope Hull	Jan. 24, 1843	Balto.
Pickett	Charles	17	Elizabeth	Donoven, Joseph S.	Jan. 2, 1850	Balto.
Pickson	Molly	50	Isaac Franklin	Kephar, George	Sept. 28, 1838	Balto.
Pie	Matilda	35	Burlington	Slatter, Hope Hull	Oct. 21, 1842	Balto.
Pie	Stephen	21	General Pinckney	Slatter, Hope Hull	Jan. 19, 1847	Balto.
Pierce	Diamond	24	Lafayette	Woolfolk, Austin	Oct. 22, 1828	Balto.
Pierce	James	30	Solomon Saltus	Slatter, Hope Hull	Oct. 7, 1839	Balto.
Pierce	John	12	General Pinckney	Donoven, Joseph S.	Nov. 10, 1845	Balto.
Pierce	Perry	19	Victorine	Slatter, Hope Hull	Sept. 12, 1846	Balto.
Pierce	Sophia	16	Billow	Woolfolk, Austin	Feb. 23, 1828	Balto.
Pierson	Maria	13	Jefferson	Woolfolk, Austin	Dec. 24, 1827	Balto.
Pike	Lucretia	19	Kirkwood	Campbell, Bernard M.	Jan. 4, 1845	Balto.
Piner	William	24	Architect	Campbell, Bernard M.	Apr. 25, 1846	Balto.
Pines	Ann	15	States	Woolfolk, Austin	Nov. 21, 1827	Balto.
Pines	Isaac	21	Elizabeth	Donoven, Joseph S.	Jan. 2, 1850	Balto.
Pines	James	20	Lafayette	Woolfolk, Austin	Oct. 18, 1828	Balto.
Pinion	Sarah	17	Henry A. Barling	Campbell, Bernard M.	Dec. 18, 1851	Balto.
Pinkett	Cristiamm	16	Paoli	Slatter, Hope Hull	Sept. 9, 1845	Balto.
Pinkett	Ralph	14	Southerner	Donoven, Joseph S.	Jan. 21, 1850	Balto.

Surname	First Name	Age	Ship	O/S	Date	Depart
Pinkney	Caroline	22	Elizabeth	Donovan, Joseph S.	Jan. 2, 1850	Balto.
Pinkney	Clenus	22	Lady Richmond	Woolfolk, Austin	Apr. 30, 1827	Balto.
Pinkney	Ellen	16	Brunswick	Woolfolk, Austin	Oct. 11, 1831	Balto.
Pinkney	James	22	Isaac Franklin	Kephart, George	Sept. 28, 1838	Balto.
Pinkney	Martha	15	Elizabeth	Campbell, Bernard M.	March 21, 1850	Balto.
Pinkney	Nelley	22	Kirkwood	Rodbind, Ebenezer	Apr. 15, 1845	Balto.
Pinkney	Sam	23	Lafayette	Woolfolk, Austin	Oct. 18, 1828	Balto.
Pinkney	Tyler	22	General Pinckney	Campbell, Bernard M.	Jan. 19, 1847	Balto.
Pipsico	Madison	22	Union	Donovan, Joseph S.	May 13, 1848	Balto.
Pitts	Charlotte	35	Kirkwood	Slatter, Hope Hull	Apr. 15, 1845	Balto.
Plater	Dolly	30	Victorine	Slatter, Hope Hull	March 1, 1845	Balto.
Plater	James	22	Elizabeth	Campbell, Bernard M.	March 21, 1850	Balto.
Plater	Jane	18	Elizabeth	Campbell, Bernard M.	March 21, 1850	Balto.
Plater	John	16	Tweed	Bowling, John D.	Oct. 20, 1836	Town Creek
Plater	Mary	15	Southerner	Campbell, Bernard M.	Jan. 5, 1852	Balto.
Plauden	Louisa	16	Victorine	Slatter, Henry F.	Dec. 31, 1846	Balto.
Pleasant	Lloyd	20	Nathaniel Hooper	Campbell, Bernard M.	Feb. 12, 1852	Balto.
Pleasant	Peter	26	Topaz	Woolfolk, Austin	Apr. 20, 1829	Balto.
Pleasants	Thomas	38	Hibernia	Woolfolk, Austin	Dec. 5, 1826	Balto.
Plowden	Henrietta	50	Isaac Franklin	Slatter, Hope Hull	Sept. 28, 1838	Balto.
Plowden	Henry	9	Arctic	Smith, Leonard J.	Jan. 29, 1828	St. Mary's
Plume	Mary	17	Kirkwood	Donovan, Joseph S.	Sept. 28, 1846	Balto.
Plummer	Billy	16	Brunswick	Woolfolk, Austin	Oct. 11, 1831	Balto.
Plummer	Frank	24	Victorine	Slatter, Hope Hull	Sept. 12, 1846	Balto.
Plummer	John	19	Southerner	Donovan, Joseph S.	Oct. 27, 1849	Balto.
Plummer	Lewis	22	Union	Donovan, Joseph S.	Dec. 16, 1848	Balto.

Surname	First Name	Age	Ship	O/S	Date	Depart
Plummer	Mary	4	Elizabeth	Donovan, Joseph S.	Jan. 2, 1850	Balto.
Plummer	Sally	6	Elizabeth	Donovan, Joseph S.	Jan. 2, 1850	Balto.
Plummer	William	19	Kirkwood	Donovan, Joseph S.	March 23, 1844	Balto.
Plythy	Henry	18	Supero	Slatter, Hope Hull	Nov. 1, 1843	Balto.
Polk	Caroline	18	Isaac Franklin	Slatter, Hope Hull	Sept. 28, 1838	Balto.
Polk	Margaret	19	Julia	Woolfolk, Austin	Jan. 8, 1829	Balto.
Pollard	Henrietta	16	Union	Donovan, Joseph S.	Dec. 16, 1848	Balto.
Pomfrey	Lou	22	Seamen	Purvis, James Franklin	Apr. 8, 1842	Balto.
Poney	Ann	infant	Kirkwood	Donovan, Joseph S.	Jan. 4, 1845	Balto.
Poney	Mary	5	Kirkwood	Donovan, Joseph S.	Jan. 4, 1845	Balto.
Popler	Elisabeth	12	Tippecanoe	Slatter, Hope Hull	Jan. 17, 1842	Balto.
Porter	Amanda	14	Helen A. Miller	Campbell, Bernard M.	Oct. 18, 1852	Balto.
Porter	Jakes	20	Intelligence	De Mapiere, Victor	Apr. 30, 1821	Balto.
Porter	Osea	22	Union	Williams, Thomas	Oct. 9, 1848	Balto.
Porter	Serepta	18	Union	Donovan, Joseph S.	Dec. 16, 1848	Balto.
Porter	Edmond	26	Union	Slatter Hope Hull	July 26, 1847	Balto.
Porter	Maria	20	Hope & Hannah	Woolfolk, Austin	March 11, 1829	Balto.
Porter	Montgomery	22	Kirkwood	Donovan, Joseph S.	Dec. 10, 1846	Balto.
Porter	Nancy	9	Kirkwood	Slatter, Hope Hull	Apr. 15, 1845	Balto.
Porter	Samuel	19	Scotia	Harker, William	Sept. 30, 1843	Balto.
Porter	Wesley	22	Union	Slatter, Hope Hull	July 26, 1847	Balto.
Potts	Caroline	9	Scotia	Slatter, Hope Hull	Sept. 30, 1843	Balto.
Powel	Louisa	30	Irad Ferry	Slatter, Hope Hull	Dec. 9, 1842	Balto.
Powell	Almira	11	Kirkwood	Donovan, Joseph S.	Sept. 28, 1846	Balto.
Powell	Columbus	17	Southerner	Donovan, Jospeh S.	Jan. 5, 1852	Balto.
Powell	Comfort	17	General Pinckney	Donovan, Joseph S.	Feb. 21, 1846	Balto.

Surname	First Name	Age	Ship	O/S	Date	Depart
Powell	Daniel	32	Margaret Hugg	Slatter, Hope Hull	Feb. 8, 1845	Balto.
Powell	Eliza	17	Lapwing	Woolfolk, Austin	Feb. 15, 1827	Balto.
Powell	Jacob	25	Kirkwood	Donovan, Joseph S.	Nov. 28, 1849	Balto.
Powell	Jinny	45	Nathaniel Hooper	Donovan, Jospeh S.	Feb. 12, 1852	Balto.
Powell	Joshua	14	General Pinckney	Donovan, Joseph S.	Nov. 10, 1845	Balto.
Powell	July ?	19	Brunswick	Woolfolk, Austin	Oct. 11, 1831	Balto.
Powell	Patience	24	Lafayette	Woolfolk, Austin	Oct. 18, 1828	Balto.
Powell	Rachel	15	States	Woolfolk, Austin	Nov. 21, 1827	Balto.
Powell	Samuel	17	Kirkwood	Donovan, Joseph S.	Oct. 26, 1847	Balto.
Powell	Thomas	21	Paoli	Slatter, Hope Hull	Sept. 9, 1845	Balto.
Powell	William	20	Southerner	Donovan, Jospeh S.	Jan. 5, 1852	Balto.
Powell	William	30	Tippecanoe	Purvis, James Franklin	Jan. 17, 1842	Balto.
Powell	William	2 mon.	Lapwing	Woolfolk, Austin	Feb. 15, 1827	Balto.
Powers	Ellen	16	St. Mary	Donovan, Joseph S.	Nov. 29, 1845	Balto.
Prater	Abigail	infant	General Pinckney	Slatter, Hope Hull	Feb. 21, 1846	Balto.
Prater	Lucinda	18	General Pinckney	Slatter, Hope Hull	Feb. 21, 1846	Balto.
Prater	Nathan	17	Northumberland	Slatter, Hope Hull	Feb. 27, 1843	Balto.
Prater	Nick	18	Union	Williams, Thomas	Oct. 9, 1848	Balto.
Praton		22	Eliza	Slatter, Hope Hull	Oct. 9, 1840	Balto.
Pratt	Alexander	17	Jefferson	Woolfolk, Austin	Dec. 24, 1827	Balto.
Pratt	Charles	20	Henry A. Barling	Campbell, Walter L.	Oct. 28, 1848	Balto.
Pratt	Ephraim	23	States	Woolfolk, Joseph B.	Nov. 21, 1827	Balto.
Pratt	Sarah	14	Abbott Lord	Campbell, Bernard M.	April 28, 1852	Balto.
Pratt	Solomon	55	Waverly	Harris, Alexander	Apr. 3, 1851	Balto.
Pratt	Washington	22	E.H.Chapin	Slatter, Hope Hull	Dec. 2, 1847	Balto.
Praverse	Eliza	16	Hermitage	Slatter, Hope Hull	Oct. 28, 1846	Balto.

Surname	First Name	Age	Ship	O/S	Date	Depart
Prentis	Frank	30	Union	Donovan, Joseph S.	Dec. 16, 1848	Balto.
Presco	Stephen	21	Eliza F. Mason	Donovan, Joseph S.	Nov. 13, 1851	Balto.
Preston	Henry	18	Brunswick	Woolfolk, Austin	Oct. 11, 1831	Balto.
Preston	John	20	Victorine	Slatter, Hope Hull	March 1, 1845	Balto.
Preston	Joshua	25	Ewarkee	Slatter, Hope Hull	March 4, 1841	Balto.
Prevost	Louisa	16	Solomon Saltus	Slatter, Hope Hull	Oct. 7, 1839	Balto.
Price	Ann	20	Solomon Saltus	Slatter, Hope Hull	Oct. 7, 1839	Balto.
Price	Betsey	11	Union	Donovan, Joseph S.	March 17, 1849	Balto.
Price	Caroline	18	Tippecanoe	Slatter, Hope Hull	Jan. 17, 1842	Balto.
Price	Charlotte	18	Seaman	Slatter, Hope Hull	Dec. 19, 1838	Balto.
Price	Emeline	5	Tweed	Tucker, J.B.	Oct. 20, 1836	Town Creek
Price	Jacob	25	Billow	Woolfolk, Austin	Feb. 23, 1828	Balto.
Price	Joseph	26	Kirkwood	Slatter, Henry F.	Dec. 10, 1846	Balto.
Price	Mitchel	15	Irad Ferry	Slatter, Hope Hull	Dec. 9, 1842	Balto.
Price	Nace	30	Tweed	Tucker, J.B.	Oct. 20, 1836	Town Creek
Price	Rachel	15	Superb	Slatter, Hope Hull	Nov. 1, 1843	Balto.
Price	Ruth	35	Tweed	Tucker, J.B.	Oct. 20, 1836	Town Creek
Price	infant		Seaman	Slatter, Hope Hull	Dec. 19, 1838	Balto.
Prier	Mary	17	Mary	Purvis, James Franklin	Feb. 8, 1841	Balto.
Primbook	Nelly	40	Scotia	Slatter, Hope Hull	Sept. 30, 1843	Balto.
Primrose	Ann	25	Intelligence	Anderson, David	May 1, 1821	Balto.
Primrose	Washington	infant	Tippecanoe	Slatter, Hope Hull	Jan. 17, 1842	Balto.
Prince	Ann	12	Victorine	Slatter, Hope Hull	March 9, 1844	Balto.
Prince	John	21	Tippecanoe	Purvis, James Franklin	Jan. 17, 1842	Balto.
Prince	Luximey	17	Tippecanoe	Purvis, James Franklin	Jan. 17, 1842	Balto.
Pringle	Moses	22	Intelligence	Anderson, David	May 1, 1821	Balto.

Surname	First Name	Age	Ship	O/S	Date	Depart
Prior	Henry	21	Victorine	Slatter, Hope Hull	Dec. 17, 1845	Balto.
Pritchard	Sidney	17	Lafayette	Woolfolk, Richard	Oct. 18, 1828	Balto.
Pritchett	Lydia	30	Isaac Franklin	Slatter, Hope Hull	Sept. 28, 1838	Balto.
Procter	Alfred	infant	Kirkwood	Donovan, Joseph S.	Oct. 14, 1848	Balto.
Procter	Ebbin	14	Lafayette	Woolfolk, Joseph B.	Oct. 18, 1828	Balto.
Procter	Edward	11	Kirkwood	Donovan, Joseph S.	Oct. 14, 1848	Balto.
Procter	Nancy	20	Kirkwood	Donovan, Joseph S.	Oct. 14, 1848	Balto.
Proctor	Alfred	22	Kirkwood	Donovan, Joseph S.	Oct. 14, 1848	Balto.
Proctor	John	25	Kirkwood	Rodbind, Ebenezer	Oct. 26, 1847	Balto.
Procttor	Louisiana	14	Victorine	Rodbind, Ebenezer	Dec. 31, 1846	Balto.
Procttor	Sophia	17	Victorine	Rodbind, Ebenezer	Dec. 31, 1846	Balto.
Proffitte	Jiles	17	Brunswick	Woolfolk, Austin	Oct. 11, 1831	Balto.
Promrose	Harriette	18	Tippecanoe	Slatter, Hope Hull	Jan. 17, 1842	Balto.
Prout	Charlotte	infant	Home	Donovan, Joseph S.	March 22, 1845	Balto.
Prout	Elizabeth	24	Home	Donovan, Joseph S.	March 22, 1845	Balto.
Prout	Horris	12	Margaret Forbs	Slatter, Hope Hull	Nov. 28, 1838	Balto.
Prout	Jacob	19	General Pinckney	Donovan, Joseph S.	Feb. 21, 1846	Balto.
Prowler	William	24	Isaac Franklin	Kephart, George	Sept. 28, 1838	Balto.
Pry	John	21	St. Mary	Donovan, Joseph S.	Nov. 29, 1845	Balto.
Pry	Madison	20	Southerner	Donovan, Joseph S.	Jan. 21, 1850	Balto.
Pry	Susan	18	Salvadora	Slatter, Hope Hull	Sept. 28, 1846	Balto.
Pulley	Isaac	21	Southerner	Donovan, Joseph S.	Oct. 27, 1849	Balto.
Pully	Matthew	40	Burlington	Slatter, Hope Hull	Oct. 21, 1842	Balto.
Pumphries	Harriett	35	Zoe	Slatter, Hope Hull	Feb. 16, 1847	Balto.
Pumphries	William	11	Zoe	Slatter, Hope Hull	Feb. 16, 1847	Balto.
Purdy	Jane	18	Burlington	Slatter, Hope Hull	Oct. 21, 1842	Balto.

Surname	First Name	Age	Ship	O/S	Date	Depart
Purdy	Milly	39	Burlington	Slatter, Hope Hull	Oct. 21, 1842	Balto.
Purnell	Harriett	26	Zoe	Slatter, Hope Hull	Feb. 16, 1847	Balto.
Purnell	Littleton	25	Victorine	Slatter, Hope Hull	Dec. 17, 1845	Balto.
Purnell	Mary Jane	15	Victorine	Slatter, Hope Hull	Dec. 17, 1845	Balto.
Purnell	Milly	28	Eliza	Slatter, Hope Hull	Oct. 9, 1840	Balto.
Purnell	Reason	25	Jefferson	Woolfolk, Austin	Dec. 24, 1827	Balto.
Purnell	Sarah	18	Kirkwood	Harker, William	March 23, 1844	Balto.
Purnell	Titus	28	Victorine	Slatter, Hope Hull	Dec. 17, 1845	Balto.
Purnell	William	19	John S. Gittings	Campbell, Bernard M.	Nov. 20, 1852	Balto.
Quaintens	Lucinda	40	Elizabeth	Donovan, Joseph S.	Nov. 18, 1848	Balto.
Quaintens	Lucy	infant	Elizabeth	Donovan, Joseph S.	Nov. 18, 1848	Balto.
Quaker	Anne	16	Hibernia	Woolfolk, Austin	Dec. 5, 1826	Balto.
Quander	Charles	23	Victorine	Donovan, Joseph S.	Sept. 29, 1845	Balto.
Quander	Nathan	18	Kirkwood	Slatter, Hope Hull	Oct. 16, 1845	Balto.
Queen	Ceney	4	Solomon Saltus	Slatter, Hope Hull	Oct. 7, 1839	Balto.
Queen	Emily	17	Catharine	Slatter, Hope Hull	Jan. 24, 1843	Balto.
Queen	George	45	Solomon Saltus	Slatter, Hope Hull	Oct. 7, 1839	Balto.
Queen	Henrietta	20	Union	Donovan, Joseph S.	May 13, 1848	Balto.
Queen	Isaac	7	Solomon Saltus	Slatter, Hope Hull	Oct. 7, 1839	Balto.
Queen	Joseph	19	Kirkwood	Campbell, Bernard M.	Oct. 14, 1848	Balto.
Queen	Mary	20	Margaret Forbs	Slatter, Hope Hull	Nov. 28, 1838	Balto.
Queen	Matthias	26	Southerner	Campbell, Bernard M.	Jan. 5, 1852	Balto.
Queen	Nicholas	18	Victorine	Donovan, Joseph S.	Oct. 25, 1844	Balto.
Queen	Susan	32	Solomon Saltus	Slatter, Hope Hull	Oct. 7, 1839	Balto.
Queen	Thomas	14	Lapwing	Woolfolk, Austin	Feb. 15, 1827	Balto.
Queen	Thomas	20	Victorine	Rodbird, Ebenezer	Dec. 31, 1846	Balto.

Surname	First Name	Age	Ship	O/S	Date	Depart
Queen		1 mon.	Margaret Forbs	Slatter, Hope Hull	Nov. 28, 1838	Balto.
Queen		infant	Solomon Saltus	Slatter, Hope Hull	Oct. 7, 1839	Balto.
Quill	Isaac	16	Superb	Slatter, Hope Hull	Nov. 1, 1843	Balto.
Quinn	Harriet	11	Union	Campbell, Bernard M.	March 17, 1849	Balto.
Quinn	Jeff	15	Elizabeth	Rodbind, Ebenezer	Nov. 18, 1848	Balto.
Quinn	Maria	19	Glasgow	Slatter, Hope Hull	Oct. 11, 1838	Balto.
Raelay	William	26	John S. Gittings	Campbell, Bernard M.	Nov. 20, 1852	Balto.
Ragan	William	21	Salvadora	Slatter, Hope Hull	Sept. 28, 1846	Balto.
Raily	Mary Ann	12	Orbit	Woolfolk, Austin	Apr. 16, 1825	Balto.
Rains	John	19	Victorine	Donovan, Joseph S.	Sept. 29, 1845	Balto.
Ramsay	Robert	35	Isaac Franklin	Kephart, George	Sept. 28, 1838	Balto.
Ramsey	Gilbert	21	Lapwing	Woolfolk, Samuel M.	Feb. 15, 1827	Balto.
Ramsey	Maria	16	Victorine	Slatter, Hope Hull	Dec. 17, 1845	Balto.
Ramsey	Milly	15	Elizabeth	Donovan, Joseph S.	Nov. 18, 1848	Balto.
Ramsey	Minta	15	Tippecanoe	Purvis, James Franklin	Jan. 17, 1842	Balto.
Randal	Susan	19	Kirkwood	Donovan, Joseph S.	Sept. 28, 1846	Balto.
Randell	Violet	25	General Pinckney	Williams, Thomas	Jan. 19, 1847	Balto.
Randolph	William	21	Budget	Purviance, William Y.	Dec. 1, 1821	Balto.
Rankin	Thomas	22	Irad Ferry	Slatter, Hope Hull	Dec. 9, 1842	Balto.
Ranking	George	2 mon.	Colonel Howard	Harker, William	Nov. 21, 1844	Balto.
Ranking	Matilda	5	Colonel Howard	Harker, William	Nov. 21, 1844	Balto.
Ranking	Nancy	12	Colonel Howard	Harker, William	Nov. 21, 1844	Balto.
Ranking	William	3	Colonel Howard	Harker, William	Nov. 21, 1844	Balto.
Ransom	Amanda	18	Elizabeth	Donovan, Joseph S.	Nov. 18, 1848	Balto.
Ransom	Martin	21	Kirkwood	Donovan, Joseph S.	Nov. 28, 1849	Balto.
Ranson	Hustina	18	Victorine	Slatter, Hope Hull	Dec. 17, 1845	Balto.

Surname	First Name	Age	Ship	O/S	Date	Depart
Ranson	Mary	16	Victorine	Donovan, Joseph S.	Dec. 31, 1846	Balto.
Rasier	Emeline	18	Burlington	Slatter, Hope Hull	Oct. 21, 1842	Balto.
Rawlins	Mordica	30	Kirkwood	Slatter, Hope Hull	Dec. 23, 1843	Balto.
Rayfield	Joshua	22	Irad Ferry	Purvis, James Franklin	Oct. 30, 1841	Balto.
Ready	Charles	35	Victorine	Donovan, Joseph S.	Sept. 29, 1845	Balto.
Ready	David	20	Louisa	Campbell, Bernard M.	March 31, 1849	Balto.
Reason	Henry	17	Victorine	Slatter, Hope Hull	March 9, 1844	Balto.
Rector	Nancy	25	Union	Donovan, Joseph S.	May 13, 1848	Balto.
Red	Anna	15	Union	Rodbinc, Ebenezer	Dec. 16, 1848	Balto.
Red	John	16	Burlington	Slatter, Hope Hull	Oct. 21, 1842	Balto.
Reddin	Hester	17	Elizabeth	Campbell, Bernard M.	Jan. 2, 1850	Balto.
Rederford	Thomas	25	Ann & Leah	Woolfolk, Austin	Nov. 1, 1831	Balto.
Redgitt	Edward	61	Helen A. Miller	Nally, William	Oct. 18, 1852	Balto.
Redman	Alfred	22	Pioneer	Slatter, Hope Hull	Sept. 15, 1847	Balto.
Redman	Charles	16	St. Mary	Donovan, Joseph S.	Nov. 29, 1845	Balto.
Redmond	Henry	21	Sabine	Donovan, Joseph S.	Feb. 10, 1844	Balto.
Redmond	James	18	Strafford	Harker, William	Nov. 22, 1843	Balto.
Reed	Ann	20	Kirkwood	Donovan, Joseph S.	Oct. 26, 1847	Balto.
Reed	Barbara	18	Southerner	Donovan, Joseph S.	Oct. 27, 1849	Balto.
Reed	Edward	infant	Kirkwood	Donovan, Joseph S.	Oct. 26, 1847	Balto.
Reed	John	18	Southerner	Donovan, Joseph S.	Oct. 27, 1849	Balto.
Reed	John	26	Superb	Slatter, Hope Hull	Nov. 1, 1843	Balto.
Reed	Moses	19	Mary	Purvis, Isaac	March 2, 1840	Balto.
Reeden		20	Victorine	Slatter, Henry F.	Dec. 31, 1846	Balto.
Reeder	Charlotte	11	Kirkwood	Slatter, Henry F.	Dec. 10, 1846	Balto.
Reeder	Jacob	19	Kirkwood	Donovan, Joseph S.	Oct. 14, 1848	Balto.

Surname	First Name	Age	Ship	O/S	Date	Depart
Reese	Edmond	18	Irad Ferry	Clendenin, A.	Jan. 16, 1840	Balto.
Reese	Maria	23	Scotia	Slatter, Hope Hull	Sept. 30, 1843	Balto.
Reese	Samuel	2	Margaret Hugg	Campbell, Bernard M.	Nov. 30, 1844	Balto.
Reese	Susan	24	Margaret Hugg	Campbell, Bernard M.	Nov. 30, 1844	Balto.
Reeves	Sophy	18	Waverly	Campbell, Bernard M.	Apr. 3, 1851	Balto.
Reeves		infant	Waverly	Campbell, Bernard M.	Apr. 3, 1851	Balto.
Regan	Bridget	16	Eliza F.Mason	Donovan, Joseph S.	Nov. 13, 1851	Balto.
Register	Ephraim	19	Ann & Leah	Woolfolk, Austin	Nov.1, 1831	Balto.
Register	Frisby	25	Tippecanoe	Slatter, Hope Hull	Jan. 17, 1842	Balto.
Reid	Robert	22	Tippecanoe	Slatter, Hope Hull	Jan. 17, 1842	Balto.
Reiley	Maria	23	Victorine	Slatter, Hope Hull	March 9, 1844	Balto.
Reiley	Mary	2	Victorine	Slatter, Hope Hull	March 9, 1844	Balto.
Reiley	Wilmer	infant	Victorine	Slatter, Hope Hull	March 9, 1844	Balto.
Reist	Ben	21	Kirkwood	Donovan, Joseph S.	Oct. 26, 1847	Balto.
Remy	Jacob	18	Union	Campbell, Bernard M.	Dec. 16, 1848	Balto.
Reynolds	Charles	19	Brunswick	Woolfolk, Austin	Oct. 11, 1831	Balto.
Reynolds	John	22	Kirkwood	Donovan, Joseph S.	Dec. 10, 1846	Balto.
Reynolds	Nancy	18	States	Woolfolk, Austin	Nov. 21, 1827	Balto.
Rhoades	Walter	19	Victorine	Slatter, Hope Hull	Dec. 17, 1845	Balto.
Rhoades	William	12	Solomon Saltus	Slatter, Hope Hull	Oct. 7, 1839	Balto.
Rice	Alexander	22	Henry A. Barling	Donovan, Joseph S.	Dec. 18, 1851	Balto.
Rice	Charles	18	Victorine	Donovan, Joseph S.	Sept. 29, 1845	Balto.
Rice	Emeline	23	Porpoise	Purvis, James Franklin	Dec. 11, 1841	Balto.
Rice	George	16	John C. Calhoun	Donovan, Joseph S.	Oct. 24, 1850	Balto.
Rice	Louis	22	Seaman	Slatter, Shadrack	March 25, 1839	Balto.
Rice	Louisa	18	Kirkwood	Slatter, Hope Hull	Jan. 4, 1845	Balto.

Surname	First Name	Age	Ship	O/S	Date	Depart
Rice	Margarett	8	Porpoise	Purvis, James Franklin	Dec. 11, 1841	Balto.
Rice	Martha	22	Margaret Hugg	Slatter, Hope Hull	Feb. 8, 1845	Balto.
Rice	Simon	22	Helen A. Miller	Campbell, Bernard M.	Oct. 18, 1852	Balto.
Rice	William	25	Virginia	Woolfork, Joseph B.	Dec. 19, 1825	Balto.
Rich	Stephen	19	Lapwing	King, Gideon T.	March 22, 1822	Balto.
Rich	Winfred	17	Frances Amy	Donovan, Joseph S.	Jan. 20, 1847	Balto.
Richard	George	13	Catharine	Slatter, Hope Hull	Jan. 24, 1843	Balto.
Richards	Ann	6	Ulysses	Richardson, Wade H.	Nov. 6, 1833	Balto.
Richards	Betsey	50	Isaac Franklin	Kephart, George	Sept. 28, 1838	Balto.
Richards	Brinton	23	Julia	Woolfork, Austin	Jan. 8, 1829	Balto.
Richards	Frances	19	Billow	Woolfork, Austin	Feb. 23, 1828	Balto.
Richards	Henry	18	Victorine	Donovan, Joseph S.	May 22, 1844	Balto.
Richards	Jane	13	Superb	Slatter, Hope Hull	Nov. 1, 1843	Balto.
Richards	Jason	22	Irad Ferry	Clenderin, A.	Jan. 16, 1840	Balto.
Richards	John	30	Isaac Franklin	Kephart, George	Sept. 28, 1838	Balto.
Richards	Kitty	22	General Pinckney	Slatter, Hope Hull	Jan. 19, 1847	Balto.
Richards	Kitty	22	Zoe	Slatter, Hope Hull	Feb. 16, 1847	Balto.
Richards	Littleton	18	Brunswick	Woolfork, Austin	Oct. 11, 1831	Balto.
Richards	Mary	13	Superb	Slatter, Hope Hull	Nov. 1, 1843	Balto.
Richards	Priscilla	16	Victorine	Donovan, Joseph S.	Dec. 31, 1846	Balto.
Richards	Thomas	23	Lafayette	Woolfork, Austin	Oct. 18, 1828	Balto.
Richardson	Aleade	18	Victorine	Donovan, Joseph S.	Sept. 29, 1845	Balto.
Richardson	Ann	16	General Pinckney	Donovan, Joseph S.	Nov. 10, 1845	Balto.
Richardson	Emily Ann	20	Tippecanoe	Slatter, Hope Hull	Jan. 17, 1842	Balto.
Richardson	James	20	Kirkwood	Campbell, Bernard M.	Dec. 10, 1846	Balto.
Richardson	Jane	15	Brunswick	Woolfork, Austin	Oct. 11, 1831	Balto.

Surname	First Name	Age	Ship	O/S	Date	Depart
Richardson	Lewis	21	Victorine	Donovan, Joseph S.	Dec. 31, 1846	Balto.
Richardson	Mary Ann	22	Ewarkee	Slatter, Hope Hull	March 4, 1841	Balto.
Richardson	Polly	40	Bostonian	Slatter, Hope Hull	Jan. 18, 1841	Balto.
Richardson	Richard	26	Abbott Lord	Campbell, Bernard M.	April 28, 1852	Balto.
Richardson	Samuel	30	Burlington	Slatter, Hope Hull	Oct. 21, 1842	Balto.
Richardson	Tom	21	States	Woolfolk, Austin	Apr. 14, 1828	Balto.
Richardson		26	Uncas	Slatter, Hope Hull	Jan. 10, 1838	Balto.
Richerson	Caroline	19	Victorine	Rodbind, Ebenezer	May 14, 1845	Balto.
Richerson	John H.	14	Nancy W. Stevens	Rodbind, Ebenezer	Feb. 18, 1845	Balto.
Richerson	Richard	23	St. Mary	Williams, Thomas	Nov. 29, 1845	Balto.
Richeson	Sarah	18	Victorine	Slatter, Hope Hull	Sept. 12, 1846	Balto.
Richie	John	21	Louisa	Slatter, Hope Hull	Oct. 11, 1847	Balto.
Richman	Benjamin	30	Victorine	Slatter, Hope Hull	Sept. 12, 1846	Balto.
Ricks	Peter	25	Union	Donovan, Joseph S.	May 13, 1848	Balto.
Ridad	Cassa	16	Hibernia	Woolfolk, Austin	Dec. 5, 1826	Balto.
Riddles	Lucinda	16	John C. Calhoun	Donovan, Joseph S.	Oct. 24, 1850	Balto.
Rideout	Emanuel	28	John C. Calhoun	Donovan, Joseph S.	Oct. 24, 1850	Balto.
Rider	John	23	Lafayette	Woolfolk, Austin	Oct. 18, 1828	Balto.
Ridgeley	John	22	Superb	Slatter, Hope Hull	Nov. 1, 1843	Balto.
Ridgely	Charles	30	Climax	Woolfolk, Austin	Dec. 6, 1828	Balto.
Ridgely	Debora	18	E.H.Chapin	Slatter, Hope Hull	Nov. 30, 1847	Balto.
Ridgey	Lucy	22	Isaac Franklin	Slatter, Hope Hull	Sept. 28, 1838	Balto.
Ridgway	Levin	23	Kirkwood	Donovan, Joseph S.	Apr. 15, 1845	Balto.
Ridoulet	Harrison	20	Brunswick	Woolfolk, Austin	Oct. 11, 1831	Balto.
Ridout	Alexander	22	Victorine	Slatter, Hope Hull	Sept. 12, 1846	Balto.
Ridout	Daniel	18	Burlington	Slatter, Hope Hull	Oct. 21, 1842	Balto.

Surname	First Name	Age	Ship	O/S	Date	Depart
Ridout	Harriet	22	Eliza	Slatter, Hope Hull	Oct. 9, 1840	Balto.
Ridout	William	20	Burlington	Slatter, Hope Hull	Oct. 21, 1842	Balto.
Ried	Elijah	24	Victorine	Donovan, Joseph S.	March 1, 1845	Balto.
Ried	George	16	Victorine	Donovan, Joseph S.	Sept. 29, 1845	Balto.
Rieston	Hinson	23	Scotia	Slatter, Hope Hull	Sept. 30, 1843	Balto.
Riggs	Mary	10	Zoe	Slatter, Hope Hull	Feb. 16, 1847	Balto.
Riggs	Remiss	21	John C. Calhoun	Donovan, Joseph S.	Oct. 24, 1850	Balto.
Right	Ann	1	Southerner	Rodbind, Ebenezer	Oct. 27, 1849	Balto.
Right	Henry	28	Northumberland	Slatter, Hope Hull	Feb. 27, 1843	Balto.
Right	Sophia	20	Southerner	Rodbind, Ebenezer	Oct. 27, 1849	Balto.
Riley	David	23	Catharine	Woolfo.k, Austin	March 3. 1829	Balto.
Riley	Henry	18	Catharine	Woolfo.k, Austin	March 3. 1829	Balto.
Riley	John	19	John C. Calhoun	Donovan, Joseph S.	Oct. 24, 1850	Balto.
Riley	Joseph	25	Tippecanoe	Slatter, Hope Hull	Jan. 17, 1842	Balto.
Riley	Maria	16	Victorine	Crozier, John R.	Sept. 12, 1846	Balto.
Riley	Mary	12	Kirkwood	Crow, William	March 23, 1844	Balto.
Riley	Nancy	23	Lady Monroe	Woolfolk, Austin	March 25, 1825	Balto.
Riley	Petra	14	Bostonian	Slatter, Hope Hull	Jan. 18, 1841	Balto.
Riley		4 weeks	Lady Monroe	Woolfolk, Austin	March 25, 1825	Balto.
Ringgold	Bill	16	Hibernia	Woolfolk, Austin	Dec. 5, 1826	Balto.
Ringgold	James	40	Kirkwood	Slatter, Hope Hull	Jan. 4, 1845	Balto.
Ringgold	Joe	37	Hibernia	Woolfolk, Austin	Dec. 5, 1826	Balto.
Ringgold	Sam	22	Eliza	Slatter, Hope Hull	Oct. 9, 1840	Balto.
Ringgold	Sewell	22	Julia	Woolfolk, Austin	Jan. 8, 1829	Balto.
Ringgold	Thomas	17	General Pinckney	Slatter, Hope Hull	Nov. 10, 1845	Balto.
Ringgold	Violet	22	Kirkwood	Donovan, Joseph S.	Jan. 14, 1846	Balto.

Surname	First Name	Age	Ship	O/S	Date	Depart
Ringo	Stansbury	16	Southerner	Campbell, Bernard M.	Jan. 5, 1852	Balto.
Ringold	Benjamin	37	Victorine	Slatter, Henry F.	Dec. 31, 1846	Balto.
Ringold	Ellenora	24	Union	Donovan, Joseph S.	May 13, 1848	Balto.
Ringold	Fanny	18	Victorine	Donovan, Joseph S.	May 22, 1844	Balto.
Ringold	Frisby	24	Margaret Hugg	Wilson, Thomas C.	Nov. 30, 1844	Balto.
Ringold	George	27	Union	Donovan, Joseph S.	May 13, 1848	Balto.
Ritchie	Fanny	11	Kirkwood	Campbell, Bernard M.	Jan. 14, 1846	Balto.
Ritchie	William	15	Kirkwood	Campbell, Bernard M.	Jan. 14, 1846	Balto.
Rite	Joshua	19	Brunswick	Woolfolk, Austin	Oct. 11, 1831	Balto.
Roach	Nathan	22	Louisa	Campbell, Bernard M.	Nov. 5, 1849	Balto.
Robbinson	Draper	22	Isaac Franklin	Slatter, Hope Hull	Sept. 28, 1838	Balto.
Roberson	Jim	30	Elizabeth	Rodbind, Ebenezer	Nov. 18, 1848	Balto.
Roberson	Nancy	28	Elizabeth	Rodbind, Ebenezer	Nov. 18, 1848	Balto.
Roberson	William	23	Tippecanoe	Slatter, Hope Hull	Jan. 17, 1842	Balto.
Robert	Edmond	18	Irad Ferry	Clendenin, A.	Jan. 16, 1840	Balto.
Robert	Henry	10	Kirkwood	Donovan, Joseph S.	Jan. 4, 1845	Balto.
Roberts	Ann	19	Harriett	Woolfolk, Austin	March 23, 1822	Balto.
Roberts	Ann	10	Zoe	Williams, Thomas	Feb. 16, 1847	Balto.
Roberts	Charlot	20	Kirkwood	Donovan, Joseph S.	Dec. 23, 1843	Balto.
Roberts	Gabriel	19	Harriett	Woolfolk, Austin	March 23, 1822	Balto.
Roberts	George	11	Seaman	Hooper, John P.	Apr. 8, 1842	Balto.
Roberts	Henry	24	Hibernia	Woolfolk, Austin	Dec. 5, 1826	Balto.
Roberts	Henry	23	Jefferson	Woolfolk, Austin	Dec. 24, 1827	Balto.
Roberts	John	19	States	Woolfolk, Austin	Nov. 21, 1827	Balto.
Roberts	Maria	17	Lady Monroe	Woolfolk, Austin	March 25, 1825	Balto.
Roberts	Nickolas	20	Brunswick	Woolfolk, Austin	Oct. 11, 1831	Balto.

Surname	First Name	Age	Ship	O/S	Date	Depart
Roberts	Robert	18	Architect	Purvis, James Franklin	Feb. 3, 1841	Balto.
Roberts	William	21	Seaman	Slatter, Shadrack	March 25, 1839	Balto.
Roberts	William	21	Seaman	Slatter, Shadrack	March 25, 1839	Balto.
Robertson	Charity	8	Lafayette	Woolfo k, Austin	Oct. 18, 1828	Balto.
Robertson	Henry	25	Charles	Campbell, Bernard M.	Dec. 18, 1850	Balto.
Robertson	Henry	45	Tangier	Campbell, Bernard M.	Nov. 26, 1853	Balto.
Robertson	Isaac		Charles	Campbell, Bernard M.	Dec. 18, 1850	Balto.
Robertson	Isaac		Charles	Campbell, Bernard M.	Dec. 18, 1850	Balto.
Robertson	Jane	32	Charles	Campbell, Bernard M.	Dec. 18, 1850	Balto.
Robertson	Mary	50	Margaret Hugg	Poindexter, T.B.	Nov. 30, 1844	Balto.
Robertson	Mina	12	Margaret Hugg	Poindexter, T.B.	Nov. 30, 1844	Balto.
Robertson	Newton	18	Charles	Campbell, Bernard M.	Dec. 18, 1850	Balto.
Robertson	Scott	14	Charles	Campbell, Bernard M.	Dec. 18, 1850	Balto.
Robertson	William	20	Charles	Campbell, Bernard M.	Dec. 18, 1850	Balto.
Robins	George	17	General Pinckney	Williams, Thomas	Jan. 19, 1847	Balto.
Robinson	Ann	15	Kirkwood	Donovan, Joseph S.	Nov. 28, 1849	Balto.
Robinson	Ann	20	Victorine	Donovan, Joseph S.	Sept. 29, 1845	Balto.
Robinson	Benjamin	30	General Pinckney	Slatter, Hope Hull	Nov. 10, 1845	Balto.
Robinson	Charles	16	Jefferson	Woolfolk, Joseph B.	Dec. 24, 1827	Balto.
Robinson	Charles		States	Woolfolk, Austin	Apr. 14, 1828	Balto.
Robinson	Charles M.	19	Uncas	Slatter, Hope Hull	Jan. 10, 1838	Balto.
Robinson	Daniel	20	Kirkwood	Donovan, Joseph S.	Sept. 28, 1846	Balto.
Robinson	Eliza	24	Kirkwood	Campbell, Bernard M.	March 9, 1847	Balto.
Robinson	Evaline	42	Southerner	Donovan, Joseph S.	Oct. 27, 1849	Balto.
Robinson	Fanny	20	States	Woolfolk, Austin	Apr. 14, 1828	Balto.
Robinson	Frank	11	Zoe	Slatter, Hope Hull	Feb. 16, 1847	Balto.

Surname	First Name	Age	Ship	O/S	Date	Depart
Robinson	George	30	Ann & Leah	Woolfolk, Austin	Nov.1, 1831	Balto.
Robinson	Griffin	24	Victorine	Donovan, Joseph S.	March 14, 1846	Balto.
Robinson	Hannah	18	Kirkwood	Campbell, Bernard M.	Oct. 14, 1848	Balto.
Robinson	Henny	22	Kirkwood	Donovan, Joseph S.	Dec. 23, 1843	Balto.
Robinson	Henry	24	Kirkwood	Campbell, Bernard M.	Oct. 14, 1848	Balto.
Robinson	Henry	infant	Louisa	Donovan, Joseph S.	Oct. 9, 1847	Balto.
Robinson	Henry	21	Victorine	Donovan, Joseph S.	Dec. 31, 1846	Balto.
Robinson	Henry	21	Victorine	Donovan, Joseph S.	May 14, 1845	Balto.
Robinson	James	21	Kirkwood	Donovan, Joseph S.	Oct. 14, 1848	Balto.
Robinson	James	24	Peru	Slatter, Hope Hull	Nov. 16, 1842	Balto.
Robinson	Jane	14	Ann & Leah	Woolfolk, Austin	Nov.1, 1831	Balto.
Robinson	John	19	Kirkwood	Donovan, Joseph S.	Oct. 14, 1848	Balto.
Robinson	Joseph	28	Emilie	Stansbury, Charles	Nov. 27, 1819	Balto.
Robinson	Joseph	21	Kirkwood	Campbell, Bernard M.	Nov. 28, 1849	Balto.
Robinson	Lewis	30	Tippecanoe	Purvis, James Franklin	Jan. 17, 1842	Balto.
Robinson	Louisa	22	General Pinckney	Slatter, Hope Hull	Nov. 10, 1845	Balto.
Robinson	Lucy	17	Henry A. Barling	Campbell, Bernard M.	Feb. 24, 1851	Balto.
Robinson	Lucy	15	Kirkwood	Donovan, Joseph S.	Dec. 10, 1846	Balto.
Robinson	Lucy	24	Louisa	Donovan, Joseph S.	Oct. 9, 1847	Balto.
Robinson	Margaret	21	Narragansett	Donovan, Joseph S.	Nov. 27, 1850	Balto.
Robinson	Martha Ellen	15	Zoe	Slatter, Hope Hull	Feb. 16, 1847	Balto.
Robinson	Mary	12	Ann & Leah	Woolfolk, Austin	Nov.1, 1831	Balto.
Robinson	Mary	15	Henry A. Barling	Campbell, Bernard M.	Apr. 19, 1849	Balto.
Robinson	Mary	11	Kirkwood	Donovan, Joseph S.	Oct. 26, 1847	Balto.
Robinson	Mary A.	40	Mary	Woolfolk, Austin	Oct. 7, 1843	Balto.
Robinson	Mary Elizabeth	4	Kirkwood	Slatter, Hope Hull	Jan. 14, 1846	Balto.

Surname	First Name	Age	Ship	O/S	Date	Depart
Robinson	Matilda	30	Irad Ferry	Clendenin, A.	Jan. 16, 1840	Balto.
Robinson	Nathan	23	Kirkwood	Donovan, Joseph S.	Nov. 28, 1849	Balto.
Robinson	Sandy	17	General Pinckney	Slatter, Hope Hull	Feb. 21, 1846	Balto.
Robinson	Simmon	33	Jefferson	Woolfolk, Austin	Dec. 24, 1827	Balto.
Robinson	Thomas	21	Colonel Howard	Harker, William	Nov. 21, 1844	Balto.
Robinson	Thomas	19	Kirkwood	Donovan, Joseph S.	Sept. 28, 1846	Balto.
Robinson	Thomas	14	Victorine	Donovan, Joseph S.	May 14, 1845	Balto.
Robinson	Washington	11	Victorine	Donovan, Joseph S.	Dec. 31, 1846	Balto.
Robinson	William	21	E.H.Chapin	Donovan, Joseph S.	Dec. 2, 1847	Balto.
Robinson	William	24	Scotia	Slatter, Hope Hull	Sept. 30, 1843	Balto.
Robinson	William	36	Solomon Saltus	Slatter, Hope Hull	Oct. 7, 1839	Balto.
Robinson		infant	Kirkwood	Campbell, Bernard M.	March 9, 1847	Balto.
Robison	Henry	25	Catharine	Donovan, Joseph S.	Jan. 18, 1845	Balto.
Robison	Henry	35	Hibernia	Woolfolk, Austin	Dec. 5, 1826	Balto.
Robison	James	15	Catharine	Donovan, Joseph S.	Jan. 18, 1845	Balto.
Robison	Jesse	21	Hibernia	Woolfolk, Austin	Dec. 5, 1826	Balto.
Roby	Bill	45	Kirkwood	Campbell, Bernard M.	Oct. 16, 1845	Balto.
Rochester	Milny	17	Catharine	Woolfolk, Austin	March 5, 1829	Balto.
Rock	Hanson	33	Victorine	Slatter, Hope Hull	Dec. 17, 1845	Balto.
Rodan	Mary Paris	16	Solomon Saltus	Slatter, Hope Hull	Oct. 7, 1839	Balto.
Rodgers	Ann Maria	18	Southerner	Donovan, Joseph S.	Oct. 27, 1849	Balto.
Roeds	Clemmut	24	Seaman	Slatter, Hope Hull	Dec. 19, 1838	Balto.
Roger	Mary	22	Isaac Franklin	Kephar, George	Sept. 28, 1838	Balto.
Rogers	Ennaly	16	Kirkwood	Campbell, Bernard M.	Jan. 4, 1845	Balto.
Rogers	Harriett	22	Uncas	Slatter, Hope Hull	Jan. 10, 1838	Balto.
Rogers	Howard	21	Paoli	Slatter, Hope Hull	Sept. 9, 1845	Balto.

Surname	First Name	Age	Ship	O/S	Date	Depart
Rogers	John	24	Southerner	Donovan, Joseph S.	Oct. 27, 1849	Balto.
Rogers	Matilda	16	States	Woolfolk, Austin	Nov. 21, 1827	Balto.
Roiston	Aquilla	13	States	Woolfolk, Austin	Nov. 21, 1827	Balto.
Roland	Joseph	24	Victorine	Slatter, Hope Hull	Dec. 17, 1845	Balto.
Rolfs	Catherine	9	Isaac Franklin	Kephart, George	Sept. 28, 1838	Balto.
Rolfs	Edmund	6	Isaac Franklin	Kephart, George	Sept. 28, 1838	Balto.
Rolfs	Henry	4	Isaac Franklin	Kephart, George	Sept. 28, 1838	Balto.
Rolfs	James	11	Isaac Franklin	Kephart, George	Sept. 28, 1838	Balto.
Rolfs		18	Isaac Franklin	Kephart, George	Sept. 28, 1838	Balto.
Rollins	Arnold	20	States	Woolfolk, Austin	Nov. 21, 1827	Balto.
Rollins	James	24	Kirkwood	Campbell, Bernard M.	Apr. 4, 1846	Balto.
Rollins	Mary		States	Woolfolk, Austin	Nov. 21, 1827	Balto.
Rollins	Sam	17	Kirkwood	Campbell, Bernard M.	Apr. 4, 1846	Balto.
Rollins	Sarah	20	Isaac Franklin	Slatter, Hope Hull	Sept. 28, 1838	Balto.
Rollins	William	22	E.H.Chapin	Donovan, Joseph S.	Dec. 2, 1847	Balto.
Rollins	William	22	Glasgow	Slatter, Hope Hull	Oct. 11, 1838	Balto.
Rook	Zachariah	45	Isaac Franklin	Kephart, George	Sept. 28, 1838	Balto.
Rose	Robinson	24	Kirkwood	Rodbind, Ebenezer	Apr. 15, 1845	Balto.
Rosier	Henrietta	14	Victorine	Slatter, Hope Hull	May 14, 1845	Balto.
Rosier	Mary Ann	14	Scotia	Slatter, Hope Hull	Sept. 30, 1843	Balto.
Ross	Brook	21	Victorine	Donovan, Joseph S.	Sept. 29, 1845	Balto.
Ross	Charles	20	Victorine	Slatter, Hope Hull	Sept. 12, 1846	Balto.
Ross	David	20	Union	Donovan, Joseph S.	May 13, 1848	Balto.
Ross	Diana	15	North America	Woolfolk, Austin	Oct. 14, 1823	Balto.
Ross	Hannah	15	Porpoise	Purvis, James Franklin	Dec. 11, 1841	Balto.
Ross	Harriett	14	Nancy W.Stevens	Harker, James	Oct. 25, 1843	Balto.

Surname	First Name	Age	Ship	O/S	Date	Depart
Ross	Jackson	20	Elizabeth	Campbell, Bernard M.	March 21, 1850	Balto.
Ross	Jacob	28	Pioneer	Slatter, Hope Hull	Sept. 15, 1847	Balto.
Ross	John	31	Scotia	Slatter, Hope Hull	Sept. 30, 1843	Balto.
Ross	Martha	13	Delawarian	Campbell, Bernard M.	Dec. 1, 1848	Balto.
Ross	Martha Jane	18	Zoe	Slatter, Hope Hull	Feb. 16, 1847	Balto.
Ross	Phebe	16	General Pinckney	Slatter, Hope Hull	Feb. 21, 1846	Balto.
Ross	Sarah	15	Eliza F. Mason	Donovan, Joseph S.	Nov. 13, 1851	Balto.
Ross	Thomas	19	St. Mary	Donovan, Joseph S.	Nov. 29, 1845	Balto.
Ross	Thomas	21	Victorine	Slatter, Hope Hull	March 1, 1845	Balto.
Ross	Thomas	24	Charles	Campbell, Bernard M.	Dec. 18, 1850	Balto.
Row	Mary Elizabeth	15	Victorine	Donovan, Joseph S.	May 22, 1844	Balto.
Roy	Ellen	18	Hermitage	Williams, Thomas	Oct. 28, 1846	Balto.
Roystin	Wesley	29	Kirkwood	Donovan, Joseph S.	Oct. 14, 1848	Balto.
Rozetta	Mary	27	Victorine	Campbell, Bernard M.	Dec. 31, 1846	Balto.
Rubin	Charles	12	Elizabeth	Donovan, Joseph S.	Nov. 18, 1848	Balto.
Rubottom	Mary	19	Kirkwood	Donovan, Joseph S.	Oct. 26, 1847	Balto.
Ruff	Abraham	18	General Pinckney	Donovan, Joseph S.	Feb. 21, 1846	Balto.
Rufus	Levin	27	Cora	Campbell, Bernard M.	Jan. 20, 1851	Balto.
Runnels	Daniel	32	Burlington	Slatter, Hope Hull	Oct. 21, 1842	Balto.
Runner	Milly	19	Isaac Franklin	Kephart, George	Sept. 28, 1838	Balto.
Rupaw	William	22	Isaac Franklin	Kephart, George	Feb. 1, 1839	Balto.
Rush	Jane	28	Isaac Franklin	Kephart, George	Sept. 28, 1838	Balto.
Russel	William	20	Home	Rodbind, Ebenezer	March 22, 1845	Balto.
Russell	Albert	infant	Union	Donovan, Joseph S.	Dec. 16, 1848	Balto.
Russell	Frank	14	Elizabeth	Rodbind, Ebenezer	Nov. 18, 1848	Balto.
Russell	Henry	9	Kirkwood	Slatter, Hope Hull	Dec. 23, 1843	Balto.

Cash For Blood

Surname	First Name	Age	Ship	O/S	Date	Depart
Russell	James	17	Victorine	Slatter, Hope Hull	March 1, 1845	Balto.
Russell	John	21	Southerner	Donovan, Joseph S.	Jan. 21, 1850	Balto.
Russell	Maria	21	Union	Donovan, Joseph S.	Dec. 16, 1848	Balto.
Russell	Nathaniel	25	Kirkwood	Donovan, Joseph S.	Oct. 26, 1847	Balto.
Russell	Samuel	14	Southerner	Donovan, Joseph S.	Jan. 21, 1850	Balto.
Russell	Thomas	40	Southerner	Donovan, Joseph S.	Jan. 21, 1850	Balto.
Russell	William	21	Tippecanoe	Slatter, Hope Hull	Apr. 15, 1844	Balto.
Russell	John	21	Nathaniel Hooper	Donovan, Jospeh S.	Feb. 12, 1852	Balto.
Rust	Alexander	18	Elizabeth	Campbell, Bernard M.	May 12, 1849	Balto.
Rustin	Becca	5	States	Woolfolk, Austin	Apr. 14, 1828	Balto.
Ruston	Samuel	14	W.H.D.C.Wright	Slatter, Hope Hull	Nov. 7, 1847	Balto.
Ruston	Wyatt	26	Pioneer	Stuart, William R.	July 20, 1848	Balto.
Sabor	Arthur	33	Architect	Slatter, Hope Hull	Feb. 13, 1843	Balto.
Sadler	Ben	6	Lafayette	Woolfolk, Austin	Oct. 18, 1828	Balto.
Sadler	Charlotte	25	Lafayette	Woolfolk, Austin	Oct. 18, 1828	Balto.
Sadler	Harry	25	Billow	Woolfolk, Joseph B.	Feb. 23, 1828	Balto.
Sadler	James	26	Kirkwood	Slatter, Hope Hull	Jan. 14, 1846	Balto.
Sadler	Julia	7	Billow	Woolfolk, Joseph B.	Feb. 23, 1828	Balto.
Sailor	Abram	21	Victorine	Slatter, Hope Hull	March 14, 1846	Balto.
Sailor	Betsy	25	Kirkwood	Slatter, Hope Hull	Dec. 23, 1843	Balto.
Sailor	Charlotte	35	Victorine	Slatter, Hope Hull	March 14, 1846	Balto.
Sailor	David	21	Victorine	Slatter, Hope Hull	March 1, 1845	Balto.
Sailor	Henry	20	Scotia	Slatter, Hope Hull	Sept. 30, 1843	Balto.
Sailor	James	19	Victorine	Slatter, Hope Hull	March 14, 1846	Balto.
Sailor	Margrett	20	Paoli	Slatter, Hope Hull	Sept. 9, 1845	Balto.
Sailor	Moses	30	Victorine	Slatter, Hope Hull	March 14, 1846	Balto.

Surname	First Name	Age	Ship	O/S	Date	Depart
Sailor	Nancy	16	Paoli	Slatter, Hope Hull	Sept. 9, 1845	Balto.
Sailor	Sarah	21	Superb	Slatter, Hope Hull	Nov. 1, 1843	Balto.
Sailor	Susan	15	Victorine	Slatter, Hope Hull	March 14, 1846	Balto.
Sampson	Ann Maria	17	Billow	Woolfolk, Joseph B.	Feb. 23, 1828	Balto.
Sampson	James	27	Scotia	Slatter, Hope Hull	Sept. 30, 1843	Balto.
Samson	Martha	25	Southerner	Campbell, Bernard M.	Oct. 27, 1849	Balto.
Samuel	Charity	15	General Pinckney	Rodbinc, Ebenezer	Feb. 21, 1846	Balto.
Sanders	Araminta	17	Splendid	Slatter, Hope Hull	Apr. 24, 1841	Balto.
Sanders	Catharine	39	Irad Ferry	Slatter, Hope Hull	Dec. 9, 1842	Balto.
Sanders	Edmond	26	E.H.Chapin	Slatter, Hope Hull	Nov. 30, 1847	Balto.
Sanders	Emeline	40	Union	Donovan, Joseph S.	May 13, 1848	Balto.
Sanders	Franklin	20	Southerner	Donovan, Joseph S.	Oct. 27, 1849	Balto.
Sanders	George	24	Abbott Lord	Campbell, Bernard M.	April 28, 1852	Balto.
Sanders	John	20	Abbott Lord	Campbell, Bernard M.	April 28, 1852	Balto.
Sanders	Sally	17	Henry A. Barling	Campbell, Bernard M.	Apr. 19, 1849	Balto.
Sanderson	Clarissa	16	Margaret Hugg	Harker, William	Nov. 30, 1844	Balto.
Sandfer	Adam	16	Jasper	Woolfolk, Austin	Apr. 7, 1827	Balto.
Sandford	Henry	23	Zoe	Slatter, Hope Hull	Feb. 16, 1847	Balto.
Sandford	Maria	9	Zoe	Slatter, Hope Hull	Feb. 16, 1847	Balto.
Sandford	Martha	4	Zoe	Slatter, Hope Hull	Feb. 16, 1847	Balto.
Sandford	Matilda	28	Zoe	Slatter, Hope Hull	Feb. 16, 1847	Balto.
Sandford	Senes	11	Zoe	Slatter, Hope Hull	Feb. 16, 1847	Balto.
Sands	George	20	John S Gittings	Campbell, Bernard M.	Nov. 20, 1852	Balto.
Sands	Milly	16	Ewarkee	Slatter, Hope Hull	March 4, 1841	Balto.
Sandy	James	18	Kirkwood	Donovan, Joseph S.	Oct. 14, 1848	Balto.
Sarah	John	25	Southerner	Campbell, Bernard M.	Jan. 5, 1852	Balto.

Surname	First Name	Age	Ship	O/S	Date	Depart
Sargent	James	11	Louisa	Donovan, Joseph S.	Oct. 9, 1847	Balto.
Sargent	Solomon	11	Louisa	Donovan, Joseph S.	Oct. 9, 1847	Balto.
Sasson	David	19	Southerner	Campbell, Bernard M.	Jan. 20, 1850	Balto.
Saucer	Felix	24	Union	Rodbind, Ebenezer	Dec. 16, 1848	Balto.
Sauenfant	Eliza	19	Lapwing	Woolfolk, Austin	Feb. 15, 1827	Balto.
Saul	Dicey	9	Victorine	Rodbind, Ebenezer	March 1, 1845	Balto.
Saul	Mary	10	Victorine	Rodbind, Ebenezer	March 1, 1845	Balto.
Saunders	Ann	25	Tweed	Forbes, George	Oct. 20, 1836	Town Creek
Saunders	George	16	Louisa	Donovan, Joseph S.	Oct. 9, 1847	Balto.
Saunders	Henry	25	Isaac Franklin	Kephart, George	Sept. 28, 1838	Balto.
Saunders	Joe	33	Tweed	Forbes, George	Oct. 20, 1836	Town Creek
Saunders	Mary	4	Tweed	Forbes, George	Oct. 20, 1836	Town Creek
Saunders	Spencer	17	Louisa	Donovan, Joseph S.	Oct. 9, 1847	Balto.
Saunders	Theodore	infant	Louisa	Donovan, Joseph S.	Oct. 9, 1847	Balto.
Savoy	Jim	16	Ann & Leah	Woolfolk, Austin	Nov. 1, 1831	Balto.
Sawyer	Rosetta	19	Jefferson	Woolfolk, Austin	Dec. 24, 1827	Balto.
Saxon	Sandy	26	Elizabeth	Campbell, Bernard M.	Jan. 2, 1850	Balto.
Saxton	Ruth	15	Victorine	Slatter, Hope Hull	March 1, 1845	Balto.
Saylor	Milly	20	Colonel Howard	Donovan, Joseph S.	Nov. 21, 1844	Balto.
Scales	Tom	16	Lapwing	Spraggins, Samuel M.	March 22, 1822	Balto.
Scarbaker	Lucy	15	Zoe	Donovan, Joseph S.	Feb. 16, 1847	Balto.
Scarborough	John	20	Union	Slatter, Hope Hull	July 26, 1847	Balto.
Schroeder	Isaac	18	States	Woolfolk, Joseph B.	Nov. 21, 1827	Balto.
Scofield	Rebeca	20	Kirkwood	Donovan, Joseph S.	Nov. 28, 1849	Balto.
Scotland	Henry	18	Elizabeth	Donovan, Joseph S.	Nov. 18, 1848	Balto.
Scotland	Rachel	20	Tippecanoe	Staples, Joshua	Jan. 17, 1842	Balto.

Surname	First Name	Age	Ship	O/S	Date	Depart
Scott	Aaron	21	Victorine	Donovan, Joseph S.	Dec. 31, 1846	Balto.
Scott	Alisan	14	Brunswick	Woolfolk, Austin	Oct. 11, 1831	Balto.
Scott	Ann R.	infant	Kirkwood	Slatter, Henry F.	Dec. 10, 1846	Balto.
Scott	Anthony	16	States	Woolfolk, Austin	Apr. 14, 1828	Balto.
Scott	Caleb	19	John C. Calhoun	Donovar, Joseph S.	Oct. 24, 1850	Balto.
Scott	Charlotte	25	Sabine	Donovan, Joseph S.	Feb. 10, 1844	Balto.
Scott	Clarissa	6	Kirkwood	Slatter, Henry F.	Dec. 10, 1846	Balto.
Scott	Dennis	23	Kirkwood	Slatter, Hope Hull	Apr. 15, 1845	Balto.
Scott	Eliza	16	John C. Calhoun	Donovan, Joseph S.	Oct. 24, 1850	Balto.
Scott	Frederick	28	Bourne	Wallis, Francis L.	Sept. 10, 1833	Balto.
Scott	George	20	Elizabeth	Campbell, Bernard M.	March 21, 1850	Balto.
Scott	Hagar	30	Brunswick	Woolfolk, Austin	Oct. 11, 1831	Balto.
Scott	Henrietta	27	Kirkwood	Slatter, Henry F.	Dec. 10, 1846	Balto.
Scott	James	19	Brunswick	Woolfolk, Austin	Oct. 11, 1831	Balto.
Scott	James	25	States	Woolfolk, Austin	Apr. 14, 1828	Balto.
Scott	Jerry	19	John C. Calhoun	Donovan, Joseph S.	Oct. 24, 1850	Balto.
Scott	John	11	John C. Calhoun	Donovan, Joseph S.	Oct. 24, 1850	Balto.
Scott	John	4	Kirkwood	Slatter, Henry F.	Dec. 10, 1846	Balto.
Scott	John	32	Kirkwood	Slatter, Henry F.	Dec. 10, 1846	Balto.
Scott	John	22	Union	Rodbird, Ebenezer	Dec. 16, 1848	Balto.
Scott	Kitty	16	Billow	Woolfolk, Austin	Feb. 23, 1828	Balto.
Scott	Linda	12	Catharine	Woolfolk, Austin	March 3. 1829	Balto.
Scott	Maria	14	Gannicleftt	Crosby Elijah R.	Nov. 25, 1840	Balto.
Scott	Mariah	17	Kirkwood	Donovan, Joseph S.	Jan. 4, 1845	Balto.
Scott	Mary	40	Louisa	Hooper, James	May 18, 1846	Balto.
Scott	Mary	11	Nathaniel Hooper	Donovan, Jospeh S.	Feb. 12, 1852	Balto.

Surname	First Name	Age	Ship	O/S	Date	Depart
Scott	Matilda	16	Henry Clay	Woolfolk, Austin	Dec. 4, 1828	Balto.
Scott	Phillip	19	Helen A. Miller	Campbell, Bernard M.	Oct. 18, 1852	Balto.
Scott	Robert	24	Kirkwood	Donovan, Joseph S.	March 9, 1847	Balto.
Scott	Robert	18	Seaman	Slatter, Shadrack	March 25, 1839	Balto.
Scott	Roberta	15	John C. Calhoun	Donovan, Joseph S.	Oct. 24, 1850	Balto.
Scott	Sam	30	Russell	Slatter, Hope Hull	March 1, 1839	Balto.
Scott	Sarah	8	Hibernia	Woolfolk, Austin	Dec. 5, 1826	Balto.
Scott	Sophia	16	Gannicleftt	Crosby, Elijah R.	Nov. 25, 1840	Balto.
Scott	Sunshine	8	Kirkwood	Slatter, Henry F.	Dec. 10, 1846	Balto.
Scott	Thornton	24	Victorine	Slatter, Hope Hull	Sept. 12, 1846	Balto.
Scott	Tom	18	Saldana	Harker, William	Feb. 27, 1844	Balto.
Scott	Walter	20	Kirkwood	Donovan, Joseph S.	Oct. 26, 1847	Balto.
Scott	William	20	Architect	Purvis, James Franklin	Feb. 3, 1841	Balto.
Scott	William	18	Brunswick	Woolfolk, Austin	Oct. 11, 1831	Balto.
Scott	William	24	Union	Rodbind, Ebenezer	Dec. 16, 1848	Balto.
Scott	William	14	John C. Calhoun	Donovan, Joseph S.	Oct. 24, 1850	Balto.
Seafus	James	26	Home	Slatter, Hope Hull	March 22, 1845	Balto.
Seal	David	19	Victorine	Slatter, Henry F.	Dec. 31, 1846	Balto.
Seals	Henrietta	17	Victorine	Slatter, Henry F.	Dec. 31, 1846	Balto.
Seals	Mary	21	Kirkwood	Slatter, Hope Hull	Jan. 4, 1845	Balto.
Sear	Ellen	16	Russell	Slatter, Hope Hull	March 1, 1839	Balto.
Sedwick	Elizabeth	18	Southerner	Donovan, Joseph S.	Oct. 27, 1849	Balto.
Seferson	Daniel	18	Union	Rodbind, Ebenezer	Dec. 16, 1848	Balto.
Seisell	James	12	Victorine	Slatter, Hope Hull	May 14, 1845	Balto.
Selby	Charlotte	3	Kirkwood	Harker, William	March 23, 1844	Balto.
Selby	Henry	21	Victorine	Donovan, Joseph S.	Oct. 25, 1844	Balto.

Surname	First Name	Age	Ship	O/S	Date	Depart
Selby	Horrace	12 mon.	Kirkwood	Harker, William	March 23, 1844	Balto.
Selby	Lloyd	22	Irad Ferry	Slatter, Hope Hull	Dec. 9, 1842	Balto.
Selby	Mary	22	Kirkwocd	Harker, William	March 23, 1844	Balto.
Selby	Patrick	17	Elizabeth	Donovan, Joseph S.	Jan. 2, 1850	Balto.
Selden	John	25	Intelligence	De Mapiere, Victor	Apr. 30, 1821	Balto.
Sellman	William	19	Victorine	Donovan, Joseph S.	May 22, 1844	Balto.
Selman	Charlotte	17	States	Woolfolk, Austin	Apr. 14, 1828	Balto.
Selman	Daniel	28	States	Woolfolk, Austin	Nov. 21, 1827	Balto.
Selman	Thomas	22	Uncas	Slatter, Hope Hull	Apr. 3, 1838	Balto.
Sephus	George	7	Henry Clay	Woolfolk, Austin	Dec. 4, 1828	Balto.
Sephus	John	26	Henry Clay	Woolfolk, Austin	Dec. 4, 1828	Balto.
Sephus	Levy	33	Henry Clay	Woolfolk, Austin	Dec. 4, 1828	Balto.
Sephus	Lucy	25	Henry Clay	Woolfolk, Austin	Dec. 4, 1828	Balto.
Sephus	Maria	1	Henry Clay	Woolfolk, Austin	Dec. 4, 1828	Balto.
Sephus	Mariah	8	Henry Clay	Woolfolk, Austin	Dec. 4, 1828	Balto.
Sephus	Mary	3	Henry Clay	Woolfolk, Austin	Dec. 4, 1828	Balto.
Sephus	Minty	23	Henry Clay	Woolfolk, Austin	Dec. 4, 1828	Balto.
Sephus	Wesley	3	Henry Clay	Woolfolk, Austin	Dec. 4, 1828	Balto.
Serges	Cornelia	17	Victorine	Donovan, Joseph S.	Oct. 25, 1844	Balto.
Serivenis	Betty	30	Kirkwood	Smith, J.M.	Nov. 28, 1849	Balto.
Serivenis	Hannah	7	Kirkwood	Smith, J.M.	Nov. 28, 1849	Balto.
Serivenis	Henry	5	Kirkwood	Smith, J.M.	Nov. 28, 1849	Balto.
Serivenis	William	3	Kirkwood	Smith, J.M.	Nov. 28, 1849	Balto.
Sevear	David	13	Union	Donovan, Joseph S.	May 13, 1848	Balto.
Sevell	Bill	16	Lady Richmond	Woolfolk, Austin	Apr. 30, 1827	Balto.
Sewell	Elizabeth	14	Eliza	Slatter, Hope Hull	Oct. 9, 1840	Balto.

Surname	First Name	Age	Ship	O/S	Date	Depart
Sewell	Harriett	16	Elizabeth	Donovan, Joseph S.	Nov. 18, 1848	Balto.
Sewell	Ignatious	16	Kirkwood	Donovan, Joseph S.	Oct. 14, 1848	Balto.
Sewell	Jefry	24	Colonel Howard	Donovan, Joseph S.	Nov. 21, 1844	Balto.
Sewell	John	17	Elizabeth	Campbell, Bernard M.	Nov. 18, 1848	Balto.
Sewell	Joshua	12	Charles	Campbell, Bernard M.	Dec. 18, 1850	Balto.
Sewell	Margaret	18	Union	Sheckles, B.O.	Nov. 17, 1849	Balto.
Sewell	Margarett	16	St. Mary	Donovan, Joseph S.	Nov. 29, 1845	Balto.
Sewell	Mary	18	General Pinckney	Slatter, Hope Hull	Nov. 10, 1845	Balto.
Sewell	Serena	40	Louisa	Donovan, Joseph S.	Oct. 9, 1847	Balto.
Sewell	Thomas	18	Scotia	Harker, William	Sept. 30, 1843	Balto.
Sewell		18	Charles	Campbell, Bernard M.	Dec. 18, 1850	Balto.
Shaddows	Jane	26	Victorine	Slatter, Hope Hull	March 9, 1844	Balto.
Shaddows	John	infant	Victorine	Slatter, Hope Hull	March 9, 1844	Balto.
Shaddows	Joshua	8	Victorine	Slatter, Hope Hull	March 9, 1844	Balto.
Shaddows	Martha	5	Victorine	Slatter, Hope Hull	March 9, 1844	Balto.
Shade	Henry	24	Victorine	Donovan, Joseph S.	Sept. 29, 1845	Balto.
Shafer	Athella	19	Victorine	Slatter, Hope Hull	March 14, 1846	Balto.
Shanklin	George	23	Union	Donovan, Joseph S.	May 13, 1848	Balto.
Shapes	Daniel	20	Lafayette	Woolfolk, Austin	Oct. 22, 1828	Balto.
Shapes	James	13	Delta	Walker, Joshua	Dec. 23, 1828	Balto.
Sharp	John	22	Charles	Donovan, Joseph S.	Apr. 23, 1851	Balto.
Sharpe	Horace	22	Architect	Donovan, Joseph S.	Apr. 25, 1846	Balto.
Shaw	Ellen	20	Victorine	Slatter, Hope Hull	Sept. 12, 1846	Balto.
Shaw	George	17	Kirkwood	Donovan, Joseph S.	Sept. 28, 1846	Balto.
Shaw	Leroy	22	Solomon Saltus	Slatter, Hope Hull	Oct. 7, 1839	Balto.
Shaw	Phill	20	General Pinckney	Rodbind, Ebenezer	Feb. 21, 1846	Balto.

Surname	First Name	Age	Ship	O/S	Date	Depart
Shawnacy	Patrick	19	Kirkwood	Slatter, Hope Hull	Apr. 15, 1845	Balto.
Sheckles	William	12	Union	Sheckles, Gannon	March 17, 1849	Balto.
Shelton	Charlotte	22	Henry A. Barling	Campbell, Walter L.	Oct. 28, 1848	Balto.
Shelton	Margarette	16	Ewarkee	Purvis, James Franklin	March 4, 1841	Balto.
Shelton	Toliver	20	Charles	Campbel, Bernard M.	Apr. 23, 1851	Balto.
Shepard	Emily	15	Victorine	Donovan, Joseph S.	May 22, 1844	Balto.
Sheppherd	William	20	Intelligence	De Mapiere, Victor	Apr. 30, 1821	Balto.
Sherman	Elizabeth	18	General Pinckney	Slatter, Hope Hull	Jan. 19, 1847	Balto.
Shields	Charlotte	18	Home	Slatter, Hope Hull	March 22, 1845	Balto.
Shields	Norman	20	General Pinckney	Slatter, Hope Hull	Feb. 21, 1846	Balto.
Shipley	Catherine	17	Elizabeth	Campbell, Bernard M.	Jan. 2, 1850	Balto.
Shipley	Mary F.	16	Uncas	Slatter, Hope Hull	Jan. 10, 1838	Balto.
Shiply	Patsy	17	Glasgow	Slatter, Hope Hull	Oct. 11, 1838	Balto.
Shockley	Ellen	18	Union	Donovan, Joseph S.	March 17, 1849	Balto.
Shore	Daniel	34	Victorine	Donovan, Joseph S.	May 22, 1844	Balto.
Short	Amos		John C. Calhoun	Donovan, Joseph S.	Oct. 24, 1850	Balto.
Short	Ellen	16	General Pinckney	Slatter, Hope Hull	Jan. 19, 1847	Balto.
Short	George	26	Kirkwood	Donovan, Joseph S.	Oct. 26, 1847	Balto.
Short	George H.	20	Superb	Slatter, Hope Hull	Nov. 1, 1843	Balto.
Short	Lucy	14	Victorine	Slatter, Hope Hull	March 1, 1845	Balto.
Short	Nathan	22	Ewarkee	Purvis, James Franklin	March 4, 1841	Balto.
Short	Rile	25	Hyperion	Kelso, George Y.	Nov. 8, 1820	Balto.
Shorter	Abraham	12	Lapwing	Woolfolk, Samuel M.	Feb. 15, 1827	Balto.
Shorter	Andrew	3	Victorine	Slatter, Hope Hull	Dec. 17, 1845	Balto.
Shorter	Andrew	35	Victorine	Slatter, Hope Hull	Dec. 17, 1845	Balto.
Shorter	Asbury	11	Home	Slatter, Hope Hull	March 22, 1845	Balto.

Surname	First Name	Age	Ship	O/S	Date	Depart
Shorter	Betty	17	Isaac Franklin	Kephart, George	Feb. 1, 1839	Balto.
Shorter	Bill	5	Victorine	Slatter, Hope Hull	Dec. 17, 1845	Balto.
Shorter	Crista	infant	Victorine	Slatter, Hope Hull	Dec. 17, 1845	Balto.
Shorter	Eliza	50	Home	Slatter, Hope Hull	March 22, 1845	Balto.
Shorter	Elizabeth	18	John C. Calhoun	Donovan, Joseph S.	Oct. 24, 1850	Balto.
Shorter	Emily	14	Southerner	Donovan, Jospeh S.	Jan. 5, 1852	Balto.
Shorter	Francis	6	Victorine	Slatter, Hope Hull	Dec. 17, 1845	Balto.
Shorter	Frederick	30	Kirkwood	Slatter, Henry F.	Dec. 10, 1846	Balto.
Shorter	Jiles	15	Kirkwood	Donovan, Joseph S.	March 23, 1844	Balto.
Shorter	John	14	John C. Calhoun	Donovan, Joseph S.	Oct. 24, 1850	Balto.
Shorter	Richard	30	Kirkwood	Slatter, Hope Hull	Apr. 4, 1846	Balto.
Shorter	Richard	26	Leda	Donovan, Joseph S.	May 30, 1846	Balto.
Shorter	Susanah	11	Home	Donovan, Joseph S.	March 22, 1845	Balto.
Shorter	William	30	Hermitage	Donovan, Joseph S.	Oct. 28, 1846	Balto.
Shorts	Harry	20	Isaac Franklin	Kephart, George	Sept. 28, 1838	Balto.
Shorts	Jose	25	Isaac Franklin	Kephart, George	Sept. 28, 1838	Balto.
Shwirel	Henry	12	Tweed	Forbes, George	Oct. 20, 1836	Town Creek
Siddens	George	18	Brunswick	Woolfolk, Austin	Oct. 11, 1831	Balto.
Sidders	Benjamin	22	Union	Donovan, Joseph S.	Dec. 16, 1848	Balto.
Sidders	Pippin	25	Tippecanoe	Purvis, James Franklin	Jan. 17, 1842	Balto.
Sidders	William	28	Union	Donovan, Joseph S.	Dec. 16, 1848	Balto.
Siddons	Henry	22	Jefferson	Woolfolk, Austin	Dec. 24, 1827	Balto.
Simber	James	24	E.H. Chapin	Donovan, Joseph S.	Aug. 26, 1848	Balto.
Simber	Nancy	16	E.H. Chapin	Donovan, Joseph S.	Aug. 26, 1848	Balto.
Simmon	Spencer	23	Victorine	Donovan, Joseph S.	Sept. 29, 1845	Balto.
Simmonds	Nickolas	22	Paoli	Slatter, Hope Hull	Sept. 9, 1845	Balto.

Surname	First Name	Age	Ship	O/S	Date	Depart
Simmons	Ellen	25	Elizabeth	Donovan, Joseph S.	Nov. 18, 1848	Balto.
Simmons	Priscilla	30	Victorire	Slatter, Henry F.	Dec. 31, 1846	Balto.
Simmons	Richard	40	Elizabeth	Donovan, Joseph S.	Nov. 18, 1848	Balto.
Simms	Alexander	22	Kirkwood	Donovan, Joseph S.	Nov. 28, 1849	Balto.
Simms	Amey	18	Kirkwood	Donovan, Joseph S.	Apr. 4, 1846	Balto.
Simms	Benjamin		Charles	Campbell, Bernard M.	Dec. 18, 1850	Balto.
Simms	Charles	20	John C. Calhoun	Donovan, Joseph S.	Oct. 24, 1850	Balto.
Simms	Charles	16	Kirkwood	Donovan, Joseph S.	Oct. 14, 1848	Balto.
Simms	Frank	24	General Pinckney	Slatter, Hope Hull	Nov. 10, 1845	Balto.
Simms	Henry	22	Catharine	Bossiere, Joseph S.	Apr. 1, 1831	Balto.
Simms	Laura	25	Waverly	Campbell, Bernard M.	Apr. 3, 1851	Balto.
Simms	Laurance	20	Architect	Harker, William	Feb. 16, 1843	Balto.
Simms	Lewis	23	Southerner	Rodbind, Ebenezer	Jan. 21, 1850	Balto.
Simms	Peter	18	Charles	Campbell, Bernard M.	Dec. 18, 1850	Balto.
Simms	Phillip	26	Union	Slatter, Hope Hull	July 26, 1847	Balto.
Simms	Sophia	17	John C. Calhoun	Donovan, Joseph S.	Oct. 24, 1850	Balto.
Simms	Thomas	23	John C. Calhoun	Donovan, Joseph S.	Oct. 24, 1850	Balto.
Simms	Warner	18	Superb	Slatter, Hope Hull	Nov. 1, 1843	Balto.
Simons	Adam	22	Mary Broughton	Campbell, Bernard M.	Nov. 18, 1851	Balto.
Simpsen	William	24	Lafayette	Woolfolk, Richard	Oct. 18, 1828	Balto.
Simpson	Betsey	10	Union	Slatter, Hope Hull	July 26, 1847	Balto.
Simpson	Henderson	22	Union	Campbell, Bernard M.	March 17, 1849	Balto.
Simpson	Rachel	17	Victorine	Donovan, Joseph S.	Dec. 31, 1846	Balto.
Sims	Abram	24	Victorine	Rodbind, Ebenezer	Dec. 31, 1846	Balto.
Sims	Adeline	13	Sabine	Donovan, Joseph S.	Feb. 10, 1844	Balto.
Sims	Harriet	25	Home	Hollins, George V.	March 19, 1845	Balto.

Surname	First Name	Age	Ship	O/S	Date	Depart
Sims	James	13	Mary	Harker, William	Feb. 10, 1844	Balto.
Sims	Jerry	20	Victorine	Donovan, Joseph S.	May 22, 1844	Balto.
Sims	Philip	25	Seaman	Rush, George Jr.	Dec. 16, 1841	Balto.
Sims	Sarah	19	Sabine	Donovan, Joseph S.	Feb. 10, 1844	Balto.
Sims	William	16	Victorine	Gardiner, Richard S.D.	Dec. 21, 1844	Balto.
Sinclair	Betsey	30	Solomon Saltus	Slatter, Hope Hull	Oct. 7, 1839	Balto.
Sinclair	Richard	15	Hibernia	Woolfolk, Austin	Dec. 5, 1826	Balto.
Singer	Theodore	19	Superb	Slatter, Hope Hull	Nov. 1, 1843	Balto.
Singer	William	38	Irad Ferry	Slatter, Hope Hull	Dec. 9, 1842	Balto.
Singleton	Henry	26	Hope & Hannah	Woolfolk, Austin	March 11, 1829	Balto.
Singleton	Joe	25	Hope & Hannah	Woolfolk, Austin	March 11, 1829	Balto.
Singleton	Henry	25	Intelligence	King, Gideon T.	Sept. 18, 1821	Balto.
Singo	Catherine	30	Kirkwood	Campbell, Bernard M.	March 23, 1844	Balto.
Sinnger	Don Carlos	10	Kirkwood	Campbell, Bernard M.	March 23, 1844	Balto.
Sinnger	Harriet Allen	8	Kirkwood	Campbell, Bernard M.	March 23, 1844	Balto.
Sinnger	Susan Ann	22	Solomon Saltus	Slatter, Hope Hull	Oct. 7, 1839	Balto.
Siters	July Ann	18	Ewarkee	Slatter, Hope Hull	March 4, 1841	Balto.
Sitters	Mary	16	Kirkwood	Donovan, Joseph S.	Oct. 14, 1848	Balto.
Sivers	Charity	19	St. Mary	Williams, Thomas	Nov. 29, 1845	Balto.
Skinner	Clement	21	Paoli	Slatter, Hope Hull	Sept. 9, 1845	Balto.
Skinner	Julia	8	Union	Williams, Thomas	Oct. 9, 1848	Balto.
Skinner	Lucy	9	Union	Williams, Thomas	Oct. 9, 1848	Balto.
Slater	Caroline	15	Victorine	Rodbind, Ebenezer	March 1, 1845	Balto.
Slater	Debby	15	Delawarian	Campbell, Bernard M.	Dec. 1, 1848	Balto.
Slatter	Samuel	21	Pioneer	Slatter, Hope Hull	Sept. 15, 1847	Balto.
Slaughter	Daniel	20	Ganniclefft	Slatter, Hope Hull	Nov. 25, 1840	Balto.

Surname	First Name	Age	Ship	O/S	Date	Depart
Slaughter	Joseph	26	Russell	Slatter, Hope Hull	March 1, 1839	Balto.
Sledney	Caroline	16	Southerner	Donovan, Joseph S.	Oct. 27, 1849	Balto.
Sluby	Benjamin	25	Cora	Donovan, Jospeh S.	Jan. 21, 1851	Balto.
Small	John	18	Hibernia	Woolfolk, Austin	Dec. 5, 1826	Balto.
Small	Lewis	26	Isaac Franklin	Slatter, Hope Hull	Sept. 28, 1838	Balto.
Small	Mary	16	Abbott Lord	Campbell, Bernard M.	April 28, 1852	Balto.
Small	Mary	20	Irad Ferry	Slatter, Hope Hull	Dec. 9, 1842	Balto.
Smalley	Cyrus	14	General Pinckney	Slatter, Hope Hull	Jan. 19, 1847	Balto.
Smallwood	Adeline	18	Sarah Bridge	Campbell, Bernard M.	Feb. 8, 1851	Balto.
Smallwood	Andrew	25	Union	Donovan, Joseph S.	May 13, 1848	Balto.
Smallwood	Ben	21	Brunswick	Woolfolk, Austin	Oct. 11, 1831	Balto.
Smallwood	Ben	24	Kirkwood	Rodbind, Ebenezer	Oct. 26, 1847	Balto.
Smallwood	Charlott	19	Victorine	Rodbind, Ebenezer	Dec. 31, 1846	Balto.
Smallwood	Eliza	17	Kirkwood	Williams, Thomas	Apr. 4, 1846	Balto.
Smallwood	Eliza	18	Tweed	Forbes, George	Oct. 20, 1836	Town Creek
Smallwood	Ellick	22	Sarah Eridge	Campbell, Bernard M.	Feb. 8, 1851	Balto.
Smallwood	Henney	40	General Pinckney	Williams, Thomas	Jan. 19, 1847	Balto.
Smallwood	Jane	25	Nancy W. Stevens	Rodbind, Ebenezer	Feb. 18, 1845	Balto.
Smallwood	Malinda	17	Billow	Woolfolk, Austin	Feb. 23, 1828	Balto.
Smallwood	Marietta	13	Kirkwood	Campbell, Bernard M.	Oct. 14, 1848	Balto.
Smallwood	Moses	16	Ann & Leah	Woolfolk, Austin	Nov. 1, 1831	Balto.
Smallwood	Moses	32	Home	Rodbind, Ebenezer	March 22, 1845	Balto.
Smallwood	Robert	18	Victorine	Donovan, Joseph S.	Sept. 29, 1845	Balto.
Smallwood	Sam	15	Billow	Woolfolk, Austin	Feb. 23, 1828	Balto.
Smallwood	Susan	20	General Pinckney	Williams, Thomas	Jan. 19, 1847	Balto.
Smallwood	Tom	21	Lady Monroe	Woolfolk, Austin	March 25, 1825	Balto.

Surname	First Name	Age	Ship	O/S	Date	Depart
Smallwood	Vincent	40	Elizabeth	Campbell, Bernard M.	March 21, 1850	Balto.
Smart	Alexander	4	Kirkwood	Harker, William	March 23, 1844	Balto.
Smart	Harriet	21	Seaman	Slatter, Shadrack	March 25, 1839	Balto.
Smart	John	26	Union	Slatter, Hope Hull	July 26, 1847	Balto.
Smart	Maria	21	Kirkwood	Harker, William	March 23, 1844	Balto.
Smart	Mary	12 mon.	Kirkwood	Harker, William	March 23, 1844	Balto.
Smith	Abraham	23	Ann & Leah	Woolfolk, Austin	Nov.1, 1831	Balto.
Smith	Abraham	12	Tweed	Sothoron, William H.	Oct. 20, 1836	Town Creek
Smith	Abram	24	Peru	Slatter, Hope Hull	Nov. 16, 1842	Balto.
Smith	Alexander	35	General Pinckney	Slatter, Hope Hull	Feb. 21, 1846	Balto.
Smith	Alexander	infant	Victorine	Slatter, Hope Hull	May 14, 1845	Balto.
Smith	Alfred	17	Kirkwood	Slatter, Hope Hull	Oct. 16, 1845	Balto.
Smith	Ann	17	Architect	Crow, William	Feb. 3, 1841	Balto.
Smith	Ann	17	Brunswick	Woolfolk, Austin	Oct. 11, 1831	Balto.
Smith	Ann	3	Elizabeth	Ireland, John	Jan. 2, 1850	Balto.
Smith	Ann	18	John C. Calhoun	Donovan, Joseph S.	Oct. 24, 1850	Balto.
Smith	Ann	20	Peru	Slatter, Hope Hull	Nov. 16, 1842	Balto.
Smith	Ann	11	Salvadora	Slatter, Hope Hull	Sept. 28, 1846	Balto.
Smith	Ann	20	Seaman	Slatter, Shadrack	March 25, 1839	Balto.
Smith	Ann M.	24	Kirkwood	Slatter, Henry F.	Dec. 10, 1846	Balto.
Smith	Anna	24	Victorine	Slatter, Hope Hull	Sept. 12, 1846	Balto.
Smith	Anthony	45	General Pinckney	Campbell, Bernard M.	Jan. 19, 1847	Balto.
Smith	Anthony	28	Kirkwood	Slatter, Hope Hull	March 9, 1847	Balto.
Smith	Archy	25	Margaret Forbs		Nov. 28, 1838	Balto.
Smith	Aron	21	Victorine	Crow, William	March 14, 1846	Balto.
Smith	Barbara	15	Elizabeth	Donovan, Joseph S.	Jan. 2, 1850	Balto.

Surname	First Name	Age	Ship	O/S	Date	Depart
Smith	Benjamin	18	Union	Rodbind, Ebenezer	Nov. 17, 1849	Balto.
Smith	Betsy	16	Kirkwood	Donovan, Joseph S.	Sept. 28, 1846	Balto.
Smith	Caleb	35	Elizabeth	Campbel, Bernard M.	Jan. 2, 1850	Balto.
Smith	Caroline	18	Margaret Forbs	Slatter, Hope Hull	Nov. 28, 1838	Balto.
Smith	Caroline	23	Victorine	Slatter, Henry F.	Dec. 31, 1846	Balto.
Smith	Cassy	15	Jefferson	Woolfolk, Austin	Dec. 24, 1827	Balto.
Smith	Charity	20	Southerner	Donovan, Joseph S.	Oct. 27, 1849	Balto.
Smith	Charles	7 mon.	Jefferson	Woolfolk, Austin	Dec. 24, 1827	Balto.
Smith	Charles	11	Julia	Woolfolk, Austin	Jan. 8, 1829	Balto.
Smith	Charles	26	Liberator	Woolfolk, Austin	Nov. 12, 1828	Balto.
Smith	Charles	21	Pioneer	Stuart, William R.	July 20, 1848	Balto.
Smith	Charlotte	7	Lafayette	Slatter, Hope Hull	March 25, 1843	Balto.
Smith	Charlotte	18	Victorine	Donovan, Joseph S.	May 14, 1845	Balto.
Smith	Chernne	28	Irad Ferry	Slatter, Hope Hull	Dec. 9, 1842	Balto.
Smith	Clarissa	25	Merrimack	Peyton, Ann Eliza	Nov. 2, 1831	Balto.
Smith	Dennis	6	Elizabeth	Ireland, John	Jan. 2, 1850	Balto.
Smith	Edward	30	Kirkwood	Donovan, Joseph S.	Nov. 28, 1849	Balto.
Smith	Edward	19	Tippecanoe	Harker, William	Dec. 16, 1840	Balto.
Smith	Edward	22	Tippecanoe	Slatter, Hope Hull	Jan. 17, 1842	Balto.
Smith	Edward	22	Victorine	Slatter, Hope Hull	March 1, 1845	Balto.
Smith	Eli	18	Kirkwood	Donovan, Joseph S.	Oct. 26, 1847	Balto.
Smith	Eliza	28	Elizabeth	Ireland, John	Jan. 2, 1850	Balto.
Smith	Elizabeth	23	Kirkwood	Slatter, Hope Hull	Dec. 23, 1843	Balto.
Smith	Elizabeth	15	Kirkwood	Campbell, Bernard M.	March 23, 1844	Balto.
Smith	Elizabeth	16	Union	Donovan, Joseph S.	Dec. 16, 1848	Balto.
Smith	Elizebeth	3	George Ross	Wilson, Thomas C.	June 18, 1847	Balto.

Surname	First Name	Age	Ship	O/S	Date	Depart
Smith	Ellen	2	Peru	Slatter, Hope Hull	Nov. 16, 1842	Balto.
Smith	Ellen	10	Salvadora	Slatter, Hope Hull	Sept. 28, 1846	Balto.
Smith	Ellen	18	Seaman	Slatter, Hope Hull	Dec. 19, 1838	Balto.
Smith	Ellen	8 mon.	States	Woolfolk, Joseph B.	Nov. 21, 1827	Balto.
Smith	Emaline	25	George Ross	Wilson, Thomas C.	June 18, 1847	Balto.
Smith	Emilie Ann	16	Solomon Saltus	Slatter, Hope Hull	Oct. 7, 1839	Balto.
Smith	Flora	17	States	Woolfolk, Austin	Nov. 21, 1827	Balto.
Smith	Frank	19	Irad Ferry	Slatter, Hope Hull	Dec. 9, 1842	Balto.
Smith	George	18	Helen A. Miller	Campbell, Bernard M.	Oct. 18, 1852	Balto.
Smith	George	30	Henry A. Barling	Donovan, Joseph S.	Dec. 18, 1851	Balto.
Smith	George	24	John C. Calhoun	Donovan, Joseph S.	Oct. 24, 1850	Balto.
Smith	George	22	Tippecanoe	Slatter, Hope Hull	Jan. 17, 1842	Balto.
Smith	Handy	19	Hope & Hannah	Woolfolk, Austin	March 11, 1829	Balto.
Smith	Hannah	20	General Pinckney	Slatter, Hope Hull	Nov. 10, 1845	Balto.
Smith	Hannah	25	Isaac Franklin	Slatter, Hope Hull	Sept. 28, 1838	Balto.
Smith	Hannah	20	Margaret Forbs	Slatter, Hope Hull	Nov. 28, 1838	Balto.
Smith	Hannah	18	Victorine	Crow, William	March 14, 1846	Balto.
Smith	Harriet	19	States	Woolfolk, Austin	Nov. 21, 1827	Balto.
Smith	Harriet	20	States	Woolfolk, Joseph B.	Nov. 21, 1827	Balto.
Smith	Harriett	20	Solomon Saltus	Slatter, Hope Hull	Oct. 7, 1839	Balto.
Smith	Harrison	24	Helen A. Miller	Campbell, Bernard M.	Oct. 18, 1852	Balto.
Smith	Henny	infant	George Ross	Wilson, Thomas C.	June 18, 1847	Balto.
Smith	Henrietta	9	Russell	Slatter, Hope Hull	March 1, 1839	Balto.
Smith	Henrietta	17	Victorine	Rodbind, Ebenezer	March 14, 1846	Balto.
Smith	Henry	17	Brunswick	Woolfolk, Austin	Oct. 11, 1831	Balto.
Smith	Henry	18	Kirkwood	Donovan, Joseph S.	March 9, 1847	Balto.

Surname	First Name	Age	Ship	O/S	Date	Depart
Smith	Henry	25	Uncas	Slatter, Hope Hull	Apr. 3, 1838	Balto.
Smith	Isaac	20	Ewarkee	Purvis, James Franklin	March 4, 1841	Balto.
Smith	Isaac	23	Margaret Hugg	Donovan, Joseph S.	Feb. 8, 1845	Balto.
Smith	Isabella	18	Eliza F.Mason	Donovan, Joseph S.	Nov. 13, 1851	Balto.
Smith	Isabella	4	Kirkwood	Slatter, Henry F.	Dec. 10, 1846	Balto.
Smith	Israel	17	Tippecanoe	Slatter, Hope Hull	Jan. 17, 1842	Balto.
Smith	Jack	27	General Pinckney	Williams, Thomas	Jan. 19, 1847	Balto.
Smith	James	17	Ann & Leah	Woolfolk, Austin	Nov. 1, 1831	Balto.
Smith	James	34	Architect	Crow, William	Feb. 3, 1841	Balto.
Smith	James	20	Isaac Franklin	Kephart, George	Feb. 1, 1839	Balto.
Smith	James	7	Jasper	Woolfolk, Austin	Apr. 7, 1827	Balto.
Smith	James	17	Kirkwood	Donovan, Joseph S.	Sept. 28, 1846	Balto.
Smith	James	3 mon.	States	Woolfolk, Austin	Nov. 21, 1827	Balto.
Smith	James	21	Superb	Slatter, Hope Hull	Nov. 1, 1843	Balto.
Smith	James	23	Victorine	Harker, William	March 14, 1846	Balto.
Smith	James	8	Russell	Slatter, Hope Hull	March 1, 1839	Balto.
Smith	Jane	14	St. Mary	Donovan, Joseph S.	Nov. 29, 1845	Balto.
Smith	Jane	27	Victorine	Donovan, Joseph S.	May 22, 1844	Balto.
Smith	Jarmotti	4	Kirkwood	Campbell, Bernard M.	March 9, 1847	Balto.
Smith	Jenny	25	Brunswick	Woolfolk, Austin	Oct. 11, 1831	Balto.
Smith	John	23	Southerner	Campbell, Bernard M.	Jan. 20, 1850	Balto.
Smith	John	26	St. Mary	Williams, Thomas	Nov. 29, 1845	Balto.
Smith	John	19	Union	Donovan, Joseph S.	Dec. 16, 1848	Balto.
Smith	John	1	Irad Ferry	Slatter, Hope Hull	Dec. 9, 1842	Balto.
Smith	Joseph	26	Northumberland	Slatter, Hope Hull	Feb. 27, 1843	Balto.
Smith	Joseph Darin	15	Architect	Crow, William	Feb. 3, 1841	Balto.
Smith	Judy					

Surname	First Name	Age	Ship	O/S	Date	Depart
Smith	Julia	20	John C. Calhoun	Donovan, Joseph S.	Oct. 24, 1850	Balto.
Smith	Julia	24	Victorine	Slatter, Hope Hull	Sept. 12, 1846	Balto.
Smith	Letty	20	Victorine	Slatter, Hope Hull	May 14, 1845	Balto.
Smith	Lewis	7 mon.	Isaac Franklin	Slatter, Hope Hull	Sept. 28, 1838	Balto.
Smith	Lewis	22	Kirkwood	Donovan, Joseph S.	Jan. 14, 1846	Balto.
Smith	Lidy	8	Russell	Slatter, Hope Hull	March 1, 1839	Balto.
Smith	Louisa	16	Kirkwood	Campbell, Bernard M.	Oct. 14, 1848	Balto.
Smith	Louisa	20	Solomon Saltus	Slatter, Hope Hull	Oct. 7, 1839	Balto.
Smith	Louisa	11	Southerner	Donovan, Joseph S.	Oct. 27, 1849	Balto.
Smith	Lucinda	25	Henry A. Barling	Donovan, Joseph S.	May 17, 1851	Balto.
Smith	Lucy	35	Architect	Crow, William	Feb. 3, 1841	Balto.
Smith	Maria	16	Union	Donovan, Joseph S.	Dec. 16, 1848	Balto.
Smith	Mariah	28	Victorine	Donovan, Joseph S.	May 22, 1844	Balto.
Smith	Mary	21	Julia	Woolfolk, Austin	Jan. 8, 1829	Balto.
Smith	Mary	18	Kirkwood	Donovan, Joseph S.	Sept. 28, 1846	Balto.
Smith	Mary	17	Louisa	Slatter, Hope Hull	Oct. 11, 1847	Balto.
Smith	Mary	23	Superb	Slatter, Hope Hull	Nov. 1, 1843	Balto.
Smith	Mary	15	Union	Donovan, Joseph S.	Dec. 16, 1848	Balto.
Smith	Mary Ann	15	States	Woolfolk, Austin	Nov. 21, 1827	Balto.
Smith	Mary Ann	17	States	Woolfolk, Austin	Nov. 21, 1827	Balto.
Smith	Mary J.	14	Victorine	Donovan, Joseph S.	March 1, 1845	Balto.
Smith	Maryann	40	Catharine	Slatter, Hope Hull	Jan. 24, 1843	Balto.
Smith	Milly	17	Arctic	Magee, Eugene	Oct. 8, 1828	Balto.
Smith	Minta	25	Kirkwood	Campbell, Bernard M.	March 9, 1847	Balto.
Smith	Moses	16	Peru	Slatter, Hope Hull	Nov. 16, 1842	Balto.
Smith	Nick	32	Hermitage	Slatter, Hope Hull	Oct. 28, 1846	Balto.

Surname	First Name	Age	Ship	O/S	Date	Depart
Smith	Nick	20	Union	Campbell, Bernard M.	Nov. 17, 1849	Balto.
Smith	Peter	19	General Pinckney	Donovan, Joseph S.	Nov. 10, 1845	Balto.
Smith	Phebe	28	Tweed	Sothoron, William H.	Oct. 20, 1836	Town Creek
Smith	Phil	12	Tweed	Sothoron, William H.	Oct. 20, 1836	Town Creek
Smith	Priscilla	15	States	Woolfolk, Austin	Nov. 21, 1827	Balto.
Smith	Rachel	6	Tweed	Sothoron, William H.	Oct. 20, 1836	Town Creek
Smith	Rachel	25	Victorine	Slatter. Hope Hull	Sept. 12, 1846	Balto.
Smith	Raymond	22	Kirkwood	Campbell, Bernard M.	Dec. 10, 1846	Balto.
Smith	Rebecca	20	Mary	Purvis James Franklin	Feb. 8, 1841	Balto.
Smith	Richard	17	Superb	Slatter Hope Hull	Nov. 1, 1843	Balto.
Smith	Robert	25	Elizabeth	Donovan, Joseph S.	Nov. 18, 1848	Balto.
Smith	Robert	3	Henry A. Barling	Donovan, Joseph S.	May 17, 1851	Balto.
Smith	Robert	17	John C. Calhoun	Donovan, Joseph S.	Oct. 24, 1850	Balto.
Smith	Robert D.	17	Virginia	Boyer, Lucy	Nov. 18, 1823	Balto.
Smith	Sam	20	States	Woolfolk, Austin	March 8, 1826	Balto.
Smith	Samuel	20	States	Woolfolk, Austin	Apr. 14, 1828	Balto.
Smith	Samuel	26	Victorine	Donovan, Joseph S.	May 22, 1844	Balto.
Smith	Sarah	18	E.H.Chapin	Slatter Hope Hull	Nov. 30, 1847	Balto.
Smith	Sarah	18	Mary Broughton	Campbell, Bernard M.	Nov. 18, 1851	Balto.
Smith	Sarah	17	Victorine	Slatter Henry F.	Dec. 31, 1846	Balto.
Smith	Sarah Ann	5	George Ross	Wilsor, Thomas C.	June 18, 1847	Balto.
Smith	Solomon	20	Kirkwood	Harker, William	March 23, 1844	Balto.
Smith	Solomon	27	Lafayette	Woolfolk, Richard	Oct. 18, 1828	Balto.
Smith	Sophia	19	Jefferson	Woolfolk, Austin	Dec. 24, 1827	Balto.
Smith	Spencer	10	Elizabeth	Ireland, John	Jan. 2, 1850	Balto.
Smith	Spencer	25	Tangier	Campbell, Bernard M.	Nov. 26, 1853	Balto.

Surname	First Name	Age	Ship	O/S	Date	Depart
Smith	Stephen	30	Helen A. Miller	Campbell, Bernard M.	Oct. 18, 1852	Balto.
Smith	Tracy	22	Irad Ferry	Slatter, Hope Hull	Dec. 9, 1842	Balto.
Smith	Trecy	15	Julia	Woolfolk, Austin	Jan. 8, 1829	Balto.
Smith	Violet	24	Billow	Woolfolk, Austin	Feb. 23, 1828	Balto.
Smith	William	25	John C. Calhoun	Donovan, Joseph S.	Oct. 24, 1850	Balto.
Smith	William	18	Julia	Woolfolk, Austin	Jan. 8, 1829	Balto.
Smith	William	37	Kirkwood	Wilson, Jonathan M.	Sept. 6, 1851	Balto.
Smith	William	12	Southerner	Donovan, Joseph S.	Jan. 21, 1850	Balto.
Smith	William	19	Tippecanoe	Slatter, Hope Hull	Jan. 17, 1842	Balto.
Smith	William	32	Victorine	Rodbind, Ebenezer	Dec. 31, 1846	Balto.
Smith	William	20	Zoe	Slatter, Hope Hull	Feb. 16, 1847	Balto.
Smith	William G.	23	John C. Calhoun	Donovan, Joseph S.	Oct. 24, 1850	Balto.
Smith	William Henry	19	John C. Calhoun	Donovan, Joseph S.	Oct. 24, 1850	Balto.
Smith	Wilma	12	Kirkwood	Donovan, Joseph S.	Oct. 26, 1847	Balto.
Smith		infant	Elizabeth	Ireland, John	Jan. 2, 1850	Balto.
Smith		infant	Kirkwood	Campbell, Bernard M.	March 9, 1847	Balto.
Smith		3 mon.	Margaret Forbs	Slatter, Hope Hull	Nov. 28, 1838	Balto.
Smith		20	Signet	Woolfolk, Austin	Nov. 12, 1831	Balto.
Smith		14	Tweed	Bowling, John D.	Oct. 20, 1836	Town Creek
Smoot	Ailsey	18	Edward Everett	Campbell, Bernard M.	Oct. 18, 1851	Balto.
Smoot	Alsey	5	Margaret Hugg	Dent, George	Nov. 30, 1844	Balto.
Smoot	Frederick	19	Helen A. Miller	Campbell, Bernard M.	Oct. 18, 1852	Balto.
Smoot	Gilbert	30	Helen A. Miller	Campbell, Bernard M.	Oct. 18, 1852	Balto.
Smoot	Leethe	20	Margaret Hugg	Dent, George	Nov. 30, 1844	Balto.
Smoot	Mathew	1	Margaret Hugg	Dent, George	Nov. 30, 1844	Balto.
Smoot	Nancy	17	Isaac Franklin	Kephart, George	Feb. 1, 1839	Balto.

Surname	First Name	Ship	Age	O/S	Date	Depart
Smoot	Rebecca	Isaac Franklin	13	Kephart, George	Feb. 1, 1839	Balto.
Smothers	Amanda	Victorine	10	Donovan, Joseph S.	May 14, 1845	Balto.
Smothers	Stephen	Isaac Franklin	25	Kephart, George	Feb. 1, 1839	Balto.
Smothers	Theophilus	Helen A. Miller	14	Campbell, Bernard M.	Oct. 18, 1852	Balto.
Smyler	George	Louisa	19	Campbell, Walter L.	July 3, 1848	Balto.
Smyler	Stephen	Louisa	21	Campbell, Walter L.	July 3, 1848	Balto.
Snapp	John	General Pinckney	22	Donovan, Joseph S.	Nov. 10, 1845	Balto.
Snell	Aaron	Solomon Saltus	16	Slatter, Hope Hull	Oct. 7, 1839	Balto.
Snell	Catherine	Solomon Saltus	9	Slatter, Hope Hull	Oct. 7, 1839	Balto.
Sniggens	Phillis	Gannclefft	16	Slatter, Hope Hull	Nov. 25, 1840	Balto.
Snoden	Basil	John C. Calhoun	20	Donovan, Joseph S.	Oct. 24, 1850	Balto.
Snowden	Caroline	Henry A. Barling	16	Donovan, Joseph S.	Feb. 24, 1851	Balto.
Snowden	Catherine	Burlington	22	Slatter, Hope Hull	Oct. 21, 1842	Balto.
Snowden	Charlotte	Victorine	18 mon.	Harke, William	March 9, 1844	Balto.
Snowden	Dennis	Pioneer	20	Stuart William R.	July 20, 1848	Balto.
Snowden	Diannah	Kirkwood	18	Slatter, Hope Hull	Jan. 4, 1845	Balto.
Snowden	Ellen	Gannclefft	14	Crosby, Elijah R.	Nov. 25, 1840	Balto.
Snowden	Emily	Peru	22	Slatter, Hope Hull	Nov. 16, 1842	Balto.
Snowden	Fanny	Eliza F. Mason	18	Donovan, Joseph S.	Nov. 13, 1851	Balto.
Snowden	Fanny	Superb	26	Slatter, Hope Hull	Nov. 1, 1843	Balto.
Snowden	George	Kirkwood	21	Donovan, Joseph S.	March 23, 1844	Balto.
Snowden	Grafton	Saldara	26	Harke, William	Feb. 27, 1844	Balto.
Snowden	Harriet	General Pinckney	17	Donovan, Joseph S.	Feb. 21, 1846	Balto.
Snowden	Harriet	Jefferson	3	Woolfolk, Austin	Dec. 24, 1827	Balto.
Snowden	Harriett	Burlington	1	Slatter Hope Hull	Oct. 21, 1842	Balto.
Snowden	Hazel	General Pinckney	28	Donovan, Joseph S.	Nov. 10, 1845	Balto.

Surname	First Name	Age	Ship	O/S	Date	Depart
Snowden	James	9	Tippecanoe	Slatter, Hope Hull	Jan. 17, 1842	Balto.
Snowden	John	32	Elizabeth	Campbell, Bernard M.	Jan. 2, 1850	Balto.
Snowden	John	25	Southerner	Donovan, Joseph S.	Jan. 21, 1850	Balto.
Snowden	Joshua	29	Lafayette	Woolfolk, Austin	Oct. 18, 1828	Balto.
Snowden	Kitty	2 mon.	Victorine	Harker, William	March 9, 1844	Balto.
Snowden	Kitty	26	Victorine	Harker, William	March 9, 1844	Balto.
Snowden	Louisa	18	Victorine	Slatter, Hope Hull	March 14, 1846	Balto.
Snowden	Loyd	18	Kirkwood	Donovan, Joseph S.	Oct. 26, 1847	Balto.
Snowden	Lucinda	17	Isaac Franklin	Kephart, George	Feb. 1, 1839	Balto.
Snowden	Nicholas	21	Kirkwood	Donovan, Joseph S.	Nov. 28, 1849	Balto.
Snowden	Peggy	10	Victorine	Harker, William	March 9, 1844	Balto.
Snowden	Peter	21	Kirkwood	Donovan, Joseph S.	Oct. 26, 1847	Balto.
Snowden	Phebe	14	Victorine	Rodbind, Ebenezer	Dec. 31, 1846	Balto.
Snowden	Raison	17	Burlington	Slatter, Hope Hull	Oct. 21, 1842	Balto.
Snowden	Richard	24	Ewarkee	Slatter, Hope Hull	March 4, 1841	Balto.
Snowden	Sabina	23	Jefferson	Woolfolk, Austin	Dec. 24, 1827	Balto.
Snowden	Stephen	18	Helen A. Miller	Campbell, Bernard M.	Oct. 18, 1852	Balto.
Snowden	William	21	Kirkwood	Donovan, Joseph S.	Sept. 28, 1846	Balto.
Snowden	William	18	Solomon Saltus	Slatter, Hope Hull	Oct. 7, 1839	Balto.
Snowden	William	19	Victorine	Donovan, Joseph S.	May 14, 1845	Balto.
Snutson	Frank	16	General Pinckney	Donovan, Joseph S.	Feb. 21, 1846	Balto.
Snyder	Philip	19	Kirkwood	Donovan, Joseph S.	Oct. 26, 1847	Balto.
Snyder	Pracilla	18	Kirkwood	Donovan, Joseph S.	Oct. 26, 1847	Balto.
Snyder	William	25	Kirkwood	Donovan, Joseph S.	Dec. 10, 1846	Balto.
Solsberry		19	Signet	Woolfolk, Austin	Nov. 12, 1831	Balto.
Somerfield	Edward	17	Elizabeth	Donovan, Joseph S.	Nov. 18, 1848	Balto.

Surname	First Name	Age	Ship	O/S	Date	Depart
Somers	Henson	21	St. Mary	Donovan, Joseph S.	Nov. 29, 1845	Balto.
Somers	Louisa	18	Kirkwood	Slatter, Hope Hull	Dec. 23, 1843	Balto.
Somerville	Ann	5	Tweed	Forbes, George	Oct. 20, 1836	Town Creek
Somerville	George H.	7	Tweed	Forbes, George	Oct. 20, 1836	Town Creek
Somerville	Jacob	32	Tweed	Forbes, George	Oct. 20, 1836	Town Creek
Somerville	James B.	6 mon.	Tweed	Forbes, George	Oct. 20, 1836	Town Creek
Somerville	Sally	32	Tweed	Forbes, George	Oct. 20, 1836	Town Creek
Sommerville	Abraham	26	Eliza	Slatter, Hope Hull	Oct. 9, 1840	Balto.
Sommerville	Ann	21	Topaz	Woolfolk, Austin	Apr. 20, 1829	Balto.
Soper	Jacob	26	Victorine	Slatter, Hope Hull	March 14, 1846	Balto.
Sorick	Aaron	26	Solomon Saltus	Slatter, Hope Hull	Oct. 7, 1839	Balto.
Sorick	Richard	13	Elizabeth	Donovan, Joseph S.	Nov. 18, 1848	Balto.
Sorrel	Robert	12	Southerner	Campbell, Bernard M.	Jan. 5, 1852	Balto.
Southern	Sarah	20	General Pinckney	Slatter, Hope Hull	Feb. 21, 1846	Balto.
Southron	John	7	Henry A. Barling	Marrictt, William H.	Oct. 28, 1848	Balto.
Spalding	Charlotte	17	Charles Henry	Burgess, F.B.F	Dec. 9, 1839	Balto.
Spalding	Maria	15	Victorine	Campbell, Bernard M.	Dec. 31, 1846	Balto.
Sparks	James	22	Victorine	Slatter Hope Hull	May 14, 1845	Balto.
Speaks	Catharine	22	Elizabeth	Donovan, Joseph S.	Oct. 6, 1849	Balto.
Spence	Draper	25	Kirkwood	Slatter, Hope Hull	Apr. 15, 1845	Balto.
Spence	Frances	19	Union	Rodbird, Ebenezer	Dec. 16, 1848	Balto.
Spence	Huldy	15	Southerner	Donovan, Joseph S.	Oct. 27, 1849	Balto.
Spence	Joshua	23	Kirkwood	Harker. William	March 23, 1844	Balto.
Spence	Wimbo	23	Union	Donovan, Joseph S.	May 13, 1848	Balto.
Spencer	Benjamin	30	Kirkwood	Slatter, Hope Hull	Apr. 4, 1846	Balto.
Spencer	Ervin	17	E.H.Chapin	Slatter, Hope Hull	Nov. 30, 1847	Balto.

Surname	First Name	Age	Ship	O/S	Date	Depart
Spencer	Henry	19	Scotia	Slatter, Hope Hull	Sept. 30, 1843	Balto.
Spencer	Jacob	26	Jefferson	Woolfolk, Joseph B.	Dec. 24, 1827	Balto.
Spencer	Jacob	21	Paoli	Slatter, Hope Hull	Sept. 9, 1845	Balto.
Spencer	James	40	Hyperion	Kelso, George Y.	Nov. 8, 1820	Balto.
Spencer	John	25	Elizabeth	Campbell, Bernard M.	Nov. 18, 1848	Balto.
Spencer	Lucinda	30	Kirkwood	Slatter, Hope Hull	Apr. 4, 1846	Balto.
Spencer	Maria	17	Catharine	Woolfolk, Austin	March 5, 1829	Balto.
Spencer	William	21	Scotia	Slatter, Hope Hull	Sept. 30, 1843	Balto.
Sphynx	Dulany	18	Helen A. Miller	Campbell, Bernard M.	Oct. 18, 1852	Balto.
Spiller	Agnes	35	Kirkwood	Slatter, Hope Hull	Apr. 4, 1846	Balto.
Spiller	Jane	15	Kirkwood	Slatter, Hope Hull	Apr. 4, 1846	Balto.
Spiller	Phebe	17	Kirkwood	Slatter, Hope Hull	Apr. 4, 1846	Balto.
Spiller	William	35	Louisa	Slatter, Hope Hull	Oct. 11, 1847	Balto.
Sprigg	Fanny	20	Margaret Hugg	Campbell, Bernard M.	Feb. 8, 1845	Balto.
Sprigg	Morris	18	Ewarkee	Purvis, James Franklin	March 4, 1841	Balto.
Sprigg	Nancy	35	Tippecanoe	Slatter, Hope Hull	Apr. 15, 1844	Balto.
Sprigg	Thomas	14	Margaret Hugg	Campbell, Bernard M.	Nov. 30, 1844	Balto.
Sprigg		infant	Margaret Hugg	Campbell, Bernard M.	Feb. 8, 1845	Balto.
Spriggs	Ambrose	19	Kirkwood	Donovan, Joseph S.	Sept. 28, 1846	Balto.
Spriggs	Dianah	20	Victorine	Rodbind, Ebenezer	Dec. 31, 1846	Balto.
Spriggs	George	15	Kirkwood	Williams, Thomas	Apr. 4, 1846	Balto.
Spriggs	Hester	18	Nathaniel Hooper	Donovan, Jospeh S.	Feb. 12, 1852	Balto.
Spriggs	Hester	9	Solomon Saltus	Slatter, Hope Hull	Oct. 7, 1839	Balto.
Spriggs	James	19	Henry A. Barling	Donovan, Joseph S.	Feb. 24, 1851	Balto.
Spriggs	Josias	8	Zoe	Williams, Thomas	Feb. 16, 1847	Balto.
Spriggs	Kitty	12	Home	Slatter, Hope Hull	March 22, 1845	Balto.

Surname	First Name	Age	Ship	O/S	Date	Depart
Spriggs	Martha	24	Union	Campbell, Bernard M.	Nov. 17, 1849	Balto.
Spriggs	Mary	infant	Nathaniel Hooper	Donovan, Jospeh S.	Feb. 12, 1852	Balto.
Spriggs	Robert	20	Home	Slatter, Hope Hull	March 22, 1845	Balto.
Spriggs	Sandra	19	Jefferson	Woolfolk, Austin	Dec. 24, 1827	Balto.
Spriggs	Sandy	9	Home	Slatter, Hope Hull	March 22, 1845	Balto.
Spriggs	Warner	21	Union	Sheckles, B.O.	Nov. 17, 1849	Balto.
Spriggs	William	19	Kirkwood	Campbell, Bernard M.	March 9, 1847	Balto.
Sprigs	Phillip	36	Kirkwood	Slatter, Hope Hull	Oct. 16, 1845	Balto.
Spurrier	Charlotte	20	Henry A. Barling	Campbell, Bernard M.	Feb. 24, 1851	Balto.
Stafford	Henny	1 mon.	Ann & Leah	Woolfolk, Austin	Nov.1, 1831	Balto.
Stafford	Hester	23	Ann & Leah	Woolfolk, Austin	Nov.1, 1831	Balto.
Stafford	Martha	2	Ann & Leah	Woolfolk, Austin	Nov.1, 1831	Balto.
Stanley	Charles	24	Brunswick	Woolfolk, Austin	Oct. 11, 1831	Balto.
Stanley	Dinah	8	Henry Clay	Woolfolk, Austin	Dec. 4, 1828	Balto.
Stanley	Harriet	10	Henry Clay	Woolfolk, Austin	Dec. 4, 1828	Balto.
Stanley	Rachel	33	Henry Clay	Woolfolk, Austin	Dec. 4, 1828	Balto.
Stanley	Robert	22	Margaret Hugg	Donovan, Joseph S.	Feb. 8, 1845	Balto.
Stansburg	Clement	30	Susan Miller	Woolfolk, Austin	Oct. 25, 1822	Balto.
Stansbury	Asbury	22	Superb	Slatter, Hope Hull	Nov. 1, 1843	Balto.
Stansbury	Charity	17	Lafayette	Woolfolk, Austin	Oct. 18, 1828	Balto.
Stansbury	Elijah	30	Lady Monroe	Woolfolk, Austin	March 25, 1825	Balto.
Stansbury	Jane	20	Lafayette	Woolfolk, Austin	Oct. 18, 1828	Balto.
Stansbury	Mingo	25	Lapwing	Woolfolk, Austin	Feb. 15, 1827	Balto.
Stansbury	Thomas	2	Lafayette	Woolfolk, Austin	Oct. 18, 1828	Balto.
Stanton	Eliza	30	Victorine	Slatter, Hope Hull	Sept. 12, 1846	Balto.
Stanwell	Ann	11	E.H.Chapin	Donovan, Joseph S.	Dec. 2, 1847	Balto.

Surname	First Name	Age	Ship	O/S	Date	Depart
Stanwell	Charlot	9	E.H.Chapin	Donovan, Joseph S.	Dec. 2, 1847	Balto.
Starling	Thomas	30	Russell	Slatter, Hope Hull	March 1, 1839	Balto.
Stawns	Rebecca	15	E.H.Chapin	Donovan, Joseph S.	Dec. 2, 1847	Balto.
Staylor	Annett	9	Ewarkee	Slatter, Hope Hull	March 4, 1841	Balto.
Steel	Thomas	28	Victorine	Rodbind, Ebenezer	Dec. 31, 1846	Balto.
Steele	Benjamin	19	Kirkwood	Slatter, Hope Hull	Jan. 4, 1845	Balto.
Stephen	Jacob	33	Helen A. Miller	Millard, J.M.	Oct. 18, 1852	Balto.
Stephen	Louisa	12	Victorine	Rodbind, Ebenezer	May 14, 1845	Balto.
Stephens	Ally	16	Isaac Franklin	Kephart, George	Sept. 28, 1838	Balto.
Stephens	George	23	Kirkwood	Donovan, Joseph S.	Oct. 26, 1847	Balto.
Stephens	Isaac	22	Eliza F.Mason	Donovan, Joseph S.	Nov. 13, 1851	Balto.
Stephens	Jacob	23	Eliza F.Mason	Donovan, Joseph S.	Nov. 13, 1851	Balto.
Stephenson	Stephen	40	Scotia	Slatter, Hope Hull	Sept. 30, 1843	Balto.
Stepheson	Daniel	28	Irad Ferry	Slatter, Hope Hull	Dec. 9, 1842	Balto.
Stephison	Milly	18	Paoli	Slatter, Hope Hull	Sept. 9, 1845	Balto.
Stepman	Lemon	23	Kirkwood	Campbell, Bernard M.	Oct. 14, 1848	Balto.
Stepney	Benjamin	infant	Elizabeth	Donovan, Joseph S.	Jan. 2, 1850	Balto.
Stepney	Elizabeth	13	Margaret Hugg	Slatter, Hope Hull	Feb. 8, 1845	Balto.
Stepney	Ellen	24	Elizabeth	Donovan, Joseph S.	Jan. 2, 1850	Balto.
Stepney	James	28	Narragansett	Campbell, Bernard M.	Nov. 27, 1850	Balto.
Sterling	Elijah	16	Southerner	Donovan, Joseph S.	Jan. 21, 1850	Balto.
Steuart	Lydia	14	Elizabeth	Campbell, Bernard M.	Nov. 18, 1848	Balto.
Stevens	Harriet	53	Harriet	Carroll, Charles	Dec. 7, 1836	Balto.
Stevenson	Eliza	15	Henry A. Barling	Campbell, Bernard M.	Apr. 19, 1849	Balto.
Stevenson	George	24	Colonel Howard	Harker, William	Nov. 21, 1844	Balto.
Stevenson	Jacob	17	Hermitage	Slatter, Hope Hull	Oct. 28, 1846	Balto.

Surname	First Name	Age	Ship	O/S	Date	Depart
Stevenson	John	10	Tippecanoe	Staples, Joshua	Jan. 17, 1842	Balto.
Stevenson	Mary	18	Tippecanoe	Staples, Joshua	Jan. 17, 1842	Balto.
Steward	Charles	26	Victorine	Slatter, Hope Hull	May 14, 1845	Balto.
Steward	Charles	18	Zoe	Williams, Thomas	Feb. 16, 1847	Balto.
Steward	David	22	Kirkwood	Slatter, Hope Hull	Oct. 16, 1845	Balto.
Steward	Dolly	30	Scotia	Slatter, Hope Hull	Sept. 30, 1843	Balto.
Steward	Elizabeth	19	Hermitage	Slatter, Hope Hull	Oct. 28, 1846	Balto.
Steward	Evelina	4	Nancy W. Stevens	Rodbird, Ebenezer	Feb. 18, 1845	Balto.
Steward	Frances	17	Kirkwood	Donovan, Joseph S.	Dec. 10, 1846	Balto.
Steward	Fredrick	18	Kirkwood	Williams, Thomas	Apr. 4, 1846	Balto.
Steward	George	12	Superb	Slatter, Hope Hull	Nov. 1, 1843	Balto.
Steward	Grace	23	Nancy W. Stevens	Rodbird, Ebenezer	Feb. 18, 1845	Balto.
Steward	Harriett	21	Home	Rodbird, Ebenezer	March 22, 1845	Balto.
Steward	Kitty	30	Victorine	Slatter, Hope Hull	March 9, 1844	Balto.
Steward	Levenia	19	Hermitage	Slatter, Hope Hull	Oct. 28, 1846	Balto.
Steward	Mary	8	Victorine	Slatter, Hope Hull	May 14, 1845	Balto.
Steward	Pius	14	Victorine	Rodbird, Ebenezer	Dec. 31, 1846	Balto.
Steward	Rachael	20	Louisa	Campbell, Bernard M.	Nov. 5, 1849	Balto.
Steward	Samuel	20	Southerner	Donovan, Joseph S.	Oct. 27, 1849	Balto.
Steward	William	24	Southerner	Donovan, Joseph S.	Oct. 27, 1849	Balto.
Stewart	Alexander	12	Kirkwood	Donovan, Joseph S.	Apr. 15, 1845	Balto.
Stewart	Ann	30	Waverly	Campbell, Bernard M.	Apr. 3, 1851	Balto.
Stewart	Anna	35	Eliza	Slatter, Hope Hull	Oct. 9, 1840	Balto.
Stewart	Caroline	1	States	Woolfolk, Austin	Nov. 21, 1827	Balto.
Stewart	Charles	21	Kirkwood	Donovan, Joseph S.	Sept. 28, 1846	Balto.
Stewart	Elanora	3	Waverly	Campbell, Bernard M.	Apr. 3, 1851	Balto.

Surname	First Name	Age	Ship	O/S	Date	Depart
Stewart	Henson	18	General Pinckney	Donovan, Joseph S.	Nov. 10, 1845	Balto.
Stewart	Hester	25	Architect	Purvis, James Franklin	Feb. 3, 1841	Balto.
Stewart	Jacob	23	Tippecanoe	Slatter, Hope Hull	Jan. 17, 1842	Balto.
Stewart	James	30	John S. Gittings	Campbell, Bernard M.	Nov. 20, 1852	Balto.
Stewart	James	30	Unicorn	Crook, Walter	Oct. 23, 1820	Balto.
Stewart	John	18	Kirkwood	Slatter, Hope Hull	Oct. 16, 1845	Balto.
Stewart	John	22	Mars	Woolfolk, Austin	Oct. 30, 1824	Balto.
Stewart	John	18	Superb	Slatter, Hope Hull	Nov. 1, 1843	Balto.
Stewart	Margaret	26	Victorine	Slatter, Hope Hull	Sept. 12, 1846	Balto.
Stewart	Maryann	18	Architect	Slatter, Hope Hull	Feb. 16, 1843	Balto.
Stewart	Nancy	18	Hibernia	Woolfolk, Austin	Dec. 5, 1826	Balto.
Stewart	Rachel	16	Eliza	Slatter, Hope Hull	Oct. 9, 1840	Balto.
Stewart	Rachel	20	States	Woolfolk, Austin	Nov. 21, 1827	Balto.
Stewart	Rezin	11	Kirkwood	Donovan, Joseph S.	Oct. 26, 1847	Balto.
Stewart	Susan	13	Architect	Slatter, Hope Hull	Feb. 16, 1843	Balto.
Stewart	York	25	Architect	Slatter, Hope Hull	Feb. 16, 1843	Balto.
Stewart		3	Architect	Purvis, James Franklin	Feb. 3, 1841	Balto.
Stewart		28	Signet	Woolfolk, Austin	Nov. 12, 1831	Balto.
Stockett	Mary	18	Paoli	Slatter, Hope Hull	Sept. 9, 1845	Balto.
Stoderd	Henry	21	Kirkwood	Slatter, Hope Hull	Oct. 16, 1845	Balto.
Stokes	Airy	18	Nathaniel Hooper	Campbell, Bernard M.	Feb. 12, 1852	Balto.
Stoner	Amelia Ann	16	Victorine	Donovan, Joseph S.	May 22, 1844	Balto.
Stoops	Rachel	9	Lady Monroe	Woolfolk, Austin	March 25, 1825	Balto.
Strange	Reuben	28	John S. Gittings	Campbell, Bernard M.	Nov. 20, 1852	Balto.
Stranger	Washington	20	Catharine	Donovan, Joseph S.	Jan. 18, 1845	Balto.
Street	Mary Jane	24	Eliza	Slatter, Hope Hull	Oct. 9, 1840	Balto.

Surname	First Name	Age	Ship	O/S	Date	Depart
Streets	Robert	17	Victorine	Rodbind, Ebenezer	March 1, 1845	Balto.
Strother	Frank	4	Helen A. Miller	Campbell, Bernard M.	Oct. 18, 1852	Balto.
Strother	Martha	18 mon.	Helen A. Miller	Campbell, Bernard M.	Oct. 18, 1852	Balto.
Strother	Phil	27	Helen A. Miller	Campbell, Bernard M.	Oct. 18, 1852	Balto.
Strother	Polly	23	Helen A. Miller	Campbell, Bernard M.	Oct. 18, 1852	Balto.
Stuart	Hannah	17	Clio	Anderson, David	March 20, 1819	Balto.
Stuart	Henry	22	Gazelle	Staples, Joseph	Feb.28, 1842	Balto.
Stuart	Huldah	12	Isaac Franklin	Kephart, George	Feb. 1, 1839	Balto.
Stuart	James	23	Victorine	Harker, William	March 14, 1846	Balto.
Stuart	Rachael	25	Victorine	Campbell, Bernard M.	March 14, 1846	Balto.
Stuart	Richard	20	Gazelle	Staples, Joseph	Feb.28, 1842	Balto.
Stubs	Thomas	45	P.R. Hazeltine	Campbell, Bernard M.	Nov. 15, 1856	Balto.
Sturgis	Eliza	19	Osprey	Tilletson, S.R.	Nov. 11, 1847	Balto.
Sturgis	Henry	17	John C. Calhoun	Donovan, Joseph S.	Oct. 24, 1850	Balto.
Sudler	Stephen	20	Algerine	Woolfolk, Joseph B.	Jan. 6, 1826	Balto.
Suison	Jacob	19	Brunswick	Woolfolk, Austin	Oct. 11, 1831	Balto.
Sulavan	Washington	20	Superb	Slatte, Hope Hull	Nov. 1, 1843	Balto.
Sullivan	Henry	15	Union	Donovan, Joseph S.	May 13, 1848	Balto.
Sumerhill	Elias	22	Narragansett	Donovan, Joseph S.	Nov. 27, 1850	Balto.
Summer	Natt	37	Elizabeth	Campbell, Bernard M.	Nov. 18, 1848	Balto.
Summers	Frances	18	Eliza F.Mason	Donovan, Joseph S.	Nov. 13, 1851	Balto.
Summers	Henry	22	States	Woolfolk, Austin	Apr. 14, 1828	Balto.
Summersell	James	22	States	Woolfolk, Austin	Apr. 14, 1828	Balto.
Susan	Rebecca	13	Tangier	Campbell, Bernard M.	Nov. 26, 1853	Balto.
Sutton	Anna	2	Waverly	Harris, Alexander	Apr. 3, 1851	Balto.
Sutton	Charles	7	Waverly	Harris, Alexander	Apr. 3, 1851	Balto.

Surname	First Name	Age	Ship	O/S	Date	Depart
Sutton	Elizebeth	18	Kirkwood	Slatter, Hope Hull	Jan. 14, 1846	Balto.
Sutton	Emory	5	Waverly	Harris, Alexander	Apr. 3, 1851	Balto.
Sutton	George	9	Kirkwood	Donovan, Joseph S.	Jan. 4, 1845	Balto.
Sutton	Harriet	28	Waverly	Harris, Alexander	Apr. 3, 1851	Balto.
Sutton	Hessey	14	Kirkwood	Donovan, Joseph S.	Jan. 14, 1846	Balto.
Sutton	Jack	10	Victorine	Donovan, Joseph S.	Sept. 29, 1845	Balto.
Sutton	Jacob	21	Kirkwood	Slatter, Hope Hull	Jan. 14, 1846	Balto.
Sutton	John	16	States	Woolfolk, Austin	Apr. 14, 1828	Balto.
Sutton	Lewis	30	Waverly	Harris, Alexander	Apr. 3, 1851	Balto.
Sutton		infant	Waverly	Harris, Alexander	Apr. 3, 1851	Balto.
Swain	Joe	22	Tippecanoe	Staples, Joshua	Jan. 17, 1842	Balto.
Swain	Kelley	13	Lafayette	Woolfolk, Richard	Oct. 18, 1828	Balto.
Swan	Charlott	20	Helen A. Miller	Campbell, Bernard M.	Oct. 18, 1852	Balto.
Swan	Delia	26	Kirkwood	Slatter, Henry F.	Dec. 10, 1846	Balto.
Swan	Harriett	infant	Kirkwood	Slatter, Henry F.	Dec. 10, 1846	Balto.
Sways	Pinkney	20	Kirkwood	Slatter, Hope Hull	Oct. 16, 1845	Balto.
Sweep	Charles	16	Jasper	Woolfolk, Austin	Apr. 7, 1827	Balto.
Sweeting	Dave	18	Victorine	Rodbind, Ebenezer	Dec. 31, 1846	Balto.
Sweetly	Phillis	14	Lafayette	Woolfolk, Austin	Oct. 18, 1828	Balto.
Syder	Eliza Jane	18	Delawarian	Campbell, Bernard M.	Dec. 1, 1848	Balto.
Sylvester	Alexander	infant	Salvadora	Slatter, Hope Hull	Sept. 28, 1846	Balto.
Sylvester	Jane	19	Salvadora	Slatter, Hope Hull	Sept. 28, 1846	Balto.
Sytus	Henry	30	Union	Donovan, Joseph S.	May 13, 1848	Balto.
Tabbs	Frances	15	Jefferson	Woolfolk, Austin	Dec. 24, 1827	Balto.
Tacket	Onpey	10 mon.	Jasper	Woolfolk, Austin	Apr. 7, 1827	Balto.
Tacket	Priscilla	17	Jasper	Woolfolk, Austin	Apr. 7, 1827	Balto.

Surname	First Name	Age	Ship	O/S	Date	Depart
Tailor	Anthony	17	Kirkwood	Slatte., Hope Hull	Jan. 14, 1846	Balto.
Tailor	Henry	24	Union	Slatte., Hope Hull	July 26, 1847	Balto.
Tailor	Kitty	18	Union	Rodbind, Ebenezer	Nov. 17, 1849	Balto.
Tailor	Mary Ann	20	Kirkwood	Slatter, Hope Hull	Apr. 15, 1845	Balto.
Tailor	Nathan	25	Victorine	Slatter, Hope Hull	Dec. 17, 1845	Balto.
Tailor	Rachel	18	Lady Richmond	Woolfolk, Austin	Apr. 30, 1827	Balto.
Talbot	Robert	24	Supero	Slatter, Hope Hull	Nov. 1, 1843	Balto.
Talbott	Elisha	18	Architect	Purvis, James Franklin	Feb. 4, 1841	Balto.
Talbott	Henry	25	Victorine	Slatter, Hope Hull	March 9, 1844	Balto.
Talbott	Lotty	24	Architect	Donovan, Joseph S.	Apr. 25, 1846	Balto.
Talbott	Michail	18	Kirkwood	Slatter Hope Hull	Oct. 16, 1845	Balto.
Taney	Lloyd	30	Seaman	Slatter Hope Hull	Dec. 19, 1838	Balto.
Tanner	John	19	Victorne	Donovan, Joseph S.	March 14, 1846	Balto.
Tarlton	Merritt	19	Louisa	Campbell, Bernard M.	March 31, 1849	Balto.
Tasco	John	30	Elizabeth	Donovan, Joseph S.	March 21, 1850	Balto.
Tasco	Lucretia	30	Elizabeth	Donovan, Joseph S.	March 21, 1850	Balto.
Taskell	Easter	16	Kirkwood	Donovan, Joseph S.	Sept. 28, 1846	Balto.
Tate	William	26	Henry A. Barling	Campbell, Bernard M.	Feb. 24, 1851	Balto.
Taylor	Ann	15	Jasper	Woolfolk, Austin	Apr. 7, 1827	Balto.
Taylor	Ann	18	Union	Campbell, Bernard M.	Dec. 16, 1848	Balto.
Taylor	Celey	25	Margaret Hugg	Slatter, Hope Hull	Feb. 8, 1845	Balto.
Taylor	Charles	19	Kirkwcod	Donovan, Joseph S.	Nov. 28, 1849	Balto.
Taylor	Edward	14	General Pinckney	Donovan, Joseph S.	Feb. 21, 1846	Balto.
Taylor	Elizabeth	20	Delawarian	Campbell, Bernard M.	Dec. 1, 1848	Balto.
Taylor	Ephraim	18	Victoria	Rodbind, Ebenezer	March 1, 1845	Balto.
Taylor	Frank	28	Pioneer	Stuart, William R.	July 20, 1848	Balto.

Surname	First Name	Age	Ship	O/S	Date	Depart
Taylor	George	23	Tippecanoe	Purvis, James Franklin	Jan. 17, 1842	Balto.
Taylor	Hannah	24	Margaret Forbs	Slatter, Hope Hull	Nov. 28, 1838	Balto.
Taylor	Harrison	28	General Pinckney	Slatter, Hope Hull	Jan. 19, 1847	Balto.
Taylor	Hester	16	Union	Donovan, Joseph S.	May 13, 1848	Balto.
Taylor	Hiram	20	Kirkwood	Donovan, Joseph S.	Oct. 14, 1848	Balto.
Taylor	Jane	11	Tippecanoe	Harker, William	Dec. 16, 1840	Balto.
Taylor	John	18	Elizabeth	Campbell, Bernard M.	Nov. 18, 1848	Balto.
Taylor	Loyd	25	Catharine	Woolfolk, Austin	March 3. 1829	Balto.
Taylor	Lucy	17	Union	Williams, Thomas	Oct. 9, 1848	Balto.
Taylor	Mary	17	General Pinckney	Donovan, Joseph S.	Feb. 21, 1846	Balto.
Taylor	Matilda	16	Catharine	Donovan, Joseph S.	Jan. 18, 1845	Balto.
Taylor	Nelson	24	Elizabeth	Campbell, Bernard M.	Jan. 2, 1850	Balto.
Taylor	Nelson	30	Union	Williams, Thomas	Oct. 9, 1848	Balto.
Taylor	Phebe	22	Tippecanoe	Purvis, James Franklin	Apr. 1, 1841	Balto.
Taylor	Rachel	22	Lafayette	Woolfolk, Austin	Oct. 18, 1828	Balto.
Taylor	Willis	25	John S. Gittings	Campbell, Bernard M.	Nov. 20, 1852	Balto.
Taylor		infant	Delawarian	Campbell, Bernard M.	Dec. 1, 1848	Balto.
Taylor		25	Lafayette	Woolfolk, Richard	Oct. 18, 1828	Balto.
Taylor		1 mon.	Margaret Forbs	Slatter, Hope Hull	Nov. 28, 1838	Balto.
Taylor		12 mon.	Tippecanoe	Purvis, James Franklin	Apr. 1, 1841	Balto.
Teackle	Levin	27	Jefferson	Woolfolk, Austin	Dec. 24, 1827	Balto.
Teaker	William	23	Lafayette	Woolfolk, Austin	Oct. 18, 1828	Balto.
Teeb	William	36	Intelligence	De Mapiere, Victor	Apr. 30, 1821	Balto.
Tellotson	Perry	22	Scotia	Harker, William	Sept. 30, 1843	Balto.
Tembels	Aaron	25	Kirkwood	Donovan, Joseph S.	Oct. 14, 1848	Balto.
Temple	Charlotte	18	Architect	Donovan, Joseph S.	Apr. 25, 1846	Balto.

Surname	First Name	Age	Ship	O/S	Date	Depart
Tennant	Margaret	19	Kirkwood	Donovan, Joseph S.	Nov. 28, 1849	Balto.
Teppett	Jerry	26	Kirkwood	Slatter, Hope Hull	Oct. 16, 1845	Balto.
Terrill	Charles	15	Helen A. Miller	Campbell, Bernard M.	Oct. 18, 1852	Balto.
Terry	Louisa	30	Phoenix	Denning, John N.	March 27, 1847	Balto.
Terry	Mariah	7	Phoenix	Denning, John N.	March 27, 1847	Balto.
Terry	Stephen	4	Phoenix	Denning, John N.	March 27, 1847	Balto.
Thadden	Heny	26	Kirkwood	Slatter, Hope Hull	Dec. 23, 1843	Balto.
Thomas	Adelaide	18	Jane Henderson	Campbell, Bernard M.	Nov. 1, 1852	Balto.
Thomas	Airis	23	Lapwing	Woolfolk, Austin	Feb. 15, 1827	Balto.
Thomas	Amy	22	Jefferson	Woolfolk, Austin	Dec. 24, 1827	Balto.
Thomas	Andrew	38	General Pinckney	Williams, Thomas	Jan. 19, 1847	Balto.
Thomas	Andrew	15	Henry A. Barling	Campbell, Bernard M.	Apr. 19, 1849	Balto.
Thomas	Ann	17	Billow	Woolfolk, Joseph B.	Feb. 23, 1828	Balto.
Thomas	Ann	17	Billow	Woolfolk, Joseph B.	Feb. 23, 1828	Balto.
Thomas	Ann	25	Elizabeth	Campbell, Bernard M.	Nov. 18, 1848	Balto.
Thomas	Ann	30	Kirkwood	Slatter, Hope Hull	Jan. 4, 1845	Balto.
Thomas	Ann	25	Louise	Donovan, Joseph S.	Oct. 9, 1847	Balto.
Thomas	Ann	17	Superb	Slatter, Hope Hull	Nov. 1, 1843	Balto.
Thomas	Ann	25	Tweed	Tucker, J.B.	Oct. 20, 1836	Town Creek
Thomas	Ann Maria	21	Solomon Saltus	Slatter, Hope Hull	Oct. 7, 1839	Balto.
Thomas	Anser	26	Algerine	Woolfolk, Joseph B.	Jan. 6, 1826	Balto.
Thomas	Benjamin	23	Edward Everett	Campbell, Bernard M.	Oct. 18, 1851	Balto.
Thomas	Betsey	20	Jefferson	Woolfolk, Joseph B.	Dec. 24, 1827	Balto.
Thomas	Betsey	9	Lafayette	Woolfolk, Austin	Oct. 18, 1828	Balto.
Thomas	Catharine	8 mon.	Jefferson	Woolfolk, Joseph B.	Dec. 24, 1827	Balto.
Thomas	Catherine	8	St. Mary	Donovan, Joseph S.	Nov. 29, 1845	Balto.

Surname	First Name	Age	Ship	O/S	Date	Depart
Thomas	Charles	8	Eliza	Slatter, Hope Hull	Oct. 9, 1840	Balto.
Thomas	Charles	16	St. Mary	Donovan, Joseph S.	Nov. 29, 1845	Balto.
Thomas	Charlott	32	Isaac Franklin	Slatter, Hope Hull	Sept. 28, 1838	Balto.
Thomas	Charlotte	14	Henry A. Barling	Campbell, Bernard M.	Feb. 24, 1851	Balto.
Thomas	Clem	25	Jefferson	Woolfolk, Austin	Dec. 24, 1827	Balto.
Thomas	Comella Ann	18	Zoe	Slatter, Hope Hull	Feb. 16, 1847	Balto.
Thomas	Daniel	17	States	Woolfolk, Austin	Apr. 14, 1828	Balto.
Thomas	Edger	11	Victorine	Donovan, Joseph S.	Sept. 29, 1845	Balto.
Thomas	Edward	35	Victorine	Slatter, Hope Hull	March 14, 1846	Balto.
Thomas	Elexius	25	Union	Campbell, Bernard M.	March 17, 1849	Balto.
Thomas	Elizabeth	20	General Pinckney	Campbell, Bernard M.	Jan. 19, 1847	Balto.
Thomas	Elizabeth	22	Victorine	Slatter, Hope Hull	March 1, 1845	Balto.
Thomas	Ellen	19	Hibernia	Woolfolk, Austin	Dec. 5, 1826	Balto.
Thomas	Ellen	13	Kirkwood	Campbell, Bernard M.	Dec. 10, 1846	Balto.
Thomas	Ellen	20	Kirkwood	Campbell, Bernard M.	March 23, 1844	Balto.
Thomas	Ellen	23	Virginia	Woolfolk, Austin	March 31, 1828	Balto.
Thomas	Euphamia	25	St. Mary	Donovan, Joseph S.	Nov. 29, 1845	Balto.
Thomas	Evan	20	Scotia	Slatter, Hope Hull	Sept. 30, 1843	Balto.
Thomas	Fanny	16	Helen A. Miller	Campbell, Bernard M.	Oct. 18, 1852	Balto.
Thomas	Francis	infant	Louisa	Donovan, Joseph S.	Oct. 9, 1847	Balto.
Thomas	Fred	18	Eliza	Slatter, Hope Hull	Oct. 9, 1840	Balto.
Thomas	George	23	Hermitage	Williams, Thomas	Oct. 28, 1846	Balto.
Thomas	George	14	Kirkwood	Campbell, Bernard M.	March 9, 1847	Balto.
Thomas	Gilbert	25	Helen A. Miller	Campbell, Bernard M.	Oct. 18, 1852	Balto.
Thomas	Hannah	18	Kirkwood	Slatter, Hope Hull	Apr. 15, 1845	Balto.
Thomas	Hariet A.	14	Union	Sheckles, B.O.	Nov. 17, 1849	Balto.

Surname	First Name	Age	Ship	O/S	Date	Depart
Thomas	Harriet	19	Seaman	Slatter, Shadrack	March 25, 1839	Balto.
Thomas	Harriett	16	General Pinckney	Donovan, Joseph S.	Nov. 10, 1845	Balto.
Thomas	Henry	26	Eliza	Slatter, Hope Hull	Oct. 9, 1840	Balto.
Thomas	Henry	18	Henry A. Barling	Campbell, Bernard M.	Apr. 19, 1849	Balto.
Thomas	Henry	14	Jasper	Woolfolk, Austin	Apr. 7, 1827	Balto.
Thomas	Henry	22	Seaman	Slatter, Shadrack	March 25, 1839	Balto.
Thomas	Henry	2	Tweed	Tucker, J.B.	Oct. 20, 1836	Town Creek
Thomas	Henson	14	Victorine	Donovan, Joseph S.	Sept. 29, 1845	Balto.
Thomas	Jacob M.	27	Uncas	Slatter, Hope Hull	Jan. 10, 1838	Balto.
Thomas	James	3 mon.	Isaac Franklin	Slatter, Hope Hull	Sept. 28, 1838	Balto.
Thomas	James	7 mon.	Jefferson	Woolfolk, Austin	Dec. 24, 1827	Balto.
Thomas	James	24	Superb	Slatter, Hope Hull	Nov. 1, 1843	Balto.
Thomas	James	30	Tweed	Tucker, J.B.	Oct. 20, 1836	Town Creek
Thomas	James Jr.	4	Tweed	Tucker, J.B.	Oct. 20, 1836	Town Creek
Thomas	Jane	30	Seaman	Slatter, Hope Hull	Dec. 19, 1838	Balto.
Thomas	Jim	17	Billow	Woolfolk, Joseph B.	Feb. 23, 1828	Balto.
Thomas	John	21	Billow	Woolfolk, Austin	Feb. 23, 1828	Balto.
Thomas	John	23	Burlington	Slatter, Hope Hull	Oct. 21, 1842	Balto.
Thomas	John	23	Charles	Campbell, Bernard M.	Apr. 23, 1851	Balto.
Thomas	John	20	Eliza F Mason	Donovan, Joseph S.	Nov. 13, 1851	Balto.
Thomas	John	23	Helen A. Miller	Campbell, Bernard M.	Oct. 18, 1852	Balto.
Thomas	John	20	Jane Henderson	Campbell, Bernard M.	Nov. 1, 1852	Balto.
Thomas	John	15	Kirkwood	Donovan, Joseph S.	Oct. 14, 1848	Balto.
Thomas	John	23	Kirkwood	Rodbird, Ebenezer	Oct. 26, 1847	Balto.
Thomas	John	7	Louisa	Donovan, Joseph S.	Oct. 9, 1847	Balto.
Thomas	John	20	Solomon Saltus	Slatter, Hope Hull	Oct. 7, 1839	Balto.

Surname	First Name	Age	Ship	O/S	Date	Depart
Thomas	John	18	Union	Slatter, Hope Hull	July 26, 1847	Balto.
Thomas	John	24	Victorine	Donovan, Joseph S.	Sept. 29, 1845	Balto.
Thomas	Judah	50	Tweed	Forbes, George	Oct. 20, 1836	Town Creek
Thomas	Kitty	7	Lafayette	Woolfolk, Richard	Oct. 18, 1828	Balto.
Thomas	Leathy	16	Seaman	Slatter, Hope Hull	Dec. 19, 1838	Balto.
Thomas	Lewis	10	Henry A. Barling	Donovan, Joseph S.	Dec. 18, 1851	Balto.
Thomas	Lidia	16	Lady Richmond	Woolfolk, Austin	Apr. 30, 1827	Balto.
Thomas	Lucy Ann	30	Tippecanoe	Slatter, Hope Hull	Dec. 16, 1840	Balto.
Thomas	Lydia	25	Lafayette	Woolfolk, Austin	Oct. 18, 1828	Balto.
Thomas	Maria	20	Hibernia	Woolfolk, Austin	Dec. 5, 1826	Balto.
Thomas	Mariah	16	Union	Campbell, Bernard M.	March 17, 1849	Balto.
Thomas	Martha	8	Kirkwood	Donovan, Joseph S.	Oct. 14, 1848	Balto.
Thomas	Martha	18	Nathaniel Hooper	Campbell, Bernard M.	Feb. 12, 1852	Balto.
Thomas	Mary	18	Union	Rodbind, Ebenezer	Dec. 16, 1848	Balto.
Thomas	Matilda	19	Southerner	Donovan, Joseph S.	Oct. 27, 1849	Balto.
Thomas	Matilda	16	Union	Sheckles, B.O.	Nov. 17, 1849	Balto.
Thomas	Melinda	20	Zoe	Campbell, Bernard M.	Feb. 16, 1847	Balto.
Thomas	Moses	21	Elizabeth	Donovan, Joseph S.	Nov. 18, 1848	Balto.
Thomas	Moses	19	Victorine	Slatter, Hope Hull	Dec. 17, 1845	Balto.
Thomas	Otho	20	Elizabeth	Donovan, Joseph S.	Nov. 18, 1848	Balto.
Thomas	Patrick	21	Victorine	Slatter, Hope Hull	March 9, 1844	Balto.
Thomas	Peter	19	Louisa	Donovan, Joseph S.	Oct. 9, 1847	Balto.
Thomas	Priscilla	16	Isaac Franklin	Slatter, Hope Hull	Sept. 28, 1838	Balto.
Thomas	Priscilla	18	Kirkwood	Harker, William	March 23, 1844	Balto.
Thomas	Rachel	18	E.H.Chapin	Donovan, Joseph S.	Dec. 2, 1847	Balto.
Thomas	Rachel	16	Hope & Hannah	Woolfolk, Austin	March 11, 1829	Balto.

Surname	First Name	Age	Ship	O/S	Date	Depart
Thomas	Ralph	51	Tweed	Forbes, George	Oct. 20, 1836	Town Creek
Thomas	Ralph	18	Union	Campbell, Bernard M.	March 17, 1849	Balto.
Thomas	Randolph	14	Seaman	Slatter, Hope Hull	Dec. 19, 1838	Balto.
Thomas	Rodo	18	Billow	Woolfolk, Joseph B.	Feb. 23, 1828	Balto.
Thomas	Rosetta	20	Eliza	Slatter, Hope Hull	Oct. 9, 1840	Balto.
Thomas	Ross	21	Victorine	Slatter, Hope Hull	March 1, 1845	Balto.
Thomas	Ruth	16	Waverly	Campbell, Bernard M.	Apr. 3, 1851	Balto.
Thomas	Sally Ann	16	Victorine	Donovan, Joseph S.	May 22, 1844	Balto.
Thomas	Sam	29	Lady Monroe	Woolfolk, Austin	March 25, 1825	Balto.
Thomas	Sam	16	States	Woolfolk, Austin	Apr. 14, 1828	Balto.
Thomas	Samuel	20	Elizabeth	Donovan, Joseph S.	March 21, 1850	Balto.
Thomas	Samuel	17	Justina	Donovan, Joseph S.	Dec. 2, 1852	Balto.
Thomas	Sarah	22	Narragansett	Campbell, Bernard M.	Nov. 27, 1850	Balto.
Thomas	Solomon	30	Victorine	Slatter, Hope Hull	March 14, 1846	Balto.
Thomas	Sophia	10	Kirkwood	Donovan, Joseph S.	Oct. 14, 1848	Balto.
Thomas	Stephen	16	Kirkwood	Campbell, Bernard M.	Dec. 10, 1846	Balto.
Thomas	Susan	7	States	Woolfolk, Austin	Apr. 14, 1828	Balto.
Thomas	Sylva	2	Narragansett	Campbell, Bernard M.	Nov. 27, 1850	Balto.
Thomas	Thomas	22	Paoli	Slatter, Hope Hull	Sept. 9, 1845	Balto.
Thomas	Uriah	15	Kirkwood	Donovan, Joseph S.	March 9, 1847	Balto.
Thomas	Westley	13	Seaman	Slatter, Hope Hull	Dec. 19, 1838	Balto.
Thomas	William	13	General Pinckney	Donovan, Joseph S.	Feb. 21, 1846	Balto.
Thomas	William	18	General Pinckney	Donovan, Joseph S.	Nov. 10, 1845	Balto.
Thomas	William	14	Henry A. Barling	Donovan, Joseph S.	Dec. 18, 1851	Balto.
Thomas	William	4	Isaac Franklin	Slatter, Hope Hull	Sept. 28, 1838	Balto.
Thomas	William	13	Kirkwood	Donovan, Joseph S.	Oct. 14, 1848	Balto.

Surname	First Name	Age	Ship	O/S	Date	Depart
Thomas	William	10	States	Woolfolk, Austin	Apr. 14, 1828	Balto.
Thomas		infant	Elizabeth	Campbell, Bernard M.	Nov. 18, 1848	Balto.
Thomas		infant	Seaman	Slatter, Hope Hull	Dec. 19, 1838	Balto.
Thomas		infant	Solomon Saltus	Slatter, Hope Hull	Oct. 7, 1839	Balto.
Thompson	Andrew	13	General Pinckney	Slatter, Hope Hull	Feb. 21, 1846	Balto.
Thompson	Benjamin	21	Pioneer	Slatter, Hope Hull	Sept. 15, 1847	Balto.
Thompson	Caroline	18	Isaac Franklin	Slatter, Hope Hull	Sept. 28, 1838	Balto.
Thompson	Chance	23	Pioneer	Slatter, Hope Hull	Sept. 15, 1847	Balto.
Thompson	Eliza	12	Lafayette	Harker, William	March 25, 1843	Balto.
Thompson	Eliza	15	Tippecanoe	Biscoe, James	March 27, 1841	Balto.
Thompson	Elizabeth	28	Hermitage	Slatter, Hope Hull	Oct. 28, 1846	Balto.
Thompson	Ellen	17	Henry A. Barling	Campbell, Bernard M.	Feb. 24, 1851	Balto.
Thompson	Emory	23	Lafayette	Woolfolk, Austin	Oct. 18, 1828	Balto.
Thompson	Evaline	12	Victorine	Slatter, Hope Hull	Dec. 17, 1845	Balto.
Thompson	Ezekiel	26	Topaz	Woolfolk, Austin	Apr. 20, 1829	Balto.
Thompson	French	22	Louisa	Campbell, Bernard M.	May 18, 1846	Balto.
Thompson	George	15	Brunswick	Woolfolk, Austin	Oct. 11, 1831	Balto.
Thompson	Hannah	5	Zoe	Slatter, Hope Hull	Feb. 16, 1847	Balto.
Thompson	Harriet	22	States	Woolfolk, Austin	Apr. 14, 1828	Balto.
Thompson	Harriett	infant	Victorine	Slatter, Hope Hull	March 14, 1846	Balto.
Thompson	Henry	23	Kirkwood	Campbell, Bernard M.	Oct. 14, 1848	Balto.
Thompson	Henry	12	Topaz	Woolfolk, Austin	Apr. 20, 1829	Balto.
Thompson	Hester Ann	21	Kirkwood	Slatter, Hope Hull	Jan. 4, 1845	Balto.
Thompson	James	26	Elizabeth	Donovan, Joseph S.	Nov. 18, 1848	Balto.
Thompson	James	23	Kirkwood	Donovan, Joseph S.	Dec. 23, 1843	Balto.
Thompson	James	24	Topaz	Woolfolk, Austin	Apr. 20, 1829	Balto.

Surname	First Name	Age	Ship	O/S	Date	Depart
Thompson	Jane	18	Tippecanoe	Wilson, William N.	May 4, 1842	Balto.
Thompson	John	22	Isaac Franklin	Slatter, Hope Hull	Sept. 28, 1838	Balto.
Thompson	John	21	Lady Monroe	Woolfolk, Austin	March 25, 1825	Balto.
Thompson	Joseph	20	Kirkwood	Donovan, Joseph S.	Oct. 26, 1847	Balto.
Thompson	Joseph	12	Tippecanoe	Biscoe, James	March 27, 1841	Balto.
Thompson	Joseph	21	Union	Slatter, Hope Hull	July 26, 1847	Balto.
Thompson	Josephine	19	Pioneer	Slatter, Hope Hull	Sept. 15, 1847	Balto.
Thompson	July ?	17	Brunswick	Woolfolk, Austin	Oct. 11, 1831	Balto.
Thompson	Leah	14	Salvadora	Slatter, Hope Hull	Sept. 28, 1846	Balto.
Thompson	Levin	22	Louisa	Slatter, Hope Hull	Oct. 11, 1847	Balto.
Thompson	Louisa	12	Liberator	Woolfolk, Austin	Nov. 12, 1828	Balto.
Thompson	Maranda	20	Victorine	Slatter, Hope Hull	March 14, 1846	Balto.
Thompson	Maria	12	Salvadora	Slatter, Hope Hull	Sept. 28, 1846	Balto.
Thompson	Mary	18	Elizabeth	Donovan, Joseph S.	Jan. 2, 1850	Balto.
Thompson	Mary	7	Lafayette	Harker, William	March 25, 1843	Balto.
Thompson	Milly	19	Brunswick	Woolfolk, Austin	Oct. 11, 1831	Balto.
Thompson	Nat	20	Porpoise	Purvis, James Franklin	Dec. 11, 1841	Balto.
Thompson	Perry	18	Justina	Donovan, Joseph S.	Dec. 2, 1852	Balto.
Thompson	Phil	14	States	Woolfolk, Austin	March 8, 1826	Balto.
Thompson	Priscilla	20	Sarah Bridge	Campbell, Bernard M.	Feb. 8, 1851	Balto.
Thompson	Rachel	24	Zoe	Slatter, Hope Hull	Feb. 16, 1847	Balto.
Thompson	Richard	infant	Zoe	Slatter, Hope Hull	Feb. 16, 1847	Balto.
Thompson	Robert	19	Southerner	Campbell, Bernard M.	Oct. 27, 1849	Balto.
Thompson	Sandy	45	Isaac Franklin	Slatter, Hope Hull	Sept. 28, 1838	Balto.
Thompson	Sarah	34	Kirkwood	Donovan, Joseph S.	Oct. 26, 1847	Balto.
Thompson	Sarah	19	St. Mary	Williams, Thomas	Nov. 29, 1845	Balto.

Surname	First Name	Age	Ship	O/S	Date	Depart
Thompson	Sarah Jane	17	Kirkwood	Slatter, Hope Hull	Jan. 4, 1845	Balto.
Thompson	Solomon	16	Glasgow	Slatter, Hope Hull	Oct. 11, 1838	Balto.
Thompson	Thomas	25	Scotia	Slatter, Hope Hull	Sept. 30, 1843	Balto.
Thompson	Washington	2	States	Woolfolk, Austin	Apr. 14, 1828	Balto.
Thompson	William	19	Kirkwood	Campbell, Bernard M.	Nov. 28, 1849	Balto.
Thorn	Hannah	16	Victorine	Slatter, Hope Hull	Dec. 17, 1845	Balto.
Thorne	Frederick	30	Tippecanoe	Harker, William	Apr. 15, 1844	Balto.
Thorne	Hannah	17	Phoenix	Slatter, Hope Hull	March 27, 1847	Balto.
Thornley	Stephen	25	Tippecanoe	Slatter, Hope Hull	Jan. 17, 1842	Balto.
Thornly	William	23	Southerner	Donovan, Joseph S.	Oct. 27, 1849	Balto.
Thornton	Ann	15	John S. Gittings	Campbell, Bernard M.	Nov. 20, 1852	Balto.
Thornton	George	20	Mary Broughton	Campbell, Bernard M.	Nov. 18, 1851	Balto.
Thornton	Henry	26	Kirkwood	Slatter, Hope Hull	Oct. 16, 1845	Balto.
Thornton	James	infant	Kirkwood	Slatter, Henry F.	Dec. 10, 1846	Balto.
Thornton	John	22	States	Woolfolk, Austin	Nov. 21, 1827	Balto.
Thornton	Lot	18	Southerner	Donovan, Joseph S.	Oct. 27, 1849	Balto.
Thornton	Mahala	16	Helen A. Miller	Campbell, Bernard M.	Oct. 18, 1852	Balto.
Thornton	Maria	19	Isaac Franklin	Slatter, Hope Hull	Sept. 28, 1838	Balto.
Thornton	Reson	27	Victorine	Slatter, Hope Hull	March 1, 1845	Balto.
Thornton	Squire	22	Kirkwood	Donovan, Joseph S.	Oct. 26, 1847	Balto.
Throdon	Andrew	16	Kirkwood	Campbell, Bernard M.	Oct. 14, 1848	Balto.
Tibbs	Jacob	17	Kirkwood	Donovan, Joseph S.	Dec. 10, 1846	Balto.
Tibett	Richard	22	Kirkwood	Rodbind, Ebenezer	Oct. 26, 1847	Balto.
Tikes	Hinson	20	Kirkwood	Donovan, Joseph S.	March 9, 1847	Balto.
Tilden	George	21	Union	Donovan, Joseph S.	Dec. 16, 1848	Balto.
Tildin	Tom	28	Lady Monroe	Woolfolk, Austin	March 25, 1825	Balto.

Surname	First Name	Age	Ship	O/S	Date	Depart
Tilghman	Charles	20	States	Woolfolk, Joseph B.	Nov. 21, 1827	Balto.
Tilghman	Emeline	19	Louise	Donovan, Joseph S.	Oct. 9, 1847	Balto.
Tilghman	Emly	20	Elizabeth	Donovan, Joseph S.	Jan. 2, 1850	Balto.
Tilghman	Frank	29	Eliza F.Mason	Donovan, Joseph S.	Nov. 13, 1851	Balto.
Tilghman	James	19	Solomon Saltus	Slatter, Hope Hull	Oct. 7, 1839	Balto.
Tilghman	James	38	Tweed	Sothoron, William H.	Oct. 20, 1836	Town Creek
Tilghman	Lucy	20	States	Woolfolk, Austin	Apr. 14, 1828	Balto.
Tilghman	Maria	20	E.H.Chapin	Slatter, Hope Hull	Nov. 30, 1847	Balto.
Tilghman	Ned	25	Hibernia	Woolfolk, Austin	Dec. 5, 1826	Balto.
Tilghman	Peggy	45	Tweed	Sothoron, William H.	Oct. 20, 1836	Town Creek
Tilghman	Pere	33	Burlington	Slatter Hope Hull	Oct. 21, 1842	Balto.
Tilghman	Rachel	28	Elizabeth	Donovan, Joseph S.	Jan. 2, 1850	Balto.
Tilghman	William	15	Hibernia	Woolfolk, Austin	Dec. 5, 1826	Balto.
Tilghman	William H.	9	Topaz	Woolfolk, Austin	Apr. 20, 1829	Balto.
Tiller	Sam	23	Julia	Woolfolk, Austin	Jan. 8, 1829	Balto.
Tillison	Chester	21	Helen A. Miller	Camptell, Bernard M.	Oct. 18, 1852	Balto.
Tillman	Maria	16	Ganniclefft	Slatter Hope Hull	Nov. 25, 1840	Balto.
Tillotson	Rosetta	11	Hibernia	Woolfolk, Austin	Dec. 5, 1826	Balto.
Tilman	Hariet	16	Lafayette	Woolfolk, Austin	Oct. 18, 1828	Balto.
Tilman	Harriett	19	Harriet	Woolfolk, Austin	March 23, 1822	Balto.
Tilman	Henny	14	Lady Monroe	Woolfolk, Austin	March 25, 1825	Balto.
Tilman	Minty	14	Margaret Forbs	Slatter, Hope Hull	Nov. 28, 1838	Balto.
Tilman	Rachel	19	Brunswick	Woolfolk, Austin	Oct. 11, 1831	Balto.
Tilman	Samuel	22	Bostorian	Slatter, Hope Hull	Jan. 18, 1841	Balto.
Tilman	Thomas	22	Lafayette	Woolfolk, Austin	Oct. 18, 1828	Balto.
Tilman	Tom	27	Lafayette	Woolfolk, Austin	Oct. 18, 1828	Balto.

Surname	First Name	Age	Ship	O/S	Date	Depart
Tilman	Wahey	12	Jefferson	Woolfolk, Austin	Dec. 24, 1827	Balto.
Timmons	Eliza Jane	14	Kirkwood	Crow, William	March 23, 1844	Balto.
Tingle	Charlotte	25	Victorine	Slatter, Hope Hull	May 14, 1845	Balto.
Tingle	Heildy	18	Victorine	Slatter, Hope Hull	May 14, 1845	Balto.
Tingle	James	4	Victorine	Slatter, Hope Hull	May 14, 1845	Balto.
Tingle	Rosetta	16	Victorine	Slatter, Hope Hull	May 14, 1845	Balto.
Tingle	Susan	4	Victorine	Slatter, Hope Hull	May 14, 1845	Balto.
Tinson	Deal	22	Victorine	Donovan, Joseph S.	Sept. 29, 1845	Balto.
Tinson	Henry		Victorine	Donovan, Joseph S.	Sept. 29, 1845	Balto.
Tinson	James		Victorine	Donovan, Joseph S.	Sept. 29, 1845	Balto.
Tinson	Minty	24	Victorine	Donovan, Joseph S.	Sept. 29, 1845	Balto.
Tison	Nancy	18	Liberator	Woolfolk, Austin	Nov. 12, 1828	Balto.
Tison	Sarah	15	Liberator	Woolfolk, Austin	Nov. 12, 1828	Balto.
Tobias	James	8	Liberator	Woolfolk, Austin	Nov. 12, 1828	Balto.
Tocas	Charles	20	Southerner	Campbell, Bernard M.	Jan. 5, 1852	Balto.
Todd	Jane	17	Burlington	Slatter, Hope Hull	Oct. 21, 1842	Balto.
Todd	Leah	15	Henry A. Barling	Campbell, Bernard M.	Dec. 18, 1851	Balto.
Tolbert	Francis	18	Southerner	Campbell, Bernard M.	Jan. 5, 1852	Balto.
Tolbert	Joshua	13	Brunswick	Woolfolk, Austin	Oct. 11, 1831	Balto.
Tolson	Daniel	35	Nathaniel Hooper	Campbell, Bernard M.	Feb. 12, 1852	Balto.
Tolson	Joseph	15	W.H.D.C.Wright	Slatter, Hope Hull	Nov. 7, 1847	Balto.
Tomes	Rebeca	22	Kirkwood	Donovan, Joseph S.	Dec. 10, 1846	Balto.
Tomey	George	20	Victorine	Harker, William	March 14, 1846	Balto.
Tomlin	Richard	12	Lafayette	Woolfolk, Richard	Oct. 18, 1828	Balto.
Tomson	Ally	19	Lafayette	Woolfolk, Austin	Oct. 18, 1828	Balto.
Tomson	Henny	18	Lafayette	Woolfolk, Austin	Oct. 18, 1828	Balto.

Surname	First Name	Age	Ship	O/S	Date	Depart
Tomson	Mary Jane	1	Lafayette	Woolfolk, Austin	Oct. 18, 1828	Balto.
Toney	Rachel	18	Kirkwood	Slatter Hope Hull	Apr. 15, 1845	Balto.
Tonizor	Thomas	24	Billow	Woolfolk, Joseph B.	Feb. 23, 1828	Balto.
Toogood	Henry	18	Irad Ferry	Purvis James Franklin	Feb. 5, 1842	Balto.
Toogood	William	23	Lafayette	Woolfolk, Austin	Oct. 18, 1828	Balto.
Torneyhill	Washington	18	Tippecanoe	Slatter Hope Hull	Jan. 17, 1842	Balto.
Town	Frances	20	Kirkwood	Slatter Hope Hull	Jan. 4, 1845	Balto.
Townes	Lexington	22	Union	Donovan, Joseph S.	Dec. 16, 1848	Balto.
Towns	Jefferson	20	Victorine	Slatter Hope Hull	May 14, 1845	Balto.
Towson	Abraham	18	Irad Ferry	Purvis James Franklin	Oct. 30, 1841	Balto.
Towson	William	17	Billow	Woolfolk, Joseph B.	Feb. 23, 1828	Balto.
Toy	Elley	21	Kirkwood	Rodbind, Ebenezer	Oct. 26, 1847	Balto.
Toy	Frederick	19	Southerner	Rodbind, Ebenezer	Jan. 21, 1850	Balto.
Toy	Henry	28	Abbott Lord	Campbell, Bernard M.	April 28, 1852	Balto.
Toyer	Henry	18	W.H.D.C.Wright	Slatter Hope Hull	Nov. 7, 1847	Balto.
Toyer	Jacob	50	Isaac Franklin	Slatter Hope Hull	Sept. 28, 1838	Balto.
Toyer	Rodney	43	Tweed	Sothoron, William H.	Oct. 20, 1836	Town Creek
Toyer	Rosanah	40	Isaac Franklin	Slatter Hope Hull	Sept. 28, 1838	Balto.
Toyer	William	18	Tweed	Sothoron, William H.	Oct. 20, 1836	Town Creek
Tracy	Albert	21	Kirkwood	Slatter. Hope Hull	Dec. 23, 1843	Balto.
Travers	Charles	24	Sarah Bridge	Campbell, Bernard M.	Feb. 8, 1851	Balto.
Travers	Levin	20	Sarah Bridge	Campbell, Bernard M.	Feb. 8, 1851	Balto.
Travers	Mary	12	Architect	Crow, William	Feb. 3, 1841	Balto.
Travers	Susan	25	Louisa	Campbell, Bernard M.	Nov. 5, 1849	Balto.
Travers	Walter	26	Mary Broughton	Campbell, Bernard M.	Nov. 18, 1851	Balto.
Travers		5	Catharine	Donovan, Joseph S.	Jan. 18, 1845	Balto.

Surname	First Name	Age	Ship	O/S	Date	Depart
Traverse	Lucinda	27	Tippecanoe	Slatter, Hope Hull	Jan. 17, 1842	Balto.
Traverse		infant	Tippecanoe	Slatter, Hope Hull	Jan. 17, 1842	Balto.
Travis	Henny	35	Kirkwood	Campbell, Bernard M.	Apr. 15, 1845	Balto.
Travis	Samuel	30	Tippecanoe	Slatter, Hope Hull	Dec. 16, 1840	Balto.
Trent	Phillip	20	Kirkwood	Donovan, Joseph S.	Dec. 10, 1846	Balto.
Trickley	Pressly	20	Charles	Campbell, Bernard M.	Apr. 23, 1851	Balto.
Trimble	George	10 mon.	Lafayette	Woolfolk, Austin	Oct. 18, 1828	Balto.
Trimble	Mary	20	Lafayette	Woolfolk, Austin	Oct. 18, 1828	Balto.
Trip	William	20	Lafayette	Woolfolk, Austin	Oct. 18, 1828	Balto.
Tripp	Debby	20	Catharine	Woolfolk, Austin	March 3. 1829	Balto.
Trippe	Emily	16	Louisa	Hooper, James	May 18, 1846	Balto.
Trippe	Jacob	26	Orbit	Woolfolk, Joseph B.	Apr. 16, 1825	Balto.
Trippe	James	20	Orbit	Woolfolk, Joseph B.	Apr. 16, 1825	Balto.
Troy	John	26	Kirkwood	Slatter, Hope Hull	Oct. 16, 1845	Balto.
Truett	James	16	Margaret Hugg	Harker, William	Nov. 30, 1844	Balto.
Trusty	Beckey	9	States	Woolfolk, Austin	Apr. 14, 1828	Balto.
Trusty	Caroline	12	States	Woolfolk, Austin	Apr. 14, 1828	Balto.
Trusty	Charity	21	States	Woolfolk, Austin	Apr. 14, 1828	Balto.
Trusty	Emily	10	Victorine	Slatter, Hope Hull	Sept. 12, 1846	Balto.
Trusty	Lewis	4	Victorine	Slatter, Hope Hull	Sept. 12, 1846	Balto.
Trusty	Maria	19	States	Woolfolk, Austin	Apr. 14, 1828	Balto.
Trusty	Rebecca	30	Victorine	Slatter, Hope Hull	Sept. 12, 1846	Balto.
Tucker	Simon	20	Abbott Lord	Campbell, Bernard M.	April 28, 1852	Balto.
Turley	Hannah	16	E.H.Chapin	Donovan, Joseph S.	Dec. 2, 1847	Balto.
Turley	Israel	21	Victorine	Donovan, Joseph S.	May 22, 1844	Balto.
Turms	Lucy	17	Kirkwood	Slatter, Hope Hull	Dec. 23, 1843	Balto.

Surname	First Name	Age	Ship	O/S	Date	Depart
Turner	Abraam	20	Mary Broughton	Campbell, Bernard M.	Nov. 18, 1851	Balto.
Turner	Abraham	24	Catharine	Donovan, Joseph S.	Jan. 18, 1845	Balto.
Turner	Albert	20	E.H.Chapin	Slatter, Hope Hull	Nov. 30, 1847	Balto.
Turner	Charles	22	Hermitage	Williams, Thomas	Oct. 28, 1846	Balto.
Turner	Charles	21	Kirkwood	Slatter, Hope Hull	Apr. 15, 1845	Balto.
Turner	Delia	14	Porpoise	Purvis, James Franklin	Dec. 11, 1841	Balto.
Turner	Enos	26	E.H.Chapin	Slatter, Hope Hull	Nov. 30, 1847	Balto.
Turner	Francis	22	Victorine	Harker, William	March 9, 1844	Balto.
Turner	Gabe	22	E.H.Chapin	Slatter, Hope Hull	Nov. 30, 1847	Balto.
Turner	Hariett	18	Kirkwood	Donovan, Joseph S.	Nov. 28, 1849	Balto.
Turner	Henry	13	Hibernia	Woolfolk, Austin	Dec. 5, 1826	Balto.
Turner	Isaac	21	Union	Donovan, Joseph S.	May 13, 1848	Balto.
Turner	James	24	Helen A. Miller	Campbell, Bernard M.	Oct. 18, 1852	Balto.
Turner	James	25	Union	Williams, Thomas	Oct. 9, 1848	Balto.
Turner	Jobe	20	Kirkwood	Campbell, Bernard M.	Nov. 28, 1849	Balto.
Turner	Joe	39	Helen A. Miller	Nally, William	Oct. 18, 1852	Balto.
Turner	Joshua	16	Supert	Slatter, Hope Hull	Nov. 1, 1843	Balto.
Turner	Kitty	17	Catharine	Slatter, Hope Hull	Jan. 24, 1843	Balto.
Turner	Lucinda	15	Victorine	Slatter, Hope Hull	Dec. 17, 1845	Balto.
Turner	Margaret	15	E.H.Chapin	Donovan, Joseph S.	Dec. 2, 1847	Balto.
Turner	Mary	18	E.H.Chapin	Slatter, Hope Hull	Nov. 30, 1847	Balto.
Turner	Mary E.	16	Kirkwood	Rodbird, Ebenezer	Oct. 26, 1847	Balto.
Turner	Moses	21	Eliza F.Mason	Donovan, Joseph S.	Nov. 13, 1851	Balto.
Turner	Paul	19	Victorine	Donovan, Joseph S.	March 1, 1845	Balto.
Turner	Perry	22	Lapwing	Woolfolk, Samuel M.	Feb. 15, 1827	Balto.
Turner	Pheba	22	Kirkwood	Donovan, Joseph S.	Oct. 14, 1848	Balto.

Surname	First Name	Age	Ship	O/S	Date	Depart
Turner	Polly	35	E.H.Chapin	Slatter, Hope Hull	Nov. 30, 1847	Balto.
Turner	Richard	19	Southerner	Donovan, Joseph S.	Oct. 27, 1849	Balto.
Turner	Sam	24	Union	Donovan, Joseph S.	May 13, 1848	Balto.
Turner	Samuel	26	Victorine	Donovan, Joseph S.	May 22, 1844	Balto.
Turner	Sarah	16	Kirkwood	Donovan, Joseph S.	Dec. 10, 1846	Balto.
Turner	Simon	9	Hibernia	Woolfolk, Austin	Dec. 5, 1826	Balto.
Turner	Stephen	30	Helen McLeod	Neale, James F.	March 28, 1846	Balto.
Turner	Stephen	8	Victorine	Harker, William	March 9, 1844	Balto.
Turner	Susan		Architect	Rodbind, Ebenezer	Feb. 12, 1840	Balto.
Turner	Thomas	22	Burlington	Slatter, Hope Hull	Oct. 21, 1842	Balto.
Turner	Thomas	18	Kirkwood	Slatter, Hope Hull	Oct. 16, 1845	Balto.
Turner	Timothy	23	Kirkwood	Donovan, Joseph S.	Oct. 26, 1847	Balto.
Turner	Truman	17	John C. Calhoun	Donovan, Joseph S.	Oct. 24, 1850	Balto.
Turner	William	26	Home	Campbell, Bernard M.	March 22, 1845	Balto.
Turner	Williuam	13	W.H.D.C.Wright	Slatter, Hope Hull	Nov. 7, 1847	Balto.
Turpin	Patience	25	General Pinckney	Slatter, Hope Hull	Jan. 19, 1847	Balto.
Tusclon	Henry	26	Algerine	Woolfolk, Austin	March 25, 1826	Balto.
Twine	Daniel	18	General Pinckney	Slatter, Hope Hull	Feb. 21, 1846	Balto.
Twine	Daniel	20	General Pinckney	Slatter, Hope Hull	Feb. 21, 1846	Balto.
Twist	Ellener	12	Kirkwood	Slatter, Hope Hull	Oct. 16, 1845	Balto.
Tyler	Harriet	24	Lady Monroe	Woolfolk, Austin	March 25, 1825	Balto.
Tyler	Harriet	10	St. Mary	Donovan, Joseph S.	Nov. 29, 1845	Balto.
Tyler	Hester	19	General Pinckney	Slatter, Hope Hull	Jan. 19, 1847	Balto.
Tyler	Mary	14	Brunswick	Woolfolk, Austin	Oct. 11, 1831	Balto.
Tyler	Philip	12	Irad Ferry	Wilson, J.W.	May 6, 1839	Balto.
Tyler	Phoeba	20	Elizabeth	Campbell, Bernard M.	Jan. 2, 1850	Balto.

Surname	First Name	Age	Ship	O/S	Date	Depart
Tyler	Plato	21	Peru	Slatter, Hope Hull	Nov. 16, 1842	Balto.
Tyler	Price	15	Lafayette	Woolfolk, Richard	Oct. 18, 1828	Balto.
Tyler	Reason	24	Kirkwood	Slatter, Hope Hull	Jan. 4, 1845	Balto.
Tyler	Robert	16	Kirkwood	Williams, Thomas	Apr. 4, 1846	Balto.
Tyler	Sinderilla	17	Brunswick	Woolfolk, Austin	Oct. 11, 1831	Balto.
Tylor	Samuel	22	Narragansett	Donovan, Joseph S.	Nov. 27, 1850	Balto.
Tyson	Elisha	20	Eros	Woolfolk, Austin	Jan. 28, 1824	Balto.
Tyson	James	9 mon.	Ann & Leah	Woolfolk, Austin	Nov. 1, 1831	Balto.
Umphries	Ellen	20	Architect	Purvis, James Franklin	Feb. 3, 1841	Balto.
Umphries		infant	Architect	Purvis, James Franklin	Feb. 3, 1841	Balto.
Upsher	Mary	20	Margaret Forbs	Slatter, Hope Hull	Nov. 28, 1838	Balto.
Upshur	Elizabeth	19	Elizabeth	Donovan, Joseph S.	Nov. 18, 1848	Balto.
Valentine	Amos	31	Phoenix	Slatter, Hope Hull	March 27, 1847	Balto.
Vance	William	3	Sarah Bridge	Campbell, Bernard M.	Feb. 8, 1851	Balto.
Vandike	George	19	Margaret Hugg	Campbell, Bernard M.	Nov. 30, 1844	Balto.
Vanhorn	Dennis	20	E.H.Chapin	Slatter, Hope Hull	Nov. 30, 1847	Balto.
Vanhorn	Peter	24	E.H.Chapin	Slatter, Hope Hull	Nov. 30, 1847	Balto.
Vanhorn	Robert	30	Uncas	Slatter, Hope Hull	Jan. 10, 1838	Balto.
Vannech	Alfred	33	Home	Hollins, George V.	March 19, 1845	Balto.
Vascan	Mary	19	Eliza	Slatter, Hope Hull	Oct. 9, 1840	Balto.
Vaughn	Henry	31	Victorine	Slatter, Henry F.	Dec. 31, 1846	Balto.
Veane	Kitty	19	General Pinckney	Slatter, Hope Hull	Jan. 19, 1847	Balto.
Vina	Betsey	18	Kirkwood	Donovan, Joseph S.	Jan. 4, 1845	Balto.
Vina	Emily	infant	Kirkwood	Donovan, Joseph S.	Jan. 4, 1845	Balto.
Vina	Mary	3	Kirkwood	Donovan, Joseph S.	Jan. 4, 1845	Balto.
Vincent	Barbary	21	Seaman	Slatter, Hope Hull	March 25, 1839	Balto.

Surname	First Name	Age	Ship	O/S	Date	Depart
Vines	Ruthy	15	Kirkwood	Donovan, Joseph S.	Dec. 10, 1846	Balto.
Vinson	Sally A.	17	Union	Williams, Thomas	Oct. 9, 1848	Balto.
Vogle	John	19	General Pinckney	Slatter, Hope Hull	Jan. 19, 1847	Balto.
Volter	Frank	20	Union	Rodbind, Ebenezer	Dec. 16, 1848	Balto.
Voss	Alfred	22	Narragansett	Donovan, Joseph S.	Nov. 27, 1850	Balto.
Waddy	Mariah	16	States	Woolfolk, Austin	Apr. 14, 1828	Balto.
Wade	George	20	Catharine	Donovan, Joseph S.	Jan. 18, 1845	Balto.
Wahles	Henry	23	Victorine	Slatter, Henry F.	Dec. 31, 1846	Balto.
Wails	William	22	Uncas	Slatter, Hope Hull	Jan. 10, 1838	Balto.
Walen	Joseph	11	Russell	Slatter, Hope Hull	March 1, 1839	Balto.
Wales	Maleese	24	Kirkwood	Donovan, Joseph S.	Nov. 28, 1849	Balto.
Walker	Ann	18	Kirkwood	Donovan, Joseph S.	Oct. 26, 1847	Balto.
Walker	Caroline	20	Margaret Hugg	Poindexter, T.B.	Nov. 30, 1844	Balto.
Walker	Daniel	24	Kirkwood	Donovan, Joseph S.	Oct. 14, 1848	Balto.
Walker	Elizabeth	17	Helen A. Miller	Campbell, Bernard M.	Oct. 18, 1852	Balto.
Walker	Emeline	17	Pioneer	Slatter, Hope Hull	Sept. 15, 1847	Balto.
Walker	George	infant	Kirkwood	Donovan, Joseph S.	Oct. 26, 1847	Balto.
Walker	Hannah	17	Helen A. Miller	Campbell, Bernard M.	Oct. 18, 1852	Balto.
Walker	Henry	18	Kirkwood	Campbell, Bernard M.	Dec. 10, 1846	Balto.
Walker	Isaac	19	Irad Ferry	Purvis, James Franklin	Oct. 30, 1841	Balto.
Walker	Jinney	18	Margaret Hugg	Poindexter, T.B.	Nov. 30, 1844	Balto.
Walker	Lewis	14	Victorine	Rodbind, Ebenezer	May 14, 1845	Balto.
Walker	Peter	20	Charles	Campbell, Bernard M.	Apr. 23, 1851	Balto.
Walker	Richard	18	Southerner	Donovan, Joseph S.	Oct. 27, 1849	Balto.
Walker	Samuel	28	Pioneer	Stuart, William R.	July 20, 1848	Balto.
Walker	William	20	Charles	Donovan, Joseph S.	Apr. 23, 1851	Balto.

Surname	First Name	Age	Ship	O/S	Date	Depart
Walker	William	20	Helen A. Miller	Campbell, Bernard M.	Oct. 18, 1852	Balto.
Wallace	Dennis	21	Liberator	Woolfolk, Austin	Nov. 12, 1828	Balto.
Wallace	Dennis	35	Tweed	Tucker J.B.	Oct. 20, 1836	Town Creek
Wallace	Elizabeth	24	Union	Campbell, Bernard M.	March 17, 1849	Balto.
Wallace	Ezekiel	34	Harriet	Carroll Charles	Dec. 7, 1836	Balto.
Wallace	Fanny	22	Superb	Slatter, Hope Hull	Nov. 1, 1843	Balto.
Wallace	Henrietta	14	Southerner	Donovan, Jospeh S.	Jan. 5, 1852	Balto.
Wallace	Henry	18	General Pinckney	Campbell, Bernard M.	Jan. 19, 1847	Balto.
Wallace	Henry	25	Seaman	Slatter, Shadrack	March 25, 1839	Balto.
Wallace	Isaac	32	Victorine	Slatter, Hope Hull	March 1, 1845	Balto.
Wallace	James	28	General Pinckney	Slatter, Hope Hull	Jan. 19, 1847	Balto.
Wallace	Jefferson	16	Kirkwood	Slatter, Hope Hull	Oct. 16, 1845	Balto.
Wallace	John	20	Zoe	Williams, Thomas	Feb. 16, 1847	Balto.
Wallace	Lucy	3	Superb	Slatter, Hope Hull	Nov. 1, 1843	Balto.
Wallace	Mason	13	Kirkwood	Donovan, Joseph S.	Oct. 26, 1847	Balto.
Wallace	Solomon	28	Paoli	Slatter, Hope Hull	Sept. 9, 1845	Balto.
Waller	Arthur	18	Kirkwood	Donovan, Joseph S.	Oct. 26, 1847	Balto.
Walley	Charity	19	Catharine	Slatter, Hope Hull	Jan. 24, 1843	Balto.
Walley	Perry	25	Ewarkee	Slatter, Hope Hull	March 4, 1841	Balto.
Wallice	Andrew	18	Union	Rodbind, Ebenezer	Nov. 17, 1849	Balto.
Wallis	Cassy	20	Brunswick	Woolfolk, Austin	Oct. 11, 1831	Balto.
Wallis	David	14	Lady Monroe	Woolfolk, Austin	March 25, 1825	Balto.
Wallis	Eliza	12	States	Woolfolk, Austin	Nov. 21, 1827	Balto.
Wallis	Hester	14	Irad Ferry	Slatter, Hope Hull	Dec. 9, 1842	Balto.
Wallis	Rachel	25	Intelligence	Miles, David M.	Apr. 4, 1823	Balto.
Walls	Margaret	18	Union	Williams, Thomas	Oct. 9, 1848	Balto.

Surname	First Name	Age	Ship	O/S	Date	Depart
Walter	Isaac	17	Kirkwood	Donovan, Joseph S.	Apr. 4, 1846	Balto.
Walters	Caroline	18	Tippecanoe	Purvis, James Franklin	Jan. 17, 1842	Balto.
Walters	Rosetta	16	Lady Monroe	Woolfolk, Austin	March 25, 1825	Balto.
Walters	William	23	Victorine	Donovan, Joseph S.	Sept. 29, 1845	Balto.
Walthan	Nicholas	24	Jasper	Woolfolk, Austin	Apr. 7, 1827	Balto.
Walton	John	24	Solomon Saltus	Slatter, Hope Hull	Oct. 7, 1839	Balto.
Walton	Peter	13	Brunswick	Woolfolk, Austin	Oct. 11, 1831	Balto.
Wan	Jacob	21	Alfred	Woolfolk, Austin	May 7, 1825	Balto.
Wands	David	22	Lafayette	Woolfolk, Austin	Oct. 18, 1828	Balto.
Wansburry	Sophia	22	Kirkwood	Slatter, Hope Hull	Apr. 15, 1845	Balto.
Waples	John	22	Tippecanoe	Slatter, Hope Hull	Jan. 17, 1842	Balto.
Ward	Harriet	9	Union	Donovan, Joseph S.	Dec. 16, 1848	Balto.
Ward	Hugh	25	Zoe	Slatter, Hope Hull	Feb. 16, 1847	Balto.
Ward	Isaac	20	Southerner	Donovan, Joseph S.	Oct. 27, 1849	Balto.
Ward	Loney	23	Catharine	Woolfolk, Austin	March 3, 1829	Balto.
Ward	Shadrick	25	Hibernia	Woolfolk, Austin	Dec. 5, 1826	Balto.
Warden	Elizabeth	24	Scotia	Slatter, Hope Hull	Sept. 30, 1843	Balto.
Warden		33	Kirkwood	Donovan, Joseph S.	Dec. 10, 1846	Balto.
Ware	Bill	28	Isaac Franklin	Kephart, George	Feb. 1, 1839	Balto.
Ware	Caroline	18	Elizabeth	Campbell, Bernard M.	March 21, 1850	Balto.
Ware	Clem	19	Elizabeth	Donovan, Joseph S.	Nov. 18, 1848	Balto.
Ware	Eliza	14	Zoe	Williams, Thomas	Feb. 16, 1847	Balto.
Ware	Horace	28	Southerner	Rodbind, Ebenezer	Oct. 27, 1849	Balto.
Ware	Samuel	20	Southerner	Donovan, Joseph S.	Oct. 27, 1849	Balto.
Warfield	Ann	14	Victorine	Donovan, Joseph S.	May 22, 1844	Balto.
Warfield	Charlotte	10	Lady Monroe	Woolfolk, Austin	March 25, 1825	Balto.

Surname	First Name	Age	Ship	O/S	Date	Depart
Warfield	Elizabeth	28	Louisa	Slatter, Hope Hull	Oct. 11, 1847	Balto.
Warfield	Ephraim	17	States	Woolfolk, Austin	Apr. 14, 1828	Balto.
Warfield	George	22	Eliza F.Mason	Donovan, Joseph S.	Nov. 13, 1851	Balto.
Warfield	Henry	11	E.H.Chapin	Slatter, Hope Hull	Nov. 30, 1847	Balto.
Warfield	Tilghman	16	Kirkwood	Slatter, Hope Hull	Dec. 23, 1843	Balto.
Warner	Andrew	21	Tippecanoe	Purvis, James Franklin	Jan. 17, 1842	Balto.
Warner	Beckey	25	Billow	Woolfolk, Joseph B.	Feb. 23, 1828	Balto.
Warner	Corscilley	18	Kirkwood	Donovan, Joseph S.	Sept. 28, 1846	Balto.
Warner	Eady	infant	Billow	Woolfolk, Joseph B.	Feb. 23, 1828	Balto.
Warner	Fanny	12	General Pinckney	Slatter, Hope Hull	Feb. 21, 1846	Balto.
Warner	Louisa	18	Kirkwood	Slatter, Hope Hull	Oct. 16, 1845	Balto.
Warner	Mary Ann	15	Home	Slatter, Hope Hull	March 22, 1845	Balto.
Warren	Agusta	12	Victorine	Rodbond, Ebenezer	May 14, 1845	Balto.
Warren	Charles	17	Margaret Hugg	Slatter, Hope Hull	Feb. 8, 1845	Balto.
Warren	Charles	19	Nathaniel Hooper	Donovan, Jospeh S.	Feb. 12, 1852	Balto.
Warren	Edward	20	Orbit	Woolfolk, Joseph B.	Apr. 16, 1825	Balto.
Warren	Harriett	11	Union	Sheckles, B.O.	Nov. 17, 1849	Balto.
Warren	Jackson	18	Nathaniel Hooper	Donovan, Jospeh S.	Feb. 12, 1852	Balto.
Warren	John	16	General Pinckney	Donovan, Joseph S.	Feb. 21, 1846	Balto.
Warren	Minty	13	Union	Sheckles, B.O.	Nov. 17, 1849	Balto.
Warren	Nancy	25	Kirkwood	Slatter, Hope Hull	Jan. 4, 1845	Balto.
Warren	Rachel	22	Southerner	Donovan, Joseph S.	Oct. 27, 1849	Balto.
Warrick	William	26	Paoli	Slatter, Hope Hull	Sept. 9, 1845	Balto.
Warrier	Sam	17	Seaman	Purvis, James Franklin	Apr. 8, 1842	Balto.
Warrington	Abraham	24	Kirkwood	Slatter, Hope Hull	Jan. 4, 1845	Balto.
Warrington	Ann Maria	infant	Kirkwood	Slatter, Hope Hull	Jan. 4, 1845	Balto.

Surname	First Name	Age	Ship	O/S	Date	Depart
Warstan	Raman	19	Union	Rodbind, Ebenezer	Dec. 16, 1848	Balto.
Warthen	Lucinda	15	Union	Campbell, Bernard M.	March 17, 1849	Balto.
Washington	Albert	26	Union	Williams, Thomas	Oct. 9, 1848	Balto.
Washington	Alexander	11	Julia	Woolfolk, Austin	Jan. 8, 1829	Balto.
Washington	Alice	15	General Pinckney	Campbell, Bernard M.	Jan. 19, 1847	Balto.
Washington	Alice	19	Scotia	Slatter, Hope Hull	Sept. 30, 1843	Balto.
Washington	Ally	16	Elizabeth	Campbell, Bernard M.	March 21, 1850	Balto.
Washington	Andrew	39	Margaret Forbs	Slatter, Hope Hull	Nov. 28, 1838	Balto.
Washington	Anne	9	Kirkwood	Harker, William	March 23, 1844	Balto.
Washington	Charles	21	Superb	Donovan, Joseph S.	Nov. 2, 1843	Balto.
Washington	Charles	17	Victorine	Donovan, Joseph S.	Sept. 29, 1845	Balto.
Washington	Courtney	26	Lafayette	Woolfolk, Richard	Oct. 18, 1828	Balto.
Washington	David	9	Elizabeth	Rodbind, Ebenezer	Nov. 18, 1848	Balto.
Washington	David	19	Jefferson	Woolfolk, Austin	Dec. 24, 1827	Balto.
Washington	Edmon	24	Architect	Donovan, Joseph S.	Apr. 25, 1846	Balto.
Washington	Eliza	4	E.H.Chapin	Slatter, Hope Hull	Nov. 30, 1847	Balto.
Washington	Emaly	9	E.H.Chapin	Slatter, Hope Hull	Nov. 30, 1847	Balto.
Washington	Emeline	14	St. Mary	Donovan, Joseph S.	Nov. 29, 1845	Balto.
Washington	Evaline	19	Scotia	Slatter, Hope Hull	Sept. 30, 1843	Balto.
Washington	George	18	Elizabeth	Campbell, Bernard M.	Nov. 18, 1848	Balto.
Washington	George	19	Helen A. Miller	Campbell, Bernard M.	Oct. 18, 1852	Balto.
Washington	George	14	John C. Calhoun	Donovan, Joseph S.	Oct. 24, 1850	Balto.
Washington	George	22	John C. Calhoun	Donovan, Joseph S.	Oct. 24, 1850	Balto.
Washington	George	11	Kirkwood	Harker, William	March 23, 1844	Balto.
Washington	George	infant	Kirkwood	Slatter, Hope Hull	Oct. 16, 1845	Balto.
Washington	George	20	Lapwing	Hall, Francis	March 22, 1822	Balto.

Surname	First Name	Age	Ship	O/S	Date	Depart
Washington	George	13	Louisa	Donovan, Joseph S.	Oct. 9, 1847	Balto.
Washington	George	20	Margaret Forbs	Slatter, Hope Hull	Nov. 28, 1838	Balto.
Washington	George	20	Osprey	Tilletson, S.R.	Nov. 11, 1847	Balto.
Washington	George	23	Scotia	Slatter, Hope Hull	Sept. 30, 1843	Balto.
Washington	George	14	Seamar	Slatter, Shadrack	March 25, 1839	Balto.
Washington	George	19	Union	Donovan, Joseph S.	Dec. 16, 1848	Balto.
Washington	George	infant	Victorine	Donovan, Joseph S.	Dec. 17, 1845	Balto.
Washington	George H.		Harriet	McCulloh, J.S.	Dec. 7, 1836	Balto.
Washington	Grace	45	Union	Campbell, Bernard M.	March 17, 1849	Balto.
Washington	Harriet	23	Brunswick	Woolfolk, Austin	Oct. 11, 1831	Balto.
Washington	Harriet	20	Helen A. Miller	Campbell, Bernard M.	Oct. 18, 1852	Balto.
Washington	Harriet	10	Victorine	Donovan, Joseph S.	Dec. 17, 1845	Balto.
Washington	Henry	22	Jasper	Woolfolk, Austin	Apr. 7, 1827	Balto.
Washington	Howard	4	Pioneer	Slatter, Hope Hull	Sept. 15, 1847	Balto.
Washington	Howard	3	Zoe	Slatter, Hope Hull	Feb. 16, 1847	Balto.
Washington	Israel	26	Mary Broughton	Campbell, Bernard M.	Nov. 18, 1851	Balto.
Washington	John	23	Kirkwood	Donovan, Joseph S.	Oct. 26, 1847	Balto.
Washington	John	6	Lapwing	Hall, Francis	March 22, 1822	Balto.
Washington	Kitty	30	Margaret Forbs	Slatter, Hope Hull	Nov. 28, 1838	Balto.
Washington	Lee	23	General Pinckney	Donovan, Joseph S.	Feb. 21, 1846	Balto.
Washington	Louisa	4	Victorine	Donovan, Joseph S.	Dec. 17, 1845	Balto.
Washington	Margaret	18	Zoe	Slatter, Hope Hull	Feb. 16, 1847	Balto.
Washington	Maria	26	Pioneer	Slatter, Hope Hull	Sept. 15, 1847	Balto.
Washington	Maria	25	Zoe	Slatter, Hope Hull	Feb. 16, 1847	Balto.
Washington	Mariah	25	Ewarkee	Slatter, Hope Hull	March 4, 1841	Balto.
Washington	Martha	10	Catharine	Donovan, Joseph S.	Jan. 18, 1845	Balto.

Surname	First Name	Age	Ship	O/S	Date	Depart
Washington	Martha	11	Phoenix	Rodbind, Ebenezer	March 27, 1847	Balto.
Washington	Mary	6	E.H.Chapin	Slatter, Hope Hull	Nov. 30, 1847	Balto.
Washington	Mary	40	Victorine	Donovan, Joseph S.	Sept. 29, 1845	Balto.
Washington	Mary Louisa	9	Tippecanoe	Slatter, Hope Hull	Jan. 17, 1842	Balto.
Washington	Media	22	Kirkwood	Slatter, Hope Hull	Oct. 16, 1845	Balto.
Washington	Nathan	20	Southerner	Donovan, Joseph S.	Oct. 27, 1849	Balto.
Washington	Peyton	18	Sarah Bridge	Campbell, Bernard M.	Feb. 8, 1851	Balto.
Washington	Philip	22	Kirkwood	Crow, William	March 23, 1844	Balto.
Washington	Philip	19	States	Woolfolk, Joseph B.	Nov. 21, 1827	Balto.
Washington	Putnum	24	Kirkwood	Donovan, Joseph S.	Oct. 26, 1847	Balto.
Washington	Rachel	26	E.H.Chapin	Slatter, Hope Hull	Nov. 30, 1847	Balto.
Washington	Rachel	37	Victorine	Donovan, Joseph S.	Dec. 17, 1845	Balto.
Washington	Rosetta	16	Kirkwood	Donovan, Joseph S.	Apr. 4, 1846	Balto.
Washington	Susan	18	General Pinckney	Donovan, Joseph S.	Feb. 21, 1846	Balto.
Washington	Thomas	23	W.H.D.C.Wright	Slatter, Hope Hull	Nov. 7, 1847	Balto.
Washington	Tusarig	18	Catharine	Woolfolk, Austin	March 3, 1829	Balto.
Washington	Warner	21	Kirkwood	Crow, William	March 23, 1844	Balto.
Washington	William	17	Margaret Hugg	Poindexter, T.B.	Nov. 30, 1844	Balto.
Washington	William	18	Union	Slatter, Hope Hull	July 26, 1847	Balto.
Washington	William	23	Victorine	Donovan, Joseph S.	Sept. 29, 1845	Balto.
Washington	Willis	20	Union	Williams, Thomas	Oct. 9, 1848	Balto.
Washington		16	Kirkwood	Donovan, Joseph S.	Dec. 10, 1846	Balto.
Washington		26	Kirkwood	Donovan, Joseph S.	Dec. 10, 1846	Balto.
Washington		3 mon.	Margaret Forbs	Slatter, Hope Hull	Nov. 28, 1838	Balto.
Waterman	Richard	22	Charles	Donovan, Joseph S.	Apr. 23, 1851	Balto.
Waters	Amy	22	Jane Henderson	Campbell, Bernard M.	Nov. 1, 1852	Balto.

Surname	First Name	Age	Ship	O/S	Date	Depart
Waters	Ann	18	Union	Campbell, Bernard M.	March 17, 1849	Balto.
Waters	Betsey	11	Topaz	Woolfolk, Austin	Apr. 20, 1829	Balto.
Waters	Binah	30	Ann & Leah	Woolfolk, Austin	Nov.1, 1831	Balto.
Waters	Caroline	16	Jane Henderson	Campbell, Bernard M.	Nov. 1, 1852	Balto.
Waters	Cassandra	18	Kirkwood	Campbell, Bernard M.	Oct. 14, 1848	Balto.
Waters	Catherine	18	Paoli	Campbell, Bernard M.	Dec. 27, 1845	Balto.
Waters	Cena	20	Jane Henderson	Campbell, Bernard M.	Nov. 1, 1852	Balto.
Waters	Charles	17	General Pinckney	Slatter, Hope Hull	Nov. 10, 1845	Balto.
Waters	Charles	16	Southerner	Donovan, Joseph S.	Oct. 27, 1849	Balto.
Waters	Daniel	12	Ann & Leah	Woolfolk, Austin	Nov.1, 1831	Balto.
Waters	Emma	5	Ann & Leah	Woolfolk, Austin	Nov.1, 1831	Balto.
Waters	Hariett	16	Narragansett	Donovan, Joseph S.	Nov. 27, 1850	Balto.
Waters	Harriet	16	Jane Henderson	Campbell, Bernard M.	Nov. 1, 1852	Balto.
Waters	Harriett	17	Louisa	Slatter, Hope Hull	Oct. 11, 1847	Balto.
Waters	Henrietta	28	Ewarkee	Slatter, Hope Hull	March 4, 1841	Balto.
Waters	Horace	17	Southerner	Donovan, Joseph S.	Oct. 27, 1849	Balto.
Waters	John	12	Ann & Leah	Woolfolk, Austin	Nov.1, 1831	Balto.
Waters	Juliett	19	Irad Ferry	Purvis, James Franklin	Feb. 5, 1842	Balto.
Waters	King	25	Edward Everett	Campbell, Bernard M.	March 10, 1851	Balto.
Waters	Louisa	15	Victorine	Slatter, Hope Hull	March 14, 1846	Balto.
Waters	Madison	20	Tweed	Bowling, John D.	Oct. 20, 1836	Town Creek
Waters	Miah	20	Kirkwcod	Slatter, Hope Hull	Dec. 23, 1843	Balto.
Waters	Murry	3	Ann & Leah	Woolfolk, Austin	Nov.1, 1831	Balto.
Waters	Nina	16	Margaret Hugg	Donovan, Joseph S.	Feb. 8, 1845	Balto.
Waters	Robert	19	Eliza F.Mason	Donovan, Joseph S.	Nov. 13, 1851	Balto.
Waters	Salina	17	Waverly	Campbell, Bernard M.	Apr. 3, 1851	Balto.

Surname	First Name	Age	Ship	O/S	Date	Depart
Watkins	Amelia	20	Ewarkee	Purvis, James Franklin	March 4, 1841	Balto.
Watkins	Caroline	14	Burlington	Slatter, Hope Hull	Oct. 21, 1842	Balto.
Watkins	Clement	26	Union	Campbell, Bernard M.	March 17, 1849	Balto.
Watkins	Elijah	16	Brunswick	Woolfolk, Austin	Oct. 11, 1831	Balto.
Watkins	Elisa	16	Burlington	Slatter, Hope Hull	Oct. 21, 1842	Balto.
Watkins	George	23	Catharine	Woolfolk, Austin	March 3. 1829	Balto.
Watkins	Harriett	9	Burlington	Slatter, Hope Hull	Oct. 21, 1842	Balto.
Watkins	Jane	5	Burlington	Slatter, Hope Hull	Oct. 21, 1842	Balto.
Watkins	Lydia	2	Burlington	Slatter, Hope Hull	Oct. 21, 1842	Balto.
Watkins	Milla	19	Isaac Franklin	Slatter, Hope Hull	Sept. 28, 1838	Balto.
Watkins	Moses	18	Catharine	Woolfolk, Austin	March 3. 1829	Balto.
Watkins	Phillip	22	E.H.Chapin	Slatter, Hope Hull	Dec. 2, 1847	Balto.
Watkins	Robert	6	Burlington	Slatter, Hope Hull	Oct. 21, 1842	Balto.
Watkins	Sophia	36	Burlington	Slatter, Hope Hull	Oct. 21, 1842	Balto.
Watson	Emily	18	General Pinckney	Slatter, Hope Hull	Nov. 10, 1845	Balto.
Watson	Emily	21	Nathaniel Hooper	Campbell, Bernard M.	Feb. 12, 1852	Balto.
Watson	Horris	16	Margaret Forbs	Slatter, Hope Hull	Nov. 28, 1838	Balto.
Watson	John	20	Elizabeth	Campbell, Bernard M.	March 21, 1850	Balto.
Watson	Margaret A.	23	Southerner	Rodbind, Ebenezer	Jan. 21, 1850	Balto.
Watson	Samuel	22	Kirkwood	Donovan, Joseph S.	Jan. 14, 1846	Balto.
Watts	Ann	18	Margaret Forbs	Slatter, Hope Hull	Nov. 28, 1838	Balto.
Watts	Hillery	infant	Kirkwood	Donovan, Joseph S.	Apr. 15, 1845	Balto.
Watts	Nancy	16	Hermitage	Donovan, Joseph S.	Oct. 28, 1846	Balto.
Watts	Sarah	16	Kirkwood	Donovan, Joseph S.	Apr. 15, 1845	Balto.
Watts	Susan	17	Topaz	Woolfolk, Austin	Apr. 20, 1829	Balto.
Watts	William	14	Topaz	Woolfolk, Austin	Apr. 20, 1829	Balto.

Surname	First Name	Age	Ship	O/S	Date	Depart
Wayne	Frank	25	Justine	Donovan, Joseph S.	Dec. 2, 1852	Balto.
Weaks	Perry	11	Lafayette	Woolfolk, Austin	Oct. 18, 1828	Balto.
Weatherly	Ferdinand	26	Mary Broughton	Campbell, Bernard M.	Nov. 18, 1851	Balto.
Weatherly	Levi	24	Mary Broughton	Campbell, Bernard M.	Nov. 18, 1851	Balto.
Weaver	Amandy	15	E.H.Chapin	Donovan, Joseph S.	Dec. 2, 1847	Balto.
Weaver	Amelia Francis	5	Tippecanoe	Slatter, Hope Hull	Jan. 17, 1842	Balto.
Weaver	Angelina	15	Kirkwood	Donovan, Joseph S.	March 9, 1847	Balto.
Weaver	Fransis	16	Kirkwood	Donovan, Joseph S.	March 9, 1847	Balto.
Weaver	Mary	18	St. Mary	Williams, Thomas	Nov. 29, 1845	Balto.
Weaver	Philop	18	Eliza F.Mason	Donovan, Joseph S.	Nov. 13, 1851	Balto.
Webb	Amy	32	Kirkwood	Donovan, Joseph S.	Oct. 26, 1847	Balto.
Webb	Araminta	23	Elizabeth	Chaplain, J. Bond	Nov. 18, 1848	Balto.
Webb	Elisa	26	Russell	Slatter, Hope Hull	March 1, 1839	Balto.
Webb	Harriet	17	Helen A. Miller	Campbell, Bernard M.	Oct. 18, 1852	Balto.
Webb	Harriet	22	Helen A. Miller	Campbell, Bernard M.	Oct. 18, 1852	Balto.
Webb	Henney	21	Kirkwood	Slatter, Henry F.	Dec. 10, 1846	Balto.
Webb	Sidney	14	Kirkwood	Donovan, Joseph S.	Oct. 26, 1847	Balto.
Webb	Thomas	22	Catharine	Donovan, Joseph S.	Jan. 18, 1845	Balto.
Webb	Cyrus	18	Elizabeth	Donovan, Joseph S.	Jan. 2, 1850	Balto.
Webster	Daniel	18	Architect	Harker, William	Feb. 16, 1843	Balto.
Webster	Eliza	18	Victorine	Slatter, Hope Hull	Sept. 12, 1846	Balto.
Webster	Harriet	9	Solomon Saltus	Slatter, Hope Hull	Oct. 7, 1839	Balto.
Webster	Henrietta	14	Victorine	Rodbind, Ebenezer	March 14, 1846	Balto.
Webster	Laura	15	Tangier	Campbell, Bernard M.	Nov. 26, 1853	Balto.
Webster	Useba	15	Tangier	Campbell, Bernard M.	Nov. 26, 1853	Balto.
Webster		17	Catharine	Donovan, Joseph S.	Jan. 18, 1845	Balto.

Surname	First Name	Age	Ship	O/S	Date	Depart
Weekes	Jerry		Eliza F. Mason	Donovan, Joseph S.	Nov. 13, 1851	Balto.
Weeks	Emaline	18	Ewarkee	Slatter, Hope Hull	March 4, 1841	Balto.
Weeks	Hannah	22	Elizabeth	Rodbind, Ebenezer	Nov. 18, 1848	Balto.
Weeks	Harriett	19	Victorine	Slatter, Hope Hull	Dec. 17, 1845	Balto.
Weeks	Henry	18	Hermitage	Donovan, Joseph S.	Oct. 28, 1846	Balto.
Weeks	Susan	8	Margaret Forbs	Slatter, Hope Hull	Nov. 28, 1838	Balto.
Weems	Augustus	20	Victorine	Slatter, Hope Hull	May 14, 1845	Balto.
Weems	Charity	16	Kirkwood	Donovan, Joseph S.	Apr. 15, 1845	Balto.
Weems	Fanny	17	Kirkwood	Donovan, Joseph S.	Dec. 23, 1843	Balto.
Weems	John	23	Elizabeth	Donovan, Joseph S.	Nov. 18, 1848	Balto.
Weems	Martha	20	Helen A. Miller	Campbell, Bernard M.	Oct. 18, 1852	Balto.
Weems	Robert	20	Kirkwood	Donovan, Joseph S.	Dec. 23, 1843	Balto.
Welch	Frank	25	Isaac Franklin	Slatter, Hope Hull	Sept. 28, 1838	Balto.
Welch	Prissilla	20	Isaac Franklin	Slatter, Hope Hull	Sept. 28, 1838	Balto.
Wellborn	Louisa	16	Henry A. Barling	Campbell, Bernard M.	Dec. 18, 1851	Balto.
Wells	Charles	28	Kirkwood	Slatter, Hope Hull	Jan. 14, 1846	Balto.
Wells	Charlotte	14	Kirkwood	Donovan, Joseph S.	Dec. 23, 1843	Balto.
Wells	Eliza	infant	Phoenix	Donovan, Joseph S.	March 27, 1847	Balto.
Wells	Henry	24	John C. Calhoun	Donovan, Joseph S.	Oct. 24, 1850	Balto.
Wells	James	27	Salvadora	Slatter, Hope Hull	Sept. 28, 1846	Balto.
Wells	Matilda	23	Seaman	Slatter, Shadrack	March 25, 1839	Balto.
Wells	Rebecca	17	Phoenix	Donovan, Joseph S.	March 27, 1847	Balto.
Wells	Sampson	30	General Pinckney	Donovan, Joseph S.	Nov. 10, 1845	Balto.
Wells	Thomas	22	Southerner	Rodbind, Ebenezer	Jan. 21, 1850	Balto.
Welsh	Charles	17	Narragansett	Donovan, Joseph S.	Nov. 27, 1850	Balto.
Welsh	Gabriel	21	General Pinckney	Donovan, Joseph S.	Nov. 10, 1845	Balto.

Surname	First Name	Age	Ship	O/S	Date	Depart
Welsh	James	21	Hermitage	Slatter, Hope Hull	Oct. 28, 1846	Balto.
Wesley	John	17	Topaz	Woolfolk, Austin	Apr. 20, 1829	Balto.
West	Ben	22	Tippecanoe	Staples, Joshua	Jan. 17, 1842	Balto.
West	David	8	Kirkwood	Slatter, Hope Hull	Dec. 23, 1843	Balto.
West	Eliza	13	Helen A. Miller	Nally, William	Oct. 18, 1852	Balto.
West	Emily	15	E.H.Chapin	Donovan, Joseph S.	Dec. 2, 1847	Balto.
West	Harriet	8 mon.	Victorine	Williams, Thomas	Dec. 20, 1844	Balto.
West	Henry	33	Elizabeth	Donovan, Joseph S.	Oct. 6, 1849	Balto.
West	James	25	Kirkwood	Slatter, Hope Hull	Jan. 4, 1845	Balto.
West	Jane	20	Victorine	Williams, Thomas	Dec. 20, 1844	Balto.
West	John	25	Elizabeth	Donovan, Joseph S.	Jan. 2, 1850	Balto.
West	Kitty	15	Elizabeth	Rodbird, Ebenezer	Nov. 18, 1848	Balto.
West	Lewis	45	P.R. Hazeltine	Campbell, Bernard M.	Nov. 15, 1856	Balto.
West	Lewis	4	Victorine	Slatter, Henry F.	Dec. 31, 1846	Balto.
West	Margaret	23	States	Woolfolk, Austin	Nov. 21, 1827	Balto.
West	Mary	11	Helen A. Miller	Nally, William	Oct. 18, 1852	Balto.
West	Mary	25	Victorine	Slatter, Henry F.	Dec. 31, 1846	Balto.
West	Minerva	35	P.R. Hazeltine	Campbell, Bernard M.	Nov. 15, 1856	Balto.
West	Patrick	22	Salvadora	Slatter, Hope Hull	Sept. 28, 1846	Balto.
West	Patsey	20	Zoe	Williams, Thomas	Feb. 16, 1847	Balto.
West	Phillippa	33	Helen A. Miller	Nally, William	Oct. 18, 1852	Balto.
West	Stephen	25	General Pinckney	Slatter, Hope Hull	Jan. 19, 1847	Balto.
West	William	22	Kirkwood	Campbell, Bernard M.	Oct. 14, 1848	Balto.
West	William	infant	Victorine	Slatter, Henry F.	Dec. 31, 1846	Balto.
Westfall	Esau	28	Uncas	Slatter, Hope Hull	Jan. 10, 1838	Balto.
Wey	Phoebe	16	Lady Monroe	Woolfolk, Austin	March 25, 1825	Balto.

Surname	First Name	Age	Ship	O/S	Date	Depart
Whalen	John	22	William and Mary	King, Gideon T.	Oct. 9, 1821	Balto.
Whaley	Hester	20	Seguin	Campbell, Bernard M.	July 12, 1853	Balto.
Wheat	Nick	9	Lady Monroe	Woolfolk, Austin	March 25, 1825	Balto.
Wheatley	Basil	16	Jasper	Woolfolk, Austin	Apr. 7, 1827	Balto.
Wheatly	Marshal	30	Burlington	Slatter, Hope Hull	Oct. 21, 1842	Balto.
Wheatly	Robert	59	Tweed	Birch, Benjamin	Oct. 15, 1836	Balto.
Wheedon	Emanuel	24	Jasper	Woolfolk, Austin	Apr. 7, 1827	Balto.
Wheeler	Charles	18	General Pinckney	Slatter, Hope Hull	Jan. 19, 1847	Balto.
Wheeler	Conelia	17	Jane Henderson	Campbell, Bernard M.	Nov. 1, 1852	Balto.
Wheeler	Emeline	10	Lapwing	Woolfolk, Austin	Feb. 15, 1827	Balto.
Wheeler	Isaac	14	Lapwing	Woolfolk, Austin	Feb. 15, 1827	Balto.
Wheeler	Jane	40	Jane Henderson	Campbell, Bernard M.	Nov. 1, 1852	Balto.
Wheeler	John	22	Louisa	Slatter, Hope Hull	Oct. 11, 1847	Balto.
Wheeler	Mary	20	Victorine	Donovan, Joseph S.	Sept. 29, 1845	Balto.
Wheeler	Matilda	20	Bostonian	Slatter, Hope Hull	Jan. 18, 1841	Balto.
Wheeler	Moses	21	Victorine	Donovan, Joseph S.	Sept. 29, 1845	Balto.
Wheeler	William	26	Paoli	Slatter, Hope Hull	Sept. 9, 1845	Balto.
Wheeler	Louisa	30	Mary Broughton	Campbell, Bernard M.	Nov. 18, 1851	Balto.
White	Alexander	21	Louisa	Campbell, Bernard M.	May 18, 1846	Balto.
White	Ambrose	21	Eliza	Slatter, Hope Hull	Oct. 9, 1840	Balto.
White	Ann Elizabeth	16	Kirkwood	Campbell, Bernard M.	March 23, 1844	Balto.
White	Becky	22	Splendid	Slatter, Hope Hull	Apr. 24, 1841	Balto.
White	Benjamin	21	Kirkwood	Donovan, Joseph S.	March 9, 1847	Balto.
White	Ellen	22	Kirkwood	Slatter, Hope Hull	Oct. 16, 1845	Balto.
White	Fanny	19	Burlington	Slatter, Hope Hull	Oct. 21, 1842	Balto.
White	Feilder	23	Victorine	Donovan, Joseph S.	May 22, 1844	Balto.

Surname	First Name	Age	Ship	O/S	Date	Depart
White	Frenetta	20	Victorine	Donovan, Joseph S.	Sept. 29, 1845	Balto.
White	Harriett	18	Burlington	Slatter, Hope Hull	Oct. 21, 1842	Balto.
White	Harry	16	Northumberland	Slatter, Hope Hull	Feb. 27, 1843	Balto.
White	Jacob	25	Ewarkee	Slatter, Hope Hull	March 4, 1841	Balto.
White	John	22	Victorine	Donovan, Joseph S.	Sept. 29, 1845	Balto.
White	Margaret	32	Margaret Forbs	Slatter, Hope Hull	Nov. 28, 1838	Balto.
White	Maria	20	Cora	Campbell, Bernard M.	Jan. 20, 1851	Balto.
White	Mariah	16	Sabine	Donovan, Joseph S.	Feb. 10, 1844	Balto.
White	Milly	16	Kirkwood	Slatter, Hope Hull	Oct. 16, 1845	Balto.
White	Rachel		Victorine	Donovan, Joseph S.	Sept. 29, 1845	Balto.
White	Solomon	25	Tippecanoe	Slatter, Hope Hull	Jan. 17, 1842	Balto.
White	Thomas	24	Union	Sheckles, Gannon	March 17, 1849	Balto.
White		infant	Burlington	Slatter, Hope Hull	Oct. 21, 1842	Balto.
Whitehead	Pleasant	25	Seaman	Slatter, Hope Hull	March 25, 1839	Balto.
Whiteing	Fanny	20	Kirkwood	Williams, Thomas	Apr. 4, 1846	Balto.
Whiteley	Alexander	26	Victorine	Slatter, Hope Hull	May 14, 1845	Balto.
Whitely	Leven	26	Pioneer	Slatter, Hope Hull	Sept. 15, 1847	Balto.
Whitely	Walter	18	Russell	Slatter, Hope Hull	March 1, 1839	Balto.
Whiting	Frank	55	Edward Everett	Ellis, A.B.	Dec. 6, 1856	Balto.
Whiting	John	22	Catharine	Donovan, Joseph S.	Jan. 18, 1845	Balto.
Whiting	John	19	Helen A. Miller	Campbell, Bernard M.	Oct. 18, 1852	Balto.
Whittenton	Alexander	21	Brunswick	Woolfolk, Austin	Oct. 11, 1831	Balto.
Whittington	Robert	22	Tangier	Campbell, Bernard M.	Nov. 26, 1853	Balto.
Whitts	Henry	19	Mars	Woolfolk, Austin	Oct. 30, 1824	Balto.
Wicham	Emaly	30	Union	Slatter, Hope Hull	July 26, 1847	Balto.
Wickersham	Robert	21	Victorine	Slatter, Hope Hull	Dec. 17, 1845	Balto.

Surname	First Name	Age	Ship	O/S	Date	Depart
Wie	Lewis	18	Kirkwood	Donovan, Joseph S.	Oct. 14, 1848	Balto.
Wiekison	Ann	16	Splendid	Slatter, Hope Hull	Apr. 24, 1841	Balto.
Wier	Hiram	20	Elizabeth	Donovan, Joseph S.	Jan. 2, 1850	Balto.
Wiley	Eliza	23	Kirkwood	Slatter, Hope Hull	Apr. 4, 1846	Balto.
Wiley	William	18	Nathaniel Hooper	Donovan, Jospeh S.	Feb. 12, 1852	Balto.
Wilkerson	John	17	Architect	Crow, William	Feb. 3, 1841	Balto.
Wilkinson	Joe	9	Lafayette	Woolfolk, Richard	Oct. 18, 1828	Balto.
Wilkinson	Mary	15	General Pinckney	Slatter, Hope Hull	Jan. 19, 1847	Balto.
Wilks	William	40	Ann & Leah	Woolfolk, Austin	Nov. 1, 1831	Balto.
William	Henson	25	Gannicleftt	Slatter, Hope Hull	Nov. 25, 1840	Balto.
Williams	Abram	15	Scotia	Slatter, Hope Hull	Sept. 30, 1843	Balto.
Williams	Abram	infant	Victorine	Slatter, Hope Hull	March 1, 1845	Balto.
Williams	Adam	18	Kirkwood	Donovan, Joseph S.	Oct. 26, 1847	Balto.
Williams	Ailey	35	Uncas	Slatter, Hope Hull	Jan. 10, 1838	Balto.
Williams	Alfred	18	States	Woolfolk, Austin	Nov. 21, 1827	Balto.
Williams	Alvina	15	Lapwing	Woolfolk, Austin	Feb. 15, 1827	Balto.
Williams	Amey	18	Seaman	Purvis, James Franklin	Apr. 8, 1842	Balto.
Williams	Angeline	19	Scotia	Slatter, Hope Hull	Sept. 30, 1843	Balto.
Williams	Ann	18	Billow	Woolfolk, Austin	Feb. 23, 1828	Balto.
Williams	Ann	21	Kirkwood	Slatter, Henry F.	Dec. 10, 1846	Balto.
Williams	Ann	17	Kirkwood	Donovan, Joseph S.	Oct. 26, 1847	Balto.
Williams	Ann	14	Sarah Bridge	Campbell, Bernard M.	Feb. 8, 1851	Balto.
Williams	Ann	15	Southerner	Donovan, Joseph S.	Oct. 27, 1849	Balto.
Williams	Ann	9	Uncas	Slatter, Hope Hull	Jan. 10, 1838	Balto.
Williams	Ann Maria	16	Frances Amy	Donovan, Joseph S.	Jan. 20, 1847	Balto.
Williams	Anne	24	Susan Miller	Woolfolk, Richard T.	Oct. 25, 1822	Balto.

Surname	First Name	Age	Ship	O/S	Date	Depart
Williams	Arena	17	Scotia	Slatter, Hope Hull	Sept. 30, 1843	Balto.
Williams	Bazil	19	Seaman	Slatter, Hope Hull	Dec. 19, 1838	Balto.
Williams	Benjamin	25	Architect	Purvis, James Franklin	Feb. 3, 1841	Balto.
Williams	Benjamin	21	Kirkwood	Donovan, Joseph S.	March 9, 1847	Balto.
Williams	Benjamin	26	Seaman	Slatter, Shadrack	March 25, 1839	Balto.
Williams	Bill	24	Victorine	Slatter, Hope Hull	Dec. 17, 1845	Balto.
Williams	Caroline	16	Kirkwood	Donovan, Joseph S.	Apr. 15, 1845	Balto.
Williams	Caroline	4	Porpoise	Purvis, James Franklin	Dec. 11, 1841	Balto.
Williams	Caroline	19	Union	Donovan, Joseph S.	Dec. 16, 1848	Balto.
Williams	Catherine	17	Victorine	Slatter, Hope Hull	March 1, 1845	Balto.
Williams	Celia	8	Victorine	Rodbird, Ebenezer	Dec. 31, 1846	Balto.
Williams	Charity	22	Uncas	Slatter, Hope Hull	Jan. 10, 1838	Balto.
Williams	Charles	12	Architect	Slatter, Hope Hull	Feb. 16, 1843	Balto.
Williams	Charles	19	Brunswick	Woolfolk, Austin	Oct. 11, 1831	Balto.
Williams	Charles	24	Delawarian	Campbell, Bernard M.	Dec. 1, 1848	Balto.
Williams	Charles	22	Elizabeth	Donovan, Joseph S.	Jan. 2, 1850	Balto.
Williams	Charles	22	Kirkwood	Crow, William	March 23, 1844	Balto.
Williams	Charles	23	Union	Donovan, Joseph S.	May 13, 1848	Balto.
Williams	Charles	19	Victorine	Donovan, Joseph S.	Sept. 29, 1845	Balto.
Williams	Charlott	19	Victorine	Rodbird, Ebenezer	Dec. 31, 1846	Balto.
Williams	Clarisa	5	Uncas	Slatter, Hope Hull	Jan. 10, 1838	Balto.
Williams	David	20	Burlington	Slatter, Hope Hull	Oct. 21, 1842	Balto.
Williams	David	18	Isaac Franklin	Kephart, George	Feb. 1, 1839	Balto.
Williams	David	17	Lafayete	Woolfolk, Austin	Oct. 18, 1828	Balto.
Williams	David	23	Lafayete	Woolfolk, Joseph B.	Oct. 18, 1828	Balto.
Williams	David	26	Paoli	Campbell, Bernard M.	Dec. 27, 1845	Balto.

Surname	First Name	Age	Ship	O/S	Date	Depart
Williams	David	21	Tippecanoe	Slatter, Hope Hull	Apr. 1, 1841	Balto.
Williams	Dennis	18	Arctic	Woolfolk, Austin	Jan. 24, 1829	Balto.
Williams	Dennis James		Victorine	Crozier, John R.	Sept. 12, 1846	Balto.
Williams	Dirk	18	Lady Richmond	Woolfolk, Austin	Apr. 30, 1827	Balto.
Williams	Edward	19	Pioneer	Slatter, Hope Hull	Sept. 15, 1847	Balto.
Williams	Eliza	18	Narragansett	Donovan, Joseph S.	Nov. 27, 1850	Balto.
Williams	Eliza	18	Superb	Slatter, Hope Hull	Nov. 1, 1843	Balto.
Williams	Eliza	18	Uncas	Slatter, Hope Hull	Jan. 10, 1838	Balto.
Williams	Eliza	23	Victorine	Donovan, Joseph S.	Sept. 29, 1845	Balto.
Williams	Eliza	34	Virginia	Barney, Lewis	May 20, 1826	Balto.
Williams	Ellen	infant	General Pinckney	Slatter, Hope Hull	Jan. 19, 1847	Balto.
Williams	Ellen	6	Victorine	Slatter, Hope Hull	March 1, 1845	Balto.
Williams	Emily	18	Paoli	Slatter, Hope Hull	Sept. 9, 1845	Balto.
Williams	Felix	22	Kirkwood	Donovan, Joseph S.	Oct. 26, 1847	Balto.
Williams	Fillis	9	Victorine	Slatter, Hope Hull	March 1, 1845	Balto.
Williams	Frisby	6	Tippecanoe	Slatter, Hope Hull	Dec. 16, 1840	Balto.
Williams	George	7	Henry A. Barling	Donovan, Joseph S.	May 17, 1851	Balto.
Williams	George	21	Hermitage	Berry, Charles H.	Oct. 28, 1846	Balto.
Williams	George	45	Isaac Franklin	Kephart, George	Sept. 28, 1838	Balto.
Williams	George	21	Kirkwood	Slatter, Hope Hull	Oct. 16, 1845	Balto.
Williams	George	22	Kirkwood	Donovan, Joseph S.	Sept. 28, 1846	Balto.
Williams	George	20	Lady Monroe	Woolfolk, Austin	March 25, 1825	Balto.
Williams	George	19	Mary Broughton	Campbell, Bernard M.	Nov. 18, 1851	Balto.
Williams	George	30	Scotia	Slatter, Hope Hull	Sept. 30, 1843	Balto.
Williams	George	24	Union	Rodbind, Ebenezer	Dec. 16, 1848	Balto.
Williams	Harriet	16	Nathaniel Hooper	Campbell, Bernard M.	Feb. 12, 1852	Balto.

Surname	First Name	Age	Ship	O/S	Date	Depart
Williams	Harriett	20	General Pinckney	Williams, Thomas	Jan. 19, 1847	Balto.
Williams	Harvey	9	Kirkwood	Donovan, Joseph S.	Oct. 26, 1847	Balto.
Williams	Hendrson	25	Billow	Woolfolk, Austin	Feb. 23, 1828	Balto.
Williams	Henna	18	Kirkwood	Donovan, Joseph S.	Oct. 26, 1847	Balto.
Williams	Henrietta	18	Sabine	Donovan, Joseph S.	Feb. 10, 1844	Balto.
Williams	Henry	21	Eliza	Slatter, Hope Hull	Oct. 9, 1840	Balto.
Williams	Henry	22	Eliza	Slatter, Hope Hull	Oct. 9, 1840	Balto.
Williams	Henry	22	Eros	Woolfolk, Austin	Jan. 28, 1824	Balto.
Williams	Henry	25	Porpoise	Purvis James Franklin	Dec. 11, 1841	Balto.
Williams	Henry	21	Salvadora	Slatter Hope Hull	Sept. 28, 1846	Balto.
Williams	Henry	25	Solomon Saltus	Slatter, Hope Hull	Oct. 7, 1839	Balto.
Williams	Henry	54	Victorine	Rodbird, Ebenezer	Dec. 31, 1846	Balto.
Williams	Hester	18	Irad Ferry	Clendenin, A.	Jan. 16, 1840	Balto.
Williams	Hilley	39	Aurilla	Warfield, Charles	Apr. 26, 1822	Balto.
Williams	Isaac	32	Kirkwood	Donovan, Joseph S.	Oct. 14, 1848	Balto.
Williams	Isaac	15	Uncas	Slatter, Hope Hull	Jan. 10, 1838	Balto.
Williams	Isabella	16	Union	Donovan, Joseph S.	March 17, 1849	Balto.
Williams	Issac	19	Brunswick	Woolfolk, Austin	Oct. 11, 1831	Balto.
Williams	Jacob	16	Salvadora	Slatter, Hope Hull	Sept. 28, 1846	Balto.
Williams	Jacob	40	Uncas	Slatter, Hope Hull	Jan. 10, 1838	Balto.
Williams	Jacob	20	Union	Donovan, Joseph S.	May 13, 1848	Balto.
Williams	Jame	6	Architect	Crow, William	Feb. 3, 1841	Balto.
Williams	James	24	Eliza F.Mason	Donovan, Joseph S.	Nov. 13, 1851	Balto.
Williams	James	12	Isaac Franklin	Kephart, George	Feb. 1, 1839	Balto.
Williams	James	18	Mary Broughton	Campbell, Bernard M.	Nov. 18, 1851	Balto.
Williams	James	8	Tippecaroe	Slatter, Hope Hull	Dec. 16, 1840	Balto.

Surname	First Name	Age	Ship	O/S	Date	Depart
Williams	Jane	18	Architect	Donovan, Joseph S.	Apr. 25, 1846	Balto.
Williams	Jane	9	Irad Ferry	Clendenin, A.	Jan. 16, 1840	Balto.
Williams	Jane	13	Kirkwood	Donovan, Joseph S.	Oct. 26, 1847	Balto.
Williams	Jane	30	Seaman	Slatter, Hope Hull	Dec. 19, 1838	Balto.
Williams	Jarvis	10	Virginia	Stone, William	Nov. 18, 1823	Balto.
Williams	Jenny	22	Tangier	Campbell, Bernard M.	Nov. 26, 1853	Balto.
Williams	John	20	General Pinckney	Slatter, Hope Hull	Feb. 21, 1846	Balto.
Williams	John	38	General Pinckney	Slatter, Hope Hull	Jan. 19, 1847	Balto.
Williams	John	23	General Pinckney	Donovan, Joseph S.	Nov. 10, 1845	Balto.
Williams	John	23	Helen A. Miller	Campbell, Bernard M.	Oct. 18, 1852	Balto.
Williams	John	19	Hortensia	Woolfolk, Austin	Dec. 14, 1836	Balto.
Williams	John	18	Kirkwood	Donovan, Joseph S.	Nov. 28, 1849	Balto.
Williams	John	21	Kirkwood	Donovan, Joseph S.	Oct. 14, 1848	Balto.
Williams	John	14	Louisa	Slatter, Hope Hull	Oct. 11, 1847	Balto.
Williams	John	16	States	Woolfolk, Austin	Nov. 21, 1827	Balto.
Williams	John	22	Union	Campbell, Bernard M.	Nov. 17, 1849	Balto.
Williams	John	16	Victorine	Slatter, Hope Hull	March 1, 1845	Balto.
Williams	John	24	Victorine	Donovan, Joseph S.	May 22, 1844	Balto.
Williams	John	30	Architect	Slatter, Hope Hull	May 20, 1841	Balto.
Williams	Joshua	22	Victorine	Slatter, Hope Hull	March 9, 1844	Balto.
Williams	Joshua	7	Uncas	Slatter, Hope Hull	Jan. 10, 1838	Balto.
Williams	Judy	18	States	Woolfolk, Austin	Nov. 21, 1827	Balto.
Williams	Kitty	26	Solomon Saltus	Slatter, Hope Hull	Oct. 7, 1839	Balto.
Williams	Leonard	20	Delawarian	Campbell, Bernard M.	Dec. 1, 1848	Balto.
Williams	Levin	22	States	Woolfolk, Austin	Nov. 21, 1827	Balto.
Williams	Lidia	17	Kirkwood	Campbell, Bernard M.	Oct. 14, 1848	Balto.
Williams	Lucretia					

Surname	First Name	Age	Ship	O/S	Date	Depart
Williams	Lucy	17	Emilie	Kerner, William	March 27, 1821	Balto.
Williams	Lucy	15	Porpoise	Purvis, James Franklin	Dec. 11, 1841	Balto.
Williams	Margaret	11	General Pinckney	Slatter, Hope Hull	Jan. 19, 1847	Balto.
Williams	Margaret	16	Henry Clay	Woolfolk, Austin	Dec. 4, 1828	Balto.
Williams	Mariah	17	Margaret Hugg	Donovan, Joseph S.	Feb. 8, 1845	Balto.
Williams	Martha	5	Kirkwood	Slatter, Hope Hull	Oct. 16, 1845	Balto.
Williams	Martha Ann	18	Tippecanoe	Purvis, James Franklin	Jan. 17, 1842	Balto.
Williams	Martin	21	General Pinckney	Donovan, Joseph S.	Nov. 10, 1845	Balto.
Williams	Mary	15	Kirkwood	Donovan, Joseph S.	Sept. 28, 1846	Balto.
Williams	Mary	13	Southerner	Donovan, Joseph S.	Oct. 27, 1849	Balto.
Williams	Mary	18	Tippecanoe	Slatter, Hope Hull	Apr. 15, 1844	Balto.
Williams	Mary	19	Uncas	Slatter, Hope Hull	Jan. 10, 1838	Balto.
Williams	Mary Jane	6	General Pinckney	Slatter, Hope Hull	Jan. 19, 1847	Balto.
Williams	Mathew	30	Scotia	Slatter, Hope Hull	Sept. 30, 1843	Balto.
Williams	Matilda	33	General Pinckney	Slatter, Hope Hull	Jan. 19, 1847	Balto.
Williams	Matilda	21	Scotia	Slatter, Hope Hull	Sept. 30, 1843	Balto.
Williams	Matilda	17	Victorine	Donovan, Joseph S.	March 1, 1845	Balto.
Williams	Mich	14	Uncas	Slatter, Hope Hull	Jan. 10, 1838	Balto.
Williams	Moriah	12	Uncas	Slatter, Hope Hull	Jan. 10, 1838	Balto.
Williams	Moses	17	Margaret Hugg	Slatter, Hope Hull	Feb. 8, 1845	Balto.
Williams	Moses	8	Victorine	Slatter, Hope Hull	March 1, 1845	Balto.
Williams	Nace	24	Lady Richmond	Woolfolk, Austin	Apr. 30, 1827	Balto.
Williams	Nancy	16	General Pinckney	Donovan, Joseph S.	Nov. 10, 1845	Balto.
Williams	Nancy	20	Kirkwood	Slatter, Hope Hull	Oct. 16, 1845	Balto.
Williams	Nancy	35	Victorine	Slatter, Hope Hull	March 1, 1845	Balto.
Williams	Nancy Ann	13	Solomon Saltus	Slatter, Hope Hull	Oct. 7, 1839	Balto.

Surname	First Name	Age	Ship	O/S	Date	Depart
Williams	Nathan	26	Kirkwood	Donovan, Joseph S.	Oct. 14, 1848	Balto.
Williams	Ned	21	Temperance	Anderson, David	Dec. 9, 1818	Balto.
Williams	Ned	18	Zoe	Williams, Thomas	Feb. 16, 1847	Balto.
Williams	Nicholas	20	Kirkwood	Donovan, Joseph S.	Oct. 26, 1847	Balto.
Williams	Oscar	18	Kirkwood	Donovan, Joseph S.	Oct. 26, 1847	Balto.
Williams	Peter	24	Brunswick	Woolfolk, Austin	Oct. 11, 1831	Balto.
Williams	Peter	23	Kirkwood	Donovan, Joseph S.	Oct. 26, 1847	Balto.
Williams	Peter	26	Tippecanoe	Slatter, Hope Hull	Jan. 17, 1842	Balto.
Williams	Philip	11	Kirkwood	Donovan, Joseph S.	Oct. 26, 1847	Balto.
Williams	Rebecca	16	Nathaniel Hooper	Donovan, Jospeh S.	Feb. 12, 1852	Balto.
Williams	Rebecca	30	Tippecanoe	Slatter, Hope Hull	Dec. 16, 1840	Balto.
Williams	Rezin	10	Ann & Leah	Woolfolk, Austin	Nov.1, 1831	Balto.
Williams	Richard	13	Narragansett	Campbell, Bernard M.	Nov. 27, 1850	Balto.
Williams	Robert	30	Victorine	Donovan, Joseph S.	May 22, 1844	Balto.
Williams	Rosetta	16	Lady Monroe	Woolfolk, Austin	March 25, 1825	Balto.
Williams	Rosy Ann	16	Victorine	Slatter, Hope Hull	March 14, 1846	Balto.
Williams	Ruth	35	Porpoise	Purvis, James Franklin	Dec. 11, 1841	Balto.
Williams	Sabe	24	Helen A. Miller	Campbell, Bernard M.	Oct. 18, 1852	Balto.
Williams	Sam	22	Home	Donovan, Joseph S.	March 22, 1845	Balto.
Williams	Sam	17	Kirkwood	Slatter, Hope Hull	Dec. 23, 1843	Balto.
Williams	Sampson	22	States	Woolfolk, Joseph B.	Nov. 21, 1827	Balto.
Williams	Samuel	16	Kirkwood	Slatter, Henry F.	Dec. 10, 1846	Balto.
Williams	Sarah	28	Cora	Campbell, Bernard M.	Jan. 20, 1851	Balto.
Williams	Sarah Jane	15	Victorine	Slatter, Hope Hull	March 9, 1844	Balto.
Williams	Sarah Louisa	11	Salvadora	Slatter, Hope Hull	Sept. 28, 1846	Balto.
Williams	Seuss	8	Architect	Slatter, Hope Hull	Feb. 16, 1843	Balto.

Surname	First Name	Age	Ship	O/S	Date	Depart
Williams	Stephen	24	Russell	Slatter, Hope Hull	March 1, 1839	Balto.
Williams	Stepney	23	Louisa	Donovan, Joseph S.	Oct. 9, 1847	Balto.
Williams	Susan	12	Victorine	Donovan, Joseph S.	May 14, 1845	Balto.
Williams	Thomas	15	Billow	Woolfolk, Austin	Feb. 23, 1828	Balto.
Williams	Thomas	21	Kirkwood	Donovan, Joseph S.	Oct. 14, 1848	Balto.
Williams	Thomas	10	Kirkwood	Slatter, Hope Hull	Oct. 16, 1845	Balto.
Williams	Thomas	19	Victorine	Williams, Thomas	Dec. 20, 1844	Balto.
Williams	Thornton	35	Elizabeth	Donovan, Joseph S.	Nov. 18, 1848	Balto.
Williams	Thornton	18	Waverly	Donovan, Joseph S.	Apr. 3, 1851	Balto.
Williams	Tobias C.	13	Billow	Woolfolk, Austin	Feb. 23, 1828	Balto.
Williams	Travers	32	Kirkwood	Slatter, Hope Hull	Jan. 14, 1846	Balto.
Williams	Wellington	22	Helen A. Miller	Campbell, Bernard M.	Oct. 18, 1852	Balto.
Williams	William	9	General Pinckney	Slatter, Hope Hull	Jan. 19, 1847	Balto.
Williams	William	20	Irad Ferry	Clendenin, A.	Jan. 16, 1840	Balto.
Williams	William	16	Kirkwood	Donovan, Joseph S.	Sept. 28, 1846	Balto.
Williams	William	30	Salvadora	Slatter, Hope Hull	Sept. 28, 1846	Balto.
Williams	Wilson	18	Northumberland	Slatter, Hope Hull	Feb. 27, 1843	Balto.
Williams		infant	Cora	Campbell, Bernard M.	Jan. 20, 1851	Balto.
Williams			Mary	Wallace, Frances	Feb. 28, 1840	Balto.
Willington	George	24	Signet	Woolfolk, Austin	Nov. 12, 1831	Balto.
Willis	Brokley	23	Uncas	Slatter, Hope Hull	Jan. 10, 1838	Balto.
Willis	Eliza	28	Architect	Donovan, Joseph S.	Apr. 25, 1846	Balto.
Willis	Joseph	18	Sarah Bridge	Campbell, Bernard M.	Feb. 8, 1851	Balto.
Willis	Lewis	21	Brunswick	Woolfolk, Austin	Oct. 11, 1831	Balto.
Willis	Malinda	30	General Pinckney	Slatter, Hope Hull	Nov. 10, 1845	Balto.
Willis		26	Victorine	Slatter, Hope Hull	March 1, 1845	Balto.

Surname	First Name	Age	Ship	O/S	Date	Depart
Willis	Margaret	18	Salvadora	Slatter, Hope Hull	Sept. 28, 1846	Balto.
Willis	Thomas	22	Southerner	Donovan, Jospeh S.	Jan. 5, 1852	Balto.
Willis	Virginia Ann	13	Victorine	Donovan, Joseph S.	May 22, 1844	Balto.
Willis		infant	Sarah Bridge	Campbell, Bernard M.	Feb. 8, 1851	Balto.
Willmer	Jacob	25	General Pinckney	Donovan, Joseph S.	Nov. 10, 1845	Balto.
Willmer	James	22	General Pinckney	Donovan, Joseph S.	Nov. 10, 1845	Balto.
Willmore	Ann	21	Liberator	Woolfolk, Austin	Nov. 12, 1828	Balto.
Willmore	Henry	8	Liberator	Woolfolk, Austin	Nov. 12, 1828	Balto.
Willmore	James	4	Liberator	Woolfolk, Austin	Nov. 12, 1828	Balto.
Willmore	Robert	18	Ann & Leah	Woolfolk, Austin	Nov. 1, 1831	Balto.
Willmore	Tom	2	Liberator	Woolfolk, Austin	Nov. 12, 1828	Balto.
Wills	Charles	22	Kirkwood	Donovan, Joseph S.	Apr. 4, 1846	Balto.
Willson	Charles	15	Lapwing	Woolfolk, Austin	Feb. 15, 1827	Balto.
Willson	Hannah	19	Lafayette	Woolfolk, Austin	Oct. 22, 1828	Balto.
Willson	Hannah	16	Scotia	Slatter, Hope Hull	Sept. 30, 1843	Balto.
Willson	John		States	Woolfolk, Austin	Nov. 21, 1827	Balto.
Willson	Moses		Virginia	Woolfolk, Joseph B.	Dec. 19, 1825	Balto.
Willson	Neel J.	27	Lady Monroe	Woolfolk, Austin	March 25, 1825	Balto.
Willson	Peter	34	Lafayette	Woolfolk, Austin	Oct. 18, 1828	Balto.
Willson	Priscilla	15	States	Woolfolk, Austin	Nov. 21, 1827	Balto.
Wilmer	Anne	22	Hibernia	Woolfolk, Austin	Dec. 5, 1826	Balto.
Wilmer	Julia	24	Paoli	Slatter, Hope Hull	Sept. 9, 1845	Balto.
Wilmington	Emerson	28	John C. Calhoun	Donovan, Joseph S.	Oct. 24, 1850	Balto.
Wilmore	Ann	16	Brunswick	Woolfolk, Austin	Oct. 11, 1831	Balto.
Wilson	Abraham	22	Southerner	Donovan, Joseph S.	Oct. 27, 1849	Balto.
Wilson	Ann	15	Billow	Woolfolk, Joseph B.	Feb. 23, 1828	Balto.

Surname	First Name	Age	Ship	O/S	Date	Depart
Wilson	Ann	18	States	Woolfolk, Austin	Nov. 21, 1827	Balto.
Wilson	Ann	16	Superb	Slatter, Hope Hull	Nov. 1, 1843	Balto.
Wilson	Anne Maria	2	Hibernia	Woolfolk, Austin	Dec. 5, 1826	Balto.
Wilson	Ben	20	Kirkwood	Campbell, Bernard M.	Oct. 14, 1848	Balto.
Wilson	Benjamin	21	Kirkwood	Donovan, Joseph S.	Dec. 23, 1843	Balto.
Wilson	Betsey	19	Hibernia	Woolfolk, Austin	Dec. 5, 1826	Balto.
Wilson	Beverly	28	Architect	Donovan, Joseph S.	Apr. 25, 1846	Balto.
Wilson	Bill	19	Billow	Woolfolk, Joseph B.	Feb. 23, 1828	Balto.
Wilson	Bill	18	Elizabeth	Campbell, Bernard M.	May 12, 1849	Balto.
Wilson	Charles	22	Lapwing	King, Gideon T.	March 22, 1822	Balto.
Wilson	Charles	32	Victorine	Slatter, Hope Hull	March 14, 1846	Balto.
Wilson	Charlotte	6	Hibernia	Woolfolk, Austin	Dec. 5, 1826	Balto.
Wilson	David	22	Union	Rodbind, Ebenezer	Dec. 16, 1848	Balto.
Wilson	Elijah	22	Zoe	Campbell, Bernard M.	Feb. 16, 1847	Balto.
Wilson	Eveline	15	Elizabeth	Donovan, Joseph S.	Jan. 2, 1850	Balto.
Wilson	Fanny	20	Solomon Saltus	Slatter, Hope Hull	Oct. 7, 1839	Balto.
Wilson	Frances	17	Tippecanoe	Purvis, James Franklin	Jan. 17, 1842	Balto.
Wilson	Frisby	12	Billow	Woolfolk, Joseph B.	Feb. 23, 1828	Balto.
Wilson	George	21	Southerner	Donovan, Joseph S.	Oct. 27, 1849	Balto.
Wilson	George	22	Union	Rodbind, Ebenezer	Nov. 17, 1849	Balto.
Wilson	Handy	24	General Pinckney	Campbell, Bernard M.	Jan. 19, 1847	Balto.
Wilson	Henry	21	Phoenix	Rodbind, Ebenezer	March 27, 1847	Balto.
Wilson	Isabella	11	Strafford	Harker, William	Nov. 22, 1843	Balto.
Wilson	Jacob	13	Agent	Jackson, John S.	June 8, 1821	Balto.
Wilson	James	9 mon.	States	Woolfolk, Austin	Nov. 21, 1827	Balto.
Wilson	Jane	8	Elizabeth	Donovan, Joseph S.	Nov. 18, 1848	Balto.

Surname	First Name	Age	Ship	O/S	Date	Depart
Wilson	Jane	18	Tippecanoe	Purvis, James Franklin	Jan. 17, 1842	Balto.
Wilson	Jerry	11	Elizabeth	Donovan, Joseph S.	Nov. 18, 1848	Balto.
Wilson	Jerry	25	Kirkwood	Donovan, Joseph S.	Dec. 10, 1846	Balto.
Wilson	Jerry	22	Elizabeth	Donovan, Joseph S.	Nov. 18, 1848	Balto.
Wilson	John	22	Nathaniel Hooper	Campbell, Bernard M.	Feb. 12, 1852	Balto.
Wilson	John	20	Victorine	Slatter, Hope Hull	Dec. 17, 1845	Balto.
Wilson	Joseph	16	Henry Clay	Woolfolk, Austin	Dec. 4, 1828	Balto.
Wilson	Joseph	20	Justina	Donovan, Joseph S.	Dec. 2, 1852	Balto.
Wilson	Kitty	18	Kirkwood	Donovan, Joseph S.	Sept. 28, 1846	Balto.
Wilson	Lewis	21	Hermitage	Donovan, Joseph S.	Oct. 28, 1846	Balto.
Wilson	Louisa	18	Kirkwood	Slatter, Hope Hull	Oct. 16, 1845	Balto.
Wilson	Louisa	12	Solomon Saltus	Slatter, Hope Hull	Oct. 7, 1839	Balto.
Wilson	Lucy	24	Nathaniel Hooper	Campbell, Bernard M.	Feb. 12, 1852	Balto.
Wilson	Margaret	11	Topaz	Woolfolk, Austin	Apr. 20, 1829	Balto.
Wilson	Mary	6	Seaman	Slatter, Shadrack	March 25, 1839	Balto.
Wilson	Mimbery	19	Billow	Woolfolk, Joseph B.	Feb. 23, 1828	Balto.
Wilson	Nace	13	Kirkwood	Slatter, Hope Hull	Jan. 4, 1845	Balto.
Wilson	Neel	20	Lady Monroe	Woolfolk, Austin	March 25, 1825	Balto.
Wilson	Norval	infant	Kirkwood	Slatter, Hope Hull	Jan. 14, 1846	Balto.
Wilson	Peter	21	Tippecanoe	Harker, William	Dec. 16, 1840	Balto.
Wilson	Pricilla	17	Victorine	Donovan, Joseph S.	Sept. 29, 1845	Balto.
Wilson	Sam	17	Billow	Woolfolk, Joseph B.	Feb. 23, 1828	Balto.
Wilson	Sarah	18	Bostonian	Slatter, Hope Hull	Jan. 18, 1841	Balto.
Wilson	Sarah	16	Victorine	Donovan, Joseph S.	Sept. 29, 1845	Balto.
Wilson	Singleton	25	Charles	Donovan, Joseph S.	Apr. 23, 1851	Balto.
Wilson	Solomon	18	Hibernia	Woolfolk, Austin	Dec. 5, 1826	Balto.

Surname	First Name	Age	Ship	O/S	Date	Depart
Wilson	Spencer	17	Kirkwood	Slatter, Hope Hull	Dec. 23, 1843	Balto.
Wilson	Susan	18	Salvadora	Slatter, Hope Hull	Sept. 28, 1846	Balto.
Wilson	Syrus	17	Colonel Howard	Harker, William	Nov. 21, 1844	Balto.
Wilson	Theodore	17	Eliza F. Mason	Donovan, Joseph S.	Nov. 13, 1851	Balto.
Wilson	Theodre	19	States	Kelso, George Y.	Nov. 25, 1825	Balto.
Wilson	Thomas Henry	18	Victorine	Slatter, Hope Hull	March 9, 1844	Balto.
Wilson	Wanda	18	Isaac Franklin	Kephart, George	Feb. 1, 1839	Balto.
Wilson	Washington	21	Irad Fery	Slatter, Hope Hull	Dec. 9, 1842	Balto.
Wilson	William	18	Elizabeth	Donovan, Joseph S.	Nov. 18, 1848	Balto.
Wilson	William	11	Hibernia	Woolfolk, Austin	Dec. 5, 1826	Balto.
Wilson		27	Kirkwood	Donovan, Joseph S.	Dec. 10, 1846	Balto.
Wilson		20	Kirkwood	Donovan, Joseph S.	Sept. 28, 1846	Balto.
Wimms		22	Tippecanoe	Slatter, Hope Hull	Jan. 17, 1842	Balto.
Winchester	Clarissa	22	Harriett	Woolfolk, Austin	March 23, 1822	Balto.
Winder	William	18	Kirkwood	Donovan, Joseph S.	Oct. 14, 1848	Balto.
Winder	Enos	21	Sarah Ann	Harrison, W.G.	Oct. 15, 1836	Balto.
Winder	George W.	infant	Kirkwood	Slatter, Henry F.	Dec. 10, 1846	Balto.
Winder	James	16	Kirkwood	Donovan, Joseph S.	Oct. 14, 1848	Balto.
Wine	Robert	22	Russell	Slatter, Hope Hull	March 1, 1839	Balto.
Winfield	Joshua	18	Victorine	Donovan, Joseph S.	May 22, 1844	Balto.
Wing	Lucy	25	Victorine	Donovan, Joseph S.	Dec. 31, 1846	Balto.
Wing	Henry	18	Solomon Saltus	Slatter, Hope Hull	Oct. 7, 1839	Balto.
Wingate	Susan	23	Brunswick	Woolfolk, Austin	Oct. 11, 1831	Balto.
Winkley	Samuel	24	Victorine	Slatter, Hope Hull	March 9, 1844	Balto.
Winson	Joseph	8	Union	Rodbind, Ebenezer	Dec. 16, 1848	Balto.
Winston	Jim		Charles	Campbel, Bernard M.	Dec. 18, 1850	Balto.
	John					

Surname	First Name	Age	Ship	O/S	Date	Depart
Winters	Daniel	24	Lapwing	Woolfolk, Samuel M.	Feb. 15, 1827	Balto.
Winwright	John	25	Helen A. Miller	Campbell, Bernard M.	Oct. 18, 1852	Balto.
Wirt	Nancy	20	Isaac Franklin	Kephart, George	Sept. 28, 1838	Balto.
Wirt	William	4	Isaac Franklin	Kephart, George	Sept. 28, 1838	Balto.
Wise	Valentine	24	Brunswick	Woolfolk, Austin	Oct. 11, 1831	Balto.
Witeker	Maranda	24	Kirkwood	Rodbind, Ebenezer	Apr. 15, 1845	Balto.
Withers	Essa	20	Elizabeth	Rodbind, Ebenezer	Nov. 18, 1848	Balto.
Wobb	John	28	John S. Gittings	Campbell, Bernard M.	Nov. 20, 1852	Balto.
Wobb	Treasey	24	John S. Gittings	Campbell, Bernard M.	Nov. 20, 1852	Balto.
Wolley	John	21	Irad Ferry	Slatter, Hope Hull	Dec. 9, 1842	Balto.
Wood	Charlotte	17	Tippecanoe	Slatter, Hope Hull	Jan. 17, 1842	Balto.
Wood	Cornelius	17	John C. Calhoun	Donovan, Joseph S.	Oct. 24, 1850	Balto.
Wood	Frank	23	Emilie	Anderson, David	Aug. 21, 1819	Balto.
Wood	Jim	12	Victorine	Rodbind, Ebenezer	May 14, 1845	Balto.
Wood	Mahaly	24	Isaac Franklin	Kephart, George	Sept. 28, 1838	Balto.
Wood	Milly	19	Victorine	Slatter, Hope Hull	March 1, 1845	Balto.
Wood	Rity	30	Kirkwood	Rodbind, Ebenezer	Apr. 15, 1845	Balto.
Wood	Sarah	17	John C. Calhoun	Donovan, Joseph S.	Oct. 24, 1850	Balto.
Wood	Sarah	24	Union	Campbell, Bernard M.	Apr. 20, 1850	Balto.
Wood	Tom	20	Union	Campbell, Bernard M.	Apr. 20, 1850	Balto.
Wood	William	22	Kirkwood	Donovan, Joseph S.	Dec. 23, 1843	Balto.
Woodard	Merscer	23	Kirkwood	Donovan, Joseph S.	Oct. 26, 1847	Balto.
Woodard	William	21	Victorine	Slatter, Hope Hull	Sept. 12, 1846	Balto.
Woodford	Obidiah	26	Kirkwood	Campbell, Bernard M.	Oct. 14, 1848	Balto.
Woodlan	John	21	Scotia	Slatter, Hope Hull	Sept. 30, 1843	Balto.
Woodland	Charles	23	Mars	Woolfolk, Austin	Oct. 30, 1824	Balto.

Surname	First Name	Age	Ship	O/S	Date	Depart
Woodland	George	16	Isaac Franklin	Kephart, George	Feb. 1, 1839	Balto.
Woodland	Margarette Ann	16	Ewarkee	Slatter, Hope Hull	March 4, 1841	Balto.
Woodland	Martha	13	Cora	Campbell, Bernard M.	Jan. 20, 1851	Balto.
Woodland	Mary	20	General Pinckney	Williams, Thomas	Jan. 19, 1847	Balto.
Woodland	Rebecca	30	General Pinckney	Slatter, Hope Hull	Nov. 10, 1845	Balto.
Woodlin	Isaac	16	Scotia	Harker, William	Sept. 30, 1843	Balto.
Woodlin	Jack	23	Lady Richmond	Woolfolk, Austin	Apr. 30, 1827	Balto.
Woodloin	Elisa	16	Burlington	Slatter, Hope Hull	Oct. 21, 1842	Balto.
Woods	Randal	11	Catharine	Donovan, Joseph S.	Jan. 18, 1845	Balto.
Woods	Thomas L.	22	Catharine	Donovan, Joseph S.	Jan. 18, 1845	Balto.
Woods	William	22	Catharine	Donovan, Joseph S.	Jan. 18, 1845	Balto.
Woodstock	Edward	26	Tippecanoe	Slatter, Hope Hull	Jan. 17, 1842	Balto.
Woodward	Moses	23	Victorine	Slatter, Hope Hull	March 1, 1845	Balto.
Woodyear	Hercules	15	Jefferson	Woolfolk, Joseph B.	Dec. 24, 1827	Balto.
Woolfolk	Jacob	9	Jasper	Woolfolk, Austin	Apr. 7, 1827	Balto.
Woolfolk	Jerry	10	Ann & Leah	Woolfolk, Austin	Nov.1, 1831	Balto.
Woolfolk	Rebecca	15	Zoe	Slatter, Hope Hull	Feb. 16, 1847	Balto.
Woolford	John	13	Home	Slatter, Hope Hull	March 22, 1845	Balto.
Word	Denis	17	Glasgow	Slatter, Hope Hull	Oct. 11, 1838	Balto.
Worly	John	8	Southerner	Campbell, Bernard M.	Jan. 5, 1852	Balto.
Worly	Ralph	32	Southerner	Campbell, Bernard M.	Jan. 5, 1852	Balto.
Worly	Sarah	28	Southerner	Campbell, Bernard M.	Jan. 5, 1852	Balto.
Wormsley	William	20	Edward Everett	Campbell, Bernard M.	March 10, 1851	Balto.
Worrell	Moses	21	Julia	Woolfolk, Austin	Jan. 8, 1829	Balto.
Worrick	Benjamin	25	Tippecanoe	Slatter, Hope Hull	Jan. 17, 1842	Balto.
Worthington	David	23	Henry Clay	Woolfolk, Austin	Dec. 4, 1828	Balto.

Surname	First Name	Age	Ship	O/S	Date	Depart
Wren	Enoch	16	Elizabeth	Donovan, Joseph S.	Nov. 18, 1848	Balto.
Wright	Bill	17	Elizabeth	Campbell, Bernard M.	May 12, 1849	Balto.
Wright	Caroline	20	Elizabeth	Donovan, Joseph S.	Jan. 2, 1850	Balto.
Wright	Charles	24	Seaman	Slatter, Hope Hull	March 25, 1839	Balto.
Wright	Edward	6 mon.	States	Woolfolk, Austin	Nov. 21, 1827	Balto.
Wright	Eliza	18	Scotia	Slatter, Hope Hull	Sept. 30, 1843	Balto.
Wright	Emory	21	Kirkwood	Slatter, Hope Hull	Oct. 16, 1845	Balto.
Wright	George	16	Isaac Franklin	Kephart, George	Sept. 28, 1838	Balto.
Wright	George	18	Jefferson	Woolfolk, Austin	Dec. 24, 1827	Balto.
Wright	Hannah	17	Kirkwood	Slatter, Hope Hull	Apr. 15, 1845	Balto.
Wright	Henrietta	20	Kirkwood	Donovan, Joseph S.	Oct. 14, 1848	Balto.
Wright	Julia	24	Victorine	Slatter, Hope Hull	May 14, 1845	Balto.
Wright	Kitty	35	Margaret Forbs	Slatter, Hope Hull	Nov. 28, 1838	Balto.
Wright	Lloyd	18	Tippecanoe	Harker, William	Dec. 16, 1840	Balto.
Wright	Margaret	19	States	Woolfolk, Austin	Apr. 14, 1828	Balto.
Wright	Maria	17	Eliza F.Mason	Donovan, Joseph S.	Nov. 13, 1851	Balto.
Wright	Maria	16	Kirkwood	Donovan, Joseph S.	Sept. 28, 1846	Balto.
Wright	Maria	34	Pompei	Donovan, Joseph S.	June 12, 1852	Balto.
Wright	Mary	17	States	Woolfolk, Austin	Apr. 14, 1828	Balto.
Wright	Matilda	14	Billow	Woolfolk, Austin	Feb. 23, 1828	Balto.
Wright	Matilda	5	Pompei	Donovan, Jospeh S.	June 12, 1852	Balto.
Wright	Nancy	18	Kirkwood	Donovan, Joseph S.	Oct. 26, 1847	Balto.
Wright	Nathan	23	General Pinckney	Donovan, Joseph S.	Feb. 21, 1846	Balto.
Wright	Perry	21	Julia	Woolfolk, Austin	Jan. 8, 1829	Balto.
Wright	Reuben	30	Salvadora	Slatter, Hope Hull	Sept. 28, 1846	Balto.
Wright	Ruben	18	Superb	Donovan, Joseph S.	Nov. 2, 1843	Balto.

Surname	First Name	Age	Ship	O/S	Date	Depart
Wright	Sam	23	Virginia	Woolfolk, Joseph B.	Dec. 19, 1825	Balto.
Wright	Susan	17	States	Woolfolk, Austin	Nov. 21, 1827	Balto.
Wright	Thomas	24	Orbit	Woolfolk, Austin	Apr. 16, 1825	Balto.
Wright	William	17	Kirkwood	Donovan, Joseph S.	Oct. 14, 1848	Balto.
Wright	William	26	Scotia	Slatter, Hope Hull	Sept. 30, 1843	Balto.
Write	Isaac	28	Kirkwood	Smith, I.M.	Nov. 28, 1849	Balto.
Wyar	John	23	Victorine	Slatter, Hope Hull	March 9, 1844	Balto.
Wye	Benjamin	20	Kirkwood	Donovan, Joseph S.	Sept. 28, 1846	Balto.
Wye	Jerry	30	Victorine	Slatter, Hope Hull	Dec. 17, 1845	Balto.
Wyett	Luke	20	Isaac Franklin	Kephar-, George	Feb. 1, 1839	Balto.
Wyett	Marcus	20	Isaac Franklin	Kephar-, George	Feb. 1, 1839	Balto.
Yates	Cealy	9 mon.	Isaac Franklin	Kephar-, George	Feb. 1, 1839	Balto.
Yates	Cealy	22	Isaac Franklin	Kephar-, George	Feb. 1, 1839	Balto.
Yates	John	30	Paoli	Slatter, Hope Hull	Sept. 9, 1845	Balto.
Yates	John	26	Uncas	Slatter, Hope Hull	Jan. 10, 1838	Balto.
Yates	Levi	22	Isaac Franklin	Kephar-, George	Feb. 1, 1839	Balto.
Yates	Marcus	18	Isaac Franklin	Kephar-, George	Feb. 1, 1839	Balto.
Yates	William	4	Isaac Franklin	Kephar-, George	Feb. 1, 1839	Balto.
Yeates	Mary Ann	22	Tippecanoe	Harker, William	Apr. 15, 1844	Balto.
Yeoman	Letha	20	Union	Rodbin-, Ebenezer	Dec. 16, 1848	Balto.
Yetto	James	9	Victorine	Donovan, Joseph S.	Dec. 17, 1845	Balto.
Young	Alexander	25	Home	Slatter, Hope Hull	March 22, 1845	Balto.
Young	Andrew	2	Tweed	Sothoron, William H.	Oct. 20, 1836	Town Creek
Young	Ben	20	Union	Campbell, Bernard M.	Oct. 9, 1848	Balto.
Young	Betsey	18	Isaac Franklin	Kephar-, George	Sept. 28, 1838	Balto.
Young	Betty	11	Victorine	Gardiner, Richard S.D.	Dec. 21, 1844	Balto.

Surname	First Name	Age	Ship	O/S	Date	Depart
Young	Bob	22	Tippecanoe	Staples, Joshua	Jan. 17, 1842	Balto.
Young	Cartoin	10	States	Woolfolk, Austin	Apr. 14, 1828	Balto.
Young	Charlotte	17	John C. Calhoun	Donovan, Joseph S.	Oct. 24, 1850	Balto.
Young	Chirely	17	Bostonian	Slatter, Hope Hull	Jan. 18, 1841	Balto.
Young	Daniel	17	Hope & Hannah	Woolfolk, Austin	March 11, 1829	Balto.
Young	Dorsey	12	Tweed	Sothoron, William H.	Oct. 20, 1836	Town Creek
Young	Edward	23	Ann & Leah	Woolfolk, Austin	Nov. 1, 1831	Balto.
Young	Eleanor	30	Tweed	Sothoron, William H.	Oct. 20, 1836	Town Creek
Young	Elias	22	General Pinckney	Campbell, Bernard M.	Jan. 19, 1847	Balto.
Young	Elisa	13	Hibernia	Woolfolk, Austin	Dec. 5, 1826	Balto.
Young	Eliza	infant	Salvadora	Slatter, Hope Hull	Sept. 28, 1846	Balto.
Young	Emily	16	Southerner	Donovan, Joseph S.	Oct. 27, 1849	Balto.
Young	Harrison	12	Tweed	Sothoron, William H.	Oct. 20, 1836	Town Creek
Young	Jack	48	Tweed	Sothoron, William H.	Oct. 20, 1836	Town Creek
Young	James	9	Nathaniel Hooper	Donovan, Joseph S.	Feb. 12, 1852	Balto.
Young	James	14	Phoenix	Donovan, Joseph S.	March 27, 1847	Balto.
Young	James	30	Scotia	Slatter, Hope Hull	Sept. 30, 1843	Balto.
Young	Jane	18	Kirkwood	Campbell, Bernard M.	Apr. 4, 1846	Balto.
Young	Joseph	17	Kirkwood	Campbell, Bernard M.	Apr. 4, 1846	Balto.
Young	Joseph	28	Lafayette	Woolfolk, Austin	Oct. 18, 1828	Balto.
Young	Julia	12	Seaman	Freeman, Theophilus	March 25, 1839	Balto.
Young	Kitty	10	Hibernia	Woolfolk, Austin	Dec. 5, 1826	Balto.
Young	Kitty	18	Tweed	Sothoron, William H.	Oct. 20, 1836	Town Creek
Young	Lewis	15	Nathaniel Hooper	Campbell, Bernard M.	Feb. 12, 1852	Balto.
Young	Lewis	20	Zoe	Campbell, Bernard M.	Feb. 16, 1847	Balto.
Young	Louisa	20	Scotia	Slatter, Hope Hull	Sept. 30, 1843	Balto.

Surname	First Name	Age	Ship	O/S	Date	Depart
Young	Luke	12	Margaret Hugg	Wilson, Thomas C.	Nov. 30, 1844	Balto.
Young	Mariah	10	States	Woolfolk, Austin	Apr. 14, 1828	Balto.
Young	Martha	20	Salvadora	Slatter, Hope Hull	Sept. 28, 1846	Balto.
Young	Mary	14	Margaret Hugg	Wilson, Thomas C.	Nov. 30, 1844	Balto.
Young	Perry	23	Helen A. Miller	Campbell, Bernard M.	Oct. 18, 1852	Balto.
Young	Phebe	18	Kirkwood	Donovan, Joseph S.	Dec. 10, 1846	Balto.
Young	Rachel	17	Victorine	Donovan, Joseph S.	Dec. 31, 1846	Balto.
Young	Ralph	22	Home	Rodbird, Ebenezer	March 22, 1845	Balto.
Young	Robert	20	Louisa	Campbell, Bernard M.	March 31, 1849	Balto.
Young	Ruth	18	Tippecanoe	Purvis, James Franklin	Jan. 17, 1842	Balto.
Young	Sarah	24	Jefferson	Woolfolk, Austin	Dec. 24, 1827	Balto.
Young	Sophia	16	Hibernia	Woolfolk, Austin	Dec. 5, 1826	Balto.
Young	Susan	18	Helen A. Miller	Campbell, Bernard M.	Oct. 18, 1852	Balto.
Young	Thomas	16	Union	Sheckles, B.O.	Nov. 17, 1849	Balto.
Young	Townly	4	Tweed	Sothoron, William H.	Oct. 20, 1836	Town Creek
Young	Vachel	19	Billow	Woolfolk, Joseph B.	Feb. 23, 1828	Balto.
Young	Washington	20	Catharine	Slatter, Hope Hull	Jan. 24, 1843	Balto.
Young	William	22	Billow	Woolfolk, Austin	Feb. 23, 1828	Balto.
Young	William	18	John C. Calhoun	Donovan, Joseph S.	Oct. 24, 1850	Balto.
Young	William B.	17	Superb	Slatter, Hope Hull	Nov. 1, 1843	Balto.
Young		infant	Tweed	Sothoron, William H.	Oct. 20, 1836	Town Creek
	Aaron	24	Catharine Jackson	Brent, George	Nov. 26, 1836	Nanjimoy
	Aaron	20	Eros	Woolfolk, Austin	Jan. 28, 1824	Balto.
	Aaron	50	Hope	Richardson, Wade H.	Dec. 3, 1833	Balto.
	Aaron	21	Kirkwood	Guyther, John	Dec. 10, 1846	Balto.
	Aaron	23	States	Woodland, James	March 7, 1826	Balto.

Surname	First Name	Age	Ship	O/S	Date	Depart
	Aaron	25	Temperance	Poumairat, John	Dec. 9, 1818	Balto.
	Abby	23	Algerine	Woolfolk, Austin	Jan. 5, 1826	Balto.
	Abigail	1 mon.	Eros	Armitage, James	June 29, 1822	Balto.
	Abigail	22	Harriett	Woolfolk, Austin	March 23, 1822	Balto.
	Abraham	24	Agent	Anderson, David	June 8, 1821	Balto.
	Abraham	22	Alfred	Woolfolk, Joseph B.	May 7, 1825	Balto.
	Abraham	23	Emilie	Anderson, David	March 27, 1821	Balto.
	Abraham	24	Eros	Armitage, James	June 29, 1822	Balto.
	Abraham	19	Harriett	Woolfolk, Austin	March 23, 1822	Balto.
	Abraham	6	Isabella	Wallis, Cornelius C.	Nov. 26, 1834	Balto.
	Abraham	17	Lady Monroe	Chabert, Leon	Sept. 29, 1825	Balto.
	Abraham	45	Mars	Woolfolk, Austin	Oct. 30, 1824	Balto.
	Abraham	22	Orbit	Pearce, James Alfred	Apr. 13, 1825	Balto.
	Abraham	20	Porpoise	Purvis, James Franklin	Dec. 11, 1841	Balto.
	Abraham	18	Robert Reade	Woolfolk, Austin	Feb. 28, 1824	Balto.
	Abraham	10	Superb	Lavelle, John F.	Apr. 7, 1819	Balto.
	Abraham	15	Susan Miller	Woolfolk, Austin	Oct. 25, 1822	Balto.
	Abraham	30	Susan Miller	Woolfolk, Austin	Oct. 25, 1822	Balto.
	Abraham	19	Susan Miller	Woolfolk, Richard T.	Oct. 25, 1822	Balto.
	Abraham	24	Triton	Heath, Dela F.	Dec. 23, 1819	Balto.
	Abram		Alfred	Woolfolk, Joseph B.	May 7, 1825	Balto.
	Abram	3	Good Hope	Woolfolk, Austin	Nov. 16, 1821	Balto.
	Abram	35	Henry Clay	Dorsett, William N.	Dec. 8, 1828	Nottingham
	Abram	infant	Intelligence	Plater, John R. Jr.	Apr. 12, 1823	St. Mary's
	Abram	22	Intelligence	Woolfolk, Austin	Apr. 5, 1823	Balto.
	Abram	25	Intelligence	Coleman, Henry E.	Nov. 4, 1820	Balto.

Surname	First Name	Age	Ship	O/S	Date	Depart
	Absalom	20	Emilie	Ferguson, Thomas	Dec. 14, 1821	Balto.
	Absalon	19	Aurilla	Chabert, Leon	Apr. 26, 1822	Balto.
	Adaline	10	Mars	Woolfolk, Austin	Oct. 30, 1824	Balto.
	Adam	22	Budget	Spraggins, Samuel M.	Nov. 27, 1821	Balto.
	Adam	11	Chatsworth	Anderson, David	Jan. 3, 1821	Balto.
	Adam	25	Creole	Allain	Oct. 19, 1833	Balto.
	Adam	34	Franklin	Somerville, Henry	Nov. 27, 1819	Balto.
	Adam	9	Gulnare	Pitts, Thomas H.	Nov. 5, 1830	Balto.
	Adam	21	Kirkwood	Donovan, Joseph S.	Dec. 10, 1846	Balto.
	Adam	13	Missouri	Little, Moses	March 2, 1819	Balto.
	Adam	20	Pilgrim	Biscoe, James	Dec. 23, 1834	Balto.
	Addison	12 mon.	States	Woolfolk, Austin	March 8, 1826	St. Mary's
	Adeline	4	Arctic	Williams, Joseph C.	Jan. 31, 1829	Balto.
	Adeline	16	North America	Woolfolk, Austin	Nov. 23, 1822	Balto.
	Adeline	16	North America	Woolfolk, Austin	Nov. 23, 1822	Balto.
	Adeline	18	Opelousas	Garland, Rice	July 5, 1836	Balto.
	Adolphus	28	Lady Monroe	Washer, J.E.	Sept. 29, 1825	Balto.
	Agnes	22	Arctic	Maddox, Thomas H.	Jan. 30, 1829	St. Mary's
	Agnes	13	Intelligence	Woolfolk, Austin	Apr. 5, 1823	Balto.
	Agnes	16	Mars	Woolfolk, Austin	Oct. 30, 1824	Balto.
	Agnes	13	Missouri	Cook, James K.	March 2, 1819	Balto.
	Ailey	12	Northumberland	Slatter, Hope Hull	Feb. 27, 1843	Balto.
	Ailsey	22	Henry Clay	Compton & Dorsett	Dec. 8, 1828	Nottingham
	Albert	8	Balloon	Knight, William	Dec. 22, 1821	Balto.
	Albert	4	Edward Everett	Bowser, Gassaway	Oct. 17, 1851	Balto.
	Albert	15	Hamlet	Woolfolk, Joseph B.	Apr. 7, 1824	Balto.

Surname	First Name	Age	Ship	O/S	Date	Depart
	Albert	23	Hortensia	Woolfolk, Austin	Dec. 14, 1836	Balto.
	Albert	14	Patrick Henry	Campbell, Bernard M.	June 1,1853	Balto.
	Albert	24	Victorine	Donovan, Joseph S.	Sept. 29, 1845	Balto.
	Alex	10	Hyperion	King, Gideon T.	Nov. 12, 1821	Balto.
	Alexander	18	Caledonia	Preston, Wm. P.	Dec. 7, 1840	Balto.
	Alexander	6 mon.	Emilie	Ferguson, Thomas	Dec. 14, 1821	Balto.
	Alexander	17	Eros	Oldham, George W.	June 29, 1822	Balto.
	Alexander	24	Hamlet	Woolfolk, Joseph B.	Apr. 7, 1824	Balto.
	Alexander	2	Hibernia	Woolfolk, Austin	Dec. 5, 1826	Balto.
	Alexander	45	Intelligence	Anderson, David	Dec. 20, 1822	Balto.
	Alexander	33	Lady Richmond	Williams, Joseph C.	Apr. 25, 1827	Balto.
	Alexander	20	Susan Miller	Woolfolk, Austin	Oct. 25, 1822	Balto.
	Alexander	9	Tweed	Bowling, John D.	Oct. 20, 1836	Town Creek
	Alferd	19	Nancy W.Stevens	Harker, James	Oct. 25, 1843	Balto.
	Alford	15	Mary	Purvis, Isaac	March 2, 1840	Balto.
	Alfred	22	Bourne	Chabert, Leon	Sept. 10, 1833	Balto.
	Alfred	14	Georgia	Brent, Robert J.	Dec. 23, 1844	Balto.
	Alfred	3	Harriett	Woolfolk, Austin	March 23, 1822	Balto.
	Alfred	9	Hibernia	Woolfolk, Austin	Dec. 5, 1826	Balto.
	Alfred	14	Tippecanoe	Simms, Benedict	Sept. 18, 1844	Balto.
	Alice	20	Arctic	Maddox, Thomas H.	Jan. 30, 1829	St. Mary's
	Alice	8	Catharine Jackson	Brent, George	Nov. 26, 1836	Nanjimoy
	Alice	infant	Hibernia	Woolfolk, Austin	Dec. 5, 1826	Balto.
	Alice	16	Hyperion	Dickey, Joseph	Nov. 12, 1821	Balto.
	Alice	16	Orion	Oldham, George W.	Dec. 30, 1822	Balto.
	Alice	24	Trafalgar	Dent, Wilfred	Jan. 13, 1827	Annapolis

Surname	First Name	Age	Ship	O/S	Date	Depart
	Allen		Caspian	Woolfolk, Austin	Nov. 26, 1836	Balto.
	Allen		Hope	Browning, Robert B.	Dec. 5, 1833	Balto.
	Alley	16	North America	Woolfolk, Austin	Nov. 23, 1822	Balto.
	Ally	8	Hope & Hannah	Woolfolk, Austin	March 11, 1829	Balto.
	Ally	15	Mars	Woolfolk, Joseph B.	Oct. 30, 1824	Balto.
	Alonzo	23	Lady Monroe	Woolfolk, Austin	Sept. 29, 1825	Balto.
	Alsey	30	Harriett	Woolfolk, Austin	March 23, 1822	Balto.
	Alvarado	23	William and Mary	King, Gideon T.	Oct. 9, 1821	Balto.
	Amanda	11	Tippecanoe	Riley, James M.	Oct. 16, 1841	Balto.
	Amanda	16	Trafalgar	Dent, Wilfred	Jan. 13, 1827	Annapolis
	Ambrose	14	Good Hope	Woolfolk, Austin	Nov. 16, 1821	Balto.
	Ambruce	6 mon.	Intelligence	Plater, John R. Jr.	Apr. 12, 1823	St. Mary's
	Ambruce	15	Intelligence	Plater, John R. Jr.	Apr. 12, 1823	St. Mary's
	Amelia	23	Kenhawa	Maddox, Thomas H.	Oct. 26, 1832	Balto.
	Amelia		Louisa	Donovan, Joseph S.	Oct. 9, 1847	Balto.
	Amelia	9	Orion	Oldharr, George W.	Dec. 30, 1822	Balto.
	Amie	17	Franklin	Williamson, David	Nov. 27, 1819	Balto.
	Ammey	18	Lady Monroe	Woolfolk, Joseph B.	March 25, 1825	Balto.
	Amos	21	Actress	Anderson, David	Nov. 8, 1819	Balto.
	Amos	60	Ajax	Richardson, Wade H.	Oct.3, 1833	Balto.
	Amos	13	Betsey	Woolfolk, Austin	Apr. 29, 1828	Balto.
	Amos	26	General Hand	Poindexter, George L.	June 1, 1832	Balto.
	Amos	14	Hamlet	Stansbury, Hammond N.	Apr. 7, 1824	Balto.
	Amos	22	Hope & Hannah	Williams, Joseph C.	Dec. 10, 1827	Balto.
	Amos	18	States	Duer, Robert	Nov. 26, 1825	Balto.
	Amy	9	Budget	Spraggns, Samuel M.	Nov. 27, 1821	Balto.

Surname	First Name	Age	Ship	O/S	Date	Depart
	Amy	14	Hope	Byrne, Walter	Dec. 5, 1833	Balto.
	Amy	19	Hope	Byrne, Walter	Dec. 5, 1833	Balto.
	Amy	28	Intelligence	Woolfolk, Austin	Dec. 20, 1822	Balto.
	Amy	10	Mars	Woolfolk, Austin	Oct. 30, 1824	Balto.
	Amy	17	Missouri	Lewis, Margaret	Feb. 25, 1819	Balto.
	Amy	18	Russell	Woolfolk, Austin	Feb. 28, 2839	Balto.
	Anan	15	Balloon	Milligan, George	Dec. 17, 1821	Balto.
	Andrew	11	Caspian	Woolfolk, Austin	Nov. 26, 1836	Balto.
	Andrew	28	Caspian	Woolfolk, Austin	Nov. 26, 1836	Balto.
	Andrew	11	Harriett	Woolfolk, Richard T.	March 6, 1823	Balto.
	Andrew	13	Henry A. Barling	Marriott, William H.	Oct. 28, 1848	Balto.
	Andrew	21	Isabella		Nov. 26, 1834	Balto.
	Andrew	10	Mars	Woolfolk, Joseph B.	Nov. 2, 1824	Balto.
	Andrew	28	North America	Woolfolk, Austin	Nov. 23, 1822	Balto.
	Andrew	28	Susan Miller	Woolfolk, Samuel M.	Oct. 25, 1822	Balto.
	Andrew	22	Virginia	Crump, R.H.	March 8, 1826	Balto.
	Anette	18	Franklin	Yeiser, John	Nov. 27, 1819	Balto.
	Aney	16	Harriett	Woolfolk, Austin	March 23, 1822	Balto.
	Angelina	22	Osceolo	Carroll, Samuel	Oct. 16, 1839	Balto.
	Angeline	18	Good Hope	Woolfolk, Austin	Nov. 16, 1821	Balto.
	Anis	17	Triton	Anderson, David	Dec. 21, 1819	Balto.
	Ann	16	Algerine	Woolfolk, Austin	Jan. 5, 1826	Balto.
	Ann	20	Arctic	Stone, John	March 16, 1827	Balto.
	Ann	10	Arctic	Kelso, George G.	Nov. 15, 1826	Balto.
	Ann	24	Aurilla	Wikoff, Stephen A.	Apr. 26, 1822	Balto.
	Ann	15	Baltimore	Hale, Colin F.	Oct. 31, 1835	Balto.

Surname	First Name	Age	Ship	O/S	Date	Depart
	Ann	24	Billow	Woolfolk, Austin	Feb. 23, 1828	Balto.
	Ann	10	Budget	Bradley, Robert	Nov. 26, 1821	Balto.
	Ann	20	Catharine	Woolfolk, Austin	Jan. 15, 1831	Balto.
	Ann	infant	Catharine Jackson	Diggs, John H.	Nov. 26, 1836	Nanjimoy
	Ann	20	Charles	Switer, Josephine P.	May 15, 1852	Balto.
	Ann	6	Creole	Allain	Oct. 19, 1833	Balto.
	Ann	12	Cumberland	Callahan, George W.	Oct. 7, 1836	Balto.
	Ann	22	Dryad	Williams, Joseph C.	Dec. 12, 1827	Balto.
	Ann	8	Dumphries	Lee, Richard H.	Sept. 25, 1828	Balto.
	Ann	20	Eros	Woolfolk, Austin	Jan. 28, 1824	Balto.
	Ann	25	Eros	Woolfolk, Austin	Jan. 28, 1824	Balto.
	Ann	2	Georgia	Brent, Robert J.	Dec. 23, 1844	Balto.
	Ann	20	Good Hope	Woolfolk, Samuel M.	Nov. 21, 1821	Balto.
	Ann	14	Hamlet	Woolfolk, Joseph B.	Apr. 7, 1824	Balto.
	Ann	13	Harriet	Carroll, Charles	Dec. 7, 1836	Balto.
	Ann	2	Harriet Cooper	Webb, W.L.	June 12, 1850	Balto.
	Ann	9	Henry Clay	Camphor, Henry	Dec. 8, 1828	Nottingham
	Ann	46	Henry Clay	Camphor, Henry	Dec. 8, 1828	Nottingham
	Ann	5	Hibernia	Chaber, Leon	Dec. 5, 1826	Balto.
	Ann	18	Hibernia	Chaber, Leon	Dec. 5, 1826	Balto.
	Ann	4	Hope	Byrne, Walter	Dec. 5, 1833	Balto.
	Ann	15	Hortensia	Woolfolk, Austin	Dec. 14, 1836	Balto.
	Ann	21	Hyperion	King, Gideon T.	Nov. 12, 1821	Balto.
	Ann	14	Irad Ferry	Clendenin, A.	Jan. 16, 1840	Balto.
	Ann	5	Isabella		Nov. 26, 1834	Balto.
	Ann	16	Julia	Woolfolk, Austin	Jan. 8, 1829	Balto.

Surname	First Name	Age	Ship	O/S	Date	Depart
	Ann	24	Kirkwood	Campbell, Bernard M.	Jan. 4, 1845	Balto.
	Ann	8	Lady Monroe	Chabert, Leon	Sept. 29, 1825	Balto.
	Ann	4	Lafayette	Slatter, Hope Hull	March 25, 1843	Balto.
	Ann	37	Mars	Woolfolk, Austin	Oct. 30, 1824	Balto.
	Ann	12	Mars	Woolfolk, Joseph B.	Oct. 30, 1824	Balto.
	Ann	18	North America	Woolfolk, Austin	Oct. 14, 1823	Balto.
	Ann	3	Orion	Oldham, George W.	Dec. 30, 1822	Balto.
	Ann	23	Palestine	Slatter, Hope Hull	Nov. 16, 1835	Balto.
	Ann	25	Russell	Woolfolk, Austin	Feb. 28, 2839	Balto.
	Ann	35	Serene	Archer, James	Oct. 19, 1836	Balto.
	Ann	21	States	Woodland, James	March 7, 1826	Balto.
	Ann	10	States	Woolfolk, Austin	Nov. 21, 1827	Balto.
	Ann	24	States	Tillotson, Giles	Nov. 22, 1827	Balto.
	Ann	20	Statira	Smith, Doctor James	March 28, 1826	Balto.
	Ann	18	Superb	Donovan, Joseph S.	Nov. 2, 1843	Balto.
	Ann	12	Susan Miller	Woolfolk, Samuel M.	Oct. 25, 1822	Balto.
	Ann	32	Tippecanoe	Purvis, James Franklin	Apr. 1, 1841	Balto.
	Ann	16	Tippecanoe	Simms, Benedict	Sept. 18, 1844	Balto.
	Ann	11	Victorine	Donovan, Joseph S.	Sept. 29, 1845	Balto.
	Ann	17	Zoe	Donovan, Joseph S.	Feb. 16, 1847	Balto.
	Ann	17	Zoe	Donovan, Joseph S.	Feb. 16, 1847	Balto.
	Ann Bailey	21	Hope	Byrne, Walter	Dec. 5, 1833	Balto.
	Ann Eliza	17	Emigrant	Somerrell, Henry S.	Apr. 29, 1836	Balto.
	Ann Elizabeth	3	Balloon	Watts, Samuel	Dec. 22, 1821	Balto.
	Ann Maria	20	Helen A. Miller	Campbell, Bernard M.	Oct. 18, 1852	Balto.
	Ann Maria	infant	Ulysses	Richardson, Wade H.	Nov. 6, 1833	Balto.

Surname	First Name	Age	Ship	O/S	Date	Depart
	Ann Mariah	26	Edward Everett	Campbell, Bernard M.	Oct. 18, 1851	Balto.
	Ann Mariah	16	Lafayette	Woolfolk, Richard	Oct. 18, 1828	Balto.
	Ann Matilda	5	Hyperion	Valcourt, Alex de	May 10, 1822	Balto.
	Anna	3	Actress	Anderson, David	Nov. 8, 1819	Balto.
	Anna	18	Alfred	Woolfolk, Austin	Jan. 18, 1825	Balto.
	Anna	3	Arctic	Williams, Joseph C.	Jan. 31, 1829	St. Mary's
	Anna	14	Balloon	Zacharie, James W.	Dec. 22, 1821	Balto.
	Anna	2	Chatsworth	Anderson, David	Jan. 3, 1821	Balto.
	Anna	6	Elizabeth	Campbell, Bernard M.	Nov. 18, 1848	Balto.
	Anna	15	Henry Clay	Bowes, Thomas F.	Dec. 8, 1828	Nottingham
	Anna	7	North America	Chabert, Leon	Apr. 24, 1826	Balto.
	Anna	25	North America	Woolfolk, Austin	Dec. 20, 1824	Balto.
	Anna	14	St. Mary	Harker, William	Nov. 29, 1845	Balto.
	Anna	20	Trafalgar	Dent, Wilfred	Jan. 13, 1827	Annapolis
	Anna	3	Virginia	Woolfolk, Joseph B.	Dec. 19, 1825	Balto.
	Anna Maria	22	Ajax	Richardson, Wade H.	Oct.3, 1833	Balto.
	Anna Maria	32	Tippecanoe	Murray, Michael	Oct. 16, 1841	Balto.
	Anne	20	Arctic	Magee, Eugene	Oct. 9, 1828	Annapolis
	Anne	15	Catharine	Woolfolk, Austin	Jan. 15, 1831	Balto.
	Anne	16	Good Hope	Woolfolk, Austin	Nov. 16, 1821	Balto.
	Anne	26	Good Hope	Woolfolk, Richard T.	Nov. 21, 1821	Balto.
	Anne	12	Intelligence	King, Gideon T.	Sept. 18, 1821	Balto.
	Anne	19	Isaac Franklin	Kephart, George	Feb. 1, 1839	Balto.
	Anne	36	North America	Thurman, William C.	Apr. 24, 1826	Balto.
	Anne	6	States	Woolfolk, Austin	Nov. 26, 1825	Balto.
	Anne	10	States	Woolfolk, Austin	Nov. 26, 1825	Balto.

Surname	First Name	Age	Ship	O/S	Date	Depart
	Anne	26	States	Woolfolk, Austin	Nov. 26, 1825	Balto.
	Anne	12	Susan Miller	Woolfolk, Austin	Oct. 25, 1822	Balto.
	Anne	18	Susan Miller	Woolfolk, Richard T.	Oct. 25, 1822	Balto.
	Anne	10	Tweed	Davis, R.	Oct. 15, 1836	Balto.
	Anne	6	Unicorn	Hynson, Robert C.	Oct. 23, 1820	Balto.
	Anne Maria	8	Hibernia	Woolfolk, Austin	Dec. 5, 1826	Balto.
	Anny	22	Aurilla	Wikoff, Stephen A.	Apr. 26, 1822	Balto.
	Anthony	24	Hibernia	Woolfolk, Austin	Dec. 5, 1826	Balto.
	Anthony	2	Isaac Franklin	Slatter, Hope Hull	Sept. 28, 1838	Balto.
	Anthony	21	North America	Price, Thomas E.	Nov. 23, 1822	Balto.
	Anthony	13	Serene	Archer, James	Oct. 19, 1836	Balto.
	Anthony	32	States	Morton, George C.	Nov. 26, 1825	Balto.
	Antionette	31	Caledonia	Barnum, Richard	Oct. 19, 1842	Balto.
	Antony	18	Lapwing	Spraggins, Samuel M.	March 22, 1822	Balto.
	Apathy	25	Alfred	Woolfolk, Austin	Jan. 18, 1825	Balto.
	Appalona	18	Elizabeth	Campbell, Bernard M.	Nov. 18, 1848	Balto.
	Appy	4	Franklin	Somerville, Henry	Nov. 27, 1819	Balto.
	Araminta	17	Eros	Knight, William	June 29, 1822	Balto.
	Araminta	2	Henry Clay	Chew, Worhtington	Dec. 8, 1828	Nottingham
	Araminta	8	Orion	Oldham, George W.	Dec. 30, 1822	Balto.
	Araminta	18	Strafford	Harker, William	Nov. 22, 1843	Balto.
	Arch	15	Betsey	Woolfolk, Austin	Apr. 29, 1828	Balto.
	Arch	26	Julia	Poindexter, George	Feb. 10, 1832	Balto.
	Aremento	16	Missouri	Little, Moses	March 2, 1819	Balto.
	Arianna	4 mon.	London	Ringold, J.	Nov. 6, 1840	Balto.
	Arilly	22	States	Duer, Robert	Nov. 26, 1825	Balto.

Surname	First Name	Age	Ship	O/S	Date	Depart
	Armintha	23	Emilie	Poncet, Louis	May 20, 1820	Balto.
	Armstead	27	Opelousas	Garland, Rice	July 5, 1836	Balto.
	Armstead	10	Tippecanoe	Purvis, James Franklin	Apr. 1, 1841	Balto.
	Arnold	15	Arctic	Williams, Joseph C.	Jan. 31, 1829	St. Mary's
	Aron	22	Superb	Donovan, Joseph S.	Nov. 2, 1843	Balto.
	Arthur	29	Emilie	Spencer, Thomas R.P.	Dec. 14, 1821	Balto.
	Arthur	17	Emilie	Anderson, David	March 27, 1821	Balto.
	Arthur	28	Emilie	Spencer, Thomas R.P.	March 27, 1821	Balto.
	Arthur	19	Pandora	Woolfolk, Austin	March 26, 1831	Balto.
	Aryanna	5	Ajax	Allain	Oct.3, 1833	Balto.
	Augusta	21	Kirkwood	Campbell, Bernard M.	Oct. 16, 1845	Balto.
	Augustus	23	Kirkwood	Donovan, Joseph S.	Dec. 10, 1846	Balto.
	Austin	21	Hamlet	Woolfolk, Joseph B.	Apr. 7, 1824	Balto.
	Avery	35	Hope	Richardson, Wade H.	Dec. 3, 1833	Balto.
	Avey	16	Lady Monroe	Woolfolk, Austin	Sept. 29, 1825	Balto.
	Barbara	30	Betsey	Woolfolk, Austin	Apr. 29, 1828	Balto.
	Barbara	24	Henry Clay	Camphor, Henry	Dec. 8, 1828	Nottingham
	Barbara	9	Home	Campbell, Bernard M.	March 22, 1845	Balto.
	Barbara	26	Intelligence	Plater, John R. Jr.	Apr. 12, 1823	St. Mary's
	Barbara	2	Unicorn	Wedenstrandt, John C.	Oct. 23, 1820	Balto.
	Barbara	10	William and Mary	Coleman, Aquila	Oct. 9, 1821	Balto.
	Barnard	6	Arctic	Hall, Joshua F.	Sept. 29, 1827	Balto.
	Barnet	40	Mars	Woolfolk, Austin	Nov. 1, 1824	Balto.
	Basil	28	Arctic	Maddox, Thomas H.	Jan. 30, 1829	St. Mary's
	Basil	4	Edward Everett	Bowser, Gassaway	Oct. 17, 1851	Balto.
	Basil	5	Georgia	Brent, Robert J.	Dec. 23, 1844	Balto.

Surname	First Name	Age	Ship	O/S	Date	Depart
	Basil	16	Hyperion	Anderson, David	May 14, 1822	Balto.
	Bassell	18	Superb	Donovan, Joseph S.	Nov. 2, 1843	Balto.
	Bazil	12	Henry Clay	Bower, Thomas F.	Dec. 8, 1828	Nottingham
	Bazil	20	Mars	Woolfolk, Austin	Oct. 30, 1824	Balto.
	Bazil	24	North America	Woolfolk, Austin	Nov. 23, 1822	Balto.
	Beal	20	Eagle	Bond, Joshua B.	Oct. 29, 1828	Balto.
	Beale	24	Susan Miller	Woolfolk, Richard T.	Oct. 25, 1822	Balto.
	Beckey	11	Betsey	Woolfolk, Austin	Apr. 29, 1828	Balto.
	Beckey	11	Intelligence	Woolfolk, Austin	Apr. 5, 1823	Balto.
	Becki	infant	North America	Woolfolk, Austin	Nov. 23, 1822	Balto.
	Becky	8	Balloon	Milligan, George	Dec. 17, 1821	Balto.
	Becky	16	Climax	Woolfolk, Austin	Dec. 6, 1828	Balto.
	Becky	10	North America	Woolfolk, Austin	Dec. 20, 1824	Balto.
	Becky Ann	8	Lafayette	Woolfolk, Austin	Oct. 18, 1828	Balto.
	Bell Jane	6 mon.	Lady Monroe	Chabert, Leon	Sept. 29, 1825	Balto.
	Ben	4	Balloon	Zacharie, James W.	Dec. 22, 1821	Balto.
	Ben	25	Betsey	Woolfolk, Austin	Apr. 29, 1828	Balto.
	Ben	13	Edward Everett	Campbell, Bernard M.	Oct. 18, 1851	Balto.
	Ben	12	Emilie	Spencer, Thomas R.P.	March 27, 1821	Balto.
	Ben	13	Henry Clay	Bower, Thomas F.	Dec. 8, 1828	Nottingham
	Ben	18	Hibernia	Chabert, Leon	Dec. 5, 1826	Balto.
	Ben	25	Hope	Purnell, Thomas R.	Dec. 3, 1833	Balto.
	Ben	21	Intelligence	Woolfolk, Austin	Apr. 5, 1823	Balto.
	Ben	14	Intelligence	Woolfolk, Austin	Dec. 20, 1822	Balto.
	Ben	21	Intelligence	Woolfolk, Austin	Dec. 20, 1822	Balto.
	Ben	24	Intelligence	Anderson, David	May 1, 1821	Balto.

Surname	First Name	Age	Ship	O/S	Date	Depart
	Ben	23	Intelligence	Ancerson, David	Nov. 3, 1820	Balto.
	Ben	24	Intelligence	Zacharie, James W.	Sept. 18, 1821	Balto.
	Ben	19	Lapwing	Hall, Francis	March 22, 1822	Balto.
	Ben	32	Leda	Nelson, James	Nov. 16, 1848	Balto.
	Ben	16	North America	Woolfolk, Austin	Nov. 23, 1822	Balto.
	Ben	18	North America	Woolfolk, Austin	Nov. 23, 1822	Balto.
	Ben	28	North America	Woolfolk, Austin	Nov. 23, 1822	Balto.
	Ben	9	P. Soule	Biscoe, James	Oct. 9, 1845	Balto.
	Ben	12	Pandora	Woolfolk, Austin	March 26, 1831	Balto.
	Ben	13	Parthenon	White, Henry	Oct. 10, 1842	Balto.
	Ben		Serene	Archer, James	Oct. 19, 1836	Balto.
	Ben	28	States	Woo folk, Austin	Nov. 26, 1825	Balto.
	Ben	28	Tippecanoe	Strohm, John F.	Jan. 17, 1842	Balto.
	Ben	19	Trafalgar	Dent, Wilfred	Jan. 13, 1827	Annapolis
	Ben	10 mon.	Virginia	Woolfolk, Joseph B.	Dec. 19, 1825	Balto.
	Benedict	6 mon.	Eros	Armiage, James	June 29, 1822	Balto.
	Benjamin	12 mon.	Actress	Anderson, David	Nov. 8, 1819	Balto.
	Benjamin	30	Alfred	Woolfolk, Austin	May 7, 1825	Balto.
	Benjamin	18	Algerine	Woolfolk, Austin	March 25, 1826	Balto.
	Benjamin	14	Alonzo	White, Philip	Nov. 8, 1822	Balto.
	Benjamin	10	Catharine	Donovan, Joseph S.	Jan. 18, 1845	Balto.
	Benjamin	25	Emilie	Stansbury, Charles	Nov. 27, 1819	Balto.
	Benjamin	23	Harriett	Woolfolk, Richard T.	March 6, 1823	Balto.
	Benjamin	2	Henry Clay	Camphor, Henry	Dec. 8, 1828	Nottingham
	Benjamin	26	Intelligence	Oldham, George W.	Nov. 4, 1820	Balto.
	Benjamin	24	Kirkwood	Donovan, Joseph S.	Dec. 10, 1846	Balto.

Surname	First Name	Age	Ship	O/S	Date	Depart
	Benjamin	12	Mars	Woolfolk, Austin	Nov. 1, 1824	Balto.
	Benjamin	2	Mars	Woolfolk, Austin	Oct. 30, 1824	Balto.
	Benjamin	21	Mechanic	Woolfolk, Austin	Jan. 1, 1831	Balto.
	Benjamin	21	Orion	Oldham, George W.	Dec. 30, 1822	Balto.
	Benjamin	23	States	Woolfolk, Austin	Nov. 21, 1827	Balto.
	Benjamin	3	States	Woolfolk, Joseph B.	Nov. 21, 1827	Balto.
	Benjamin	26	Statira	Smith, Doctor James	March 28, 1826	Balto.
	Benjamin	4 weeks	Susan Miller	Woolfolk, Richard T.	Oct. 25, 1822	Town Creek
	Benjamin	13	Tweed	Bowling, John D.	Oct. 20, 1836	Balto.
	Bennett	32	Elizabeth	Campbell, Walter L.	Oct. 6, 1849	Balto.
	Bernard	19	Dumphries	Lee, Richard H.	Sept. 25, 1828	Balto.
	Bet	17	Orbit	Chabert, Leon	Apr. 16, 1825	Balto.
	Beth	24	Intelligence	Anderson, David	Nov. 3, 1820	Balto.
	Betsey	14	Ajax	Richardson, Wade H.	Oct.3, 1833	Balto.
	Betsey	7	Arctic	Smith, Leonard J.	Jan. 29, 1828	St. Mary's
	Betsey	33	Arctic	Smith, Leonard J.	Jan. 29, 1828	St. Mary's
	Betsey	15	Arctic	Etchberger, Sarah	Sept. 29, 1827	Balto.
	Betsey	9	Arctic	McConnell, Alex	Sept. 29, 1827	Balto.
	Betsey	20	Catharine	Woolfolk, Austin	Apr. 14, 1831	Balto.
	Betsey	9	Eagle	Bond, Joshua B.	Oct. 29, 1828	Balto.
	Betsey	23	Eros	Woolfolk, Austin	Jan. 28, 1824	Balto.
	Betsey	1	Good Hope	Woolfolk, Samuel M.	Nov. 21, 1821	Balto.
	Betsey	18	Gulnare	Pitts, Thomas H.	Nov. 5, 1830	Balto.
	Betsey	6	Harriett	Pierce, Levi	Oct. 29, 1822	Balto.
	Betsey	40	Henry Clay	Bower, Thomas F.	Dec. 8, 1828	Nottingham
	Betsey	2	Henry Clay	Chew, Worthington	Dec. 8, 1828	Nottingham

Surname	First Name	Age	Ship	O/S	Date	Depart
	Betsey	26	Hope	Byrne, Walter	Dec. 5, 1833	Balto.
	Betsey	16	Intelligence	Woolfolk, Austin	Apr. 5, 1823	Balto.
	Betsey	7	Intelligence	Anderson, David	Dec. 20, 1822	Balto.
	Betsey	28	Intelligence	Woolfolk, Austin	Dec. 20, 1822	Balto.
	Betsey	18	Julia	Woolfolk, Austin	Feb. 10, 1832	Balto.
	Betsey	13	Kenhawa	Madcox, Thomas H.	Oct. 26, 1832	Balto.
	Betsey	2	Lady Monroe	Woolfolk, Austin	March 25, 1825	Balto.
	Betsey	16	Lapwing	Spraggins, Samuel M.	March 22, 1822	Balto.
	Betsey	16	Lawrence	Woolfolk, Austin	May 9, 1823	Balto.
	Betsey	9	Mars	Woolfolk, Austin	Nov. 1, 1824	Balto.
	Betsey	11	North America	Hixon, Lucas	Apr. 24, 1826	Balto.
	Betsey	15	North America	Woolfolk, Austin	Nov. 23, 1822	Balto.
	Betsey	8	Orbit	Woolfolk, Joseph B.	Apr. 16, 1825	Balto.
	Betsey	25	Palestine	Slatter, Hope Hull	Nov. 16, 1835	Balto.
	Betsey	25	Pilgrim	Carr, S.J.	Dec. 22, 1834	Balto.
	Betsey	17	States	Woolfolk, Joseph B.	Nov. 21, 1827	Balto.
	Betsey	15	Susan Miller	Woolfolk, Samuel M.	Oct. 25, 1822	Balto.
	Betsey	35	Susan Miller	Woolfolk, Samuel M.	Oct. 25, 1822	Balto.
	Betsey	14	Triton	Anderson, David	Dec. 20, 1819	Balto.
	Betsy	14	Balloon	Knight, William	Dec. 22, 1821	Balto.
	Betsy	12	Henry Clay	Dorsett, William N.	Dec. 8, 1828	Nottingham
	Betsy	12	Isabella		Nov. 26, 1834	Balto.
	Betsy	13	Mechanic	Woolfolk, Austin	Jan. 1, 1831	Balto.
	Betsy	14	Tippecanoe	Bangs, Theopilus	Apr. 15, 1844	Balto.
	Bett	13	Nelson Clark	Pascault, Lewis F.	May 17, 1836	Balto.
	Betty	15	Aurilla	Warfield, Charles	Apr. 26, 1822	Balto.

Surname	First Name	Age	Ship	O/S	Date	Depart
	Betty	18	Decatur	Stansburg, Mrs.	May 20, 1820	Balto.
	Betty	12	Franklin	Anderson, David	Nov. 27, 1819	Balto.
	Betty	22	Gulnare	Kelso, George G.	Nov. 3, 1830	Balto.
	Betty	13	Harriet	Carroll, Charles	Dec. 7, 1836	Balto.
	Betty	9	Julia	Woolfolk, Austin	Jan. 8, 1829	Balto.
	Betty	15	Mars	Woolfolk, Austin	Oct. 30, 1824	Balto.
	Betty	28	Orion	Oldham, George W.	Dec. 30, 1822	Balto.
	Betty	33	States	Woolfolk, Austin	March 8, 1826	Balto.
	Betty	34	Trafalgar	Dent, Wilfred	Jan. 13, 1827	Annapolis
	Betty Ann	18	Victorine	Slatter, Henry F.	Dec. 31, 1846	Balto.
	Betzy	30	Caspian	Woolfolk, Austin	Nov. 26, 1836	Balto.
	Biby	23	Franklin	Somerville, Henry	Nov. 27, 1819	Balto.
	Bicey	22	Algerine	Woolfolk, Austin	Jan. 5, 1826	Balto.
	Bidely	20	Brunswick	Woolfolk, Austin	Oct. 11, 1831	Balto.
	Bill	17	Agent	Anderson, David	June 8, 1821	Balto.
	Bill	7 mon.	Alfred	Woolfolk, Austin	Jan. 18, 1825	Balto.
	Bill	50	Ann Wayne	Guyton, Elisha	Sept. 2, 1836	Balto.
	Bill	13	Arctic	Stone, John	Jan. 24, 1828	Balto.
	Bill	34	Arctic	Maddox, Thomas H.	Jan. 30, 1829	St. Mary's
	Bill	3	Arctic	Kelso, George G.	Nov. 15, 1826	Balto.
	Bill	11	Arctic	Magee, Eugene	Oct. 9, 1828	Annapolis
	Bill	19	Aurilla	Wikoff, Stephen A.	Apr. 26, 1822	Balto.
	Bill	12	Balloon	Penieres, Emile	Dec. 22, 1821	Balto.
	Bill	21	Balloon	Zacharie, James W.	Dec. 22, 1821	Balto.
	Bill	20	Baltimore	Hale, Colin F.	Oct. 31, 1835	Balto.
	Bill	20	Bourne	Woolfolk, Austin	Sept. 10, 1833	Balto.

Surname	First Name	Age	Ship	O/S	Date	Depart
	Bill	21	Bourne	Rogers, Selemachus	Sept. 9, 1833	Balto.
	Bill	3	Budget	Spraggins, Samuel M.	Nov. 27, 1821	Balto.
	Bill	25	Caspian	Woolfolk, Austin	Nov. 26, 1836	Balto.
	Bill	10	Hamlet	Stansbury, Hammond N.	Apr. 7, 1824	Balto.
	Bill	4	Henry Clay	Waring, E.M.	Dec. 8, 1828	Nottingham
	Bill	11	Hibernia	Chabert, Leon	Dec. 5, 1826	Balto.
	Bill	11	Hope & Hannah	Williams, Joseph C.	Dec. 10, 1827	Balto.
	Bill	20	Hyperion	Anderson, David	May 14, 1822	St. Mary's
	Bill	26	Intelligence	Plater, John R. Jr.	Apr. 12, 1823	Balto.
	Bill	15	Intelligence	Anderson, David	Dec. 20, 1822	Balto.
	Bill	30	Intelligence	Somerville, Alexander	Dec. 20, 1822	Balto.
	Bill	12	Intelligence	Coleman, Henry E.	Nov. 4, 1820	Balto.
	Bill	19	Irad Ferry	Clencenin, A.	Jan. 16, 1840	Balto.
	Bill	16	Kirkwood	Campbell, Bernard M.	Oct. 16, 1845	Balto.
	Bill	15	Lady Monroe	Woolfolk, Austin	Sept. 29, 1825	Balto.
	Bill	46	Lion	Garwood, Richard	March 16, 1845	Balto.
	Bill	23	Mars	Woolfolk, Austin	Oct. 30, 1824	Balto.
	Bill	30	Merrimack	Kelso, George G.	Nov. 2, 1831	Balto.
	Bill	12	North America	Hixon, Lucas	Apr. 24, 1826	Balto.
	Bill	22	North America	Woolfolk, Austin	Dec. 20, 1824	Balto.
	Bill	16	Palestine	Slatter, Hope Hull	Nov. 16, 1835	Balto.
	Bill	38	States	Kelso, George G.	March 8, 1826	Balto.
	Bill	16	Susan Miller	Bibbs, John T.	Oct. 25, 1822	Balto.
	Billy	8	Gulnare	Pitts, Thomas H.	Nov. 5, 1830	Balto.
	Billy	20	North America	Woolfolk, Austin	Dec. 20, 1824	Balto.
	Biner	15	Susan Miller	Woolfolk, Austin	Oct. 25, 1822	Balto.

Surname	First Name	Age	Ship	O/S	Date	Depart
	Blanch	18	Mars	Woolfolk, Austin	Oct. 30, 1824	Balto.
	Bob	21	Aurilla	Wikoff, Stephen A.	Apr. 26, 1822	Balto.
	Bob	25	Betsey	Woolfolk, Austin	Apr. 29, 1828	Balto.
	Bob	10	Budget	Spraggins, Samuel M.	Nov. 27, 1821	Balto.
	Bob	22	Emilie	Bratten, William	March 29, 1821	Balto.
	Bob	20	Franklin	Anderson, David	Nov. 27, 1819	Balto.
	Bob	20	General Hand	Poindexter, George L.	June 1, 1832	Balto.
	Bob	28	Globe	Campbell, Bernard M.	Sept. 7, 1846	Balto.
	Bob	25	Hibernia	Chabert, Leon	Dec. 5, 1826	Balto.
	Bob	16	Hyperion	Anderson, David	May 14, 1822	Balto.
	Bob	14	Intelligence	Woolfolk, Austin	Dec. 20, 1822	Balto.
	Bob		Isabella		Nov. 26, 1834	Balto.
	Bob	14	North America	Woolfolk, Joseph B.	Apr. 29, 1826	Balto.
	Bob	16 mon.	North America	Woolfolk, Austin	Nov. 23, 1822	Balto.
	Bob		Plutarch	Johnson, M.	Sept. 17, 1834	Balto.
	Bob	10	Schuylkill	Cliffe, Henry	Oct. 25, 1822	Balto.
	Bob	8	Serene	Archer, James	Oct. 19, 1836	Balto.
	Bob	16	States	Woolfolk, Austin	March 8, 1826	Balto.
	Bob	14	States	Morton, George C.	Nov. 26, 1825	Balto.
	Bob	16	Trafalgar	Dent, Wilfred	Jan. 13, 1827	Annapolis
	Bridget	24	Caspian	Woolfolk, Austin	Nov. 26, 1836	Balto.
	Bridget	8	Merrimack	Kelso, George G.	Nov. 2, 1831	Balto.
	Brily	2	Arctic	Smith, Leonard J.	Jan. 29, 1828	St. Mary's
	Brister	18	Hyperion	Anderson, David	May 14, 1822	Balto.
	Brown	infant	Victorine	Slatter, Henry F.	Dec. 31, 1846	Balto.
	Butcher	30	Patrick Henry	Campbell, Bernard M.	June 1,1853	Balto.

Surname	First Name	Age	Ship	O/S	Date	Depart
	Caesar	19	Hamlet	Woolfolk, Austin	Jan. 2, 1824	Balto.
	Caesar	25	Virginia	Morton, George C.	Dec. 19, 1825	Balto.
	Cain	12	Triton	Farrow, Nimrod	Dec. 18, 1819	Balto.
	Caleb	26	Hope	Byrne, Walter	Dec. 5, 1833	Balto.
	Caleb	24	Robert Reade	Woolfolk, Austin	Feb. 28, 1824	Balto.
	Caleb	10	Shepcerdiss	Williams, Joseph C.	March 27, 1827	Balto.
	Caleb	13	States	Duer, Robert	Nov. 26, 1825	Balto.
	Calvin	18	Caledonia	Barnun, Richard	Oct. 19, 1842	Balto.
	Camy Ann	16	Hope	Byrne, Walter	Dec. 5, 1833	Balto.
	Carlos	15 mon.	Eros	Anderson, David	June 29, 1822	Balto.
	Carlus	18 mon.	States	Woolfolk, Austin	Nov. 21, 1827	Balto.
	Carolina	6	Emilie	Anderson, David	Jan. 5, 1819	Balto.
	Caroline	21 mon.	Betsey	Woolfolk, Austin	Apr. 29, 1828	Balto.
	Caroline	8 mon.	Betsey	Woolfolk, Austin	Apr. 29, 1828	Balto.
	Caroline	5	Brunswick	Woolfolk, Austin	Oct. 11, 1831	Balto.
	Caroline	10	Elizabeth	Campbell, Bernard M.	Nov. 18, 1848	Balto.
	Caroline	12	Emilie	Ford, Josiah L.	Dec. 14, 1821	Balto.
	Caroline	10	Emilie	Anderson, David	Jan. 5, 1819	Balto.
	Caroline	17	Eros	Woolfolk, Austin	Jan. 28, 1824	Balto.
	Caroline	13	Forester	Garland, Rice	May 26, 1836	Balto.
	Caroline	13	General Hand	Poindexter, George L.	June 1, 1832	Balto.
	Caroline	8	Hamlet	Woolfolk, Austin	Jan. 2, 1824	Balto.
	Caroline	14	Harriett	Woolfolk, Austin	March 23, 1822	Balto.
	Caroline	13	Henry A. Barling	Marriott, William H.	Oct. 28, 1848	Balto.
	Caroline	8	Henry Clay	Compton & Dorsett	Dec. 8, 1828	Nottingham
	Caroline	19	Henry Clay	Dorsett, William N.	Dec. 8, 1828	Nottingham

Surname	First Name	Age	Ship	O/S	Date	Depart
	Caroline	17	Hermann	Rowe, Ralph	June 21, 1851	Balto.
	Caroline	9	Hibernia	Chabert, Leon	Dec. 5, 1826	Balto.
	Caroline	6 mon.	Intelligence	King, Gideon T.	Sept. 18, 1821	Balto.
	Caroline	8	Julia	Woolfolk, Austin	Feb. 10, 1832	Balto.
	Caroline	11	Kirkwood	Campbell, Bernard M.	Oct. 16, 1845	Balto.
	Caroline	14	Lady Monroe	Woolfolk, Joseph B.	March 25, 1825	Balto.
	Caroline	16	Lady Monroe	Woolfolk, Austin	Sept. 29, 1825	Balto.
	Caroline	8	Lapwing	Spraggins, Samuel M.	March 22, 1822	Balto.
	Caroline	12 mon.	Lawrence	Woolfolk, Austin	May 9, 1823	Balto.
	Caroline	12	Mars	Woolfolk, Austin	Oct. 30, 1824	Balto.
	Caroline	18	Nancy W. Stevens	Harker, James	Oct. 25, 1843	Balto.
	Caroline	10	North America	Woolfolk, Austin	Dec. 20, 1824	Balto.
	Caroline	16	Palestine	Slatter, Hope Hull	Nov. 16, 1835	Balto.
	Caroline	17	Superb	Donovan, Joseph S.	Nov. 2, 1843	Balto.
	Caroline	6	Tippecanoe	Bangs, Theopilus	Apr. 15, 1844	Balto.
	Caroline	24	Union	Campbell, Bernard M.	Dec. 16, 1848	Balto.
	Caroline	14	Virginia	Woolfolk, Joseph B.	Dec. 19, 1825	Balto.
	Caroline	19	Caspian	Woolfolk, Austin	Nov. 26, 1836	Balto.
	Carrol	10	Catharine	Bossiere, Joseph S.	Apr. 1, 1831	Balto.
	Caroline		Kirkwood	Donovan, Joseph S.	Dec. 10, 1846	Balto.
	Carroll		Kirkwood	Donovan, Joseph S.	Dec. 10, 1846	Balto.
	Carroll	3	Mary Broughton	Chaplain, J. Bond	Nov. 18, 1851	Balto.
	Casey	8	Chatsworth	Anderson, David	Jan. 3, 1821	Balto.
	Cassan	25	Southerner	Campbell, Bernard M.	Jan. 20, 1850	Balto.
	Cassandra	12	Alonzo	Oldham, George W.	Nov. 7, 1822	Balto.
	Cassandra	3	Balloon	Penieres, Emile	Dec. 22, 1821	Balto.

Surname	First Name	Age	Ship	O/S	Date	Depart
	Cassy	17	Robert Reade	Woolfolk, Austin	Feb. 28, 1824	Balto.
	Caster	27	Mars	Woolfolk, Austin	Nov. 1, 1824	Balto.
	Catharine	7	Actress	Garsieles, James	Nov. 6, 1819	Balto.
	Catharine	12	Brunswick	Woolfolk, Austin	Oct. 11, 1831	Balto.
	Catharine	27	Creole	Allain	Oct. 19, 1833	Balto.
	Catharine	20	Eros	Knight, William	June 29, 1822	Balto.
	Catharine	8 mon.	Henry Clay	Compron & Dorsett	Dec. 8, 1828	Nottingham
	Catharine	23	Signet	Woolfolk, Austin	Nov. 17, 1831	Balto.
	Catherine	19	Aurilla	Wikoff, Stephen A.	Apr. 26, 1822	Balto.
	Catherine	8	Cumberland	Callahan, George W.	Oct. 7, 1836	Balto.
	Catherine	15	Harriet	Carroll, Charles	Dec. 7, 1836	Balto.
	Catherine	16	Harriet	Carroll, Charles	Dec. 7, 1836	Balto.
	Catherine	4	Osceolo	Carroll Samuel	Oct. 16, 1839	Balto.
	Catherine	12	Seguin	Campbell, Bernard M.	July 12, 1853	Balto.
	Cato	65	Charles	Carter, John A.	Sept. 29, 1849	Balto.
	Cato	20	Gulnare	Kelso, George G.	Nov. 3, 1830	Balto.
	Cato	18	Henry Clay	Chew, Worhtington	Dec. 8, 1828	Nottingham
	Caty	22	North America	Woolfolk, Austin	Dec. 20, 1824	Balto.
	Ceanna	5	P. Soule	Biscoe, James	Oct. 9, 1845	Balto.
	Cecilia	4	Balloon	Zacharie, James W.	Dec. 22, 1821	Balto.
	Cecilia		Dumphries	Lee, Richard H.	Sept. 25, 1828	Balto.
	Ceciline	9	Orbit	Pearce, James Alfred	Apr. 13, 1825	Balto.
	Cecily	13	Eros	Armitage, James	June 29, 1822	Balto.
	Celia	4	Balloon	Penieres, Emile	Dec. 22, 1821	Balto.
	Celia	24	Henry Clay	Waring, E.M.	Dec. 8, 1828	Nottingham
	Celia	12	Hyperion	King, Gideon T.	Nov. 12, 1821	Balto.

Surname	First Name	Age	Ship	O/S	Date	Depart
	Celia	18	Isabella	Woolfolk, Austin	Nov. 26, 1834	Balto.
	Celia	12	Mars	Dent, Wilfred	Oct. 30, 1824	Balto.
	Celia	16	Trafalgar	Hall, Francis	Jan. 13, 1827	Annapolis
	Cene	3	Lapwing	Carroll, Charles	March 22, 1822	Balto.
	Cesar	26	Harriet	Carroll, Charles	Dec. 7, 1836	Balto.
	Chance	18	Superb	Donovan, Joseph S.	Nov. 2, 1843	Balto.
	Chany	17	Tweed	Woolfolk, Austin	Oct. 15, 1836	Balto.
	Charity	20	Caspian	Woolfolk, Austin	Nov. 26, 1836	Balto.
	Charity	16	Eros	Woolfolk, Austin	Jan. 28, 1824	Balto.
	Charity	12	Georgia	Brent, Robert J.	Dec. 23, 1844	Balto.
	Charity	8	Mars	Woolfolk, Joseph B.	Oct. 30, 1824	Balto.
	Charity	22	Mechanic	Woolfolk, Austin	Jan. 1, 1831	Balto.
	Charity	35	Serene	Arman, John	Oct. 20, 1836	Balto.
	Charity	14	St. Mary	Campbell, Bernard M.	Nov. 29, 1845	Balto.
	Charity	1	Susan Miller	Woolfolk, Austin	Oct. 25, 1822	Balto.
	Charles	10	Alfred	Woolfolk, Joseph B.	May 7, 1825	Balto.
	Charles	19	Algerine	Woolfolk, Austin	Jan. 5, 1826	Balto.
	Charles	7	Alonzo	White, Philip	Nov. 8, 1822	Balto.
	Charles	35	Arctic	Smith, Leonard J.	Jan. 29, 1828	St. Mary's
	Charles	2	Arctic	Williams, Joseph C.	Jan. 31, 1829	St. Mary's
	Charles	18	Arctic	McConnell, Alex	Sept. 29, 1827	Balto.
	Charles	16 mon.	Aurilla	Warfield, Charles	Apr. 26, 1822	Balto.
	Charles	23	Balloon	Milligan, George	Dec. 17, 1821	Balto.
	Charles	38	Balloon	Zacharie, James W.	Dec. 22, 1821	Balto.
	Charles	22	Bourne	Rogers, Selemachus	Sept. 9, 1833	Balto.
	Charles	7	Emilie	Ford, Josiah L.	Dec. 14, 1821	Balto.

Surname	First Name	Age	Ship	O/S	Date	Depart
	Charles	21	Emilie	Anderson, David	Jan. 5, 1819	Balto.
	Charles	19	Emilie	Spencer, Thomas R.P.	March 27, 1821	Balto.
	Charles	20	Eros	Woolfolk, Austin	Jan. 28, 1824	Balto.
	Charles	30	Franklin	Someville, Henry	Nov. 27, 1819	Balto.
	Charles	5	Georgia	Brent Robert J.	Dec. 23, 1844	Balto.
	Charles	21	Georgia	Brent Robert J.	Dec. 23, 1844	Balto.
	Charles	12	Good Hope	Woolfolk, Austin	Nov. 16, 1821	Balto.
	Charles	16	Good Hope	Woolfolk, Austin	Nov. 16, 1821	Balto.
	Charles	15	Good Hope	Woolfolk, Samuel M.	Nov. 21, 1821	Balto.
	Charles	16	Harriet	Carroll, Charles	Dec. 7, 1836	Balto.
	Charles	21	Harriett	Woolfolk, Austin	March 23, 1822	Balto.
	Charles	19	Helen McLeod	Cox, P. Landale	Nov. 18, 1843	Balto.
	Charles	30	Henry Clay	Camphor, Henry	Dec. 8, 1828	Nottingham
	Charles	20	Henry Clay	Chew, Worthington	Dec. 8, 1828	Nottingham
	Charles	4	Henry Clay	Dorsett, William N.	Dec. 8, 1828	Nottingham
	Charles	17	Hibernia	Kelso, John M.	Dec. 5, 1826	Balto.
	Charles	4	Hibernia	Woolfolk, Austin	Dec. 5, 1826	Balto.
	Charles	14	Hibernia	Woolfolk, Austin	Dec. 5, 1826	Balto.
	Charles	3	Home	Campbell, Bernard M.	March 22, 1845	Balto.
	Charles	4	Hope	Purnel, Thomas R.	Dec. 3, 1833	Balto.
	Charles	5 mon.	Hope	Byrne, Walter	Dec. 5, 1833	Balto.
	Charles	20	Hyperion	Anderson, David	May 14, 1822	Balto.
	Charles	20	Hyperion	Anderson, David	May 14, 1822	Balto.
	Charles	22	Hyperion	King, Gideon T.	Nov. 12, 1821	Balto.
	Charles	9	Intelligence	Plater, John R. Jr.	Apr. 12, 1823	St. Mary's
	Charles	35	Intelligence	Plater, John R. Jr.	Apr. 12, 1823	St. Mary's

Surname	First Name	Age	Ship	O/S	Date	Depart
	Charles	11	Intelligence	Woolfolk, Austin	Dec. 20, 1822	Balto.
	Charles	10	Intelligence	Anderson, David	March 14, 1820	Balto.
	Charles	17	Intelligence	Coleman, Henry E.	Nov. 4, 1820	Balto.
	Charles	10	Jefferson	Woolfolk, Austin	Dec. 24, 1827	Balto.
	Charles	21	Julia	Poindexter, George	Feb. 10, 1832	Balto.
	Charles	21	Lawrence	Woolfolk, Austin	May 9, 1823	Balto.
	Charles	2	Leda	Nelson, James	Nov. 16, 1848	Balto.
	Charles		London	Ringold, J.	Nov. 6, 1840	Balto.
	Charles	5	Mars	Woolfolk, Austin	Nov. 1, 1824	Balto.
	Charles	13	Mars	Woolfolk, Austin	Oct. 30, 1824	Balto.
	Charles	18	Mars	Woolfolk, Austin	Oct. 30, 1824	Balto.
	Charles	3	Mechanic	Woolfolk, Austin	Jan. 1, 1831	Balto.
	Charles	17	Merrimack	Kelso, George G.	Nov. 2, 1831	Balto.
	Charles	2	Missouri	Cook, James K.	March 2, 1819	Balto.
	Charles	6	Nancy W. Stevens	Baker, William	Oct. 23, 1843	Balto.
	Charles	4	North America	Thurman, William C.	Apr. 24, 1826	Balto.
	Charles	15	North America	Thompson, Henry	Dec. 20, 1824	Balto.
	Charles	17	North America	Woolfolk, Austin	Dec. 20, 1824	Balto.
	Charles	17	North America	Woolfolk, Austin	Dec. 20, 1824	Balto.
	Charles	23	North America	Woolfolk, Austin	Nov. 23, 1822	Balto.
	Charles	16	North America	Woolfolk, Austin	Oct. 14, 1823	Balto.
	Charles	20	Palestine	Slatter, Hope Hull	Nov. 16, 1835	Balto.
	Charles	43	Plutarch	Johnson, M.	Sept. 17, 1834	Balto.
	Charles	9	States	Woolfolk, Austin	March 8, 1826	Balto.
	Charles		States	Woolfolk, Austin	Nov. 21, 1827	Balto.
	Charles	9	Statira	Smith, Doctor James	March 28, 1826	Balto.

Surname	First Name	Age	Ship	O/S	Date	Depart
	Charles	24	Susan Miller	Woolfolk, Austin	Oct. 25, 1822	Balto.
	Charles	27	Susan Miller	Woolfolk, Samuel M.	Oct. 25, 1822	Balto.
	Charles	30	Temperance	Duprantier, Guy	Dec. 9, 1818	Balto.
	Charles	22	Trafalgar	Deny, Wilfred	Jan. 13, 1827	Annapolis
	Charles	4	Union	Campbell, Bernard M.	Dec. 16, 1848	Balto.
	Charles	28	Victorine	Woolfolk, Austin	Sept. 12, 1846	Balto.
	Charles	12	Virginia	Chabert, Leon	Dec. 19, 1825	Balto.
	Charles	31	Zuline	Penillant, Stephen	Dec. 15, 1823	Balto.
	Charles Henry	6 mon.	Emilie	Anderson, David	March 27, 1821	Balto.
	Charley	18	Chatsworth	Anderson, David	Jan. 3, 1821	Balto.
	Charlott	20	Caspian	Woolfolk, Austin	Nov. 26, 1836	Balto.
	Charlott	25	Peru	Cruckshanks, J.D.	Nov. 17, 1842	Balto.
	Charlott Jane	10	Kirkwood	Campbell, Bernard M.	Oct. 14, 1848	Balto.
	Charlotte	18	Alfred	Woolfolk, Austin	Jan. 18, 1825	Balto.
	Charlotte	1	Algerine	Woolfolk, Austin	Jan. 5, 1826	Balto.
	Charlotte	13	Algerine	Woolfolk, Joseph B.	Jan. 6, 1826	Balto.
	Charlotte	13	Algerine	Woolfolk, Joseph B.	Jan. 6, 1826	Balto.
	Charlotte	1	Alonzo	White, Philip	Nov. 8, 1822	Balto.
	Charlotte	9	Arctic	Maddox, Thomas H.	Jan. 30, 1829	St. Mary's
	Charlotte	18	Balloon	Milligan, George	Dec. 17, 1821	Balto.
	Charlotte	7	Balloon	Penieres, Emile	Dec. 22, 1821	Balto.
	Charlotte	8	Bourne	Chabert, Leon	Sept. 10, 1833	Balto.
	Charlotte	11	Bourne	Rogers, Selemachus	Sept. 9, 1833	Balto.
	Charlotte	16	Budge	Spraggins, Samuel M.	Nov. 27, 1821	Balto.
	Charlotte	6	E.H. Chapin	Tyson, A.H.	Aug. 25, 1848	Balto.
	Charlotte	25	Eagle	Bond, Joshua B.	Oct. 29, 1828	Balto.

Surname	First Name	Age	Ship	O/S	Date	Depart
	Charlotte	17	Emilie	Anderson, David	March 27, 1821	Balto.
	Charlotte	10	Franklin	Anderson, David	Nov. 27, 1819	Balto.
	Charlotte	18	Gulnare	Kelso, George G.	Nov. 3, 1830	Balto.
	Charlotte	19	Hamlet	Woolfolk, Joseph B.	Apr. 7, 1824	Balto.
	Charlotte	20	Harriett	Arnest, John	March 23, 1822	Balto.
	Charlotte	16	Harriett	Woolfolk, Austin	March 23, 1822	Balto.
	Charlotte	2	Hibernia	Woolfolk, Austin	Dec. 5, 1826	Balto.
	Charlotte	10	Home	Campbell, Bernard M.	March 22, 1845	Balto.
	Charlotte	22	Intelligence	Purviance, William F.	Dec. 29, 1821	Balto.
	Charlotte	2	Isabella	Wallis, Cornelius C.	Nov. 26, 1834	Balto.
	Charlotte	18	Jasper	Woolfolk, Austin	Apr. 7, 1827	Balto.
	Charlotte	6 mon.	Julia	Woolfolk, Austin	Feb. 10, 1832	Balto.
	Charlotte	16	Lafayette	Woolfolk, Richard	Oct. 18, 1828	Balto.
	Charlotte	17	Lapwing	Woolfolk, Joseph B.	Feb. 15, 1827	Balto.
	Charlotte	8	Mars	Woolfolk, Austin	Oct. 30, 1824	Balto.
	Charlotte	18	Mars	Woolfolk, Austin	Oct. 30, 1824	Balto.
	Charlotte	15	Mechanic	Woolfolk, Austin	Jan. 1, 1831	Balto.
	Charlotte	26	Missouri	Gilmore, John	March 1, 1819	Balto.
	Charlotte	19	North America	Woolfolk, Joseph B.	Apr. 26. 1826	Balto.
	Charlotte	17	Orbit	Chabert, Leon	Apr. 16, 1825	Balto.
	Charlotte	6	P. Soule	Biscoe, James	Oct. 9, 1845	Balto.
	Charlotte	24	Sarah	Scotti, Lewis F.	Sept. 8, 1831	Balto.
	Charlotte	32	Serene	Archer, James	Oct. 19, 1836	Balto.
	Charlotte	1	Signet	Woolfolk, Austin	Nov. 17, 1831	Balto.
	Charlotte	23	States	Woolfolk, Austin	Nov. 21, 1827	Balto.
	Charlotte	6 mon.	Susan Miller	Woolfolk, Samuel M.	Oct. 25, 1822	Balto.

Surname	First Name	Age	Ship	O/S	Date	Depart
	Charlotte	14	Ulysses	Richardson, Wade H.	Nov. 6, 1833	Balto.
	Charlotte	6	William and Mary	King, Gideon T.	Oct. 9, 1821	Balto.
	Charlotte Ann	14	Abbot Lord	Campbell, Bernard M.	April 28, 1852	Balto.
	Charry	13	Lady Monroe	Woolfolk, Austin	Sept. 29, 1825	Balto.
	Chasity	11	Betsey	Woolfolk, Austin	Apr. 29, 1828	Balto.
	Chester	19	North America	Woolfolk, Austin	Apr. 24, 1826	Balto.
	Chester	23	Robert Reade	Woolfolk, Austin	Feb. 28, 1824	Balto.
	Chloe	28	Mars	Woolfolk, Austin	Nov. 1, 1824	Balto.
	Chloe Ann	2	Henry Clay	Chew, Worhtington	Dec. 8, 1828	Nottingham
	Chris	2	Nancy W. Stevens	Harp, W.B.	Oct. 23, 1843	Balto.
	Christopher	22	Hope	Byrne, Walter	Dec. 5, 1833	Balto.
	Christopher	20	Hyperion	Woolfolk, Austin	May 10, 1822	Balto.
	Cicelia	6	Catharine Jackson	Diggs, John H.	Nov. 26, 1836	Nanjimoy
	Cicely	21	Aurilla	Wikoff Stephen A.	Apr. 26, 1822	Balto.
	Cirus	18	Kirkwood	Donovan, Joseph S.	Dec. 10, 1846	Balto.
	Cis	54	Harriet	Carroll. Charles	Dec. 7, 1836	Balto.
	Claiborne	16	Opelousas	Garlanc, Rice	July 5, 1836	Balto.
	Clanssa	2	Kirkwood	Campbell, Bernard M.	Jan. 14, 1846	Balto.
	Clara	14	Aurilla	Chabert Leon	Apr. 26, 1822	Balto.
	Clara	23	Balloon	Knight, William	Dec. 22, 1821	Balto.
	Clara	6	Gulnare	Pitts, Thomas H.	Nov. 5, 1830	Balto.
	Clara	45	Louisa	Pendleton, George W.	Nov. 5, 1849	Balto.
	Clara	16	Mars	Woolfolk, Joseph B.	Oct. 30, 1824	Balto.
	Clara	8	Nancy W. Stevens	Baker, William	Oct. 23, 1843	Balto.
	Clare	4	Aurilla	Wikoff, Stephen A.	Apr. 26, 1822	Balto.
	Clarend	12	Superb	Lavelle, John F.	Apr. 7, 1819	Balto.

Surname	First Name	Age	Ship	O/S	Date	Depart
	Clarissa	19	Ann & Leah	Woolfolk, Austin	Nov. 1, 1831	Balto.
	Clarissa	20	Brunswick	Woolfolk, Austin	Oct. 11, 1831	Balto.
	Clarissa	20	Hyperion	King, Gideon T.	Nov. 12, 1821	Balto.
	Clarissa	infant	States	Woolfolk, Austin	Nov. 21, 1827	Balto.
	Clarissa	11	Sultana	Coskery, Bernard	Oct. 31, 1827	Balto.
	Clarissa	27	Trafalgar	Dent, Wilfred	Jan. 13, 1827	Annapolis
	Clarissa	22	Balloon	Penieres, Emile	Dec. 22, 1821	Balto.
	Clary	5	Henry Clay	Chew, Worhtington	Dec. 8, 1828	Nottingham
	Clay	13	Shepderdiss	Williams, Joseph C.	March 27, 1827	Balto.
	Clem	21	Aurilla	Woolfolk, Austin	Apr. 26, 1822	Balto.
	Clem	35	Mars	Woolfolk, Joseph B.	Oct. 30, 1824	Balto.
	Clem	infant	P. Soule	Biscoe, James	Oct. 9, 1845	Balto.
	Clem	11	Trafalgar	Dent, Wilfred	Jan. 13, 1827	Annapolis
	Clif	22	Georgia	Brent, Robert J.	Dec. 23, 1844	Balto.
	Cloe	28	Arctic	Donaldson, Priscilla	Oct. 7, 1828	Balto.
	Cloe	45	Catharine Jackson	Brent, George	Nov. 26, 1836	Nanjimoy
	Cloe	36	Orion	Oldham, George W.	Dec. 30, 1822	Balto.
	Cloe Ann	14	Betsey	Woolfolk, Austin	Apr. 29, 1828	Balto.
	Cloe Ann	20	Charles	Campbell, Bernard M.	Dec. 18, 1850	Balto.
	Collins	26	Intelligence	Anderson, David	Dec. 20, 1822	Balto.
	Comfort	20	Hope	Richardson, Wade H.	Dec. 3, 1833	Balto.
	Comfort	18	States	Woolfolk, Austin	Nov. 21, 1827	Balto.
	Cordelia	19	Mechanic	Woolfolk, Austin	Jan. 1, 1831	Balto.
	Cornelia	5	Catharine Jackson	Diggs, John H.	Nov. 26, 1836	Nanjimoy
	Cornelius	6	Opelousas	Garland, Rice	July 5, 1836	Balto.
	Cory	2	States	Woolfolk, Austin	Apr. 14, 1828	Balto.

Surname	First Name	Age	Ship	O/S	Date	Depart
	Crawley	20	Intelligence	Zacharie, James W.	Sept. 18, 1821	Balto.
	Cressy	19	Susan Miller	Bibbs, John T.	Oct. 25, 1822	Balto.
	Cuffry	26	Hope	Byrne, Walter	Dec. 5, 1833	Balto.
	Cyms	21	Serene	Archer, James	Oct. 19, 1836	Balto.
	Cyrus	16	Balloon	Knight, William	Dec. 22, 1821	Balto.
	Cyrus	12 mon.	Harriet	Woolfolk, Austin	March 23, 1822	Balto.
	Cyrus	30	Mary	W. Taylor	Oct. 6, 1838	Balto.
	Dabby	19	Lady Monroe	Chabert, Leon	Sept. 29, 1825	Balto.
	Dafenney	8	Lady Monroe	Woolfolk, Joseph B.	March 25, 1825	Balto.
	Daisy	31	Patrick Henry	Campbell, Bernard M.	June 1, 1853	Balto.
	Dan	6	Balloon	Milligan, George	Dec. 17, 1821	Balto.
	Dan	20	Caspian	Woolfolk, Austin	Nov. 26, 1836	Balto.
	Dan	21	North America	Woolfolk, Austin	Apr. 24, 1826	Balto.
	Daniel	14	Ajax	Richardson, Wade H.	Oct. 3, 1833	Balto.
	Daniel	23	Algerine	Woolfolk, Austin	Jan. 5, 1826	Balto.
	Daniel	23	Brunswick	Woolfolk, Austin	Oct. 11, 1831	Balto.
	Daniel	18	Chatsworth	Anderson, David	Jan. 3, 1821	Balto.
	Daniel	2	Dumphries	Lee, Richard H.	Sept. 25, 1828	Balto.
	Daniel	14	Emilie	Ferguson, Thomas	Dec. 14, 1821	Balto.
	Daniel	22	Emilie	Anderson, David	March 27, 1821	Balto.
	Daniel	10	Eros	Woolfolk, Austin	Jan. 28, 1824	Balto.
	Daniel	40	Eros	Armitage, James	June 29, 1822	Balto.
	Daniel	12	Franklin	Anderson, David	Nov. 27, 1819	Balto.
	Daniel	7	Hibernia	Chabert, Leon	Dec. 5, 1826	Balto.
	Daniel	18	Hyperion	Anderson, David	May 14, 1822	Balto.
	Daniel	23	Kirkwood	Campbell, Bernard M.	Oct. 16, 1845	Balto.

Surname	First Name	Age	Ship	O/S	Date	Depart
	Daniel	19	Lady Monroe	Chabert, Leon	Sept. 29, 1825	Balto.
	Daniel	13	Lawrence	Woolfolk, Austin	May 9, 1823	Balto.
	Daniel	18	Mars	Woolfolk, Austin	Oct. 30, 1824	Balto.
	Daniel	26	Merrimack	Kelso, George G.	Nov. 2, 1831	Balto.
	Daniel	16	North America	Woolfolk, Austin	Dec. 20, 1824	Balto.
	Daniel	19	North America	Woolfolk, Austin	Dec. 20, 1824	Balto.
	Daniel	17	North America	Woolfolk, Austin	Oct. 14, 1823	Balto.
	Daniel	23	P. Soule	Biscoe, James	Oct. 9, 1845	Balto.
	Daniel	12	Seaman	Davis, J.L.	Dec. 20, 1838	Balto.
	Daniel	19	Signet	Woolfolk, Austin	Nov. 17, 1831	Balto.
	Daniel	25	States	Kelso, George G.	March 8, 1826	Balto.
	Daniel	19	States	Woolfolk, Austin	Nov. 21, 1827	Balto.
	Daniel	24	States	Woolfolk, Austin	Nov. 21, 1827	Balto.
	Daniel	infant	Ulysses	Richardson, Wade H.	Nov. 6, 1833	Balto.
	Daniel	38	Virginia	Woolfolk, Austin	Nov. 18, 1823	Balto.
	Daphne	23	States	Woolfolk, Austin	March 8, 1826	Balto.
	Daphny	10	Aurilla	Woolfolk, Austin	Apr. 26, 1822	Balto.
	Darkey	14	Hyperion	Dickey, Joseph	Nov. 12, 1821	Balto.
	Darkey	16	Intelligence	McElderry, Hugh	Apr. 4, 1823	Balto.
	Darkey	12	Intelligence	King, Gideon T.	Sept. 18, 1821	Balto.
	Darkey	23	Serene	Archer, James	Oct. 19, 1836	Balto.
	Dary	14	Clio	Starnsburg, William	March 22, 1819	Balto.
	Dave	3	Clio	Anderson, David	March 20, 1819	Balto.
	Dave	23	Missouri	Mulhocan, Hugh	March 2, 1819	Balto.
	David	20	Ajax	Richardson, Wade H.	Oct.3, 1833	Balto.
	David	2	Arctic	Kelso, George G.	Nov. 15, 1826	Balto.

Surname	First Name	Age	Ship	O/S	Date	Depart
	David	19	Balloon	Knight, William	Dec. 22, 1821	Balto.
	David	23	Balloon	Penieres, Emile	Dec. 22, 1821	Balto.
	David	17	Balloon	Zacharie, James W.	Dec. 22, 1821	Balto.
	David	23	Balloon	Zacharie, James W.	Dec. 22, 1821	Balto.
	David	4	Caledonia	Barnum, Richard	Oct. 19, 1842	Balto.
	David	26	Catharine	Woolfolk, Austin	Jan. 15, 1831	Balto.
	David	17	Catharine	Woolfolk, Austin	March 3. 1829	Balto.
	David	3	Cumberland	Callahan, George W.	Oct. 7, 1836	Balto.
	David	22	Emilie	Spencer, Thomas R.P.	Dec. 14, 1821	Balto.
	David	22	Emilie	Thompson, Henry	Jan. 5, 1819	Balto.
	David	25	Harriett	Woolfolk, Austin	March 23, 1822	Nottingham
	David	10	Henry Clay	Waring, E.M.	Dec. 8, 1828	Balto.
	David	25	Hortensia	Woolfolk, Austin	Dec. 14, 1836	Balto.
	David	13	Hyperion	Gassaway, Henry	May 10, 1822	Balto.
	David	26	Intelligence	Woolfolk, Austin	Apr. 5, 1823	Balto.
	David	11	Jefferson	Woolfolk, Austin	Dec. 24, 1827	Balto.
	David	24	Kirkwood	Campbell, Bernard M.	Oct. 16, 1845	Balto.
	David	9	Lady Monroe	Woolfolk, Joseph B.	March 25, 1825	Balto.
	David	35	Lapwing	King, Gideon T.	March 22, 1822	Balto.
	David	18	Mars	Woolfolk, Austin	Nov. 1, 1824	Balto.
	David	23	Mechanic	Woolfolk, Austin	Jan. 1, 1831	Balto.
	David	30	Palestine	Slatter, Hope Hull	Nov. 16, 1835	Balto.
	David	30	Plutarch	Mosse, Henry	Sept. 17, 1834	Balto.
	David	3	Serene	Archer, James	Oct. 19, 1836	Balto.
	David	22	Susan Miller	Woolfolk, Samuel M.	Oct. 25, 1822	Balto.
Davis	David	14	Schuylkill	Cliffe, Henry	Oct. 25, 1822	Balto.

Surname	First Name	Age	Ship	O/S	Date	Depart
	Davis	14	St. Mary	Harker, William	Nov. 29, 1845	Balto.
	Davy	7	Henry Clay	Camphor, Henry	Dec. 8, 1828	Nottingham
	Davy	17	Henry Clay	Dorsett, William N.	Dec. 8, 1828	Nottingham
	Davy	15	Hibernia	Chabert, Leon	Dec. 5, 1826	Balto.
	Davy	3	Lapwing	Spraggins, Samuel M.	March 22, 1822	Balto.
	Davy	17	States	Woolfolk, Austin	Nov. 26, 1825	Balto.
	Debby	3	Hibernia	Chabert, Leon	Dec. 5, 1826	Balto.
	Debby	18	Robert Reade	Woolfolk, Austin	Feb. 28, 1824	Balto.
	Debby	4	States	Woolfolk, Joseph B.	Nov. 21, 1827	Balto.
	Deborah	17	Lady Monroe	Chabert, Leon	Sept. 29, 1825	Balto.
	Deborah	15	William and Mary	Coleman, Aquila	Oct. 9, 1821	Balto.
	Decatur	7	Franklin	Yeiser, John	Nov. 27, 1819	Balto.
	Delia	15	Ajax	Richardson, Wade H.	Oct.3, 1833	Balto.
	Delia	26	Arctic	Kelso, George G.	Nov. 15, 1826	Balto.
	Delia	16	Balloon	Zacharie, James W.	Dec. 22, 1821	Balto.
	Delia	8	Burlington	Stout, G.H.	Oct. 22, 1842	Balto.
	Delia	30	Caspian	Woolfolk, Austin	Nov. 26, 1836	Balto.
	Delia	10	Gulnare	Pitts, Thomas H.	Nov. 5, 1830	Balto.
	Delia	18	Intelligence	Woolfolk, Austin	Dec. 20, 1822	Balto.
	Delia		Isabella		Nov. 26, 1834	Balto.
	Delia		Isabella		Nov. 26, 1834	Balto.
	Delia	18	Lapwing	Hall, Francis	March 22, 1822	Balto.
	Delia	8	Orleans	Stout, G.H.	Oct. 22, 1842	Balto.
	Deliah	7	Billow	Woolfolk, Austin	Feb. 23, 1828	Balto.
	Deliah	25	States	Woolfolk, Austin	Apr. 14, 1828	Balto.
	Delila	1	Balloon	Penieres, Emile	Dec. 22, 1821	Balto.

Surname	First Name	Age	Ship	O/S	Date	Depart
	Dellia	15	Baltimore	Hale, Colin F.	Oct. 31, 1835	Balto.
	Delphi Ann	20	Tangier	Campbell, Bernard M.	Nov. 26, 1853	Balto.
	Delphy	12	Henry Clay	Chew, Worthington	Dec. 8, 1828	Nottingham
	Delphy	4	Missouri	Cook, James K.	March 2, 1819	Balto.
	Denis	11	P. Soule	Biscoe, James	Oct. 9, 1845	Balto.
	Dennis	9	Caspian	Woolfolk, Austin	Nov. 26, 1836	Balto.
	Dennis	22	Charles	Campbell, Bernard M.	Dec. 18, 1850	Balto.
	Dennis	39	Emilie	Hollingsworth, W.Samuel	Aug. 21, 1819	Balto.
	Dennis	35	Henry A. Barling	Campbell, Walter L.	Aug. 11, 1849	Balto.
	Dennis	21	Intelligence	Woolfolk, Austin	Apr. 5, 1823	Balto.
	Dennis	12	Intelligence	Woolfolk, Austin	Dec. 20, 1822	Balto.
	Dennis	20	Intelligence	Anderson, David	March 14, 1820	Balto.
	Dennis	20	Intelligence	Anderson, David	Nov. 3, 1820	Balto.
	Dennis	35	Intelligence	Oldham, George W.	Nov. 4, 1820	Balto.
	Dennis	21	Isaac Franklin	Kephart, George	Sept. 28, 1838	Balto.
	Dennis	26	Kirkwood	Donovan, Joseph S.	Sept. 28, 1846	Balto.
	Dennis	20	Mary Broughton	Chaplain, J. Bond	Nov. 18, 1851	Balto.
	Dennis	23	Signet	Woolfolk, Austin	Nov. 17, 1831	Balto.
	Diana	9	Harriet	Carroll, Charles	Dec. 7, 1836	Balto.
	Diana	3	Hibernia	Woolfolk, Austin	Dec. 5, 1826	Balto.
	Diana	20	Lady Monroe	Woolfolk, Austin	Sept. 29, 1825	Balto.
	Diana	15	North America	Woolfolk, Austin	Nov. 23, 1822	Balto.
	Diana	16	North America	Woolfolk, Austin	Oct. 14, 1823	Balto.
	Diana	25	Orion	Woolfolk, Austin	Dec. 30, 1822	Balto.
	Diana	28	Pilgrim	Williams, George W.	Dec. 22, 1834	Balto.
	Dick	11	Alonzo	Oldham, George W.	Nov. 7, 1822	Balto.

Surname	First Name	Age	Ship	O/S	Date	Depart
	Dick	12	Alonzo	White, Philip	Nov. 8, 1822	Balto.
	Dick	6	Aurilla	Woolfolk, Austin	Apr. 26, 1822	Balto.
	Dick	20	Balloon	Milligan, George	Dec. 17, 1821	Balto.
	Dick	30	Betsey	Woolfolk, Austin	Apr. 29, 1828	Balto.
	Dick	23	Commodore Pattersc	Thompson, Henry	March 20, 1819	Balto.
	Dick	17	Emilie	Jacobs, Charles A.	Nov. 27, 1819	Balto.
	Dick	11	Harriet	Carroll, Charles	Dec. 7, 1836	Balto.
	Dick	24	Henry Clay	Camphor, Henry	Dec. 8, 1828	Nottingham
	Dick	27	Henry Clay	Ghyeler, Robert	Dec. 8, 1828	Nottingham
	Dick		Hope	Browning, Robert B.	Dec. 5, 1833	Balto.
	Dick	17	Intelligence	Woolfolk, Austin	Apr. 5, 1823	Balto.
	Dick	11	Intelligence	Anderson, David	March 14, 1820	Balto.
	Dick	8	Kenhawa	Maddox, Thomas H.	Oct. 26, 1832	Balto.
	Dick	22	North America	Woolfolk, Austin	Oct. 14, 1823	Balto.
	Dick	22	Serene	Archer, James	Oct. 19, 1836	Balto.
	Dick	18	Shepderdiss	Williams, Joseph C.	March 27, 1827	Balto.
	Dick	12	Statira	Smith, Doctor James	March 28, 1826	Balto.
	Dick	12	Susan Miller	Woolfolk, Austin	Oct. 25, 1822	Balto.
	Dick	25	Temperance	Lafitte, John Jr.	Dec. 9, 1818	Balto.
	Dido	30	Missouri	Mulhocan, Hugh	March 2, 1819	Balto.
	Dilvy	13	North America	Woolfolk, Austin	Oct. 14, 1823	Balto.
	Dinah	26	Actress	Anderson, David	Nov. 8, 1819	Balto.
	Dinah	23	Alfred	Woolfolk, Austin	Jan. 18, 1825	Balto.
	Dinah	12	Budget	Spraggins, Samuel M.	Nov. 27, 1821	Balto.
	Dinah	6	Emilie	Anderson, David	Jan. 5, 1819	Balto.
	Dinah	15	Eros	Woolfolk, Austin	Jan. 28, 1824	Balto.

Surname	First Name	Age	Ship	O/S	Date	Depart
	Dinah	40	Franklin	Anderson, David	Nov. 27, 1819	Balto.
	Dinah	20	Isabella	Wall s, Cornelius C.	Nov. 26, 1834	Balto.
	Dinah	12	Lapwing	King, Gideon T.	March 22, 1822	Balto.
	Dinah	32	Nancy W. Stevens	Harp. W.B.	Oct. 23, 1843	Balto.
	Dinah	19	Plutarch	Mosse, Henry	Sept. 17, 1834	Balto.
	Dodson	17	Oscar	O'Bean, Thomas	Sept. 29, 1827	Balto.
	Doll	23	Henry Clay	Waring, E.M.	Dec. 8, 1828	Nottingham
	Dolly	25	Alonzo	White, Philip	Nov. 8, 1822	Balto.
	Dora	18	General Hand	Poindexter, George L.	June 1, 1832	Balto.
	Dorcas	10	Emilie	Spencer, Thomas R.P.	March 27, 1821	Balto.
	Dorcas	34	Lapwing	King, Gideon T.	March 22, 1822	Balto.
	Easter	18	States	Woolfolk, Joseph B.	Nov. 21, 1827	Balto.
	Eban	14	Aurilla	Warfield, Charles	Apr. 26, 1822	Balto.
	Ebben	24	Brunswick	Woolfolk, Austin	Oct. 11, 1831	Balto.
	Ebbin	5	Union	Campbell, Bernard M.	Oct. 9, 1848	Balto.
	Eben	22	Balloon	Watts, Samuel	Dec. 22, 1821	Balto.
	Eben	6	Virginia	Woolfolk, Joseph B.	Dec. 19, 1825	Balto.
	Ebenezer	20	Jefferson	Woolfolk, Austin	Dec. 24, 1827	Balto.
	Eden	12	Intelligence	Anderson, David	March 14, 1820	Balto.
	Edmon	19	Supert	Donovan, Joseph S.	Nov. 2, 1843	Balto.
	Edmond	16	Henry Clay	Dorset, William N.	Dec. 8, 1828	Nottingham
	Edmond	22	Mars	Woolfolk, Austin	Nov. 1, 1824	Balto.
	Edmonds	3	Isabella		Nov. 26, 1834	Balto.
	Edmonia	14	Patrick Henry	Campbell, Bernard M.	June 1,1853	Balto.
	Edmund	3	Hortensia	Woolfolk, Austin	Dec. 14, 1836	Balto.
	Edward		Algerine	Woolfolk, Austin	Jan. 5, 1826	Balto.

Surname	First Name	Ship	Age	O/S	Date	Depart
	Edward	Arctic	13	McConnell, Alex	Sept. 29, 1827	Balto.
	Edward	Balloon	10	Knight, William	Dec. 22, 1821	Balto.
	Edward	Balloon	18	Knight, William	Dec. 22, 1821	Balto.
	Edward	Brunswick	18	Woolfolk, Austin	Oct. 11, 1831	Balto.
	Edward	Harriet	4	Carroll, Charles	Dec. 7, 1836	Balto.
	Edward	Hope	23	Purnell, Thomas R.	Dec. 3, 1833	Balto.
	Edward	Hyperion	3	Anderson, David	May 14, 1822	Balto.
	Edward	Hyperion	12	Anderson, David	May 14, 1822	Balto.
	Edward	Hyperion	22	Anderson, David	May 14, 1822	Balto.
	Edward	Hyperion	25	King, Gideon T.	Nov. 12, 1821	Balto.
	Edward	Intelligence	14	De Mapiere, Victor	Apr. 30, 1821	Balto.
	Edward	Jupiter	10		March 25, 1836	Balto.
	Edward	Margaret Forbs	12	Slatter, Hope Hull	Nov. 28, 1838	Balto.
	Edward	Missouri	14	Andrews, Joseph	March 2, 1819	Balto.
	Edward	Virginia	18	Stone, William	Nov. 18, 1823	Balto.
	Edwin	Eros	21	Anderson, David	June 29, 1822	Balto.
	Edwin	Virginia	1	Woolfolk, Joseph B.	Dec. 19, 1825	Balto.
	Edy	States	16	Tillotson, Giles	Nov. 22, 1827	Balto.
	Eleanor	Alonzo	18	Oldham, George W.	Nov. 7, 1822	Balto.
	Eleanor	Catharine Jackson	18	Brent, George	Nov. 26, 1836	Nanjimoy
	Eleanor	Catharine Jackson	16	Diggs, John H.	Nov. 26, 1836	Nanjimoy
	Eleanor	Hyperion	28	Valcourt, Alex de	May 10, 1822	Balto.
	Eleanora	Arctic	15	Smith, Leonard J.	Jan. 29, 1828	St. Mary's
	Elen	Caledonia	10	Woolfolk, Austin	Oct. 27, 1841	Balto.
	Elen	Julia	15	Woolfolk, Austin	Feb. 10, 1832	Balto.
	Eley	Arctic	7	Magee, Eugene	Oct. 9, 1828	Annapolis

Surname	First Name	Age	Ship	O/S	Date	Depart
	Eley	4	Patriot	Simms, Edward	July 13, 1836	Balto.
	Elias	23	Balloon	Milligan, George	Dec. 17, 1821	Balto.
	Elias	8	Harriett	Woolfolk, Austin	March 23, 1822	Balto.
	Elias	15	Mars	Woolfolk, Austin	Nov. 1, 1824	Balto.
	Elias	16	Strafford	Harker, William	Nov. 22, 1843	Balto.
	Elick	22	Harriett	Woolfolk, Austin	March 23, 1822	Balto.
	Elick	22	Lady Monroe	Woolfolk, Joseph B.	March 25, 1825	Balto.
	Elijah	21	Arctic	Bond, Francis A.	May 15, 1828	Balto.
	Elijah	2	Georgia	Brent, Robert J.	Dec. 23, 1844	Balto.
	Elijah	47	Georgia	Brent, Robert J.	Dec. 23, 1844	Balto.
	Elijah	4	Henry Clay	Camphor, Henry	Dec. 8, 1828	Nottingham
	Elijah	21	Intelligence	Plater, John R. Jr.	Apr. 12, 1823	St. Mary's
	Elijah	37	States	Duer, Robert	Nov. 26, 1825	Balto.
	Elin	17	Caspian	Woolfolk, Austin	Nov. 26, 1836	Balto.
	Elisa	7	Arctic	Kelso, George G.	Nov. 15, 1826	Balto.
	Elisa	16	Georgia	Brent, Robert J.	Dec. 23, 1844	Balto.
	Elisa	10	Hibernia	Chabert, Leon	Dec. 5, 1826	Balto.
	Elisa	13	Hibernia	Chabert, Leon	Dec. 5, 1826	Balto.
	Elisa	18	Hibernia	Chabert, Leon	Dec. 5, 1826	Balto.
	Elisa	15	Lady Monroe	Chabert, Leon	Sept. 29, 1825	Balto.
	Elisa	22	Virginia	Woolfolk, Joseph B.	Dec. 19, 1825	Balto.
	Elisa Ann	5	Lady Monroe	Chabert, Leon	Sept. 29, 1825	Balto.
	Elisabeth	11	Brunswick	Woolfolk, Austin	Oct. 11, 1831	Balto.
	Eliza	9	Alfred	Davidson, george	Jan. 18, 1825	Balto.
	Eliza	23	Alfred	Woolfolk, Austin	May 7, 1825	Balto.
	Eliza	18 mon.	Alonzo	White, Philip	Nov. 8, 1822	Balto.

Surname	First Name	Age	Ship	O/S	Date	Depart
	Eliza	20	Arctic	Maddox, Thomas H.	Jan. 30, 1829	St. Mary's
	Eliza	18	Arctic	Kelso, George G.	Nov. 15, 1826	Balto.
	Eliza	12	Aurilla	Chabert, Leon	Apr. 26, 1822	Balto.
	Eliza	7 mon.	Aurilla	Wikoff, Stephen A.	Apr. 26, 1822	Balto.
	Eliza	8 mon.	Aurilla	Wikoff, Stephen A.	Apr. 26, 1822	Balto.
	Eliza	16	Betsey	Woolfolk, Austin	Apr. 30, 1828	Balto.
	Eliza	8	Billow	Woolfolk, Austin	Feb. 23, 1828	Balto.
	Eliza		Bourne	Handy, Samuel	Oct. 13, 1832	Balto.
	Eliza	10	Bourne	Rogers, Selemachus	Sept. 9, 1833	Balto.
	Eliza	16	Budget	Spraggins, Samuel M.	Nov. 27, 1821	Balto.
	Eliza	18	Caspian	Woolfolk, Austin	Nov. 26, 1836	Balto.
	Eliza	18	Catharine	Woolfolk, Austin	Jan. 15, 1831	Balto.
	Eliza	16	Catharine Jackson	Diggs, John H.	Nov. 26, 1836	Nanjimoy
	Eliza	5	Dumphries	Lee, Richard H.	Sept. 25, 1828	Balto.
	Eliza	17	Elizabeth	Campbell, Bernard M.	Nov. 18, 1848	Balto.
	Eliza	18	Eros	Woolfolk, Austin	Jan. 28, 1824	Balto.
	Eliza	11	Forester	Garland, Rice	May 26, 1836	Balto.
	Eliza	8	Franklin	Anderson, David	Nov. 27, 1819	Balto.
	Eliza	8	General Hand	Poindexter, George L.	June 1, 1832	Balto.
	Eliza	16	Hamlet	Stansbury, Hammond N.	Apr. 7, 1824	Balto.
	Eliza	9	Harriet	Carroll, Charles	Dec. 7, 1836	Balto.
	Eliza	2 mon.	Harriett	Woolfolk, Austin	March 23, 1822	Balto.
	Eliza	16	Harriett	Woolfolk, Austin	March 23, 1822	Balto.
	Eliza	6 mon.	Harriett	Woolfolk, Richard T.	March 6, 1823	Balto.
	Eliza	19	Harriett	Woolfolk, Richard T.	March 6, 1823	Balto.
	Eliza	12	Hector	Woolfolk, Austin	Nov. 4, 1835	Balto.

Surname	First Name	Age	Ship	O/S	Date	Depart
	Eliza	3	Henry A. Barling	Campbell, Bernard M.	Dec. 18, 1851	Balto.
	Eliza	8	Henry Clay	Chew, Worthington	Dec. 8, 1828	Nottingham
	Eliza	14	Hibernia	Woolfolk, Austin	Dec. 5, 1826	Balto.
	Eliza	7	Hope	Byrne, Walter	Dec. 5, 1833	Balto.
	Eliza	27	Hope	Byrne, Walter	Dec. 5, 1833	Balto.
	Eliza	24	Hyperion	Valcourt, Alex de	May 10, 1822	Balto.
	Eliza	17	Hyperion	Dickey, Joseph	Nov. 12, 1821	Balto.
	Eliza	4	Hyperion	Kelso, George Y.	Nov. 8, 1820	Balto.
	Eliza	4	Intelligence	Plater, John R. Jr.	Apr. 12, 1823	St. Mary's
	Eliza	14	Intelligence	Woolfolk, Austin	Dec. 20, 1822	Balto.
	Eliza	18	Intelligence	Anderson, David	Nov. 3, 1820	Balto.
	Eliza	23	Isabella		Nov. 26, 1834	Balto.
	Eliza	16	Julia	Woolfolk, Austin	Feb. 10, 1832	Balto.
	Eliza	42	Kirkwood	Guythe, John	Dec. 10, 1846	Balto.
	Eliza	4	Mars	Woolfolk, Austin	Nov. 1, 1824	Balto.
	Eliza	43	Mars	Woolfolk, Austin	Nov. 1, 1824	Balto.
	Eliza	7	Mars	Woolfolk, Austin	Oct. 30, 1824	Balto.
	Eliza	15	Mars	Woolfolk, Austin	Oct. 30, 1824	Balto.
	Eliza	18	Mecharic	Woolfolk, Austin	Jan. 1, 1831	Balto.
	Eliza	19	North America	Woolfolk, Austin	Dec. 20, 1824	Balto.
	Eliza	14	North America	Woolfolk, Austin	Nov. 23, 1822	Balto.
	Eliza	18	Orion	Oldham, George W.	Dec. 30, 1822	Balto.
	Eliza	20	Osprey	Tilletson, S.R.	Nov. 11, 1847	Balto.
	Eliza	16	Palestine	Slatter, Hope Hull	Nov. 16, 1835	Balto.
	Eliza	17	Palestine	Slatter, Hope Hull	Nov. 16, 1835	Balto.
	Eliza	33	Seaman	Biscoe, James	March 20, 1840	Balto.

Surname	First Name	Age	Ship	O/S	Date	Depart
	Eliza	11	Statira	Smith, Doctor James	March 28, 1826	Balto.
	Eliza	12	Susan Miller	Woolfolk, Austin	Oct. 25, 1822	Balto.
	Eliza	7	Susan Miller	Woolfolk, Samuel M.	Oct. 25, 1822	Balto.
	Eliza	4	Tangier	Campbell, Bernard M.	Nov. 26, 1853	Balto.
	Eliza	20	Temperance	Wikoff, Steven W.	Dec. 12, 1818	Balto.
	Eliza	11	Trafalgar	Dent, Wilfred	Jan. 13, 1827	Annapolis
	Eliza	28	Victorine	Campbell, Bernard M.	Dec. 17, 1845	Balto.
	Eliza	11	Victorine	Campbell, Bernard M.	March 1, 1845	Balto.
	Eliza	18	Virginia	Chabert, Leon	Dec. 19, 1825	Balto.
	Eliza	2 mon.	Virginia	Woolfolk, Austin	Nov. 18, 1823	Balto.
	Eliza	18	William and Mary	King, Gideon T.	Oct. 9, 1821	Balto.
	Eliza Ann	18	Helen A. Miller	Campbell, Bernard M.	Oct. 18, 1852	Balto.
	Eliza Ann	23	Helen A. Miller	Campbell, Bernard M.	Oct. 18, 1852	Balto.
	Eliza Ann	4	Lafayette	Slatter, Hope Hull	March 25, 1843	Balto.
	Eliza Ann	9	Tippecanoe	Purvis, James Franklin	Jan. 17, 1842	Balto.
	Eliza Ann	17	Union	Campbell, Bernard M.	Dec. 16, 1848	Balto.
	Eliza Ann	20	Union	Campbell, Bernard M.	Dec. 16, 1848	Balto.
	Eliza Jane	20	Jane Henderson	Campbell, Bernard M.	Nov. 1, 1852	Balto.
	Eliza Jane	17	Victorine	Slatter, Henry F.	Dec. 31, 1846	Balto.
	Eliza Jane	10	Zoe	Slatter, Hope Hull	Feb. 16, 1847	Balto.
	Elizabeth	13	Aurilla	Warfield, Charles	Apr. 26, 1822	Balto.
	Elizabeth	24	Balloon	Knight, William	Dec. 22, 1821	Balto.
	Elizabeth	19	Balloon	Watts, Samuel	Dec. 22, 1821	Balto.
	Elizabeth	23	Charles	Glavarry, Francis R.	July 10, 1819	Balto.
	Elizabeth	10	Eros	Woolfolk, Austin	Jan. 28, 1824	Balto.
	Elizabeth	30	General Hand	Poindexter, George L.	June 1, 1832	Balto.

Surname	First Name	Age	Ship	O/S	Date	Depart
	Elizabeth	8	Hamlet	Woolfolk, Austin	Jan. 2, 1824	Balto.
	Elizabeth	24	Leda	Nelson, James	Nov. 16, 1848	Balto.
	Elizabeth	14	North America	Woolfolk, Austin	Nov. 23, 1822	Balto.
	Elizabeth	13	Seguin	Campbell, Bernard M.	July 12, 1853	Balto.
	Elizabeth	12	Serene	Archer, James	Oct. 19, 1836	Balto.
	Elizabeth	4	Strafford	Wilson, Thomas C.	Nov. 21, 1843	Balto.
	Elizabeth	16	Supero	Donovan, Joseph S.	Nov. 2, 1843	Balto.
	Elizabeth	1	Susan Miller	Woolfolk, Austin	Oct. 25, 1822	Balto.
	Elizabeth	3	Trafalgar	Dent, Wilfred	Jan. 13, 1827	Annapolis
	Elizabeth Ann	16	Cora	Campbell, Bernard M.	Jan. 20, 1851	Balto.
	Elizabeth Ann	10	Kirkwood	Campbell, Bernard M.	March 23, 1844	Balto.
	Elizabeth Jane	24	Union	Campbell, Bernard M.	Dec. 16, 1848	Balto.
	Elizabeth Jane	9	Union	Sheckles, B.O.	Nov. 17, 1849	Balto.
	Ellen	4	Arctic	Kelso, George G.	Nov. 15, 1826	Balto.
	Ellen	2	Arletta	Carr, Labney S.	July 18, 1826	Balto.
	Ellen	6 mon.	Balloon	Zacharde, James W.	Dec. 22, 1821	Balto.
	Ellen	11	Baltimore	Hale, Colin F.	Oct. 31, 1835	Balto.
	Ellen		Dumphries	Lee, Richard H.	Sept. 25, 1828	Balto.
	Ellen	16	Eros	Woolfolk, Austin	Jan. 28, 1824	Balto.
	Ellen	17	Eros	Woolfolk, Austin	Jan. 28, 1824	Balto.
	Ellen	4	Gulnare	Pitts, Thomas H.	Nov. 5, 1830	Balto.
	Ellen	1 mon.	Harriet Cooper	Webb, W.L.	June 12, 1850	Balto.
	Ellen	20	Hibernia	Chabert, Leon	Dec. 5, 1826	Balto.
	Ellen	infant	Home	Campbell, Bernard M.	March 22, 1845	Balto.
	Ellen	10 mon.	Intelligence	Woolfolk, Austin	Apr. 5, 1823	Balto.
	Ellen	16	Kirkwood	Donovan, Joseph S.	March 9, 1847	Balto.

Surname	First Name	Age	Ship	O/S	Date	Depart
	Ellen	17	Kirkwood	Donovan, Joseph S.	Sept. 28, 1846	Balto.
	Ellen	17	Kirkwood	Donovan, Joseph S.	Sept. 28, 1846	Balto.
	Ellen	19	Lafayette	Woolfolk, Richard	Oct. 18, 1828	Balto.
	Ellen	18	Orbit	Chabert, Leon	Apr. 16, 1825	Balto.
	Ellen	4	Scotia	Woolfolk, Austin	Sept. 30, 1843	Balto.
	Ellen	40	Serene	Archer, James	Oct. 19, 1836	Balto.
	Ellen	14	Shepderdiss	Williams, Joseph C.	March 27, 1827	Balto.
	Ellen	5	Susan Miller	Woolfolk, Samuel M.	Oct. 25, 1822	Balto.
	Ellen	10	Temperance	Wikoff, Steven W.	Dec. 12, 1818	Balto.
	Ellen	16	Zoe	Donovan, Joseph S.	Feb. 16, 1847	Balto.
	Ellenor	22	Hyperion	King, Gideon T.	Nov. 12, 1821	Balto.
	Ellick	11	Caspian	Woolfolk, Austin	Nov. 26, 1836	Balto.
	Ellick	29	Robert Reade	Woolfolk, Austin	Feb. 28, 1824	Balto.
	Ellick	22	Russell	Williams, John G.	Feb. 27, 1839	Balto.
	Ellinore	26	Serene	Archer, James	Oct. 19, 1836	Balto.
	Ellis	19	Temperance	Anderson, David	Dec. 9, 1818	Balto.
	Eloisa	14	Intelligence	De Mapiere, Victor	Apr. 30, 1821	Balto.
	Elsa	15	Calagari	Nelson, George S.	Nov. 7, 1832	Balto.
	Elsa	29	Georgia	Brent, Robert J.	Dec. 21, 1844	Balto.
	Elsey	16	Cumberland	Callahan, George W.	Oct. 7, 1836	Balto.
	Elsey	18	Intelligence	King, Gideon T.	Sept. 18, 1821	Balto.
	Elsey	1	Virginia	Woolfolk, Joseph B.	Dec. 19, 1825	Balto.
	Elusia	9	States	Woolfolk, Austin	Apr. 14, 1828	Balto.
	Emaline	5	Mars	Woolfolk, Austin	Oct. 30, 1824	Balto.
	Emaline	18	Orion	Oldham, George W.	Dec. 30, 1822	Balto.
	Emanuel	27	Balloon	Knight, William	Dec. 22, 1821	Balto.

Surname	First Name	Age	Ship	O/S	Date	Depart
	Emelie	14	Lady Monroe	Chabert, Leon	Sept. 29, 1825	Balto.
	Emeline	18	Alfred	Woolfolk, Austin	Jan. 18, 1825	Balto.
	Emeline	2	Alfred	Woolfolk, Austin	May 7, 1825	Balto.
	Emeline	12	Algerine	Woolfolk, Austin	March 25, 1826	Balto.
	Emeline	9	Arctic	Williams, Joseph C.	Jan. 31, 1829	St. Mary's
	Emeline	15	Clio	Coalman, Henry E.	March 20, 1819	Balto.
	Emeline	2	Emilie	Ferguson, Thomas	Dec. 14, 1821	Balto.
	Emeline	4	Emilie	Ford, Josiah L.	Dec. 14, 1821	Balto.
	Emeline	4	Emilie	Anderson, David	Jan. 5, 1819	Balto.
	Emeline	17	Gulnare	Kelso, George G.	Nov. 3, 1830	Balto.
	Emeline	16	Harriet	Woolfolk, Austin	March 23, 1822	Balto.
	Emeline	18	Hortersia	Woolfolk, Austin	Dec. 14, 1836	Balto.
	Emeline	10 mon.	Mars	Woolfolk, Austin	Oct. 30, 1824	Balto.
	Emeline	15	Mars	Woolfolk, Joseph B.	Oct. 30, 1824	Balto.
	Emeline	16	Orbit	Woolfolk, Joseph B.	Apr. 16, 1825	Balto.
	Emeline	8	Signet	Woolfolk, Austin	Nov. 12, 1831	Balto.
	Emeline	8	Mars	Woolfolk, Joseph B.	Oct. 30, 1824	Balto.
	Emery	12	Arctic	Phillips, Elizabeth	Oct. 4, 1828	Balto.
	Emily	16	Caspian	Woolfolk, Austin	Nov. 26, 1836	Balto.
	Emily	1	Franklin	Yeiser, John	Nov. 27, 1819	Balto.
	Emily	27	Hope	Byrne, Walter	Dec. 5, 1833	Balto.
	Emily	29	Julia	Poindexter, George	Feb. 10, 1832	Balto.
	Emily	20	Orion	Oldham, George W.	Dec. 30, 1822	Balto.
	Emily	13	Palestine	Slatter, Hope Hull	Nov. 16, 1835	Balto.
	Emily		Pilgrim	Williams, George W.	Dec. 22, 1834	Balto.
	Emily	10	Plutarch	Crane, Andrew E.	Sept. 17, 1834	Balto.

Surname	First Name	Age	Ship	O/S	Date	Depart
	Emily	13	Seguin	Campbell, Bernard M.	July 12, 1853	Balto.
	Emily	35	Serene	Archer, James	Oct. 19, 1836	Balto.
	Emily	17	Triton	Lee, Thomas	Dec. 18, 1819	Balto.
	Emma	4	Charles	Campbell, Bernard M.	Dec. 18, 1850	Balto.
	Emma	20	Lafayette	Harker, William	March 25, 1843	Balto.
	Emma	9	States	Woolfolk, Austin	March 8, 1826	Balto.
	Emma	15	States	Woolfolk, Austin	March 8, 1826	Balto.
	Emmanuel	36	Clio	Turner, John S.	March 20, 1819	Balto.
	Emmanuel	24	Good Hope	Woolfolk, Austin	Nov. 16, 1821	Balto.
	Emmos	20	North America	Woolfolk, Austin	Nov. 23, 1822	Balto.
	Emmy	10	Peru	Cruckshanks, J.D.	Nov. 17, 1842	Balto.
	Emory	6 mon.	Baltimore	Hale, Colin F.	Oct. 31, 1835	Balto.
	Emory	12	Budget	Bradley, Robert	Nov. 26, 1821	Balto.
	Emory	9	Leda	Peacock, William W.	Nov. 15, 1848	Balto.
	Empson	11	Mars	Woolfolk, Austin	Oct. 30, 1824	Balto.
	Ennalds	28	Lady Monroe	Woolfolk, Austin	Sept. 29, 1825	Balto.
	Ennison	13	Balloon	Penieres, Emile	Dec. 22, 1821	Balto.
	Ennolds	12	Hector	Woolfolk, Austin	Nov. 4, 1835	Balto.
	Ephraim	infant	Hibernia	Kelso, John M.	Dec. 5, 1826	Balto.
	Ephraim	24	Hortensia	Woolfolk, Austin	Dec. 14, 1836	Balto.
	Ephraim	27	States	Duer, Robert	Nov. 26, 1825	Balto.
	Ephraim	25	Susan Miller	Woolfolk, Richard T.	Oct. 25, 1822	Balto.
	Esherson	20	Lapwing	Hall, Francis	March 22, 1822	Balto.
	Esther	13	Alfred	Stansbury, Hammond N.	Nov. 6, 1824	Balto.
	Esther	13	Aurilla	Warfield, Charles	Apr. 26, 1822	Balto.
	Esther	10	Chatsworth	Anderson, David	Jan. 3, 1821	Balto.

Surname	First Name	Age	Ship	O/S	Date	Depart
	Esther	23	Eros	Armitage, James	June 29, 1822	Balto.
	Esther	17	Hope	Richardson, Wade H.	Dec. 3, 1833	Balto.
	Esther	23	Hyperion	Anderson, David	May 14, 1822	Balto.
	Esther	6	Lapwing	King, Gideon T.	March 22, 1822	Balto.
	Esther	23	Mars	Woolfolk, Austin	Oct. 30, 1824	Balto.
	Esther	14	North America	Woolfolk, Austin	Nov. 23, 1822	Balto.
	Esther	30	Palestine	Slatter, Hope Hull	Nov. 16, 1835	Balto.
	Esther	20	States	Duer, Robert	Nov. 26, 1825	Balto.
	Esther	4	States	Morton, George C.	Nov. 26, 1825	Balto.
	Esther	22	Virginia	Woolfolk, Joseph B.	Dec. 19, 1825	Balto.
	Eugenia	12	Isabella	Wallis, Cornelius C.	Nov. 26, 1834	Balto.
	Evan	28	Susan Miller	Woolfolk, Samuel M.	Oct. 25, 1822	Balto.
	Eve	30	Eros	Oldham, George W.	June 29, 1822	Balto.
	Evelina	21	Tippecanoe	Wallis, Philip	Oct. 16, 1841	Balto.
	Fanny	18	Alfred	Woolfolk, Austin	Jan. 18, 1825	Balto.
	Fanny	22	Architect	Campbell, Bernard M.	Apr. 25, 1846	Balto.
	Fanny	30	Bourne	Chaille, W.H.	Oct. 15, 1832	Balto.
	Fanny	18	Caspian	Woolfolk, Austin	Nov. 26, 1836	Balto.
	Fanny	15	Commodore Patterson	Thompson, Henry	March 20, 1819	Balto.
	Fanny	17	Eros	Woolfolk, Austin	Jan. 28, 1824	Balto.
	Fanny	27	Eros	Armitage, James	June 29, 1822	Balto.
	Fanny	28	Franklin	Anderson, David	Nov. 27, 1819	Balto.
	Fanny	18	Hamlet	Woolfolk, Joseph B.	Apr. 7, 1824	Balto.
	Fanny	19	Harriet	Woolfolk, Austin	March 23, 1822	Balto.
	Fanny	19	Harriet	Woolfolk, Richard T.	March 6, 1823	Balto.
	Fanny	12	Hibernia	Chaber, Leon	Dec. 5, 1826	Balto.

Surname	First Name	Age	Ship	O/S	Date	Depart
	Fanny	8	Hibernia	Woolfolk, Austin	Dec. 5, 1826	Balto.
	Fanny	9	Intelligence	Anderson, David	May 1, 1821	Balto.
	Fanny	19	Lady Monroe	Chabert, Leon	Sept. 29, 1825	Balto.
	Fanny	9	Lady Richmond	Woolfolk, Austin	Apr. 30, 1827	Balto.
	Fanny	16	Lawrence	Woolfolk, Austin	May 9, 1823	Balto.
	Fanny	24	Mechanic	Woolfolk, Austin	Jan. 1, 1831	Balto.
	Fanny	15	North America	Woolfolk, Austin	Dec. 20, 1824	Balto.
	Fanny	9	Russell	Woolfolk, Austin	Feb. 28, 2839	Balto.
	Fanny	16	States	Woolfolk, Austin	Nov. 26, 1825	Balto.
	Fanny	19	States	Woolfolk, Austin	Nov. 26, 1825	Balto.
	Fanny	11	Statira	Smith, Doctor James	March 28, 1826	Balto.
	Fanny	17	Susan Miller	Woolfolk, Richard T.	Oct. 25, 1822	Balto.
	Felix	20	Hyperion	Anderson, David	May 14, 1822	Balto.
	Felix	15	Solomon Saltus	Henderson, Henry	March 1, 1841	Balto.
	Fenson		Missouri	Little, Moses	March 2, 1819	Balto.
	Ferdinand	9	General Pinckney	Slatter, Hope Hull	Jan. 19, 1847	Balto.
	Ferdinand	18	Victorine	Campbell, Bernard M.	March 1, 1845	Balto.
	Ferris	6 mon.	Superb	Anderson, David	Apr. 6, 1819	Balto.
	Ferris Lea	24	Superb	Anderson, David	Apr. 6, 1819	Balto.
	Flora	5	Actress	Anderson, David	Nov. 8, 1819	Balto.
	Flora	23	States	Woolfolk, Austin	Nov. 21, 1827	Balto.
	Flora	13	Susan Miller	Woolfolk, Austin	Oct. 25, 1822	Balto.
	Frances	16	Aurilla	Woolfolk, Austin	Apr. 26, 1822	Balto.
	Frances	19	Balloon	Watts, Samuel	Dec. 22, 1821	Balto.
	Frances	3	Catharine Jackson	Brent, George	Nov. 26, 1836	Nanjimoy
	Frank	23	Alonzo	Oldham, George W.	Nov. 7, 1822	Balto.

Surname	First Name	Age	Ship	O/S	Date	Depart
	Frank	2	Arctic	Smith, Leonard J.	Jan. 29, 1828	St. Mary's
	Frank	15	Arctic	Smith, Leonard J.	Jan. 29, 1828	St. Mary's
	Frank	22	Balloon	Zacharie, James W.	Dec. 22, 1821	Balto.
	Frank	4	Betsey	Woolfolk, Austin	Apr. 29, 1828	Balto.
	Frank	9	Betsey	Woolfolk, Austin	Apr. 29, 1828	Balto.
	Frank	23	Emile	Anderson, David	Jan. 5, 1819	Balto.
	Frank	8	Forester	Garland, Rice	May 26, 1836	Balto.
	Frank	7	Franklin	Yeiser, John	Nov. 27, 1819	Balto.
	Frank	14	Harriett	Woolfolk, Austin	March 23, 1822	Balto.
	Frank	23	Harriett	Woolfolk, Austin	March 23, 1822	Balto.
	Frank	20	Henry Clay	Dorset, William N.	Dec. 8, 1828	Nottingham
	Frank	23	North America	Woolfolk, Austin	Oct. 14, 1823	Balto.
	Frank	3	Serene	Archer, James	Oct. 19, 1836	Balto.
	Frank	16	Serene	Archer, James	Oct. 19, 1836	Balto.
	Frank	25	Susan Miller	Bibbs, John T.	Oct. 25, 1822	Balto.
	Frank	14	Susan Miller	Woolfolk, Austin	Oct. 25, 1822	Balto.
	Frank	11	Virginia	Woolfolk, Austin	March 31, 1828	Balto.
	Fred	46	Caledonia	Barnum, Richard	Oct. 19, 1842	Balto.
	Fred	12	Sarah Ann	Keene, Wallace	Oct. 14, 1836	Balto.
	Frederick	12	Arctic	Magee, Eugene	Oct. 9, 1828	Annapolis
	Frederick	25	Balloon	Zacharie, James W.	Dec. 22, 1821	Balto.
	Frederick	8	Baltimore	Hale, Colin F.	Oct. 31, 1835	Balto.
	Frederick	36	Georgia	Brent, Robert J.	Dec. 21, 1844	Balto.
	Frederick	35	Good Hope	Woolfolk, Richard T.	Nov. 21, 1821	Balto.
	Frederick	20	Intelligence	Lee, William	Dec. 20, 1822	Balto.
	Frederick	16	Intelligence	Anderson, David	Nov. 3, 1820	Balto.

Surname	First Name	Age	Ship	O/S	Date	Depart
	Frederick	18	Isabella	Wallis, Cornelius C.	Nov. 26, 1834	Balto.
	Frederick	5	North America	Chabert, Leon	Apr. 24, 1826	Balto.
	Frederick	22	Orion	Oldham, George W.	Dec. 30, 1822	Balto.
	Frisby	13	Agent	Anderson, David	June 8, 1821	Balto.
	Frisby	13	Ajax	Allain	Oct.3, 1833	Balto.
	Frisby	20	Balloon	Knight, William	Dec. 22, 1821	Balto.
	Frisby	10	Henry Clay	Bower, Robert W.	Dec. 8, 1828	Nottingham
	Frisby	9	Orion	Oldham, George W.	Dec. 30, 1822	Balto.
	Gabe	28	Leda	Nelson, James	Nov. 16, 1848	Balto.
	Gabriel	20	Alfred	Woolfolk, Joseph B.	May 7, 1825	Balto.
	Gabriel	26	Gulnare	Kelso, George G.	Nov. 3, 1830	Balto.
	Gabriel	2	Henry Clay	Chew, Worhtington	Dec. 8, 1828	Nottingham
	Garretson	4	Orion	Oldham, George W.	Dec. 30, 1822	Balto.
	Garrett	25	Eagle	Bond, Joshua B.	Oct. 29, 1828	Balto.
	Gary	23	Henry Clay	Chew, Worhtington	Dec. 8, 1828	Nottingham
	Gatty	17	Emilie	Anderson, David	March 27, 1821	Balto.
	Gelson	40	Mars	Woolfolk, Austin	Nov. 1, 1824	Balto.
	General	35	Kirkwood	Campbell, Bernard M.	March 23, 1844	Balto.
	George	5	Actress	Garsicles, James	Nov. 6, 1819	Balto.
	George		Ajax	Allain	Oct.3, 1833	Balto.
	George	25	Alonzo	Oldham, George W.	Nov. 7, 1822	Balto.
	George	13	Alonzo	White, Philip	Nov. 8, 1822	Balto.
	George	21	Alonzo	White, Philip	Nov. 8, 1822	Balto.
	George	29	Arctic	Maddox, Thomas H.	Jan. 30, 1829	St. Mary's
	George	28	Arctic	Williams, Joseph C.	Jan. 31, 1829	St. Mary's
	George	7	Arletta	Carr, Dabney S.	July 18, 1826	Balto.

Surname	First Name	Age	Ship	O/S	Date	Depart
	George	14	Aurilla	Wikoff, Stephen A.	Apr. 26, 1822	Balto.
	George	9	Balloon	Milligan, George	Dec. 17, 1821	Balto.
	George	30	Balloon	Penieres, Emile	Dec. 22, 1821	Balto.
	George	20	Bourne	Chailie, W.H.	Oct. 15, 1832	Balto.
	George	19	Bourne	Rogers, Selemachus	Sept. 9, 1833	Balto.
	George	7	Brunswick	Woolfolk, Austin	Oct. 11, 1831	Balto.
	George	14	Brunswick	Woolfolk, Austin	Oct. 12, 1831	Balto.
	George	30	Caledonia	Barnun, Richard	Oct. 19, 1842	Balto.
	George	20	Caspian	Woolfolk, Austin	Nov. 26, 1836	Balto.
	George	19	Catharine	Donovan, Joseph S.	Jan. 18, 1845	Balto.
	George	21	Catharine	Donovan, Joseph S.	Jan. 18, 1845	Balto.
	George	16	Catharine Jackson	Brent, George	Nov. 26, 1836	Nanjimoy
	George	14	Charles	Carter, John A.	Sept. 29, 1849	Balto.
	George	13	Creole	Zacharie, Theodore	Oct. 19, 1833	Balto.
	George	22	Eagle	Bond, Joshua B.	Oct. 28, 1828	Balto.
	George	19	Emilie	Ford, Josiah L.	Dec. 14, 1821	Balto.
	George	17	Emilie	Spencer, Thomas R.P.	Dec. 14, 1821	Balto.
	George	28	Emilie	Coalman, Henry E.	Nov. 27, 1819	Balto.
	George	10	Eros	Woolfolk, Austin	Jan. 28, 1824	Balto.
	George	20	Eros	Woolfolk, Austin	Jan. 28, 1824	Balto.
	George	30	Eros	Woolfolk, Austin	Jan. 28, 1824	Balto.
	George	30	Eros	Woolfolk, Austin	Jan. 28, 1824	Balto.
	George	10	Georgia	Brent, Robert J.	Dec. 23, 1844	Balto.
	George	13	Hamlet	Stansbury, Hammond N.	Apr. 7, 1824	Balto.
	George	17	Hamlet	Woolfolk, Austin	Jan. 2, 1824	Balto.
	George	13	Harriett	Woolfolk, Austin	March 23, 1822	Balto.

Surname	First Name	Age	Ship	O/S	Date	Depart
	George	14	Harriett	Woolfolk, Austin	March 23, 1822	Balto.
	George	3	Henry Clay	Camphor, Henry	Dec. 8, 1828	Nottingham
	George	3	Henry Clay	Camphor, Henry	Dec. 8, 1828	Nottingham
	George	2	Henry Clay	Compton & Dorsett	Dec. 8, 1828	Nottingham
	George	16	Henry Clay	Dorsett, William N.	Dec. 8, 1828	Nottingham
	George	11	Hibernia	Chabert, Leon	Dec. 5, 1826	Balto.
	George	16	Hibernia	Chabert, Leon	Dec. 5, 1826	Balto.
	George	infant	Hibernia	Woolfolk, Austin	Dec. 5, 1826	Balto.
	George	22	Hope	Byrne, Walter	Dec. 5, 1833	Balto.
	George	23	Hortensia	Woolfolk, Austin	Dec. 14, 1836	Balto.
	George	4 days	Hyperion	Valcourt, Alex de	May 10, 1822	Balto.
	George	23	Hyperion	Anderson, David	May 14, 1822	Balto.
	George	12	Intelligence	Plater, John R. Jr.	Apr. 12, 1823	St. Mary's
	George	14	Intelligence	Anderson, David	March 14, 1820	Balto.
	George	20	Intelligence	Anderson, David	March 14, 1820	Balto.
	George	24	Isabella	Wallis, Cornelius C.	Nov. 26, 1834	Balto.
	George	20	Isabella		Nov. 26, 1834	Balto.
	George	24	James Ramsay	Thompson, James	Sept. 30, 1831	Balto.
	George	19	John C. Calhoun	Donovan, Joseph S.	Oct. 24, 1850	Balto.
	George	11	Kirkwood	Donovan, Joseph S.	Dec. 10, 1846	Balto.
	George	11	Kirkwood	Campbell, Bernard M.	Oct. 16, 1845	Balto.
	George	36	Lafayette	Slatter, Hope Hull	March 25, 1843	Balto.
	George	25	Lapwing	Anderson, David	March 22, 1822	Balto.
	George	16	Lapwing	King, Gideon T.	March 22, 1822	Balto.
	George	20	Lapwing	Spraggins, Samuel M.	March 22, 1822	Balto.
	George	16	Mars	Woolfolk, Austin	Oct. 30, 1824	Balto.

Surname	First Name	Age	Ship	O/S	Date	Depart
	George	24	Mars	Woolfolk, Austin	Oct. 30, 1824	Balto.
	George	13	Missouri	Little, Moses	March 2, 1819	Balto.
	George	22	North America	Woolfolk, Joseph B.	Aor. 25, 1826	Balto.
	George	7 mon.	North America	Woolfolk, Austin	Nov. 23, 1822	Balto.
	George	26	North America	Woolfolk, Austin	Oct. 14, 1823	Balto.
	George	26	Orion	Woolfolk, Richard	Dec. 30, 1822	Balto.
	George	16	Phoenix	Donovan, Joseph S.	March 27, 1847	Balto.
	George	21	Phoenix	Donovan, Joseph S.	March 27, 1847	Balto.
	George	24	Sarah	Woolfolk, Austin	Apr. 2, 1831	Balto.
	George	9	Shamrock	Guyton, Elisha	March 11, 1840	Balto.
	George	10	Snow	Willis	Feb 5, 1835	Balto.
	George	17	States	Chabert, Leon	March 8, 1826	Balto.
	George	16	States	Woolfolk, Austin	March 8, 1826	Balto.
	George		States	Woolfolk, Austin	Nov. 21, 1827	Balto.
	George	4	States	Woolfolk, Joseph B.	Nov. 21, 1827	Balto.
	George	7	States	Duer, Robert	Nov. 26, 1825	Balto.
	George	8	Statira	Smith, Doctor James	March 28, 1826	Balto.
	George	26	Susan Miller	Woolfolk, Austin	Oct. 25, 1822	Balto.
	George	22	Susan Miller	Woolfolk, Samuel M.	Oct. 25, 1822	Balto.
	George	2	Tangier	Campbell, Bernard M.	Nov. 26, 1853	Balto.
	George	24	Temperance	Anderson, David	Dec. 9, 1818	Balto.
	George	13	Trafalgar	Dent, Wilfred	Jan. 13, 1827	Annapolis
	George	1 mon.	Tweed	Bowling, John D.	Oct. 20, 1836	Town Creek
	George	1	Victorine	Campbell, Bernard M.	March 1, 1845	Balto.
	George	16	Victorine	Campbell, Bernard M.	March 1, 1845	Balto.
	George	21	Victorine	Donovan, Joseph S.	Sept. 29, 1845	Balto.

Surname	First Name	Age	Ship	O/S	Date	Depart
	George	25	Virginia	Woolfolk, Joseph B.	Dec. 19, 1825	Balto.
	George	5	Virginia	Woolfolk, Austin	March 31, 1828	Balto.
	Georgianna Louisa	11	John C. Calhoun	Donovan, Joseph S.	Oct. 24, 1850	Balto.
	Gerard	2	Catharine Jackson	Diggs, John H.	Nov. 26, 1836	Nanjimoy
	Gerard	17	Kenhawa	Maddox, Thomas H.	Oct. 26, 1832	Balto.
	Gidron	11	Alfred	Cross, William S.	Feb. 10, 1827	Balto.
	Ginney	19	Hope	Purnell, Thomas R.	Dec. 3, 1833	Balto.
	Gould	17	Lady Monroe	Chabert, Leon	Sept. 29, 1825	Balto.
	Gowan	22	Schuylkill	Rogers, G.	Oct. 25, 1822	Balto.
	Grace	19	Mary	Short, Hugh	Feb. 9, 1844	Balto.
	Grace	12	Mary	Smith, E.J.	Nov. 30, 1841	Balto.
	Grace	19	States	Woolfolk, Austin	March 8, 1826	Balto.
	Grace	18	States	Duer, Robert	Nov. 26, 1825	Balto.
	Grace Ann	6 mon.	Balloon	Zacharie, James W.	Dec. 22, 1821	Balto.
	Gracy	3	Trafalgar	Dent, Wilfred	Jan. 13, 1827	Annapolis
	Grandison	12	Arctic	Maddox, Thomas H.	Jan. 30, 1829	St. Mary's
	Grandison	13	Kirkwood	Guyther, John	Dec. 10, 1846	Balto.
	Greenbury	22	Lady Monroe	Woolfolk, Austin	Sept. 29, 1825	Balto.
	Griffin	16	Cumberland	Callahan, George W.	Oct. 7, 1836	Balto.
	Gulliver	17	Good Hope	Woolfolk, Samuel M.	Nov. 21, 1821	Balto.
	Gustavus	12	Balloon	Zacharie, James W.	Dec. 22, 1821	Balto.
	Gusty	25	Henry Clay	Dorsett, William N.	Dec. 8, 1828	Nottingham
	Gusty	16	Trafalgar	Dent, Wilfred	Jan. 13, 1827	Annapolis
	Guy	14	Harriett	Woolfolk, Austin	March 23, 1822	Balto.
	Haelany	3 mon.	Mars	Woolfolk, Austin	Oct. 30, 1824	Balto.
	Hagar	24	Hyperion	Kelso, George Y.	Nov. 8, 1820	Balto.

Surname	First Name	Age	Ship	O/S	Date	Depart
	Hagar	15	Lady Monroe	Woolfolk, Austin	March 25, 1825	Balto.
	Hagar	27	Lawrence	Woolfolk, Austin	May 9, 1823	Balto.
	Haggar	23	William and Mary	King, Gideon T.	Oct. 9, 1821	Balto.
	Ham	19	Hyperion	Dickey, Joseph	Nov. 12, 1821	Balto.
	Hamilton	18	Kirkwood	Wheeler, A.C.	July 19, 1845	Balto.
	Hamp	9	Orbit	Chabert, Leon	Apr. 16, 1825	Balto.
	Hampton	11	Susan Miller	Woolfolk, Austin	Oct. 25, 1822	Balto.
	Hampton	26	Unicorn	Wedenstrandt, John C.	Oct. 23, 1820	Balto.
	Hanah		Dumphries	Lee, Richard H.	Sept. 25, 1828	Balto.
	Handle	24	North America	Woolfolk, Austin	Dec. 20, 1824	Balto.
	Handy	2	Mary	Short, Hugh	Feb. 9, 1844	Balto.
	Handy	17	States	Tillotson, Giles	Nov. 22, 1827	Balto.
	Hannah	10	Alfred	Woolfolk, Austin	Jan. 18, 1825	Balto.
	Hannah	21	Alonzo	Oldham, George W.	Nov. 7, 1822	Balto.
	Hannah	16	Arctic	Williams, Joseph C.	Jan. 31, 1829	St. Mary's
	Hannah	7	Arctic	Kelso, George G.	Nov. 15, 1826	Balto.
	Hannah	14	Aurilla	Warfield, Charles	Apr. 26, 1822	Balto.
	Hannah	40	Balloon	Milligan, George	Dec. 17, 1821	Balto.
	Hannah	1	Balloon	Penieres, Emile	Dec. 22, 1821	Balto.
	Hannah	7	Balloon	Penieres, Emile	Dec. 22, 1821	Balto.
	Hannah	9	Balloon	Watts, Samuel	Dec. 22, 1821	Balto.
	Hannah	45	Bourne	Chaille. W.H.	Oct. 15, 1832	Balto.
	Hannah	20	Eros	Woolfolk, Austin	Jan. 28, 1824	Balto.
	Hannah	28	Good Hope	Woolfolk, Samuel M.	Nov. 21, 1821	Balto.
	Hannah	28	Henry Clay	Bower, Thomas F.	Dec. 8, 1828	Nottingham
	Hannah	25	Hope	Purnell Thomas R.	Dec. 3, 1833	Balto.

Surname	First Name	Age	Ship	O/S	Date	Depart
	Hannah	20	Intelligence	Anderson, David	Nov. 3, 1820	Balto.
	Hannah	11	Isabella	Wallis, Cornelius C.	Nov. 26, 1834	Balto.
	Hannah	6	Isabella		Nov. 26, 1834	Balto.
	Hannah	28	Leda	Nelson, James	Nov. 16, 1848	Balto.
	Hannah		London	Hopp, H.B.	Nov. 6, 1840	Balto.
	Hannah	13	Mars	Woolfolk, Austin	Oct. 30, 1824	Balto.
	Hannah	19	Missouri	Little, Moses	March 2, 1819	Balto.
	Hannah	27	North America	Chabert, Leon	Apr. 24, 1826	Balto.
	Hannah	20	Pandora	Woolfolk, Austin	March 26, 1831	Balto.
	Hannah	3	Serene	Archer, James	Oct. 19, 1836	Balto.
	Hannah	14	States	Woolfolk, Austin	Nov. 26, 1825	Balto.
	Hannah	25	Statira	Smith, Doctor James	March 28, 1826	Balto.
	Hannah	1	Susan Miller	Woolfolk, Austin	Oct. 25, 1822	Balto.
	Hannah	36	Temperance	Poumairat, John	Dec. 9, 1818	Balto.
	Hannah	38	Ulysses	Richardson, Wade H.	Nov. 6, 1833	Balto.
	Hannah	18	Victorine	Campbell, Bernard M.	March 1, 1845	Balto.
	Hannah	15	William and Mary	Coleman, Aquila C.	Oct. 9, 1821	Balto.
	Hannah Ann	2	Emilie	Ford, Josiah L.	Dec. 14, 1821	Balto.
	Hanner	25	Isaac Franklin	Kephart, George	Sept. 28, 1838	Balto.
	Hannibal	16	Algerine	Woolfolk, Austin	March 25, 1826	Balto.
	Hanson	22	Bourne	Woolfolk, Austin	Sept. 10, 1833	Balto.
	Hanson	21	Caroline	Ferguson, Thomas	March 2, 1821	Balto.
	Happy	17	Hyperion	Anderson, David	May 14, 1822	Balto.
	Hariet	11	Home	Donovan, Joseph S.	March 22, 1845	Balto.
	Harney	infant	Victorine	Slatter, Henry F.	Dec. 31, 1846	Balto.
	Harriet	15	Actress	Anderson, David	Nov. 8, 1819	Balto.

Surname	First Name	Age	Ship	O/S	Date	Depart
	Harriet	16	Agent	Anderson, David	June 8, 1821	Balto.
	Harriet	17	Agent	Anderson, David	June 8, 1821	Balto.
	Harriet	19	Algerine	Woolfolk, Austin	March 25, 1826	Balto.
	Harriet	22	Arctic	Kelso, George G.	Nov. 15, 1826	Balto.
	Harriet	24	Aurilla	Warfield, Charles	Apr. 26, 1822	Balto.
	Harriet	10	Balloon	Milligan, George	Dec. 17, 1821	Balto.
	Harriet	2	Balloon	Knight William	Dec. 22, 1821	Balto.
	Harriet	7	Balloon	Zacharie, James W.	Dec. 22, 1821	Balto.
	Harriet	42	Baltimore	Hale, Colin F.	Oct. 31, 1835	Balto.
	Harriet	27	Bourne	Handy, Samuel	Oct. 13, 1832	Balto.
	Harriet	11	Bourne	Chabert, Leon	Sept. 10, 1833	Balto.
	Harriet	3	Brunswick	Woolfolk, Austin	Oct. 11, 1831	Balto.
	Harriet	2	Budget	King, Gideon T.	Dec. 1, 1821	Balto.
	Harriet	20	Commodore Patterson	Thompson, Henry	March 20, 1819	Balto.
	Harriet	6	Dryad	Williams, Joseph C.	Dec. 12, 1827	Balto.
	Harriet	22	Emilie	Ford, Josiah L.	Dec. 14, 1821	Balto.
	Harriet	10 mon.	Emilie	Spence, Thomas R.P.	March 27, 1821	Balto.
	Harriet	6 mon.	Eros	Oldham, George W.	June 29, 1822	Balto.
	Harriet	10	Good Hope	Woolfolk, Samuel M.	Nov. 21, 1821	Balto.
	Harriet	30	Gulnare	Pitts, Thomas H.	Nov. 5, 1830	Balto.
	Harriet	2	Harriet	Carroll, Charles	Dec. 7, 1836	Balto.
	Harriet	17	Harriet	Woolfolk, Austin	March 23, 1822	Balto.
	Harriet	11	Harriet	Pierce, Levi	Oct. 29, 1822	Balto.
	Harriet	6	Henry Clay	Compton & Dorsett	Dec. 8, 1828	Nottingham
	Harriet	6	Hope & Hannah	Williams, Joseph C.	Dec. 10, 1827	Balto.
	Harriet	14	Hyperion	Anderson, David	May 14, 1822	Balto.

Surname	First Name	Age	Ship	O/S	Date	Depart
	Harriet	8	Hyperion	King, Gideon T.	Nov. 12, 1821	Balto.
	Harriet	2	Hyperion	Lee, Thomas	Nov. 9, 1821	Balto.
	Harriet	23	Intelligence	Barron, John	Apr. 30, 1821	Balto.
	Harriet	14	Lady Monroe	Woolfolk, Joseph B.	March 25, 1825	Balto.
	Harriet		Lady Monroe	Woolfolk, Joseph B.	March 25, 1825	Balto.
	Harriet	9 mon.	Lafayette	Woolfolk, Joseph B.	Oct. 18, 1828	Balto.
	Harriet	6 mon.	Lafayette	Woolfolk, Richard	Oct. 18, 1828	Balto.
	Harriet	8	Mars	Woolfolk, Joseph B.	Nov. 1, 1824	Balto.
	Harriet	16	Missouri	Little, Moses	March 2, 1819	Balto.
	Harriet	17	North America	Chabert, Leon	Apr. 24, 1826	Balto.
	Harriet	19	North America	Woolfolk, Joseph B.	Apr. 25, 1826	Balto.
	Harriet	17	Orbit	Woolfolk, Austin	Apr. 16, 1825	Balto.
	Harriet	13	P. Soule	Biscoe, James	Oct. 9, 1845	Balto.
	Harriet	15	Sarah	Woolfolk, Austin	Apr. 2, 1831	Balto.
	Harriet	8	Seaman	Biscoe, James	March 20, 1840	Balto.
	Harriet	6 weeks	Serene	Archer, James	Oct. 19, 1836	Balto.
	Harriet		Signet	Woolfolk, Austin	Nov. 17, 1831	Balto.
	Harriet	18	Southerner	Campbell, Bernard M.	Jan. 20, 1850	Balto.
	Harriet	1	States	Duer, Robert	Nov. 26, 1825	Balto.
	Harriet	9	States	Woolfolk, Austin	Nov. 26, 1825	Balto.
	Harriet	25	Susan Miller	Bibbs, John T.	Oct. 25, 1822	Balto.
	Harriet	20	Susan Miller	Woolfolk, Richard T.	Oct. 25, 1822	Balto.
	Harriet	16	Virginia	Woolfolk, Austin	March 31, 1828	Balto.
	Harriet Ann	13	Charles	Campbell, Bernard M.	Dec. 18, 1850	Balto.
	Harriett	26	Alfred	Woolfolk, Joseph B.	May 7, 1825	Balto.
	Harriett	23	Arctic	Smith, Leonard J.	Jan. 29, 1828	St. Mary's

Surname	First Name	Age	Ship	O/S	Date	Depart
	Harriett	8	Arctic	Bond, Francis A.	May 15, 1828	Balto.
	Harriett	25	Arctic	Cliffe, Henry	Oct. 4, 1828	Balto.
	Harriett	4	E.H. Chapin	Tyson, A.H.	Aug. 25, 1848	Balto.
	Harriett	30	Frances Amy	Donovan, Joseph S.	Jan. 20, 1847	Balto.
	Harriett	16	Franklin	Somerville, Henry	Nov. 27, 1819	Balto.
	Harriett	15	Georgia	Brent, Robert J.	Dec. 23, 1844	Balto.
	Harriett	4	Good Hope	Woolfolk, Austin	Nov. 16, 1821	Balto.
	Harriett	35	Henry A. Barling	Marriott, William H.	Oct. 28, 1848	Balto.
	Harriett	2	Hope	Purnell, Thomas R.	Dec. 3, 1833	Balto.
	Harriett	1	Hyperion	Dickey, Joseph	Nov. 12, 1821	Balto.
	Harriett	40	Intelligence	Andersen, David	Dec. 20, 1822	Balto.
	Harriett	11	Intelligence	Andersen, David	Nov. 3, 1820	Balto.
	Harriett	18	Mars	Woolfolk, Austin	Oct. 30, 1824	Balto.
	Harriett	18	Nancy W.Stevens	Harker, James	Oct. 25, 1843	Balto.
	Harriett	13	Nelson Clark	Pascault, Lewis F.	May 17, 1836	Balto.
	Harriett	14	Palestine	Slatter, Hope Hull	Nov. 16, 1835	Balto.
	Harriett	14	Palestine	Slatter, Hope Hull	Nov. 16, 1835	Balto.
	Harriett	16	Palestine	Slatter, Hope Hull	Nov. 16, 1835	Balto.
	Harriett	23	Robert Reade	Woolfolk, Austin	Feb. 28, 1824	Balto.
	Harriett	35	Sarah	Winter, Gabriel	Sept. 8, 1831	Balto.
	Harriett	5	Strafford	Wilson, Thomas C.	Nov. 21, 1843	Balto.
	Harriett	13	Triton	Anderson, David	Dec. 20, 1819	Balto.
	Harriett	19	Virginia	Stone, William	Nov. 18, 1823	Balto.
	Harriett Ann	20	Elizabeth	Rodbird, Ebenezer	Nov. 18, 1848	Balto.
	Harriot	20	Catharine Jackson	Brent, George	Nov. 26, 1836	Nanjimoy
	Harriott	27	Ajax	Richardson, Wade H.	Oct.3, 1833	Balto.

Surname	First Name	Age	Ship	O/S	Date	Depart
	Harriott	16	Arctic	Williams, Joseph C.	Jan. 31, 1829	St. Mary's
	Harris	20	Ajax	Richardson, Wade H.	Oct.3, 1833	Balto.
	Harris	6	Eliza	Slatter, Hope Hull	Oct. 9, 1840	Balto.
	Harris	19	Intelligence	King, Gideon T.	Sept. 18, 1821	Balto.
	Harris	4	Temperance	Wikoff, Steven W.	Dec. 12, 1818	Balto.
	Harrison	9 mon.	Budget	Bradley, Robert	Nov. 26, 1821	Balto.
	Harrison	17	Tippecanoe	Simms, Benedict	Sept. 18, 1844	Balto.
	Harriss	17	Victorine	Donovan, Joseph S.	Sept. 29, 1845	Balto.
	Harry	16	Agent	Anderson, David	June 8, 1821	Balto.
	Harry	20	Alonzo	White, Philip	Nov. 8, 1822	Balto.
	Harry	27	Anice	Lee, John	May 24, 1830	Balto.
	Harry	16	Arctic	Dunham, John	Jan. 24, 1828	Balto.
	Harry	25	Arctic	Smith, Leonard J.	Jan. 29, 1828	St. Mary's
	Harry	28	Arctic	Williams, Joseph C.	Jan. 31, 1829	St. Mary's
	Harry	6	Balloon	Milligan, George	Dec. 17, 1821	Balto.
	Harry	15	Balloon	Penieres, Emile	Dec. 22, 1821	Balto.
	Harry	23	Bourne	Rogers, Selemachus	Sept. 9, 1833	Balto.
	Harry	36	Catharine Jackson	Diggs, John H.	Nov. 26, 1836	Nanjimoy
	Harry	7	Dumphries	Lee, Richard H.	Sept. 25, 1828	Balto.
	Harry	32	Emilie	Briscoe, Frederick G.	Dec. 14, 1821	Balto.
	Harry	28	Emilie	Spencer, Thomas R.P.	Dec. 14, 1821	Balto.
	Harry	17	Emilie	Spencer, Thomas R.P.	March 27, 1821	Balto.
	Harry	10	Eros	Woolfolk, Austin	Jan. 28, 1824	Balto.
	Harry	40	Eros	Woolfolk, Austin	Jan. 28, 1824	Balto.
	Harry	18 mon.	Eros	Armitage, James	June 29, 1822	Balto.
	Harry	16	Franklin	Somerville, Henry	Nov. 27, 1819	Balto.

Surname	First Name	Age	Ship	O/S	Date	Depart
	Harry	30	Harriett	King, John	March 23, 1822	Balto.
	Harry	24	Intelligence	Woolfolk, Austin	Apr. 5, 1823	Balto.
	Harry	23	Intelligence	Anderson, David	Dec. 20, 1822	Balto.
	Harry	19	Intelligence	Woolfolk, Austin	Dec. 20, 1822	Balto.
	Harry	16	Intelligence	Anderson, David	May 1, 1821	Balto.
	Harry	28	Intelligence	Anderson, David	Nov. 3, 1820	Balto.
	Harry	20	Lady Monroe	Woolfolk, Austin	March 25, 1825	Balto.
	Harry	20	Mars	Woolfolk, Joseph B.	Nov. 2, 1824	Balto.
	Harry	23	Mars	Woolfolk, Joseph B.	Oct. 30, 1824	Balto.
	Harry	22	Mechanic	Woolfolk, Austin	Jan. 1, 1831	Balto.
	Harry	19	Merrimack	Kelso, George G.	Nov. 2, 1831	Balto.
	Harry	20	North America	Chabert, Leon	Apr. 24, 1826	Balto.
	Harry	20	North America	Woolfolk, Austin	Dec. 20, 1824	Balto.
	Harry	23	North America	Woolfolk, Austin	Dec. 20, 1824	Balto.
	Harry	22	Palestine	Slatter, Hope Hull	Nov. 16, 1835	Balto.
	Harry	23	States	Woolfolk, Austin	March 8, 1826	Balto.
	Harry	15	States	Morton, George C.	Nov. 26, 1825	Balto.
	Harry	5	Statira	Smith, Doctor James	March 28, 1826	Balto.
	Harry	11	Superb	Lavelle, John F.	Apr. 7, 1819	Balto.
	Haywood	infant	St. Mary	Williams, Thomas	Nov. 29, 1845	Balto.
	Hector	17	Good Hope	Woolfolk, Austin	Nov. 16, 1821	Balto.
	Helen	19	Kenhewa	Maddox, Thomas H.	Oct. 26, 1832	Balto.
	Helen	16	Victorine	Campbell, Bernard M.	March 1, 1845	Balto.
	Hemsley	21	Aurilla	Woolfolk, Austin	Apr. 26, 1822	Balto.
	Hemsley	17	Palestine	Slatter, Hope Hull	Nov. 16, 1835	Balto.
	Hendley	17	North America	Chabert, Leon	Apr. 24, 1826	Balto.

Surname	First Name	Age	Ship	O/S	Date	Depart
	Henly	20	Hamlet	Woolfolk, Austin	Apr. 7, 1824	Balto.
	Hennay	17	Alonzo	Oldham, George W.	Nov. 7, 1822	Balto.
	Henney	16	Forester	Garland, Rice	May 26, 1836	Balto.
	Henney	8	Harriett	Pierce, Levi	Oct. 29, 1822	Balto.
	Henney	25	Kirkwood	Guytan, Elisha	Dec. 10, 1846	Balto.
	Henney	3	Lapwing	King, Gideon T.	March 22, 1822	Balto.
	Henney	10	Actress	Anderson, David	Nov. 8, 1819	Balto.
	Henny	17	Agent	Anderson, David	June 8, 1821	Balto.
	Henny	3 mon.	Alfred	Woolfolk, Austin	Jan. 18, 1825	Balto.
	Henny	20	Alfred	Woolfolk, Austin	Jan. 18, 1825	Balto.
	Henny	22	Alonzo	White, Philip	Nov. 8, 1822	Balto.
	Henny	12	Ann & Leah	Woolfolk, Austin	Nov.1, 1831	Balto.
	Henny	5	Arctic	Cliffe, Henry	Oct. 4, 1828	Balto.
	Henny	17	Arctic	Magee, Eugene	Oct. 9, 1828	Annapolis
	Henny	32	Catharine Jackson	Diggs, John H.	Nov. 26, 1836	Nanjimoy
	Henny	5	Dumphries	Lee, Richard H.	Sept. 25, 1828	Balto.
	Henny	13	Dumphries	Lee, Richard H.	Sept. 25, 1828	Balto.
	Henny	16	Eros	Woolfolk, Austin	Jan. 28, 1824	Balto.
	Henny	18	Hamlet	Woolfolk, Austin	Jan. 2, 1824	Balto.
	Henny	14	Harriet	Carroll, Charles	Dec. 7, 1836	Balto.
	Henny	2	Harriett	Woolfolk, Austin	March 23, 1822	Balto.
	Henny	16	Henry Clay	Bower, Thomas F.	Dec. 8, 1828	Nottingham
	Henny	30	Henry Clay	Camphor, Henry	Dec. 8, 1828	Nottingham
	Henny	22	Hibernia	Chabert, Leon	Dec. 5, 1826	Balto.
	Henny	33	Hibernia	Chabert, Leon	Dec. 5, 1826	Balto.
	Henny	16	Hyperion	King, Gideon T.	Nov. 12, 1821	Balto.

Surname	First Name	Age	Ship	O/S	Date	Depart
	Henny	26	Hyperion	Davis, H.	Oct. 13, 1835	Balto.
	Henny	17	Intelligence	Anderson, David	Dec. 20, 1822	Balto.
	Henny	14	Mars	Woolfolk, Austin	Oct. 30, 1824	Balto.
	Henny	18	Mars	Woolfolk, Austin	Oct. 30, 1824	Balto.
	Henny	18	Mars	Woolfolk, Joseph B.	Oct. 30, 1824	Balto.
	Henny	16	Missouri	Cook, James K.	March 2, 1819	Balto.
	Henny	26	North America	Woolfolk, Joseph B.	Apr. 26. 1826	Balto.
	Henny	13	North America	Woolfolk, Austin	Nov. 23, 1822	Balto.
	Henny	21	North America	Woolfolk, Austin	Nov. 23, 1822	Balto.
	Henny	14	Oscar	O'Bean, Thomas	Sept. 29, 1827	Balto.
	Henny	42	Pilgrim	Carr, S.J.	Dec. 22, 1834	Balto.
	Henny	30	Shepderdiss	Williams, Joseph C.	March 27, 1827	Balto.
	Henny	2	Susan Miller	Bibbs, John T.	Oct. 25, 1822	Balto.
	Henny	4	Susan Miller	Bibbs, John T.	Oct. 25, 1822	Balto.
	Henny	15	Susan Miller	Woolfolk, Richard T.	Oct. 25, 1822	Balto.
	Henny	18	Susan Miller	Woolfolk, Richard T.	Oct. 25, 1822	Balto.
	Henny	9	Susan Miller	Woolfolk, Samuel M.	Oct. 25, 1822	Balto.
	Henny	38	Triton	Lee, Thomas	Dec. 18, 1819	Balto.
	Henny	16	Virginia	Chabert, Leon	Dec. 19, 1825	Balto.
	Henny	20	Virginia	Woolfolk, Austin	Nov. 18, 1823	Balto.
	Henrietta	25	Balloon	Penieres, Emile	Dec. 22, 1821	Balto.
	Henrietta	5	Betsey	Woolfolk, Austin	Apr. 29, 1828	Balto.
	Henrietta	infant	Calagari	Nelson, George S.	Nov. 7, 1832	Balto.
	Henrietta	32	Catharine Jackson	Brent, George	Nov. 26, 1836	Nanjimoy
	Henrietta	4	Catharine Jackson	Diggs, John H.	Nov. 26, 1836	Nanjimoy
	Henrietta	infant	Charles	Campbell, Bernard M.	Dec. 18, 1850	Balto.

Surname	First Name	Age	Ship	O/S	Date	Depart
	Henrietta	6	Chatsworth	Anderson, David	Jan. 3, 1821	Balto.
	Henrietta	35	Delawarian	Campbell, Bernard M.	Dec. 1, 1848	Balto.
	Henrietta	18 mon.	Emigrant	Somerrell, Henry S.	Apr. 29, 1836	Balto.
	Henrietta	21	Hibernia	Chabert, Leon	Dec. 5, 1826	Balto.
	Henrietta	25	Kirkwood	Donovan, Joseph S.	Sept. 28, 1846	Balto.
	Henrietta	17	Nancy W. Stevens	Harker, James	Oct. 25, 1843	Balto.
	Henrietta	7 mon.	North America	Woolfolk, Joseph B.	Apr. 26. 1826	Balto.
	Henrietta	25	St. Mary	Campbell, Bernard M.	Nov. 29, 1845	Balto.
	Henriette	8	Harriet	Carroll, Charles	Dec. 7, 1836	Balto.
	Henry	22	Alfred	Woolfolk, Austin	Jan. 18, 1825	Balto.
	Henry	10	Algerine	Woolfolk, Austin	March 25, 1826	Balto.
	Henry	30	Anice	Lee, John	May 24, 1830	Balto.
	Henry	20	Ann Wayne	Guyton, Elisha	Sept. 2, 1836	Balto.
	Henry	8	Arctic	Smith, Leonard J.	Jan. 29, 1828	St. Mary's
	Henry	24	Arctic	Maddox, Thomas H.	Jan. 30, 1829	St. Mary's
	Henry	2	Arctic	Magee, Eugene	Oct. 9, 1828	Annapolis
	Henry	13	Balloon	Milligan, George	Dec. 17, 1821	Balto.
	Henry	35	Balloon	Knight, William	Dec. 22, 1821	Balto.
	Henry	1	Balloon	Watts, Samuel	Dec. 22, 1821	Balto.
	Henry	7	Betsey	Woolfolk, Austin	Apr. 29, 1828	Balto.
	Henry	17	Betsey	Woolfolk, Austin	Apr. 29, 1828	Balto.
	Henry	23	Betsey	Woolfolk, Austin	Apr. 29, 1828	Balto.
	Henry	24	Bourne	Rogers, Selemachus	Sept. 9, 1833	Balto.
	Henry	24	Bourne	Rogers, Selemachus	Sept. 9, 1833	Balto.
	Henry	16	Budget	Spraggins, Samuel M.	Nov. 27, 1821	Balto.
	Henry	infant	Burlington	Stout, G.H.	Oct. 22, 1842	Balto.

Surname	First Name	Ship	Age	O/S	Date	Depart
	Henry	Calagari	5	Nelson, George S.	Nov. 7, 1832	Balto.
	Henry	Caledonia	20	Preston, Wm. P.	Dec, 7, 1840	Balto.
	Henry	Chatsworth	35	Anderson, David	Jan. 3, 1821	Balto.
	Henry	Cumberland	13	Callahan, George W.	Oct. 7, 1836	Balto.
	Henry	Dumphries	3	Lee, Richard H.	Sept. 25, 1828	Balto.
	Henry	Dumphries	31	Lee, Richard H.	Sept. 25, 1828	Balto.
	Henry	Eliza	6	Slatter, Hope Hull	Oct. 9, 1840	Balto.
	Henry	Elizabeth	23	Campbell, Walter L.	Oct. 6, 1849	Balto.
	Henry	Eros	5	Woolfolk, Austin	Jan. 28, 1824	Balto.
	Henry	Franklin	12	Somerville, Henry	Nov. 27, 1819	Balto.
	Henry	Gulnare	12	Howard, William	Nov. 5, 1830	Balto.
	Henry	Gulnare	3	Pitts, Thomas H.	Nov. 5, 1830	Balto.
	Henry	Harriet	14	Carrol, Charles	Dec, 7, 1836	Balto.
	Henry	Harriet	21	Carroll, Charles	Dec. 7, 1836	Balto.
	Henry	Harriett	20	Woolfolk, Austin	March 23, 1822	Balto.
	Henry	Harriett	5	Pierce, Levi	Oct. 29, 1822	Balto.
	Henry	Henry A. Barling	14	Marrictt, William H.	Oct. 28, 1848	Nottingham
	Henry	Henry Clay	4 mon.	Waring, E.M.	Dec. 8, 1828	Balto.
	Henry	Hermann	9	Rowe, Ralph	June 21, 1851	Balto.
	Henry	Hibernia	7 mon.	Chabert, Leon	Dec. 5, 1826	Balto.
	Henry	Hibernia	25	Chaber, Leon	Dec. 5, 1826	Balto.
	Henry	Hibernia	3	Woolfolk, Austin	Dec. 5, 1826	Balto.
	Henry	Hibernia	11	Woolfolk, Austin	Dec. 5, 1826	Balto.
	Henry	Hope	10	Byrne, Walter	Dec. 5, 1833	Balto.
	Henry	Hortensia	20	Woolfolk, Austin	Dec. 14, 1836	Balto.
	Henry	Intelligence	23	Woolfolk, Austin	Apr, 5, 1823	Balto.

Surname	First Name	Age	Ship	O/S	Date	Depart
	Henry	17	Isabella	Wallis, Cornelius C.	Nov. 26, 1834	Balto.
	Henry	11	Kirkwood	Donovan, Joseph S.	Dec. 10, 1846	Balto.
	Henry	16	Kirkwood	Donovan, Joseph S.	March 9, 1847	Balto.
	Henry	22	Kirkwood	Campbell, Bernard M.	Oct. 16, 1845	Balto.
	Henry	30	Kirkwood	Donovan, Joseph S.	Sept. 28, 1846	Balto.
	Henry		Lady Monroe	Woolfolk, Joseph B.	March 25, 1825	Balto.
	Henry	16	Lady Monroe	Chabert, Leon	Sept. 29, 1825	Balto.
	Henry	10	Lady Richmond	Williams, Joseph C.	Apr. 25, 1827	Balto.
	Henry	18	Lady Richmond	Williams, Joseph C.	Apr. 25, 1827	Balto.
	Henry	1	Lafayette	Woolfolk, Joseph B.	Oct. 18, 1828	Balto.
	Henry	18	Lafayette	Woolfolk, Richard	Oct. 18, 1828	Balto.
	Henry	26	Lafayette	Woolfolk, Richard	Oct. 18, 1828	Balto.
	Henry	14	Lapwing	King, Gideon T.	March 22, 1822	Balto.
	Henry	20	Lapwing	Spraggins, Samuel M.	March 22, 1822	Balto.
	Henry	38	Mary	Jones, Frances J.	Nov. 30, 1841	Balto.
	Henry	6	Mechanic	Woolfolk, Austin	Jan. 1, 1831	Balto.
	Henry	35	Merrimack	Hoffman, William C.	Nov. 2, 1831	Balto.
	Henry	2	Missouri	Mulhocan, Hugh	March 2, 1819	Balto.
	Henry	3	Nancy W. Stevens	Baker, William	Oct. 23, 1843	Balto.
	Henry	9	North America	Chabert, Leon	Apr. 24, 1826	Balto.
	Henry	26	North America	Thurman, William C.	Apr. 24, 1826	Balto.
	Henry	9	North America	Woolfolk, Joseph B.	Apr. 26. 1826	Balto.
	Henry	19	North America	Woolfolk, Austin	Dec. 20, 1824	Balto.
	Henry	21	North America	Woolfolk, Austin	Dec. 20, 1824	Balto.
	Henry	14	Orbit	Chabert, Leon	Apr. 16, 1825	Balto.
	Henry	15	Orbit	Chabert, Leon	Apr. 16, 1825	Balto.

Surname	First Name	Age	Ship	O/S	Date	Depart
	Henry	infant	Orleans	Stout, G.H.	Oct. 22, 1842	Balto.
	Henry	3	Palestine	Slater, Hope Hull	Nov. 16, 1835	Balto.
	Henry	16	Palestine	Slater, Hope Hull	Nov. 16, 1835	Balto.
	Henry	22	Parthenon	White, Henry	Oct. 10, 1842	Balto.
	Henry	12	Seaman	Honsey, L.H.	March 25, 1839	Balto.
	Henry	1 mon.	Serene	Archer, James	Oct. 19, 1836	Balto.
	Henry	20	St. Mary	Campbell, Bernard M.	Nov. 29, 1845	Balto.
	Henry	2	States	Woolfolk, Austin	Apr. 14, 1828	Balto.
	Henry	25	States	Woolfolk, Jospeh B.	March 10, 1826	Balto.
	Henry	20	States	Duer, Robert	Nov. 26, 1825	Balto.
	Henry	14	States	Morton, George C.	Nov. 26, 1825	Balto.
	Henry	7	States	Woolfolk, Austin	Nov. 26, 1825	Balto.
	Henry	15	Statira	Smith, Doctor James	March 28, 1826	Balto.
	Henry	16	Strafford	Wilson, Thomas C.	Nov. 21, 1843	Balto.
	Henry	21	Strafford	Wilson, Thomas C.	Nov. 21, 1843	Balto.
	Henry	7	Susan Miller	Woolfolk, Richard T.	Oct. 25, 1822	Balto.
	Henry	14	Susan Miller	Woolfolk, Samuel M.	Oct. 25, 1822	Balto.
	Henry	5	Tangier	Campbell, Bernard M.	Nov. 26, 1853	Balto.
	Henry	3 mon.	Temperance	Wikoff, Steven W.	Dec. 12, 1818	Balto.
	Henry	6	Trafalgar	Dent, Wilfred	Jan. 13, 1827	Annapolis
	Henry	10	Trafalgar	Dent, Wilfred	Jan. 13, 1827	Annapolis
	Henry	23	Trafalgar	Dent, Wilfred	Jan. 13, 1827	Annapolis
	Henry	18	Virginia	Morton, George C.	Dec. 19, 1825	Balto.
	Henry	3	William and Mary	King, Gideon T.	Oct. 9, 1821	Balto.
	Henry Thomas		Kirkwood	Donovan, Joseph S.	Dec. 10, 1846	Balto.
	Henson	7	Balloon	Zacharie, James W.	Dec. 22, 1821	Balto.

Surname	First Name	Age	Ship	O/S	Date	Depart
	Henson	5	Mars	Woolfolk, Austin	Oct. 30, 1824	Balto.
	Henson	18	Palestine	Slatter, Hope Hull	Nov. 16, 1835	Balto.
	Herbert	2	Architect	Crow, William	Feb. 3, 1841	Balto.
	Hercules	14	Lady Richmond	Woolfolk, Austin	Apr. 30, 1827	Balto.
	Herman	35	States	Tillotson, Giles	Nov. 22, 1827	Balto.
	Hessy	14	Henry Clay	Bower, Thomas F.	Dec. 8, 1828	Nottingham
	Hessy	15	Henry Clay	Waring, E.M.	Dec. 8, 1828	Nottingham
	Hester	15	Ajax	Allain	Oct.3, 1833	Balto.
	Hester	4	Arctic	Kelso, George G.	Nov. 15, 1826	Balto.
	Hester	3	Arctic	Cliffe, Henry	Oct. 4, 1828	Balto.
	Hester	17	Elizabeth	Campbell, Bernard M.	May 12, 1849	Balto.
	Hester	33	Emilie	Laurenson, Andrew U.	Dec. 14, 1821	Balto.
	Hester	3	Julia	Poindexter, George	Feb. 10, 1832	Balto.
	Hester	5	Lafayette	Woolfolk, Joseph B.	Oct. 18, 1828	Balto.
	Hester	11mon.	Opelousas	Abercombie, James	July 6, 1836	Balto.
	Hester	58	Seaman	Hooper, John	Dec. 18, 1838	Balto.
	Hester	25	States	Woolfolk, Austin	March 8, 1826	Balto.
	Hester Ann	13	Helen A. Miller	Campbell, Bernard M.	Oct. 18, 1852	Balto.
	Hetty	45	Franklin	Anderson, David	Nov. 27, 1819	Balto.
	Hetty	18 mon.	Hyperion	Valcourt, Alex de	May 10, 1822	Balto.
	Hetty	2 mon.	Jasper	Woolfolk, Austin	Apr. 7, 1827	Balto.
	Hetty	22	Jasper	Woolfolk, Austin	Apr. 7, 1827	Balto.
	Hetty	22	Mars	Woolfolk, Austin	Oct. 30, 1824	Balto.
	Hetty	23	Nelson Clark	Tongue, Thomas R.	Nov. 20, 1835	Balto.
	Hetty	22	Ulysses	Richardson, Wade H.	Nov. 6, 1833	Balto.
	Hillery	30	Kirkwood	Campbell, Bernard M.	Oct. 16, 1845	Balto.

Surname	First Name	Age	Ship	O/S	Date	Depart
	Hinson	14	Hope	Byrne, Walter	Dec. 5, 1833	Balto.
	Hiram	9	Ajex	Richardson, Wade H.	Oct.3, 1833	Balto.
	Hison	8	Mars	Woolfolk, Austin	Oct. 30, 1824	Balto.
	Holesworth	26	Susan Miller	Woolfolk, Austin	Oct. 25, 1822	Balto.
	Holly	13	Home	Donovan, Joseph S.	March 22, 1845	Balto.
	Hope	55	Seaman	Hooper, John	Dec. 18, 1838	Balto.
	Horace	9 mon.	Alfred	Woolfolk, Austin	Jan. 18, 1825	Balto.
	Horace	8	Bourne	Chaille, W.H.	Oct. 15, 1832	Balto.
	Horace	19	Brunswick	Woolfolk, Austin	Oct. 11, 1831	Balto.
	Horace	22	Elizabeth	Campbell, Walter L.	Oct. 6, 1849	Balto.
	Horace	15	Good Hope	Woolfolk, Austin	Nov. 16, 1821	Balto.
	Horace	20	Hibernia	Chabert, Leon	Dec. 5, 1826	Balto.
	Horace	21	Mars	Woolfolk, Joseph B.	Oct. 30, 1824	Balto.
	Horace	8	North America	Woolfolk, Joseph B.	Apr. 29, 1826	Balto.
	Horace	20	North America	Woolfolk, Austin	Oct. 14, 1823	Balto.
	Horace	3	Virginia	Woolfolk, Austin	March 31, 1828	Balto.
	Horation	15	Susan Miller	Bibbs, John T.	Oct. 25, 1822	Balto.
	Humphrey	1	Jasper	Woolfolk, Austin	Apr. 7, 1827	Balto.
	Hyland	21	Balloon	Knight, William	Dec. 22, 1821	Balto.
	Ibby	25	Lady Monroe	Woolfolk, Austin	Sept. 29, 1825	Balto.
	India	13	Intelligence	Coalman, Henry E.	March 14, 1820	Balto.
	Irena	6	Hope	Byrne, Walter	Dec. 5, 1833	Balto.
	Isaac	17	Aurille	Warfield, Charles	Apr. 26, 1822	Balto.
	Isaac	18	Aurilla	Woolfolk, Austin	Apr. 26, 1822	Balto.
	Isaac	40	Aurilla	Woolfolk, Austin	Apr. 26, 1822	Balto.
	Isaac	4	Bourne	Handy, Samuel	Oct. 13, 1832	Balto.

Surname	First Name	Age	Ship	O/S	Date	Depart
	Isaac	19	Bourne	Rogers, Selemachus	Sept. 9, 1833	Balto.
	Isaac	36	Calagari	Nelson, George S.	Nov. 7, 1832	Balto.
	Isaac	35	Charles	Campbell, Bernard M.	Dec. 18, 1850	Balto.
	Isaac	19	Dumphries	Lee, Richard H.	Sept. 25, 1828	Balto.
	Isaac	19	E.H. Chapin	Campbell, Walter L.	June 7, 1848	Balto.
	Isaac	25	Emilie	Yejser, John	Aug. 21, 1819	Balto.
	Isaac	29	Emilie	Coalman, Henry E.	Nov. 27, 1819	Balto.
	Isaac	59	Franklin	Somerville, Henry	Nov. 27, 1819	Balto.
	Isaac	5	Good Hope	Woolfolk, Samuel M.	Nov. 21, 1821	Balto.
	Isaac	17	Harriett	Woolfolk, Richard T.	March 6, 1823	Balto.
	Isaac	18	Home	Campbell, Bernard M.	March 22, 1845	Balto.
	Isaac	14	Hortensia	Woolfolk, Austin	Dec. 14, 1836	Balto.
	Isaac	21	Isabella		Nov. 26, 1834	Balto.
	Isaac	22	Kirkwood	Campbell, Bernard M.	Oct. 16, 1845	Balto.
	Isaac	23	Lady Monroe	Woolfolk, Joseph B.	March 25, 1825	Balto.
	Isaac	20	Missouri	Little, Moses	March 2, 1819	Balto.
	Isaac	19	North America	Woolfolk, Austin	Dec. 20, 1824	Balto.
	Isaac	16	North America	Woolfolk, Austin	Oct. 14, 1823	Balto.
	Isaac	15	Orbit	Chabert, Leon	Apr. 16, 1825	Balto.
	Isaac	23	Orion	Woolfolk, Richard	Dec. 30, 1822	Balto.
	Isaac	15	Palestine	Slatter, Hope Hull	Nov. 16, 1835	Balto.
	Isaac	18	Pandora	Wpolfolk, Austin	March 26, 1831	Balto.
	Isaac	13	Shamrock	Guyton, Elisha	March 13, 1840	Balto.
	Isaac	20	Signet	Woolfolk, Austin	Nov. 17, 1831	Balto.
	Isaac	23	States	Woolfolk, Austin	March 8, 1826	Balto.
	Isaac	20	States	Tillotson, Giles	Nov. 22, 1827	Balto.

Surname	First Name	Age	Ship	O/S	Date	Depart
	Isaac	14	States	Morton, George C.	Nov. 26, 1825	Balto.
	Isaac	28	States	Woolfolk, Austin	Nov. 26, 1825	Balto.
	Isaac	10	Strafford	Wilson, Thomas C.	Nov. 21, 1843	Balto.
	Isaac	23	Susan Miller	Windsor, Robert M.	Oct. 25, 1822	Balto.
	Isaac	15	Victorine	Campbell, Bernard M.	Dec. 17, 1845	Balto.
	Isaac	17	Virginia	Morton, George C.	Dec. 19, 1825	Balto.
	Isaac	18	Virginia	Woolfolk, Joseph B.	Dec. 19, 1825	Balto.
	Isaac	27	William and Mary	Coleman, Aquila C.	Oct. 9, 1821	Balto.
	Isaac		Zoe	Donovan, Joseph S.	Feb. 16, 1847	Balto.
	Isiah	15	Lafayette	Woolfolk, Joseph B.	Oct. 18, 1828	Balto.
	Israel	2	Edward Everett	Bowser, Gassaway	Oct. 17, 1851	Balto.
	Israel	12	Lady Monroe	Wascherr, J.E.	Sept. 29, 1825	Balto.
	Israel	14	States	Duer, Robert	Nov. 26, 1825	Balto.
	Isreal	20	Bourne	Handy Samuel	Oct. 13, 1832	Balto.
	Jack	33	Alonzo	Oldham, George W.	Nov. 7, 1822	Balto.
	Jack	40	Arctic	Magee Eugene	Oct. 9, 1828	Annapolis
	Jack	35	Budget	Spragains, Samuel M.	Nov. 27, 1821	Balto.
	Jack	40	Eros	Woolfolk, Austin	Jan. 28, 1824	Balto.
	Jack	22	Franklin	Anderson, David	Nov. 27, 1819	Balto.
	Jack	23	Good Hope	Woolfolk, Samuel M.	Nov. 21, 1821	Balto.
	Jack	33	Henry Clay	Bower, Robert W.	Dec. 8, 1828	Nottingham
	Jack	13	Hope	Randolph, Isaac	March 25, 1834	Balto.
	Jack	24	Intelligence	Woolfolk, Austin	Dec. 20, 1822	Balto.
	Jack	37	Intelligence	Butler, Thomas	Nov. 3, 1820	Balto.
	Jack	17	Isabelle	Wallis, Cornelius C.	Nov. 26, 1834	Balto.
	Jack	23	Lady Monroe	Woolfolk, Austin	Sept. 29, 1825	Balto.

Surname	First Name	Age	Ship	O/S	Date	Depart
	Jack	55	Lapwing	Hall, Francis	March 22, 1822	Balto.
	Jack	22	Mars	Woolfolk, Joseph B.	Oct. 30, 1824	Balto.
	Jack	30	Mars	Woolfolk, Joseph B.	Oct. 30, 1824	Balto.
	Jack	22	Mechanic	Woolfolk, Austin	Jan. 1, 1831	Balto.
	Jack	27	North America	Thurman, William C.	Apr. 24, 1826	Balto.
	Jack	20	North America	Woolfolk, Austin	Dec. 20, 1824	Balto.
	Jack	35	Snow	Willis	Feb 5, 1835	Balto.
	Jack	22	Triton	Anderson, David	Dec. 20, 1819	Balto.
	Jack	28	Virginia	Morton, George C.	Dec. 19, 1825	Balto.
	Jack	24	Virginia	Woolfolk, Joseph B.	Dec. 19, 1825	Balto.
	Jackee	26	Emilie	Spencer, Thomas R.P.	Dec. 14, 1821	Balto.
	Jacob	21	Alfred	Woolfolk, Austin	Jan. 18, 1825	Balto.
	Jacob	51	Ann Wayne	Guyton, Elisha	Sept. 2, 1836	Balto.
	Jacob	12	Aurilla	Chabert, Leon	Apr. 26, 1822	Balto.
	Jacob	1	Balloon	Penieres, Emile	Dec. 22, 1821	Balto.
	Jacob	24	Betsey	Woolfolk, Austin	Apr. 29, 1828	Balto.
	Jacob	20	Bourne	Rogers, Selemachus	Sept. 9, 1833	Balto.
	Jacob	17	Caroline	Ferguson, Thomas	March 2, 1821	Balto.
	Jacob	35	Emilie	Robinson, Abner	Dec. 14, 1821	Balto.
	Jacob	23	Emilie	Fortin, Charles	May 19, 1820	Balto.
	Jacob	28	Eros	Anderson, David	June 29, 1822	Balto.
	Jacob	12	Eros	Armitage, James	June 29, 1822	Balto.
	Jacob	22	Eros	Knight, William	June 29, 1822	Balto.
	Jacob	20	Good Hope	Woolfolk, Austin	Nov. 16, 1821	Balto.
	Jacob	30	Good Hope	Woolfolk, Samuel M.	Nov. 21, 1821	Balto.
	Jacob	5	Hyperion	Valcourt, Alex de	May 10, 1822	Balto.

Surname	First Name	Age	Ship	O/S	Date	Depart
	Jacob	35	Hyperion	Anderson, David	May 14, 1822	Balto.
	Jacob	3	Intelligence	Woolfolk, Austin	Apr. 5, 1823	Balto.
	Jacob	23	Intelligence	Anderson, David	Dec. 20, 1822	Balto.
	Jacob	21	Isabella		Nov. 26, 1834	Balto.
	Jacob		Kirkwood	Donovan, Joseph S.	March 9, 1847	Balto.
	Jacob	18	Kirkwood	Donovan, Joseph S.	Sept. 28, 1846	Balto.
	Jacob	23	Lady Monroe	Chabert, Leon	Sept. 29, 1825	Balto.
	Jacob	18	Lady Monroe	Woolfolk, Austin	Sept. 29, 1825	Balto.
	Jacob	22	Lapwing	King, Gideon T.	March 22, 1822	Balto.
	Jacob	27	London	Waller, Francis	Nov. 5, 1840	Balto.
	Jacob	33	Mars	Woolfolk, Joseph B.	Oct. 30, 1824	Balto.
	Jacob	6	Missouri	Gilmore, John	March 1, 1819	Balto.
	Jacob	13	North America	Woolfolk, Austin	Nov. 23, 1822	Balto.
	Jacob	23	North America	Woolfolk, Austin	Oct. 14, 1823	Balto.
	Jacob	4	Palestine	Slatter, Hope Hull	Nov. 16, 1835	Balto.
	Jacob	13	Pandora	Woolfolk, Austin	March 26, 1831	Balto.
	Jacob	22	States	Woolfolk, Austin	March 8, 1826	Balto.
	Jacob	22	Statira	Smith, Doctor James	March 28, 1826	Balto.
	Jacob	12	Superb	Donovan, Joseph S.	Nov. 2, 1843	Balto.
	Jacob	20	Susan Miller	Woolfolk, Austin	Oct. 25, 1822	Balto.
	Jacob	11	Susan Miller	Woolfolk, Richard T.	Oct. 25, 1822	Balto.
	Jacob	21	Susan Miller	Woolfolk, Richard T.	Oct. 25, 1822	Balto.
	Jacob	52	Victorine	Campbell, Bernard M.	March 1, 1845	Balto.
	Jacob		Zoe	Donovan, Joseph S.	Feb. 16, 1847	Balto.
	Jake	3	Julia	Poindexter, George	Feb. 10, 1832	Balto.
	James	5	Alonzo	White, Philip	Nov. 8, 1822	Balto.

Surname	First Name	Age	Ship	O/S	Date	Depart
	James	20	Alonzo	White, Philip	Nov. 8, 1822	Balto.
	James	21	Alonzo	White, Philip	Nov. 8, 1822	Balto.
	James	21	Alonzo	White, Philip	Nov. 8, 1822	Balto.
	James	10 mon.	Arctic	Smith, Leonard J.	Jan. 29, 1828	St. Mary's
	James	6	Arctic	Smith, Leonard J.	Jan. 29, 1828	St. Mary's
	James	5	Arletta	Carr, Dabney S.	July 18, 1826	Balto.
	James	33	Aurilla	Woolfolk, Austin	Apr. 26, 1822	Balto.
	James	13	Balloon	Penieres, Emile	Dec. 22, 1821	Balto.
	James	4	Bostonian	Slatter, Hope Hull	Jan. 18, 1841	Balto.
	James	28	Clio	Starnsburg, William	March 22, 1819	Balto.
	James	24	E.H.Chapin	Slatter, Hope Hull	Nov. 30, 1847	Balto.
	James	15	Eagle	Sterett, Harrison	Oct. 28, 1828	Balto.
	James	25	Emilie	Ferguson, Thomas	Dec. 14, 1821	Balto.
	James	20	Emilie	Anderson, David	March 27, 1821	Balto.
	James	25	Emilie	Mercer, William D.	March 27, 1821	Balto.
	James	21	Good Hope	Woolfolk, Austin	Nov. 16, 1821	Balto.
	James	17	Harriett	Woolfolk, Austin	March 23, 1822	Balto.
	James	23	Henry Clay	Camphor, Henry	Dec. 8, 1828	Nottingham
	James	11	Hibernia	Chabert, Leon	Dec. 5, 1826	Balto.
	James	9	Hope	Richardson, Wade H.	Dec. 3, 1833	Balto.
	James	21	Hyperion	King, Gideon T.	Nov. 12, 1821	Balto.
	James	22	Hyperion	King, Gideon T.	Nov. 12, 1821	Balto.
	James	20	Intelligence	Plater, John R. Jr.	Apr. 12, 1823	St. Mary's
	James	30	Intelligence	Woolfolk, Austin	Apr. 5, 1823	Balto.
	James	8 mon.	Intelligence	Anderson, David	Dec. 20, 1822	Balto.
	James	22	Intelligence	Anderson, David	March 14, 1820	Balto.

Surname	First Name	Age	Ship	O/S	Date	Depart
	James	27	Isabella	Wallis, Cornelius C.	Nov. 26, 1834	Balto.
	James	19	Julia	Woolfolk, Austin	Feb. 10, 1832	Balto.
	James	16	Kirkwood	Donovan, Joseph S.	Dec. 10, 1846	Balto.
	James	1	Kirkwood	Campbell, Bernard M.	Jan. 4, 1845	Balto.
	James	16	Kirkwood	Campbell, Bernard M.	Oct. 16, 1845	Balto.
	James	23	Lady Monroe	Chabert, Leon	Sept. 29, 1825	Balto.
	James	24	Lady Monroe	Wascherr, J.E.	Sept. 29, 1825	Balto.
	James	22	Mars	Woolfolk, Austin	Oct. 30, 1824	Balto.
	James	2	Mechanic	Woolfolk, Austin	Jan. 1, 1831	Balto.
	James	6	North America	Thurman, William C.	Apr. 24, 1826	Balto.
	James	27	North America	Woolfolk, Austin	Nov. 23, 1822	Balto.
	James	16	Pandora	Woolfolk, Austin	March 26, 1831	Balto.
	James	22	Signet	Woolfolk, Austin	Nov. 17, 1831	Balto.
	James		States	Woolfolk, Austin	Nov. 21, 1827	Balto.
	James	24	Susan Miller	Woolfolk, Richard T.	Oct. 25, 1822	Balto.
	James	23	Susan Miller	Woolfolk, Samuel M.	Oct. 25, 1822	Balto.
	James	5	Temperance	Duplantier, Guy	Dec. 9, 1818	Balto.
	James	15	Tippecanoe	Harker, William	Dec. 16, 1840	Balto.
	James	28	Triton	Heath, Dela F.	Dec. 23, 1819	Balto.
	James	24	Victorine	Donovan, Joseph S.	Sept. 29, 1845	Balto.
	James	10	Virginia	Chabert, Leon	Dec. 19, 1825	Balto.
	James	30	Virginia	Purviance, W.G.	March 29, 1828	Balto.
	James	24	Zoe	Donovan, Joseph S.	Feb. 16, 1847	Balto.
	James		Zoe	Donovan, Joseph S.	Feb. 16, 1847	Balto.
	James Henry	11	Patrick Henry	Campbell, Bernard M.	June 1,1853	Balto.
	Jamy	25	Chatsworth	Anderson, David	Jan. 3, 1821	Balto.

Surname	First Name	Age	Ship	O/S	Date	Depart
	Janay	13	Hope	Byrne, Walter	Dec. 5, 1833	Balto.
	Jane	14	Agent	Anderson, David	June 8, 1821	Balto.
	Jane	16	Ajax	Richardson, Wade H.	Oct. 3, 1833	Balto.
	Jane	17	Alfred	Woolfolk, Austin	May 7, 1825	Balto.
	Jane	12 mon.	Ann Wayne	Guyton, Elisha	Sept. 2, 1836	Balto.
	Jane	10	Architect	Purvis, James Franklin	Feb. 3, 1841	Balto.
	Jane	2	Arctic	Smith, Leonard J.	Jan. 29, 1828	St. Mary's
	Jane	16	Arctic	Maddox, Thomas H.	Jan. 30, 1829	St. Mary's
	Jane	30	Arctic	Williams, Joseph C.	Jan. 31, 1829	St. Mary's
	Jane	2	Aurilla	Wikoff, Stephen A.	Apr. 26, 1822	Balto.
	Jane	2	Balloon	Zacharie, James W.	Dec. 22, 1821	Balto.
	Jane	3	Balloon	Zacharie, James W.	Dec. 22, 1821	Balto.
	Jane	7	Bostonian	Slatter, Hope Hull	Jan. 18, 1841	Balto.
	Jane	17	Bourne	Chabert, Leon	Sept. 10, 1833	Balto.
	Jane	9	Caspian	Woolfolk, Austin	Nov. 26, 1836	Balto.
	Jane	16	Caspian	Woolfolk, Austin	Nov. 26, 1836	Balto.
	Jane	45	Charles	Switer, Josephine P.	May 15, 1852	Balto.
	Jane	5	Charles	Carter, John A.	Sept. 29, 1849	Balto.
	Jane	20	Eros	Woolfolk, Austin	Jan. 28, 1824	Balto.
	Jane	25	General Pinckney	Duffel, H.L.	Nov. 8, 1845	Balto.
	Jane	24	Good Hope	Woolfolk, Austin	Nov. 16, 1821	Balto.
	Jane	45	Harriett	Woolfolk, Austin	March 23, 1822	Balto.
	Jane	17	Harriett	Woolfolk, Richard T.	March 6, 1823	Balto.
	Jane	5	Henry Clay	Bower, Thomas F.	Dec. 8, 1828	Nottingham
	Jane	20	Hope	Richardson, Wade H.	Dec. 3, 1833	Balto.
	Jane		Hope	Richardson, Wade H.	Dec. 3, 1833	Balto.

Surname	First Name	Age	Ship	O/S	Date	Depart
	Jane	13	Intelligence	Woolfolk, Austin	Dec. 20, 1822	Balto.
	Jane	12	Isabella	Wallis, Cornelius C.	Nov. 26, 1834	Balto.
	Jane	3	Isabella		Nov. 26, 1834	Balto.
	Jane	5	Isabella		Nov. 26, 1834	Balto.
	Jane	7	Isabella		Nov. 26, 1834	Balto.
	Jane	11	Isabella		Nov. 26, 1834	Balto.
	Jane	18	Lafayette	Slatter, Hope Hull	March 25, 1843	Balto.
	Jane	8	Lafayette	Woolfolk, Austin	Oct. 18, 1828	Balto.
	Jane	16	Mary	Campbell, Bernard M.	Aug. 23, 1845	Balto.
	Jane	9	Missouri	Shields, Thomas	March 2, 1819	Balto.
	Jane	17	Nelson Clark	Tongue, Thomas R.	Nov. 20, 1835	Balto.
	Jane	18	North America	Woolfolk, Austin	Dec. 20, 1824	Balto.
	Jane	8	Orbit	Woolfolk, Joseph B.	Apr. 16, 1825	Balto.
	Jane	4	States	Duer, Robert	Nov. 26, 1825	Balto.
	Jane	7 mon.	Susan Miller	Woolfolk, Richard T.	Oct. 25, 1822	Balto.
	Jane	16	Ulysses	Richardson, Wade H.	Nov. 6, 1833	Balto.
	Jane	25	Unicorn	Hynson, Robert C.	Oct. 23, 1820	Balto.
	Jane	1	Victorine	Campbell, Bernard M.	March 1, 1845	Balto.
	Jane	22	William and Mary	King, Gideon T.	Oct. 9, 1821	Balto.
	Jane	19	Zoe	Donovan, Joseph S.	Feb. 16, 1847	Balto.
	Janet	25	Serene	Archer, James	Oct. 19, 1836	Balto.
	Janson	3	Orion	Oldham, George W.	Dec. 30, 1822	Balto.
	Janty	35	Ann Wayne	Guyton, Elisha	Sept. 2, 1836	Balto.
	Janty	16	Orbit	Woolfolk, Austin	Apr. 16, 1825	Balto.
	Jared	20	Sultana	Kelso, George G.	Oct. 31, 1827	Balto.
	Jaret	14	Hyperion	Anderson, David	May 14, 1822	Balto.

Surname	First Name	Age	Ship	O/S	Date	Depart
	Jarrett	25	Agent	Anderson, David	June 8, 1821	Balto.
	Jarrett	16	Balloon	Zacharie, James W.	Dec. 22, 1821	Balto.
	Jarrett	25	Charles	Carter, John A.	Sept. 29, 1849	Balto.
	Jarrett	17	Good Hope	Woolfolk, Richard T.	Nov. 21, 1821	Balto.
	Jarrett	40	Hyperion	Kelso, George Y.	Nov. 8, 1820	Balto.
	Jarrette	22	Isabella		Nov. 26, 1834	Balto.
	Jarrot	5	Intelligence	Plater, John R. Jr.	Apr. 12, 1823	St. Mary's
	Jarvis	35	Caledonia	Woolfolk, Austin	Oct. 27, 1841	Balto.
	Jarvis	18	North America	Woolfolk, Austin	Oct. 14, 1823	Balto.
	Jean Baptiste	3	Actress	Garsicles, James	Nov. 6, 1819	Balto.
	Jefferson	20	Pandora	Woolfolk, Austin	March 26, 1831	Balto.
	Jeffrey	10	Lapwing	King, Gideon T.	March 22, 1822	Balto.
	Jenkins	25	Franklin	Anderson, David	Nov. 27, 1819	Balto.
	Jenny	22	Actress	Anderson, David	Nov. 8, 1819	Balto.
	Jenny	38	Arletta	Carr, Dabney S.	July 18, 1826	Balto.
	Jenny	14	Bourne	Handy, Samuel	Oct. 13, 1832	Balto.
	Jenny	16	Commodore Pattersc	Thompson, Henry	March 20, 1819	Balto.
	Jenny	11	Franklin	Somerville, Henry	Nov. 27, 1819	Balto.
	Jenny	15	Hyperion	Anderson, David	May 14, 1822	Balto.
	Jenny	14	Intelligence	Anderson, David	March 14, 1820	Balto.
	Jenny	35	Jupiter		March 25, 1836	Balto.
	Jenny	20	Lady Monroe	Chabert, Leon	Sept. 29, 1825	Balto.
	Jenny	17	Statira	Smith, Doctor James	March 28, 1826	Balto.
	Jenny	14	Triton	Woolfolk, Austin	Dec. 22, 1819	Balto.
	Jenny	30	William and Mary	McCulloh, Samuel	Oct. 4, 1821	Balto.
	Jeny	23	Kirkwood	Wilson, Jonathan M.	Sept. 6, 1851	Balto.

Surname	First Name	Age	Ship	O/S	Date	Depart
	Jeremiah	2 mon.	Hyperion	Woolfolk, Austin	May 10, 1822	Balto.
	Jeremiah	21	States	Chabert, Leon	March 8, 1826	Balto.
	Jerry	48	Arctic	Maddox, Thomas H.	Jan. 30, 1829	St. Mary's
	Jerry	16	Aurilla	Woolfolk, Austin	Apr. 26, 1822	Balto.
	Jerry	20	Balloon	Millgan, George	Dec. 17, 1821	Balto.
	Jerry	3	Betsey	Woolfolk, Austin	Apr. 29, 1828	Balto.
	Jerry	19	Budget	Spraggins, Samuel M.	Nov. 27, 1821	Balto.
	Jerry	9	Eagle	Steret, Harrison	Oct. 28, 1828	Balto.
	Jerry	10	Georgia	Bren-, Robert J.	Dec. 23, 1844	Balto.
	Jerry	3	Hyperion	King, Gideon T.	Nov. 12, 1821	Balto.
	Jerry	20	Intelligence	Plate-, John R. Jr.	Apr. 12, 1823	St. Mary's
	Jerry	18	Intelligence	De Mapiere, Victor	Apr. 30, 1821	Balto.
	Jerry	28	Kirkwood	Slatter, Hope Hull	Dec. 23, 1843	Balto.
	Jerry	20	Mars	Woolfolk, Austin	Oct. 30, 1824	Balto.
	Jerry	21	Russell	Woolfolk, Austin	Feb. 27, 1839	Balto.
	Jerry	25	States	Chabert, Leon	March 9, 1826	Balto.
	Jesse	13	Arletta	Carr, Dabney S.	July 18, 1826	Balto.
	Jesse	32	Budget	Spraggins, Samuel M.	Nov. 27, 1821	Balto.
	Jesse	5	Intelligence	Plater John R. Jr.	Apr. 12, 1823	St. Mary's
	Jesse	11	Orion	Oldham, George W.	Dec. 30, 1822	Balto.
	Jesse	33	States	Duer, Robert	Nov. 26, 1825	Balto.
	Jesse	22	Susan Miller	Woolfolk, Samuel M.	Oct. 25, 1822	Balto.
	Jesse	22	Union	Campbell, Bernard M.	Oct. 9, 1848	Balto.
	Jessy	24	Hortensia	Woolfolk, Austin	Dec. 14, 1836	Balto.
	Jetson	13	Elizabeth	Campbell, Bernard M.	Nov. 18, 1848	Balto.
	Jim	15	Algerine	Woolfolk, Austin	Jan. 5, 1826	Balto.

Surname	First Name	Age	Ship	O/S	Date	Depart
	Jim	15	Algerine	Woolfolk, Austin	Jan. 5, 1826	Balto.
	Jim	10	Arctic	Bond, Francis A.	May 15, 1828	Balto.
	Jim	4	Aurilla	Wikoff, Stephen A.	Apr. 26, 1822	Balto.
	Jim	16	Bourne	Chaille, W.H.	Oct. 15, 1832	Balto.
	Jim	19	Bourne	Rogers, Selemachus	Sept. 9, 1833	Balto.
	Jim	17	Caspian	Woolfolk, Austin	Nov. 26, 1836	Balto.
	Jim		Caspian	Woolfolk, Austin	Nov. 26, 1836	Balto.
	Jim	11	Creole	Allain	Oct. 19, 1833	Balto.
	Jim	21	Eros	Knight, William	June 29, 1822	Balto.
	Jim	21	Gulnare	Kelso, George G.	Nov. 3, 1830	Balto.
	Jim	16	Hamlet	Woolfolk, Austin	Apr. 7, 1824	Balto.
	Jim	23	Hamlet	Woolfolk, Joseph B.	Apr. 7, 1824	Balto.
	Jim	5	Henry A. Barling	Campbell, Bernard M.	Dec. 18, 1851	Balto.
	Jim	13	Hermann	Rowe, Ralph	June 21, 1851	Balto.
	Jim	14	Hope	Randolph, Isaac	March 25, 1834	Balto.
	Jim	16	Isabella		Nov. 26, 1834	Balto.
	Jim	25	Isabella		Nov. 26, 1834	Balto.
	Jim	9	Mars	Woolfolk, Austin	Oct. 30, 1824	Balto.
	Jim	15	Mars	Woolfolk, Austin	Oct. 30, 1824	Balto.
	Jim	22	Mary	Chaplain, Charles	Nov. 30, 1841	Balto.
	Jim	23	Merrimack	Kelso, George G.	Nov. 2, 1831	Balto.
	Jim	30	Missouri	Little, Moses	March 2, 1819	Balto.
	Jim	20	North America	Woolfolk, Joseph B.	Apr. 26, 1826	Balto.
	Jim	22	Palestine	Slatter, Hope Hull	Nov. 16, 1835	Balto.
	Jim	11	States	Woolfolk, Austin	Nov. 26, 1825	Balto.
	Jim	27	Tippecanoe	McNuly, Samuel	Sept. 18, 1844	Balto.

Surname	First Name	Age	Ship	O/S	Date	Depart
	Jim	18	Virginia	Morton, George C.	Dec. 19, 1825	Balto.
	Jim	18	Virginia	Woolfolk, Joseph B.	Dec. 19, 1825	Balto.
	Jim	19	Virginia	Woolfolk, Joseph B.	Dec. 19, 1825	Balto.
	Jimmy	2	Georgia	Brent, Robert J.	Dec. 23, 1844	Balto.
	Jinney	27	Lapwing	King, Gideon T.	March 22, 1822	Balto.
	Jinny	18 mon.	Irad Ferry	Clendenin, A.	Jan. 16, 1840	Balto.
	Joanna	6	Edward Everett	Campbell, Bernard M.	Oct. 18, 1851	Balto.
	Jobe	23	Superb	Donovan, Joseph S.	Nov. 2, 1843	Balto.
	Joe	20	Alonzo	White, Philip	Nov. 8, 1822	Balto.
	Joe	9	Dryad	Williams, Joseph C.	Dec. 12, 1827	Balto.
	Joe	17	Emigrant	Somerell, Henry S.	Apr. 29, 1836	Balto.
	Joe	27	Emilie	Ferguson, Thomas	Dec. 14, 1821	Balto.
	Joe	9	Hamlet	Stansbury, Hammond N.	Apr. 7, 1824	Balto.
	Joe	9	Hope & Hannah	Williams, Joseph C.	Dec. 10, 1827	Balto.
	Joe	16	Intelligence	Plater, John R. Jr.	Apr. 12, 1823	St. Mary's
	Joe	9	Intelligence	De Mapiere, Victor	Apr. 30, 1821	Balto.
	Joe	20	Intelligence	Coleman, Henry E.	Nov. 4, 1820	Balto.
	Joe	15	Mars	Woolfolk, Austin	Oct. 30, 1824	Balto.
	Joe	17	Missouri	Barrow, John H.	March 2, 1819	Balto.
	Joe	24	North America	Woolfolk, Austin	Dec. 20, 1824	Balto.
	Joe	25	States	Woolfolk, Austin	March 8, 1826	Balto.
	Joe	17	Trafalgar	Dent, Wilfred	Jan. 13, 1827	Annapolis
	Joe	9	Ulysses	Richardson, Wade H.	Nov. 6, 1833	Balto.
	Joe	19	Virgin a	Woolfolk, Austin	Nov. 18, 1823	Balto.
	John	4	Agent	Anderson, David	June 8, 1821	Balto.
	John	19	Agent	Anderson, David	June 8, 1821	Balto.

Surname	First Name	Age	Ship	O/S	Date	Depart
	John		Ajax	Richardson, Wade H.	Oct.3, 1833	Balto.
	John	21	Alfred	Woolfolk, Austin	May 7, 1825	Balto.
	John	45	Alfred	Mann, William	Nov. 6, 1824	Balto.
	John	20	Algerine	Woolfolk, Austin	Jan. 5, 1826	Balto.
	John	10 mon.	Arctic	Smith, Leonard J.	Jan. 29, 1828	St. Mary's
	John	15	Arctic	Williams, Joseph C.	Jan. 31, 1829	St. Mary's
	John	15	Arctic	Williams, Joseph C.	Jan. 31, 1829	St. Mary's
	John	8	Arctic	Kelso, George G.	Nov. 15, 1826	Balto.
	John	5	Arctic	Cliffe, Henry	Oct. 4, 1828	Balto.
	John	2	Arctic	McConnell, Alex	Sept. 29, 1827	Balto.
	John	11	Balloon	Milligan, George	Dec. 17, 1821	Balto.
	John	14	Balloon	Zacharie, James W.	Dec. 22, 1821	Balto.
	John	12	Betsey	Woolfolk, Austin	Apr. 29, 1828	Balto.
	John	13	Betsey	Woolfolk, Austin	Apr. 29, 1828	Balto.
	John	17	Bourne	Chaille, W.H.	Oct. 15, 1832	Balto.
	John	19	Bourne	Rogers, Selemachus	Sept. 9, 1833	Balto.
	John	5 mon.	Brunswick	Woolfolk, Austin	Oct. 11, 1831	Balto.
	John	25	Brunswick	Woolfolk, Austin	Oct. 11, 1831	Balto.
	John	12	Budget	Spraggins, Samuel M.	Nov. 27, 1821	Balto.
	John	3	Burlington	Stout, G.H.	Oct. 22, 1842	Balto.
	John	2	Caledonia	Barnum, Richard	Oct. 19, 1842	Balto.
	John	21	Caroline	Ferguson, Thomas	March 2, 1821	Balto.
	John	22	Caspian	Woolfolk, Austin	Nov. 26, 1836	Balto.
	John	33	Caspian	Woolfolk, Austin	Nov. 26, 1836	Balto.
	John	14	Commodore Patterso	Thompson, Henry	March 20, 1819	Balto.
	John	5	Dryad	Williams, Joseph C.	Dec. 12, 1827	Balto.

Surname	First Name	Age	Ship	O/S	Date	Depart
	John	3	Dumphries	Lee, Richard H.	Sept. 25, 1828	Balto.
	John	9	Dumphries	Lee, Richard H.	Sept. 25, 1828	Balto.
	John	25	Dumphries	Lee, Richard H.	Sept. 25, 1828	Balto.
	John		Dumphries	Lee, Richard H.	Sept. 25, 1828	Balto.
	John	20	Elizabeth	Campbell, Walter L.	Oct. 6, 1849	Balto.
	John	5	Emilie	Ferguson, Thomas	Dec. 14, 1821	Balto.
	John	20	Emilie	Ferguson, Thomas	Dec. 14, 1821	Balto.
	John	22	Eros	Woolfolk, Austin	Jan. 28, 1824	Balto.
	John	8	Franklin	Somerville, Henry	Nov. 27, 1819	Balto.
	John	13	Good Hope	Woolfolk, Austin	Nov. 16, 1821	Balto.
	John	19	Hamlet	Woolfolk, Austin	Apr. 7, 1824	Balto.
	John	21	Hamlet	Woolfolk, Joseph B.	Apr. 7, 1824	Balto.
	John	15	Harriet	Carroll, Charles	Dec. 7, 1836	Balto.
	John	20	Harriet	Carroll, Charles	Dec. 7, 1836	Balto.
	John	23	Harriett	Woolfolk, Austin	March 23, 1822	Balto.
	John	5	Hector	Woolfolk, Austin	Nov. 4, 1835	Balto.
	John		Helen A. Miller	Campbell, Bernard M.	Oct. 18, 1852	Balto.
	John	20	Henry A. Barling	Donovan, Joseph S.	Dec. 18, 1851	Balto.
	John	13	Henry Clay	Bower, Robert W.	Dec. 8, 1828	Nottingham
	John	6	Henry Clay	Bower, Thomas F.	Dec. 8, 1828	Nottingham
	John	16	Henry Clay	Chew, Worthington	Dec. 8, 1828	Nottingham
	John	18	Henry Clay	Compton & Dorsett	Dec. 8, 1828	Nottingham
	John	2	Hermann	Rowe, Ralph	June 21, 1851	Balto.
	John	20	Hibernia	Chaber, Leon	Dec. 5, 1826	Balto.
	John	24	Hibernia	Chaber, Leon	Dec. 5, 1826	Balto.
	John	30	Hibernia	Chaber, Leon	Dec. 5, 1826	Balto.

Surname	First Name	Age	Ship	O/S	Date	Depart
	John	14	Home	Campbell, Bernard M.	March 22, 1845	Balto.
	John	4	Hope	Purnell, Thomas R.	Dec. 3, 1833	Balto.
	John	20	Hope	Byrne, Walter	Dec. 5, 1833	Balto.
	John	50	Hope	Byrne, Walter	Dec. 5, 1833	Balto.
	John	5	Hope & Hannah	Williams, Joseph C.	Dec. 10, 1827	Balto.
	John	20	Hortensia	Woolfolk, Austin	Dec. 14, 1836	Balto.
	John	9	Intelligence	Plater, John R. Jr.	Apr. 12, 1823	St. Mary's
	John	11	Intelligence	Plater, John R. Jr.	Apr. 12, 1823	St. Mary's
	John	24	Intelligence	Woolfolk, Austin	Apr. 5, 1823	Balto.
	John	20	Intelligence	Anderson, David	Dec. 20, 1822	Balto.
	John	20	Intelligence	Anderson, David	Dec. 20, 1822	Balto.
	John	27	Intelligence	Somerville, Alexander	Dec. 20, 1822	Balto.
	John	8	Intelligence	Woolfolk, Austin	Dec. 20, 1822	Balto.
	John	25	Julia	Poindexter, George	Feb. 10, 1832	Balto.
	John	19	Kirkwood	Campbell, Bernard M.	Jan. 4, 1845	Balto.
	John	16	Kirkwood	Wheeler, A.C.	July 19, 1845	Balto.
	John	18	Lady Monroe	Chabert, Leon	Sept. 29, 1825	Balto.
	John	12	Lady Monroe	Woolfolk, Austin	Sept. 29, 1825	Balto.
	John	25	Lady Monroe	Woolfolk, Austin	Sept. 29, 1825	Balto.
	John	17	Lafayette	Slatter, Hope Hull	March 25, 1843	Balto.
	John	18	Lafayette	Woolfolk, Richard	Oct. 18, 1828	Balto.
	John	29	Lafayette	Woolfolk, Richard	Oct. 18, 1828	Balto.
	John	8	Mars	Woolfolk, Austin	Nov. 1, 1824	Balto.
	John	26	Mars	Woolfolk, Joseph B.	Nov. 1, 1824	Balto.
	John	14	Mars	Woolfolk, Austin	Oct. 30, 1824	Balto.
	John	9	Mary Broughton	Chaplain, J. Bond	Nov. 18, 1851	Balto.

Surname	First Name	Age	Ship	O/S	Date	Depart
	John	18	Mechanic	Woolfolk, Austin	Jan. 1, 1831	Balto.
	John	20	Mechanic	Woolfolk, Austin	Jan. 1, 1831	Balto.
	John	10 mon.	Merrimack	Kelso, George G.	Nov. 2, 1831	Balto.
	John	10	Merrimack	Kelso, George G.	Nov. 2, 1831	Balto.
	John	7	Missouri	Gilmore, John	March 1, 1819	Balto.
	John	17	Napier	Hammond, T.G.	Nov. 3, 1842	Balto.
	John	11	North America	Thurman, William C.	Apr. 24, 1826	Balto.
	John	17	North America	Woolfolk, Austin	Nov. 23, 1822	Balto.
	John	21	North America	Woolfolk, Austin	Nov. 23, 1822	Balto.
	John	23	North America	Woolfolk, Austin	Nov. 23, 1822	Balto.
	John	3	Orleans	Stout, J.H.	Oct. 22, 1842	Balto.
	John	12	Palestine	Slatter, Hope Hull	Nov. 16, 1835	Balto.
	John	9	Pandora	Woolfolk, Austin	March 26, 1831	Balto.
	John	17	Pandora	Woolfolk, Austin	March 26, 1831	Balto.
	John	17	Seaman	Hooper, John	Dec. 18, 1838	Balto.
	John	1	Serene	Archer, James	Oct. 19, 1836	Balto.
	John	13	Serene	Archer, James	Oct. 19, 1836	Balto.
	John	35	Serene	Archer, James	Oct. 19, 1836	Balto.
	John	6	Shamrock	Guyton, Elisha	March 11, 1840	Balto.
	John	15	Shepherdiss	Williams, Joseph C.	March 27, 1827	Balto.
	John	21	St. Mary	Campbell, Bernard M.	Nov. 29, 1845	Balto.
	John	24	States	Chaber, Leon	March 8, 1826	Balto.
	John	25	States	Woolfolk, Austin	March 8, 1826	Balto.
	John	9	States	Duer, Robert	Nov. 26, 1825	Balto.
	John	13	States	Morton, George C.	Nov. 26, 1825	Balto.
	John	35	States	Woolfolk, Austin	Nov. 26, 1825	Balto.

Surname	First Name	Age	Ship	O/S	Date	Depart
	John	18	Strafford	Wilson, Thomas C.	Nov. 21, 1843	Balto.
	John	28	Susan Miller	Woolfolk, Richard T.	Oct. 25, 1822	Balto.
	John	15	Susan Miller	Woolfolk, Samuel M.	Oct. 25, 1822	Balto.
	John	3 mon.	Temperance	Wikoff, Steven W.	Dec. 12, 1818	Balto.
	John	40	Temperance	Woolfolk, Austin	Dec. 9, 1818	Balto.
	John	17	Tippecanoe	Harker, William	Dec. 16, 1840	Balto.
	John	20	Triton	Anderson, David	Dec. 20, 1819	Balto.
	John	13	Tweed	Bowling, John D.	Oct. 20, 1836	Town Creek
	John	24	Tweed	Bowling, John D.	Oct. 20, 1836	Town Creek
	John	26	Virginia	Woolfolk, Joseph B.	Dec. 19, 1825	Balto.
	John	10	Virginia	Pearce, James Alfred	March 27, 1828	Balto.
	John	21	William and Mary	King, Gideon T.	Oct. 9, 1821	Balto.
	John		Zoe	Donovan, Joseph S.	Feb. 16, 1847	Balto.
	John Benjamin	4	Leda	Nelson, James	Nov. 16, 1848	Balto.
	John Henry	12	Kirkwood	Campbell, Bernard M.	Oct. 14, 1848	Balto.
	John Henry	8	Lafayette	Woolfolk, Joseph B.	Oct. 18, 1828	Balto.
	John Henry	19	Leda	Nelson, James	Nov. 16, 1848	Balto.
	John Henry	13	Mary	Harker, William	March 3, 1842	Balto.
	John Henry	5	Union	Campbell, Bernard M.	Dec. 16, 1848	Balto.
	Johnson	18	Isabella		Nov. 26, 1834	Balto.
	Jonah	5	Eros	Woolfolk, Austin	Jan. 28, 1824	Balto.
	Jonas	16	Intelligence	Coleman, Henry E.	Nov. 4, 1820	Balto.
	Jonas	38	North America	Woolfolk, Austin	Dec. 20, 1824	Balto.
	Jonas	21	Susan Miller	Woolfolk, Richard T.	Oct. 25, 1822	Balto.
	Joney	15	Mars	Woolfolk, Austin	Oct. 30, 1824	Balto.
	Joseph	16	Ajax	Richardson, Wade H.	Oct.3, 1833	Balto.

Surname	First Name	Age	Ship	O/S	Date	Depart
	Joseph	5	Alfred	Woolfolk, Austin	Jan. 18, 1825	Balto.
	Joseph	23	Algerine	Woolfolk, Joseph B.	Jan. 6, 1826	Balto.
	Joseph	22	Betsey	Woolfolk, Austin	Apr. 29, 1828	Balto.
	Joseph	50	Caledonia	Woolfolk, Austin	Oct. 27, 1841	Balto.
	Joseph	19	Good Hope	Woolfolk, Austin	Nov. 16, 1821	Balto.
	Joseph	23	Hamlet	Woolfolk, Austin	Apr. 7, 1824	Balto.
	Joseph	27	Hamlet	Woolfolk, Joseph B.	Apr. 7, 1824	Balto.
	Joseph	21	Intelligence	Jenkins, Benedict J.	Apr. 27, 1821	Balto.
	Joseph	14	Intelligence	Wallace, Joseph A.	Apr. 27, 1821	Balto.
	Joseph	16	Lady Monroe	Woolfolk, Austin	March 25, 1825	Balto.
	Joseph	24	Lady Monroe	Wascher, J.E.	Sept. 29, 1825	Balto.
	Joseph	20	Lady Monroe	Woolfolk, Austin	Sept. 29, 1825	Balto.
	Joseph	23	Mars	Woolfolk, Austin	Oct. 30, 1824	Balto.
	Joseph	25	Mars	Woolfolk, Joseph B.	Oct. 30, 1824	Balto.
	Joseph	25	Mechanic	Woolfolk, Austin	Jan. 1, 1831	Balto.
	Joseph	24	Missouri	Little, Moses	March 2, 1819	Balto.
	Joseph	20	North America	Woolfolk, Austin	Nov. 23, 1822	Balto.
	Joseph	21	North America	Woolfolk, Austin	Oct. 14, 1823	Balto.
	Joseph	18	Orbit	Woolfolk, Austin	Apr. 16, 1825	Balto.
	Joseph	4	Signet	Woolfolk, Austin	Nov. 17, 1831	Balto.
	Joseph		States	Woolfolk, Austin	Nov. 21, 1827	Balto.
	Joseph		States	Woolfolk, Austin	Nov. 21, 1827	Balto.
	Joseph	7	Statira	Smith, Doctor James	March 28, 1826	Balto.
	Joseph	14	Susan Miller	Woolfolk, Austin	Oct. 25, 1822	Balto.
	Joseph	16	Susan Miller	Woolfolk, Austin	Oct. 25, 1822	Balto.
	Josephine	15	General Pinckney	Duffel, H.L.	Nov. 8, 1845	Balto.

Surname	First Name	Age	Ship	O/S	Date	Depart
	Josephine	infant	States	Morton, George C.	Nov. 26, 1825	Balto.
	Josephus	30	Victorine	Campbell, Walter L.	Sept. 12, 1846	Balto.
	Josh	19	Bourne	Rogers, Selemachus	Sept. 9, 1833	Balto.
	Josh	18	Russell	Woolfolk, Austin	Feb. 27, 1839	Balto.
	Joshua	45	Baltimore	Hale, Colin F.	Oct. 31, 1835	Balto.
	Joshua	23	Betsey	Woolfolk, Austin	Apr. 29, 1828	Balto.
	Joshua	19	Caspian	Woolfolk, Austin	Nov. 26, 1836	Balto.
	Joshua	16	Good Hope	Woolfolk, Austin	Nov. 21, 1821	Balto.
	Joshua	23	Harriett	Woolfolk, Richard T.	March 6, 1823	Balto.
	Joshua	26	Hibernia	Woolfolk, Austin	Dec. 5, 1826	Balto.
	Joshua	18	Mars	Woolfolk, Austin	Oct. 30, 1824	Balto.
	Joshua	15	Mars	Woolfolk, Joseph B.	Oct. 30, 1824	Balto.
	Joshua	25	Merrimack	Kelso, George G.	Nov. 2, 1831	Balto.
	Joshua	22	Missouri	Little, Moses	March 2, 1819	Balto.
	Joshua	25	States	Woolfolk, Austin	March 8, 1826	Balto.
	Joshua	11	Statira	Smith, Doctor James	March 28, 1826	Balto.
	Joshua	20	Susan Miller	Woolfolk, Austin	Oct. 25, 1822	Balto.
	Josiah	4	Emilie	Spencer, Thomas R.P.	March 27, 1821	Balto.
	Josiah		Hope	Browning, Robert B.	Dec. 5, 1833	Balto.
	Jube	14	Harriett	King, John	March 23, 1822	Balto.
	Juda	14	Intelligence	Anderson, David	Dec. 20, 1822	Balto.
	Judah		Bourne	Handy, Samuel	Oct. 13, 1832	Balto.
	Judah	26	Henry A. Barling	Campbell, Bernard M.	Dec. 18, 1851	Balto.
	Judah	19	Susan Miller	Bibbs, John T.	Oct. 25, 1822	Balto.
	Judith		Snow	Willis	Feb 5, 1835	Balto.
	Judy	19	Budget	Spraggins, Samuel M.	Nov. 27, 1821	Balto.

Surname	First Name	Age	Ship	O/S	Date	Depart
	Judy	24	Orion	Oldham, George W.	Dec. 30, 1822	Balto.
	Julia	6	Ann Wayne	Guyton, Elisha	Sept. 2, 1836	Balto.
	Julia	3	Hyperion	Valcourt, Alex de	May 10, 1822	Balto.
	Julia	14	Hyperion	King, Gideon T.	Nov. 12, 1821	Balto.
	Julia	30	Kirkwood	Campbell, Bernard M.	Oct. 16, 1845	Balto.
	Julia	18	Mars	Woolfolk, Austin	Oct. 30, 1824	Balto.
	Julia	22	Nancy W. Stevens	Harp, W.B.	Oct. 23, 1843	Balto.
	Julia	9	States	Woolfolk, Joseph B.	Nov. 21, 1827	Balto.
	Julia	16	Statira	Smith, Doctor James	March 28, 1826	Balto.
	Julia	30	Tippecanoe	Pearce, Greenbury W.?	Dec. 15, 1840	Balto.
	Julia	14	William and Mary	King, Gideon T.	Oct. 9, 1821	Balto.
	Julia	12	Harriett	Woolfolk, Austin	March 23, 1822	Balto.
	Julia Ann	11	North America	Chabert, Leon	Apr. 24, 1826	Balto.
	Julia Ann	18	Union	Campbell, Bernard M.	Dec. 16, 1848	Balto.
	Julia Ann	11	Henry A. Barling	Marriott, William H.	Oct. 28, 1848	Balto.
	Julian	8	Margaret Hugg	Campbell, Bernard M.	Feb. 8, 1845	Balto.
	Julian	19	North America	Woolfolk, Austin	Nov. 23, 1822	Balto.
	Julian	22	Pilgrim	Williams, George W.	Dec. 22, 1834	Balto.
	Juliann	4	Arctic	Smith, Leonard J.	Jan. 29, 1828	St. Mary's
	Juliann	2	Balloon	Penieres, Emile	Dec. 22, 1821	Balto.
	Juliann	10	Mars	Woolfolk, Austin	Oct. 30, 1824	Balto.
	Juliann	18	Mars	Woolfolk, Austin	Oct. 30, 1824	Balto.
	Julianne	26	Gulnae	Kelso, George G.	Nov. 3, 1830	Balto.
	Julianne	27	Lapwing	King, Gideon T.	March 22, 1822	Balto.
	Juliet	13	Henry Clay	Camphor, Henry	Dec. 8, 1828	Nottingham
	Juliett	8	Balloon	Zacharie, James W.	Dec. 22, 1821	Balto.

Surname	First Name	Age	Ship	O/S	Date	Depart
	Juliett Ann	27	Balloon	Zacharie, James W.	Dec. 22, 1821	Balto.
	Julius	25	States	Tillotson, Giles	Nov. 22, 1827	Balto.
	July ?	15	Algerine	Woolfolk, Joseph B.	Jan. 6, 1826	Balto.
	July ?	24	Harriet	Carroll, Charles	Dec. 7, 1836	Balto.
	July ?	23	Julia	Poindexter, George	Feb. 10, 1832	Balto.
	July Ann	16	Hortensia	Woolfolk, Austin	Dec. 14, 1836	Balto.
	Kate	29	Aurilla	Warfield, Charles	Apr. 26, 1822	Balto.
	Kate	13	Dumphries	Lee, Richard H.	Sept. 25, 1828	Balto.
	Kate	2	Tangier	Campbell, Bernard M.	Nov. 26, 1853	Balto.
	Kemmy	23	Mars	Woolfolk, Austin	Nov. 1, 1824	Balto.
	Kesiah	20	Emilie	Spencer, Thomas R.P.	Dec. 14, 1821	Balto.
	Kesiah	22	Emilie	Spencer, Thomas R.P.	March 27, 1821	Balto.
	Kesiah	16	Harriett	Woolfolk, Austin	March 23, 1822	Balto.
	Kesiah	17	Mars	Woolfolk, Austin	Oct. 30, 1824	Balto.
	Kezant	20	Hermann	Rowe, Ralph	June 21, 1851	Balto.
	Kittty	18	Pandora	Woolfolk, Austin	March 26, 1831	Balto.
	Kitty	24	Arctic	Smith, Leonard J.	Jan. 29, 1828	St. Mary's
	Kitty	10	Arctic	Kelso, George G.	Nov. 15, 1826	Balto.
	Kitty	8	Balloon	Zacharie, James W.	Dec. 22, 1821	Balto.
	Kitty	32	Balloon	Zacharie, James W.	Dec. 22, 1821	Balto.
	Kitty	21	Betsey	Woolfolk, Austin	Apr. 29, 1828	Balto.
	Kitty	5	Budget	Bradley, Robert	Nov. 26, 1821	Balto.
	Kitty	25	Catharine Jackson	Diggs, John H.	Nov. 26, 1836	Nanjimoy
	Kitty	7	Henry Clay	Chew, Worthington	Dec. 8, 1828	Nottingham
	Kitty	12	Hope	Byrne, Walter	Dec. 5, 1833	Balto.
	Kitty	8	Intelligence	Plater, John R. Jr.	Apr. 12, 1823	St. Mary's

Surname	First Name	Age	Ship	O/S	Date	Depart
	Kitty	12	Intelligence	Woolfolk, Austin	Dec. 20, 1822	Balto.
	Kitty	2	Intelligence	Anderson, David	Nov. 3, 1820	Balto.
	Kitty		Lady Monroe	Woolfolk, Austin	March 25, 1825	Balto.
	Kitty	22	Lafayette	Woolfolk, Richard	Oct. 18, 1828	Balto.
	Kitty	40	Lapwing	Thompson, Henry	Nov. 28, 1827	Balto.
	Kitty	10	Mars	Woolfolk, Austin	Oct. 30, 1824	Balto.
	Kitty	26	Mary	Chaplain, Charles	Nov. 30, 1841	Balto.
	Kitty	19	Missouri	Lewis, Margaret	Feb. 25, 1819	Balto.
	Kitty	16	North America	Woolfolk, Austin	Nov. 23, 1822	Balto.
	Kitty	4	Opelousas	Garland, Rice	July 5, 1836	Balto.
	Kitty	32	Opelousas	Abercombie, James	July 6, 1836	Balto.
	Kitty	33	Orion	Oldham, George W.	Dec. 30, 1822	Balto.
	Kitty	15	Palestine	Slatter, Hope Hull	Nov. 16, 1835	Balto.
	Kitty	25	Palestine	Slatter, Hope Hull	Nov. 16, 1835	Balto.
	Kitty	5	Signet	Woolfolk, Austin	Nov. 12, 1831	Balto.
	Kitty	18	States	Woolfolk, Austin	Nov. 26, 1825	Balto.
	Kitty	5	Susan Miller	Woolfolk, Austin	Oct. 25, 1822	Balto.
	Kitty	18	Susan Miller	Woolfolk, Samuel M.	Oct. 25, 1822	Balto.
	Kitty	4	Trafalgar	Dent, Wilfred	Jan. 13, 1827	Annapolis
	Kitty Ann	14	Arctic	Maddox, Thomas H.	Jan. 30, 1829	St. Mary's
	Kitty Ann	9	Lafayette	Woolfolk, Austin	Oct. 18, 1828	Balto.
	Kitty Ann	16	Superb	Slatter Hope Hull	Nov. 1, 1843	Balto.
	Lafayette	10	Caspian	Woolfolk, Austin	Nov. 26, 1836	Balto.
	Larkin	18	General Hand	Poindexter, George L.	June 1, 1832	Balto.
	Larney	16	Hyperion	Anderson, David	May 14, 1822	Balto.
	Laura	5	Margaret Hugg	Campbell, Bernard M.	Feb. 8, 1845	Balto.

Surname	First Name	Age	Ship	O/S	Date	Depart
	Sarah	20	Mars	Woolfolk, Austin	Nov. 1, 1824	Balto.
	Sarah	11	Nancy W.Stevens	Baker, William	Oct. 23, 1843	Balto.
	Sarah	4	North America	Chabert, Leon	Apr. 24, 1826	Balto.
	Sarah	11	North America	Chabert, Leon	Apr. 24, 1826	Balto.
	Sarah	13	Orbit	Chabert, Leon	Apr. 16, 1825	Balto.
	Sarah	3	Orion	Woolfolk, Austin	Dec. 30, 1822	Balto.
	Sarah	17	Palestine	Slatter, Hope Hull	Nov. 16, 1835	Balto.
	Sarah	9	Serene	Arman, John	Oct. 20, 1836	Balto.
	Sarah	15 mon.	States	Woolfolk, Austin	March 8, 1826	Balto.
	Sarah	7	States	Woolfolk, Joseph B.	Nov. 21, 1827	Balto.
	Sarah	3	States	Duer, Robert	Nov. 26, 1825	Balto.
	Sarah	11	States	Duer, Robert	Nov. 26, 1825	Balto.
	Sarah	35	States	Duer, Robert	Nov. 26, 1825	Balto.
	Sarah	10	Tippecanoe	Riley, James M.	Oct. 16, 1841	Balto.
	Sarah Ann	5	Arctic	Smith, Leonard J.	Jan. 29, 1828	St. Mary's
	Sarah Ann	2	Arctic	Williams, Joseph C.	Jan. 31, 1829	St. Mary's
	Sarah Ann	20	Catharine Jackson	Brent, George	Nov. 26, 1836	Nanjimoy
	Sarah Ann	19	Cicero	Guyton, Elisha	Aug. 31, 1835	Balto.
	Sarah Ann	4	Harriett	Woolfolk, Austin	March 23, 1822	Balto.
	Sarah Ann	16	Helen A. Miller	Campbell, Bernard M.	Oct. 18, 1852	Balto.
	Sarah Ann	30	Leda	Nelson, James	Nov. 16, 1848	Balto.
	Sarah Ann	8	Missouri	Cook, James K.	March 2, 1819	Balto.
	Sarah Ann	8	Seaman	Hooper, John	Dec. 18, 1838	Balto.
	Sarah Ann	9	Tippecanoe	Simms, Benedict	Sept. 18, 1844	Balto.
	Sarah Ann	14	Union	Campbell, Bernard M.	Dec. 16, 1848	Balto.
	Sarah Anne	17	Pandora	Woolfolk, Austin	March 26, 1831	Balto.

Surname	First Name	Age	Ship	O/S	Date	Depart
	Sarah Ellen	20	Jane Henderson	Campbell, Bernard M.	Nov. 1, 1852	Balto.
	Sarah Ellen	10	Southerner	Donovan, Jospeh S.	Jan. 5, 1852	Balto.
	Sarah Jane	20	Helen A. Miller	Campbell, Bernard M.	Oct. 18, 1852	Balto.
	Sarah Jane	19	Union	Campbell, Bernard M.	Dec. 16, 1848	Balto.
	Sarah Jane	20	Union	Campbell, Bernard M.	Dec. 16, 1848	Balto.
	Sary Ann	14	Peru	Cruckshanks, J.D.	Nov. 17, 1842	Balto.
	Saul	11	Balloon	Milligan, George	Dec. 17, 1821	Balto.
	Saul	24	Lawrence	Woolfolk, Austin	May 9, 1823	Balto.
	Scipio	14	Agent	Anderson, David	June 8, 1821	Balto.
	Scipio	17	Mars	Woolfolk, Austin	Nov. 1, 1824	Balto.
	Scipio	19	Susan Miller	Woolfolk, Austin	Oct. 25, 1822	Balto.
	Scylla	35	Opelousas	Garlard, Rice	July 5, 1836	Balto.
	Sefy	11	Baltimore	Hale, Colin F.	Oct. 31, 1835	Balto.
	Selina	20	Zuline	Guestier, P.A.	Dec. 17, 1823	Balto.
	Seneca	23	Palestine	Slatter Hope Hull	Nov. 16, 1835	Balto.
	Seny	33	Mars	Woolfolk, Austin	Oct. 30, 1824	Balto.
	Sephora	32	Agent	Condir, Lewis	June 8, 1821	Balto.
	Serena	6 mon.	Hyperion	King, Gideon T.	Nov. 12, 1821	Balto.
	Sewell	1	Emilie	Laurenson, Andrew U.	Dec. 14, 1821	Balto.
	Shadrach	22	Billow	Woolfolk, Austin	Feb. 23, 1828	Balto.
	Shadrack	21	Emilie	Mercer William D.	March 27, 1821	Balto.
	Shadrack	24	Jasper	Woolfolk, Austin	Apr. 7, 1827	Balto.
	Shadrack	15	Susan Miller	Bibbs, John T.	Oct. 25, 1822	Balto.
	Sidney	17	Hortensia	Woolfolk, Austin	Dec. 14, 1836	Balto.
	Sidney	10	Lawrence	Woolfolk, Austin	May 9, 1823	Balto.
	Silas	8	Herman	Rowe, Ralph	June 21, 1851	Balto.

Surname	First Name	Age	Ship	O/S	Date	Depart
	Silvy	15	Harriett	Woolfolk, Austin	March 23, 1822	Balto.
	Simon	40	Aurilla	Chabert, Leon	Apr. 26, 1822	Balto.
	Simon	29	Budget	Spraggins, Samuel M.	Nov. 27, 1821	Balto.
	Simon	20	Charles	Glavary, Francis R.	Apr. 30, 1820	Balto.
	Simon	20	Intelligence	Woolfolk, Austin	Dec. 20, 1822	Balto.
	Simon	6	Mary	Lee, John	March 3, 1840	Balto.
	Simon	9	North America	Chabert, Leon	Apr. 24, 1826	Balto.
	Simon	20	States	Woolfolk, Austin	March 8, 1826	Balto.
	Simpson	22	Aurilla	Warfield, Charles	Apr. 26, 1822	Balto.
	Sissy	7	Brunswick	Woolfolk, Austin	Oct. 11, 1831	Balto.
	Solomon	3	Ann Wayne	Guyton, Elisha	Sept. 2, 1836	Balto.
	Solomon	8	Caledonia	Barnum, Richard	Oct. 19, 1842	Balto.
	Solomon		Caspian	Woolfolk, Austin	Nov. 26, 1836	Balto.
	Solomon	33	Emilie	Bratten, William	March 29, 1821	Balto.
	Solomon	22	Eros	Knight, William	June 29, 1822	Balto.
	Solomon	21	Good Hope	Woolfolk, Austin	Nov. 16, 1821	Balto.
	Solomon	20	Intelligence	Anderson, David	May 1, 1821	Balto.
	Solomon	18	Isabella		Nov. 26, 1834	Balto.
	Solomon	5	Lady Monroe	Woolfolk, Austin	March 25, 1825	Balto.
	Solomon	17	Lady Monroe	Woolfolk, Austin	Sept. 29, 1825	Balto.
	Solomon	22	Mars	Woolfolk, Austin	Oct. 30, 1824	Balto.
	Solomon	28	Susan Miller	Woolfolk, Austin	Oct. 25, 1822	Balto.
	Somerfield	3	Tippecanoe	Bangs, Theopilus	Apr. 15, 1844	Balto.
	Sophia	8	Arctic	Smith, Leonard J.	Jan. 29, 1828	St. Mary's.
	Sophia	16	Arctic	Maddox, Thomas H.	Jan. 30, 1829	St. Mary's.
	Sophia	5	Arctic	Kelso, George G.	Nov. 15, 1826	Balto.

Surname	First Name	Age	Ship	O/S	Date	Depart
	Sophia	16	Balloon	Zachare, James W.	Dec. 22, 1821	Balto.
	Sophia	22	Baltimore	Woolfolk, Austin	Nov. 2, 1835	Balto.
	Sophia	19	Elizabeth	Campbell, Bernard M.	Nov. 18, 1848	Balto.
	Sophia	13	Henry Clay	Bower, Thomas F.	Dec. 8, 1828	Nottingham
	Sophia	18	Hyperion	Woolfolk, Austin	May 10, 1822	Balto.
	Sophia	20	Hyperion	King, Gideon T.	Nov. 12, 1821	Balto.
	Sophia	15	Intelligence	Woolfolk, Austin	Dec. 20, 1822	Balto.
	Sophia	8	Irad Ferry	Clendenin, A.	Jan. 16, 1840	Balto.
	Sophia	25	Kirkwood	Campbell, Bernard M.	Apr. 4, 1846	Balto.
	Sophia	15	Merrimack	Kelso, George G.	Nov. 2, 1831	Balto.
	Sophia	22	Signet	Woolfolk, Austin	Nov. 17, 1831	Balto.
	Sophia	23	Superb	Anderson, David	Apr. 6, 1819	Balto.
	Sophia	19	Triton	Anderson, David	Dec. 20, 1819	Balto.
	Sophia	13	Ulysses	Harwood, James	Nov. 9, 1833	Balto.
	Sophia	11	Union	Campbell, Bernard M.	Oct. 9, 1848	Balto.
	Sophia	10	Victorine	Campbell, Bernard M.	March 1, 1845	Balto.
	Sophia	24	Victorine	Campbell, Bernard M.	March 1, 1845	Balto.
	Sophia	19	Virginia	Chabert, Leon	Dec. 19, 1825	Balto.
	Sophia	22	William and Mary	King, Gideon T.	Oct. 9, 1821	Balto.
	Sophy	20	Emilie	Anderson, David	March 27, 1821	Balto.
	Sophy	17	Henry Clay	Chew, Worthington	Dec. 8, 1828	Nottingham
	Sophy	18	Intelligence	Anderson, David	Nov. 3, 1820	Balto.
	Sophy	26	Jefferson	Woolfolk, Austin	Dec. 24, 1827	Balto.
	Sophy	23	Temperance	Woolfolk, Austin	Dec. 9, 1818	Balto.
	Soshy	3	Mars	Woolfolk, Austin	Oct. 30, 1824	Balto.
	Spencer	13	Agent	Anderson, David	June 8, 1821	Balto.

Surname	First Name	Age	Ship	O/S	Date	Depart
	Spencer	20	Aurilla	Woolfolk, Austin	Apr. 26, 1822	Balto.
	Spencer	17	Balloon	Penieres, Emile	Dec. 22, 1821	Balto.
	Spencer	45	Bourne	Chaille, W.H.	Oct. 15, 1832	Balto.
	Spencer	20	Henry Clay	Chew, Worthington	Dec. 8, 1828	Nottingham
	Spencer	20	Lady Monroe	Woolfolk, Austin	Sept. 29, 1825	Balto.
	Spenser	30	Mars	Woolfolk, Austin	Oct. 30, 1824	Balto.
	Stanley	11	Betsey	Woolfolk, Austin	Apr. 29, 1828	Balto.
	Stansbury	7	Lady Monroe	Chabert, Leon	Sept. 29, 1825	Balto.
	Stella	30	Mary	W.Taylor	Oct. 6, 1838	Balto.
	Stephen	16	Aurilla	Warfield, Charles	Apr. 26, 1822	Balto.
	Stephen	3	Balloon	Milligan, George	Dec. 17, 1821	Balto.
	Stephen	10	Balloon	Knight, William	Dec. 22, 1821	Balto.
	Stephen	18	Balloon	Penieres, Emile	Dec. 22, 1821	Balto.
	Stephen	22	Bourne	Rogers, Selemachus	Sept. 9, 1833	Balto.
	Stephen	22	Brunswick	Woolfolk, Austin	Oct. 11, 1831	Balto.
	Stephen	18	Dumphries	Lee, Richard H.	Sept. 25, 1828	Balto.
	Stephen	24	Emilie	Anderson, David	Jan. 5, 1819	Balto.
	Stephen	10	Emilie	Anderson, David	March 27, 1821	Balto.
	Stephen	16	Emilie	Anderson, David	March 27, 1821	Balto.
	Stephen	19	Emilie	Fortin, Charles	May 19, 1820	Balto.
	Stephen	45	Franklin	Somerville, Henry	Nov. 27, 1819	Balto.
	Stephen	21	Good Hope	Woolfolk, Samuel M.	Nov. 21, 1821	Balto.
	Stephen	20	Hyperion	Woolfolk, Austin	May 10, 1822	Balto.
	Stephen	25	Hyperion	Anderson, David	May 14, 1822	Balto.
	Stephen	23	Intelligence	Woolfolk, Austin	Dec. 20, 1822	Balto.
	Stephen	30	Intelligence	King, Gideon T.	Sept. 18, 1821	Balto.

Surname	First Name	Age	Ship	O/S	Date	Depart
	Stephen	21	Julia	Woolfolk, Austin	Feb. 10, 1832	Balto.
	Stephen	19	Kenhawa	Maddox, Thomas H.	Oct. 26, 1832	Balto.
	Stephen	21	Lady Monroe	Chaber, Leon	Sept. 29, 1825	Balto.
	Stephen	16	Missouri	Marrass, John	March 1, 1819	Balto.
	Stephen	9	Nancy W. Stevens	Baker, William	Oct. 23, 1843	Balto.
	Stephen	22	North America	Woolfolk, Austin	Oct. 14, 1823	Balto.
	Stephen	20	Seaman	Hooper, John	Dec. 18, 1838	Balto.
	Stephen	28	States	Chaber, Leon	March 8, 1826	Balto.
	Stephen	16	States	Kelso, George Y.	Nov. 25, 1825	Balto.
	Stephen	45	Statira	Smith, Doctor James	March 28, 1826	Balto.
	Stephen	4	Unicorn	Wedenstrandt, John C.	Oct. 23, 1820	Balto.
	Stephen	27	Virginia	Woolfolk, Joseph B.	Dec. 19, 1825	Balto.
	Sterling	19	States	Woolfolk, Austin	March 8, 1826	Balto.
	Stess	2	Emilie	Anderson, David	March 27, 1821	Balto.
	Stewart	14	Harriett	Arnest, John	March 23, 1822	Balto.
	Suckey	25	Aurilla	Wikoff, Stephen A.	Apr. 26, 1822	Balto.
	Suckey	31	Intelligence	Plater, John R. Jr.	Apr. 12, 1823	St. Mary's
	Suke	34	Franklin	Yeiser, John	Nov. 27, 1819	Balto.
	Sukey	24	Balloon	Zacharie, James W.	Dec. 22, 1821	Balto.
	Susan	22	Alonzo	White, Philip	Nov. 8, 1822	Balto.
	Susan	18	Aurilla	Woolfolk, Austin	Apr. 26, 1822	Balto.
	Susan	40	Balloon	Milligan, George	Dec. 17, 1821	Balto.
	Susan	1	Brunswick	Woolfolk, Austin	Oct. 11, 1831	Balto.
	Susan	5	Caspian	Woolfolk, Austin	Nov. 26, 1836	Balto.
	Susan	23	Caspian	Woolfolk, Austin	Nov. 26, 1836	Balto.
	Susan	22	Catharine Jackson	Brent, George	Nov. 26, 1836	Nanjimoy

Surname	First Name	Age	Ship	O/S	Date	Depart
	Susan	25	Delta	Jones, Nicholas S.	Dec. 19, 1828	Balto.
	Susan	3	Dumphries	Lee, Richard H.	Sept. 25, 1828	Balto.
	Susan	22	Dumphries	Lee, Richard H.	Sept. 25, 1828	Balto.
	Susan	24	Dumphries	Lee, Richard H.	Sept. 25, 1828	Balto.
	Susan	16	Emilie	Weddenstrande, John C.	Jan. 5, 1819	Balto.
	Susan	1	General Hand	Poindexter, George L.	June 1, 1832	Balto.
	Susan	10	General Pinckney	Slatter, Hope Hull	Jan. 19, 1847	Balto.
	Susan	7	Harriet	Carroll, Charles	Dec. 7, 1836	Balto.
	Susan	7	Harriet	Carroll, Charles	Dec. 7, 1836	Balto.
	Susan	11	Harriet	Carroll, Charles	Dec. 7, 1836	Balto.
	Susan	16	Henry A. Barling	Marriott, William H.	Oct. 28, 1848	Balto.
	Susan		Hope	Richardson, Wade H.	Dec. 3, 1833	Balto.
	Susan	24	Hyperion	Woolfolk, Austin	May 10, 1822	Balto.
	Susan	9 mon.	Intelligence	Woolfolk, Austin	Dec. 20, 1822	Balto.
	Susan	24	Intelligence	Woolfolk, Austin	Dec. 20, 1822	Balto.
	Susan	17	Jefferson	Woolfolk, Austin	Dec. 24, 1827	Balto.
	Susan	5	Julia	Poindexter, George	Feb. 10, 1832	Balto.
	Susan	6	Lady Monroe	Woolfolk, Austin	Sept. 29, 1825	Balto.
	Susan	28	Lady Monroe	Woolfolk, Austin	Sept. 29, 1825	Balto.
	Susan	14	Lafayette	Slatter, Hope Hull	March 25, 1843	Balto.
	Susan		Lafayette	Slatter, Hope Hull	March 25, 1843	Balto.
	Susan	20	Lapwing	King, Gideon T.	March 22, 1822	Balto.
	Susan	13	Orion	Oldham, George W.	Dec. 30, 1822	Balto.
	Susan	43	Patriot	White, Charles	July 14, 1836	Balto.
	Susan	20	States	Woodland, James	March 7, 1826	Balto.
	Susan	21	Unicorn	Wedenstrandt, John C.	Oct. 23, 1820	Balto.

Surname	First Name	Age	Ship	O/S	Date	Depart
	Syas	17	Arctic	Smith, Leonard J.	Jan. 29, 1828	St. Mary's
	Syas	25	Arctic	Smith, Leonard J.	Jan. 29, 1828	St. Mary's
	Sylvester	4 mon.	Dumphries	Lee, R chard H.	Sept. 25, 1828	Balto.
	Sylvester	19	Mars	Woolfolk, Austin	Oct. 30, 1824	Balto.
	Sylvia	24	Alonzo	Oldham, George W.	Nov. 7, 1822	Balto.
	Sylvia	33	Henry Clay	Chew, Worhtington	Dec. 8, 1828	Nottingham
	Tabby	12	Patrick Henry	Campbell, Bernard M.	June 1, 1853	Balto.
	Talbott	8	Aurille	Warfield, Charles	Apr. 26, 1822	Balto.
	Tamal	13	Hermitage	Slatter, Hope Hull	Oct. 28, 1846	Balto.
	Tanney	15	Harrie-	Carroll, Charles	Dec. 7, 1836	Balto.
	Tarey	30	Susan Miller	Woolfolk, Austin	Oct. 25, 1822	Balto.
	Ted	30	Henry Clay	Camp-or, Henry	Dec. 8, 1828	Nottingham
	Temperance	24	Alonzo	Oldham, George W.	Nov. 7, 1822	Balto.
	Temperance	18	Hamlet	Woolfolk, Austin	Jan. 2, 1824	Balto.
	Tenna	18	Balloon	Penieres, Emile	Dec. 22, 1821	Balto.
	Teresa	9	Balloon	Zacharie, James W.	Dec. 22, 1821	Balto.
	Teresa	28	Betsey	Woolfolk, Austin	Apr. 29, 1828	Balto.
	Teresa	5	Leda	Nelson, James	Nov. 16, 1848	Balto.
	Teresa	2	Susan Miller	Woolfolk, Samuel M.	Oct. 25, 1822	Balto.
	Teressa	10	Betsey	Woolfolk, Austin	Apr. 29, 1828	Balto.
	Terry	10	Eros	Armitage, James	June 29, 1822	Balto.
	Terry	19	Intelligence	Plater, John R. Jr.	Apr. 12, 1823	St. Mary's
	Terry	14	Triton	Anderson, David	Dec. 20, 1819	Balto.
	Thaddeus	18 mon.	Snow	Willis	Feb 5, 1835	Balto.
	Theodore	22	Good Hope	Woolfolk, Austin	Nov. 16, 1821	Balto.
	Theodore	21	Hiberria	Kelso, John M.	Dec. 5, 1826	Balto.

Surname	First Name	Age	Ship	O/S	Date	Depart.
	Thomas	12 mon.	Actress	Anderson, David	Nov. 8, 1819	Balto.
	Thomas	23	Alonzo	Oldham, George W.	Nov. 7, 1822	Balto.
	Thomas		Alonzo	White, Philip	Nov. 8, 1822	Balto.
	Thomas	9	Arctic	Hollins, John Smith	Oct. 3, 1828	Balto.
	Thomas	3	Billow	Woolfolk, Joseph B.	Feb. 23, 1828	Balto.
	Thomas	5	Catharine Jackson	Diggs, John H.	Nov. 26, 1836	Nanjimoy
	Thomas	4	Dumphries	Lee, Richard H.	Sept. 25, 1828	Balto.
	Thomas	21	Dumphries	Lee, Richard H.	Sept. 25, 1828	Balto.
	Thomas		Dumphries	Lee, Richard H.	Sept. 25, 1828	Balto.
	Thomas	8	Emilie	Anderson, David	Jan. 5, 1819	Balto.
	Thomas	22	Emilie	Coalman, Henry E.	Nov. 27, 1819	Balto.
	Thomas	25	Emilie	Coalman, Henry E.	Nov. 27, 1819	Balto.
	Thomas	17	General Hand	Poindexter, George L.	June 1, 1832	Balto.
	Thomas	32	General Hand	Poindexter, George L.	June 1, 1832	Balto.
	Thomas	35	General Hand	Poindexter, George L.	June 1, 1832	Balto.
	Thomas	4	Georgia	Brent, Robert J.	Dec. 23, 1844	Balto.
	Thomas	7	Harriet	Carroll, Charles	Dec. 7, 1836	Balto.
	Thomas	19	Henry Clay	Camphor, Henry	Dec. 8, 1828	Nottingham
	Thomas	21	Henry Clay	Dorsett, William N.	Dec. 8, 1828	Nottingham
	Thomas	9	Kirkwood	Donovan, Joseph S.	Apr. 15, 1845	Balto.
	Thomas	21	Kirkwood	Campbell, Bernard M.	Oct. 16, 1845	Balto.
	Thomas	17	Kirkwood	Donovan, Joseph S.	Sept. 28, 1846	Balto.
	Thomas	6 mon.	Mary Broughton	Chaplain, J. Bond	Nov. 18, 1851	Balto.
	Thomas	15	Missouri	Cook, James K.	March 2, 1819	Balto.
	Thomas	2 mon.	North America	Thurman, William C.	Apr. 24, 1826	Balto.
	Thomas	20	Pandora	Woolfolk, Austin	March 26, 1831	Balto.

Surname	First Name	Age	Ship	O/S	Date	Depart
	Thomas	2	Pilgrim	Williams, George W.	Dec. 22, 1834	Balto.
	Thomas	18	Russell	Woolfolk, Austin	Feb. 27, 1839	Balto.
	Thomas	5	Statira	Smith, Doctor James	March 28, 1826	Balto.
	Thomas	36	Statira	Smith, Doctor James	March 28, 1826	Balto.
	Thomas		Supero	Slatter, Hope Hull	Nov. 1, 1843	Balto.
	Thomas	20	Susan Miller	Woolfolk, Austin	Oct. 25, 1822	Balto.
	Thomas	21	Triton	Farrow, Nimrod	Dec. 18, 1819	Balto.
	Thomas	14	Triton	Anderson, David	Dec. 20, 1819	Balto.
	Thomas	24	Unicorn	Hynson, Robert C.	Oct. 23, 1820	Balto.
	Thomas	18	Victorine	Campbell, Bernard M.	March 1, 1845	Balto.
	Thornton	21	London	Kelly, Alex D.Jr	Nov. 6, 1840	Balto.
	Tilly	19	Hope	Richardson, Wade H.	Dec. 3, 1833	Balto.
	Tilly	17	Orion	Oldham, George W.	Dec. 30, 1822	Balto.
	Tim	21	Alonzo	Oldham, George W.	Nov. 7, 1822	Balto.
	Tim	5	Hope	Craig, John	Dec. 5, 1833	Balto.
	Tim	12	Isabella		Nov. 26, 1834	Balto.
	Tim	22	Lawrence	Woolfolk, Austin	May 9, 1823	Balto.
	Titus	23	Eros	Woolfolk, Austin	Jan. 28, 1824	Balto.
	Tobey	13	Hibernia	Woolfolk, Austin	Dec. 5, 1826	Balto.
	Tobias	25	Susan Miller	Woolfolk, Samuel M.	Oct. 25, 1822	Balto.
	Toby	50	Agent	Pierce, Levi	June 8, 1821	Balto.
	Toby	25	Caspian	Woolfolk, Austin	Nov. 26, 1836	Balto.
	Toby	15	Franklin	Somerville, Henry	Nov. 27, 1819	Balto.
	Toim	7 mon.	Lafayette	Woolfolk, Richard	Oct. 18, 1828	Balto.
	Tom	5 weeks	Alfred	Woolfolk, Austin	Jan. 18, 1825	Balto.
	Tom	18	Alfred	Woolfolk, Austin	Jan. 18, 1825	Balto.

Surname	First Name	Age	Ship	O/S	Date	Depart
	Tom	4	Arctic	Kelso, George G.	Nov. 15, 1826	Balto.
	Tom	14	Balloon	Milligan, George	Dec. 17, 1821	Balto.
	Tom	15	Budget	Spraggins, Samuel M.	Nov. 27, 1821	Balto.
	Tom	7	Charles	Carter, John A.	Sept. 29, 1849	Balto.
	Tom	12	Climax	Woolfolk, Austin	Dec. 6, 1828	Balto.
	Tom	8	Dryad	Williams, Joseph C.	Dec. 12, 1827	Balto.
	Tom	4	E.H. Chapin	Tyson, A.H.	Aug. 25, 1848	Balto.
	Tom	46	Emigrant	Somerrell, Henry S.	Apr. 29, 1836	Balto.
	Tom	19	Eros	Armitage, James	June 29, 1822	Balto.
	Tom	30	Franklin	Somerville, Henry	Nov. 27, 1819	Balto.
	Tom	6	Harriet	Carroll, Charles	Dec. 7, 1836	Balto.
	Tom	17	Harriett	Woolfolk, Richard T.	March 6, 1823	Balto.
	Tom	38	Henry Clay	Chew, Worhtington	Dec. 8, 1828	Nottingham
	Tom	16	Hibernia	Chabert, Leon	Dec. 5, 1826	Balto.
	Tom	23	Hibernia	Chabert, Leon	Dec. 5, 1826	Balto.
	Tom	8	Hope & Hannah	Williams, Joseph C.	Dec. 10, 1827	Balto.
	Tom	24	Intelligence	Woolfolk, Austin	Apr. 5, 1823	Balto.
	Tom	25	Intelligence	Woolfolk, Austin	Apr. 5, 1823	Balto.
	Tom	11	Intelligence	Anderson, David	Dec. 20, 1822	Balto.
	Tom	22	Intelligence	Woolfolk, Austin	Dec. 20, 1822	Balto.
	Tom	8	Intelligence	Anderson, David	March 14, 1820	Balto.
	Tom	11	Intelligence	Coalman, Henry E.	March 14, 1820	Balto.
	Tom	30	Isabella	Wallis, Cornelius C.	Nov. 26, 1834	Balto.
	Tom	12	Isabella		Nov. 26, 1834	Balto.
	Tom	40	Lady Monroe	Woolfolk, Austin	Sept. 29, 1825	Balto.
	Tom	24	Lawrence	Woolfolk, Austin	May 9, 1823	Balto.

Surname	First Name	Age	Ship	O/S	Date	Depart
	Tom	22	Mars	Woolfolk, Joseph B.	Oct. 30, 1824	Balto.
	Tom	8	North America	Woolfolk, Joseph B.	Apr. 26. 1826	Balto.
	Tom	19	North America	Woolfolk, Austin	Dec. 20, 1824	Balto.
	Tom	25	North America	Woolfolk, Austin	Dec. 20, 1824	Balto.
	Tom	23	North America	Woolfolk, Austin	Nov. 23, 1822	Balto.
	Tom	22	Palestine	Slatter, Hope Hull	Nov. 16, 1835	Balto.
	Tom	25	Palestine	Slatter, Hope Hull	Nov. 16, 1835	Balto.
	Tom	30	Palestine	Slatter, Hope Hull	Nov. 16, 1835	Balto.
	Tom	17	Sarah Ann	Keene, Wallace	Oct. 14, 1836	Balto.
	Tom	24	States	Woolfolk, Austin	March 8, 1826	Balto.
	Tom	1	Trafalgar	Dent, Wilfred	Jan. 13, 1827	Annapolis
	Tom	19	Trafalgar	Dent, Wilfred	Jan. 13, 1827	Annapolis
	Tommy	34	Georgia	Brent, Robert J.	Dec. 21, 1844	Balto.
	Tona	4	Balloon	Peniers, Emile	Dec. 22, 1821	Balto.
	Toney	6	Henry Clay	Bower, Thomas F.	Dec. 8, 1828	Nottingham
	Toney	30	Orbit	Chabert, Leon	Apr. 16, 1825	Balto.
	Tony		Caspian	Woolfolk, Austin	Nov. 26, 1836	Balto.
	Tony	4	Trafalgar	Dent, Wilfred	Jan. 13, 1827	Annapolis
	Torey	12	North America	Woolfolk, Austin	Dec. 20, 1824	Balto.
	Travers	32	Henry Clay	Compton & Dorsett	Dec. 8, 1828	Nottingham
	Tredus	19	Emilie	Mercer, William D.	March 27, 1821	Balto.
	Tusank	22	Intelligence	Woolfolk, Austin	Dec. 20, 1822	Balto.
	Ulysses	9 mon.	Charles	Carter John A.	Sept. 29, 1849	Balto.
	Vach	48	Balloon	Peniers, Emile	Dec. 22, 1821	Balto.
	Van Buren	11 mon.	Henry Clay	Chew, Worthington	Dec. 8, 1828	Nottingham
	Victoire	26	Actress	Garsicles, James	Nov. 6, 1819	Balto.

Surname	First Name	Age	Ship	O/S	Date	Depart
	Victory	58	Harriet	Carroll, Charles	Dec. 7, 1836	Balto.
	Vincent	20	Kirkwood	Campbell, Bernard M.	Oct. 16, 1845	Balto.
	Vincent	11	Lady Monroe	Chabert, Leon	Sept. 29, 1825	Balto.
	Vincent	20	Susan Miller	Woolfolk, Richard T.	Oct. 25, 1822	Balto.
	Vindy	18	Hibernia	Chabert, Leon	Dec. 5, 1826	Balto.
	Vine	14	Emilie	Spencer, Thomas R.P.	March 27, 1821	Balto.
	Violet	17	Actress	Anderson, David	Nov. 8, 1819	Balto.
	Violet		Hope	Browning, Robert B.	Dec. 5, 1833	Balto.
	Violet	18	North America	Woolfolk, Austin	Dec. 20, 1824	Balto.
	Violet	9	Robert Reade	Woolfolk, Austin	Feb. 28, 1824	Balto.
	Violet	13	Southerner	Campbell, Bernard M.	Jan. 5, 1852	Balto.
	Violet	16	States	Woolfolk, Austin	March 8, 1826	Balto.
	Violette	22	Alonzo	White, Philip	Nov. 8, 1822	Balto.
	Violette	17	Hyperion	Anderson, David	May 14, 1822	Balto.
	Violette	13	Intelligence	Woolfolk, Austin	Apr. 5, 1823	Balto.
	Violette	19	Lapwing	King, Gideon T.	March 22, 1822	Balto.
	Virginia	4	Georgia	Brent, Robert J.	Dec. 23, 1844	Balto.
	Virginia	infant	Pharsalia	Daniel, Edward	Jan. 10, 1855	Balto.
	Walter	2	Isabella	Wallis, Cornelius C.	Nov. 26, 1834	Balto.
	Walter	13	Kenhawa	Maddox, Thomas H.	Oct. 26, 1832	Balto.
	Warner	16	Margaret Hugg	Dent, George	Nov. 30, 1844	Balto.
	Warner	15	Palestine	Slatter, Hope Hull	Nov. 16, 1835	Balto.
	Warren	22	Mary	Campbell, Bernard M.	Aug. 23, 1845	Balto.
	Warwick	16	Good Hope	Woolfolk, Austin	Nov. 16, 1821	Balto.
	Washington	8	Betsey	Woolfolk, Austin	Apr. 29, 1828	Balto.
	Washington	9	Betsey	Woolfolk, Austin	Apr. 29, 1828	Balto.

Surname	First Name	Age	Ship	O/S	Date	Depart
	Washington	12	Catharine Jackson	Diggs, John H.	Nov. 26, 1836	Nanjimoy
	Washington	24	Emilie	Yeiser, John	Aug. 21, 1819	Balto.
	Washington	18 mon.	Gulnare	Kelso, George G.	Nov. 3, 1830	Balto.
	Washington	21	Intelligence	Plater, John R. Jr.	Apr. 12, 1823	St. Mary's
	Washington	25	Intelligence	Woolfolk, Austin	Apr. 5, 1823	Balto.
	Washington	20	Lady Monroe	Woolfolk, Austin	Sept. 29, 1825	Balto.
	Washington	22	Lawrence	Woolfolk, Austin	May 9, 1823	Balto.
	Washington	8	Pandora	Woolfolk, Austin	March 26, 1831	Balto.
	Washington	11	Serene	Arman, John	Oct. 20, 1836	Balto.
	Washington	19	States	Woolfolk, Austin	March 8, 1826	Balto.
	Washington	12	Tippecanoe	Bangs, Theopilus	Apr. 15, 1844	Balto.
	Washington	11	Victorine	Williams, Thomas	Dec. 20, 1844	Balto.
	Washington	21	Zoe	Donovan, Joseph S.	Feb. 16, 1847	Balto.
	Wesley	18	Brunswick	Woolfolk, Austin	Oct. 11, 1831	Balto.
	Wesley	12	Irad Ferry	Warfield, Daniel	Dec. 4, 1843	Balto.
	West	19	Mars	Woolfolk, Austin	Nov. 1, 1824	Balto.
	Whiting	28	Shamrock	Guyton, Elisha	March 13, 1840	Balto.
	Wilfred	25	Kirkwood	Donovan, Joseph S.	Sept. 28, 1846	Balto.
	Wilhelmina	13	Susan Miller	Woolfolk, Samuel M.	Oct. 25, 1822	Balto.
	Wilks	21	Lapwing	King, Gideon T.	March 22, 1822	Balto.
	Will	18	Isabella		Nov. 26, 1834	Balto.
	William	8	Alfred	Woolfolk, Joseph B.	May 7, 1825	Balto.
	William	17	Anice	Lee, John	May 24, 1830	Balto.
	William	24	Architect	Rodbine, Ebenezer	Feb. 12, 1840	Balto.
	William	9	Arctic	Maddox, Thomas H.	Jan. 30, 1829	St. Mary's
	William	16	Arctic	Maddox, Thomas H.	Jan. 30, 1829	St. Mary's

Surname	First Name	Age	Ship	O/S	Date	Depart
	William	7	Arctic	Magee, Eugene	Oct. 9, 1828	Annapolis
	William	15	Arctic	Hall, Joshua F.	Sept. 29, 1827	Balto.
	William	10	Arletta	Carr, Dabney S.	July 18, 1826	Balto.
	William	16 mon.	Aurilla	Warfield, Charles	Apr. 26, 1822	Balto.
	William	4	Balloon	Penieres, Emile	Dec. 22, 1821	Balto.
	William		Balloon	Zacharie, James W.	Dec. 22, 1821	Balto.
	William	2	Betsey	Woolfolk, Austin	Apr. 29, 1828	Balto.
	William	5	Betsey	Woolfolk, Austin	Apr. 29, 1828	Balto.
	William	8	Budget	King, Gideon T.	Dec. 1, 1821	Balto.
	William	15	Budget	Spraggins, Samuel M.	Nov. 27, 1821	Balto.
	William	21	Budget	Spraggins, Samuel M.	Nov. 27, 1821	Balto.
	William	15	Catharine Jackson	Brent, George	Nov. 26, 1836	Nanjimoy
	William	5	Columbus	Cayenove, Cecelia	Nov. 1, 1827	Balto.
	William	17	Commodore Pattersc	Thompson, Henry	March 20, 1819	Balto.
	William	12	Elizabeth	Campbell, Bernard M.	Nov. 18, 1848	Balto.
	William	15	Emigrant	Somerrell, Henry S.	Apr. 29, 1836	Balto.
	William	7 mon.	Emilie	Ferguson, Thomas	Dec. 14, 1821	Balto.
	William	22	Eros	Oldham, George W.	June 29, 1822	Balto.
	William	14	Good Hope	Woolfolk, Austin	Nov. 16, 1821	Balto.
	William	19	Hamlet	Woolfolk, Austin	Apr. 7, 1824	Balto.
	William	23	Hamlet	Woolfolk, Austin	Apr. 7, 1824	Balto.
	William	1	Harriet	Carroll, Charles	Dec. 7, 1836	Balto.
	William	18	Harriet	Carroll, Charles	Dec. 7, 1836	Balto.
	William	8 mon.	Harriett	Woolfolk, Austin	March 23, 1822	Balto.
	William	14	Harriett	Woolfolk, Austin	March 23, 1822	Balto.
	William	13	Harriett	Pierce, Levi	Oct. 29, 1822	Balto.

Surname	First Name	Age	Ship	O/S	Date	Depart
	William	5	Henry A. Barling	Marriott, William H.	Oct. 28, 1848	Balto.
	William	20	Henry Clay	Campior, Henry	Dec. 8, 1828	Nottingham
	William	11	Henry Clay	Compton & Dorsett	Dec. 8, 1828	Nottingham
	William	2	Henry Clay	Dorset, William N.	Dec. 8, 1828	Nottingham
	William	3	Hibernia	Woolfolk, Austin	Dec. 5, 1826	Balto.
	William	3	Hope	Purnell, Thomas R.	Dec. 3, 1833	Balto.
	William		Hope	Browning, Robert B.	Dec. 5, 1833	Balto.
	William	17	Hortensia	Woolfolk, Austin	Dec. 14, 1836	Balto.
	William	5	Hyperion	Anderson, David	May 14, 1822	Balto.
	William	35	Hyperion	Daniels, J.D.	Oct. 14, 1835	Balto.
	William	13	Intelligence	De Mapiere, Victor	Apr. 30, 1821	Balto.
	William	11	Intelligence	Anderson, David	May 1, 1821	Balto.
	William	8	Intelligence	Oldhan, George W.	Nov. 4, 1820	Balto.
	William	3	Isabel a		Nov. 26, 1834	Balto.
	William	6	Isabel a		Nov. 26, 1834	Balto.
	William	11	Kirkwood	Donovan, Joseph S.	Dec. 10, 1846	Balto.
	William	22	Kirkwood	Donovan, Joseph S.	Dec. 10, 1846	Balto.
	William	26	Kirkwood	Donovan, Joseph S.	Dec. 10, 1846	Balto.
	William	16	Kirkwood	Donovan, Joseph S.	Sept. 28, 1846	Balto.
	William	22	Lady Monroe	Woolfolk, Austin	Sept. 29, 1825	Balto.
	William	23	Lafayette	Slatter, Hope Hull	March 25, 1843	Balto.
	William	9 mon.	Lafayette	Woolfolk, Richard	Oct. 18, 1828	Balto.
	William	4	Mars	Woolfolk, Austin	Oct. 30, 1824	Balto.
	William	20	Mars	Woolfolk, Austin	Oct. 30, 1824	Balto.
	William	35	Mary	Chaplain, Charles	Nov. 30, 1841	Balto.
	William	11	Mary Broughton	Chaplain, J. Bond	Nov. 18, 1851	Balto.

Surname	First Name	Age	Ship	O/S	Date	Depart
	William	13	Missouri	Cook, James K.	March 2, 1819	Balto.
	William	4	North America	Chabert, Leon	Apr. 24, 1826	Balto.
	William	20	North America	Woolfolk, Austin	Dec. 20, 1824	Balto.
	William	23	North America	Woolfolk, Austin	Dec. 20, 1824	Balto.
	William	24	North America	Woolfolk, Austin	Dec. 20, 1824	Balto.
	William	22	North America	Woolfolk, Austin	Nov. 23, 1822	Balto.
	William	6	Orion	Oldham, George W.	Dec. 30, 1822	Balto.
	William	12	Orion	Oldham, George W.	Dec. 30, 1822	Balto.
	William	6	Orion	Woolfolk, Austin	Dec. 30, 1822	Balto.
	William	19	Oscar	O'Bean, Thomas	Sept. 29, 1827	Balto.
	William	22	Pandora	Woolfolk, Austin	March 26, 1831	Balto.
	William	10	Pilgrim	Carr, S.J.	Dec. 22, 1834	Balto.
	William	11	Shepderdiss	Williams, Joseph C.	March 27, 1827	Balto.
	William	20	States	Woolfolk, Austin	March 8, 1826	Balto.
	William	23	States	Woolfolk, Austin	March 8, 1826	Balto.
	William	28	States	Woolfolk, Austin	March 8, 1826	Balto.
	William		States	Woolfolk, Austin	Nov. 21, 1827	Balto.
	William	3	Statira	Smith, Doctor James	March 28, 1826	Balto.
	William	13	Statira	Smith, Doctor James	March 28, 1826	Balto.
	William	8	Susan Miller	Woolfolk, Austin	Oct. 25, 1822	Balto.
	William	25	Susan Miller	Woolfolk, Austin	Oct. 25, 1822	Balto.
	William	20	Susan Miller	Woolfolk, Richard T.	Oct. 25, 1822	Balto.
	William	22	Temperance	Anderson, David	Dec. 9, 1818	Balto.
	William	1	Temperance	Woolfolk, Austin	Dec. 9, 1818	Balto.
	William	1	Topaz	Woolfolk, Austin	Apr. 20, 1829	Balto.
	William	23	Triton	Farrow, Nimrod	Dec. 18, 1819	Balto.

Surname	First Name	Age	Ship	O/S	Date	Depart
	William	16	Virginia	Woolfolk, Joseph B.	Dec. 19, 1825	Balto.
	William	39	Virginia	Woolfolk, Austin	Nov. 18, 1823	Balto.
	William	24	William and Mary	King, Gideon T.	Oct. 9, 1821	Balto.
	William Allen	35	Ulysses	Richardson, Wade H.	Nov. 6, 1833	Balto.
	William Henry	infant	Kirkwood	Slatter, Hope Hull	Dec. 23, 1843	Balto.
	Wilmina	4	Mary Ann Jones	Bass, Vincent	Sept. 16, 1848	Balto.
	Wilson	3	Mars	Woolfolk, Austin	Nov. 1, 1824	Balto.
	Winney	5	Henry A. Barling	Campbell, Bernard M.	Dec. 18, 1851	Balto.
	Winney	20	Kirkwood	Donovan, Joseph S.	Dec. 10, 1846	Balto.
	Yacinthe	22	Hibernia	Chabert, Leon	Dec. 5, 1826	Balto.
	Zachariah	11	Jupiter		March 25, 1836	Balto.
	Zachariah	20	Palestine	Slatter, Hope Hull	Nov. 16, 1835	Balto.
		3 mon.	Actress	Anderson, David	Nov. 8, 1819	Balto.
		1	Ajax	Richardson, Wade H.	Oct.3, 1833	Balto.
		2	Ajax	Richardson, Wade H.	Oct.3, 1833	Balto.
		12	Ajax	Richardson, Wade H.	Oct.3, 1833	Balto.
		17	Ajax	Richardson, Wade H.	Oct.3, 1833	Balto.
		23	Ajax	Richardson, Wade H.	Oct.3, 1833	Balto.
		23	Ajax	Richardson, Wade H.	Oct.3, 1833	Balto.
		18	Architect	Rodbind, Ebenezer	Feb. 12, 1840	Balto.
		22	Architect	Rodbind, Ebenezer	Feb. 12, 1840	Balto.
		25	Architect	Rodbind, Ebenezer	Feb. 12, 1840	Balto.
		31	Architect	Rodbind, Ebenezer	Feb. 12, 1840	Balto.
			Architect	Rodbind, Ebenezer	Feb. 12, 1840	Balto.
			Architect	Rodbind, Ebenezer	Feb. 12, 1840	Balto.
			Architect	Rodbind, Ebenezer	Feb. 12, 1840	Balto.

Surname	First Name	Age	Ship	O/S	Date	Depart
			Architect	Rodbind, Ebenezer	Feb. 12, 1840	Balto.
			Architect	Harker, William	Feb. 15, 1840	Balto.
		6 weeks	Arctic	Maddox, Thomas H.	Jan. 30, 1829	St. Mary's
		3 mon.	Arctic	Williams, Joseph C.	Jan. 31, 1829	St. Mary's
		8 mon.	Arctic	Williams, Joseph C.	Jan. 31, 1829	St. Mary's
		infant	Billow	Woolfolk, Austin	Feb. 23, 1828	Balto.
		infant	Billow	Woolfolk, Austin	Feb. 23, 1828	Balto.
			Bourne	Handy, Samuel	Oct. 13, 1832	Balto.
			Bourne	Handy, Samuel	Oct. 13, 1832	Balto.
			Bourne	Handy, Samuel	Oct. 13, 1832	Balto.
			Brunswick	Woolfolk, Austin	Oct. 11, 1831	Balto.
		9 mon.	Budget	Spraggins, Samuel M.	Nov. 27, 1821	Balto.
		infant	Budget	Spraggins, Samuel M.	Nov. 27, 1821	Balto.
		11	Calagari	Nelson, George S.	Nov. 7, 1832	Balto.
			Calagari	Nelson, George S.	Nov. 7, 1832	Balto.
			Calagari	Nelson, George S.	Nov. 7, 1832	Balto.
			Calagari	Nelson, George S.	Nov. 7, 1832	Balto.
		1	Caspian	Woolfolk, Austin	Nov. 26, 1836	Balto.
		16	Caspian	Woolfolk, Austin	Nov. 26, 1836	Balto.
		19	Caspian	Woolfolk, Austin	Nov. 26, 1836	Balto.
		19	Caspian	Woolfolk, Austin	Nov. 26, 1836	Balto.
		21	Caspian	Woolfolk, Austin	Nov. 26, 1836	Balto.
		23	Caspian	Woolfolk, Austin	Nov. 26, 1836	Balto.
		23	Caspian	Woolfolk, Austin	Nov. 26, 1836	Balto.
		25	Caspian	Woolfolk, Austin	Nov. 26, 1836	Balto.
		26	Caspian	Woolfolk, Austin	Nov. 26, 1836	Balto.

Surname	First Name	Age	Ship	O/S	Date	Depart
		26	Caspian	Woolfolk, Austin	Nov. 26, 1836	Balto.
			Caspian	Woolfolk, Austin	Nov. 26, 1836	Balto.
			Caspian	Woolfolk, Austin	Nov. 26, 1836	Balto.
			Caspian	Woolfolk, Austin	Nov. 26, 1836	Balto.
			Caspian	Woolfolk, Austin	Nov. 26, 1836	Balto.
			Caspian	Woolfolk, Austin	Nov. 26, 1836	Balto.
			Caspian	Woolfolk, Austin	Nov. 26, 1836	Balto.
			Caspian	Woolfolk, Austin	Nov. 26, 1836	Balto.
			Caspian	Woolfolk, Austin	Nov. 26, 1836	Balto.
			Caspian	Woolfolk, Austin	Nov. 26, 1836	Balto.
			Caspian	Woolfolk, Austin	Nov. 26, 1836	Balto.
			Caspian	Woolfolk, Austin	Nov. 26, 1836	Balto.
			Caspian	Woolfolk, Austin	Nov. 26, 1836	Balto.
			Caspian	Woolfolk, Austin	Nov. 26, 1836	Balto.
			Caspian	Woolfolk, Austin	Nov. 26, 1836	Balto.
			Caspian	Woolfolk, Austin	Nov. 26, 1836	Balto.
			Caspian	Woolfolk, Austin	Nov. 26, 1836	Balto.
		43	Catharine Jackson	Diggs, John H.	Nov. 26, 1836	Nanjimoy
		3	Dumphries	Lee, Richard H.	Sept. 25, 1828	Balto.
		3	Dumphries	Lee, Richard H.	Sept. 25, 1828	Balto.
		4	Dumphries	Lee, Richard H.	Sept. 25, 1828	Balto.
		4	Dumphries	Lee, Richard H.	Sept. 25, 1828	Balto.
		5	Dumphries	Lee, Richard H.	Sept. 25, 1828	Balto.
		6	Dumphries	Lee, Richard H.	Sept. 25, 1828	Balto.
		11	Dumphries	Lee, Richard H.	Sept. 25, 1828	Balto.
		16	Dumphries	Lee, Richard H.	Sept. 25, 1828	Balto.
		17	Dumphries	Lee, Richard H.	Sept. 25, 1828	Balto.

Surname	First Name	Age	Ship	O/S	Date	Depart
		17	Dumphries	Lee, Richard H.	Sept. 25, 1828	Balto.
		19	Dumphries	Lee, Richard H.	Sept. 25, 1828	Balto.
		30	Dumphries	Lee, Richard H.	Sept. 25, 1828	Balto.
		31	Dumphries	Lee, Richard H.	Sept. 25, 1828	Balto.
		33	Dumphries	Lee, Richard H.	Sept. 25, 1828	Balto.
		41	Dumphries	Lee, Richard H.	Sept. 25, 1828	Balto.
			Dumphries	Lee, Richard H.	Sept. 25, 1828	Balto.
			Dumphries	Lee, Richard H.	Sept. 25, 1828	Balto.
			Dumphries	Lee, Richard H.	Sept. 25, 1828	Balto.
			Dumphries	Lee, Richard H.	Sept. 25, 1828	Balto.
			Dumphries	Lee, Richard H.	Sept. 25, 1828	Balto.
			Dumphries	Lee, Richard H.	Sept. 25, 1828	Balto.
			Dumphries	Lee, Richard H.	Sept. 25, 1828	Balto.
			Dumphries	Lee, Richard H.	Sept. 25, 1828	Balto.
			Dumphries	Lee, Richard H.	Sept. 25, 1828	Balto.
			Dumphries	Lee, Richard H.	Sept. 25, 1828	Balto.
			Dumphries	Lee, Richard H.	Sept. 25, 1828	Balto.
			Dumphries	Lee, Richard H.	Sept. 25, 1828	Balto.
			Dumphries	Lee, Richard H.	Sept. 25, 1828	Balto.
			Dumphries	Lee, Richard H.	Sept. 25, 1828	Balto.
			Dumphries	Lee, Richard H.	Sept. 25, 1828	Balto.
			Dumphries	Lee, Richard H.	Sept. 25, 1828	Balto.
		22	E.H.Chapin	Slatter, Hope Hull	Nov. 30, 1847	Balto.
		infant	Eliza	Slatter, Hope Hull	Oct. 9, 1840	Balto.
		17	Eliza	Slatter, Hope Hull	Oct. 9, 1840	Balto.
		22	Eliza	Slatter, Hope Hull	Oct. 9, 1840	Balto.
		22	Eliza	Slatter, Hope Hull	Oct. 9, 1840	Balto.
		22	Eliza	Slatter, Hope Hull	Oct. 9, 1840	Balto.
		26	Eliza	Slatter, Hope Hull	Oct. 9, 1840	Balto.

Surname	First Name	Age	Ship	O/S	Date	Depart
		30	Eliza	Slatter, Hope Hull	Oct. 9, 1840	Balto.
			Eliza	Slatter, Hope Hull	Oct. 9, 1840	Balto.
			Eliza	Slatter, Hope Hull	Oct. 9, 1840	Balto.
			Eliza	Slatter, Hope Hull	Oct. 9, 1840	Balto.
			Eliza	Slatter, Hope Hull	Oct. 9, 1840	Balto.
			Eliza	Slatter, Hope Hull	Oct. 9, 1840	Balto.
			Eliza	Slatter, Hope Hull	Oct. 9, 1840	Balto.
			Eliza	Slatter, Hope Hull	Oct. 9, 1840	Balto.
			Eliza	Slatter, Hope Hull	Oct. 9, 1840	Balto.
		infant	Elizabeth	Rodbird, Ebenezer	Nov. 18, 1848	Balto.
			Emilie	Mercer, William D.	March 27, 1821	Balto.
		6	Frances Amy	Donovan, Joseph S.	Jan. 20, 1847	Balto.
		6	Frances Amy	Donovan, Joseph S.	Jan. 20, 1847	Balto.
			Frances Amy	Donovan, Joseph S.	Jan. 20, 1847	Balto.
			Frances Amy	Donovan, Joseph S.	Jan. 20, 1847	Balto.
			Frances Amy	Donovan, Joseph S.	Jan. 20, 1847	Balto.
			Frances Amy	Donovan, Joseph S.	Jan. 20, 1847	Balto.
			Frances Amy	Donovan, Joseph S.	Jan. 20, 1847	Balto.
			Frances Amy	Donovan, Joseph S.	Jan. 20, 1847	Balto.
			Frances Amy	Donovan, Joseph S.	Jan. 20, 1847	Balto.
			Frances Amy	Donovan, Joseph S.	Jan. 20, 1847	Balto.
			Frances Amy	Donovan, Joseph S.	Jan. 20, 1847	Balto.
			Frances Amy	Donovan, Joseph S.	Jan. 20, 1847	Balto.
			Frances Amy	Donovan, Joseph S.	Jan. 20, 1847	Balto.
			Frances Amy	Donovan, Joseph S.	Jan. 20, 1847	Balto.
			Frances Amy	Donovan, Joseph S.	Jan. 20, 1847	Balto.

Surname	First Name	Age	Ship	O/S	Date	Depart
			Frances Amy	Donovan, Joseph S.	Jan. 20, 1847	Balto.
			Frances Amy	Donovan, Joseph S.	Jan. 20, 1847	Balto.
			Frances Amy	Donovan, Joseph S.	Jan. 20, 1847	Balto.
			Frances Amy	Donovan, Joseph S.	Jan. 20, 1847	Balto.
			Frances Amy	Donovan, Joseph S.	Jan. 20, 1847	Balto.
			Frances Amy	Donovan, Joseph S.	Jan. 20, 1847	Balto.
			Frances Amy	Donovan, Joseph S.	Jan. 20, 1847	Balto.
			Frances Amy	Donovan, Joseph S.	Jan. 20, 1847	Balto.
			Frances Amy	Donovan, Joseph S.	Jan. 20, 1847	Balto.
			Frances Amy	Donovan, Joseph S.	Jan. 20, 1847	Balto.
			Frances Amy	Donovan, Joseph S.	Jan. 20, 1847	Balto.
			Frances Amy	Donovan, Joseph S.	Jan. 20, 1847	Balto.
			Frances Amy	Donovan, Joseph S.	Jan. 20, 1847	Balto.
			Frances Amy	Donovan, Joseph S.	Jan. 20, 1847	Balto.
			Frances Amy	Donovan, Joseph S.	Jan. 20, 1847	Balto.
			Frances Amy	Donovan, Joseph S.	Jan. 20, 1847	Balto.
			Frances Amy	Donovan, Joseph S.	Jan. 20, 1847	Balto.
			Frances Amy	Donovan, Joseph S.	Jan. 20, 1847	Balto.
			Frances Amy	Donovan, Joseph S.	Jan. 20, 1847	Balto.
			Frances Amy	Donovan, Joseph S.	Jan. 20, 1847	Balto.
			Frances Amy	Donovan, Joseph S.	Jan. 20, 1847	Balto.
			Frances Amy	Donovan, Joseph S.	Jan. 20, 1847	Balto.
			Frances Amy	Donovan, Joseph S.	Jan. 20, 1847	Balto.
			Frances Amy	Donovan, Joseph S.	Jan. 20, 1847	Balto.
			Frances Amy	Donovan, Joseph S.	Jan. 20, 1847	Balto.
			Frances Amy	Donovan, Joseph S.	Jan. 20, 1847	Balto.
			Frances Amy	Donovan, Joseph S.	Jan. 20, 1847	Balto.

Surname	First Name	Age	Ship	O/S	Date	Depart
			Frances Amy	Donovan, Joseph S.	Jan. 20, 1847	Balto.
			Frances Amy	Donovan, Joseph S.	Jan. 20, 1847	Balto.
			Frances Amy	Donovan, Joseph S.	Jan. 20, 1847	Balto.
			Frances Amy	Donovan, Joseph S.	Jan. 20, 1847	Balto.
			Frances Amy	Donovan, Joseph S.	Jan. 20, 1847	Balto.
			Frances Amy	Donovan, Joseph S.	Jan. 20, 1847	Balto.
			Frances Amy	Donovan, Joseph S.	Jan. 20, 1847	Balto.
			Frances Amy	Donovan, Joseph S.	Jan. 20, 1847	Balto.
			Frances Amy	Donovan, Joseph S.	Jan. 20, 1847	Balto.
			Frances Amy	Donovan, Joseph S.	Jan. 20, 1847	Balto.
			Frances Amy	Donovan, Joseph S.	Jan. 20, 1847	Balto.
			Frances Amy	Donovan, Joseph S.	Jan. 20, 1847	Balto.
		12 mon.	Franklin	Somerville, Henry	Nov. 27, 1819	Balto.
		4 mon.	Franklin	Somerville, Henry	Nov. 27, 1819	Balto.
		40	Franklin	Somerville, Henry	Nov. 27, 1819	Balto.
		10 mon.	General Pinckney	Rodbird, Ebenezer	Feb. 21, 1846	Balto.
		infant	General Pinckney	Williams, Thomas	Jan. 19, 1847	Balto.
		infant	General Pinckney	Williams, Thomas	Jan. 19, 1847	Balto.
		17	George Ross	Handy, J.	June 18, 1847	Balto.
			George Ross	Handy, J.	June 18, 1847	Balto.
		infant	Georgia	Brent, Robert J.	Dec. 21, 1844	Balto.
		infant	Georgia	Brent, Robert J.	Dec. 21, 1844	Balto.
		infant	Georgia	Brent, Robert J.	Dec. 21, 1844	Balto.
		infant	Glasgow	Slatter Hope Hull	Dec. 19, 1838	Balto.
		infant	Glasgow	Slatter Hope Hull	Dec. 19, 1838	Balto.

Surname	First Name	Age	Ship	O/S	Date	Depart
		20	Good Hope	Woolfolk, Austin	Nov. 16, 1821	Balto.
		3 mon.	Harriet	Carroll, Charles	Dec. 7, 1836	Balto.
		19	Harriet	Carroll, Charles	Dec. 7, 1836	Balto.
			Helen A. Miller	Campbell, Bernard M.	Oct. 18, 1852	Balto.
		infant	Henry A. Barling	Campbell, Bernard M.	Dec. 18, 1851	Balto.
		infant	Henry A. Barling	Campbell, Bernard M.	Dec. 18, 1851	Balto.
		infant	Hermann	Rowe, Ralph	June 21, 1851	Balto.
		infant	Hermitage	Berry, Charles H.	Oct. 28, 1846	Balto.
		infant	Hermitage	Slatter, Hope Hull	Oct. 28, 1846	Balto.
		infant	Hermitage	Slatter, Hope Hull	Oct. 28, 1846	Balto.
		infant	Hermitage	Slatter, Hope Hull	Oct. 28, 1846	Balto.
		5	Hibernia	Woolfolk, Austin	Dec. 5, 1826	Balto.
		7	Hibernia	Woolfolk, Austin	Dec. 5, 1826	Balto.
		12	Hibernia	Woolfolk, Austin	Dec. 5, 1826	Balto.
		16	Hibernia	Woolfolk, Austin	Dec. 5, 1826	Balto.
		16	Hibernia	Woolfolk, Austin	Dec. 5, 1826	Balto.
		17	Hibernia	Woolfolk, Austin	Dec. 5, 1826	Balto.
		18	Hibernia	Woolfolk, Austin	Dec. 5, 1826	Balto.
		19	Hibernia	Woolfolk, Austin	Dec. 5, 1826	Balto.
		27	Hibernia	Woolfolk, Austin	Dec. 5, 1826	Balto.
			Hibernia	Woolfolk, Austin	Dec. 5, 1826	Balto.
			Hibernia	Woolfolk, Austin	Dec. 5, 1826	Balto.
			Hibernia	Woolfolk, Austin	Dec. 5, 1826	Balto.
			Hibernia	Woolfolk, Austin	Dec. 5, 1826	Balto.

Surname	First Name	Age	Ship	O/S	Date	Depart
			Hibernia	Woolfolk, Austin	Dec. 5, 1826	Balto.
			Hibernia	Woolfolk, Austin	Dec. 5, 1826	Balto.
			Hibernia	Woolfolk, Austin	Dec. 5, 1826	Balto.
			Hibernia	Woolfolk, Austin	Dec. 5, 1826	Balto.
		infant	Hope	Browning, Robert B.	Dec. 5, 1833	Balto.
			Hope	Browning, Robert B.	Dec. 5, 1833	Balto.
			Hope	Browning, Robert B.	Dec. 5, 1833	Balto.
			Hope	Browning, Robert B.	Dec. 5, 1833	Balto.
			Hope	Browning, Robert B.	Dec. 5, 1833	Balto.
			Hope	Browning, Robert B.	Dec. 5, 1833	Balto.
			Hope	Browning, Robert B.	Dec. 5, 1833	Balto.
			Hope	Browning, Robert B.	Dec. 5, 1833	Balto.
			Hope	Browning, Robert B.	Dec. 5, 1833	Balto.
			Hope	Browning, Robert B.	Dec. 5, 1833	Balto.
			Hope	Browning, Robert B.	Dec. 5, 1833	Balto.
			Hope	Byrne, Walter	Dec. 5, 1833	Balto.
			Hyperion		Oct. 17, 1835	Balto.
		22	Intelligence	Somerville, Alexander	Dec. 20, 1822	Balto.
		3 mon.	Intelligence	Colt, R.L.	Sept. 18, 1821	Balto.
		2	Intelligence	Colt, R.L.	Sept. 18, 1821	Balto.
		infant	Irad Ferry	Clendenin, A.	Jan. 16, 1840	Balto.
		12	Isabella		Nov. 26, 1834	Balto.
		14	Isabella		Nov. 26, 1834	Balto.
		15	Isabella		Nov. 26, 1834	Balto.
		16	Isabella		Nov. 26, 1834	Balto.
		21	Isabella		Nov. 26, 1834	Balto.

Surname	First Name	Age	Ship	O/S	Date	Depart
		35	Isabella		Nov. 26, 1834	Balto.
			Isabella		Nov. 26, 1834	Balto.
			Isabella		Nov. 26, 1834	Balto.
		23	John C. Calhoun	Donovan, Joseph S.	Oct. 24, 1850	Balto.
		15	Kenhawa	Maddox, Thomas H.	Oct. 26, 1832	Balto.
		15	Kenhawa	Maddox, Thomas H.	Oct. 26, 1832	Balto.
		20	Kenhawa	Maddox, Thomas H.	Oct. 26, 1832	Balto.
		28	Kenhawa	Maddox, Thomas H.	Oct. 26, 1832	Balto.
		infant	Kirkwood	Campbell, Bernard M.	Apr. 4, 1846	Balto.
		infant	Kirkwood	Campbell, Bernard M.	Apr. 4, 1846	Balto.
		11	Kirkwood	Donovan, Joseph S.	Dec. 10, 1846	Balto.
		15	Kirkwood	Donovan, Joseph S.	Dec. 10, 1846	Balto.
		15	Kirkwood	Donovan, Joseph S.	Dec. 10, 1846	Balto.
		21	Kirkwood	Donovan, Joseph S.	Dec. 10, 1846	Balto.
		22	Kirkwood	Donovan, Joseph S.	Dec. 10, 1846	Balto.
		24	Kirkwood	Donovan, Joseph S.	Dec. 10, 1846	Balto.
		31	Kirkwood	Donovan, Joseph S.	Dec. 10, 1846	Balto.
			Kirkwood	Donovan, Joseph S.	Dec. 10, 1846	Balto.
			Kirkwood	Donovan, Joseph S.	Dec. 10, 1846	Balto.
			Kirkwood	Donovan, Joseph S.	Dec. 10, 1846	Balto.
			Kirkwood	Donovan, Joseph S.	Dec. 10, 1846	Balto.
			Kirkwood	Donovan, Joseph S.	Dec. 10, 1846	Balto.
			Kirkwood	Donovan, Joseph S.	Dec. 10, 1846	Balto.
			Kirkwood	Donovan, Joseph S.	Dec. 10, 1846	Balto.
			Kirkwood	Donovan, Joseph S.	Dec. 10, 1846	Balto.

Surname	First Name	Age	Ship	O/S	Date	Depart
			Kirkwood	Donovan, Joseph S.	Dec. 10, 1846	Balto.
			Kirkwood	Donovan, Joseph S.	Dec. 10, 1846	Balto.
			Kirkwood	Donovan, Joseph S.	Dec. 10, 1846	Balto.
			Kirkwood	Donovan, Joseph S.	Dec. 10, 1846	Balto.
			Kirkwood	Donovan, Joseph S.	Dec. 10, 1846	Balto.
			Kirkwood	Donovan, Joseph S.	Dec. 10, 1846	Balto.
			Kirkwood	Donovan, Joseph S.	Dec. 10, 1846	Balto.
		infant	Kirkwood	Slatter, Hope Hull	Jan. 4, 1845	Balto.
		10	Kirkwood	Donovan, Joseph S.	Oct. 26, 1847	Balto.
		infant	Kirkwood	Rodbird, Ebenezer	Oct. 26, 1847	Balto.
		infant	Kirkwood	Rodbird, Ebenezer	Oct. 26, 1847	Balto.
		9	Lady Monroe	Woolfolk, Austin	March 25, 1825	Balto.
		29	Lady Monroe	Woolfolk, Austin	March 25, 1825	Balto.
			Lady Monroe	Woolfolk, Austin	March 25, 1825	Balto.
		6	Lady Monroe	Woolfolk, Joseph B.	March 25, 1825	Balto.
		19	Lady Monroe	Woolfolk, Joseph B.	March 25, 1825	Balto.
		infant	Lady Monroe	Chabert, Leon	Sept. 29, 1825	Balto.
		6 mon.	Lady Monroe	Wascherr, J.E.	Sept. 29, 1825	Balto.
		13	Lafayette	Slatter, Hope Hull	March 25, 1843	Balto.
		17	Lafayette	Slatter, Hope Hull	March 25, 1843	Balto.
		17	Lafayette	Slatter, Hope Hull	March 25, 1843	Balto.
		18	Lafayette	Slatter, Hope Hull	March 25, 1843	Balto.
		18	Lafayette	Slatter, Hope Hull	March 25, 1843	Balto.
		19	Lafayette	Slatter, Hope Hull	March 25, 1843	Balto.
		21	Lafayette	Slatter, Hope Hull	March 25, 1843	Balto.
		21	Lafayette	Slatter, Hope Hull	March 25, 1843	Balto.

Surname	First Name	Age	Ship	O/S	Date	Depart
		23	Lafayette	Slatter, Hope Hull	March 25, 1843	Balto.
		25	Lafayette	Slatter, Hope Hull	March 25, 1843	Balto.
		29	Lafayette	Slatter, Hope Hull	March 25, 1843	Balto.
		30	Lafayette	Slatter, Hope Hull	March 25, 1843	Balto.
		40	Lafayette	Slatter, Hope Hull	March 25, 1843	Balto.
			Lafayette	Slatter, Hope Hull	March 25, 1843	Balto.
			Lafayette	Slatter, Hope Hull	March 25, 1843	Balto.
			Lafayette	Slatter, Hope Hull	March 25, 1843	Balto.
			Lafayette	Slatter, Hope Hull	March 25, 1843	Balto.
		18	Lafayette	Woolfolk, Richard	Oct. 18, 1828	Balto.
		21	Lafayette	Woolfolk, Richard	Oct. 18, 1828	Balto.
		23	Lafayette	Woolfolk, Richard	Oct. 18, 1828	Balto.
		25	Lafayette	Woolfolk, Richard	Oct. 18, 1828	Balto.
		25	Lafayette	Woolfolk, Richard	Oct. 18, 1828	Balto.
		26	Lafayette	Woolfolk, Richard	Oct. 18, 1828	Balto.
		30	Lafayette	Woolfolk, Richard	Oct. 18, 1828	Balto.
		32	Lafayette	Woolfolk, Richard	Oct. 18, 1828	Balto.
		40	Lafayette	Woolfolk, Richard	Oct. 18, 1828	Balto.
			Lafayette	Woolfolk, Richard	Oct. 18, 1828	Balto.
			Lafayette	Woolfolk, Richard	Oct. 18, 1828	Balto.
			Lafayette	Woolfolk, Richard	Oct. 18, 1828	Balto.
			Lafayette	Woolfolk, Richard	Oct. 18, 1828	Balto.
			Lafayette	Woolfolk, Richard	Oct. 18, 1828	Balto.
			Lafayette	Woolfolk, Richard	Oct. 18, 1828	Balto.

Surname	First Name	Age	Ship	O/S	Date	Depart
			Lafayette	Woolfolk, Richard	Oct. 18, 1828	Balto.
			Lafayette	Woolfolk, Richard	Oct. 18, 1828	Balto.
			London	Palmer, J.W.	Nov. 5, 1840	Balto.
			London	Palmer, J.W.	Nov. 5, 1840	Balto.
			London	Palmer, J.W.	Nov. 5, 1840	Balto.
			London	Palmer, J.W.	Nov. 5, 1840	Balto.
			London	Palmer, J.W.	Nov. 5, 1840	Balto.
			London	Palmer, J.W.	Nov. 5, 1840	Balto.
		infant	London	Hope, H.B.	Nov. 6, 1840	Balto.
		23	Louisa	Donovan, Joseph S.	Oct. 9, 1847	Balto.
		infant	Mars	Woolfolk, Austin	Nov. 1, 1824	Balto.
		6 mon.	Mars	Woolfolk, Joseph B.	Oct. 30, 1824	Balto.
		15	Mary	Wallace, Frances	Feb. 28, 1840	Balto.
			Mary	Marston, Thomas	Jan. 6, 1845	Balto.
		14	Merrimack	Kelso, George G.	Nov. 2, 1831	Balto.
		17	Merrimack	Kelso, George G.	Nov. 2, 1831	Balto.
		1	Missouri	Little, Moses	March 2, 1819	Balto.
		16	Missouri	Mulhocan, Hugh	March 2, 1819	Balto.
		infant	Nathaniel Hooper	Campbell, Bernard M.	Feb. 12, 1852	Balto.
		infant	Nathaniel Hooper	Campbell, Bernard M.	Feb. 12, 1852	Balto.
		infant	Nelson Clark	Tongue, Thomas R.	Nov. 20, 1835	Balto.
		2 mon.	North America	Woolfolk, Austin	Nov. 23, 1822	Balto.
		14	North America	Stile, George	Oct. 14, 1823	Balto.
		infant	Opelousas	Garland, Rice	July 5, 1836	Balto.
		infant	Opelousas	Garland, Rice	July 5, 1836	Balto.
		9 mon.	Orbit	Chabert, Leon	Apr. 16, 1825	Balto.

Surname	First Name	Age	Ship	O/S	Date	Depart
		3	Orbit	Chabert, Leon	Apr. 16, 1825	Balto.
		10 mon.	P. Soule	Biscoe, James	Oct. 9, 1845	Balto.
		infant	Palestine	Slatter, Hope Hull	Nov. 16, 1835	Balto.
		infant	Patrick Henry	Campbell, Bernard M.	June 1,1853	Balto.
		infant	Patrick Henry	Campbell, Bernard M.	June 1,1853	Balto.
		15	Phillipi?	Byrn, Thomas	Feb. 8, 1829	Balto.
		2 mon.	Pilgrim	Smith, R.J.	Dec. 12, 1835	Balto.
		2	Pilgrim	Smith, R.J.	Dec. 12, 1835	Balto.
		4	Pilgrim	Smith, R.J.	Dec. 12, 1835	Balto.
		13	Pilgrim	Smith, R.J.	Dec. 12, 1835	Balto.
		15	Pilgrim	Smith, R.J.	Dec. 12, 1835	Balto.
		16	Pilgrim	Smith, R.J.	Dec. 12, 1835	Balto.
		23	Pilgrim	Smith, R.J.	Dec. 12, 1835	Balto.
		infant	Plutarch	Johnson, M.	Sept. 17, 1834	Balto.
			Plutarch	Johnson, M.	Sept. 17, 1834	Balto.
			Plutarch	Johnson, M.	Sept. 17, 1834	Balto.
			Plutarch	Mosse, Henry	Sept. 17, 1834	Balto.
			Plutarch	Mosse, Henry	Sept. 17, 1834	Balto.
			Plutarch	Mosse, Henry	Sept. 17, 1834	Balto.
			Plutarch	Mosse, Henry	Sept. 17, 1834	Balto.
			Plutarch	Mosse, Henry	Sept. 17, 1834	Balto.
			Plutarch	Mosse, Henry	Sept. 17, 1834	Balto.
			Plutarch	Mosse, Henry	Sept. 17, 1834	Balto.
		infant	Sarah Bridge	Campbell, Bernard M.	Feb. 8, 1851	Balto.
			Scotland		Oct. 21, 1840	Balto.
			Scotland		Oct. 21, 1840	Balto.

Surname	First Name	Age	Ship	O/S	Date	Depart
			Scotland		Oct. 21, 1840	Balto.
			Scotland		Oct. 21, 1840	Balto.
			Scotland		Oct. 21, 1840	Balto.
			Scotland		Oct. 21, 1840	Balto.
		infant	Seguin	Campbell, Bernard M.	July 12, 1853	Balto.
		infant	Seguin	Campbell, Bernard M.	July 12, 1853	Balto.
		infant	Seguin	Campbell, Bernard M.	July 12, 1853	Balto.
		1	Seguin	Campbell, Bernard M.	July 12, 1853	Balto.
		6	Serene	Archer, James	Oct. 19, 1836	Balto.
		12	Shamrock	Guyton, Elisha	March 11, 1840	Balto.
			Snow	Willis	Feb 5, 1835	Balto.
		28	States	Woolfolk, Austin	Nov. 21, 1827	Balto.
			States	Woolfolk, Austin	Nov. 21, 1827	Balto.
			States	Woolfolk, Austin	Nov. 21, 1827	Balto.
			States	Woolfolk, Austin	Nov. 21, 1827	Balto.
			States	Woolfolk, Austin	Nov. 21, 1827	Balto.
			States	Woolfolk, Austin	Nov. 21, 1827	Balto.
			States	Woolfolk, Austin	Nov. 21, 1827	Balto.
		25	States	Morton, George C.	Nov. 26, 1825	Balto.
		9 mon.	Strafford	Harker William	Nov. 22, 1843	Balto.
		infant	Tangier	Campbell, Bernard M.	Nov. 26, 1853	Balto.
		infant	Tangier	Campbell, Bernard M.	Nov. 26, 1853	Balto.
		infant	Tippecanoe	Wilson, Wm. N.	May 4, 1842	Balto.
		1	Topaz	Woolfolk, Austin	Apr. 20, 1829	Balto.
		11	Topaz	Woolfolk, Austin	Apr. 20, 1829	Balto.

Surname	First Name	Age	Ship	O/S	Date	Depart
		21	Topaz	Woolfolk, Austin	Apr. 20, 1829	Balto.
		3 mon.	Trafalgar	Dent, Wilfred	Jan. 13, 1827	Annapolis
		infant	Trafalgar	Dent, Wilfred	Jan. 13, 1827	Annapolis
		21	Trafalgar	Dent, Wilfred	Jan. 13, 1827	Annapolis
		22	Trafalgar	Dent, Wilfred	Jan. 13, 1827	Annapolis
		32	Trafalgar	Dent, Wilfred	Jan. 13, 1827	Annapolis
		8 mon.	Triton	Lee, Thomas	Dec. 18, 1819	Balto.
		10 mon.	Triton	Anderson, David	Dec. 20, 1819	Balto.
		19	Tweed	Bowling, John D.	Oct. 20, 1836	Town Creek
		infant	Union	Campbell, Bernard M.	Dec. 16, 1848	Balto.
		infant	Union	Campbell, Bernard M.	Dec. 16, 1848	Balto.
		infant	Union	Campbell, Bernard M.	Dec. 16, 1848	Balto.
		infant	Union	Rodbind, Ebenezer	Nov. 17, 1849	Balto.
		infant	Union	Campbell, Bernard M.	Oct. 9, 1848	Balto.
			Union	Williams, Thomas	Oct. 9, 1848	Balto.
			Union	Williams, Thomas	Oct. 9, 1848	Balto.
			Union	Williams, Thomas	Oct. 9, 1848	Balto.
			Union			
		3 mon.	Victorine	Rodbind, Ebenezer	March 14, 1846	Balto.
		infant	Victorine	Slatter, Hope Hull	Sept. 12, 1846	Balto.
		infant	Victorine	Slatter, Hope Hull	Sept. 12, 1846	Balto.
		infant	Victorine	Slatter, Hope Hull	Sept. 12, 1846	Balto.
		infant	Victorine	Slatter, Hope Hull	Sept. 12, 1846	Balto.
		20	Victorine	Donovan, Joseph S.	Sept. 29, 1845	Balto.
		20	Victorine	Donovan, Joseph S.	Sept. 29, 1845	Balto.
		21	Victorine	Donovan, Joseph S.	Sept. 29, 1845	Balto.
		22	Zoe	Donovan, Joseph S.	Feb. 16, 1847	Balto.

Surname	First Name	Age	Ship	O/S	Date	Depart
			Zoe	Donovan, Joseph S.	Feb. 16, 1847	Balto.
			Zoe	Donovan, Joseph S.	Feb. 16, 1847	Balto.
			Zoe	Donovan, Joseph S.	Feb. 16, 1847	Balto.
			Zoe	Donovan, Joseph S.	Feb. 16, 1847	Balto.
			Zoe	Donovan, Joseph S.	Feb. 16, 1847	Balto.
			Zoe	Donovan, Joseph S.	Feb. 16, 1847	Balto.
			Zoe	Donovan, Joseph S.	Feb. 16, 1847	Balto.
			Zoe	Donovan, Joseph S.	Feb. 16, 1847	Balto.
			Zoe	Donovan, Joseph S.	Feb. 16, 1847	Balto.
			Zoe	Donovan, Joseph S.	Feb. 16, 1847	Balto.
			Zoe	Donovan, Joseph S.	Feb. 16, 1847	Balto.
		infant	Zoe	Williams, Thomas	Feb. 16, 1847	Balto.

Surname	First Name	Age	Ship	O/S	Date	Depart
	Laura	1	Tippecanoe	Purvis, James Franklin	Jan. 17, 1842	Balto.
	Lavinia	28	Charles	Carter, John A.	Sept. 29, 1849	Balto.
	Leah	9	Ann Wayne	Guyton, Elisha	Sept. 2, 1836	Balto.
	Leah	13	Budget	Bradley, Robert	Nov. 26, 1821	Balto.
	Leah	8	Caspian	Woolfolk, Austin	Nov. 26, 1836	Balto.
	Leah	15	Hector	Woolfolk, Austin	Nov. 4, 1835	Balto.
	Leah	15	Hope	Purnell, Thomas R.	Dec. 3, 1833	Balto.
	Leah	16	North America	Woolfolk, Austin	Oct. 14, 1823	Balto.
	Leah	26	Susan Miller	Woolfolk, Richard T.	Oct. 25, 1822	Balto.
	Leander	7	Arctic	Kelso, George G.	Nov. 15, 1826	Balto.
	Lear	24	Eros	Oldham, George W.	June 29, 1822	Balto.
	Lectius	12	Betsey	Woolfolk, Austin	Apr. 29, 1828	Balto.
	Lemo	27	Alonzo	White, Philip	Nov. 8, 1822	Balto.
	Lemon	15 mon.	Harriett	King, John	March 23, 1822	Balto.
	Leney	20	Emilie	Ford, Josiah L.	Dec. 14, 1821	Balto.
	Lennox	20	Palestine	Slatter, Hope Hull	Nov. 16, 1835	Balto.
	Leon	19	North America	Woolfolk, Austin	Nov. 23, 1822	Balto.
	Leonard	22	Balloon	Zacharie, James W.	Dec. 22, 1821	Balto.
	Leonard	17	Dumphries	Lee, Richard H.	Sept. 25, 1828	Balto.
	Leonard	30	Intelligence	Anderson, David	Dec. 20, 1822	Balto.
	Leonard	19	Serene	Arman, John	Oct. 20, 1836	Balto.
	Lesley	20	Plutarch	Johnson, M.	Sept. 17, 1834	Balto.
	Letha	18	St. Mary	Campbell, Bernard M.	Nov. 29, 1845	Balto.
	Letty	18	Colonel Howard	Harker, William	Nov. 21, 1844	Balto.
	Letty	16	Henry A. Barling	Marriott, William H.	Oct. 28, 1848	Balto.
	Levey	26	General Hand	Poindexter, George L.	June 1, 1832	Balto.

Surname	First Name	Age	Ship	O/S	Date	Depart
	Levi	2	Emilie	Laurenson, Andrew U.	Dec. 14, 1821	Balto.
	Levi	14	Hibernia	Woolfolk, Austin	Dec. 5, 1826	Balto.
	Levi	24	Lawrence	Woolfolk, Austin	May 9, 1823	Balto.
	Levi	8	Mars	Woolfolk, Joseph B.	Oct. 30, 1824	Balto.
	Levi	38	States	Woolfolk, Austin	March 8, 1826	Balto.
	Levia Ann	9	Kirkwood	Campbell, Bernard M.	Jan. 14, 1846	Balto.
	Levin	9	Budget	Bradley, Robert	Nov. 26, 1821	Balto.
	Levin	27	Lapwing	Robbins, Daniel G.	March 22, 1822	Balto.
	Levin	13	Lawrence	Woolfolk, Austin	May 9, 1823	Balto.
	Levin	21	Temperance	Wikoff, Steven W.	Dec. 12, 1818	Balto.
	Levy	18	Agent	Anderson, David	June 8, 1821	Balto.
	Levy	25	Alonzo	White, Philip	Nov. 8, 1822	Balto.
	Lewellin	16	Frances Amy	Donovan, Joseph S.	Jan. 20, 1847	Balto.
	Lewis	26	Alfred	Woolfolk, Austin	Jan. 18, 1825	Balto.
	Lewis	10	Alfred	Woolfolk, Joseph B.	May 7, 1825	Balto.
	Lewis	11	Algerine	Woolfolk, Austin	March 25, 1826	Balto.
	Lewis	18	Alonzo	White, Philip	Nov. 8, 1822	Balto.
	Lewis	25	Arletta	Carr, Dabney S.	July 18, 1826	Balto.
	Lewis	2	Betsey	Woolfolk, Austin	Apr. 29, 1828	Balto.
	Lewis	35	Betsey	Woolfolk, Austin	Apr. 29, 1828	Balto.
	Lewis	22	Catharine	Woolfolk, Austin	Jan. 15, 1831	Balto.
	Lewis	24	Catharine Jackson	Diggs, John H.	Nov. 26, 1836	Nanjimoy
	Lewis	12	E.H.Chapin	Penn, Alexander	Nov. 30, 1847	Balto.
	Lewis	33	Emigrant	Somerell, Henry S.	Apr. 29, 1836	Balto.
	Lewis	17	Franklin	Somerville, Henry	Nov. 27, 1819	Balto.
	Lewis	21	Good Hope	Woolfolk, Samuel M.	Nov. 21, 1821	Balto.

Surname	First Name	Age	Ship	O/S	Date	Depart
	Lewis	3	Henry Clay	Compton & Dorsett	Dec. 8, 1828	Nottingham
	Lewis	8	Intelligence	Plater, John R. Jr.	Apr. 12, 1823	St. Mary's
	Lewis	25	Intelligence	Plater, John R. Jr.	Apr. 12, 1823	St. Mary's
	Lewis	16	Julia	Poindexter, George	Feb. 10, 1832	Balto.
	Lewis	16	Jupiter		March 25, 1836	Balto.
	Lewis	19	Kirkwood	Campbell, Bernard M.	Oct. 16, 1845	Balto.
	Lewis	22	Lady Monroe	Woolfolk, Austin	Sept. 29, 1825	Balto.
	Lewis	24	North America	Woolfolk, Austin	Dec. 20, 1824	Balto.
	Lewis	22	Russell	Woolfolk, Austin	Feb. 27, 1839	Balto.
	Lewis	18 mon.	Seaman	Biscoe, James	March 20, 1840	Balto.
	Lewis	9	States	Woolfolk, Austin	March 8, 1826	Balto.
	Lewis	13	Virginia	Pearce, James Alfred	March 27, 1828	Balto.
	Liddy	20	Clio	Anderson, David	March 20, 1819	Balto.
	Liddy	35	Emilie	Stansbury, Charles	Nov. 27, 1819	Balto.
	Lidia	15	Billow	Woolfolk, Austin	Feb. 23, 1828	Balto.
	Lige	24	Russell	Woolfolk, Austin	Feb. 27, 1839	Balto.
	Linday	22	Kirkwood	Donovan, Joseph S.	March 9, 1847	Balto.
	Lindsey	infant	Leda	Nelson, James	Nov. 16, 1848	Balto.
	Lindy	17	Orbit	Chabert, Leon	Apr. 16, 1825	Balto.
	Linny	16	Georgia	Brent, Robert J.	Dec. 21, 1844	Balto.
	Lisbon	24	Mars	Woolfolk, Austin	Oct. 30, 1824	Balto.
	Lissy	9	Arctic	Smith, Leonard J.	Jan. 29, 1828	St. Mary's
Littleton		19	Emilie	Anderson, David	March 27, 1821	Balto.
Littleton		6	States	Duer, Robert	Nov. 26, 1825	Balto.
Littleton		14	Strafford	Wilson, Thomas C.	Nov. 21, 1843	Balto.
Littleton		16	Tippecanoe	Wallis, Philip	Oct. 16, 1841	Balto.

Surname	First Name	Age	Ship	O/S	Date	Depart
	Littleton	16	Ulysses	Richardson, Wade H.	Nov. 6, 1833	Balto.
	Liva	18	Agent	Anderson, David	June 8, 1821	Balto.
	Lives	14	Hope & Hannah	Williams, Joseph C.	Dec. 10, 1827	Balto.
	Liza	17	Julia	Poindexter, George	Feb. 10, 1832	Balto.
	Liza	16	Lapwing	Spraggins, Samuel M.	March 22, 1822	Balto.
	Liza	17	Missouri	Mulhocan, Hugh	March 2, 1819	Balto.
	Lloyd	10	Betsey	Woolfolk, Austin	Apr. 29, 1828	Balto.
	Lloyd	19	Emilie	Mercer, William D.	March 27, 1821	Balto.
	Lloyd	19	Emilie	Johnson, Thomas	May 19, 1820	Balto.
	Lloyd	8	Intelligence	Wallace, Joseph A.	Apr. 27, 1821	Balto.
	Lloyd	23	Lady Monroe	Woolfolk, Austin	Sept. 29, 1825	Balto.
	Lloyd	23	Lafayette	Slatter, Hope Hull	March 25, 1843	Balto.
	Lloyd	4	Serene	Archer, James	Oct. 19, 1836	Balto.
	Long Tom	21	Intelligence	Anderson, David	Dec. 20, 1822	Balto.
	Loretta Jane	infant	General Pinckney	Slatter, Hope Hull	Jan. 19, 1847	Balto.
	Lornhill	21	Intelligence	Anderson, David	March 14, 1820	Balto.
	Lorris	13	Orion	Oldham, George W.	Dec. 30, 1822	Balto.
	Lou	4	Arctic	Hall, Joshua F.	Sept. 29, 1827	Balto.
	Louis	16	Arctic	Stone, John	Jan. 24, 1828	Balto.
	Louis	7	Balloon	Zacharie, James W.	Dec. 22, 1821	Balto.
	Louis	11	Intelligence	Wallace, Joseph A.	Apr. 27, 1821	Balto.
	Louisa	18	Alfred	Woolfolk, Austin	Jan. 18, 1825	Balto.
	Louisa	3	Alonzo	White, Philip	Nov. 8, 1822	Balto.
	Louisa	16	Arctic	Maddox, Thomas H.	Jan. 30, 1829	St. Mary's.
	Louisa	8	Arctic	Kelso, George G.	Nov. 15, 1826	Balto.
	Louisa	17	Caspian	Woolfolk, Austin	Nov. 26, 1836	Balto.

Surname	First Name	Age	Ship	O/S	Date	Depart
	Louisa	7	Catharine Jackson	Diggs, John H.	Nov. 26, 1836	Nanjimoy
	Louisa	18	E.H. Chapin	Tyson, A.H.	Aug. 25, 1848	Balto.
	Louisa	30	Elizabeth	Campbell, Walter L.	Oct. 6, 1849	Balto.
	Louisa	9	Eros	Armitage, James	June 29, 1822	Balto.
	Louisa	11	Eros	Armitage, James	June 29, 1822	Balto.
	Louisa	10	Good Hope	Woolfolk, Richard T.	Nov. 21, 1821	Balto.
	Louisa	8	Hamlet	Woolfolk, Austin	Jan. 2, 1824	Balto.
	Louisa	18 mon.	Isabella	Wallis, Cornelius C.	Nov. 26, 1834	Balto.
	Louisa	35	Kirkwood	Donovan, Joseph S.	Dec. 10, 1846	Balto.
	Louisa	11	Lady Monroe	Chabert, Leon	Sept. 29, 1825	Balto.
	Louisa	18	Lady Monroe	Woolfolk, Austin	Sept. 29, 1825	Balto.
	Louisa	12	Orbit	Woolfolk, Austin	Apr. 16, 1825	Balto.
	Louisa	2	Orion	Oldham, George W.	Dec. 30, 1822	Balto.
	Louisa	17	Sarah	Woolfolk, Austin	Apr. 2, 1831	Balto.
	Louisa	17	Susan Miller	Woolfolk, Austin	Oct. 25, 1822	Balto.
	Louisa	18	Susan Miller	Woolfolk, Samuel M.	Oct. 25, 1822	Balto.
	Louisa	17	Tweed	Bowling, John D.	Oct. 20, 1836	Town Creek
	Louisa	infant	Victorine	Slatter, Henry F.	Dec. 31, 1846	Balto.
	Loves	20	Aurilla	Woolfolk, Austin	Apr. 26, 1822	Balto.
	Luce	35	Hamlet	Woolfolk, Austin	Apr. 7, 1824	Balto.
	Lucinda	34	Pensacola	Coskery, Bernard	Apr. 9, 1832	Balto.
	Lucinda		Snow	Willis	Feb 5, 1835	Balto.
	Lucinda	18	St. Mary	Harker, William	Nov. 29, 1845	Balto.
	Lucretia	10	Kirkwood	Campbell, Bernard M.	Oct. 16, 1845	Balto.
	Lucretia	19	North America	Woolfolk, Austin	Dec. 20, 1824	Balto.
	Lucy	10	Alfred	Davidson, george	Jan. 18, 1825	Balto.

Surname	First Name	Age	Ship	O/S	Date	Depart
Lucy	17	Aurilla	Warfield, Charles	Apr. 26, 1822	Balto.
Lucy	1	Balloon	Knight, William	Dec. 22, 1821	Balto.
Lucy	27	Bourne	Chabert, Leon	Sept. 10, 1833	Balto.
Lucy	16	Caspian	Woolfolk, Austin	Nov. 26, 1836	Balto.
Lucy	14	Dryad	Williams, Joseph C.	Dec. 12, 1827	Balto.
Lucy	41	Dumphries	Lee, Richard H.	Sept. 25, 1828	Balto.
Lucy	18	Emilie	Anderson, David	Jan. 5, 1819	Balto.
Lucy	16	Georgia	Bren, Robert J.	Dec. 23, 1844	Balto.
Lucy	11	Gulnare	Pitts, Thomas H.	Nov. 5, 1830	Balto.
Lucy	20	Harriet	Carrell, Charles	Dec. 7, 1836	Balto.
Lucy	44	Harriet	Carrell, Charles	Dec. 7, 1836	Balto.
Lucy	18	Hyperion	King, Gideon T.	Nov. 12, 1821	Balto.
Lucy	infant	Intelligence	Plater, John R. Jr.	Apr. 12, 1823	St. Mary's
Lucy	26	Intelligence	De Mapiere, Victor	Apr. 30, 1821	Balto.
Lucy	2	Intelligence	Somerville, Alexander	Dec. 20, 1822	Balto.
Lucy	18	Lady Monroe	Woolfolk, Joseph B.	March 25, 1825	Balto.
Lucy	18	Lafayette	Woolfolk, Richard	Oct. 18, 1828	Balto.
Lucy	30	Lapwing	Thomson, Henry	Nov. 28, 1827	Balto.
Lucy	10	Orbit	Chabert, Leon	Apr. 16, 1825	Balto.
Lucy	18	Russell	Woolfolk, Austin	Feb. 28, 2839	Balto.
Lucy	22	States	Morton, George C.	Nov. 26, 1825	Balto.
Lucy	40	Statira	Smith, Doctor James	March 28, 1826	Balto.
Lucy Ann	21	Helen A. Miller	Campbell, Bernard M.	Oct. 18, 1852	Balto.
Lucy Ann	16	Nathaniel Hooper	Campbell, Bernard M.	Feb. 12, 1852	Balto.
Lucy Ann	17	Union	Campbell, Bernard M.	Dec. 16, 1848	Balto.
Luke	25	Catharine	Woolfolk, Austin	Jan. 15, 1831	Balto.

Surname	First Name	Age	Ship	O/S	Date	Depart
	Luke	17	Robert Reade	Woolfolk, Austin	Feb. 28, 1824	Balto.
	Lula	18	Zoe	Donovan, Joseph S.	Feb. 16, 1847	Balto.
	Lydia	35	Arctic	Smith, Leonard J.	Jan. 29, 1828	St. Mary's
	Lydia	18	Bourne	Rogers, Selemachus	Sept. 9, 1833	Balto.
	Lydia	16	Intelligence	Woolfolk, Austin	Apr. 5, 1823	Balto.
	Lydia	18	Jasper	Woolfolk, Austin	Apr. 7, 1827	Balto.
	Lydia	14	Lapwing	Woolfolk, Austin	Feb. 16, 1827	Balto.
	Lydia	17	Mars	Woolfolk, Austin	Oct. 30, 1824	Balto.
	Lydia	22	Mars	Woolfolk, Austin	Oct. 30, 1824	Balto.
	Lydia	infant	St. Mary	Campbell, Bernard M.	Nov. 29, 1845	Balto.
	Lydia	2	Statira	Smith, Doctor James	March 28, 1826	Balto.
	Lydia	18	Phoenix	Slatter, Hope Hull	March 27, 1847	Balto.
	Lydia Ann	18	Southerner	Rodbind, Ebenezer	Jan. 21, 1850	Balto.
	Lydia Ann	17	Mars	Woolfolk, Joseph B.	Nov. 1, 1824	Balto.
	Macey	38	Globe	Campbell, Bernard M.	Sept. 7, 1846	Balto.
	Mack	10	Catharine Jackson	Diggs, John H.	Nov. 26, 1836	Nanjimoy
	Madison	22	Georgia	Brent, Robert J.	Dec. 23, 1844	Balto.
	Mag	15	Balloon	Penieres, Emile	Dec. 22, 1821	Balto.
	Mahala	6	Henry Clay	Camphor, Henry	Dec. 8, 1828	Nottingham
	Major	25	Intelligence	Anderson, David	Nov. 3, 1820	Balto.
	Major	22	Merrimack	Kelso, George G.	Nov. 2, 1831	Balto.
	Major	13	Caspian	Woolfolk, Austin	Nov. 26, 1836	Balto.
	Manny	20	Algerine	Woolfolk, Austin	March 25, 1826	Balto.
	Manuel	35	Good Hope	Woolfolk, Samuel M.	Nov. 21, 1821	Balto.
	Manuel	28	Harriett	Woolfolk, Austin	March 23, 1822	Balto.
	Manuel	24	North America	Woolfolk, Austin	Dec. 20, 1824	Balto.

Surname	First Name	Age	Ship	O/S	Date	Depart
	Manuel	8	Patriot	Simms, Edward	July 13, 1836	Balto.
	Maranda	1 mon.	Isabella		Nov. 26, 1834	Balto.
	Marandy	25	Strafford	Wilsor, Thomas C.	Nov. 21, 1843	Balto.
	Marceller	16	Betsey	Woolfolk, Austin	Apr. 29, 1828	Balto.
	Marcia	20	Lapwing	Hall, Francis	March 22, 1822	Balto.
	Mareen	16	Missouri	Little, Moses	March 2, 1819	Balto.
	Margaret	7	Architect	Hannan McHiane	Nov. 23, 1838	Balto.
	Margaret	6	Arctic	Maddox, Thomas H.	Jan. 30, 1829	St. Mary's
	Margaret	12	Arctic	Kelso, George G.	Nov. 15, 1826	Balto.
	Margaret	20	Aurilla	Chabert, Leon	Apr. 26, 1822	Balto.
	Margaret	26	Aurilla	Warfield, Charles	Apr. 26, 1822	Balto.
	Margaret	25	E.H. Chapin	Tyson. A.H.	Aug. 25, 1848	Balto.
	Margaret	18	General Hand	Poindexter, George L.	June 1, 1832	Balto.
	Margaret	19	Henry Clay	Bowen, Robert W.	Dec. 8, 1828	Nottingham
	Margaret	7	Henry Clay	Camphor, Henry	Dec. 8, 1828	Nottingham
	Margaret	16	Hyperion	King, Gideon T.	Nov. 12, 1821	Balto.
	Margaret	9	Intelligence	Anderson, David	Dec. 20, 1822	Balto.
	Margaret	22	Kirkwood	Campbell, Bernard M.	Oct. 14, 1848	Balto.
	Margaret		Mars	Woolfolk, Austin	Oct. 30, 1824	Balto.
	Margaret	14	North America	Woolfolk, Austin	Oct. 14, 1823	Balto.
	Margaret	12	Orbit	Chabert, Leon	Apr. 16, 1825	Balto.
	Margaret	13	Pioneer	Baggett, Elizabeth A.	Sept. 9, 1847	Balto.
	Margaret	13	Serene	Archer, James	Oct. 19, 1836	Balto.
	Margaret		Signer	Woolfolk, Austin	Nov. 12, 1831	Balto.
	Margaret	16	States	Woolfolk, Austin	Apr. 14, 1828	Balto.
	Margaret	2	Susan Miller	Woolfolk, Richard T.	Oct. 25, 1822	Balto.

Surname	First Name	Age	Ship	O/S	Date	Depart
	Margaret Ann	17	Seaman	Purvis, James Franklin	Apr. 8, 1842	Balto.
	Margaret Jane	infant	Kirkwood	Slatter, Hope Hull	Dec. 23, 1843	Balto.
	Margarett	28	Caledonia	Woolfolk, Austin	Oct. 27, 1841	Balto.
	Margarett	9	Georgia	Brent, Robert J.	Dec. 23, 1844	Balto.
	Margrett	6	Isabella		Nov. 26, 1834	Balto.
	Maria	23	Ajax	Richardson, Wade H.	Oct.3, 1833	Balto.
	Maria	15	Alfred	Woolfolk, Austin	Jan. 18, 1825	Balto.
	Maria	16	Algerine	Woolfolk, Austin	Jan. 5, 1826	Balto.
	Maria	17	Alonzo	White, Philip	Nov. 8, 1822	Balto.
	Maria	22	Alonzo	White, Philip	Nov. 8, 1822	Balto.
	Maria	22	Architect	Harker, William	Feb. 15, 1840	Balto.
	Maria	19	Arctic	Woolfolk, Austin	Jan. 28, 1829	Annapolis
	Maria	7 mon.	Arctic	Williams, Joseph C.	Jan. 31, 1829	St. Mary's
	Maria	12	Arctic	Magee, Eugene	Oct. 9, 1828	Annapolis
	Maria	3	Aurilla	Woolfolk, Austin	Apr. 26, 1822	Balto.
	Maria	16	Balloon	Milligan, George	Dec. 17, 1821	Balto.
	Maria	26	Balloon	Knight, William	Dec. 22, 1821	Balto.
	Maria	8	Balloon	Penieres, Emile	Dec. 22, 1821	Balto.
	Maria	13	Balloon	Zacharie, James W.	Dec. 22, 1821	Balto.
	Maria	14	Betsey	Woolfolk, Austin	Apr. 29, 1828	Balto.
	Maria	16	Betsey	Woolfolk, Austin	Apr. 29, 1828	Balto.
	Maria	14	Bourne	Handy, Samuel	Oct. 13, 1832	Balto.
	Maria	5	Brunswick	Woolfolk, Austin	Oct. 11, 1831	Balto.
	Maria	26	Budget	Bradley, Robert	Nov. 26, 1821	Balto.
	Maria	6	Budget	Spraggins, Samuel M.	Nov. 27, 1821	Balto.
	Maria	8	Caspian	Woolfolk, Austin	Nov. 26, 1836	Balto.

Surname	First Name	Age	Ship	O/S	Date	Depart
	Maria	3	Catharine Jackson	Brent, George	Nov. 26, 1836	Nanjimoy
	Maria	15	Catharine Jackson	Diggs John H.	Nov. 26, 1836	Nanjimoy
	Maria	2	Chatsworth	Anderson, David	Jan. 3, 1821	Balto.
	Maria	4	Chatsworth	Anderson, David	Jan. 3, 1821	Balto.
	Maria	13	Emilie	Ferguson, Thomas	Dec. 14, 1821	Balto.
	Maria	23	Emilie	Levells, William H.	Jan. 4, 1819	Balto.
	Maria	16	Eros	Woolfolk, Austin	Jan. 28, 1824	Balto.
	Maria	18	General Hand	Poindexter, George L.	June 1, 1832	Balto.
	Maria	19	General Hand	Poindexter, George L.	June 1, 1832	Balto.
	Maria	18	Georgia	Brent, Robert J.	Dec. 23, 1844	Balto.
	Maria	13	Good Hope	Woolfolk, Austin	Nov. 16, 1821	Balto.
	Maria	14	Good Hope	Woolfolk, Austin	Nov. 16, 1821	Balto.
	Maria	24	Gulnare	Kelso George G.	Nov. 3, 1830	Balto.
	Maria	17	Hamlet	Woolfolk, Austin	Apr. 7, 1824	Balto.
	Maria	18	Hamlet	Woolfolk, Austin	Jan. 2, 1824	Balto.
	Maria	17	Harriett	King, John	March 23, 1822	Balto.
	Maria	16	Harriett	Woolfolk, Austin	March 23, 1822	Balto.
	Maria	13	Henry Clay	Chew Worthington	Dec. 8, 1828	Nottingham
	Maria	40	Hermann	Rowe Ralph	June 21, 1851	Balto.
	Maria	20	Hope	Purnell, Thomas R.	Dec. 3, 1833	Balto.
	Maria	20	Hope	Byrne, Walter	Dec. 5, 1833	Balto.
	Maria	7	Hyperion	Valcourt, Alex de	May 10, 1822	Balto.
	Maria	16	Hyperion	Anderson, David	May 14, 1822	Balto.
	Maria	24	Hyperion	Anderson, David	May 14, 1822	Balto.
	Maria	18	Intelligence	Anderson, David	Nov. 3, 1820	Balto.
	Maria	15	Intelligence	Coleman, Henry E.	Nov. 4, 1820	Balto.

Surname	First Name	Age	Ship	O/S	Date	Depart
	Maria	19	Isabella	Wallis, Cornelius C.	Nov. 26, 1834	Balto.
	Maria	3	Julia	Poindexter, George	Feb. 10, 1832	Balto.
	Maria	5	Kirkwood	Guyther, John	Dec. 10, 1846	Balto.
	Maria	20	Lady Monroe	Woolfolk, Joseph B.	March 25, 1825	Balto.
	Maria	2	Lapwing	King, Gideon T.	March 22, 1822	Balto.
	Maria	3	Liberator	Woolfolk, Austin	Nov. 12, 1828	Balto.
	Maria	2	Mars	Woolfolk, Austin	Oct. 30, 1824	Balto.
	Maria	19	Mars	Woolfolk, Austin	Oct. 30, 1824	Balto.
	Maria	10	Mars	Woolfolk, Joseph B.	Oct. 30, 1824	Balto.
	Maria	38	Mary Broughton	Chaplain, J. Bond	Nov. 18, 1851	Balto.
	Maria	33	Missouri	Gilmore, John	March 1, 1819	Balto.
	Maria	35	Nancy W. Stevens	Baker, William	Oct. 23, 1843	Balto.
	Maria	28	North America	Chabert, Leon	Apr. 24, 1826	Balto.
	Maria	8	North America	Thurman, William C.	Apr. 24, 1826	Balto.
	Maria	8	North America	Woolfolk, Austin	Dec. 20, 1824	Balto.
	Maria	9	North America	Woolfolk, Austin	Dec. 20, 1824	Balto.
	Maria	11	Opelousas	Abercombie, James	July 6, 1836	Balto.
	Maria	13	Orbit	Pearce, James Alfred	Apr. 13, 1825	Balto.
	Maria	25	P. Soule	Unquahart, David	Oct. 10, 1845	Balto.
	Maria	19	Palestine	Slatter, Hope Hull	Nov. 16, 1835	Balto.
	Maria	35	Plutarch	Johnson, M.	Sept. 17, 1834	Balto.
	Maria	22	Russell	Woolfolk, Austin	Feb. 28, 2839	Balto.
	Maria	14	Shamrock	Guyton, Elisha	March 11, 1840	Balto.
	Maria	11	States	Woolfolk, Joseph B.	Nov. 21, 1827	Balto.
	Maria	5	States	Woolfolk, Austin	Nov. 26, 1825	Balto.
	Maria	15	Susan Miller	Woolfolk, Austin	Oct. 25, 1822	Balto.

Surname	First Name	Age	Ship	O/S	Date	Depart
	Maria	18	Susan Miller	Woolfolk, Samuel M.	Oct. 25, 1822	Balto.
	Maria	12	Temperance	Wikoff, Steven W.	Dec. 12, 1818	Balto.
	Maria	6	Triton	Lee, Thomas	Dec. 18, 1819	Balto.
	Maria	16	Virginia	Tiernan, Charles	Dec. 12, 1825	Balto.
	Maria	22	Virginia	Tiernan, Charles	Dec. 12, 1825	Balto.
	Maria	17	Virginia	Woolfolk, Joseph B.	Dec. 19, 1825	Balto.
	Maria	16	Zoe	Donovan, Joseph S.	Feb. 16, 1847	Balto.
	Mariah	16	Caspian	Woolfolk, Austin	Nov. 26, 1836	Balto.
	Mariah	3	Lafayette	Woolfolk, Joseph B.	Oct. 18, 1828	Balto.
	Mariah	12	Lafayette	Woolfolk, Richard	Oct. 18, 1828	Balto.
	Mariah	13	Seguin	Campbell, Bernard M.	July 12, 1853	Balto.
	Mariah	16	Supero	Donovan, Joseph S.	Nov. 2, 1843	Balto.
	Mariah	18	Victorine	Campbell, Bernard M.	March 1, 1845	Balto.
	Marian	19	Isabella		Nov. 26, 1834	Balto.
	Marinda	1	Gulnare	Pitts, Thomas H.	Nov. 5, 1830	Balto.
	Mark	18	Mars	Woolfolk, Austin	Oct. 30, 1824	Balto.
	Marry Ellin	16	Southerner	Campbell, Bernard M.	Jan. 5, 1852	Balto.
	Martha	24	Hope	Purnel, Thomas R.	Dec. 3, 1833	Balto.
	Martha	18	Isabella	Wallis, Cornelius C.	Nov. 26, 1834	Balto.
	Martha	24	Lafayette	Slatter, Hope Hull	March 25, 1843	Balto.
	Martha	11	Leda	Nelson, James	Nov. 16, 1848	Balto.
	Martha	17 mon.	Osceolo	Carroll, Samuel	Oct. 16, 1839	Balto.
	Martha	7 mon.	States	Woolfolk, Joseph B.	Nov. 21, 1827	Balto.
Martha Ann		8	Bostonian	Slatter, Hope Hull	Jan. 18, 1841	Balto.
Martha Ann		14	General Pinckney	Rodbind, Ebenezer	Feb. 21, 1846	Balto.
Martha Ann		3 mon.	Lafayette	Woolfolk, Austin	Oct. 18, 1828	Balto.

Surname	First Name	Age	Ship	O/S	Date	Depart
	Martha Ann	15	Tangier	Campbell, Bernard M.	Nov. 26, 1853	Balto.
	Martha Ellen	7	Architect	Crow, William	Feb. 3, 1841	Balto.
	Martha Ellen	4	Seaman	Hooper, John	Dec. 18, 1838	Balto.
	Martin	1	Ajax	Richardson, Wade H.	Oct.3, 1833	Balto.
	Martin	5	Harriet	Carroll, Charles	Dec. 7, 1836	Balto.
	Martin	17	Intelligence	Woolfolk, Austin	Dec. 20, 1822	Balto.
	Martin	18	Lapwing	Spraggins, Samuel M.	March 22, 1822	Balto.
	Mary	24	Ajax	Richardson, Wade H.	Oct.3, 1833	Balto.
	Mary	21	Alonzo	Oldham, George W.	Nov. 7, 1822	Balto.
	Mary	19	Alonzo	White, Philip	Nov. 8, 1822	Balto.
	Mary	20	Arctic	Woolfolk, Austin	Jan. 28, 1829	Annapolis
	Mary	22	Arctic	Williams, Joseph C.	Jan. 31, 1829	St. Mary's
	Mary	30	Arctic	Williams, Joseph C.	Jan. 31, 1829	St. Mary's
	Mary	36	Arctic	Hall, Joshua F.	Sept. 29, 1827	Balto.
	Mary	infant	Aurilla	Warfield, Charles	Apr. 26, 1822	Balto.
	Mary	15	Aurilla	Wikoff, Stephen A.	Apr. 26, 1822	Balto.
	Mary	17	Aurilla	Woolfolk, Austin	Apr. 26, 1822	Balto.
	Mary	1	Balloon	Penieres, Emile	Dec. 22, 1821	Balto.
	Mary	1	Balloon	Penieres, Emile	Dec. 22, 1821	Balto.
	Mary	2	Baltimore	Hale, Colin F.	Oct. 31, 1835	Balto.
	Mary	18	Bourne	Handy, Samuel	Oct. 13, 1832	Balto.
	Mary	9	Bourne	Rogers, Selemachus	Sept. 9, 1833	Balto.
	Mary	2	Brunswick	Woolfolk, Austin	Oct. 11, 1831	Balto.
	Mary	18	Brunswick	Woolfolk, Austin	Oct. 11, 1831	Balto.
	Mary	2	Budget	Bradley, Robert	Nov. 26, 1821	Balto.
	Mary	30	Calagari	Nelson, George S.	Nov. 7, 1832	Balto.

Surname	First Name	Age	Ship	O/S	Date	Depart
	Mary	9	Caspian	Woolfolk, Austin	Nov. 26, 1836	Balto.
	Mary	16	Catharine Jackson	Brent, George	Nov. 26, 1836	Nanjimoy
	Mary	9	Catharine Jackson	Diggs, John H.	Nov. 26, 1836	Nanjimoy
	Mary	4	Charles	Carter, John A.	Sept. 29, 1849	Balto.
	Mary	18	Cumberland	Callahan, George W.	Oct. 7, 1836	Balto.
	Mary	5	Dumpfries	Lee, Richard H.	Sept. 25, 1828	Balto.
	Mary	17	E.H.Chapin	Penn, Alexander	Nov. 30, 1847	Balto.
	Mary	5	Eliza	Slatter, Hope Hull	Oct. 9, 1840	Balto.
	Mary	27	Emilie	Ferguson, Thomas	Dec. 14, 1821	Balto.
	Mary	4	Emilie	Anderson, David	March 27, 1821	Balto.
	Mary	20	Eros	Woolfolk, Austin	Jan. 28, 1824	Balto.
	Mary	17	Eros	Armitage, James	June 29, 1822	Balto.
	Mary	18	Eros	Armitage, James	June 29, 1822	Balto.
	Mary	16	Frances Amy	Donovan, Joseph S.	Jan. 20, 1847	Balto.
	Mary	10	Franklin	Yeiser, John	Nov. 27, 1819	Balto.
	Mary	20	Franklin	Yeiser, John	Nov. 27, 1819	Balto.
	Mary	22	General Hand	Poindexter, George L.	June 1, 1832	Balto.
	Mary	18 mon.	Good Hope	Woolfolk, Austin	Nov. 16, 1821	Balto.
	Mary	14	Good Hope	Woolfolk, Austin	Nov. 16, 1821	Balto.
	Mary	18 mon.	Gulnare	Kelso, George G.	Nov. 3, 1830	Balto.
	Mary	18	Hamlet	Woolfolk, Austin	Jan. 2, 1824	Balto.
	Mary	12 mon.	Harriett	Woolfolk, Austin	March 23, 1822	Balto.
	Mary	14	Harriett	Woolfolk, Austin	March 23, 1822	Balto.
	Mary	20	Harriett	Woolfolk, Austin	March 23, 1822	Balto.
	Mary	24	Harriett	Woolfolk, Austin	March 23, 1822	Balto.
	Mary	20	Henry Clay	Bower, Robert W.	Dec. 8, 1828	Nottingham

Surname	First Name	Age	Ship	O/S	Date	Depart
	Mary	3	Henry Clay	Chew, Worhtington	Dec. 8, 1828	Nottingham
	Mary	12	Hibernia	Woolfolk, Austin	Dec. 5, 1826	Balto.
	Mary	23	Home	Campbell, Bernard M.	March 22, 1845	Balto.
	Mary	15	Hope	Richardson, Wade H.	Dec. 3, 1833	Balto.
	Mary	10	Hope	Byrne, Walter	Dec. 5, 1833	Balto.
	Mary	15	Hope	Byrne, Walter	Dec. 5, 1833	Balto.
	Mary	14	Hope	Knight, James M.	March 26, 1834	Balto.
	Mary	15	Hortensia	Woolfolk, Austin	Dec. 14, 1836	Balto.
	Mary	24	Hyperion	Woolfolk, Austin	May 10, 1822	Balto.
	Mary	25	Hyperion	Anderson, David	May 14, 1822	Balto.
	Mary	21	Hyperion	Dickey, Joseph	Nov. 12, 1821	Balto.
	Mary	19	Hyperion	Lee, Thomas	Nov. 9, 1821	Balto.
	Mary	16	Intelligence	Woolfolk, Austin	Dec. 20, 1822	Balto.
	Mary	13	Intelligence	Oldham, George W.	Nov. 4, 1820	Balto.
	Mary	14	Isabella		Nov. 26, 1834	Balto.
	Mary	17	John R. Gardner	Page, Mrs.	Jan. 8, 1840	Balto.
	Mary	26	Julia	Poindexter, George	Feb. 10, 1832	Balto.
	Mary	8 mon.	Lafayette	Woolfolk, Richard	Oct. 18, 1828	Balto.
	Mary	21	Lawrence	Woolfolk, Austin	May 9, 1823	Balto.
	Mary	23	Lawrence	Woolfolk, Austin	May 9, 1823	Balto.
	Mary	11	Lion	Garwood, Richard	March 16, 1845	Balto.
	Mary	24	London	Hopp, H.B.	Nov. 6, 1840	Balto.
	Mary	3	Mars	Woolfolk, Austin	Nov. 1, 1824	Balto.
	Mary	8	Mars	Woolfolk, Austin	Oct. 30, 1824	Balto.
	Mary	19	Mars	Woolfolk, Austin	Oct. 30, 1824	Balto.
	Mary	24	Mars	Woolfolk, Austin	Oct. 30, 1824	Balto.

Surname	First Name	Age	Ship	O/S	Date	Depart
	Mary	7	Mary Broughton	Chaplain, J. Bond	Nov. 18, 1851	Balto.
	Mary	20	Mechanic	Woolfolk, Austin	Jan. 1, 1831	Balto.
	Mary	22	Merrimack	Kelso George G.	Nov. 2, 1831	Balto.
	Mary	17	Nancy W.Stevens	Harker, James	Oct. 25, 1843	Balto.
	Mary	3	North America	Thurman, William C.	Apr. 24, 1826	Balto.
	Mary	19	Opelousas	Garland, Rice	July 5, 1836	Balto.
	Mary	32	Orbit	McLanahan, William	Apr. 15, 1825	Balto.
	Mary	3	Orion	Oldham, George W.	Dec. 30, 1822	Balto.
	Mary	17	Palestine	Slatter, Hope Hull	Nov. 16, 1835	Balto.
	Mary	14	Pandora	Woolfolk, Austin	March 26, 1831	Balto.
	Mary		Plutarch	Mosse, Henry	Sept. 17, 1834	Balto.
	Mary	11	Russell	Woolfolk, Austin	Feb. 28, 2839	Balto.
	Mary	16	Sarah	Winn, George	Sept. 8, 1831	Balto.
	Mary	1	Sarah Ann	Keene, Wallace	Oct. 14, 1836	Balto.
	Mary	27	Schuylkill	McKee, William	Oct. 25, 1822	Balto.
	Mary	10	Serene	Archer, James	Oct. 19, 1836	Balto.
	Mary	2	Signet	Woolfolk, Austin	Nov. 12, 1831	Balto.
	Mary	5	Signet	Woolfolk, Austin	Nov. 17, 1831	Balto.
	Mary	12	States	Woolfolk, Joseph B.	Nov. 21, 1827	Balto.
	Mary	18	States	Duer, Robert	Nov. 26, 1825	Balto.
	Mary	3	States	Woolfolk, Austin	Nov. 26, 1825	Balto.
	Mary	15	States	Woolfolk, Austin	Nov. 26, 1825	Balto.
	Mary	36	Statira	Smith, Doctor James	March 28, 1826	Balto.
	Mary	2	Susan Miller	Woolfolk, Samuel M.	Oct. 25, 1822	Balto.
	Mary	3	Tangier	Campbell, Bernard M.	Nov. 26, 1853	Balto.
	Mary	19	Temperance	Wikoff, Steven W.	Dec. 12, 1818	Balto.

Surname	First Name	Age	Ship	O/S	Date	Depart
	Mary	8	Tippecanoe	Purvis, James Franklin	Jan. 17, 1842	Balto.
	Mary	16	Tippecanoe	Simms, Benedict	Sept. 18, 1844	Balto.
	Mary	16	Triton	Anderson, David	Dec. 20, 1819	Balto.
	Mary	12	Ulysses	Richardson, Wade H.	Nov. 6, 1833	Balto.
	Mary	16	Ulysses	Harwood, James	Nov. 9, 1833	Balto.
	Mary	15	Venus	Cromwell, Richard Jr.	Nov. 13, 1845	Balto.
	Mary	16	Victorine	Campbell, Bernard M.	March 1, 1845	Balto.
	Mary	16	Victorine	Campbell, Bernard M.	March 1, 1845	Balto.
	Mary	12	William and Mary	Coleman, Aquila C.	Oct. 9, 1821	Balto.
	Mary	21	William and Mary	King, Gideon T.	Oct. 9, 1821	St. Mary's
	Mary Ann	10 mon.	Arctic	Smith, Leonard J.	Jan. 29, 1828	Balto.
	Mary Ann	10	Arctic	Hall, Joshua F.	Sept. 29, 1827	Balto.
	Mary Ann	24	Budget	King, Gideon T.	Dec. 1, 1821	Balto.
	Mary Ann	14	Harriett	Woolfolk, Austin	March 23, 1822	Balto.
	Mary Ann	22	Henry A. Barling	Campbell, Bernard M.	Dec. 18, 1851	Balto.
	Mary Ann	15	Hermitage	Slatter, Hope Hull	Oct. 28, 1846	Balto.
	Mary Ann	9	Hyperion	Lanahan, J.J.M.	Nov. 9, 1821	Balto.
	Mary Ann	1	Intelligence	Somerville, Alexander	Dec. 20, 1822	Balto.
	Mary Ann	2	Intelligence	Somerville, Alexander	Dec. 20, 1822	Balto.
	Mary Ann	10	Lady Richmond	Woolfolk, Austin	Apr. 30, 1827	Balto.
	Mary Ann	13	Leda	Meekins, J.S.	Oct. 1, 1846	Balto.
	Mary Ann	25	P. Soule	Biscoe, James	Oct. 9, 1845	Balto.
	Mary Ann	3	Pilgrim	Carr, S.J.	Dec. 22, 1834	Balto.
	Mary Ann	5	Statira	Smith, Doctor James	March 28, 1826	Balto.
	Mary Ann	17	Superb	Anderson, David	Apr. 6, 1819	Balto.
	Mary Ann	6	Union	Campbell, Bernard M.	Dec. 16, 1848	Balto.

Surname	First Name	Age	Ship	O/S	Date	Depart
	Mary Ann	3	Victorine	Slatter, Henry F.	Dec. 31, 1846	Balto.
	Mary Anne	16	North America	Woolfolk, Austin	Nov. 23, 1822	Balto.
	Mary Eliza	16	Eliza	Slatter, Hope Hull	Oct. 9, 1840	Balto.
	Mary Eliza	9	Henry A. Barling	Marriott, William H.	Oct. 28, 1848	Balto.
	Mary Eliza	15	John S. Gittings	Campbell, Bernard M.	Nov. 20, 1852	Balto.
	Mary Eliza	16	Mary Broughton	Campbell, Bernard M.	Nov. 18, 1851	Balto.
	Mary Eliza	10	Victorine	Campbell, Bernard M.	Dec. 31, 1846	Balto.
	Mary Elizabeth	6	Leda	Nelson, James	Nov. 16, 1848	Balto.
	Mary Elizabeth	14	Phoenix	Slatter, Hope Hull	March 27, 1847	Balto.
	Mary Elizabeth	8	Topaz	Woolfolk, Austin	Apr. 20, 1829	Balto.
	Mary Elizabethy	16	Tangier	Campbell, Bernard M.	Nov. 26, 1853	Balto.
	Mary Ellen	infant	General Pinckney	Slatter, Hope Hull	Jan. 19, 1847	Balto.
	Mary Ellen	infant	General Pinckney	Slatter, Hope Hull	Jan. 19, 1847	Balto.
	Mary Ellen	6	Georgia	Brent, Robert J.	Dec. 23, 1844	Balto.
	Mary Ellen	1 mon.	Mary	Purvis, James Franklin	Feb. 8, 1841	Balto.
	Mary Jane	infant	Edward Everett	Campbell, Bernard M.	Oct. 18, 1851	Balto.
	Mary Jane	20	Elizabeth	Campbell, Walter L.	Oct. 6, 1849	Balto.
	Mary Jane	17	Kirkwood	Campbell, Bernard M.	Oct. 16, 1845	Balto.
	Mary Jane	28	Osprey	Tilletson, S.R.	Nov. 11, 1847	Balto.
	Mary Josephine	6	States	Woolfolk, Austin	Nov. 26, 1825	Balto.
	Massy	55	Statira	Smith, Doctor James	March 28, 1826	Balto.
	Mathew	12	Intelligence	De Mapiere, Victor	Apr. 30, 1821	Balto.
	Mathew	15	Kirkwood	Donovan, Joseph S.	Dec. 10, 1846	Balto.
	Matilda	21	Alfred	Woolfolk, Austin	Jan. 18, 1825	Balto.
	Matilda	infant	Arctic	Kelso, George G.	Nov. 15, 1826	Balto.
	Matilda	8 mon.	Auril a	Wikoff, Stephen A.	Apr. 26, 1822	Balto.

Surname	First Name	Age	Ship	O/S	Date	Depart
	Matilda	20	Aurilla	Woolfolk, Austin	Apr. 26, 1822	Balto.
	Matilda	9	Balloon	Zacharie, James W.	Dec. 22, 1821	Balto.
	Matilda	13	Balloon	Zacharie, James W.	Dec. 22, 1821	Balto.
	Matilda	20	Balloon	Zacharie, James W.	Dec. 22, 1821	Balto.
	Matilda		Bourne	Handy, Samuel	Oct. 13, 1832	Balto.
	Matilda		Brunswick	Woolfolk, Austin	Oct. 11, 1831	Balto.
	Matilda	16	Budget	Spraggins, Samuel M.	Nov. 27, 1821	Balto.
	Matilda	18	Calagari	Nelson, George S.	Nov. 7, 1832	Balto.
	Matilda	35	Catharine Jackson	Brent, George	Nov. 26, 1836	Nanjimoy
	Matilda	6	Catharine Jackson	Diggs, John H.	Nov. 26, 1836	Nanjimoy
	Matilda	45	Charles	Carter, John A.	Sept. 29, 1849	Balto.
	Matilda	3	Clio	Starnsburg, William	March 22, 1819	Balto.
	Matilda	31	Dumphries	Lee, Richard H.	Sept. 25, 1828	Balto.
	Matilda	16	Emilie	Ferguson, Thomas	Dec. 14, 1821	Balto.
	Matilda	23	Eros	Woolfolk, Austin	Jan. 28, 1824	Balto.
	Matilda	48	Georgia	Brent, Robert J.	Dec. 23, 1844	Balto.
	Matilda	19	Harriett	Woolfolk, Austin	March 23, 1822	Balto.
	Matilda	5	Henry Clay	Compton & Dorsett	Dec. 8, 1828	Nottingham
	Matilda	14	Hope	Knight, James M.	March 26, 1834	Balto.
	Matilda	23	Intelligence	Woolfolk, Austin	Dec. 20, 1822	Balto.
	Matilda	18	Julia	Poindexter, George	Feb. 10, 1832	Balto.
	Matilda	12	Julia	Woolfolk, Austin	Jan. 8, 1829	Balto.
	Matilda	21	Lafayette	Slatter, Hope Hull	March 25, 1843	Balto.
	Matilda	17	Mars	Woolfolk, Austin	Oct. 30, 1824	Balto.
	Matilda	19	Mars	Woolfolk, Austin	Oct. 30, 1824	Balto.
	Matilda	11	North America	Woolfolk, Austin	Nov. 23, 1822	Balto.

Surname	First Name	Age	Ship	O/S	Date	Depart
	Matilda	25	Palestine	Slatter, Hope Hull	Nov. 16, 1835	Balto.
	Matilda	16	Shamrock	Guyton, Elisha	March 11, 1840	Balto.
	Matilda	5	Virginia	Woolfolk, Joseph B.	Dec. 19, 1825	Balto.
	Matilda	13	William and Mary	Coleman, Aquila	Oct. 9, 1821	Balto.
	Matilda Ann	18	Charles	Campbell, Bernard M.	Dec. 18, 1850	Balto.
	Matthew	28	General Hand	Poindexter, George L.	June 1, 1832	Balto.
	Matthew	17	North America	Woolfolk, Austin	Dec. 20, 1824	Balto.
	Maty	24	Henry Clay	Bower, Thomas F.	Dec. 8, 1828	Nottingham
	Maty	19	Intelligence	Anderson, David	May 1, 1821	Balto.
	Melcha	15	States	Duer, Robert	Nov. 26, 1825	Balto.
	Metus	24	Susan Miller	Woolfolk, Austin	Oct. 25, 1822	Balto.
	Michael	8	Arctic	McConnell, Alex	Sept. 29, 1827	Balto.
	Michael	16	Balloon	Knight, William	Dec. 22, 1821	Balto.
	Michael	25	Balloon	Knight, William	Dec. 22, 1821	Balto.
	Michael	33	Dumphries	Lee, Richard H.	Sept. 25, 1828	Balto.
	Michael	44	Dumphries	Lee, Richard H.	Sept. 25, 1828	Balto.
	Michael		Emilie	Mercer, William D.	March 27, 1821	Balto.
	Michael	50	Georgia	Brent, Robert J.	Dec. 21, 1844	Balto.
	Michael	25	Lady Monroe	Woolfolk, Austin	Sept. 29, 1825	Balto.
	Michael	19	Merrimack	Kelso, George G.	Nov. 2, 1831	Balto.
	Middleton	22	Bourne	Rogers, Selemachus	Sept. 9, 1833	Balto.
	Mike	40	Aurilla	Chabert, Leon	Apr. 26, 1822	Balto.
	Mike	23	Good Hope	Woolfolk, Samuel M.	Nov. 21, 1821	Balto.
	Mike	14	Superb	Donovan, Joseph S.	Nov. 2, 1843	Balto.
	Mike	25	Virginia	Woolfolk, Joseph B.	Dec. 19, 1825	Balto.
	Milby	22	Agent	Anderson, David	June 8, 1821	Balto.

Surname	First Name	Age	Ship	O/S	Date	Depart
	Milby	29	Emilie	Spencer, Thomas R.P.	Dec. 14, 1821	Balto.
	Miles	25	Charles	Campbell, Bernard M.	Dec. 18, 1850	Balto.
	Miles	17	Copia	Blow, Richard	Dec. 27, 1838	Balto.
	Milicent	13	Lady Monroe	Chabert, Leon	Sept. 29, 1825	Balto.
	Milkey	19	North America	Hixon, Lucas	Apr. 24, 1826	Balto.
	Milky	13	Clio	Poumairat, John	March 20, 1819	Balto.
	Milley	18	Pensacola	Martin, James	Apr. 9, 1832	Balto.
	Milly	7	Ajax	Richardson, Wade H.	Oct.3, 1833	Balto.
	Milly	12	Ann Wayne	Guyton, Elisha	Sept. 2, 1836	Balto.
	Milly	6	Arctic	Kelso, George G.	Nov. 15, 1826	Balto.
	Milly	28	Balloon	Penieres, Emile	Dec. 22, 1821	Balto.
	Milly	12	Caspian	Woolfolk, Austin	Nov. 26, 1836	Balto.
	Milly	23	Caspian	Woolfolk, Austin	Nov. 26, 1836	Balto.
	Milly	8	Eros	Armitage, James	June 29, 1822	Balto.
	Milly	31	Georgia	Brent, Robert J.	Dec. 21, 1844	Balto.
	Milly	28	Good Hope	Woolfolk, Austin	Nov. 16, 1821	Balto.
	Milly	20	Henry Clay	Chew, Worhtington	Dec. 8, 1828	Nottingham
	Milly	12	Hibernia	Woolfolk, Austin	Dec. 5, 1826	Balto.
	Milly	18	Hyperion	Anderson, David	May 14, 1822	Balto.
	Milly	17	Hyperion	Dickey, Joseph	Nov. 12, 1821	Balto.
	Milly	3	Jasper	Woolfolk, Austin	Apr. 7, 1827	Balto.
	Milly	10	Kenhawa	Maddox, Thomas H.	Oct. 26, 1832	Balto.
	Milly	17	Lady Monroe	Woolfolk, Joseph B.	March 25, 1825	Balto.
	Milly	4	Lady Monroe	Woolfolk, Austin	Sept. 29, 1825	Balto.
	Milly	17	Lady Monroe	Woolfolk, Austin	Sept. 29, 1825	Balto.
	Milly	19	Lafayette	Woolfolk, Richard	Oct. 18, 1828	Balto.

Surname	First Name	Age	Ship	O/S	Date	Depart
	Milly	17	Mechanic	Woolfolk, Austin	Jan. 1, 1831	Balto.
	Milly	13	Missouri	Marrash, John	March 1, 1819	Balto.
	Milly	25	Missouri	Cook, James K.	March 2, 1819	Balto.
	Milly	18	Palestine	Slater, Hope Hull	Nov. 16, 1835	Balto.
	Milly	18	Sarah Ann	Keene, Wallace	Oct. 14, 1836	Balto.
	Milly	22	States	Woolfolk, Austin	March 8, 1826	Balto.
	Milly	23	States	Tillotson, Giles	Nov. 22, 1827	Balto.
	Milly	48	Strafford	Wilson, Thomas C.	Nov. 21, 1843	Balto.
	Milly	11	Susan Miller	Bibbs, John T.	Oct. 25, 1822	Balto.
	Milly	19	William and Mary	King, Gideon T.	Oct. 9, 1821	Balto.
	Mima	22	Alfred	Woolfolk, Austin	Jan. 18, 1825	Balto.
	Mima	46	Georgia	Brent, Robert J.	Dec. 23, 1844	Balto.
	Mima	40	Hortensia	Woolfolk, Austin	Dec. 14, 1836	Balto.
	Mima	20	Intelligence	Plater, John R. Jr.	Apr. 12, 1823	St. Mary's
	Mimi	23	P. Soule	Biscoe, James	Oct. 9, 1845	Balto.
	Mint	5	Orbit	Chabert, Leon	Apr. 16, 1825	Balto.
	Minta	35	Ajax	Allain	Oct.3, 1833	Balto.
	Minta	25	Aurilla	Warfield, Charles	Apr. 26, 1822	Balto.
	Minta	11	Bourne	Chaille, W.H.	Oct. 15, 1832	Balto.
	Minta	15	Lady Monroe	Chabert, Leon	Sept. 29, 1825	Balto.
	Minta	22	Lady Monroe	Wasmerr, J.E.	Sept. 29, 1825	Balto.
	Minta	7	Palestine	Slater, Hope Hull	Nov. 16, 1835	Balto.
	Minta Elizabeth	4	Charles	Campbell, Bernard M.	Dec. 18, 1850	Balto.
	Mintey	20	Hyperion	King, Gideon T.	Nov. 12, 1821	Balto.
	Minty	35	Eros	Armitage, James	June 29, 1822	Balto.
	Minty	43	Forester	Garland, Rice	May 26, 1836	Balto.

Surname	First Name	Age	Ship	O/S	Date	Depart
	Minty	18	General Hand	Poindexter, George L.	June 1, 1832	Balto.
	Minty	9 mon.	Georgia	Brent, Robert J.	Dec. 23, 1844	Balto.
	Minty	23	Good Hope	Woolfolk, Austin	Nov. 16, 1821	Balto.
	Minty	18	Hibernia	Chabert, Leon	Dec. 5, 1826	Balto.
	Minty	40	Lapwing	Spraggins, Samuel M.	March 22, 1822	Balto.
	Minty	22	Mars	Woolfolk, Joseph B.	Oct. 30, 1824	Balto.
	Minty	11	Superb	Lavelle, John F.	Apr. 7, 1819	Balto.
	Minty	16	Topaz	Woolfolk, Austin	Apr. 20, 1829	Balto.
	Mirabelle	55	Agent	Condin, Lewis	June 8, 1821	Balto.
	Miranda	21	Henry A. Barling	Campbell, Bernard M.	Dec. 18, 1851	Balto.
	Miranda	10	Susan Miller	Woolfolk, Samuel M.	Oct. 25, 1822	Balto.
	Mitchel	35	Charles	Wright, Thomas	Apr. 30, 1820	Balto.
	Mitchell	14	States	Kelso, George G.	March 8, 1826	Balto.
	Molly	20	Pilgrim	Carr, S.J.	Dec. 22, 1834	Balto.
	Montgomery	12	Serene	Archer, James	Oct. 19, 1836	Balto.
	Morris	30	Betsey	Woolfolk, Austin	Apr. 29, 1828	Balto.
	Moses	4	Arctic	Kelso, George G.	Nov. 15, 1826	Balto.
	Moses	24	Balloon	Milligan, George	Dec. 17, 1821	Balto.
	Moses	22	Budget	Spraggins, Samuel M.	Nov. 27, 1821	Balto.
	Moses	23	Eagle	Bond, Joshua B.	Oct. 29, 1828	Balto.
	Moses	1	Emilie	Anderson, David	Jan. 5, 1819	Balto.
	Moses	18	Eros	Anderson, David	June 29, 1822	Balto.
	Moses	1	Harriet	Carroll, Charles	Dec. 7, 1836	Balto.
	Moses	22	Harriett	Woolfolk, Richard T.	March 6, 1823	Balto.
	Moses	25	Intelligence	Woolfolk, Austin	Apr. 5, 1823	Balto.
	Moses	35	Intelligence	Woolfolk, Austin	Dec. 20, 1822	Balto.

Surname	First Name	Age	Ship	O/S	Date	Depart
	Moses	19	Mechanic	Woolfolk, Austin	Jan. 1, 1831	Balto.
	Moses	20	Mechanic	Woolfolk, Austin	Jan. 1, 1831	Balto.
	Moses	14	Merrmack	Kelso, George G.	Nov. 2, 1831	Balto.
	Moses	20	Missouri	Thompson, Henry	March 2, 1819	Balto.
	Moses	17	Orbit	Woolfolk, Joseph B.	Apr. 16, 1825	Balto.
	Moses	23	Russell	Woolfolk, Austin	Feb. 27, 1839	Balto.
	Moses	24	Signet	Woolfolk, Austin	Nov. 12, 1831	Balto.
	Moses	31	Splendid	Kelly, John P.	Apr. 24, 1841	Balto.
	Moses	4	States	Woolfolk, Austin	March 8, 1826	Balto.
	Moses	25	Superb	Donovan, Joseph S.	Nov. 2, 1843	Balto.
	Murry	12	Merrimack	Kelso, George G.	Nov. 2, 1831	Balto.
	Nace	42	Arctic	Hall, Joshua F.	Sept. 29, 1827	Balto.
	Nace	19	Budget	Spraggins, Samuel M.	Nov. 27, 1821	Balto.
	Nace	29	Henry Clay	Camphor, Henry	Dec. 8, 1828	Nottingham
	Nace	27	Lapwing	Spraggins, Samuel M.	March 22, 1822	Balto.
	Nacey	14	Henry Clay	Chew, Worthington	Dec. 8, 1828	Nottingham
	Nacky	20	Robert Reade	Woolfolk, Austin	Feb. 28, 1824	Balto.
	Nancy	15	Alfred	Davison, george	Jan. 18, 1825	Balto.
	Nancy	17	Alonzo	White, Philip	Nov. 8, 1822	Balto.
	Nancy	23	Arctic	Smith, Leonard J.	Jan. 29, 1828	St. Mary's
	Nancy	14	Aurilia	Warfield, Charles	Apr. 26, 1822	Balto.
	Nancy	10	Balloon	Penieres, Emile	Dec. 22, 1821	Balto.
	Nancy	32	Balloon	Zacherie, James W.	Dec. 22, 1821	Balto.
	Nancy	12	Brunswick	Woolfolk, Austin	Oct. 12, 1831	Balto.
	Nancy	8	Chatsworth	Anderson, David	Jan. 3, 1821	Balto.
	Nancy	16	Dumphries	Lee, Richard H.	Sept. 25, 1828	Balto.

Surname	First Name	Age	Ship	O/S	Date	Depart
	Nancy	14	Eagle	Sterett, Harrison	Oct. 28, 1828	Balto.
	Nancy	27	Edward Everett	Bowser, Gassaway	Oct. 17, 1851	Balto.
	Nancy	22	Emilie	Anderson, David	Jan. 5, 1819	Balto.
	Nancy	21	Eros	Oldham, George W.	June 29, 1822	Balto.
	Nancy	4	Franklin	Somerville, Henry	Nov. 27, 1819	Balto.
	Nancy	9 mon.	Gulnare	Pitts, Thomas H.	Nov. 5, 1830	Balto.
	Nancy	65	Gulnare	Pitts, Thomas H.	Nov. 5, 1830	Balto.
	Nancy	1	Harriet	Carroll, Charles	Dec. 7, 1836	Balto.
	Nancy	39	Harriet	Carroll, Charles	Dec. 7, 1836	Balto.
	Nancy	6	Harriett	Pierce, Levi	Oct. 29, 1822	Balto.
	Nancy		Helen A. Miller	Campbell, Bernard M.	Oct. 18, 1852	Nottingham
	Nancy	3	Henry Clay	Bower, Thomas F.	Dec. 8, 1828	Balto.
	Nancy	30	Hibernia	Chabert, Leon	Dec. 5, 1826	Balto.
	Nancy	22	Hyperion	Anderson, David	May 14, 1822	Balto.
	Nancy	34	Isabella	Wallis, Cornelius C.	Nov. 26, 1834	Balto.
	Nancy	10	Kirkwood	Guyther, John	Dec. 10, 1846	Balto.
	Nancy	14	Lady Monroe	Woolfolk, Joseph B.	March 25, 1825	Balto.
	Nancy	19	Lady Monroe	Chabert, Leon	Sept. 29, 1825	Balto.
	Nancy	2 mon.	Lapwing	Woolfolk, Austin	Feb. 15, 1827	Balto.
	Nancy	26	Margaret Hugg	Campbell, Bernard M.	Feb. 8, 1845	Balto.
	Nancy	22	Mechanic	Woolfolk, Austin	Jan. 1, 1831	Balto.
	Nancy	11	Missouri	Marrash, John	March 1, 1819	Balto.
	Nancy	22	Orbit	Chabert, Leon	Apr. 16, 1825	Balto.
	Nancy	14	Shepderdiss	Williams, Joseph C.	March 27, 1827	Balto.
	Nancy	20	States	Woolfolk, Austin	March 8, 1826	Balto.
	Nancy	9 mon.	Virginia	Woolfolk, Joseph B.	Dec. 19, 1825	Balto.

Surname	First Name	Age	Ship	O/S	Date	Depart
	Nancy	17	Virginia	Woolfolk, Joseph B.	Dec. 19, 1825	Balto.
	Nanny	35	Franklin	Somerville, Henry	Nov. 27, 1819	Balto.
	Nat	21	Franklin	Somerville, Henry	Nov. 27, 1819	Balto.
	Nat	22	Lawrence	Woolfolk, Austin	May 9, 1823	Balto.
	Nat	26	Lawrence	Woolfolk, Austin	May 9, 1823	Balto.
	Nat	8	Mars	Woolfolk, Austin	Nov. 1, 1824	Balto.
	Nat	48	Mars	Woolfolk, Austin	Nov. 1, 1824	Balto.
	Nat	19	North America	Woolfolk, Austin	Nov. 23, 1822	Annapolis
	Nat	15	Trafalgar	Dent, Wilfred	Jan. 13, 1827	Balto.
	Nat	17	Unicorn	McNeal, Catherine	Oct. 23, 1820	Balto.
	Nathan	27	Aurilla	Woolfolk, Austin	Apr. 26, 1822	Balto.
	Nathan	22	Gulnare	Kelso. George G.	Nov. 3, 1830	Nottingham
	Nathan	26	Henry Clay	Ghyelzr, Robert	Dec. 8, 1828	Balto.
	Nathan	24	Hope	Richardson, Wade H.	Dec. 3, 1833	Balto.
	Nathan	20	Lady Monroe	Chabert, Leon	Sept. 29, 1825	Balto.
	Nathan	20	Lady Monroe	Wascherr, J.E.	Sept. 29, 1825	Balto.
	Nathan	28	Lapwing	Spraggins, Samuel M.	March 22, 1822	Balto.
	Nathan	14	Mars	Woolfolk, Austin	Oct. 30, 1824	Balto.
	Nathan	20	Mars	Woolfolk, Austin	Oct. 30, 1824	Balto.
	Nathan	25	Robert Reade	Woolfolk, Austin	Feb. 28, 1824	Balto.
	Nathan	35	Serere	Archer, James	Oct. 19, 1836	Balto.
	Nathan	21	States	Woolfolk, Austin	March 8, 1826	Balto.
	Nathan	21	Alfred	Woolfolk, Austin	Jan. 18, 1825	Balto.
	Natt	24	Merrimack	Kelsc, George G.	Nov. 2, 1831	Balto.
	Neal	31	Arctic	Madcox, Thomas H.	Jan. 30, 1829	St. Mary's
	Neatty	22	Alfred	Woolfolk, Austin	Jan. 18, 1825	Balto.
	Ned					

Surname	First Name	Age	Ship	O/S	Date	Depart
	Ned	16	Alfred	Woolfolk, Joseph B.	May 7, 1825	Balto.
	Ned	12	Alonzo	Oldham, George W.	Nov. 7, 1822	Balto.
	Ned	14	Arctic	Cliffe, Henry	Oct. 4, 1828	Balto.
	Ned	3	Franklin	Anderson, David	Nov. 27, 1819	Balto.
	Ned	11	Gulnare	Kelso, George G.	Nov. 3, 1830	Balto.
	Ned	4	Hermann	Rowe, Ralph	June 21, 1851	Balto.
	Ned	21	Intelligence	Woolfolk, Austin	Apr. 5, 1823	Balto.
	Ned	23	Intelligence	Woolfolk, Austin	Apr. 5, 1823	Balto.
	Ned	16	Kenhawa	Maddox, Thomas H.	Oct. 26, 1832	Balto.
	Ned	23	Lapwing	Hall, Francis	March 22, 1822	Balto.
	Ned	23	Mars	Woolfolk, Austin	Oct. 30, 1824	Balto.
	Ned	34	Missouri	Little, Moses	March 2, 1819	Balto.
	Ned	13	North America	Woolfolk, Austin	Nov. 23, 1822	Balto.
	Ned	19	North America	Woolfolk, Austin	Oct. 14, 1823	Balto.
	Ned	22	Palestine	Slatter, Hope Hull	Nov. 16, 1835	Balto.
	Ned	12	Shamrock	Guyton, Elisha	March 13, 1840	Balto.
	Neddy	14	Georgia	Brent, Robert J.	Dec. 23, 1844	Balto.
	Neice	20	General Hand	Poindexter, George L.	June 1, 1832	Balto.
	Nell	13	Balloon	Knight, William	Dec. 22, 1821	Balto.
	Nell	22	Budget	Spraggins, Samuel M.	Nov. 27, 1821	Balto.
	Nell	20	Henry Clay	Chew, Worhtington	Dec. 8, 1828	Nottingham
	Nelly	23	Aurilla	Woolfolk, Austin	Apr. 26, 1822	Balto.
	Nelly	14	Emilie	Anderson, David	Jan. 5, 1819	Balto.
	Nelly	15	Emilie	Anderson, David	Jan. 5, 1819	Balto.
	Nelly	20	Eros	Anderson, David	June 29, 1822	Balto.
	Nelly	35	Georgia	Brent, Robert J.	Dec. 23, 1844	Balto.

Surname	First Name	Age	Ship	O/S	Date	Depart
	Nelly	24	Harriett	Woolfolk, Richard T.	March 6, 1823	Balto.
	Nelly	16	Henry Clay	Bower, Thomas F.	Dec. 8, 1828	Nottingham
	Nelly	10	Intelligence	Anderson, David	Dec. 20, 1822	Balto.
	Nelly	18	Intelligence	Somerville, Alexander	Dec. 20, 1822	Balto.
	Nelly	30	States	Woolfolk, Austin	Nov. 26, 1825	Balto.
	Nelly	28	Susan Miller	Woolfolk, Austin	Oct. 25, 1822	Balto.
	Nelly	50	Susan Miller	Woolfolk, Samuel M.	Oct. 25, 1822	Balto.
	Nelly	4	Tippecanoe	Murray, Michael	Oct. 16, 1841	Balto.
	Nelson	20	Caspien	Woolfolk, Austin	Nov. 26, 1836	Balto.
	Nelson	22	Caspien	Woolfolk, Austin	Nov. 26, 1836	Balto.
	Nelson	17	Copia	Blow, Richard	Dec. 27, 1838	Balto.
	Nelson	15	Elizabeth	Campbell, Bernard M.	Nov. 18, 1848	Balto.
	Nelson	20	Henry Clay	Dorset, William N.	Dec. 8, 1828	Nottingham
	Nelson	2	Opelousas	Garlard, Rice	July 5, 1836	Balto.
	Nelson		Plutarch	Mosse, Henry	Sept. 17, 1834	Balto.
	Nero	3	Arctic	Kelso, George G.	Nov. 15, 1826	Balto.
	Netty	35	Orbit	Chabert, Leon	Apr. 16, 1825	Balto.
	Nic	19	Catharine	Woolfolk, Austin	Jan. 15, 1831	Balto.
	Nicholas	4	Lady Monroe	Woolfolk, Austin	March 25, 1825	Balto.
	Nicholas	1	Lafayette	Slatter, Hope Hull	March 25, 1843	Balto.
	Nick	25	Arctic	Smith Leonard J.	Jan. 29, 1828	St. Mary's
	Nick	19	Mechanic	Woolfolk, Austin	Jan. 1, 1831	Balto.
	Nick	24	North America	Woolfolk, Austin	Nov. 23, 1822	Balto.
	Nickolas	23	Phoenix	Donovan, Joseph S.	March 27, 1847	Balto.
	Nicky	18	Betsey	Woolfolk, Austin	Apr. 29, 1828	Balto.
	Nicy	24	Mechanic	Woolfolk, Austin	Jan. 1, 1831	Balto.

Surname	First Name	Age	Ship	O/S	Date	Depart
	Noah	21	Bourne	Cottman, James S.	Apr. 6, 1833	Balto.
	Noble	6	Arctic	Kelso, George G.	Nov. 15, 1826	Balto.
	Octavius	2	Union	Campbell, Bernard M.	Dec. 16, 1848	Balto.
	Oliver	5	Hibernia	Chabert, Leon	Dec. 5, 1826	Balto.
	Oliver	9	Intelligence	Wallace, Joseph A.	Apr. 27, 1821	Balto.
	Oliver	18	Intelligence	Anderson, David	Nov. 3, 1820	Balto.
	Oliver	4	Solomon Saltus	Slatter, Hope Hull	Oct. 7, 1839	Balto.
	Oliver	29	States	Woodland, James	March 7, 1826	Balto.
	Olivia	3	Arctic	Maddox, Thomas H.	Jan. 30, 1829	St. Mary's
	Olla	14	Lady Monroe	Wascher, J.E.	Sept. 29, 1825	Balto.
	Ozwald	11	Trafalgar	Dent, Wilfred	Jan. 13, 1827	Annapolis
	Pack	22	Merrimack	Kelso, George G.	Nov. 2, 1831	Balto.
	Page	17	Susan Miller	Woolfolk, Samuel M.	Oct. 25, 1822	Balto.
	Pallace	26	Lafayette	Woolfolk, Richard	Oct. 18, 1828	Balto.
	Palmer	11	Victorine	Campbell, Bernard M.	March 1, 1845	Balto.
	Paris	19	Clio	Starnsburg, William	March 22, 1819	Balto.
	Parker	18	Henry Clay	Dorsett, William N.	Dec. 8, 1828	Nottingham
	Parker	9	North America	Woolfolk, Austin	Dec. 20, 1824	Balto.
	Parmela	15	Lapwing	Spraggins, Samuel M.	March 22, 1822	Balto.
	Passote	42	Orion	Clery, M.A.	Dec. 30, 1822	Balto.
	Pat		Balloon	Milligan, George	Dec. 17, 1821	Balto.
	Pat	23	Henry Clay	Chew, Worhtington	Dec. 8, 1828	Nottingham
	Pat	13	Intelligence	Coleman, Henry E.	Nov. 4, 1820	Balto.
	Patience	17	Balloon	Penieres, Emile	Dec. 22, 1821	Balto.
	Patience	22	Eros	Woolfolk, Austin	Jan. 28, 1824	Balto.
	Patience	12	Eros	Anderson, David	June 29, 1822	Balto.

Surname	First Name	Age	Ship	O/S	Date	Depart
	Patience	10	Henry Clay	Chew, Worthington	Dec. 8, 1828	Nottingham
	Patience	21	Virginia	Woolfolk, Joseph B.	Dec. 19, 1825	Balto.
	Patrick	38	Arctic	Smith, Leonard J.	Jan. 29, 1828	St. Mary's
	Patrick	11	Elizabeth	Campbell, Bernard M.	Nov. 18, 1848	Balto.
	Patrick	16	Harriet	Carroll, Charles	Dec. 7, 1836	Balto.
	Patrick	14	Shepderdiss	Williams, Joseph C.	March 27, 1827	Balto.
	Patsey	28	Arctic	McCornell, Alex	Sept. 29, 1827	Balto.
	Patsy	19	Susan Miller	Woolfolk, Austin	Oct. 25, 1822	Balto.
	Patty	17	Hamlet	Woolfolk, Austin	Apr. 7, 1824	Balto.
	Patty	15	Hope	Purnel, Thomas R.	Dec. 3, 1833	Balto.
	Patty	24	Hope	Byrne, Walter	Dec. 5, 1833	Balto.
	Patty	27	Lapwing	Woolfolk, Samuel M.	Feb. 15, 1827	Balto.
	Patty	32	Missouri	Cook, James K.	March 2, 1819	Balto.
	Patty	18	North America	Woolfolk, Austin	Nov. 23, 1822	Balto.
	Patty	17	States	Woolfolk, Austin	March 8, 1826	Balto.
	Patty Ellen	6 mon.	Balloon	Zacharie, James W.	Dec. 22, 1821	Balto.
	Paul	6	Emilie	Ponce, Louis	May 20, 1820	Balto.
	Paul	39	Leda	Nelson, James	Nov. 16, 1848	Balto.
	Paul	13	Missouri	Gilmore, John	March 1, 1819	Balto.
	Pauline	26	General Pinckney	Duffel, H.L.	Nov. 8, 1845	Balto.
	Peggy	28	Arctic	Magee, Eugene	Oct. 9, 1828	Annapolis
	Peggy	15	Aurilla	Woolfolk, Austin	Apr. 26, 1822	Balto.
	Peggy	18	Balloon	Penieres, Emile	Dec. 22, 1821	Balto.
	Peggy	17	Commodore Patterso	Thompson, Henry	March 20, 1819	Balto.
	Peggy	28	Good Hope	Woolfolk, Austin	Nov. 16, 1821	Balto.
	Peggy	28	Good Hope	Woolfolk, Samuel M.	Nov. 21, 1821	Balto.

Surname	First Name	Age	Ship	O/S	Date	Depart
	Penny	5	Leda	Brown, J.L.	Oct. 1, 1846	Balto.
	Perry	10	Alfred	Woolfolk, Austin	May 7, 1825	Balto.
	Perry	1	Aurilla	Chabert, Leon	Apr. 26, 1822	Balto.
	Perry	14	Aurilla	Warfield, Charles	Apr. 26, 1822	Balto.
	Perry	19	Balloon	Penieres, Emile	Dec. 22, 1821	Balto.
	Perry	22	Emilie	Anderson, David	Jan. 5, 1819	Balto.
	Perry	20	Eros	Woolfolk, Austin	Jan. 28, 1824	Balto.
	Perry	2	Franklin	Somerville, Henry	Nov. 27, 1819	Balto.
	Perry	22	Harriett	Woolfolk, Austin	March 23, 1822	Balto.
	Perry	19	Harriett	Woolfolk, Richard T.	March 6, 1823	Balto.
	Perry	13	Hibernia	Woolfolk, Austin	Dec. 5, 1826	Balto.
	Perry	25	Hope	Byrne, Walter	Dec. 5, 1833	St. Mary's
	Perry	6	Intelligence	Plater, John R. Jr.	Apr. 12, 1823	Balto.
	Perry	3	Lady Monroe	Chabert, Leon	Sept. 29, 1825	Balto.
	Perry	3	Lady Monroe	Chabert, Leon	Sept. 29, 1825	Balto.
	Perry	5	Leda	Brown, J.L.	Oct. 1, 1846	Balto.
	Perry	20	Mechanic	Woolfolk, Austin	Jan. 1, 1831	Balto.
	Perry	15	North America	Chabert, Leon	Apr. 24, 1826	Balto.
	Perry	22	North America	Chabert, Leon	Apr. 24, 1826	Balto.
	Perry	9	Orion	Oldham, George W.	Dec. 30, 1822	Balto.
	Perry	6	Palestine	Slatter, Hope Hull	Nov. 16, 1835	Balto.
	Perry	24	Sarah Ann	Keene, Wallace	Oct. 14, 1836	Balto.
	Perry	40	Sarah Ann	Keene, Wallace	Oct. 14, 1836	Balto.
	Perry	18	Signet	Woolfolk, Austin	Nov. 12, 1831	Balto.
	Perry	29	States	Woodland, James	March 7, 1826	Balto.
	Perry	24	States	Woolfolk, Austin	March 8, 1826	Balto.

Surname	First Name	Age	Ship	O/S	Date	Depart
	Perry	17	States	Tillotson, Giles	Nov. 22, 1827	Balto.
	Perry	23	Virginia	Woolfolk, Austin	Nov. 18, 1823	Balto.
	Peter	22	Agent	Anderson, David	June 8, 1821	Balto.
	Peter	36	Algerine	Robbins, Daniel G.	March 25, 1826	Balto.
	Peter	13	Aurilla	Warfield, Charles	Apr. 26, 1822	Balto.
	Peter	16	Aurilla	Wikoff, Stephen A.	Apr. 26, 1822	Balto.
	Peter	21	Aurilla	Woolfolk, Austin	Apr. 26, 1822	Balto.
	Peter	10	Balloon	Zacharie, James W.	Dec. 22, 1821	Balto.
	Peter	10	Bourne	Handy, Samuel	Oct. 13, 1832	Balto.
	Peter	26	Budget	Spraggins, Samuel M.	Nov. 27, 1821	Balto.
	Peter	23	Clio	Coleman, Daniel J.	March 20, 1819	Balto.
	Peter	25	Commodore Patterso	Thompson, Henry	March 20, 1819	Balto.
	Peter	31	Dumphries	Lee, Richard H.	Sept. 25, 1828	Balto.
	Peter	25	Eros	Anderson, David	June 29, 1822	Balto.
	Peter	17	Eros	Armitage, James	June 29, 1822	Balto.
	Peter	33	Georgia	Brent, Robert J.	Dec. 21, 1844	Balto.
	Peter	30	Good Hope	Woolfolk, Richard T.	Nov. 21, 1821	Balto.
	Peter	22	Hibernia	Chaber, Leon	Dec. 5, 1826	Balto.
	Peter	40	Intelligence	Anderson, David	Dec. 20, 1822	Balto.
	Peter	32	Intelligence	Coalman, Henry E.	March 14, 1820	Balto.
	Peter	21	Lady Monroe	Woolfolk, Joseph B.	March 25, 1825	Balto.
	Peter	23	Lapwing	King, Gideon T.	March 22, 1822	Balto.
	Peter	45	Lapwing	Spraggins, Samuel M.	March 22, 1822	Balto.
	Peter	20	Mars	Woolfolk, Joseph B.	Oct. 30, 1824	Balto.
	Peter	12	Palestine	Slatter, Hope Hull	Nov. 16, 1835	Balto.
	Peter	30	Patriot	White, Charles	July 14, 1836	Balto.

Surname	First Name	Age	Ship	O/S	Date	Depart
	Peter	11	Pilgrim	Williams, George W.	Dec. 22, 1834	Balto.
	Peter	9	Shepderdiss	Williams, Joseph C.	March 27, 1827	Balto.
	Peter	27	Susan Miller	Woolfolk, Austin	Oct. 25, 1822	Balto.
	Peter	37	William and Mary	Crawford, Alexander	Oct. 9, 1821	Balto.
	Peter	26	William and Mary	Dessin, Nicholas	Oct. 9, 1821	Balto.
	Peyton	22	Henry A. barling	Campbell, Walter L.	Aug. 11, 1849	Balto.
	Phebe	22	Ajax	Richardson, Wade H.	Oct.3, 1833	Balto.
	Pheebe	17	Missouri	Gilmore, John	March 1, 1819	Balto.
	Phil	12	Agent	Anderson, David	June 8, 1821	Balto.
	Phil	12	Balloon	Zacharie, James W.	Dec. 22, 1821	Balto.
	Phil	30	Balloon	Zacharie, James W.	Dec. 22, 1821	Balto.
	Phil	9	Budget	Spraggins, Samuel M.	Nov. 27, 1821	Balto.
	Phil	23	Emilie	Stansbury, Charles	Nov. 27, 1819	Balto.
	Phil	29	Franklin	Somerville, Henry	Nov. 27, 1819	Balto.
	Phil	22	Hyperion	King, Gideon T.	Nov. 12, 1821	Balto.
	Phil	22	Hyperion	Lee, Thomas	Nov. 9, 1821	Balto.
	Phil	18	Triton	Anderson, David	Dec. 20, 1819	Balto.
	Philip	30	Agent	Anderson, David	June 8, 1821	Balto.
	Philip	18	Alonzo	White, Philip	Nov. 8, 1822	Balto.
	Philip	15	Aurilla	Warfield, Charles	Apr. 26, 1822	Balto.
	Philip	8	Balloon	Milligan, George	Dec. 17, 1821	Balto.
	Philip	10	Harriett	King, John	March 23, 1822	Balto.
	Philip	22	Harriett	Woolfolk, Austin	March 23, 1822	Balto.
	Philip	14	Kirkwood	Campbell, Bernard M.	Oct. 16, 1845	Balto.
	Philip	23	Lady Monroe	Wascherr, J.E.	Sept. 29, 1825	Balto.
	Philip	26	Lady Monroe	Wascherr, J.E.	Sept. 29, 1825	Balto.

Surname	First Name	Age	Ship	O/S	Date	Depart
	Philip	28	Lapwing	Spraggins, Samuel M.	March 22, 1822	Balto.
	Philip	18	Mechanic	Woolfolk, Austin	Jan. 1, 1831	Balto.
	Philip	31	North America	Thurman, William C.	Apr. 24, 1826	Balto.
	Philip	27	States	Woolfolk, Austin	Nov. 21, 1827	Balto.
	Philip	24	Temperance	Woolfolk, Austin	Dec. 9, 1818	Balto.
	Philip	20	William and Mary	Colemar, Aquila C.	Oct. 9, 1821	Balto.
	Phill	50	Ajax	Richardson, Wade H.	Oct.3, 1833	Balto.
	Phill	15	Budget	Spraggins, Samuel M.	Nov. 27, 1821	Balto.
	Phill	22	Hibernia	Chabert, Leon	Dec. 5, 1826	Balto.
	Phill	6	Hibernia	Woolfolk, Austin	Dec. 5, 1826	Balto.
	Phill	18	Hibernia	Woolfolk, Austin	Dec. 5, 1826	Balto.
	Phill	22	Isabella		Nov. 26, 1834	Balto.
	Phill	4	Lady Monroe	Woolfolk, Austin	Sept. 29, 1825	Balto.
	Phill	24	Mars	Woolfolk, Austin	Oct. 30, 1824	Balto.
	Phill	19	Merrimack	Kelso, George G.	Nov. 2, 1831	Balto.
	Phillip	27	Dumphries	Lee, Richard H.	Sept. 25, 1828	Balto.
	Phillip	25	Lafayette	Slatter, Hope Hull	March 25, 1843	Balto.
	Phillip		Zoe	Donovan, Joseph S.	Feb. 16, 1847	Balto.
	Phillis	20	Algerine	Woolfolk, Austin	March 25, 1826	Balto.
	Phillis	24	Ballocn	Peniers, Emile	Dec. 22, 1821	Balto.
	Phillis	18	Catharine	Woolfolk, Austin	March 3. 1829	Balto.
	Phillis	16	Emilie	Mercer, William D.	March 27, 1821	Balto.
	Phillis	5	Georgia	Brent, Robert J.	Dec. 23, 1844	Balto.
	Phillis	21	Good Hope	Woolfolk, Samuel M.	Nov. 21, 1821	Balto.
	Phillis	12	Hamlet	Stansbury, Hammond N.	Apr. 7, 1824	Balto.
	Phillis	28	Hibernia	Kelso, John M.	Dec. 5, 1826	Balto.

Surname	First Name	Age	Ship	O/S	Date	Depart
	Phillis	27	Home	Campbell, Bernard M.	March 22, 1845	Balto.
	Phillis	25	Intelligence	Woolfolk, Austin	Apr. 5, 1823	Balto.
	Phillis	25	Intelligence	Somerville, Alexander	Dec. 20, 1822	Balto.
	Phillis	6	Pilgrim	Carr, S.J.	Dec. 22, 1834	Balto.
	Phillis	16	States	Woolfolk, Joseph B.	Nov. 21, 1827	Balto.
	Phillis	33	Virginia	Woolfolk, Joseph B.	Dec. 19, 1825	Balto.
	Phobe	7	Arctic	Bond, Francis A.	May 15, 1828	Balto.
	Phoebe	14	Hibernia	Chabert, Leon	Dec. 5, 1826	Balto.
	Phoebe	25	Intelligence	King, Gideon T.	Sept. 18, 1821	Balto.
	Phoebe	19	Lion	Higlehart, Thomas	March 21, 1835	Balto.
	Phoebe	38	Tippecanoe	Connally, Pierce	Sept. 4, 1843	Balto.
	Phoeby	19	Caspian	Woolfolk, Austin	Nov. 26, 1836	Balto.
	Pina	10 mon.	North America	Chabert, Leon	Apr. 24, 1826	Balto.
	Pinkney	17	Susan Miller	Woolfolk, Austin	Oct. 25, 1822	Balto.
	Pippin	16	Arctic	Bond, Francis A.	May 15, 1828	Balto.
	Poe	22	Merrimack	Kelso, George G.	Nov. 2, 1831	Balto.
	Polly	4 mon.	Chatsworth	Anderson, David	Jan. 3, 1821	Balto.
	Polly	22	Chatsworth	Anderson, David	Jan. 3, 1821	Balto.
	Polly	30	Clio	Starnsburg, William	March 22, 1819	Balto.
	Polly	12	Dumphries	Lee, Richard H.	Sept. 25, 1828	Balto.
	Polly	18	General Hand	Poindexter, George L.	June 1, 1832	Balto.
	Polly	11	Mary Broughton	Chaplain, J. Bond	Nov. 18, 1851	Balto.
	Polly	15	Susan Miller	Woolfolk, Richard T.	Oct. 25, 1822	Balto.
	Polydore	18	Unicorn	Wedenstrandt, John C.	Oct. 23, 1820	Balto.
	Pompey	35	George Ross	Elder, Frances W.	June 18, 1847	Balto.
	Pondore	23	Mars	Woolfolk, Austin	Oct. 30, 1824	Balto.

Surname	First Name	Age	Ship	O/S	Date	Depart
	Precilia Ann	8	Union	Sheckles, B.O.	Nov. 17, 1849	Balto.
	Pricilla	infant	Strafford	Wilson, Thomas C.	Nov. 21, 1843	Balto.
	Primus	14	States	Woolfolk, Austin	March 8, 1826	Balto.
	Prince	17	Henry Clay	Bower, Thomas F.	Dec. 8, 1828	Nottingham
	Prince	15	Lapwing	Robbins, Daniel G.	March 22, 1822	Balto.
	Priscilla	9	Arctic	Magee, Eugene	Oct. 9, 1828	Annapolis
	Priscilla	27	Emilie	Ferguson, Thomas	Dec. 14, 1821	Balto.
	Priscilla	17	Henry Clay	Bower, Thomas F.	Dec. 8, 1828	Nottingham
	Priscilla	4 mon.	Henry Clay	Chew, Worthington	Dec. 8, 1828	Nottingham
	Priscilla	11	Henry Clay	Chew, Worhtington	Dec. 8, 1828	Nottingham
	Priscilla	23	Julia	Woolfolk, Austin	Jan. 8, 1829	Balto.
	Priscilla	19	North America	Woolfolk, Austin	Dec. 20, 1824	Balto.
	Priscilla	2	Sarah	Winter Gabriel	Sept. 8, 1831	Balto.
	Priscilla	45	Scotia	Woolfolk, Austin	Sept. 30, 1843	Balto.
	Priscilla	40	Statira	Smith, Doctor James	March 28, 1826	Balto.
	Priscilla	9	Zoe	Slatter, Hope Hull	Feb. 16, 1847	Balto.
	Prisilla	19	Aurilla	Wikoff, Stephen A.	Apr. 26, 1822	Balto.
	Prissey	14	Good Hope	Woolfolk, Austin	Nov. 16, 1821	Balto.
	Prissy	23	Harriett	Woolfolk, Austin	March 23, 1822	Balto.
	Prissy	3	States	Tillotson, Giles	Nov. 22, 1827	Balto.
	Prudence	27	Intelligence	Plater, John R. Jr.	Apr. 12, 1823	St. Mary's
	Pryer	3	Hope	Byrne, Walter	Dec. 5, 1833	Balto.
	Purnell	30	Kirkwood	Guytan, Elisha	Dec. 10, 1846	Balto.
	Rachael	3	Balloon	Milligan, George	Dec. 17, 1821	Balto.
	Rachael	33	Baltimore	Hale, Colin F.	Oct. 31, 1835	Balto.
	Rachael	14	Caspian	Woolfolk, Austin	Nov. 26, 1836	Balto.

Surname	First Name	Age	Ship	O/S	Date	Depart
	Rachael	13	E.H.Chapin	Penn, Alexander	Nov. 30, 1847	Balto.
	Rachael	20	Emilie	Ferguson, Thomas	Dec. 14, 1821	Balto.
	Rachael	16	Emilie	Poncet, Louis	May 20, 1820	Balto.
	Rachael	18	Eros	Oldham, George W.	June 29, 1822	Balto.
	Rachael	52	Georgia	Brent, Robert J.	Dec. 21, 1844	Balto.
	Rachael	10	Georgia	Brent, Robert J.	Dec. 23, 1844	Balto.
	Rachael	22	Good Hope	Woolfolk, Austin	Nov. 16, 1821	Balto.
	Rachael	44	Harriet	Carroll, Charles	Dec. 7, 1836	Balto.
	Rachael	3 mon.	Hope	Byrne, Walter	Dec. 5, 1833	Balto.
	Rachael	15	Hope	Byrne, Walter	Dec. 5, 1833	Balto.
	Rachael	19	Hyperion	Dickey, Joseph	Nov. 12, 1821	Balto.
	Rachael	12	Intelligence	Anderson, David	March 14, 1820	Balto.
	Rachael	20	Kirkwood	Campbell, Bernard M.	Apr. 4, 1846	Balto.
	Rachael	5	Kirkwood	Campbell, Bernard M.	Jan. 4, 1845	Balto.
	Rachael	22	Palestine	Slatter, Hope Hull	Nov. 16, 1835	Balto.
	Rachael	40	Sarah Bridge	Campbell, Bernard M.	Feb. 8, 1851	Balto.
	Rachael	3	Serene	Archer, James	Oct. 19, 1836	Balto.
	Rachael	21	States	Woolfolk, Austin	March 8, 1826	Balto.
	Rachael	19	States	Kelso, George Y.	Nov. 25, 1825	Balto.
	Rachael	24	Temperance	Anderson, David	Dec. 9, 1818	Balto.
	Rachael	4	Ulysses	Richardson, Wade H.	Nov. 6, 1833	Balto.
	Rachael	20	Union	Campbell, Bernard M.	Oct. 9, 1848	Balto.
	Rachael Ann	15	Elizabeth	Campbell, Bernard M.	March 21, 1850	Balto.
	Rachael Ann	19	Union	Campbell, Bernard M.	Dec. 16, 1848	Balto.
	Rachel	14	Balloon	Penieres, Emile	Dec. 22, 1821	Balto.
	Rachel	16	Betsey	Woolfolk, Austin	Apr. 29, 1828	Balto.

Surname	First Name	Age	Ship	O/S	Date	Depart
	Rachel	11	Caledonia	Barnum, Richard	Oct. 19, 1842	Balto.
	Rachel	25	Charles	Carter, John A.	Sept. 29, 1849	Balto.
	Rachel	20	Clio	Crouch, William	March 20, 1819	Balto.
	Rachel	33	Dumphries	Lee, Richard H.	Sept. 25, 1828	Balto.
	Rachel	35	General Hand	Poindexter, George L.	June 1, 1832	Balto.
	Rachel	4	Good Hope	Woolfolk, Samuel M.	Nov. 21, 1821	Balto.
	Rachel	18	Hamlet	Woolfolk, Austin	Apr. 7, 1824	Balto.
	Rachel	7	Hibernia	Chaber, Leon	Dec. 5, 1826	Balto.
	Rachel	8	Hibernia	Chaber, Leon	Dec. 5, 1826	Balto.
	Rachel	28	Hibernia	Woolfolk, Austin	Dec. 5, 1826	Balto.
	Rachel	17	Hortensia	Woolfolk, Austin	Dec. 14, 1836	Balto.
	Rachel	18	Hyperion	Woolfolk, Austin	May 10, 1822	Balto.
	Rachel	6	Intelligence	Anderson, David	Dec. 20, 1822	Balto.
	Rachel	36	Intelligence	Anderson, David	Dec. 20, 1822	Balto.
	Rachel	8	Intelligence	Woolfolk, Austin	Dec. 20, 1822	Balto.
	Rachel	25	Intelligence	Woolfolk, Austin	Dec. 20, 1822	Balto.
	Rachel	8 mon.	Julia	Poindexter, George	Feb. 10, 1832	Balto.
	Rachel	24	Lady Monroe	Woolfolk, Joseph B.	March 25, 1825	Balto.
	Rachel	29	Lady Monroe	Chabert, Leon	Sept. 29, 1825	Balto.
	Rachel	4	Lapwing	Woolfolk, Samuel M.	Feb. 15, 1827	Balto.
	Rachel	37	Lapwing	Hall, Francis	March 22, 1822	Balto.
	Rachel	23	London	Palmer, J.W.	Nov. 5, 1840	Balto.
	Rachel	18	Mars	Woolfolk, Austin	Oct. 30, 1824	Balto.
	Rachel	32	North America	Thurman, William C.	Apr. 24, 1826	Balto.
	Rachel	16	North America	Woolfolk, Austin	Dec. 20, 1824	Balto.
	Rachel		Orion	Oldham, George W.	Dec. 30, 1822	Balto.

Surname	First Name	Age	Ship	O/S	Date	Depart
	Rachel	16	Pandora	Woolfolk, Austin	March 26, 1831	Balto.
	Rachel	10	Snow	Willis	Feb 5, 1835	Balto.
	Rachel	15	Superb	Donovan, Joseph S.	Nov. 2, 1843	Balto.
	Rachel	15	Unicorn	Wedenstrandt, John C.	Oct. 23, 1820	Balto.
	Rachel Ann	20	Billow	Woolfolk, Austin	Feb. 23, 1828	Balto.
	Rachel Jane	6	Hyperion	Lanahan, J.J.M.	Nov. 9, 1821	Balto.
	Rachell	40	Irad Ferry	Maddox, C.T.	Jan. 14, 1840	Balto.
	Ralph	5	Arctic	Smith, Leonard J.	Jan. 29, 1828	St. Mary's
	Ralph	5	Leda	Nelson, James	Nov. 16, 1848	Balto.
	Randal	6	Missouri	Cook, James K.	March 2, 1819	Balto.
	Randle	22	Mars	Woolfolk, Austin	Oct. 30, 1824	Balto.
	Randolph	5	Henry Clay	Chew, Worhtington	Dec. 8, 1828	Nottingham
	Randolph	6	P. Soule	Biscoe, James	Oct. 9, 1845	Balto.
	Raney	30	Lady Monroe	Chabert, Leon	Sept. 29, 1825	Balto.
	Rausby	4	Franklin	Somerville, Henry	Nov. 27, 1819	Balto.
	Raymond	14	North America	Woolfolk, Austin	Nov. 23, 1822	Balto.
	Reason	13	Intelligence	Anderson, David	March 14, 1820	Balto.
	Rebecca	3	Arctic	Smith, Leonard J.	Jan. 29, 1828	St. Mary's
	Rebecca	5	Aurilla	Chabert, Leon	Apr. 26, 1822	Balto.
	Rebecca	20	Eros	Woolfolk, Austin	Jan. 28, 1824	Balto.
	Rebecca	8	Henry Clay	Compton & Dorsett	Dec. 8, 1828	Nottingham
	Rebecca	6	Hermann	Rowe, Ralph	June 21, 1851	Balto.
	Rebecca	18	Intelligence	Somerville, Alexander	Dec. 20, 1822	Balto.
	Rebecca	18	Kirkwood	Donovan, Joseph S.	Sept. 28, 1846	Balto.
	Rebecca	16	Unicorn	Wedenstrandt, John C.	Oct. 23, 1820	Balto.
	Rebecca Ann	8	Liberator	Woolfolk, Austin	Nov. 12, 1828	Balto.

Surname	First Name	Age	Ship	O/S	Date	Depart
	Reizen	13	Intelligence	Anderson, David	Dec. 20, 1822	Balto.
	Resin	13	Alonzo	White, Philip	Nov. 8, 1822	Balto.
	Reuben		Good Hope	Woolfolk, Austin	Nov. 16, 1821	Balto.
	Reuben	24	States	Woolfolk, Austin	March 8, 1826	Balto.
	Rezin	23	Lapwing	Hall, Francis	March 22, 1822	Balto.
	Rhoda	10	Chatsworth	Anderson, David	Jan. 3, 1821	Balto.
	Rhoda	21	States	Woolfolk, Joseph B.	Nov. 21, 1827	Balto.
	Rhody	14 mon.	Henry Clay	Waring E.M.	Dec. 8, 1828	Nottingham
	Rice	16	Lapwing	Spraggins, Samuel M.	March 22, 1822	Balto.
	Richard	7	Alfred	Davidson, george	Jan. 18, 1825	Balto.
	Richard	16	Algerine	Woolfolk, Austin	March 25, 1826	Balto.
	Richard	2	Arctic	Kelso, George G.	Nov. 15, 1826	Balto.
	Richard	4 mon.	Arctic	Magee, Eugene	Oct. 9, 1828	Annapolis
	Richard	12	Aurilla	Warfield, Charles	Apr. 26, 1822	Balto.
	Richard	11	Balloon	Peniers, Emile	Dec. 22, 1821	Balto.
	Richard	14	Betsey	Woolfolk, Austin	Apr. 29, 1828	Balto.
	Richard	19	Budget	King, Gideon T.	Dec. 1, 1821	Balto.
	Richard	6	Eros	Armitage, James	June 29, 1822	Balto.
	Richard	25	Irad Ferry	Clendenin, A.	Jan. 16, 1840	Balto.
	Richard	17	Kirkwood	Wheeler, A.C.	July 19, 1845	Balto.
	Richard	20	Lady Monroe	Woolfolk, Joseph B.	March 25, 1825	Balto.
	Richard	7	Louisa	Donovan, Joseph S.	Oct. 9, 1847	Balto.
	Richard	16	Mars	Woolfolk, Austin	Nov. 1, 1824	Balto.
	Richard	3	Mars	Woolfolk, Austin	Oct. 30, 1824	Balto.
	Richard	35	Mars	Woolfolk, Austin	Oct. 30, 1824	Balto.
	Richard	14	Orion	Oldham, George W.	Dec. 30, 1822	Balto.

Surname	First Name	Age	Ship	O/S	Date	Depart
	Richard	3	P. Soule	Biscoe, James	Oct. 9, 1845	Balto.
	Richard		Signet	Woolfolk, Austin	Nov. 17, 1831	Balto.
	Richard		States	Woolfolk, Austin	March 8, 1826	Balto.
	Richard	25	Temperance	Wikoff, Steven W.	Dec. 12, 1818	Balto.
	Riley	25	Triton	Farrow, Nimrod	Dec. 18, 1819	Balto.
	Rob	23	Hope	Randolph, Isaac	March 25, 1834	Balto.
	Robert	20	Alfred	Woolfolk, Joseph B.	May 7, 1825	Annapolis
	Robert	25	Arctic	Magee, Eugene	Oct. 9, 1828	Balto.
	Robert	9	Arctic	Hall, Joshua F.	Sept. 29, 1827	Balto.
	Robert	2	Arctic	McConnell, Alex	Sept. 29, 1827	Balto.
	Robert	5	Betsey	Woolfolk, Austin	Apr. 29, 1828	Balto.
	Robert	19	Brunswick	Woolfolk, Austin	Oct. 11, 1831	Balto.
	Robert	14	Budget	Bradley, Robert	Nov. 26, 1821	Balto.
	Robert	21	Cumberland	Callahan, George W.	Oct. 7, 1836	Balto.
	Robert	17	Dryad	Williams, Joseph C.	Dec. 12, 1827	Balto.
	Robert	11	Elizabeth	Campbell, Bernard M.	Nov. 18, 1848	Balto.
	Robert	17	Hamlet	Woolfolk, Joseph B.	Apr. 7, 1824	Balto.
	Robert	25	Hope & Hannah	Williams, Joseph C.	Dec. 10, 1827	Balto.
	Robert	11	Hyperion	Dickey, Joseph	Nov. 12, 1821	Balto.
	Robert	12	Hyperion	Dickey, Joseph	Nov. 12, 1821	Balto.
	Robert	16	Intelligence	De Mapiere, Victor	Apr. 30, 1821	Balto.
	Robert	14	Kirkwood	Campbell, Bernard M.	March 23, 1844	Balto.
	Robert	3	Lafayette	Woolfolk, Richard	Oct. 18, 1828	Balto.
	Robert	33	Lapwing	Hall, Francis	March 22, 1822	Balto.
	Robert	28	Mary Broughton	Chaplain, J. Bond	Nov. 18, 1851	Balto.
	Robert	5	Mary Broughton	Chaplain, J. Bond	Nov. 18, 1851	Balto.
	Robert	18				

Surname	First Name	Age	Ship	O/S	Date	Depart
	Robert	15	Missouri	Marrash, John	March 1, 1819	Balto.
	Robert	33	Missouri	Cook, James K.	March 2, 1819	Balto.
	Robert	22	Missouri	Little, Moses	March 2, 1819	Balto.
	Robert	20	Nelson Clark	Tongue, Thomas R.	Nov. 20, 1835	Balto.
	Robert	2	Orion	Oldham, George W.	Dec. 30, 1822	Balto.
	Robert	5	Pilgrim	Carr, S.J.	Dec. 22, 1834	Balto.
	Robert	28	Pioneer	Stuart, William R.	July 20, 1848	Balto.
	Robert	9	Seaman	Hamilton, P.M.	March 25, 1839	Balto.
	Robert	24	States	Tillotson, Giles	Nov. 22, 1827	Balto.
	Robert	13	Statira	Smith, Doctor James	March 28, 1826	Balto.
	Robert	46	Statira	Smith, Doctor James	March 28, 1826	Balto.
	Robert	23	Susan Miller	Woolfolk, Richard T.	Oct. 25, 1822	Balto.
	Robert	33	Susan Miller	Woolfolk, Richard T.	Oct. 25, 1822	Balto.
	Robert	19	Virginia	Morton, George C.	Dec. 19, 1825	Balto.
	Robert	11	Virginia	Woolfolk, Joseph B.	Dec. 19, 1825	Balto.
	Robert	6 mon.	William and Mary	King, Gideon T.	Oct. 9, 1821	Balto.
	Robison	23	States	Morton, George C.	Nov. 26, 1825	Balto.
	Rody	15	Harriett	Woolfolk, Austin	March 23, 1822	Balto.
	Romulus	8	Catherine Jackson	Brent, George	Nov. 26, 1836	Nanjimoy
	Ronsby	19	Emigrant	Somerell, Henry S.	Apr. 29, 1836	Balto.
	Rooth	11	Clio	Crouch, William	March 20, 1819	Balto.
	Rosa	6	Georgia	Brent, Robert J.	Dec. 23, 1844	Balto.
	Rosa	24	Serene	Archer, James	Oct. 19, 1836	Balto.
	Rose	11	Emilie	Spencer, Thomas R.P.	March 27, 1821	Balto.
	Rose	25	Emilie	Coalman, Henry E.	Nov. 27, 1819	Balto.
	Rose	21	Eros	Armitage, James	June 29, 1822	Balto.

Surname	First Name	Age	Ship	O/S	Date	Depart
	Rose	10	Harriett	Pierce, Levi	Oct. 29, 1822	Balto.
	Rose	15	Hope	Purnell, Thomas R.	Dec. 3, 1833	Balto.
	Rose	3	Hope	Richardson, Wade H.	Dec. 3, 1833	Balto.
	Rose	17	Lawrence	Woolfolk, Austin	May 9, 1823	Balto.
	Rose	20	Missouri	Little, Moses	March 2, 1819	Balto.
	Rose	15	North America	Woolfolk, Austin	Dec. 20, 1824	Balto.
	Rose	9	States	Woolfolk, Austin	March 8, 1826	Balto.
	Rose	22	States	Woolfolk, Joseph B.	Nov. 21, 1827	Balto.
	Rose	4	Virginia	Woolfolk, Joseph B.	Dec. 19, 1825	Balto.
	Rose	2	Balloon	Zacharie, James W.	Dec. 22, 1821	Balto.
	Rosella	14	Patrick Henry	Campbell, Bernard M.	June 1, 1853	Balto.
	Rosete	7	Ajax	Richardson, Wade H.	Oct. 3, 1833	Balto.
	Rosetta	7	Arctic	Cliffe, Henry	Oct. 4, 1828	Balto.
	Rosetta	6 mon.	Hibernia	Chabert, Leon	Dec. 5, 1826	Balto.
	Rosetta	14	Lapwing	King, Gideon T.	March 22, 1822	Balto.
	Rosetta	13	Mars	Woolfolk, Austin	Oct. 30, 1824	Balto.
	Rosetta	20	Mars	Woolfolk, Austin	Oct. 30, 1824	Balto.
	Rosetta	28	Patriot	Simms, Edward	July 13, 1836	Balto.
	Rosetta	28	Signet	Woolfolk, Austin	Nov. 17, 1831	Balto.
	Rosetta	21 mon.	States	Woolfolk, Austin	Nov. 21, 1827	Balto.
	Rosetta	15	Susan Miller	Woolfolk, Austin	Oct. 25, 1822	Balto.
	Rosey	7 mon.	Franklin	Somerville, Henry	Nov. 27, 1819	Balto.
	Rosine	60	Actress	Garsicles, James	Nov. 6, 1819	Balto.
	Roswell	6	Intelligence	Somerville, Alexander	May 1, 1821	Balto.
	Rousby	36	Balloon	Zacharie, James W.	Dec. 22, 1821	Balto.
	Rozena Ann		Edward Everett	Campbell, Bernard M.	Oct. 18, 1851	Balto.

Surname	First Name	Age	Ship	O/S	Date	Depart
	Ruben	12	Superb	Donovan, Joseph S.	Nov. 2, 1843	Balto.
	Ruth	35	Burlington	Stout, G.H.	Oct. 22, 1842	Balto.
	Ruth	3	Hope	Byrne, Walter	Dec. 5, 1833	Balto.
	Ruth	22	Lady Monroe	Woofolk, Austin	March 25, 1825	Balto.
	Ruth	16	Orion	Woofolk, Austin	Dec. 30, 1822	Balto.
	Ruth	35	Orleans	Stout, G.H.	Oct. 22, 1842	Balto.
	S.	45	Franklin	Somerville, Henry	Nov. 27, 1819	Balto.
	Sabery	35	Virginia	Woofolk, Austin	Nov. 18, 1823	Balto.
	Sabina	19	Intelligence	Woofolk, Austin	Dec. 20, 1822	Balto.
	Sabina	28	Orion	Oldham, George W.	Dec. 30, 1822	Balto.
	Sabrina	16	Isabella	Wallis, Cornelius C.	Nov. 26, 1834	Balto.
	Sal	21	Hibernia	Kelso, John M.	Dec. 5, 1826	Balto.
	Sal	16	Intelligence	Woofolk, Austin	Dec. 20, 1822	Balto.
	Salina	5	Alfred	Woofolk, Austin	Jan. 18, 1825	Balto.
	Salina	10	Hope	Byrne, Walter	Dec. 5, 1833	Balto.
	Sally	12	Alfred	Woofolk, Austin	Jan. 18, 1825	Balto.
	Sally	14	Arctic	McSban, Hannah	Nov. 16, 1826	Balto.
	Sally	7	Arctic	McConnell, Alex	Sept. 29, 1827	Balto.
	Sally	4	Brunswick	Woofolk, Austin	Oct. 11, 1831	Balto.
	Sally	16	Dryad	Williams, Joseph C.	Dec. 12, 1827	Balto.
	Sally	14	Henry Clay	Bower, Thomas F.	Dec. 8, 1828	Nottingham
	Sally	12	Hibernia	Woofolk, Austin	Dec. 5, 1826	Balto.
	Sally	16	Hope & Hannah	Williams, Joseph C.	Dec. 10, 1827	Balto.
	Sally	21	Intelligence	Woofolk, Austin	Apr. 5, 1823	Balto.
	Sally	40	Leda	Nelson, James	Nov. 16, 1848	Balto.
	Sally	infant	Mars	Woofolk, Austin	Nov. 1, 1824	Balto.

Surname	First Name	Age	Ship	O/S	Date	Depart
	Sally	20	Mars	Woolfolk, Austin	Oct. 30, 1824	Balto.
	Sally	21	Mary	Lee, John	March 3, 1840	Balto.
	Sally	15	Mary	William Hooper	Nov. 6, 1839	Balto.
	Sally	14	Opelousas	Garland, Rice	July 5, 1836	Balto.
	Sally	14	Orion	Oldham, George W.	Dec. 30, 1822	Balto.
	Sally	17	Orion	Woolfolk, Richard	Dec. 30, 1822	Balto.
	Sally	17	States	Woolfolk, Austin	Nov. 21, 1827	Balto.
	Sally	16	Victorine	Campbell, Bernard M.	March 1, 1845	Balto.
	Sally Ann	14 mon.	Emilie	Mercer, William D.	March 27, 1821	Balto.
	Sam	23	Alfred	Woolfolk, Austin	Jan. 18, 1825	Balto.
	Sam	25	Alfred	Woolfolk, Austin	Jan. 18, 1825	Balto.
	Sam	29	Alfred	Woolfolk, Austin	Jan. 18, 1825	Balto.
	Sam	18	Algerine	Woolfolk, Austin	Jan. 5, 1826	Balto.
	Sam	24	Algerine	Woolfolk, Austin	March 25, 1826	Balto.
	Sam	11	Arctic	Maddox, Thomas H.	Jan. 30, 1829	St. Mary's
	Sam	16	Aurilla	Woolfolk, Austin	Apr. 26, 1822	Balto.
	Sam		Billow	Woolfolk, Austin	Feb. 23, 1828	Balto.
	Sam	23	Bourne	Rogers, Selemachus	Sept. 9, 1833	Balto.
	Sam	23	Bourne	Rogers, Selemachus	Sept. 9, 1833	Balto.
	Sam	28	Budget	King, Gideon T.	Dec. 1, 1821	Balto.
	Sam	23	Budget	Spraggins, Samuel M.	Nov. 27, 1821	Balto.
	Sam	36	Catharine	Woolfolk, Austin	Jan. 15, 1831	Balto.
	Sam	22	Eagle	Bond, Joshua B.	Oct. 29, 1828	Balto.
	Sam	11	Emilie	Ferguson, Thomas	Dec. 14, 1821	Balto.
	Sam	24	Emilie	Anderson, David	Jan. 5, 1819	Balto.
	Sam	21	Eros	Anderson, David	June 29, 1822	Balto.

Surname	First Name	Age	Ship	O/S	Date	Depart
	Sam	21	Hamlet	Woolfolk, Austin	Apr. 7, 1824	Balto.
	Sam	13	Harriett	King, John	March 23, 1822	Balto.
	Sam	19	Harriett	Woolfolk, Austin	March 23, 1822	Balto.
	Sam	19	Hibernia	Woolfolk, Austin	Dec. 5, 1826	Balto.
	Sam	2	Home	Campbell, Bernard M.	March 22, 1845	Balto.
	Sam	22	Hyperion	Anderson, David	May 14, 1822	Balto.
	Sam	30	Intelligence	Woolfolk, Austin	Apr. 5, 1823	Balto.
	Sam	14	Intelligence	Anderson, David	Dec. 20, 1822	Balto.
	Sam	22	Intelligence	Anderson, David	Dec. 20, 1822	Balto.
	Sam	22	Intelligence	Anderson, David	Nov. 3, 1820	Balto.
	Sam	23	Intelligence	Anderson, David	Nov. 3, 1820	Balto.
	Sam	14	Irad Ferry	Maddox, C.T.	Jan. 14, 1840	Balto.
	Sam	19	Isabella		Nov. 26, 1834	Balto.
	Sam	5	Lady Monroe	Woolfolk, Joseph B.	March 25, 1825	Balto.
	Sam	24	Lady Monroe	Chabert, Leon	Sept. 29, 1825	Balto.
	Sam	9	Leda	Nelson, James	Nov. 16, 1848	Balto.
	Sam	22	Mars	Woolfolk, Joseph B.	Oct. 30, 1824	Balto.
	Sam	35	Misscuri	Gilmore, John	March 1, 1819	Balto.
	Sam	30	Nelson Clark	Pascault, Lewis F.	May 17, 1836	Balto.
	Sam	20	Schuylkill	Rogers, G.	Oct. 25, 1822	Balto.
	Sam	27	Shamrock	Guyton, Elisha	March 13, 1840	Balto.
	Sam	28	St. Mary	Campbell, Bernard M.	Nov. 29, 1845	Balto.
	Sam	18 mon.	States	Woolfolk, Austin	Nov. 21, 1827	Balto.
	Sam	22	States	Woolfolk, Austin	Nov. 21, 1827	Balto.
	Sam	22	Susan Miller	Woolfolk, Austin	Oct. 25, 1822	Balto.
	Sam	9 mon.	Susan Miller	Woolfolk, Samuel M.	Oct. 25, 1822	Balto.

Surname	First Name	Age	Ship	O/S	Date	Depart
	Sam	25	Susan Miller	Woolfolk, Samuel M.	Oct. 25, 1822	Balto.
	Sam	25	Temperance	Lafitte, John Jr.	Dec. 9, 1818	Balto.
	Sam	28	Triton	Ricaud, John	Dec. 22, 1819	Balto.
	Sam	infant	Victorine	Donovan, Joseph S.	Sept. 29, 1845	Balto.
	Sam	24	Virginia	Williamson, David	March 11, 1826	Balto.
	Sampson	18	Lapwing	Spraggins, Samuel M.	March 22, 1822	Balto.
	Sampson	2	Mars	Woolfolk, Austin	Nov. 1, 1824	Balto.
	Samuel	25	Architect	Rodbind, Ebenezer	Feb. 12, 1840	Balto.
	Samuel	22	Hyperion	King, Gideon T.	Nov. 12, 1821	Balto.
	Samuel	infant	Intelligence	Plater, John R. Jr.	Apr. 12, 1823	St. Mary's
	Samuel	18	Lady Monroe	Chabert, Leon	Sept. 29, 1825	Balto.
	Samuel	22	Lady Monroe	Wascherr, J.E.	Sept. 29, 1825	Balto.
	Samuel	2	London	Hopp, H.B.	Nov. 6, 1840	Balto.
	Samuel	10	Mars	Woolfolk, Austin	Oct. 30, 1824	Balto.
	Samuel	22	Nelson Clark	Tongue, Thomas R.	Nov. 20, 1835	Balto.
	Samuel	7	North America	Chabert, Leon	Apr. 24, 1826	Balto.
	Samuel	8	States	Duer, Robert	Nov. 26, 1825	Balto.
	Samuel	10	States	Duer, Robert	Nov. 26, 1825	Balto.
	Samuel	35	Superb	Donovan, Joseph S.	Nov. 2, 1843	Balto.
	Sandy	22	Arctic	Maddox, Thomas H.	Jan. 30, 1829	St. Mary's
	Sandy	2	Dryad	Williams, Joseph C.	Dec. 12, 1827	Balto.
	Sandy	22	Hamlet	Woolfolk, Austin	Apr. 7, 1824	Balto.
	Sandy	2	Hope & Hannah	Williams, Joseph C.	Dec. 10, 1827	Balto.
	Sandy	22	Intelligence	Plater, John R. Jr.	Apr. 12, 1823	St. Mary's
	Sandy	4	Intelligence	Anderson, David	Dec. 20, 1822	Balto.
	Sandy	40	Lady Monroe	Woolfolk, Austin	Sept. 29, 1825	Balto.

Surname	First Name	Age	Ship	O/S	Date	Depart
	Sandy	7	Seaman	Biscoe, James	March 20, 1840	Balto.
	Santa	22	Eros	Woolfolk, Austin	Jan. 28, 1824	Balto.
	Sarah	14	Ajax	Richardson, Wade H.	Oct.3, 1833	Balto.
	Sarah	1 mon.	Alfred	Woolfolk, Austin	Jan. 18, 1825	Balto.
	Sarah	9	Alfred	Woolfolk, Austin	Jan. 18, 1825	Balto.
	Sarah	17	Alfred	Woolfolk, Austin	May 7, 1825	Balto.
	Sarah	40	Algerne	Woolfolk, Austin	March 25, 1826	Balto.
	Sarah	21	Aurilla	Wikoff, Stephen A.	Apr. 26, 1822	Balto.
	Sarah	21	Aurilla	Woolfolk, Austin	Apr. 26, 1822	Balto.
	Sarah	30	Aurilla	Woolfolk, Austin	Apr. 26, 1822	Balto.
	Sarah	13	Betsey	Woolfolk, Austin	Apr. 29, 1828	Balto.
	Sarah	30	Betsey	Woolfolk, Austin	Apr. 29, 1828	Balto.
	Sarah	45	Bourre	Handy, Samuel	Oct. 13, 1832	Balto.
	Sarah	1	Brunswick	Woolfolk, Austin	Oct. 11, 1831	Balto.
	Sarah	13	Caledonia	Barnum, Richard	Oct. 19, 1842	Balto.
	Sarah	16	Caspian	Woolfolk, Austin	Nov. 26, 1836	Balto.
	Sarah	12	Catharine	Woolfolk, Austin	March 3, 1829	Balto.
	Sarah	16	Clio	Walker, John W.	March 20, 1819	Balto.
	Sarah	30	Emilie	Dorney, Patrick	Dec. 14, 1821	Balto.
	Sarah	30	Emilie	Dorney, Patrick	Dec. 14, 1821	Balto.
	Sarah	30	Emilie	Ferguson, Thomas	Dec. 14, 1821	Balto.
	Sarah	2	Emilie	Anderson, David	Jan. 5, 1819	Balto.
	Sarah	infant	Franklin	Anderson, David	Nov. 27, 1819	Balto.
	Sarah	14	Good Hope	Woolfolk, Austin	Nov. 16, 1821	Balto.
	Sarah	22	Good Hope	Woolfolk, Austin	Nov. 16, 1821	Balto.
	Sarah	40	Gulnare	Pitts, Thomas H.	Nov. 5, 1830	Balto.

Surname	First Name	Age	Ship	O/S	Date	Depart
	Sarah	18	Hamlet	Woolfolk, Joseph B.	Apr. 7, 1824	Balto.
	Sarah	17	Harriett	King, John	March 23, 1822	Balto.
	Sarah	23	Harriett	Woolfolk, Richard T.	March 6, 1823	Balto.
	Sarah	10	Harriett	Pierce, Levi	Oct. 29, 1822	Balto.
	Sarah	41	Henry Clay	Chew, Worhtington	Dec. 8, 1828	Nottingham
	Sarah	35	Henry Clay	Compton & Dorsett	Dec. 8, 1828	Nottingham
	Sarah	20	Hermann	Rowe, Ralph	June 21, 1851	Balto.
	Sarah	15	Hibernia	Chabert, Leon	Dec. 5, 1826	Balto.
	Sarah	18	Hibernia	Chabert, Leon	Dec. 5, 1826	Balto.
	Sarah	9	Hope	Purnell, Thomas R.	Dec. 3, 1833	Balto.
	Sarah	12	Hope	Richardson, Wade H.	Dec. 3, 1833	Balto.
	Sarah	18	Hope	Richardson, Wade H.	Dec. 3, 1833	Balto.
	Sarah	6 mon.	Hope	Byrne, Walter	Dec. 5, 1833	Balto.
	Sarah	29	Hope	Byrne, Walter	Dec. 5, 1833	Balto.
	Sarah	33	Hyperion	Saul, Joseph	Nov. 8, 1820	Balto.
	Sarah	6 mon.	Hyperion	Lee, Thomas	Nov. 9, 1821	Balto.
	Sarah	30	Intelligence	Woolfolk, Austin	Dec. 20, 1822	Balto.
	Sarah	8	Intelligence	Oldham, George W.	Nov. 4, 1820	Balto.
	Sarah	17	Isabella		Nov. 26, 1834	Balto.
	Sarah	18	Julia	Woolfolk, Austin	Feb. 10, 1832	Balto.
	Sarah	3	Kirkwood	Campbell, Bernard M.	Jan. 4, 1845	Balto.
	Sarah	2	Kirkwood	Campbell, Bernard M.	Oct. 16, 1845	Balto.
	Sarah	9	Lafayette	Woolfolk, Austin	Oct. 18, 1828	Balto.
	Sarah	11	Lapwing	Hall, Francis	March 22, 1822	Balto.
	Sarah	40	Leda	Brown, J.L.	Oct. 1, 1846	Balto.
	Sarah	40	Leda	Brown, J.L.	Oct. 1, 1846	Balto.

Index to Vessels Transporting Slaves

The following index was created using several sources in tandem with one another. The primary document was the inward bound slave manifests into the port of New Orleans stored in record group 36 of the manuscript division of the National Archives. The second source, used to determine docks or wharves where slaves were boarded, was the newspaper entitled The American and Baltimore Daily Advertiser. The index is organized as follows:

Column 1: dates: Indicates the date of the latest roll call of slaves placed on the vessel in Baltimore (or other Maryland port)

Column 2: vessel: The name of the vessel or packet ship

Column 3: vessel type: although brigs and barques were the vessels of choice ships, sloops, schooners, and on rare occasions, steamers were used for transport. This column indicates the type of vessel and weight (or tons burthen) when the information was available.

Column 4: Dock: the dock or wharf where the vessel was loaded was occasionally indicated in advertisements placed in local newspapers. This is an important source of information in that it assists the researcher in determining possible trends in shipping. It appears that both the northern end of the inner harbor basin as well as the entire length of Fells Point docks were used on a regular basis for the shipments. By referring to this source of information one can determine what contemporary structure stands on the original site of disembarkation.

Column 5: Ship's master: students of maritime history can use this category of information to determine a number of facts about the ship's captain when used in conjunction with other sources of information. Census records and city directories afford us the potential to locate the trends in geographical residence, particularly when the captain resided in the port of disembarkation. By using a variety of records we can study the area of habitation, not only as it appeared during the period of shipments, but also as it appears today. A number of captains lived within easy walking distance of the docks. This information allows the historian the potential to enrich his or her study of the overall maritime history of the region.

Column 6: Number: this indicated the total number of slaves taken on board vessel from Baltimore. On a small number of occasions the vessel made additional stops in Maryland ports, particularly in St. Mary's and Anne Arundel counties. On these occasions the number of slaves boarded were separately recorded.

Column 7: Arrival: By carefully studying the inward bound slave manifests one can often determine the time of the Customs Official's roll call of the slaves in Balize or New Orleans. The date entered in this column is either the New Orleans or Balize dates. It is important to note that the dates may differ by one to three days at times. Nevertheless this category of information gives us the opportunity to study the length of time the slaves spent traveling on board the vessels and to narrow that period to within a one or two day span. By using this technique we can clearly see that vessels making a straight run, and in perfect sailing conditions, would make the trip in under two weeks. Other vessels hampered by poor weather, incursion by pirates, and stop-offs, occasionally required as much as six or seven weeks for the journey.

Column 8: Duration: This column indicates the total number of days elapsed between the final roll call in Baltimore and the roll call in New Orleans.

(B) placed next to vessel's name indicates that it was Baltimore built.

Dates	Vessel	Vessel Type	Dock	Ship's Master	#	Arrival	#days
June 29, 1850	Abbott Lord	barque	Henderson's Wharf	Ruark, Alex	1	July 31, 1850	32
Oct. 4, 1851	Abbott Lord	barque	Henderson's Wharf	Collier, George W.	1	Oct. 17, 1851	13
April 28, 1852	Abbott Lord	barque	Henderson's Wharf	Knowles, A.	37	May 7, 1852	9
Nov. 8, 1819	Actress	brig 176t		Parker, Thomas	16	Nov. 28, 1819	20
June 8, 1821	Agent	brig	Frederick Street Dock	VanLorn	23	July 27, 1821	49
Oct. 3, 1833	Ajax	brig		Rawlins, W.M.?	31		
Nov.6, 1824	Alfred	brig 260t	Ramsay's Wharf	Oliver, Paul A.	3	Dec. 1, 1824	25
Jan.18, 1825	Alfred	brig 260t	Ramsay's Wharf	Oliver, Paul A.	34	Feb.11, 1825	24
May 7, 1825	Alfred	brig 260t	Ramsay's Wharf	Oliver, Paul A.	23	May 30, 1825	23
Feb.10, 1827	Alfred	brig 260t		Oliver, Paul A.	1	March 20, 1827	38
Jan.6, 1826	Algerine	brig 145t		Foster, Herman	20	Feb. 2, 1826	27
Mar.25, 1826	Algerine	brig 145t		Foster, Herman	15	April 9, 1826	15
Nov.8, 1822	Alonzo	brig		Gold, Joseph	42	Nov. 22, 1822	14
Sept.23, 1852	America	ship	Henderson's Wharf	Saunders, ?	1	Oct. 16, 1852	23
May 24, 1830	Anice	schooner 51t		Pascal, Peter	3	July 23, 1820	60
Nov.1, 1831	Ann and Leah	brig 150t		Goldsmith, Samuel	85	Nov. 21, 1831	20
Sept.2, 1836	Ann Wayne	brig 195t	Spear's Wharf	Longcope, William?	9	Oct. 3, 1836	31
May 2, 1838	Architect	brig 163t	Spear's Wharf	Grey, Albert	1	May 30, 1838	28
Nov. 23, 1838	Architect	brig 163t	Spear's Wharf	Grey, Adams	1		
Feb.15, 1840	Architect	brig 163t	Frederick Street Dock	Gary, Albert	16	March 22, 1840	40
May 25, 1840	Architect	brig 163t	Frederick Street Dock	Gray, Albert	1	June 27, 1840	33
Feb. 4, 1841	Architect	brig 163t	Frederick Street Dock	Gray, Albert	27	March 9, 1841	33
May 20, 1841	Architect	brig 163t	Frederick Street Dock	Gray, Albert	15	July 1, 1841	42
Feb. 16, 1843	Architect	brig 163t			24	March 19, 1843	31
April 25, 1846	Architect	brig 163t	Flanigan's Wharf	Gray, A	25	May 22, 1846	27
Nov. 16, 1826	Arctic	brig 231t		Soule, Elijah	24	Dec. 11, 1826	25

Dates	Vessel	Vessel Type	Dock	Ship's Master	#	Arrival	#days
Oct. 5, 1827	Arctic	brig 231t		Soule, Elijah	18	Oct. 29, 1827	24
Oct. 8, 1828	Arctic	brig 231t	Gibson's Wharf	Phillips, William	10	Oct. 26, 1828	22
Jan. 28, 1829	Arctic	brig 231t	Gibson's Wharf		15	March 3, 1829	34
Mar. 16, 1827	Arctic	brig 231t		Soule, Elijah	1	April 14, 1827	29
Jan. 24, 1828	Arctic	brig 231t	Gibson's Wharf	Soule, Elijah	3	Feb. 19, 1828	26
May 15, 1828	Arctic	brig 231t		Soule, Elijah	25	June 14, 1828	30
Jan. 29, 1828	Arctic*	brig 231t	St. Mary's	Soule, Elijah	30	Feb. 19, 1828	21
Oct. 9, 1828	Arctic*	brig 231t	Gibson's Wharf		14	Oct. 26, 1828	17
Jan. 31, 1829	Arctic*	brig 231t	St Mary's	Phillips, William	40	March 3, 1829	31
July 18, 1826	Arletta	brig 177t	Frederick Street Dock	Coulbourn, E.	7	Sept. 1, 1826	45
April 26, 1822	Aurilla	brig 111t	Frederick Street Dock	Howland, Wing	74	June 11, 1822	46
Dec. 22, 1821	Balloon	ship		Smith, John A.	128	Jan. 18, 1822	27
Nov. 2, 1835	Baltimore	brig 167t	Spear's Wharf	C.	12	Nov.25, 1835	23
April 30, 1828	Betsey (B)	schooner 120t		Andrews, William	47	May 19, 1828	19
Feb. 23, 1828	Billow	brig 182t	Frederick Street Dock	Sampson, Thomas B.	93	March 13, 1828	19
Jan. 18, 1841	Bostonian	barque 267t		Gillchrist, L.B.	32	March 8, 1841	49
July 21, 1832	Bourne	brig 195t		Benthall, Robert	1	Aug. 12, 1832	22
Oct. 15, 1832	Bourne	brig 195t		Benthall, Robert	22	Nov. 13, 1832	29
April 6, 1833	Bourne	brig 195t		Benthall, Robert	1	May 1, 1833	25
Sept. 10, 1833	Bourne	brig 195t		Benthall, Robert	27	Oct. 7, 1833	27
Oct. 15, 1852	Brandywine	ship 729t		Merryman, P.	6	Oct. 29, 1852	14
Oct. 12, 1831	Brunswick	ship 295t	Water's Wharf	Merryman, Jacob	148	Oct. 28, 1831	16
Dec. 1, 1921	Budget	ship 280t	Ramsay's Wharf		45	Jan. 3, 1822	34
Oct. 22, 1842	Burlington	ship 534t		Thing, Abram	80	Nov. 12, 1842	34
Nov. 7, 1832	Calagari	schooner 110t		Cozens, H.	10		21

Dates	Vessel	Vessel Type	Dock	Ship's Master	#	Arrival	#days
Dec. 7, 1840	Caledonia	ship 540t	Ramsay's Wharf	Massicott	2	Jan. 4, 1841	28
Oct. 27, 1841	Caledonia	ship 540t	Ramsay's Wharf	Marriott, William	4	Nov. 15, 1841	19
Oct. 19, 1842	Caledonia	ship 540t	Ramsay's Wharf	Marriott, William	9	Nov. 10, 1842	22
March 2, 1821	Caroline	ship 280t	Water's Wharf	Serrell, James	4	March 20, 1821	18
Nov. 26, 1836	Caspian	ship 531t	Kerr's Wharf	Patton, D.	70		
March 5, 1829	Catharine (B)	brig 199t	Tenant's Wharf	Stephens, Reuben	23	March 28, 1829	23
Jan. 15, 1831	Catharine (B)	brig 199t		Stevens, Reuben	8	Feb. 12, 1831	28
Apr. 14, 1831	Catharine (B)	brig 199t		Stevens, Reuben	4	May 4, 1831	20
Jan. 24, 1843	Catharine (B)	brig 199t		Vespir, ?	32	Feb. 11, 1843	18
Jan. 18, 1845	Catharine (B)	brig 199t	Smith's Dock	Wingate, Thomas	49	Feb. 7, 1845	20
Nov. 26, 1836	Catharine Jackson*	ship 456t	Nanjimoy*	Peabody, John	34	Dec. 9, 1836	13
Sept. 29, 1849	Charles	ship 381t	Flanigan's Wharf	Collier, George W.	10	Oct. 20, 1849	21
Dec. 18, 1850	Charles	ship 381t	Henderson's Wharf	Collier, George W.	32	Jan. 15, 1851	28
Apr. 23, 1851	Charles	ship 381t	Henderson's Wharf	Ruark, Alex	25	May 12, 1851	19
May 15, 1852	Charles	ship 381t	Henderson's Wharf	Ruark, Alex	2		
July 10, 1819	Charles	schooner 93t		Glavarry, Francis R.	1		
Apr. 30, 1820	Charles	schooner 93t		Glavarry, Francis R.	2		
Dec. 9, 1839	Charles Henry	schooner 94t.		Brewster, Charles	2	Jan. 16, 1840	38
Jan. 3, 1821	Chatsworth	brig		Davidson, John	15	Feb. 15, 1821	43
Aug. 31, 1835	Cicero			Watts	1		
Dec. 6, 1828	Climax	schooner 58t	Spear's Wharf	Parker, Peter	3	Jan. 9, 1829	33
March 22, 1819	Clio	brig		Starnsburg, William	24	April 17, 1819	26
Nov. 21, 1844	Colonel Howard	barque 322t		Prentiss, S.H.G.	36	Dec. 15, 1844	24
Nov. 1, 1827	Columbus	brig 209t	Water's Wharf	Lake, John	1	Dec. 2, 1827	31
March 20, 1819	Comm. Patterson	sloop		Myrick, John R.	8	April 20, 1819	31

Dates	Vessel	Vessel Type	Dock	Ship's Master	#	Arrival	#days
Dec. 27, 1838	Copia	barque 431t	Henderson's Wharf	Horton, Hiram	2	Jan. 25, 1839	29
Jan. 21, 1851	Cora	schooner 125t	Frederick Street Dock	Connier, Lewis	16	Feb. 13, 1851	23
Oct. 19, 1833	Creole	ship	Chase's Wharf	Harty, ?	5	Nov. 5, 1833	17
Oct. 7, 1836	Cumberland				8		
Oct. 24, 1819	Decatur	brig 183t		Stansburg, Tobias E.	3	Nov.26, 1819	33
May 20, 1820	Decatur	brig 183t	Ramsay's Wharf	Andrews, William	1	June 29, 1820	40
Dec. 1, 1848	Delawarian	barque 223t	Frederick Street Dock	Haynie, John F.	26	Jan. 2, 1849	32
Dec. 23, 1828	Delta	brig 224t		Knight, James	2	Jan. 26, 1829	34
Dec. 12, 1827	Dryad	brig 262t		Scott, John G.	9	Jan. 3, 1827	22
Sept. 25, 1828	Dumfries	ship 325t (B)		Harvey, Joseph	65		
Dec, 2, 1847	E.H.Chapin	barque 424t	Flannigan's Wharf	Collier, George W.	101	Dec.25, 1847	23
June 7, 1848	E.H.Chapin	barque 424t	Flanigan's Wharf	Collier, George W.	5	June 29, 1848	22
Aug. 26, 1848	E.H.Chapin	barque 424t	Flanigan's Wharf	Collier, George W.	7	Sept. 22, 1848	27
Oct. 28, 1828	Eagle	ship 282t		Powell, Thomas	10		
March 10, 1851	Edward Everett	ship 622t	Henderson's Wharf	Vigures, Isaac L.	22	April 2, 1851	23
Oct. 18, 1851	Edward Everett	ship 622t	Henderson's Wharf	Gunby, F.A.	12	Nov. 5, 1851	18
Dec. 6, 1856	Edward Everett	ship 622t		Gunby, F.A.	2		
Oct. 9, 1840	Eliza	barque 295t	Frederick Street Dock	Talbot, R.	48	Oct. 30, 1840	21
Nov. 13, 1851	Eliza F. Mason	ship 581t		Jones, William N.	57		
Nov. 18, 1848	Elizabeth	barque 230t	Flanigan's Wharf	Jones, Alexander	139	Dec. 3, 1848	15
May 12, 1849	Elizabeth	barque 230t	Flanigan's Wharf	Long, S.	12	June 4, 1849	23
Oct. 6, 1849	Elizabeth	barque 230t	Flanigan's Wharf	Jones, Alexander	18	Oct. 18, 1849	12
Jan. 2, 1850	Elizabeth	barque 230t	Jackson's Wharf	Jones, Alexander	65	Jan. 21, 1850	19
March 21, 1850	Elizabeth	barque 230t	Flanigan's Wharf	Jones, Alexander	47	April 10, 1850	20
Apr.29, 1836	Emigrant	schooner 83t		Rouse, George L.	7	June 8, 1836	40
Jan. 5, 1819	Emilie (B)	brig 116t		Godfrey, Benjamin	20	Jan.29, 1819	24

Dates	Vessel	Vessel Type	Dock	Ship's Master	#	Arrival	#days
May 20, 1820	Emilie (B)	brig 116t	Kerr's Wharf	Godfrey, Benjamin	6	June 26, 1820	37
March 27, 1821	Emilie (B)	brig 116t	Tenants wharf	Godfrey, Benjamin	37	May 13, 1821	47
Dec. 14, 1821	Emilie (B)	brig 116t		Gocfrey, Benjamin	37	Jan. 19, 1822	36
Aug. 21, 1819	Emilie (B)	brig 116t	Kerr's Wharf	Gocfrey. ?	5	Sept. 20, 1819	31
Nov. 27, 1819	Emilie (B)	brig 116t		Gocfrey, Benjamin	10	Dec. 14, 1819	17
June 29, 1822	Eros (B)	brig 127t		Darneron, John	40	Sept. 3, 1822	66
Jan. 28, 1824	Eros (B)	brig 127t	Ramsay's Wharf	Carns, John	37	April 3, 1824	35
March 4, 1841	Ewarkee	schooner 119t	Fenby's Wharf	Morton, John	63	March 31, 1841	27
May 13, 1843	Fidelia	brig		Small, ?	1	June 4, 1843	22
May 26, 1836	Forester	schooner 95t		Russell, Ephraim H.	5	July 28, 1836	63
Jan. 20, 1847	Francis Amy	brig	Flanigan's Wharf	Guxby, F.A.	66	Feb. 12, 1847	23
Nov. 27, 1819	Franklin	brig 119t	Wharf	Baxter, J.A.	46	Dec. 15, 1819	15
Nov. 25, 1840	Gannicleft	brig 200t	O'Dornell's Wharf	Levy, James P.	39	Dec. 21, 1840	26
Feb, 28, 1842	Gazelle	brig 145t	Bowly's Wharf	Thomas, Caleb	6	March 21, 1842	21
June 1, 1832	General Hand	ship 318t	Ramsay's Wharf	W.	21	Aug. 13, 1832	73
Nov. 10, 1845	General Pinckney	brig 194t		Hobbs, George	77	Nov. 24, 1845	14
Feb. 21, 1846	General Pinckney	brig 194t		Hobbs, George	74	March 12, 1846	19
Jan. 19, 1847	General Pinckney	brig 194t		Gayle, ?	140	Feb. 2, 1847	14
June 18, 1847	George Ross	schooner 86t	Wate-'s Wharf	Stirling, ?	7	July 16, 1847	28
Dec. 23, 1844	Georgia	barque 363t		Ots, James	40	Jan. 29, 1845	37
Oct. 11, 1838	Glasgow	ship		Litle, ?	20	Nov. 1, 1838	21
Dec. 19, 1838	Glasgow	ship			2		
Sept. 7, 1846	Globe	brig 239t	Flanigan's Wharf	Young, H.W.	2	Sept. 30, 1846	23
Nov. 21, 1821	Good Hope	sloop 81t	Bowly's Wharf	Wing, Paul	54	Dec. 17, 1821	26
Nov. 5, 1830	Gulnane (B)	ship 324t		Griffith, David	27	Dec. 1, 1830	26
April 7, 1824	Hamlet	ship 340t	Ramsay's Wharf	Pnce, Peter	30	April 28, 1824	21

Dates	Vessel	Vessel Type	Dock	Ship's Master	#	Arrival	#days
Jan. 2, 1824	Hamlet	ship 340t	Ramsay's Wharf	Price, Peter	9	Jan. 23, 1824	21
Dec. 7, 1836	Harriet	brig 286t	Ramsay's Wharf	Collins, William	52	Dec. 30, 1836	23
June 12, 1850	Harriet Cooper	brig 235t		Rees, Thomas H.	4	July 7, 1850	25
March 23, 1822	Harriett (B)	brig 141t	Jackson's Wharf	Diamond, William	65	April 26, 1822	34
March 7, 1823	Harriett (B)	brig 141t	Ramsay's Wharf	Diamond, William	16	April 4, 1823	28
Oct. 29, 1822	Harriett (B)	brig 141t	Smith's Dock	Dino, William	8	Nov. 20, 1822	22
Nov. 4, 1835	Hector	brig 198t	Spear's Wharf	Farrow, John	4		
Oct. 18, 1852	Helen A. Miller	ship 510t		Galt, W.	114	Oct. 29, 1852	11
March 28, 1846	Helen McCleod	brig 268t	Flannigan's Wharf	Marston, Thomas	1	April 13, 1846	16
Nov. 18, 1843	Helen McLeod	brig 268t		Landis, D.C.	1		
Oct. 28, 1848	Henry A. Barling	schooner 160t	Flanigan's Wharf	Haynie, ?	20		
Apr. 19, 1849	Henry A. Barling	schooner 160t	Flanigan's Wharf	Galt, W.	13	May 7, 1849	18
Aug. 11, 1849	Henry A. Barling	schooner 160t		Galt, W.	2	Aug. 31, 1849	20
Feb. 24, 1851	Henry A. Barling	schooner 160t	Henderson's Wharf	Gunby, F.A.	36	March 14, 1851	18
May 17, 1851	Henry A. Barling	schooner 160t	Henderson's Wharf	Marshall, P.J.	4		
Dec. 18, 1851	Henry A. Barling	schooner 160t	Henderson's Wharf	Mercy, Edward A.	50	Jan. 12, 1852	25
Dec. 4, 1828	Henry Clay (B)	ship 371t	Price's Wharf	Parker, Thomas	41	Jan. 8, 1829	35
Dec. 8, 1828	Henry Clay* (B)	ship 371t	Nottingham	Parker, Thomas	103	Jan. 8, 1829	31
July 14, 1832	Hercules	barque	Ramsay's Wharf	Longscope, William	1	Aug. 12, 1832	29
June 21, 1851	Hermann	ship 419t	Henderson's Wharf	Skinner, ?	11		
Oct. 28, 1846	Hermitage	barque 317t	Frederick Street Dock	Fry, John H.	90	Nov. 23, 1846	26
Dec. 5, 1826	Hibernia (B)	ship 327t	Water's Wharf	Robinson, Matthew	188	Jan. 24, 1827	50
Dec. 5, 1833	Hope	brig 235t	Craig's Wharf	Galt, Henry	79	Dec. 31, 1833	26
March 26, 1834	Hope	brig 235t	Craig's Wharf	Galt, Henry	6	April 30, 1834	35
Sept. ?, 1834	Hope	brig 235t			1		
Dec. 10, 1827	Hope and Hannah	schooner 93t			10		

Dates	Vessel	Vessel Type	Dock	Ship's Master	#	Arrival	#days
March 11, 1829	Hope and Hannah	schooner 93t	Frederick Street Dock	Chase, Jonathan	15	April 4, 1829	24
March 22, 1845	Home	barque 377t		Watts, W.J.	99	April 9, 1845	18
Dec. 14, 1836	Hortensia	barque		Massicott, ?	18	Jan. 12, 1837	29
Nov. 12, 1821	Hyperion	brig 413t		Forbes, James	37	Dec. 12, 1821	30
May 14, 1822	Hyperion	brig		Forbes, James	44	June 18, 1822	35
Oct. 17, 1835	Hyperion	ship 413t	Tenant's Wharf	Janney, Joseph	3		
Nov. 8, 1820	Hyperion (B)	brig		Blackwell, Francis	6	Dec. 5, 1820	27
Nov. 4, 1820	Intelligence (B)	brig 152t		Jenkins, B.J.	28	Dec. 4, 1820	30
May 1, 1821	Intelligence (B)	brig 152t	Kerr's Wharf	Jenkins, B.J.	32	June 11, 1821	41
Dec. 20, 1822	Intelligence (B)	brig 152t	Jackson's Wharf	Godfrey, Benjamin	70	Jan. 21, 1823	32
April 5, 1823	Intelligence (B)	brig 152t	Jackson's Wharf	Godfrey, Benjamin	29	May 11, 1823	36
March 14, 1820	Intelligence (B)	brig 152t	Jackson's Wharf	Wilkinson, Shubal	15	April 6, 1820	23
Sept. 18, 1821	Intelligence (B)	brig 152t	Frederick Street Dock	Jenkins, B.J.	19	Oct. 17, 1821	29
Dec. 29, 1821	Intelligence (B)	brig 152t		Godfrey, Benjamin	1	Feb. 2, 1822	35
April 12, 1823	Intelligence (B)*	brig 152t	St. Mary's	Godfrey, Benjamin	29	May 11, 1823	29
May 6, 1839	Irad Ferry	barque 299t		Stevens, J.J	20	May 30, 1839	24
Jan. 22, 1840	Irad ferry	barque 299t	Frederick Street Dock	Stevens, J.J.	37	Feb. 18, 1840	27
Oct. 31, 1841	Irad Ferry	barque 299t	Fenby's Wharf	Chase, J.	4	Nov. 19, 1841	19
Feb. 5, 1842	Irad ferry	barque 299t	Chase's Wharf	Chase, J.	11	March 8, 1842	31
Dec. 9, 1842	Irad Ferry	barque 299t	Fenby's Wharf	Chase, Stephen	44	Jan. 6, 1843	28
Dec. 4, 1843	Irad Ferry	barque 299t	Frederick Street Dock	Chase, Stephen	1		
Sept. 28, 1838	Isaac Franklin	brig	Craig's Wharf	Smith, William	170	Oct. 17, 1838	19
Feb.1, 1839	Isaac Franklin	brig			54		
Nov. 26, 1834	Isabella	brig 165t		Faunie, John	60	Dec. 26, 1834	30
Sept. 30, 1831	James Ramsay	brig 153t		Ginby, James	2	Oct. 16, 1831	16
Nov. 1, 1952	Jane Henderson	ship 637t	Henderson's Wharf	Collier, George W.	18	Nov. 26, 1852	25

Dates	Vessel	Vessel Type	Dock	Ship's Master	#	Arrival	#days
Apr. 7, 1827	Jasper	brig 191t	Tenant's Wharf	Colbourn, Oliver	35	May 14, 1827	37
Dec. 24, 1827	Jefferson (B)	ship 306t	Price's New Wharf	Leslie, Robert	97	Jan. 26, 1828	33
Oct. 24, 1850	John C. Calhoun	ship 708t	Henderson's Wharf		93		
Jan. 8, 1840	John R. Gardner	brig 190t		Neill, F.	1	Feb. 3, 1840	36
Nov. 20, 1852	John S. Gittings	brig 165t		Hearn, ?	36	Dec. 14, 1852	24
Feb. 10, 1832	Julia	brig 166t	Smith's Dock	Bourne, Silas J.	25	March 12, 1832	31
Jan. 8, 1829	Julia	brig 166t	Smith's Dock	Kimball, Nathaniel	44	Jan. 30, 1829	22
March 25, 1836	Jupiter	ship 316t	Water's Wharf	Webb, Michael	4		
Dec. 2, 1852	Justina	barque 248t	Chase's Wharf	Block, James G.	22	Dec. 27, 1852	25
Oct. 26, 1832	Kenhawa	brig 174t	Ramsay's Wharf	Ransdell, H.W.	13	Nov. 16, 1832	21
March 9, 1847	Kirkwood	brig 211t	Frederick Street Dock	Haynie, John F.	57	March 29, 1847	20
Oct. 14, 1848	Kirkwood	barque 343t	Flanigan's Wharf	Martin, O.R.	147	Nov. 2, 1848	19
Nov. 28, 1849	Kirkwood	barque 343t	Flanigan's Wharf	Martin, Hugh	59	Dec. 13, 1849	15
Sept. 6, 1851	Kirkwood	barque 343t			2		
Dec. 23, 1843	Kirkwood (B)	brig 211t	Smith's Dock	Martin, Hugh	91	Jan. 13, 1844	21
March 23, 1844	Kirkwood (B)	brig 211t	Smith's Dock	Martin, Hugh	69	April 5, 1844	13
Jan. 4, 1845	Kirkwood (B)	brig 211t		Martin, Hugh	110	Jan. 25, 1845	21
Apr. 15, 1845	Kirkwood (B)	brig 211t	Frederick Street Dock	Haynie, John F.	127	April 29, 1845	14
July 19, 1845	Kirkwood (B)	brig 211t	Frederick Street Dock	Haynie, John F.	3	Aug. 21, 1845	33
Oct. 16, 1845	Kirkwood (B)	brig 211t	Frederick Street Dock	Martin, Hugh	117	Oct. 31, 1845	15
Jan. 14, 1846	Kirkwood (B)	brig 211t	Frederick Street Dock	Haynie, John F.	71	Jan. 31, 1846	17
Apr. 4, 1846	Kirkwood (B)	brig 211t	Frederick Street Dock	Haynie, John F.	68	April 23, 1846	19
Sept. 28, 1846	Kirkwood (B)	brig 211t	Frederick Street Dock	Haynie, John F.	82	Oct. 12, 1846	14
Dec. 10, 1846	Kirkwood (B)	brig 211t	Frederick Street Dock	Haynie, John F.	158	Dec. 28, 1846	18
Oct. 26, 1847	Kirkwood (B)	barque 343t	Flanigan's Wharf	Martin, Hugh	168	Nov. 8, 1847	13
March 25, 1825	Lady Monroe	brig 239t		Bailey, Edwin	97	April 17, 1825	23

Dates	Vessel	Vessel Type	Dock	Ship's Master	#	Arrival	#days
Sept. 29, 1825	Lady Monroe	brig 239t		Bailey, Edwin	74	Oct. 22, 1825	23
Apr. 30, 1827	Lady Richmond	brig 207t		Freeman, Frederick	17	May 27, 1827	27
Oct. 22, 1828	Lafayette	ship 260t		Hardie, Robert	211	Nov. 13, 1828	22
March 25, 1843	Lafayette	schooner 140t	Frederick Street Dock	Winchester, F.	42	April 25, 1843	31
March 22, 1822	Lapwing	schooner 107t		Kennedy, Thomas	61	April 14, 1822	23
Feb. 16, 1827	Lapwing	schooner 107t		Kennedy, Thomas	50	March 15, 1827	27
Nov. 28, 1827	Lapwing	schooner 107t		Kennedy, Thomas	2	Dec. 23, 1827	25
May 9, 1823	Lawrence	schooner		Bourne, Elisha	22	June 1, 1823	23
May 30, 1846	Leda	barque 254t	Flannigan's Wharf	Ruark, Alex	5	June 23, 1846	24
Oct. 1, 1846	Leda	barque 258t	Flanigan's Wharf	Ruark, Alex	5	Oct. 26, 1846	25
Nov. 16, 1848	Leda	barque 258t	Flanigan's Wharf	Ruark, Alex	20	Dec. 4, 1848	18
Nov. 12, 1828	Liberator	brig 279t	Chases Wharf	Jefferson, S.	27	Dec. 8, 1828	26
March 21, 1835	Lion	brig	Frederick Street Dock	Morrell, ?	1		
March 16, 1845	Lion	brig			2		
Nov. 6, 1840	London	ship 637t		Patton, J.F.	19	Nov. 24, 1840	18
May 18, 1846	Louisa	barque 316t	Flannigan's Wharf	Galt, W.	8	June 18, 1846	31
Oct. 11, 1847	Louisa	barque 316t	Flanigan's Wharf	Gunby, F.A.	74	Nov. 8, 1847	29
July 3, 1848	Louisa	barque 316t	Flanigan's Wharf	Gunby, F.A.	3	July 27, 1848	24
March 31, 1849	Louisa	barque 316t	Flanigan's Wharf	Gunby, F.A.	16	April 12, 1849	12
Nov. 5, 1849	Louisa	barque 316t	Flanigan's Wharf	Gunby, F.A.	18	Nov. 25, 1849	20
June 14, 1848	Manchester	barque 290t		Fairchild, Lucius H.	2		
Nov. 28, 1838	Margaret Forbs	ship	Chases Wharf	King, ?	35		
Nov. 30, 1844	Margaret Hugg	barque 327t	Corner's Wharf	Liton, William H.	64	Dec. 21, 1844	21
Feb. 8, 1845	Margaret Hugg	barque 327t	Corner's Wharf	Liton, William H.	53	March 1, 1845	23
Nov. 2, 1824	Mars	brig 190t	Water's Wharf	Ford, Clement	139	Dec. 4, 1824	32
Oct. 6, 1838	Mary	barque 244t	Frederick Street Dock	Nickerson, ?	2	Oct. 29, 1838	23

Dates	Vessel	Vessel Type	Dock	Ship's Master	#	Arrival	#days
Nov. 7, 1839	Mary	barque 244t	Frederick Street Dock	Myrick, Joseph	2	Nov. 28, 1839	21
March 3, 1840	Mary	barque 244t	Frederick Street Dock	Myrick, Joseph	8	March 30, 1840	27
Feb. 8, 1841	Mary	barque 244t	Fenby's Wharf	Myrick, Joseph	7	March 6, 1841	26
Nov. 30, 1841	Mary	barque 244t	Fenby's Wharf	Crosby, Edmund	5	Dec. 31, 1841	31
March 3, 1842	Mary	barque 244t	Fenby's Wharf	Crosby, Edmund	1	April 23, 1842	51
Oct. 7, 1843	Mary	barque 244t	Frederick Street Dock	Myrick, Joseph	4	Oct. 27, 1843	20
Feb. 10, 1844	Mary	barque 244t	Frederick Street Dock	Myrick, Joseph	11		
Jan. 6, 1845	Mary	barque 244t	Fenby's Wharf		1	Feb. 28, 1845	53
Aug. 23, 1845	Mary	barque 244t	Flanigan's Wharf	Marston, ?	2	Sept. 26, 1845	34
Sept. 16, 1848	Mary Ann Jones	brig		Hooper, Edward	1	Oct. 7, 1848	21
Nov. 18, 1851	Mary Broughton	barque 330t	Henderson's Wharf	Prior, Henry	46	Dec. 10, 1851	22
Jan. 1, 1831	Mechanic	brig 218t	Frederick Street Dock		26	Feb. 9, 1831	39
Nov. 2, 1831	Merrimack	ship 288t	Ramsay's Wharf	Brown, Nicholas	23	Dec. 6, 1831	34
May 22, 1832	Milton	brig 122t	Chase's Wharf	Pearse, H.H.	1	June 10, 1832	19
March 2, 1819	Missouri	ship	Water's Wharf	Hart, Robert	51	April 2, 1819	31
Oct. 25, 1843	Nancy W. Stevens	barque 345t	Frederick Street Dock	Stevens, J.J.	17	Nov. 14, 1843	20
Feb. 18, 1845	Nancy W. Stevens	barque 345t	McElderry's Dock	Stevens, J.J.	7	March 19, 1845	29
Nov. 3, 1842	Napier	ship 470t	Jackson's Wharf	Sanford, John L.	2	Nov. 25, 1842	22
Nov. 27, 1850	Narragansett	ship 620t	Henderson's Wharf	Edmunds, John	50		
Feb. 12, 1852	Nathaniel Hooper	ship 427t	Brown's Wharf	Rains, Lewis	51	March 10, 1852	27
Nov. 20, 1835	Nelson Clark	brig 187t	Spear's Wharf	Smith, John A.	5	Dec. 12, 1835	22
May 17, 1836	Nelson Clark	brig 187t	Smith's Dock	Smith, John A.	3	June 28, 1836	42
Apr. 26. 1826	North America	ship 284t	Mezick's Wharf	Child, Christopher	43	May 20, 1826	24
Nov. 23, 1822	North America	ship 284t	Water's Wharf	Child, Samuel C.	40	Dec. 30, 1822	37
Oct. 14, 1823	North America	ship 284t	Ramsay's Wharf	Child, Samuel C.	20	Nov. 18, 1823	35
Dec. 20, 1824	North America	ship 284t	Water's Wharf	Martin, Henry	40	Feb. 5, 1825	47

Dates	Vessel	Vessel Type	Dock	Ship's Master	#	Arrival	#days
Feb.27, 1843	Northumberland	brig 167t		Nason, William C.	34	March 19, 1843	20
July 6, 1836	Opelousas	brig 160t		Collins, R.	14	Aug. 5, 1836	30
Apr.16, 1825	Orbit	brig 199t		Riley, Philip	48	May 11, 1825	25
Dec. 30, 1822	Orion	brig 204t	Spear's Wharf	Mayhew, ?	38	Jan. 27, 1823	28
Oct. 22, 1842	Orleans	brig		Lewis, William J.	4		
Sept. 29, 1827	Oscar	schooner		Byrne, Thomas	3		
Oct. 16, 1839	Osceola	ship 549t	Frederick Street Dock	Childs, A.	3	Oct. 28, 1839	12
Nov. 11, 1847	Osprey	brig 236t	Corner's Wharf	Gibbons	13		
Oct. 10, 1845	P. Soule	brig 177t	Flanigan's Wharf	Delville, A.	19	Oct. 27, 1845	17
Nov. 15, 1856	P.R. Hazeltine	barque 399t		McCullis, ?	8	Dec. 14, 1856	29
Nov. 16, 1835	Palestine	ship 470t	Water's Wharf	Littlefield, A.M.	47	Dec. 18, 1835	32
March 30, 1853	Pamphylia	barque 252t	Henderson's Wharf	Shald, Saul	1	April 23, 1853	24
March 26, 1831	Pandora	brig 210t		Ewell, James	16	May 3, 1831	38
Sept. 9, 1845	Paoli	barque 309t	Frederick Street Dock	Welsh, James	61	Oct. 6, 1845	27
Dec. 27, 1845	Paoli	barque 310t	Chase's Wharf	Welsh, James	9	Jan. 24, 1846	28
Oct. 10, 1842	Parthenon	ship 536t	Chase's Wharf	Woodbury, J.T.	2	Oct. 23, 1842	13
June 1, 1853	Patrick Henry	schooner 211t	Henderson's Wharf	Kendson, ?	15	July 21, 1853	50
July 14, 1836	Patriot	brig 124t	Spear's Wharf	Hammond, Oliver	5	Aug. 5, 1836	22
Apr. 9, 1832	Pensacola	brig 237t	Chase's Wharf	Gregory, John Jr.	2	May 1, 1832	22
Nov. 17, 1842	Peru	barque 271t		Bailey, James G.	21	Dec. 5, 1842	18
Jan. 10, 1855	Pharsalia	ship 617t	Henderson's Wharf	Dreyer, John	7	Feb. 11, 1855	32
Feb. 8, 1829	Phillipi				1	March 6, 1829	26
March 27, 1827	Phoenix	barque 244t		Bcush, Nathaniel	56	April 22, 1847	26
Dec. 23, 1834	Pilgrim	brig 199t	Spear's Wharf	Stevens, J.J,	13	Jan. 27, 1835	35
Dec. 12, 1835	Pilgrim	brig 199t	Spear's Wharf	Martin, H.	7	Jan. 10, 1836	29
Dec. 4, 1837	Pilgrim	brig 199t	Spear's Wharf	Stevens, ?	1	Jan. 2, 1838	29

Dates	Vessel	Vessel Type	Dock	Ship's Master	#	Arrival	#days
Sept. 15, 1847	Pioneer	barque 346t	Flanigan's Wharf	Galt, W.	50	Oct. 7, 1847	22
July 20, 1848	Pioneer	barque 346t	Flanigan's Wharf	Galt, W.	18	Aug. 14, 1848	25
Sept. 17, 1834	Plutarch	ship 359t	Ramsay's Wharf	Johnson, Samuel M.	19	Oct. 17, 1834	30
June 12, 1852	Pompei	Steamer			2		
Dec. 11, 1841	Porpoise	brig 160t	Smith's Dock	Jordan, Washington	20	Jan. 7, 1842	27
Feb. 28, 1824	Robert Reade	brig 185t	Water's Wharf	Smith, Samuel	11	March 22, 1824	23
	Russell	brig	Bowly's Wharf	Matthews, '?	48	March 16, 1839	15
Feb. 10, 1844	Sabine	brig 164t	Frederick Street Dock	Blockington, J.M.	20		
Feb. 27, 1844	Saldana	brig 220t		Stubbs, J.S.	10	March 13, 1844	15
Sept. 28, 1846	Salvadora	brig 182t	Bowly's Wharf	Hobbs, George	51	Oct. 17, 1846	19
Apr. 2, 1831	Sarah	brig 137t		Rollins, William	3	April 30, 1831	28
Sept. 8, 1831	Sarah (B)	brig 137t		Rollins, William	4	Oct.14, 1831	36
Oct. 15, 1836	Sarah Ann	schooner	O'Donnell's Wharf	Bontemp, J.	8	Oct. 29, 1836	14
Feb. 8, 1851	Sarah Bridge	barque 483t	Henderson's Wharf	Stout, ?	38	Feb. 28, 1851	20
Oct. 25, 1822	Schuylkill	ship		Greaves, John	6		
Sept. 30, 1843	Scotia	ship 560t		Leslie, Henry	97	Oct. 16, 1843	16
Oct. 21, 1840	Scotland				6		
Dec. 20, 1838	Seaman	ship 240t	Frederick Street Dock		32		
March 25, 1839	Seaman	ship 240t	Bowly's Wharf	Crowell, James	55	April 18, 1839	24
Nov. 26, 1839	Seaman	ship 240t	Frederick Street Dock		1	Dec. 20, 1839	24
March 20, 1840	Seaman	ship 240t	Frederick Street Dock	Nickerson, ?	4	April 15, 1840	26
Dec. 16, 1841	Seaman	ship 240t	Spear's Wharf	Myrick, Joseph	14	Jan. 16, 1842	31
Apr. 8, 1842	Seaman	ship 240t	Fenby's Wharf	Myrick, Joseph	8	May 3, 1842	25
July 12, 1853	Sequin	brig 198t		Hubel, James A.	17		
Oct. 20, 1836	Serene	brig 313t	Tenant's Wharf	Cooksey, C.H.	34	Nov. 20, 1836	31
March 13, 1840	Shamrock	brig 195t	Frederick Street Dock	Goodrich, ?	13	April 10, 1840	28

Dates	Vessel	Vessel Type	Dock	Ship's Master	#	Arrival	#days
March 27, 1827	Shepherdess	ship 274t	Gibson's Wharf	Cook, Enoch	10	June 10, 1827	75
Nov. 14, 1853	Sherwood	barque	Henderson's Wharf	Foster ?	1	Dec. 7, 1853	23
Nov. 17, 1831	Signet	sloop 75t		Griffin, E.	33	Dec. 14, 1831	27
Feb. 5, 1835	Snow	brig 197t	O'Donnell's Wharf	Snow, Israel	7		
Oct. 7, 1839	Solomon Saltus	barque 316t	Frederick Street Dock	Nickerson, S.R.	114	Nov. 7, 1839	31
March 1, 1841	Solomon Saltus	barque 316t	Fenby's Wharf	Gray, Joshua	1	March 29, 1841	28
March 18, 1842	Solomon Saltus	barque 316t	Fenby's Wharf	Gray, Joshua	1	April 5, 1842	18
Oct. 27, 1849	Southerner	barque 338t	Frederick Street Dock	Hooper, Edward	94	Nov. 11, 1849	15
Jan. 21, 1850	Southerner	barque 338t	Frederick Street Dock	Hooper, Edward	46	Feb. 7, 1850	17
Jan. 5, 1852	Southerner	barque 338t	Brown's Wharf	Hooper, Edward	52	Jan. 29, 1852	24
Apr. 24, 1841	Splendid	brig 226t	Fenby's Wharf	McKensie, Reuben	27	May 21, 1841	27
Nov. 29, 1845	St. Mary	brig 188t		White, R.D.	73	Dec. 19, 1845	20
Nov. 26, 1825	States (B)	ship 290t	Mezick's Wharf	Child, Samuel C.	60	Dec. 23, 1825	27
March 10, 1826	States (B)	ship 290t	Mezick's Wharf	Child, Samuel C.	57	April 8, 1826	29
Nov. 22, 1827	States (B)	ship 290t			149	Dec. 23, 1827	31
Apr. 14, 1828	States (B)	ship 290t	Mezick's Wharf	Hipkins, J.L.	76	May 2, 1828	18
March 28, 1825	Statira	brig 183t	Smith's Dock	Patton, William	28	April 14, 1825	17
Nov. 21, 1843	Strafford	barque 314t	Jackson's Wharf	Robson, William H.	20	Dec. 10, 1843	19
Oct. 31, 1827	Sultana	brig 230t	Gibson's Wharf	Stansbury, Robert	3		
Apr. 7, 1819	Superb	ship 523t	Baron's Wharf	Weems, Charles	15	April 29, 1819	22
Nov. 2, 1843	Superb	ship 523t	Tenart's Wharf	Gatchell, John G.	117	Nov. 19, 1843	17
Oct. 25, 1822	Susan Miller	schooner		Davis, Francis	102	Nov. 25, 1822	31
Nov. 26, 1853	Tangier	barque 373t		Switzer, ?	25	Dec. 22, 1853	26
Dec. 12, 1818	Temperance	brig 441t		Beard, James	24	Jan.12, 1819	31
Dec. 16, 1840	Tippecanoe	ship 444t	Chase's Wharf		23	Jan. 4, 1841	19
Apr. 1, 1841	Tippecanoe	ship 444t	Fenby's Wharf	Gray, Adams	23	April 23, 1841	22

Dates	Vessel	Vessel Type	Dock	Ship's Master	#	Arrival	#days
Oct. 16, 1841	Tippecanoe	ship 444t	Fenby's Wharf	Gray, Adams	6	Oct. 29, 1841	13
Jan. 18, 1842	Tippecanoe	ship 444t	Chase's Wharf	Gray, Adams	115	Feb. 4, 1842	17
May 4, 1842	Tippecanoe	ship 444t			4		
Sept. 4, 1843	Tippecanoe	ship 444t	Chase's Wharf	Gray, Adams	1	Sept. 25, 1843	21
Apr. 15, 1844	Tippecanoe	ship 444t	Chase's Wharf	Gray, Adams	41	May 4, 1844	19
Sept. 18. 1844	Tippecanoe	ship 244t	Fenby's Wharf	Gray, Adams	7	Oct. 6, 1844	18
Apr. 20, 1829	Topaz	brig 193t	O'Donnell's Wharf	Brown, Stephen	39	May 20, 1829	30
Jan. 13, 1827	Trafalgar*	brig 160t		Winsor, Isaac	30	Feb.1, 1827	19
Dec. 23, 1819	Triton (B)	ship 324t	Kerr's Wharf	Jenkins, B.J.	27	Feb.1, 1820	40
Oct. 15, 1836	Tweed	brig 306t		Robinson, R.	3	Nov. 15, 1836	26
Oct. 20, 1836	Tweed*	brig 306t	Town Creek	Robinson, R.	111	Nov. 15, 1836	26
Nov. 9, 1833	Ulysees	ship	Tenant's Wharf	Kennedy, Thomas	14		
Jan. 10, 1838	Uncas	brig 155t		Boush, ?	43	Feb. 1, 1838	22
Apr. 3, 1838	Uncas	brig 155t			5	April 26, 1838	23
Oct. 23, 1820	Unicorn (B)	ship		McKowen, S.W.	12	Nov. 16, 1820	24
July 26, 1847	Union	brig 180t	O'Donnell's Wharf	Hooper, Edward	50	Aug. 21, 1847	26
May 13, 1848	Union	brig 180t	O'Donnell's Wharf	Hooper, Edward	46	June 14, 1848	32
Oct. 9, 1848	Union	brig 180t	Frederick Street Dock	Hooper, Edward	64	Oct. 29, 1848	20
Dec. 16, 1848	Union	brig 180t	Frederick Street Dock	Hooper, Edward	139	Jan. 13, 1849	28
March 17, 1849	Union	brig 180t	Frederick Street Dock	Goodmanson, John	42	April 9, 1849	23
Nov. 17, 1849	Union	brig 180t	Frederick Street Dock	H.	65	Dec. 5, 1849	18
Apr. 20, 1850	Union	brig 180t	Frederick Street Dock	Goodwin, ?	9	May 17, 1850	27
Nov. 17, 1845	Venus	brig 195t	Flanigan's Wharf	Saul, Francis	2	Dec. 16, 1845	29
Dec. 9, 1843	Victorine	brig 239t		Jones, Alexander	1		
March 9, 1844	Victorine	brig 239t	Smith's Dock	Jones, Alexander	60	March 26, 1844	17

Dates	Vessel	Vessel Type	Dock	Ship's Master	#	Arrival	#days
May 24, 1844	Victorine	brig 239t		Jones, Alexander	60	June 29, 1844	38
Oct. 25, 1844	Victorine	brig 239t			8	Nov. 11, 1844	17
Dec. 21, 1844	Victorine	brig 239t		Sanner, J.B.	24	Jan. 12, 1845	22
March 1, 1845	Victorine	brig 239t	Smith's Dock	Davis, T.D.	82	March 25, 1845	24
May 14, 1845	Victorine	brig 239t		Davis, Thomas D.	90	June 4, 1845	21
Sept. 29, 1845	Victorine	brig 239t	Smith's Dock	Davis, T.D.	108	Oct. 19, 1845	20
Dec. 17, 1845	Victorine	brig 239t		Forest, James F.	96	Jan. 2, 1846	16
March 14, 1846	Victorine	brig 239t		Forest, James F.	62	April 3, 1846	20
Sept. 12, 1846	Victorine	brig 239t	Smith's Dock	Forest, James F.	71	Sept. 26, 1846	14
Dec. 31, 1846	Victorine	brig 239t	Smith's Dock	Hobbs, George	138	Jan. 27, 1847	27
Dec. 19, 1825	Virginia	brig 171t		Doggett, ?	49	Jan. 10, 1826	22
March 11, 1826	Virginia	brig 171t		Doggett, ?	2	April 2, 1826	22
March 31, 1828	Virginia	brig 234t	Gibsor's Wharf	Ancrews, William	9	April 23, 1828	23
Nov. 18, 1823	Virginia	brig 234t		Staples, John	14	Dec. 10, 1823	22
May 20, 1826	Virginia	brig 272t		Weeks, Alexander	1	June 11, 1826	22
Nov. 7, 1847	W.H.D.C. Wright	barque 371t	Flannigan's Wharf	Jackson	9	Nov. 30, 1847	23
Apr. 3, 1851	Waverly	brig 192t	Henderson's Wharf	Anderson, ?	33	April 29, 1851	26
Oct. 9, 1821	William and Mary				25		
Feb. 16, 1847	Zoe	brig 196t		Phillips, William	133	March 15, 1847	27
Dec. 17, 1823	Zuline	schooner 144t		Pascal, Peter	2	Jan. 8, 1824	22

Appendix 1

The Largest New Orleans Shipments

Balloon-December 22, 1821
(128 slaves)

Several days before Christmas, 1822, on board the ship *Balloon*, the final Baltimore roll call of slaves occurred. Those preparing the vessel, captained by John A. Smith, had now boarded 128 human beings for shipment. Two indicators lead to the probability that this entire shipment was scheduled for transmigration (re-settlement) and not for sale. First, the owners were private shippers, appearing on a one-time basis in the records. Secondly, the number of children twelve years of age and under on board was fifty-six. This would have been uncustomary for the trader. The slave traders with the largest percentage of children shipped for sale in the Southern market rarely reached a number larger than 20 percent of the whole.

The final roll call in New Orleans occurred on January 18th, twenty-seven days after the roll call in Baltimore.

Susan Miller- October 25, 1822
(102 slaves)

During the latter portion of October 1822 the schooner *Susan Miller*, captained by Francis Davis, was prepared for departure bound from Baltimore to New Orleans. On board the schooner the Custom's Official performed the roll call of slaves. With several exceptions, the Woolfolk family shipped all of the slaves with the intention of re-sale within the Southern market. Twenty-six of the one hundred-two slaves on board were twelve years of age and under.

The New Orleans final roll call of the slaves occurred thirty-one days after the roll call in Baltimore (November 25, 1822).

The Mars- November 2, 1824
(139 slaves)

Moored at Water's Wharf on the southeast end of Pitt Street, The one hundred-ninety ton brig *Mars* received merchandise, passengers and slaves during the latter part of October 1824. The sole shippers of the one 139 slaves on board were Austin and Joseph Biggers Woolfolk of Pratt Street. Seventy-four of the one hundred-thirty-five slaves, whose sex was discernable, were males. Forty-one of the slaves on board were children, twelve years of age and under. Typically the Woolfolk's family business shipped a very high percentage of children south, probably as a result of their known substantial shipments of entire families.

The total duration between roll call in Baltimore and final roll call in New Orleans covered a period of 32 days.

Hibernia-December 5, 1826
(188 slaves)

In early December 1826 the 327-ton Baltimore built ship *Hibernia* lie moored at Water's Wharf. By December 5th the New Orleans merchant Leon Chabert as well as Austin Woolfolk had brought on board the vast majority of the 188 slaves slated for shipment. With Matthew Robinson as captain the vessel was prepared to weigh anchor. Among the slaves on board 55 of the 188 whose ages were discernable were 12 years of age or under, an unusually high number of children slated for sale in New Orleans.

Between the roll call on December 5th and the final roll call in New Orleans the slaves had spent fifty days in transit.

States-November 22, 1827
(149 slaves)

The 290-ton Baltimore built ship states departed for New Orleans during the beginning of the fourth week of November. All but eleven of the slaves on board were being shipped for Austin Woolfolk and his brother Joseph. Of the one 122 Woolfolk slaves whose ages were discernible, 30 were children 12 years of age and under. Among some off the youngest on board were 3 month-old James Smith, 6 month-old Edward Wright, 8 month-old Ellen Smith and 9 month-old James Wilson.

The thirty-one day journey ended with the final roll call in New Orleans on December 23rd.

Lafayette-October 22, 1828
(211 slaves)

Little is known about this particular shipment other than that it was the largest manifest of slaves (amongst the surviving manifests) ever shipped to New Orleans from Baltimore. The 260 ton ship, captained by veteran Robert Hardie, carried slaves for Joseph, Austin and Richard Woolfolk, placed on board in several installments over a period of five days. Of the 200 slaves whose ages were discernable, 47 were 12 years of age and under.

The period between the roll call in Baltimore and the final roll call in New Orleans was twenty-two days.

Henry Clay-December 4th through 8th, 1828
(144 slaves)

When the forty-one slaves of Austin Woolfolk were roll called on December 4th, 1828 they were placed below deck for their final passage to New Orleans. Eight members of the Sephus family, some of whom would surely have been separated by sale in New Orleans, were segregated in the belly of the Baltimore built 371 ton ship *Henry Clay* moored at Price's Wharf. Also placed on board were four members of the Haman family, Ann Guy and her two children, Ann and Mariah Finley (both 19), Bill and Margaret Heath, Rachel Stanley and her children Harriet and Dinah, Fanny and Jack Brown, Sinah Gibson and her children Henry and James. James W. Bennett (12 years old) and Neal Boyer (11 years old), despite their age, were shipped without accompanying family members as were a number of young adults.

What made this shipment particularly unusual is that the **Henry Clay** was scheduled to dock at Nottingham, Anne Arundel County, and pick up additional slaves. After the final roll call in Baltimore on December 4th the additional human cargo was roll called four days later at Nottingham. There 103 slaves, all being shipped as a result of transmigration (and not for sale) were boarded and mixed together below deck with Woolfolk's slaves for the Southern market.

Sixty-one of the slaves on board were twelve years of age or under.

Their thirty-five day journey ended with the final roll call in New Orleans on January 8th.

Brunswick-October 12, 1831
(148 slaves)

The 295-ton ship weighed anchor from Water's Wharf at the southeast end of Pitt Street during the end of the second week of October carrying a manifest of slaves owned entirely by the Woolfolk family. Twenty-six, or more than one in every six slaves on board were children twelve years of age and under. Among the children on board were fifteen that were five years of age or under.

The slaves whose surnames were discernible seem to indicate that a substantial number of those on board were families of two or more members. Considering the fact that Woolfolk often purchased entire families or portions of families this finding is representative of the norm more often than not in his family business.

The journey to New Orleans was one of sixteen days duration. The *Brunswick's* manifest was roll called in New Orleans on October 28, 1831.

Tweed-October 20, 1836
(111 slaves)

When the 306 ton brig *Tweed* was pulled by steamer into Baltimore's harbor for its' departure during the third week of

October only three slaves had been placed on board the vessel. Captain Robinson's orders required him to proceed to Town Creek, Annapolis, where an additional manifest was to be loaded on board.

Upon arrival in Town Creek 108 slaves, owned by four slaveholders, were boarded for the journey to New Orleans. Close scrutiny of those moving their slaves confirms the probability that these slaves were being shipped as a result of transmigration and not for sale in the Southern market. Thirty-seven of the slaves on board were twelve years of age or under.

The total voyage of the *Tweed* constituted a journey of twenty-six days duration. The Tweed arrived in New Orleans for final roll call on November 15th.

Isaac Franklin-September 28, 1838
(170 slaves)

The 187-ton brig **Isaac Franklin** was constructed by Levin Dunkin in his Baltimore shipyard and completed in 1835. The vessel, with a seventy-three foot keel, was commissioned by the Alexandria based slave traders Isaac Franklin and John Armfield specifically for the domestic slave trade. This particular shipment brought together two of the nation's leading traders. One of the traders, Hope Hull Slatter, whose slave jail had been completed three months earlier, loaded eighty-eight of the total number of slaves on board. The slaves had been marched down Pratt Street from the pen's location on Pratt, several doors east of Howard Street.

The second trader, George Kephart, who had not long since purchased a portion of the Franklin-Armfield business, placed the remaining eighty-two slaves on board. Kephart's slaves were probably kept at the pen of James Franklin Purvis until shipment. Purvis, whose pen was on Harford Road near Aisquith Street, was the nephew and one time agent for Isaac

Franklin. In light of the fact that he had previous business relations with Kephart and was managing this particular shipment along with Slatter it would have been the likely choice.

Thirty-three of the slaves on board were children twelve years of age or under.

The *Isaac Franklin* was moored in fells Point, at the foot of Thames and Lancaster at what was then known as Craig's Wharf. When captain William Smith weighed anchor with his precious cargo on board during the last week of September he began what was destined to be a nineteen-day journey to New Orleans. The final roll call was initiated in New Orleans on October 17, 1838.

Solomon Saltus-October 7, 1839
(114 slaves)

All 114 slaves on board this 316-ton barque were the property of Hope Hull Slatter and, consequently, destined for sale in the New Orleans market. Twenty-nine of Slatter's slaves were twelve years of age or under. The vessel, captained by S. R. Nickerson, was moored at the Frederick Street Dock. There appears to be at least fourteen families aboard the vessel among those being shipped.

This thirty-one day journey ended with the final roll call on November 7th.

Tippecanoe-January 18, 1842
(115 slaves)

Chase's Wharf, South of Thames Street in Fells Point, was a popular shipping location during the height of the domestic slave trade. At least 297 slaves were shipped in 13 separate shipments from Chase's Wharf to the city of New Orleans. Present on three of those voyages was popular Fells Point resident and captain Adams Gray. Of the 115 slaves on board the **Tippecanoe** during this shipment 97 were owned by slave trader Hope Hull Slatter.

The 444-ton ship **Tippecanoe** weighed anchor during the third week of January, arriving in New Orleans on February 4th after a journey of seventeen days.

Superb-November 2, 1843
(117 slaves)

Baltimore Shipbuilder John Robb completed this 523-ton ship in 1834 on behalf of a number of merchants. This particular vessel appears only once in slave manifests. The early November shipment was significant in size and carried the slaves of Baltimore traders Hope Hull Slatter and Joseph Donovan. Slatter shipped eighty-eight of the human chattels, while the remaining thirty-five sent on their "final passage" by Donovan. Only five children, twelve years of age or under, were placed on the **Superb**.

The two-decked, one hundred-twelve foot keeled ship, captained by John G. Gatchell disembarked from Tenant's Wharf on its seventeen-day voyage shortly after roll call. The final roll call occurred in New Orleans on November 19th.

Kirkwood-January 4, 1845
(110 slaves)

Another popular captain sailing packet ships from Baltimore to New Orleans was Hugh Martin. When Martin weighed anchor from Smith's Wharf (currently the site of Baltimore's national aquarium) the 110 slaves on board brought his twelve-month total to 277 human captives carried south.

The captain was a popular choice in the packet trade. Over a six-year period vessels he captained carried 614 slaves to the port of New Orleans alone.

This shipment was significant in that three of the top five traders in Baltimore's history were represented on board. Bernard Moore Campbell, whose pen was on Conway Street, shipped twelve slaves. Hope Hull Slatter shipped thirty-six of the captives. The bulk of the slaves on board, sixty-two in number, were shipped by Joseph Donovan who was still using the pen of Austin Woolfolk on Pratt Street, west of Cove Street.

Of the total, twenty-eight of the slaves were twelve years of age and under.

The 211 ton Baltimore built brig's journey to New Orleans lasted twenty-one days arriving in New Orleans on January 25th.

Kirkwood-April 15, 1845
(127 slaves)

John F. Haynie was another popular captain sailing packets to the Southern market. His New Orleans shipments of slaves transported almost 600 human captives to the southern city on behalf of Baltimore traders. This shipment proved to be unusual in that four major traders, including one traveling trader, placed their human cargo on board. The only non Baltimore based trader on board was Ebenezer Rodbind whose property numbered twenty-three slaves, or about 19% of the total. Also on board were Bernard Moore Campbell (5 slaves), Hope Hull Slatter (60 slaves), and Joseph Donovan (39 slaves).

The vessel was moored at the Frederick Street dock, popular wharves for the shipment of slaves during the busy 1840's period. The current site of this dock lies between the National Aquarium and the mammal building at the foot of

Frederick Street. The *Kirkwood's* final voyage before the 1845 growing season required a total of only fourteen days, landing in New Orleans on April 29th.

Victorine-September 29, 1845
(108 slaves)

The current site of the west end of the National Aquarium, once known as Smith's Dock, has two important connections to slavery. It was the site where young Frederick Bailey (Alias Frederick Douglass) landed when shipped from the Eastern Shore to Baltimore as a young boy. Secondly, it was one of the most popular sites for the shipments of slaves on board packet vessels, particularly during the 1840's.

The *Victorine* shipped on a number of occasions from Smith's Dock. On this occasion Thomas D. Davis was the captain of the vessel. In less than three years the *Victorine* was to carry 799 slaves to the New Orleans market.

On this particular journey of twenty days Joseph Donovan was the major slave trader shipping his cargo. Only twelve of the slaves on board were twelve years of age or under. Donovan liked to ship adults or older children, as he was a major supplier of labor for Southern plantation owners.

The final roll call took place in the New Orleans harbor on October 19th.

Kirkwood-October 16, 1845
(117 slaves)

When the brig *Kirkwood*, captained by Hugh Martin, departed the Frederick Street Dock on its fourteen-day journey to New Orleans there were slaves belonging to three major traders on board. Hope Hull Slatter had 89 slaves, Joseph Donovan 5 slaves, and Bernard Moore Campbell 23 slaves.

Nineteen of the one hundred-seventeen on board were children twelve years of age and under.

The final roll call in New Orleans took place on October 31st.

Kirkwood-December 10, 1846
(158 slaves)

When the brig **Kirkwood**, captained by John F. Haynie, was pulled by steamer from the Frederick Street Dock 32 of the 139 slaves whose ages were discernible were children 12 years of age or under. Hope Slatter's son Henry shipped 42 slaves, Bernard Moore Campbell 18, and Joseph Donovan 91. Two citizens not in the trade shipped the remaining seven slaves.

The eighteen-day journey ended with the final roll call on December 28th.

Victorine-December 31, 1846
(138 slaves)

When the 239-ton brig **Victorine**, captained by George Hobbs, was pulled from its berth the last of December the trader with the greatest number of slaves on board was traveling trader Ebenezer Rodbind (52 slaves). Henry F. Slatter shipped 45 slaves, Joseph S. Donovan 33, and Bernard Moore Campbell 8.

The journey from Smith's Dock in the inner harbor basin to New Orleans was twenty-seven days in duration. A journey of this duration could indicate troubled seas, a stop-off, or both.

The vessel arrived in New Orleans for final roll call on January 27th.

General Pinckney-January 19, 1847
(140 slaves)

The 194-ton brig was moored at Smith's Dock before weighing anchor near the end of the third week of January. Hope Hull Slatter, as was typical of his shipments for several years, had moved his eighty-three slaves down Pratt Street to the waiting vessel in a series of omnibuses.

The scene was a horrifying one (as it often was) as family members, weeping with sorrow, followed the moving caravan down Baltimore's Trail of Tears. Their attempts for one last hug or kiss from their enslaved family members were defeated by Slatter's whip.

Also marching his slaves (thirty-two in number) down Pratt Street that day, from his pen on Conway Street, was Bernard Moore Campbell. Traveling trader Thomas Williams brought his twenty-five slaves to the dock and placed them on board for roll call.

Of the 140 humans placed on board that day 38 (nearly 39 percent) were children 12 years of age and under.

The vessel's fourteen-day journey ended in New Orleans with a final roll call on February 2nd.

Zoe-February 16, 1847
(133 slaves)

The 196 ton brig, captained by William Phillips, carried slaves for Bernard Moore Campbell (9 slaves), Joseph S. Donovan (35 slaves), Hope Hull Slatter (71 slaves), and Thomas Williams (18 slaves).

Of the 115 slaves whose ages were discernible 33 were children 12 years of age and under.

The brig's journey of twenty-seven days ended with the final roll call in New Orleans on March 15th

Kirkwood-October 26, 1847
(168 slaves)

The 343-ton barque **Kirkwood** (not to be confused with the brig Kirkwood) carried the fourth largest cargo of slaves ever shipped to the New Orleans market from Baltimore. With Hugh Martin on board as captain the vessel made the journey south in short order (thirteen days). One hundred forty-one slaves on board belonged to Joseph S. Donovan. The remaining twenty-seven slaves belonged to New Orleans traveling trader Ebenezer Rodbind.

Twenty-one of the slaves on board were children twelve years of age and under.

The final roll call on board the **Kirkwood** was made at New Orleans on November 8th.

E. H. Chapin-December 2, 1847
(101 slaves)

Of the three journeys in nine months the 424-ton barque made from Baltimore this voyage carried the largest shipment of slaves. Captained by George W. Collier, the vessel was pulled into the harbor from Flannigan's Wharf on the beginning of a twenty-three day journey to New Orleans. Traders Hope Hull Slatter and Joseph S. Donovan shipped the vast majority of slaves on board.

Thirty-one of the human cargo were children twelve years of age and under.

The final roll call occurred on Christmas day in the New Orleans harbor.

Kirkwood-October 14, 1848
(147 slaves)

The 343-ton barque, moored at Flannigan's Wharf, was loaded with fifty-two slaves belonging to Bernard Moore

Campbell as well as ninety-five slaves belonging to Joseph S. Donovan. Twenty-two of the total numbers of slaves on board were twelve years of age and under.

The nineteen-day journey ended with a final roll call in New Orleans on November 2nd.

Elizabeth-November 18, 1848
(139 slaves)

With the exception of three slaves, Joseph S. Donovan, Bernard Moore Campbell, and Ebenezer Rodbind shipped all on board. Campbell had purchased Hope Slatter's pen and now operated from its Pratt Street location. Donovan's pen was now located on Camden Street near Light Street. The 230-ton barque, sailing from Flanigan's Wharf during the third week of November, made the journey to New Orleans in fifteen days.

Twenty-seven of the slaves on board were children twelve years of age and under.

The final roll call was held on December 3rd.

Union-December 16, 1848
(139 slaves)

This shipment of the 180-ton brig moored at the Frederick Street Dock carried slaves for Ebenezer Rodbind, Bernard Moore Campbell, and Joseph S. Donovan.

Twenty-five of the slaves on board were children twelve years of age and under.

The twenty-eight day journey ended with the final roll call in New Orleans' harbor on January 13th.

Helen A. Miller–October 18, 1852
(114 slaves)

With the Campbell brothers' rise to prominence in the slave trade in the 1850's their names became a household word throughout the South. This 510 ton ship, captained by W. Galt, carried 114 slaves to New Orleans, all but 9 of which were owned by the Campbells.

The vessel made the journey in an amazing period of eleven days, one of the fastest on record.

Only 2 of the 105 slaves owned by the Campbells were 12 years of age and under. This type of shipment was almost certainly as a result of a special order to supply adult field laborers to plantations in the South. Children above six years of age who were kept from such shipments would sometimes be sold through advertisements in local papers.

The final roll call in New Orleans occurred on October 29th.

Appendix 2

Wharves and Docks of Baltimore

The following is a list of Wharves and Docks lining the inner harbor and Fells Point areas of the northern coastline of Baltimore's harbor. These were the wharves and docks commonly used for the loading of packet vessels that regularly made their return to New Orleans with passengers, merchandise, and slaves.

The listings are gleaned from several decades of city directory entries. The author indicates, whenever possible, the current site of the wharf or dock.

I.H indicates inner harbor
F.P indicates Fells Point

Bowly's Wharf- South end of South Street (currently west of the Constellation) *I.H.*

Smith's Wharf- East side of Gay Street Dock (currently Pier 3 National Aquarium) *I.H.*

O'Donnell's Wharf- East side of the Frederick Street Dock. (currently between The National Aquarium and Marine mammal building) *I.H.*

Kerr's Wharf- Foot of Wills Street *F.P.*

Chase's Wharf- South from Thames between Ramsay's Wharf and Fenby's Wharf- Fells Point *F.P.*

Spears Wharf- West side of Gay Street Dock (current site of the U.S.S Torsk and Chesapeake Light Ship) *I.H.*

Corner's Wharf- Lower end of Frederick Street Dock (see O'Donnell's Wharf) *I.H.*

Wilson's Wharf- South of Fell Street between County and Sheppard *F.P.*

Craiggs' Wharf- East from Wolfe Street (current site of boat slips at the foot of Thames and Lancaster) *F.P.*

Barron's Wharf- see Craigg's Wharf *F.P.*

Waters Wharf- Between Fell and Thames *F.P.*

Kerr's Wharf- Between Bond and Market (Broadway) *F.P.*

Mezick's Wharf- Between Market (Broadway) and Ann *F.P.*

Jackson's Wharf- Foot of Bond, south of Thames *F.P.*

County Wharf- South end of Market (Broadway) *F.P.*

Commerce Street Wharf- South end of Commerce Street *I.H.*

Price's Wharf- East from the south end of Wolfe, between Thames and Fell *F.P*

Gibson's Wharf- South of Thames from 43 Fell *F.P.*

Tenant's Wharf- Between Market (Broadway) and Ann, south of Thame *F.P.*

McElderry's Wharf- East side of Long Dock (currently the site of the Power Plant) *I.H.*

Buchanan's Wharf- West side of the Frderick Street Dock. (currently the east end of the National Aquarium) *I.H.*

Brown's Wharf- The Foot of Market (Broadway) *F.P.*

Ramsay's Wharf- Between Caroline and Bond. (South of Thames) *F.P.*

Henderson's Wharf- Foot of Fell. *F.P*

Notes

Chapter 1 - **Auctions**

1. Account by author information in the Genius of Universal Emancipation May 13, 1826, p.292.
2. National Anti-Slavery Standard, March 17, 1853, p.170
3. Walter Johnson, *Soul by Soul: Life Inside the Antebellum Slave Market* (Cambridge, Mass. 1999) p.141
4. Frederic Bancroft, *Slave Trading in the Old South* (South Carolina, reprinted 1996) p. 108
5. National Anti-Slavery Standard, March 17, 1853 p.170
6. American and Commercial Daily Advertiser, September 10,1822, p.4
7. Ibid, September 30, 1813, p.3
8. Ibid, September 30, 1813, p.3
9. Ibid, October 5, 1813, p.3
10. Ibid, October 5, 1813, p.3
11. Ibid, October 12, 1813, p.3
12. Ibid, October 15, 1813, p.3
13. Ibid, November 23, 1813, p.1
14. Ibid, December 3, 1813, p.3
15. Ibid, December 17, 1813, p.3
16. Ibid, December 20, 1813, p.3
17. Ibid, December 30, 1813, p.3
18. Ibid, December 1, 1814, p.3
19. Ibid, December 7, 1814, p.3
20. Ibid, December 9, 1814, p.3
21. Ibid, January 6, 1815, p.3
22. Ibid, January 15, 1816, p.3
23. Ibid, February 5, 1816, p.3
24. Ibid, March 12, 1816, p.2
25. Ibid, November 5, 1816, p.2
26. Ibid, December 11, 1816, p.3
27. Ibid, December 17, 1816, p.3
28. Ibid, January 24, 1817, p.3
29. Ibid, July 27, 1816, p.1

30. Ibid, July 8, 1818, p.4
31. Ibid, July 19, 1816, p.3
32. Ibid, December 7, 1818, p.3
33. Ibid, January 28, 1823, p.3
34. Ibid, January 8, 1824, p.1
35. Ibid, April 9, 1824, p.3
36. Ibid, June 4, 1824, p.1
37. Ibid, September 16, 1824, p.1
38. Ibid, July 20, 1825, p.3

Chapter 2 - Agencies and Intelligence Offices

1. American and Commercial daily Advertiser July 21, 1821, p.3
2. Ibid, January 11, 1822, p.3
3. Ibid, August 21, 1822, p.3
4. Ibid, October 7, 1822, p.3
5. Ibid, September 26, 1822, p.3
6. Ibid, October 1, 1822, p.3
7. Ibid, October 30, 1822, p.2
8. Ibid, October 16, 1822, p.2
9. Ibid, August 5, 1825, p.3
10. Ibid, September 14, 1825, p.3
11. Ibid, September 24, 1825, p.3
12. Ibid, September 23, 1826, p.4
13. Ibid, January 15, 1833, p.3
14. Matchett's Baltimore City Directory 1849-50 and Baltimore Sun, January 9, 1849, p.3
15. Baltimore Sun, October 24, 1851, p.3
16. Pilot and Transcript, January 16, 1841, p.3
17. Baltimore Sun, June 10, 1844, p.2
18. Ibid, January 3, 1842, p.3
19. American and Commercial Daily Advertiser, October 20, 1828, p.3
20. Ibid, September 13, 1828, p.4
21. Ibid, September 22, 1828, p.4
22. Pilot and Transcript, January 16, 1841, p.3
23. Ibid
24. Ibid
25. Ibid, p.4

Chapter 3 - Dockside Sales

1. The Slave Narratives (Maryland), Federal Writers Project September 27, 1937 (Rezin Williams)
2. American and Commercial daily advertiser, December 2, 1815, p.3
3. Ibid, February 28, 1816, p.4

4. Ibid, March 5, 1816, p.3
5. Ibid, March 14, 1816, p.3
6. Ibid, December 16, 1816, p.3
7. Ibid, December 18, 1816, p.3
8. Ibid, December 21, 1818, p.3
9. Ibid, August 8, 1823, p.3
10. Ibid, July 21, 1825, p.3
11. Ibid, September 16, 1826, p.1
12. Ibid, September 13, 1828, p.4
13. Ibid, October 10, 1828, p.2
14. Ibid, October 18, 1828, p.4
15. Ibid, December 22, 1828, p.3
16. Ibid, September 10, 1829, p.4
17. Ibid, September 18, 1828, p.2
18. Ibid, September 19, 1828, p.4

Chapter 4 - **Hotels, Taverns, and Inns**

1. Bancroft, *Slave Trading in the Old South*, p.102
2. Baltimore Sun, February 28, 1855, p.1. The slave's name was actually Alexander Burns (incorrectly reported as Arthur Burns).
3. American and Commercial Daily Advertiser, December 1, 1815, p.4
4. Ibid, December 1, 1815, p.3
5. Ibid, December 19, 1815, p.4
6. Ibid, January 1, 1816, p.4
7. Ibid, April 23, 1816, p.3
8. Ibid, January 8, 1817, p.4
9. Ibid, July 1, 1817, p.4
10. Ibid, July 27, 1822, p.1
11. Ibid, January 12, 1824, p.3
12. Ibid, January 20, 1824, p.1
13. Ibid, January 21, 1824, p.3
14. Ibid, January 29, 1824, p.3
15. Ibid, February 7, 1824, p.4
16. Ibid, September 10, 1824, p.1
17. Ibid, November 9, 1829, p.1
18. Ibid, November 11, 1829, p.3
19. Hagerstown Mail, April 22, 1831, p.4
20. Frederick-town Herald, Apr. 23, 1831, p.4
21. Maryland Gazette, December 18, 1834, p.1
22. Frederick-town Herald, January 31, 1835, p.4
23. Port Tobacco Times and Charles County Advertiser, August 7, 1845, p.3
24. Cambridge Chronicle, October 10, 1846, p.3
25. Johnson, *Soul by Soul,* p.52

Note: This is an additional list sampling hotel/slave sale ads from local newspapers. In the following list all entries under acda signify *American and Commercial Daily Advertiser*. Entries listed Sun are the *Baltimore Sun*: the bar of the Washington Hotel acda-4/18/20-4;the bar of the New Bridge hotel (also known as Joseph Hart's Hotel acda-11/6/18-1, acda-10/29/21-3; the bar of the Globe Hotel (opposite the exchange) acda-1/14/24-4; the Cross Keys Tavern (corner of Lombard and South Howard Streets) acda-1/8/17-3; the United States Hotel (opposite the depot...Pratt Street) Pilot and Transcript-9/16/40-3; Barnum's Hotel Pilot and Transcript-9/2/40-3; Miller's Hotel Sun-5/14/50-4; General Wayne Hotel Sun-2/29/60-4; the Eastern and Western Hotel Sun-4/1/52-4; the Union Hotel Sun-1/7/50-3; Howard House Sun-3/31/56-3; The Eagle Hotel acda-9/8/42-3; Cugles Tavern, head of market Street acda-7/5/23-4; The Three Tuns Tavern acda-7/5/24-4; The Exchange Hotel, Water Street acda-4/20/24-3; Pamphilion's Hotel, Fells Point acda-7/18/16-3; Fowler's Tavern, near the market on Lexington Street acda- 12/4/15-4; Renshaw's Tavern, High St. Old Town, acda-12/9/16-1

Chapter 5 - **Children as victims of the Trade**

1. American and Commercial Daily Advertiser, December 9, 1820, p.1
2. Ibid, June 21, 1824, p.4
3. Ibid, October 1, 1827, p.3
4. Baltimore Sun, April 9, 1847, p.4
5. Ibid, January 9, 1849, p.3
6. Ibid, March 13, 1852, p.2
7. American and Commercial Daily Advertiser, March 1, 1824, p.1
8. Baltimore Sun, February 12, 1859, p.3
9. Ibid, April 6, 1857, p.2
10. Ibid, March 21, 1855, p.3
11. American and Commercial Daily advertiser, September 23, 1826, p.4
12. Baltimore Sun, March 26, 1853, p.3
Note: For other examples of the sale or hiring out of children 16 and under see Sun 1/11/47-4; 11/25/58-2; 2/6/57-2; 7/31/54-2; 4/13/54-3; 8/3/49-3; 11/20/55-3).
13. Inward Bound Slave Manifests (Record group #36) Baltimore to New Orleans May 14, 1822
14. Ibid, December 24, 1827
15. Ibid, January 28, 1829
16. Ibid, November 1, 1831
17. Ibid, April 13, 1825
18. American and Commercial Daily Advertiser, August 22, 1823, p.4
19. Ibid, May 1, 1824, p.4
20. Ibid, July 31, 1824, p.4
21. Ibid, July 14, 1828, p.4
22. Ibid, September 8, 1835, p.3
23. Ibid, April 22, 1836, p.1
24. Baltimore Sun, January 8, 1853, p.3

25. Inward Bound Slave Manifests (Record group #36) Baltimore to New Orleans March 22, 1822

26. Ibid, November 27, 1819

27. Baltimore Sun, august 17, 1847, p.2

28. Genius of Universal Emancipation, December 1821, p.85

Note: For additional information on kidnapping in Baltimore see *Baltimore, the Nineteenth Century Black Capital*, by Leroy Graham and *Slavery, Slaveholding, and the Free Black Population of Antebellum Baltimore*, by Ralph Clayton.

Chapter 6 - **Baltimore's Early Coastwise Domestic Slave Trade**

1.In November of 1821 the Woolfolk family shipped 52 slaves from Baltimore to New Orleans. Inward Bound Slave Manifests (Record group#36) Baltimore to New Orleans, November 21, 1821.

2. American and Commercial Daily Advertiser, October 29, 1816, p.2

3. Ibid, July 8, 1818, p.1

4. Inward Bound Slave Manifests (Record Group #36), Baltimore to New Orleans, December 9- 12, 1818

5. Ibid, January 6, 1819

6. Ibid, April 7, 1819

7. Ibid, November 8, 1819

Note: Some other examples of early shipments (1819-1821) include the *Triton*, 40 days; the *Franklin*, 18 days; the *Clio*, 26 days; the *Missouri*, 31 days; *Commodore Patterson*, 31 days; the *Intelligence*, 23 days; the *Unicorn*, 24 days; the *Agent*, 49 days; the *Hyperion*, 30 days; the *Good Hope*, 26 days; the *Superb*, 22 days;

8. Ibid, March 27, 1821

9. Ibid, March 20, 1819

10. Ibid, March 22, 1822

11. Ibid, Norfolk to New Orleans, February 19, 1819

12. Ibid, Richmond to New Orleans, February 19, 1820

13. Ibid, Baltimore to New Orleans, June 29, 1822

14. Ibid, December 17, 1821

15. Ibid, June 29, 1822

16. Ibid, April 26, 1822

17. Ibid, April 5, 1823

18. American and Commercial Daily Advertiser, October 26, 1820, p.1

19. Inward Bound Slave Manifests (Record group #36), Baltimore to New Orleans, November 8, 1820

20. American and Commercial Daily Advertiser, October 21, 1819, p.1

21. Inward Bound Slave Manifests (Record group #36), Baltimore to New Orleans, October 24, 1819

22. American and Commercial Daily Advertiser, December 23, 1822, p.1

23. Ibid, February 10, 1824, p.3

24. Ibid, October 16, 1827, p.1

25. Ibid, October 1, 1841, p.3
26. Inward Bound Slave Manifests (Record group #36), Baltimore to New Orleans, December 15, 1840
27. Ibid, March 27, 1841
28. Ibid, January 15, 1842
29. Ibid, April 15, 1844
30. Ibid, November 28, 1838
31. American and Commercial Daily Advertiser, November 19, 1838, p.3
32. Inward Bound Slave Manifests (Record group #36), Baltimore to New Orleans, January 14-22, 1840
33. American and Commercial Daily Advertiser, January 11, 1840, p.1
34. Inward Bound Slave Manifests (Record group #36), Baltimore to New Orleans, October 26, 1847
35. American and Commercial Daily Advertiser, October 2, 1847, p.2

Chapter 7 - **The Baltimore/Alexandria Market**

1. Bancroft *Slave Trading in the Old South* p.58
2. Andrews, *Slavery and the Domestic Slave Trade in the United States* p.142, 148
3. Jay, *Miscellaneous Writings on Slavery,* p.157, 158
4. Register of Vessels, port of New Orleans, Book #7 (1831-36) p.501.
The Isaac Franklin was built in Baltimore by the firm of Levin H. Dunkin in 1835 on behalf of John Armfield. *See Design Makes a Difference: Shipbuilding in Baltimore 1795-1835* by Toni Ahrens, p.151.
5. Account by author based on Inward Bound Slave Manifests (Record group #36) Baltimore to New Orleans, September 28, 1838
6. National Anti-Slavery Standard, June 3, 1841, p.206
7. Michel and Co. New Orleans City Directory 1838 and 1846
8. Cohen's New Orleans City Directory 1851
9. Ibid
10. Ibid
11. Pitts and Clarke New Orleans City Directory 1842
12. Michel and Co. New Orleans City Directory 1838

Chapter 8 - **Baltimore's Slave Traders**
Austin Woolfolk, Early King of the Trade

1. American and Commercial daily Advertiser, May 8, 1816, p.3
2. Ibid, January 31, 1817, p.1
3. Ibid, July 10, 1817, p.1
4. July 17, 1818, p.3
5. Genius of Universal Emancipation, November 6, 1829, p.67
6. Inward Bound Slave Manifests (Record group #36), Baltimore to New Orleans, November 21, 1821

7. Carolyn Greenfield Adams, *Hunter Sutherland's Slave Manumissions and Sales in Harford County, Md. 1775-1865* (Heritage Press, Bowie, Md.) p.75-78

8. American and Commercial Daily Advertiser, January 16, 1822, p.4

9. Inward Bound Slave Manifests (Record Group #36), Baltimore to New Orleans, March 23, 1822

10. Genius of Universal Emancipation, September 1822, p.47-48

11. American and Commercial Daily Advertiser, January 1, 1824, p.1

12. Inward Bound Slave manifests (Record Group #36), Baltimore to New Orleans, January 2, 1824

13. American and Commercial Daily Advertiser, March 1, 1824, p.4

14. Ibid, March 20, 1824, p.4

15. Inward Bound Slave manifests (Record Group #36), Baltimore to New Orleans, April 7, 1824

16. American and Commercial Daily Advertiser, April 17, 1824, p.3

17. Ibid, May 19, 1824, p.4

18. Ibid, June 17, 1824, p.1

19. Genius of Universal Emancipation, June 1825, p.129-130

20. Inward Bound Slave Manifests (Record Group #36), Baltimore to New Orleans, March 25, 1825

21. Genius of Universal Emancipation, July 1825, p.149-151

22. Genius of Universal Emancipation, June, 1825, p.130; also Inward Bound Slave Manifests (Record group #36), Baltimore to New Orleans, March 28, 1825

23. Inward Bound Slave Manifests (Record Group #36), Baltimore to New Orleans, April 16, 1825

24. Ibid, Baltimore to New Orleans, May 7, 1825

25. Johnson, *Soul by Soul*, p.25-26

26. Ibid, p.26

Austin Woolfolk's Rise to Supremacy

1. Genius of Universal Emancipation, September 12, 1825, p.17

2. Adams, *Hunter Sutherland's Slave Manumissions and sales in Harford County, Md. 1775-1865,* p.70-86

3. Inward Bound Slave Manifests (Record group #36), Baltimore to New Orleans, October 15, 1822

4. Adams, *Hunter Sutherland's Slave Manumissions and sales in Harford County, Md. 1775-1865,* p.75-78

5. Ibid, p.81-82

6. Inward Bound Slave Manifests (Record group #36), Baltimore to New Orleans, April 16, 1825

7. An account recited by Bowser shortly before his execution may be seen in the Genius of Universal Emancipation, January 2, 1827, p.109-110. An additional source of interest is the Niles Weekly Register, May 20, 1826, p. 202.

8. Inward Bound Slave Manifests (Record group #36), Baltimore to New Orleans, December 5, 1826

9. Ibid, Baltimore to New Orleans, February 16, 1827

10. Ibid, Baltimore to New Orleans, April 7, 1827

11. Ibid, Baltimore to New Orleans, April 30, 1827

12. Ibid, Baltimore to New Orleans, November 22, 1827

13. American and Commercial Daily Advertiser, November 28, 1827, p.3

14. Account by author based on Inward Bound Slave Manifests (Record group #36), Baltimore to New Orleans, December 24, 1827. Austin Woolfolk's trend was to ship before sunrise when possible.

15. Ethan Allan Andrews, *Slavery and the Domestic Slave Trade in the United States* (Freeport, N.Y. Books for Libraries Press, 1971) Reprint of 1836 ed., p.80

16. Inward Bound Slave Manifests (Record group #36) Baltimore to New Orleans, September 12, 1846

17. Letter from John Woolfolk to Emily Woolfolk, February 13, 1847. Reprinted in the *Slack Family Papers*, University of North Carolina at Chapel Hill, p.126

18. Columbus Times (Georgia), February 23, 1847. Reprinted in the *Slack Family Papers*, Louisiana State University, p.126

Chapter 9 - **Hope Hull Slatter, Heir to the Throne**

1. *Central Georgia Genealogical Society Quarterly, v.18-20, 1996-1998,* Bibb County deed books Book O, April 26, 1828 and July 2, 1828.

2. Bancroft, *Slave Trading in the Old South,* p.37

3. Matchett's Baltimore City directory, 1837.

4. Andrews, *Slavery and the Domestic Slave Trade in the United States,* p.78

5. Ibid

6. Petition #129, 1837. Baltimore City Archives

7. Baltimore Sun, July 9, 1838, p.3

8. Ibid

9. National Anti-Slavery Standard, June 25, 1840, p.10

10. Inward Bound Slave Manifests (Record Group #36) Baltimore to New Orleans, March 4, 1841.

11. Applications for Certificates of Freedom, 1808-1864, Basil Tyler (Anne Arundel County) was manumitted by Hope Hull Slatter July 1848. For details on the visit by Sturge and Whittier see *A Visit to the United States in 1841* by Joseph Sturge (London 1842).

12. Inward Bound Slave Manifests (Record group #36) Baltimore to New Orleans, November 2, 1843

13. National Anti-Slavery Standard, November 16, 1843, p.94

14. Ibid

15. Henry Stockbridge Jr. *Baltimore in 1846* Maryland Historical Magazine, v.6, 1911, p.27

16. New York Daily Tribune, July 30, 1863. Although this article post- dates Slatter's reign it offers patterns of lifestyles in the pens that were common to the trade throughout the South.

17. The Slave Narratives (Maryland), Federal Writer's Project 1936-1938 (Rezin Williams)

18. Baltimore Evening Sun, September 18, 1937, p.3

Note: Although the account of the discovery of the tunnel as reported in the Baltimore Sunday American (September 19, 1937 p.16) indicated that it was three feet in circumference, a photograph in the Baltimore Evening Sun clearly shows that it was larger. There does appear to be inadequate height for adults to walk through the tunnel. This probably explains the terror that some of those present felt and their hesitation to crawl into the darkness of the orifice.

19. Ibid

20. The Liberator, November 29, 1839, p.1.See also Inward Bound Slave Manifests (Record group #36) Baltimore to New Orleans, October 7, 1839

21. National Anti-Slavery Standard, December 28, 1843, p.2

22. Inward Bound Slave Manifests (Record group #36) Baltimore to New Orleans, December 23, 1843

23. Baltimore Sun, November 25, 1844, p.2

24. Leeds Anti-Slavery Series, No.9 (1847)

25. American and Commercial Daily Advertiser, December 30, 1846, p.3

26. Inward Bound Slave Manifests (Record group #36) Baltimore to New Orleans, January 19, 1847

27. Ibid

28. Baltimore Sun, April 20, 1848, p.4 and April 19, 1848, p.4

29. Port Tobacco Times and Charles County Advertiser, April 27, 1848, p.2

30. National Anti-Slavery Standard, May 4, 1848, p.2

31. Inward Bound Slave Manifests (Record group #36) Baltimore to New Orleans, May 13, 1848. The National Anti-Slavery Standard of June 29, 1848 (page 1) confirms the story that fugitive Ellen Stewart was purchased from Campbell before her intended shipment to New Orleans.

32. Ibid

33. National Anti-Slavery Society, September 28, 1848, p.1

34. Ibid

35. Harriet Beecher Stowe A Key to Uncle Tom's Cabin New York, Arno Press 1968 (originally published in 1853) p.155-168 and National Anti-Slavery Standard September 28, 1848, p.1

Note: Numerous newspapers printed accounts of the Pearl incident. The most thorough coverage, however, was that of the National Anti-Slavery Standard.

Chapter 10 - **Other Local Traders**

1. Inward Bound Slave Manifests (Record group #36) Baltimore to New Orleans, November 2, 1843

2. Baltimore Sun, October 9, 1843, p.3

3. Baltimore Sun, October 26, 1846, p.3

4. Ibid

5. Baltimore Sun, October 8, 1849, p.4

6. Baltimore Sun, November 30, 1858, p.3

7. Baltimore Sun, July 10, 1847, p.4

8. Inward Bound Slave Manifests (Record group #36) Baltimore to New Orleans, October 26, 1847

9. Cambridge Chronicle, November 23, 1850, p.4

10. Baltimore Sun, August 2, 1849, p.2

11. Baltimore Sun, April 16, 1861, p.1

12. Bancroft, *Slave Trading in the Old South*, p.59

13. Matchett's Baltimore City Directory, 1835/36

14. Baltimore Sun, June 21, 1841, p.3

15. Baltimore Clipper, September 10, 1839, p.1

16. Inward Bound Slave Manifests (Record group #36) Baltimore to New Orleans, February 3, 1841

17. Bancroft, *Slave Trading in the Old South*, p.120

18. Baltimore Sun, April 26, 1880, p.1

19. Baltimore Sun, January 2, 1849, p.4

20. Baltimore Sun, January 16, 1850, p.4

21. Baltimore Sun, December 17, 1850, p.4

22. Baltimore Sun, December 22, 1849, p.4

23. Baltimore Sun, October 12, 1849, p.4

24. Ibid, August 2, 1849, p.2

25. Ibid, June 21, 1856, p.4

26. Ibid, January 3, 1857, p.4

27. Ibid, May 30, 1861, p.4

28. Inward Bound Slave Manifests (Record group #36) Baltimore to New Orleans, September 6, 1851

29. Ibid, March 23, 1844

30. Baltimore Sun, June 21, 1844, p.4

31. Port Tobacco Times and Charles County Advertiser, November 27, 1845, p.3

32. Ibid

33. Baltimore Sun, November 20, 1852, p.4

34. Bancroft, *Slave Trading in the Old South*, p.121

35. Ibid, p.317

36. Mitchell, *Divided Town*, p.60

37. Ibid, p.75

38. Ibid, p.75

39. Baltimore Sun, June 2, 1862, p.1 and Baltimore American and Commercial Advertiser, June 2, 1862, p.4

40. Baltimore American and Commercial Advertiser, June 2, 1862, p.4

41. Ibid,

42. Mary Mitchell, *Divided Town*, p.75

43. Account by author based on information in the Baltimore Sun, July 28, 1863, p.1; Baltimore American and Commercial Advertiser, July 28, 1863, p.4; Ibid, July 29, 1863, p.4

44. New York Daily Tribune, July 39, 1863

Chapter 11 - **Baltimore Traders' Banner Years 1840-1849**

1. Inward Bound Slave Manifests (Record group #36) Baltimore to New Orleans, January 18, 1842
2. Ibid, October 22, 1842
3. Ibid, September 30, 1843
4. Ibid, November 2, 1843
5. Ibid, December 23, 1843
6. Ibid, December 21, 1844
7. Ibid, December 23, 1844
8. Ibid, January 4, 1845
9. Ibid, January 18, 1845
10. Ibid, February 8, 1845
11. Ibid, February 18, 1845
12. Ibid, March 1, 1845
13. Ibid, March 22, 1845
14. Ibid, April 15, 1845
15. Ibid, May 14, 1845
16. Baltimore Sun, January 7, 1845, p.2
17. Inward Bound Slave Manifests (Record group #36) Baltimore to New Orleans, October 28, 1846
18. Ibid, July 26, 1847
19. Ibid, September 15, 1847
20. Ibid, October 11, 1847
21. Stowe, *A Key to Uncle Tom's Cabin*, p. 149

Bibliography

Newspapers

American and Commercial Daily Advertiser 1813-1847
Baltimore American and Commercial Advertiser 1862-1863
Baltimore Clipper 1839
Baltimore Evening Sun 1937
Baltimore Sun 1838-1861
Cambridge Chronicle 1846-1850
Columbus Times (Georgia) 1847
Fredericktown Herald 1831-1835
Genius of Universal Emancipation 1821-1829
Hagerstown Mail 1831
Lee's Anti-Slavery Series 1847
Liberator 1839
Maryland Gazette (Annapolis) 1834
National Anti-Slavery Standard 1840-1853
New York Daily Tribune 1863
Pilot and Transcript 1831
Port Tobacco Times and Charles County Advertiser 1845-1848

Journals

Stockbridge, Henry Jr. "Baltimore in 1846" *Maryland Historical Magazine* v.6 (1911)

Manuscripts

Baltimore City Petitions 1837
Slave Narratives (WPA project) 1937
Register of Vessels New Orleans 1831-1836
Inward Bound Slave Manifests New Orleans 1818-1856

New Orleans City Directories 1838-1851
Bibb County Deeds (Georgia) 1828
The Slack Family Papers, (Unpublished family genealogy by William
Samuel Slack). Louisiana State University 1930

Books

Adams, Carolyn Greenfield. *Slave Manumissions and Sales in Harford
County, Maryland 1775-1865.* Bowie, Md., Heritage Books Inc.

Ahrens, Toni. *Design Makes a Difference: Shipbuilding in Baltimore
1795-1835.* Bowie, Md., Heritage Books Inc.

Andrews, Ethan Allen. *Slavery and the Domestic Slave Trade in the
United States.* Freeport, N.Y. Books For Libraries Press, 1971
(reprint of 1836 edition).

Bancroft, Frederic. *Slave Trading in the Old South.* South Carolina,
University of South Carolina Press, 1996 (originally published 1931
by J.H Furst Co.)

Drayton, Daniel. *Personal Memoir of Daniel Drayton.* New York,
American and Anti-Slavery Society 1855

Graham, Leroy, *Baltimore, The Nineteenth Century Black Capital.*
Washington, D.C., University Press of America 1982

Jay, William. *Miscellaneous Writings on Slavery.* Boston, J. P. Jewett &
Co, 1853.

Johnson, Walter. *Soul By Soul. Life Inside the Antebellum Slave Market.*
Cambridge, Mass., Harvard University Press, 1999

Mitchel, Mary. *Divided Town.* Barre, Mass. Barre Publishers, 1968

Stowe, Harriet Beecher. *The Key to Uncle Tom's Cabin.* New York, Arno
Press, 1968

Stephenson, Wendle Holmes. *Isaac Franklin, Slave Trader and Planter
of the Old South.* University, University of Louisiana Press, 1938

Index

This index contains the names and subjects from the main text and appendices. It does not contain the names from the alphabetical Slave Manifest roster nor the Vessels roster.

----, Abraham 70 Andrew 47 93
Augusta 94 Betty 49 70 Bob 70
Carlos 47 Caroline 93 Clary 56
Copely 115 Elizabeth 94 Ellen
93-94 Emily 94 Ephraim 94
Frank 94 George 47 Grace 94
Hamp 70 Hannah 47 70
Hannibal 94 Harriet 48 93-94
Henny 40 Hetty 40 Isaac 70 94
Jacob 70 Jane 94 Joe 94 John 47
70 Kitty 94 Lucy 70 Manuel 56
Margaret 70 Maria 70 Mary 93-
94 Mary Ann 94 Matthew 94
Mint 70 Moses 38 Nancy 48 Nat
94 Newman 95 Old Ben 126
Pinkey 70 Precilla 94 Reuben
94 Robert 70 Rosetta 70 Sam 94
Sara 94 Sarah 49 William 94-95
118 Winston 70
ABBOTT, E G 83
ABRAMS, 129
ACCINELLY, Barthalomew 45
ADVERTISEMENTS
    7 9 15 19 20 25 27 30 32 33 60
    63 65 103 105
AGENCIES 15
ALBY, James H 119
ALLENDER, Michael 120
AMMISON, William 118 120

ANDERSON, David 40 44-47
    Levin 41 William 118
ARMFIELD, 55 John 54 646
ARMISTEAD, Mr 93 Mrs 93
ARTHUR, Mary 56
AUCTIONS
    Description Of 3
    Merchandise For Sale 6-10
    Locations Of 13
AULD, Capt 26
AUSTIN, Nat 83
BADEN, Sophia 118
BAILEY, Edwin 64 Frederick 650
BAKER, 56 Claiborne 56 Nicholas
    37
BALDWIN, Thomas 119
BALTIMORE/ALEXANDRIA
    MARKET 53
BANGS, Theophilus 51
BANKS, Dan 118
BARNEY, John H 30
BARNUM, David 32
BARRON, 40
BATES, J Jr 83
BEAL, Mr 24
BEARD, James 45
BEECHER, Henry W 97

BELL, 97 Daniel 92-93 Edward 118
George 93 Henry C 54 Mary 93
Mr 95 Washington 119
BENNET, George 37
BENNETT, James W 644
BERRY, Lindy 37 76 Phillip E 118
Thomas E 118
BIRCH, James H 53
BIRNEY, Col 116 William 116
BISCOE, James 51
BLAKE, Priscilla 39
BOND, Henrietta 118
BOURROUGHS, H J 33
BOUSH, Nathaniel 54 Samuel C 54
BOWEN, Charles 12
BOWSER, William 71 73
BOYD, 76 Margaret 37
BOYER, Neal 644
BRADSHAW, John 34 105
BRANILL, James 95
BRENT, Jane 94 Robert J 127
BRERETON, S 94
BRICE, Judge 74
BRIGHT, Emily 56 Harriet 56 Mary
56
BRODGEN, William 120
BROOKE, John B B 94
BROOKS, Jane 118 Samuel E 120
BROWN, Fanny 644 Jack 644
James 72 O B 94
BRUIN, 97 Mr 97
BRUNER, Cora 56 Elias 56
BUCK, B 52
BUN, Dealy 56
BURNETT, Garland 5
BURNS, Anthony 30 Arthur 30
BUSK, John 83
BUTLER, Charles 37 Mary 37
CALVERT, John 94
CAMBELL, Gabriel 94
CAMPBELL, 655 B M 113 Bernard
18 33 57-58 95 118 125 127-
128 Bernard Moore 45 53 91 98
112 114 116 120 123 128 649-
652-654 John 113 John G 113
Lewis 57 91 95 Walter 125
Walter Lewis 107-108 112 116
123

CARTER, Col 95 John 26
CAUSIN, Dr 94
CHABERT, Leon 48 70 643
CHALBUT, James 118
CHAMBERS, Ann 91 Benjamin 32
Charlotte 91
CHASE, 6 Augustus 94 Emeline 37
Thomas 5 8 9
CHENOWITH, J W 51 126
CHEW, Alfred 37 Beverly 48 Lear
56

CHILDREN
Kidnapping Of 38-40
CHILDS, Samuel 40
CHISLER, James C 118
CLAGGET, William H 118
CLAGGETT, William 120
CLARK, 50 52 Daniel 118 Martha
118 Robert 118
CLAY, John 47
CLENDENIN, A 52
CLOUD, Justice 19
COBBS, David 31
COLBOURN, Oliver 74
COLE, John 11 Samuel 9-11
COLLIER, George W 653
COLLINS, Susan 117-118 Willie
117-118
CONNELLY, Mr 95
CONTEE, William 118
COOK, A L 32
COOKE, John C 118
COOPER, 129 John 36 Judy 37
Perry 39 Rachel 39
CORCORAN, Mrs 94
CORNISH, Delia 91 Samuel 91
COUCH, Bob 37
COUCY, Jane 118
COUNTER, Nancy 120
CRAIG, George 94
CRAIGG, 40
CRANE, Sarah 94
CROWLEY, Philip 94
CUGLE, John 31
CULVER, Ms 94
DALY, John 47

DAVIS, Elijah 70 Francis 656 Jon
31 Minn 94 Samuel 118 Thomas
D 650
DAWES, Harrison 12
DAY, A R 19-20 Mary 94
DEBTOR, Martha 118
DENNING, John N 53 111 John S
125
DENT, James 118
DEVALCOURT, Alex 37
DIAMOND, William 62
DICK, Ms 94
DICKSON, Andrew 118
DIGGS, Gabriel 61
DODGE, F 94
DOLLERHIDE, J A 31
DONOVAN, J S 105 Joseph 96 98
106 112 648-651 Joseph S 45
52-53 103-104 106 109 125 130
652-654
DORM, Harriett 118
DORRY, Charles 119
DORSEY, Charles 119 Mary 56
Samuel 119 Thomas 56
DOTSON, Mary 94
DOUCY, Hammond 118
DOUGLASS, Frederick 650
DOWNING, John 94
DRAYTON, Daniel 92
DRIVER, John 37
DUFFIN, Harriett 91 Joe 91
DUKE, G H 33 112
DUNBAR, George T 12
DUNKIN, Levin 646
DUTTON, Dennis 37
DUVAL, Washington 118 120
DUVALL, Charles R 119
DYER, Betty Ann 91 Lucy 91 Mary
91
EDMONDSON, 92 96 Amelia 96
Emily 96-97 Emly 96 Ephrim 96
John 96 Mary 96-98 Paul 96
Richard 96 Samuel 96-97
EGAN, Anthony 59
EICHELBERGER, George S 40
ELLIOTT, Elizabeth 12 Mary 119
ENGLISH, Chester 92
EUBANK, Caleb 31

EVANS, John 94
EVARD, Dolly 91 Frank 91 Jane 91
Mary Jane 91
EXAMINATION
Of Male Slaves 3-5
Of Female Slaves 4 5
FINLEY, Ann 644 Mariah 644
FLETCHER, Charles 94 Michael
119 Samuel 119
FLURRY, Benjamin A 119
FOOTE, Charles 119 Perry 119
FOSTER, Jane 119 Louisa 119
Philip 119
FOWLER, William 31 59
FRANKLIN, 55 George 56 Isaac
53-54 109 646-647
FREE BLACKS
Kidnapping Of 18 38-41 62
Shipped To New Orleans With
Papers 40
FREEMAN, John 30
FREY, John H 129
FROZEL, Mr 95
FRY, Elizabeth 11
FUGITIVE SLAVES
Escapes Of 71-73 92-98
Roster From The Pearl 93-95
GALLOWAY, Capt 72 Walter R 71
GALT, W 655
GANT, 56
GARDINER, Richard S D 127
GARDNER, Owen 118
GARSICLES, James 46
GARY, Adam 51
GATCHEL, John G 126
GATCHELL, John G 648
GAYLE, Capt 91
GIBSON, Henry 644 James 644
Sinah 644
GODFREY, Benjamin 46 48
GOLDSMITH, Samuel 37
GORHAM, William T 45
GRAHAM, Henry 94
GRAY, Adam 51 Adams 126 648
GREEN, 11 Charles R 10 Jackson
37 Jesse 37 Mrs 60 Rachel 37
GREENE, Edward M 17
GRIFFIN, Charlotte 76

GRIMES, Lloyd A 30
GROSS, Perry 94
GUNBY, F A 129
GUSTAW, James C 118
GUY, Ann 644
HALL, 127 Edward 70
HAMAN, 644
HAMMOND, George 119 Reese 119
HARDIE, Robert 644
HARKER, William 51 53 110 126-127
HARRIS, 56 Dolly 126 Jane 40 John 18-19
HARRISON, 8
HARROD, Lenah 119 Rachel 119 Thomas 72
HAYES, Talbot 39
HAYNIE, John F 649 651
HEATH, Bill 644 Margaret 644
HENDERSON, George 70
HESSETT, Uriah 119
HIGGINS, John 118
HILL, 97 Charles 119 William 71 119 William B 120
HINDES, Moses 53 112
HOBBS, George 651
HOLLINS, George V 128 Hannah 49
HOOPER, Edward 129 William 33
HOOVER, A 94
HORMAN, W 94
HORTON, James 12
HOTEL, TAVERNS AND INNS
    Meeting Places 27 29
    Bartenders Used As Agents 29 34
    Anthony Egan's 59
    Barnum's Hotel 30
    The City Hotel 32
    Columbian Hotel 31
    Cugle's Tavern 32
    Fowler's Tavern 30
    Globe Hotel 31
    J H Burroughs Hotel 33
    James Hunter's Hotel 33
    John Bradshaw's Hotel 34

John H. Barneys Fountain Inn 30
    Knight's Tavern 31
    Mr Lilly's Tavern 30
    Mrs Green's Tavern 60
    Mrs Kirk's 31
    New Bridge Hotel 44
    Sign Of General Wayne 31
    Sign Of The Green Tree 60
    Sign Of The Three Kegs 31
    Sinner's Tavern 30 31
    Three Tuns Tavern 60
    Turnbutt's Hotel 33
    Union Tavern 33
    Western Inn 33
    William Fowler's 31 59
HOUSTON, Col 30
HOWARD, George C 95
HUNTER, Gen 95
HUTCHERSON, John S 31
HYNSON, Jacob P 18 Nathaniel 11
INTELLIGENCE OFFICES 15
    General Intelligence Office 15
    Register Office 16
    Maryland Intelligence Office 17 37
    Scott's General Slave Agency And Intelligence Office 17 18
    City Agency 19
    Real Estate And Intelligence Office 20
IRWIN, Mrs 95
ISNARD, Joseph 45
IVENS, Jane 119
JACKSON, 56 W 95
JARBOE, Capt 24
JAY, William 54
JOHNS, Hercules 49 Louisa 49
JOHNSON, 56 76 Eliza 119 John 37 Walter 4 68
KARTHAUS, Charles W 75
KEAN, John 70
KELLOG, 50 52
KELSO, George Y 49
KENNARD, George 56 Richard 56 Samuel 26
KENNEDY, Thomas 47
KENNY, John Sr 70

KEPHART, 647 George 53 55-56
646
KIDNAPPING 18 38-41 62
KING, 19 Edward 94 Gideon T 44
Leonard 94 Mary Letha 94
Priscilla 94 Vincent 94
KIRK, Mrs 31
KIRKWOOD, Mr 94
KITTLE, Maria 119
KNIGHT, William 47
KNOX, John 94
LANGLY, Henry 119 Mary Jane
119
LEAKIN, Sheppard C 61 Sheriff 62
LEE, Edwin 45 Pat 119
LEGG, Henry 25 Lemeul 24
LESLIE, Henry 126
LEWIS, Fortune 62
LILLY, Mr 30
LINCOLN, Abraham 119 Dan 119
Pres 114
LINN, Ned 11
LISLE, Mrs 94
LITTON, William H 127
LLOYD, Edward 26
LOUISE-PHILLIPE, Of France 92
LOWE, Henry 33
LUNDY, Benjamin 64 71 73
LYONS, Mr 95
MADDOX, C T 52
MADISON, Mrs 94
MAGRUDER, John Read 61
MAKEL, S 119
MARSHALL, Anderson 94
MARTIN, Hugh 126-127 648 650
653
MATTHEWS, Plumer 94 William H
37
MAYO, W 94
MCCAUGHAN, Daniel 12 Davis 12
MCCLEAN, Hector 44 46
MCCLELLAN, Rupel 119
MCCOMAS, Acquilla 70
MCDANIEL, Mr 30 Mrs 94
MCNEIL, Patrick 36
MEEK, Joseph 31
MIDDLETON, B F 94
MILES, Catherine 56

MILLER, Edward 40
MILLIGAN, George 47
MITCHELL, Abram 37 Sarah 70
MOORE, Dennis 37
MORRIS, Nancy 56
MORTON, Nathaniel 126
MUDD, Ignatius 94
MULLIGAN, James 120
NALLY, R B 94
NEAL, Joseph W 53
NEGRO, Charles 11 George 37
NEILSON, O H 9
NELSON, Aquilla 70
NEW ORLEANS
Merchant Hector Mclean 44 46
Merchant William T Gorham 45
Merchant John Clay 47
NICKERSON, S R 647
OAKS, Samuel 18
OLDHAM, George W 47 50
OLIVER, Paul A 66
OSBORNE, Alfred 118
OTIS, James 127
OWENS, Emeline 37
PARKER, Mary J 119 Thomas 46
PATTON, William 65
PAVRE, Daphne 95
PEARCE, Greenbury 51
PENNINGTON, Justice 18
PETERS, J 89
PHILLIPS, William 652
PITTS, Madison 95
PLATER, John R Jr 49
POPE, Alfred 95
PORTER, William 72
PURVIS, James Franklin 51 53 69
83 109-110 126 646
QUEEN, Ellen 119 Pricella 94
RAGLAND, Thomas 30
RANDALL, Elisha 12 John K 91
RANKING, George 37
RANSKIN, George 120
READING BODIES 3, 4
REYNOLDS, James 119
RILEY, Philip 37 66 70
RISTAR, Thomas 119
RIX, Peter 95
ROBB, John 648

ROBERTSON, Ellen J 119
ROBINSON, Capt 646 Matthew 74 643
ROBY, Alfred 119
RODBIND, Ebenezer 52 127-128 649 651 653 654
ROLFS, 56
SANNER, J B 127
SAUL, Joseph 49
SAYRES, Edward 92
SCHWARTZ, George 40
SCOTT, 20 Francis 119 Lewis F 17-18 21
SEPHUS, 644
SHANKLIN, George 95
SHIPLEY, Henry 117 120 Matilda 117 120
SIMMONS, Sophia 120
SIMMS, William 120
SIMPSON, W 10
SLATTER, 55 647 Henry 57 98 665 Henry F 100 651 Hope 57 91 95 112 130 651 654 Hope H 88-89 Hope Henry 101 Hope Hull 40 45 51-53 83-84 91 98 109 125-129 646-649 652 653 Mr 85 Nancy 83 Shadrack 57 98-99 Solomon 83
SLAVES
    Brought Over From The Eastern Shore 23 24
    Children Sale Of 35
    Children Born During Shipment 46 47
    Children Percentage Shipped By Traders 81 101 104 109 123
    Deaths During Shipment 47
    Examination Of 3-5
    Occupations Of 10
    Sales Of, In Hotels 27
    Sales Of, By Administrators Of Estates 11 12 31 32
    Sales Of, By Orphans' Court 5 7 9 12
    Sales Of, In Trader's Pens 5
    Sales Of, By Exchange 17 37
    Sold For Bad Behavior 11
    Value Of, In Advertisements 11
    Transportation Of, By Caravan 89
    Suspected Runaways 61 62
SLAVE JAILS (PENS)
    Description Of 56 84 86 87 110
    Incarceration In 18 114 115
    Cost Of Housing Slaves In 57 84
    Slaves Incarcerated In, As Runaways 57 61 62
    Slaves Released By Col Birney 118-120
SLAVE TRADERS
    Major Competitors 125
    Pen Of, Auctions Held 5
SLAVE TRADING
    Shipping Cycle 45
SMALLWOOD, Henry 95
SMITH, Dr 65 Elizabeth 12 Ellen 643 James 37 65 643 John A 641 John H 94 Samuel 50 William 54 646
SMOOT, John N 120
SNOW, Hannah 120
SNOWDEN, Kitty 37
SNYDER, Dr 120
SPARR, Willis 120
STAFFORD, Henry 37
STANLEY, Dinah 644 Harriet 644 Rachel 644
STANSBURG, Tobias E 49
STAPLES, Joshua 51 126
STEVENS, J J 52
STEVENSON, Elisa 120
STORM, L 95
STOWE, Harriet Beecher 97 130
STRIKE, Nicholas 5 11
STROHN, John F 51 126
STULL, J J 94
STURGE, Joseph 85
SWANN, Mr 94
SWELL, Marwin 119
TALBOT, Frederick 119 John 119
TENANT, Thomas 49
TENNANT, Thomas 65

THOMAS, Amy 76 Charlott 55
  Clem 76 James 37 55 120
  Priscilla 55 William 55
THOMPSON, Caroline 55 Henry
  48-49 John 55 Sandy 55
  William 95
THOMSON, Phillip 120
TOODLES, Henry 120 John F 120
TRIPLETT, Dr 94
TURNER, Robert E 118 Samuel 95
TYLER, Basil 86
UPPERMAN, William H 94
VANCE, William 8
VESSELS
  Actress 46
  Alfred 66
  Ann And Leah 37
  Araminta Elizabeth 26
  Arctic 37
  Aurilla 48
  Balloon 47 641
  Brunswick 645
  Budget 45
  Burlington 126
  Catherine 127
  Chestertown Packet 25
  Clio 46
  Constitution 72
  Decatur 49 71 72
  E. H. Chapin 130 653
  Easton Packet 23-26
  Elizabeth 130 654
  Emilie 46
  Eros 47
  Ewarkee 85
  European 19
  Fanny And Mary Seabury 47
  Franklin 40
  General Pinckney 89 90 652
  Georgia 127
  Good Hope 43 61
  Hamlet 63 64
  Harriet 62
  Helen A. Miller 655
  Henry Clay 644
  Hermitage 129
  Hibernia 74 643
  Horne 128
  Hyperion 37 49
  Intelligence 48
  Irad Ferry 51
  Isaac Franklin 54 55 646 647
  Jasper 74
  Jefferson 37 75
  Kirkwood 52 89 105 113 126-
    128 130 648-651 653
  Lady Monroe 64 65
  Lady Richmond 75
  Lafayette 644
  Lapwing 40 47 74
  Louisa 129 130
  Margaret Forbs 51
  Margaret Hugg 127
  Mars 642
  Nancy W. Stevens 127
  Orbit 37 66 70
  Orion 50
  P. Soule 128
  Paoli 128
  Pearl 91-93 95-97
  Pioneer 129
  Planter 47
  Queenstown Packet 24
  Robert Reade 50
  Rooke 73
  Sally And Betsey 24
  Scotia 126
  Solomon Saltus 88 647
  Southerner 130
  States 75 643
  Statira 65
  Sultana 50
  Superb 44 46 86 103 126 648
  Susan Miller 69 642
  Temperance 44 45
  Tippecanoe 50 51 125 647 648
  Tribune 54
  Tweed 645 646
  Uncas 54
  Union 97 129 130 654
  United States 54
  Victorine 127 128 650 651
  Types Preferred 49 125
  Zoe 652
VICKARS, 24 Capt 23
WADE, Emanuel 120

WALKER, James 120
WALTER, John 36
WARD, Betsey 120
WARFIELD, Charles 48
WASHINGTON, Louisa 94
    Minerva 94
WATERS, Mr 94
WATTS, W J 128
WELCH, Thomas T 119
WELD, Charles R 4
WELLS, Mother 120
WEST, Virginia 120
WHEELER, A C 33
WHITE, David H 83
WHITING, Mary 40-41
WHITTIER, John Greenleaf 85
WIKOFF, Stephen A 48
WILLIAMS, 118 Rezin 87 Thomas
    91 127 129 652 William H 53
WILLIGMAN, Charles 33

WILSON, Isaac 70 James 643
    Jonathan M 33 57 106 125
    Jonathan Means 53 112 Manuel
    72 Robert B 31
WING, Paul 61
WIRT, William 56
WOOD, 6-7 Henry H 20 John 6 8-9
WOOLFOLK, 45 53 642 645
    Austin 48 50 58-60 62-63 66 69
    71 73 75 77 81 83 98 103 642-
    644 649 John 65 77 Joseph 64
    75 643-644 Joseph B 64 Joseph
    Biggers 66 78-80 642 Richard
    50 644 Richard T 61 78 80
    Samuel M 61 78 79
WORTHINGTON, Thomas 119
WRIGHT, Edward 643
YATES, 8
YOUNG, John M 94 Jonathan Y 94
    Madison 95
ZACHARIE, James W 51

Ralph Clayton is a library research assistant and freelance writer living in Baltimore. His articles on the antebellum experience of African Americans have appeared in numerous newspapers and journals in Baltimore. In 1992 the Enoch Pratt Free Library honored Mr. Clayton with the William G. Baker Award for his excellent public service and proficiency as a writer while a member of the staff.

Mr. Clayton is currently developing tours that accurately reflect the African American experience in Baltimore before the Civil War. His next project, the role of the underground railroad in the city, will put his twenty-five years of research experience to its' greatest test.

CPSIA information can be obtained
at www.ICGtesting.com
Printed in the USA
LVHW080724281021
701668LV00017B/304